The Letters and Diaries
of
John Henry Newman

The Letters and Diaries
of
John Henry Newman

Edited at the Birmingham Oratory
with notes and an introduction

by

Charles Stephen Dessain
of the same Oratory

and

Thomas Gornall, S.J.

Volume XXX
A Cardinal's Apostolate
October 1881 to December 1884

CLARENDON PRESS · OXFORD
1976

Oxford University Press, Ely House, London W.1

GLASGOW NEW YORK TORONTO MELBOURNE WELLINGTON
CAPE TOWN IBADAN NAIROBI DAR ES SALAAM LUSAKA ADDIS ABABA
DELHI BOMBAY CALCUTTA MADRAS KARACHI LAHORE DACCA
KUALA LUMPUR SINGAPORE HONG KONG TOKYO

ISBN 0 19 920060 2

Printed in Great Britain by
Cox & Wyman Ltd,
London, Fakenham and Reading

Preface

WITHOUT the gradual building up at the Birmingham Oratory of a very full collection of Cardinal Newman's correspondence (an account of which will be found in the Introduction to Volume XI), the present work could not have been undertaken. Its aim is to provide an exhaustive edition of Newman's letters; with explanatory notes, which are often summaries of or quotations from the other side of the correspondence. Some of these letters *to* Newman, when they appear to have particular importance, or to be necessary for following a controversy, are inserted in the text. Every one of the letters written *by* Newman is included there, in chronological sequence. Should there eventually be any of his letters, whose existence is known to the editor, but of which he has failed to obtain a copy, this will be noted in its place. On the other hand, no attempt has been made to include a list of letters written by Newman and now lost, nor the brief précis he occasionally made of his reply, on the back of a correspondent's letter, although these are utilised for the annotation.

In order that the text of each letter may be as accurate as possible, the original autograph, when it still exists, or at least a photographic copy of it, has been used by the editor as his source. (The very few cases in which he has been content with an authenticated copy will be noted as they occur.) Always the text of the autograph is reproduced, or, when the autograph has disappeared, that of the copy that appears most reliable. When only Newman's draft exists, that is printed. The source used in each case is to be found in the list of letters by correspondents.

Such alterations as are made in transcribing the letters aim, without sacrifice of accuracy, at enabling them to be read with ease. Newman writes simply and has none of those idiosyncrasies which sometimes need to be reproduced for the sake of the evidence of one kind or another which they provide.

The following are the only alterations made in transcription:

ADDRESS AND DATE are always printed on the same line, and at the head of the letter, even when Newman puts them at the end. When he omits or gives an incomplete date, the omission is supplied in square brackets, and justified in a note unless the reason for it is obvious. The addresses, to which letters were sent, are included in the list of letters by correspondents. The information derived from postmarks is matter for annotation.

THE CONCLUSION of the letter is made to run on, irrespective of Newman's separate lines, and all postscripts are placed at the end.

NEWMAN'S CORRECTIONS AND ADDITIONS are inserted in their intended place. His interlinear explanations are printed in the text in angle brackets ⟨ ⟩, after the word or phrase they explain. His erasures are given in footnotes when they appear to be of sufficient interest to warrant it. Square brackets are reserved for editorial additions. All Newman's brackets are printed as rounded ones (the kind most usual with him).

NEWMAN'S PARAGRAPHS AND PUNCTUATION are preserved, except that single quotation marks are printed throughout, and double ones for quotations within them. (Newman generally used the latter in both cases.) Further, a parenthesis or quotation that he began with the proper mark but failed to complete, or completed but did not begin, is supplied. All other punctuation marks supplied by the editor are enclosed in square brackets. Newman's dashes, which frequently do duty either for a full stop, a semicolon or a comma (especially when he is tired or writing hurriedly), are represented by a '—' with a space before and after. His spelling and use of capitals are left unchanged, but 'raised' letters are lowered in every case.

NEWMAN'S ABBREVIATIONS are retained in the case of proper names, and in the address and conclusion of each letter, since these are sometimes useful indications of his attitude at the time. In all other cases, abbreviations are printed out in full, where Newman employs them.

When he uses the initials of proper names, the full name is normally inserted in square brackets after the initials, at the first occurrence in each letter, and more often if it seems advisable in order to avoid confusion. No addition of the full name is made in the case of Newman's correspondent, whether his initials occur at the beginning of the letter or in the course of it.

When Newman uses only a Christian name, the surname is sometimes added in square brackets for the reader's convenience. The Christian names of members of the Oratory, since they are of frequent occurrence, are listed in the index of proper names and the reader is referred to surnames.

When transcription is made from a PRINTED SOURCE, typographical alterations clearly due to editor or printer are disregarded.

Sometimes Newman made HOLOGRAPH copies of his letters or of portions of them, when they were returned to him long after they had been written. In order that the reader may be able to see how much he copied and what changes he introduced, the copied passages are placed in quarter brackets ⌐ ⌐, and all additions of any importance included in the text in double square brackets, or, where this is impracticable, in the annotation.

Newman's letters are printed in CHRONOLOGICAL ORDER, with the name of his correspondent at the head (except that those of each day are arranged alphabetically), and, when more than one is written to the same person on the same day, numbered I, II. In the headings the name of the correspondent is given in its most convenient form, sometimes with Christian names in full, sometimes only with initials.

THE LIST OF LETTERS BY CORRESPONDENTS, at the end of each volume, shows whether the source used was an autograph, draft, printed source or copy, and in the last case, whether a holograph made by Newman later; and gives the present location of the source, as well as of any additional holograph copies or drafts. When a letter, or a considerable portion of it, has been printed in a standard work, references are given; but mistakes or omissions in these previous publications are noticed, if at all, in the annotation.

THE LETTERS WRITTEN TO NEWMAN, when inserted in the text, are printed in type smaller than that used for Newman's own letters, and headed by the name of the correspondent. These letters are not arranged in chronological order, but are placed either just before or just after the letter of Newman to which they are related. A list of them is given at the end of each volume in which they occur. These and the quotations from letters in the annotation are always, unless otherwise stated, printed from autographs at the Birmingham Oratory, and are transcribed in the same way as Newman's letters.

NEWMAN'S DIARIES COVER THE YEARS 1824 to 1879 (with a gap from July 1826 to March 1828). They are written in a series of mottled copy books, 12 × 18½ centimetres, printed for a year each, and entitled *The Private Diary: arranged, printed, and ruled, for receiving an account of every day's employment . . .*' with the exception of the four periods July 1847–May 1850, January 1854–January 1861, January 1861–March 1871, March 1871– October 1879, each of which is contained in a somewhat thicker copy book.

These diaries are printed complete for each day in which Newman has made an entry, except that the lists of people to whom he has written or from whom he has received letters are omitted, as not being of sufficient general interest. The original diaries are, of course, available for consultation. At the end of each diary book are various notes, lists of addresses, of people to be prayed for, accounts, etc. These, also, are omitted, except for occasional dated notes of events, which are inserted in their proper place. Of the rest of the notes, some are theological and will be reserved for a volume of Newman's theological papers, and others will perhaps have room found for them in any fuller edition of *Autobiographical Writings*.

Newman compiled with his own hands, on quarto sheets sewn together, a book of *Chronological Notes*, drawn largely from the diaries. Any new matter in these *Notes* is printed in italics with the appropriate diary entry. (It should be noted that the diary entries themselves were sometimes written up considerably later than the events they record).

Each volume is preceded by a brief summary of the period of Newman's life that it covers. Summary, diaries and annotation give a roughly biographical form to the whole, and will, it is hoped, enable the ordinary reader to treat it as a continuous narrative.

THE BIOGRAPHIES OF PERSONS are collected in the index of proper names at the end of each volume, in order to simplify the annotation of the letters. Occasionally, when a person is mentioned only once or twice, and a note is required in any case, biographical details have been given in the notes, and a reference in the index. Volume XXI, being the first of a new period in Newman's life, contains an account of every person mentioned, with the exception of a few for whom a notice seemed unnecessary, and of still fewer who have not yet been identified. The indexes of Volume XXII and of subsequent volumes will contain notices of persons who appear in them for the first time, and references back, in the case of those who have been noticed in an earlier volume. (The editor will be grateful for information as to persons not identified.)

These notices have been compiled from such various sources — books of reference, letters at the Oratory, information supplied by the families or religious communities of the persons concerned, and by librarians and archivists — that the giving of authorities would be a very complicated and lengthy process. Like others faced with the same problem, the editor has decided usually to omit them. References are given, however, to *The Dictionary of National Biography*, or *The Dictionary of American Biography*, in all cases where there is an article there, and failing them, to Boase's *Modern English Biography* or Gillow's *Bibliographical Dictionary of the English Catholics*. When all the volumes of letters have been issued, a final index volume will be compiled for the whole work.

Contents

Contents

Abbreviations in Volume XXX

THE abbreviations used for Newman's works are those listed in Joseph Rickaby, S.J., *Index to the Works of John Henry Cardinal Newman*, London 1914, with a few additions.

References to works included by Newman in his uniform edition are always, unless otherwise stated, to that edition, which was begun in 1868 with *Parochial and Plain Sermons*, and concluded in 1881 with *Select Treatises of St Athanasius*. From 1886, until the stock was destroyed in the 1939–45 war, all the volumes were published by Longmans, Green and Co. They are distinguished from other, usually posthumous, publications by having their date of inclusion in the uniform edition in brackets after the title, in the list of abbreviations below. The unbracketed date is, in every case, the date of the edition (or impression) used for giving references. (Once volumes were included in the uniform edition the pagination usually remained unchanged, but there are exceptions and minor alterations.)

Add.	*Addresses to Cardinal Newman with His Replies etc. 1879–82* ed. W. P. Neville, 1905.
Apo.	*Apologia pro Vita Sua* (1873) 1905.
Ari.	*The Arians of the Fourth Century* (1871) 1908.
Ath. I, II	*Select Treatises of St Athanasius*, two volumes (1881) 1920.
A.W.	*John Henry Newman : Autobiographical Writings*, ed. Henry Tristram 1956.
Call.	*Callista, a Tale of the Third Century* (1876) 1923.
Campaign	*My Campaign in Ireland, Part I* (printed for private circulation only), 1896.
D.A.	*Discussions and Arguments on Various Subjects* (1872) 1911.
Dev.	*An Essay on the Development of Christian Doctrine* (1878) 1908.
Diff. I, II	*Certain Difficulties felt by Anglicans in Catholic Teaching*, two volumes (1879, 1876) 1908.
Ess. I, II	*Essays Critical and Historical*, two volumes (1871) 1919.
G.A.	*An Essay in aid of a Grammar of Assent* (1870) 1913.
H.S., I, II, III	*Historical Sketches*, three volumes (1872) 1908, 1912, 1909
Idea	*The Idea of a University defined and illustrated* (1873) 1902.
Jfc.	*Lectures on the Doctrine of Justification* (1874) 1908.
K.C.	*Correspondence of John Henry Newman with John Keble and Others, 1839–45*, ed. at the Birmingham Oratory, 1917.
L.G.	*Loss and Gain: the Story of a Convert* (1874) 1911.
M.D.	*Meditations and Devotions of the late Cardinal Newman*, 1893.
Mir.	*Two Essays on Biblical and on Ecclesiastical Miracles* (1870) 1907.
Mix.	*Discourses addressed to Mixed Congregations* (1871) 1909.
Moz I, II	*Letters and Correspondence of John Henry Newman*, ed. Anne Mozley, two volumes, 1891.

O.S.	*Sermons preached on Various Occasions* (1870) 1927.
P.S. I–VIII	*Parochial and Plain Sermons* (1868) 1907–10.
Prepos.	*Present Position of Catholics* (n.d. 1872) 1913.
S.D.	*Sermons bearing on Subjects of the Day* (1869) 1902.
S.E.	*Stray Essays on Controversial Points* (private) 1890.
S.N.	*Sermon Notes of John Henry Cardinal Newman, 1849–1878*, ed. Fathers of the Birmingham Oratory, 1913.
T.T.	*Tracts Theological and Ecclesiastical* (1874) 1908.
U.S.	*Fifteen Sermons preached before the University of Oxford* (1872) 1909.
V.M. I, II	*The Via Media* (1877) 1908, 1911.
V.V.	*Verses on Vaious Occasions* (1874) 1910.

*   *   *

Boase	Frederick Boase, *Modern English Biography*, six volumes, Truro 1892–1921.
Butler	Cuthbert Butler, *The Life and Times of Bishop Ullathorne*, two volumes, London 1926.
de Lisle	E. S. Purcell, *Life and Letters of Ambrose Phillipps de Lisle*, two volumes, London 1900.
D A B	*Dictionary of American Biography*, London, 1928–36.
D N B	*Dictionary of National Biography*, to 1900, London, reprinted in 1937–8 in twenty-two volumes, the last being a Supplement *D N B*, Suppl.
D N B, 1901–11	*Dictionary of National Biography*, 1901–11, three volumes in one.
DR	*Dublin Review.*
D T C	*Dictionnaire de Théologie Catholique*, Paris, 1903–50.
Gillow	Joseph Gillow, *Bibliographical Dictionary of the English Catholics*, five volumes, London 1885 and later.
Liddon's *Pusey* I–IV	H. P. Liddon, *Life of Edward Bouverie Pusey*, four volumes, London 1893–7
Newman and Bloxam	R. D. Middleton, *Newman and Bloxam*, London 1947.
Purcell	E. S. Purcell, *The Life of Cardinal Manning*, two volumes, London 1895.
Trevor I	Meriol Trevor, *Newman the Pillar of the Cloud*, London 1962.
Trevor II	Meriol Trevor, *Newman Light in Winter*, London 1962.
Ward I, II	Wilfrid Ward, *The Life of John Henry Cardinal Newman*, two volumes, London 1912.

Introductory Note

NEWMAN was now established as a Cardinal, and although well into his eighties with the natural infirmities of old age, still remained extremely active. One of the gravest of the problems facing a Christian pastor seemed to be the general undermining of faith in Holy Scripture, discredited alike by modern science and historical research. Newman was too old to deal at due length with these matters, but he could use the weight of his name to suggest the limits of Inspiration, and above all to keep questions open. He wanted especially 'to preserve the inward peace of religious Catholics'. A letter in which he had tried to do this, written some time before the first Vatican Council, was published in the American *Century Magazine* for June 1882. Newman explained that very little had been formally decided as to the Bible except that the saving truths of the Christian faith came to us by means of it. He was taken to task by William Barry, a young theologian returned from Rome, who quoted the more stringent definitions of the recent Council. Newman saw that, no matter how delicate and dangerous, the question of Inspiration must be faced. He set to work early in 1883, consulting Archbishop Errington and Bishop Clifford. The latter had been arguing in the *Dublin Review* that the first verses of *Genesis* were a religious hymn and not a scientific treatise. His correspondence with these bishops shows how carefully Newman prepared his article 'On the Inspiration of Scripture' which appeared in the *Nineteenth Century* for February 1884. This time he was attacked by John Healy, a professor at Maynooth, while Ignatius Ryder in the Oratory became alarmed at his Superior's audacity. The views Newman put forward, however, as to the extent of biblical Inspiration are remarkably close to those laid down at the Second Vatican Council. He replied to the Maynooth theologian with a 'Postscript', whose purpose was to show that the question remained an open one. Already in April 1883, while still engaged upon this task, he had written to Lord Emly: 'My own difficulty in attempting it is because, as I think, theologians decide many questions about Scripture which the Church has not decided'. He wished the Bible to be read as a religious book and regretted that, in spite of papal encouragement of this, the *Catechism* authorised by the English bishops contained 'no reference to Scripture as a book given us by God, inspired, a guide — and a comfort.'

The young Friedrich von Hügel wrote to thank Newman for the articles on Inspiration which had helped him personally and which he had read and reread. He also recounted how he had met at the Institut Catholique in Paris, d'Hulst, de Broglie and Duchesne, 'all three, while discussing your papers, agree to their conclusions and maintain that their subject was the burning religious question of the hour, and that our Apologetics would cease to fail of their due effect only when the concessions you would allow can be fully applied and explicitly proclaimed'.

Another problem for which Newman years earlier had tried to provide a solution remained acute. There was still no provision for the university education of English Catholics. The bishops' prohibition of the universities was renewed in even stronger terms in the Spring of 1882. Newman urged the Jesuits to make more of their presence at Oxford and encouraged the efforts of Bishop Hedley, who had the support of Bishop Clifford, of Lord Braye and others, at least to secure some mitigation of the prohibition. On 2 November 1882 he wrote to Lord Braye: 'The cardinal question for the moment is the Oxford question . . . The undergraduates and Junior Fellows are as sheep without a shepherd. They are sceptics or inquirers, quite open to religious influences . . . The Liberals are sweeping along in triumph, without any Catholic or religious influence to stem them now that Pusey and Liddon are gone.' Newman continued: 'Alas it is only one out of various manifestations of what may be called Nihilism in the Catholic Body, and its rulers. They forbid, but they do not direct or create'. When Bishop Hedley and Lord Braye had an audience in April 1883, this letter was read to Leo XIII in Italian translation. The Pope depended on his advisers and could only reply that he would consult Cardinal Manning. In 1884 the English bishops were again asked for their views, and in 1885 the ban on Protestant universities was once more renewed.

At his death in 1879 William Palmer of Magdalen had left Newman all his papers. One of the most interesting was the account of his visit to Russia in 1840–1. Palmer was a Tractarian and he wished to prove that the Anglican and Russian Churches were integral portions of the one Catholic Church, by receiving communion in the Russian Church. As Newman explained to Anne Mozley in July 1882, 'His main object is to be recognized as a member of the Holy Catholic Church, and to be admitted to communion as such. In this he was unsuccessful — as for other reasons, so for this, that the Russian Ecclesiastics are not quite sure that any one Catholic Church now remains in the world. There was once, but it has died, and the Russo-Greek Church is all that remains of it — so that Palmer is indeed at liberty to become a Russo-Greek, but not to remain an Anglican.' In 1881 and 1882 Newman was preparing *Notes of a Visit to the Russian Church* for publication. He explained in his preface, that although Palmer's appeal for recognition and the answer it received was the main subject of the volume it was not the main object of its publication. 'It is published for the vivid picture it presents to us, for better or for worse, of the Russian Church, gained as it was, without effort by the author's intercourse with priests and laymen, and with the population generally.' The sale of the book did not fulfil Newman's hopes, but the subsequent history of Russia and the rise of the Ecumenical Movement give it an added interest today.

Newman was involved in less immediately religious problems. In the autumn of 1881 the land war was raging in Ireland, with evictions by landlords and widespread agrarian crime. Newman wrote to his nephew in October, 'judging by what I saw in Ireland twenty years ago, the question between the two countries is not one of land or property, but of *union*.' The Irish had never condoned the English occupation. How differently Scotland had been treated, with its own religion and its own universities. 'I have long thought the Irish would gain Home Rule in some shape' although it would be 'a blow on the power of England as great as it is retributive.' In December Gladstone, who was Prime Minister, sent Newman evidence that priests in Ireland had been encouraging sedition, and appealed to him to bring this to the notice of the Pope, whom the decrees of 1870 had made so powerful. Before replying, Newman asked a question of William J. Walsh, President of Maynooth and a Home Ruler, promising to burn his answer. 'I want to ask you as an Irish theologian, whether you think the following position tenable . . . It is a probable opinion and therefore may be acted on by an individual, that the Irish people has never recognized . . . the sovereignty of England . . . and therefore it is no sin to be what is commonly called a rebel'. A few days later Newman reminded Gladstone that he had overrated the Pope's power in political and social matters. It was for bishops to deal with their priests. He did not feel he could intervene in the affairs of another country and returned Gladstone's papers, telling him that 'a firm friend of the civil powers', probably Lord O'Hagan, was anyhow about to put the English Government's views before the Holy See. Six months later Newman was writing to the daughter of an Irish landlord, 'Your account of Ireland is dreadful — but you had no need to tell me that. But as to the future! It seems as if at last a judgment was coming down on England for its centuries of pride and self confidence.'

Newman became involved publicly in the controversy over Gladstone's Affirmation Bill of 1883, which would have allowed the atheist Charles Bradlaugh, elected member for Northampton, to make an affirmation before taking his seat, instead of being sworn. Some of the Conservative opposition saw their opportunity of rallying religious people, nonconformists and Irish Catholics, against the Government, in defence of the official recognition of God by the state. Petitions were widely signed against the Bill, with the full encouragement of Anglican bishops and other Church leaders, not least Cardinal Manning. To Newman they seemed 'a piece of humbug', but if one of the petitions came his way, he felt it would have been difficult to refuse to sign and thus appear different from all other religious people. However, when the *Morning Post* said it was 'authorised' to state that Newman did not approve 'in any sense of the word' of the Affirmation Bill, he was obliged to make known that he saw no religious principle involved in it. The God sworn by in the political world was not the Personal God of the Jewish religion and those derived from it. 'Hence it as little concerns religion whether Mr Bradlaugh swears by no God with the Government or swears by an Impersonal or Material, or abstract Ideal Something or other, which is all that is secured to us by the opposition.'

Newman found himself much against his will, drawn into other newspaper controversy. Emily Fortey, a schoolgirl at Clifton, wrote of her determination to become a Catholic in spite of parental opposition. He advised her to consult the Jesuits where she lived, and his letter found its way into *The Times*. Lord Malmesbury in his *Memoirs* confused Newman with another Oriel tutor and depicted him as tormented by his pupils and helpless. Here Lord Blachford came to his defence, but when Lord Malmesbury took no notice of this, Newman was unwillingly obliged to intervene as well. The issue had its importance because, far from being helpless, Newman had withstood the privileged young aristocrats, and protested against the custom by which those who were living disorderly lives took the Sacrament regularly as a matter of course. In 1884, however, attacks on Newman were the exception. More typical was R. H. Hutton's account of the reception of his lecture on Newman to working men, in January 1884, which showed 'how heartily you are admired and loved and reverenced even among the Protestants of the working class.' When Hutton referred to 'Lead kindly Light', 'there was a perfect thunder of applause'.

In 1882 E. B. Pusey died, and in 1884 after a long illness, Mark Pattison. Newman insisted on paying him a visit at Lincoln College when it was known that he was dying, in the hope of reviving the Christian faith he had lost. After his death, his wife wrote to Newman: 'The Rector spoke to Mrs Pattison in terms of strong feeling of Cardinal Newman's visit to him last January: he recapitulated every little incident of the meeting and turn of the conversation with a keen sense of the real meaning of the effort and deep gratitude for the affection which had prompted it.'

Summary of Events covered by this Volume

22 March	Death of Charles Robert Newman.
May	Newman publishes a 'Postscript' on Inspiration, in reply to John Healy.
30 July	Death of Mark Pattison at Harrogate.
1–5 September	Newman's portrait is painted at the Oratory by Emmeline Deane.
9–10 October	Hon. Charles Lindley Wood (later Lord Halifax) stays at the Oratory.
13 October	Lord Blachford's letter defending Newman against Lord Malmesbury is published in the *Daily News*.

The Letters and Diaries
of
John Henry Newman

Bm Oct 2. 1881

My dear Dr Bloxam,

Thank you, our Library *has* a copy of Palmer's unpublished 'Appeal'.[1]

The pamphlet which is not in your list, is the 'Letter to a Protestant Catholic.' One copy is in our Library, another I have offered to Archdeacon Palmer, and don't know of a third[2]

I had noticed some of your false prints[3]

As I am writing, I would ask you, whether you can tell me the authors of any of the Lives of Saints in Toovey's Series.[4]

Yours affly John H Card. Newman

TO WILLIAM LOCKHART

Birm Oct 2. 1881

My dear Fr Lockhart,

I have been asked who were the authors of the Saints' etc Lives in Toovey's Series. I do not know, and no wonder, as I ceased to be Editor almost at once, though I saw various of them in MS.

Various names are given, and some, even by so accurate a man as Canon Estcourt, wrongly.

Can you help me in answering

St Stephen and St Aelred, St Helier, St Bettelin and others were by Fr Dalgairns[5].

St Richard and his Three children by Fr Meyrick[6]

St Augustine by Canon Oakeley

Was St Gilbert by you?[7]

St Germanus by Fr Coffin?[8]

St Richard of Chichester by whom?[9]

St Wilfrid by Fr Faber

Stephen Langton by Pattison?[10]

[1] Bloxam wrote on 30 Sept. about W. Palmer, 'You are probably aware that he gives a long account of his Russian Expedition in . . . "An Appeal to the Scottish Bishops and Clergy," if you have not the Volume I will gladly send it to you.'

[2] See letter of 2 Aug. to Edwin Palmer.

[3] In the *Magdalen College Register*. See Letter of 28 Sept. to Bloxam.

[4] See next letter. According to S. L. Ollard, 'The Littlemore "Lives of the English Saints,"' *St Edmund Hall Magazine* (1933), p. 82, Newman sent an incomplete list of the authors of the *Lives* to G. R. Adam, Vicar of Shoulden, near Deal, on 31 March 1881. This letter of Newman's was then in Ollard's possession. Francis Joseph Bacchus wished to know the authors of the *Lives*. See letter of 6 Oct. to him.

[5] According to the accurate list drawn up by S. L. Ollard in the *St. Edmund Hall Magazine* (1933), pp. 82–3, these attributions were correct, except that only the verse of St Bettelin was by J. D. Dalgairns, the prose being by Newman. Dalgairns also wrote the lives of St Bartholomew, St Richard of Chichester, Waltheof and Robert of Newminster.

[6] Thomas Meyrick. The attributions of St Augustine and St Wilfrid below are correct.

[7] According to Ollard St Gilbert of Sempringham was by Lockhart, finished by Dalgairns.

[8] This was by J. Walker.

[9] By Dalgairns.

[10] This is correct.

I am writing to Dr Bloxam, he being so skilled an antiquarian, for the chance of his knowing some.

Would Toovey know any?[1]

Who would?

While I am writing, let me know, if you can, whether Mr Kirwan Brown is alive or dead, and, if alive, how he fares. Some one said that he had met him in the street, looking very ill

Yours affly John H Card. Newman

TO THOMAS ALDER POPE

Rednall Oct 5. 1881

My dear Fr Thomas

Thank you for the trouble you have taken. I quite agree with you.

I have no notion what can be the origin of what I never should dream of sanctioning.[2]

From time to time I have cuttings from the Newspapers sent me, with favorable notices of me — and I return civil answers.

What has happened lately in the case of Mr Purcell, brother of the Priest, *may* be at the bottom of it, but I don't think it possible. He said he was putting a Life of me in 'Celebrities of the Day'. It was already printing and he sent a portion of it me in MS. I found it not only inaccurate and fulsome in its praise — but reviving old stories of the opposition made to me by Catholics. I wrote him 'Let by gones be by-gones' — and he sent me the proof of *part* of it with corrections. I let him do so because, since it *was* to appear, I thought it the better alternative that it should appear with certain passages cut out, than as he originally sent it me. When the time of publication came, he sent me the August instalment of it. For what I know, the rest has not been published.[3]

I cannot accuse him of taking so great a liberty with me — and I don't suppose he knows any thing of Messrs Haughton [sic] and Jennings

---

[1] For his list Ollard made use of the letters of the authors of the *Lives* to James Toovey the publisher. The letters are at St Edmund Hall, Oxford.

[2] The reference is to Henry J. Jennings, *Cardinal Newman: The Story of his Life*, Birmingham and London 1882; 2nd edition, same year; new and revised edition 1888. The Birmingham publishers were Houghton and Co., the London Simpkin, Marshall and Co.

Thomas Pope wrote to Newman on 4 Oct. 1881 that he had heard from Kegan Paul about the projected Life, and had discouraged him from publishing it since it would not be of high enough quality, and had not received Newman's approval. On 6 Oct. Jennings wrote to Newman inviting him to read the proofs, ard to 'strike out . . . anything which you think unsuitable, or inadequately put, or of which you in any way disapprove.' Newman's reply is not to be found, but it was evidently a refusal, see letter of 26 Oct. to Houghton and Co., also letter of 13 Dec. 1881 to Gladstone.

[3] It was published in *Celebrities of the Day* (Sept. and Oct.). See letter of 22 June 1881 to Edmund Sheridan Purcell, brother of Arthur Dillon Purcell the priest at Hampstead.

I now recollect that a Birmingham publisher has asked for a photograph of me — and I think means to follow it up with a notice[1]

Yrs affly J. H. Card Newman

TO FRANCIS JOSEPH BACCHUS

Rednall Oct 6. 1881

My dear Joseph

The inclosed is from Dr Bloxam. You may rely on it, as far as it goes. Take a copy for yourself, and give it me back, when I return[2]

Yrs affectly John H. Card. Newman

TO WILLIAM NEVILLE

Oct 6/81

My dear W

Unless it rains badly I should like the brougham to come out for me tomorrow (Friday) morning.

I said Mass for you today instead of the 29th

I grieve you should be ill. The inclosed for Joseph

Yrs affly J H Card N.

TO EMILY BOWLES

Birmingham Oct 9. 1881

My dear Child

I was much disappointed to find that an arrangement, which seemed so natural and desirable for you, had been impossible — but is it really so? it seems too suitable not to revive.[3]

I think it must have been while you were here, that the MS of Hope Scott's Life came to me. It has been done with great care, and brings out H S's character very strikingly.

Since then I have taken up W. Palmer's papers, and have found them most interesting. He was very kindly received at Peterburg, but from the climate, gout, his fare, and his lodgings he went through a good deal.

[1] See letter of 31 March 1881 to Messrs Houghton and Hammond. The photograph was later used in Jennings's *Cardinal Newman*. See letter of 5 Nov. to the Editor of the *Birmingham Daily Gazette*.
[2] This was Bloxam's list of authors of *Lives of the English Saints*. See letters of 2 Oct. Bacchus's copy is at the Birmingham Oratory. Bloxam's is at Magdalen College, Bloxam Papers I, 517. Magd. MSS. 304.
[3] This was a plan that Emily Bowles should live with one of her brothers. She gave up her work at the Oratory School in July 1881, on which occasion Newman sent her to the Birmingham station in his own carriage and followed later with Neville, to see her off.

What took me by surprise was that a year *before* Number 90, and a year and a half before I knew him, he wrote a Latin Dissertation on the Articles with the same drift as Number 90, to take to Russia with him, and showed it to the President of Magdalen.[1] The Row about Number 90 took place when he had been some six months in Russia, as if purposely intended to undo his attempt to prove that the Anglican Church was sufficiently near the Greek Church to allow the priests of the latter to give him Communion.

I should think the narrative would interest various circles of readers[2]

Yours affectly John H Card. Newman

TO EDWIN PALMER

The Oratory Octr 9. 1881

My dear Archdeacon Palmer,

Your most welcome present came quite right. The books are as useful as they are handsome to look upon.[3]

I shall send you the duplicate pamphlets, if you do not hinder me.[4] I have *got into* your brother's journals, and they are most interesting, not only from the exact account they give of the state of the Russian Church, but to me they come home intimately as finding I was unconsciously defeating all he was doing, or wishing to do, in Petersburg. He went there with his Dissertation on the 39 Articles[5] in August 1840, and just when he had succeeded in creating a great sensation, I came out in February 1841 with Number 90, undoing by the fierce opposition it elicited what he was labouring after in his conversations with the Greek ecclesiastics.

Yet I cannot help thinking he did a real work there. He introduced among them the idea and the desirableness of Unity, and made them understand that the action of the Anglican establishment was not the measure of the Catholic religious feeling in this country.

And I wonder at his spirit. He was certainly most kindly received, and so far had not the trials of a missionary — but his lodgings and fare, the climate, his gout, his wearisome use of two languages not his own, and that in difficult controversy, and his great patience, which all who personally knew him, must discern in exercise throughout his narrative, make me think of him with great admiration.

Is Mr Blackmore alive? If so, I should like to write to him.[6]

Very sincerely Yours John H. Card. Newman

---

[1] See next letter. Martin Routh was the President of Magdalen College.
[2] i.e. *Notes of a Visit to the Russian Church.*
[3] See letter of 27 Aug. to Palmer.
[4] See letter of 1 Sept. to Palmer.
[5] *In XXXIX Articulos.* See letter of 2 Aug. to Palmer.
[6] See last note to letter of 29 July to Palmer and letter of 16 Dec. 1881 to R. W. Blackmore.

TO GEORGE GILBERT SCOTT

Bm Oct 9. 1884

My dear Mr Scott

I fear we have given you a great deal of trouble about [our] apse[1] but I hope that[2]

when we came

your design, that it made the slab of the Altar come forward far more than it does at present; this would involve the throwing the Predella forward, and this would involve moving the *altar rails* forward which we could not do. Hence we have been making trial after trial how we could select such portion of the whole design, as would not require this impossibility, yet not exceed our

quite lately

slicing of[f]

the front of the slab and throwing the front of the altar back by the same number of inches, will obviate the difficulty, yet not interfere with your design.

It follows, that, with many thanks for the trouble to which you have put yourself for us, we are enabled to use your plans at once, without going out of our way to trouble you more

Very faithfully Yours John H Card Newman

TO THOMAS SCRATTON

Birmingham Oct. 9. 1881

My dear Scratton

Your letter has so seriously perplexed and pained me, that I have delayed answering from my difficulty in doing so.[3]

Neither Ornsby nor Stewart has asked me in their own case for a letter such as that which you desire, and since I have not done so in their behalf, I do not see I can act differently as regards others under like circumstances.

Then again the Classics have been their Province so long, that to contemplate others as Professors in that Province seems unfair to them.

And then again what can I say that Lord O'Hagan does not know? He knows that you are an Oxford man and about your claims far better than I can, considering I have been from Dublin above 20 years.

---

[1] See letter of 17 July to Scott.
[2] The autograph has been damaged and in two places about a line and a half are illegible.
[3] The rest of this letter shows that Scratton wanted Newman to recommend him to Lord O'Hagan, one of the Senators of the new Royal University of Ireland, for a Professorship in Classics. cf. letter to Scratton placed at beginning of June 1880.

And indeed I know not what Professorships are to be given away, what are still open, or what qualifications they require, and what I can say which will really be to the purpose, as regards a particular Professorship

I hope you will see from that I have said, that I could not without impropriety address Lord O'Hagan as you wish

Very truly Yours John H. Card. Newman[1]

Thos Scratton Esqr

TO AN UNKNOWN CORRESPONDENT

The Oratory Bm Oct 12. 1881

Dear Sir

I beg to say, in answer to your question, that I made no personal allusion when I spoke of Phaeton and the Sun.

By Phaeton I meant liberalism in Religion — by the Sun the Secular Power, the National Government viewed in its Action.[2]

Your faithful Servant John H. Card. Newman

TO SISTER MARY GABRIEL DU BOULAY

The Oratory Octr. 15. 1881

My dear Sister M.G.

I have just received your bewildering news.[3]

How wonderful are the way of God! — Mother Margaret's lingering death, and her dear Successor's abrupt removal!

We all send you our heartfelt sorrow, and affectionate condolements and commiserations on so overpowering an affliction.

May God be with us all, and make as fit, as she was, to meet his sudden call!

Many prayers will be said for her from all in this place. I trust to say Mass for her, and for all of you tomorrow morning.

[1] Ornsby wrote to Newman on 23 April 1882, 'I don't know whether you have heard from Scratton. He is *sadly cut up* about his being passed over in the recent election in which he was a Candidate for a Fellowship in the Department of English. Perhaps a line from your Eminence would be a comfort to him, only please don't let it appear that I hinted this.' In Nov. 1882 Newman interceded with Cardinal MacCabe on behalf of Scratton, who wrote on 21 Nov. 1882 to Newman: 'I am very grateful to you for your kind letter and thank you heartily for it. In my present gloom and depression, it has given me no little consolation . . .' In 1885 Scratton sued the Irish bishops and was awarded £300 compensation for dismissal from his post as Secretary to the Catholic University. See letter of 5 Nov. 1885 to him.
[2] After describing R. D. Hampden's pamphlet of Nov. 1834 *Observations on Religious Dissent* . . . in which 'the Trinitarian doctrine' was a 'Theological Opinion' and not to be identified 'with the simple religion of Christ', Newman added, *Apo.* p. 58, 'Since that time Phaeton has got into the chariot of the sun; we, alas! can only look on, and watch him down the steep of heaven. Meanwhile, the lands, which he is passing over, suffer from his driving.'
[3] Mary Imelda Poole, Provincial of the English Dominican nuns died at their Torquay convent on 14 Oct.

Only this very day, I have had occasion to write to her on a matter of business. I shall keep the letter back for some days.[1]

Yours affectly John H. Card. Newman

The Oratory Oct. 16. 1881

My dear Mother Prioress

Yesterday I heard from Sister M. Gabriel your immense trial. But He who is immensity itself will enable you to bear it, and will turn it to good. And, while your hearts are torn, you will feel (I speak from keen experience) that you would not have it otherwise. God prepares us all for that Day, which must come for every one of us, whether suddenly or with warning, whether soon or late.

I said Mass this morning for dear Sister Imilda, and for all of you

Yours affectly in our Lord John H Card. Newman

Birmingham Oct 17. 1881

Cardinal Newman requests Sign. Liverziani to send him, as before, the Christmas letters to be sent to Sovereigns and Cardinals, with the envelopes and addresses, as soon as possible. They were not written so clearly and neatly last year, as they ought to have been.[2]

Birmingham Octr 20. 1881

My dear John,

I am anything but a politician, whether in grasp of principles or knowledge of facts. As to Ireland, judging by what I saw in Ireland 20 years ago, the question between the countries is not one of land or property, but of *union*.

Cromwell and others have, by their conduct to the Irish, burned into the national heart a deep hatred of England, and, if the population perseveres, the sentiment of patriotism and the latent sense of historical wrongs will hinder even the more rational, and calm judging, the most friendly to England, from separating themselves from their countrymen. They are abundantly warmhearted and friendly to individual Englishmen, of that I have clear

[1] On 20 Oct. Sister Mary Gabriel asked Newman to send his letter. See that of 27 Oct. to Augusta Theodosia Drane.
[2] For these letters see at 25 Nov. 1879, 1880, and later. On 12 Sept. Liverziani sent drafts for Newman's approval, addressed to sixty Cardinals and nine royal persons, but not the King of Rumania, nor the King of the Belgians with whom diplomatic relations had not been restored.

experience in my own case, but what I believe, though I have no large experience to appeal to, is, that there is not one *Anglo-philist* in the nation.

Observe, Gladstone the other day at Leeds complained of the little support given him by the middle class and gentry in Ireland. I think it was at the time of the Fenian rising that the Times had an article to the same effect. (Gladstone seemed to think them cowards; no, they are patriots.)[1]

I knew, when in Ireland, one of the leaders of the Smith O'Brien movement in 1848:[2] his boast was that from Henry ii's time, the people had *never* condoned the English occupation. They by a succession of risings, from then till now, protested against it.

Our rule has been marked by a persistent forcing on them English usages. Such, I suppose, was our law of property, founded on the feudal system, instead of their own communism.

About this I know very little. What I do know is the stupid forcing on their catholicism our godless education. Since 1845 all English parties have been resolved that primary education and University education in Ireland should be without religion, except that ... the Bible without comment, should be allowed in the primary — .....[3] But to conclude. We are suffering partly for 'delicta majorum', partly for our own. Is it too late, *for one thing*, to give Ireland a Catholic University?

Yrs afftly J H Card. Newman.

Recollect Belgium, Greece, Hungary, Bulgaria, Lombardy; all have got free in my lifetime. Please always write to your discretion.[4]

TO THOMAS MOZLEY

The Oratory Bm Oct. 21. 1881

My dear Tom

I am sure no one is in a better position to write an account of the Oxford Movement than yourself.[5] Perhaps you know that Copeland has long been

[1] In his speech at Leeds on 7 Oct. Gladstone complained of 'the incapacity of the healthier portion of society in Ireland to do anything whatever for themselves', and accused them of cowardice in not supporting the law. *The Times* (8 Oct.), p. 7. He was defending his Land Act, and denounced Parnell, who still encouraged agrarian violence, and who was imprisoned a week later.

[2] Charles Gavan Duffy.

[3] First about half a dozen and then about twenty words were erased here by J. R. Mozley who made a note as to this letter and those which follow, of 24 Oct. and 3 Nov., which explains the omissions:

'The three preceding letters were written in the most excited period of the Irish Home Rule agitation, and I wished my uncle to allow them to be published at the time. He did in the end refuse his consent; but he seriously thought of giving permission; and as well as I can judge, he would have wished the general bearing of their contents to be known, but he felt that the verification of all the details, at his age, was too much for him. Before deciding against publication, he had directed that a few words in the first letter should be crossed out; and I think I am acting in accordance with his wishes in crossing them out now.' Mozley added that Newman 'was a little sensitive as to the style of the letters; but it will be obvious that they were written without any view *to publication.*'

[4] J. R. Mozley made a note on his copy of this letter, 'These last words are difficult to read, and I am not quite sure of their purport.'

[5] Mozley wrote on 20 Oct. from 7 Lansdown Terrace, Cheltenham: 'I am writing "Reminiscences of Oriel College, and of the Oxford Movement," and the MS nearly complete is in

collecting materials with the same purpose, but I think he would rather aim at a documentary history (if even a writer's self can prophesy the outcome of his intentions) whereas yours would be the narrative of your own experience. Few men could bring to the work such literary power, such observation such a command of detail, such memory as yourself. I think you are likely to be caustic, and wanting in tenderness — (I am not thinking of myself, for I have full confidence in your affection for me, but of such as Blanco White and Tony Buller, (supposing him alive)) and what I *fear* is *controversy*[1] Recollect how very sore people may be on points one least suspects — For instance, as to Sidney Herbert — his widow is still alive, and, as I cannot guess what you are to say of him, so you cannot guess what will afflict his near relatives.[2]

The only exception I observe to my above remark about your writing from *experience*, is your first chapter, 'Newman, London and Trinity.' What can you know of me accurately before 1825–6?

I welcome with great pleasure and full trust your anticipation that as to your *whole* work 'I shall find your intention kind and the result at least harmless.' I know how very interesting your book will be, but you are so powerful a writer that against your wish your little finger can wound.

I hope I have said nothing to trouble you

Yours affectionately John H Card. Newman

TO ARTHUR WOLLASTON HUTTON [?]

Oct 24/81[3]

I was much surprised and frightened to see that proposed additions would amount to £2000 even as the Architect calculated the cost, which at the very least would be £2500.

Then, I asked myself who is to pay, if there is any money to be borrowed or debt? The property is ours; ours will be the responsibility of the addition.

Longman's hands.' Mozley began in the Spring and his work had grown from one volume to two. 'I need not say that you are inevitably the most prominent, and central figure in it. Now I know that you have perfect confidence in my affection, and some confidence in my truth and justice; but you certainly have good reason not to repose too confidently in my discretion So I have only to say that I feel very sure there is not a line, or a word to give you pain. The work is exceedingly miscellaneous, as you will see from the List of Chapters I enclose. As I have been writing for the Times more than usually since I began the book, and my eye sight does not allow of long spells of writing or reading even by candle light, I have not been able to consult books, and a large pile lies beside me wholly un-utilized. In truth, as you must long have been aware, I am no theologian.' Longman was printing from the manuscript, without sending proofs. 'The work has been a growing pleasure to me, perhaps because it did not ever strain my mind, running out into circumstances and trifles. Some of the headings will startle you, but you will find my intention kind, and the result at least harmless.' See letter of 9 June 1882 to T. Mozley for Newman's remarks on reading *Reminiscences chiefly of Oriel College and the Oxford Movement*, London 1882.

[1] Anthony Buller died on 13 Aug. 1881. Chapter LXXXVIII was devoted to him, and Chapter VII to Blanco White.
[2] Sidney Herbert appeared in Chapter XCVI. His widow was Lady Herbert of Lea.
[3] This was perhaps a memorandum for Arthur Hutton, who was proposing to build on a Middle School for older children to the Oratory parish schools. He had been given permission on this day by the Oratorian Community to do so, and to collect funds for the purpose.

Then if we are to spend a large sum, the Oratory School, and the Oratorium Parvum have more claims than a middle school.

Then again I should have liked to have had a voice in determining the architect of a work which would require so great an outlay[1]

J H N.

TO JOHN RICKARDS MOZLEY

Bm Oct 24/81

My dear John

If I did not write to you at once, perhaps I should not write to you for a month.

I am no politician. I have long thought that the Irish would gain Home Rule in some shape, and that both because of the issue of the series of past conflicts with Great Britain, which seems to portend it, and because of Greece, Belgium, Lombardy, Hungary, and Bulgaria. But I am no advocate for such issue, rather it seems to me a blow on the power of England as great as it is retributive

As to the University question; it opens a question larger than itself. Why has not England acted towards Ireland as it has treated Scotland? Scotland had its own religion, and, after a short time the attempt to impose Episcopacy on it was given up, and so indulgent has been England to Scotland, that even the Queen, the head of the Anglican Church, goes to Kirk and listens to Presbyterian preachers. On the contrary, not only great sums have been poured through centuries into Ireland from England by the state and by the people, to force Protestantism on the Irish, but there were the persecuting laws, of which I say nothing because the question you have asked is one of property. The Irish people consider the sums which the Anglo-Irish Establishment took year by year from the Irish population, as the property of their own Church, which Church was proscribed by English law. In asking back a small portion of these confiscations (I think one or two of the Anglican Irish Archbishops in my day left behind them towards 500,000 apiece on their death)[2] they have not acted unreasonably. The sums given for Protestant education were as prodigious as those for religion.

Now what was done as regards the University. First Peel set up his godless colleges, aided by public yearly grants, I am almost sure, or quite sure. Then our Bishops set up in opposition their University — not at once, but after it had been much and long discussed both in Catholic Ireland and at Rome. We were obliged to raise £5000 a year from the peasantry, and this

---

[1] The architect was Mr Naden. In the following month the advice of two other architects was sought. See letter of 21 Nov. to Hutton.

[2] See letter of 20 Oct. with J. R. Mozley's note on this correspondence. About the present letter he adds: 'I have retained the parenthesis in the second of the three letters, which he would not have published in any case *at that time*, but still thought a matter of interest and importance, and one that deserved investigation.'

we did for 20 years! There was no cry for money from us then. All we asked, and what we could not get, little as it was, was the power of granting degrees. No — we were not even to have a *fair stage*. At length the Irish took, in defence of the peasantry to ask for *money*.

By a Catholic University I mean one in which the *officers* and Teachers are Catholics. And I demand it for Ireland because the country is Catholic. This would be secured by the Bishops having a *Veto* on appointments.

Yrs afftely J.H.N.

TO HENRY BITTLESTON

Bm Oct 26/81

My dear Henry

I meant long before this to thank you for your kind congratulations. Thank you very much for your Masses.

Fr Bampfield, I fear, [has] been forced to retire from Kelvedon, by your writing from Barnet.[1] This is true wisdom tho' it is so difficult to practise, when the Sacrifice is great, but it only becomes a greater sacrifice, when delayed. I do not know whether you were acquainted with a great friend and pupil of mine T. Stevens who set up the school at Bradfield, about the same time as Sewell set up Radley. Sewell, you know, failed — and now St. is bankrupt, his debts being £100.000. There is something very piteous in such being the issue of a generous and munificent undertaking.[2]

I forget whether you know that W. Palmer left me all his papers and I am trying to put into shape a volume relating his adventures in Russia

I hope you are fairly well

Yours affectly John H Card. Newman

TO MESSRS HOUGHTON AND CO.

The Oratory, Oct. 26, 1881[3]

Private

Cardinal Newman presents his compliments to Messrs Houghton and Co, and thanks them for the interest in him which is implied in their proposing to publish a Life of him, and the considerate and courteous language in which they communicate with him on the subject. He is sure that the memoir is written carefully and conscientiously, and kindly towards him; but every narrative is made up of details; and at the present time it is as impossible that details, whether statements and assumptions of fact, or the inevitable

[1] Bittleston was assisting George Bampfield, the priest at Barnet. Bampfield tried to establish a boarding school at Kelvedon.
[2] See letter of 17 July 1881 to Anne Mozley.
[3] The date is that on the letter as sent to the *Birmingham Daily Gazette* (8 Nov.), the rest of the letter is taken from Newman's draft.

colouring of the whole, should be exact, as it is certain that they may be impartial and friendly to him, as he believes they will be.

The Cardinal then cannot directly or indirectly make himself responsible for the work. As he said in a former letter, the time has not come for a Memoir of him. He is very sorry for the necessity of declining, but he is obliged to return to this second proposal, as he returned to the first, a distinct negative.[1]

JHN

TO HENRIETTA WOODGATE

The Oratory Octr 26. 1881

My dear Child

I shall be very glad to see you, as you propose, on Thursday about 3.

Yours affectly John H. Card. Newman

TO AUGUSTA THEODOSIA DRANE

The Oratory Octr 27. 1881

My dear Mother Prioress

It is thirty years today since the Achilli process began — a day which brings before me how much I owed then to dear Mother Margaret and all of you.

And now, though I did not mean to throw upon you the necessity of your doing a new kindness to me, I consider your kindness to Dr Neve such an act — for 'justice' does not, as his sisters think, come into it.[2] I told them in the letter I wrote that in thirty years bodies are no longer made up of the same members, and that nothing could be claimed of them as a right, but what was formally committed to writing. Indeed, I did not know the Sisters of Penance had any part in the Clifton convent now, and did not introduce their name into my letter, thinking that the Miss Neves ought to apply to the present occupiers of the Convent. And even now I don't know why I

[1] See letter of 5 Oct. to T. A. Pope and first note there. On 25 Oct. Messrs Houghton wrote asking Newman to read the proofs of Henry Jennings's life. Messrs Houghton published this letter of Newman's omitting the final paragraph. See letter of 4 Nov. to the Editor of the *Birminghan Daily Gazette.*
[2] Frederick Robert Neve's health had broken down and he suffered from loss of memory. He had retired into lodgings at Clifton, with an attendant to look after him. His sisters wrote to Newman on 13 Oct. that he had contributed to the building of the Dominican nuns' convent at Clifton, now the property of the Bishop and occupied by Franciscans, with the promise that if he were infirm the nuns would take care of him. This was the matter mentioned at the end of Newman's letter of 15 Oct. to Sister Mary Gabriel. He wrote about it on 25 Oct. to Augusta Drane, who replied next day that Neve was simply a benefactor to whom no promise had been made. The nuns, howover, had always felt and said they were in duty bound to take care of him in old age. They had offered to take him into one of their convents, but he preferred to live in lodgings. When a fund was being got together for his support, they asked how much they should contribute and Neve had replied '£30'. This they gave, promising that if necessary they would gladly give more to one they so loved and respected. They now promised him £50 a year for life, which more than represented his original benefaction. Neve's sisters, who were well off, appear to have contributed £10 a year.

should not write to them (the occupants) in Miss N's name, except that you by your letter to Dr Neve have anticipated my so acting.

You may be sure that in the letter which I shall now write to Miss Neve, I shall explain to her your generosity.

I have been going to ask you ever since dear Mother Provincial was taken away, whether I might come and say Mass some morning for her and all of you in your Church, If you let me, I must come in my own way, and should not take a bed at the priest's house, but come to you in the morning. But the difficulty is naming the day. I don't know what days your rule allows as black days, and then if on the day appointed the weather should be very bad[1]

Yours affectly in Xt   John H Card. Newman

TO HENRIETTA WOODGATE

Bm Oct. 28/81

My dear Child

I hope you understood me yesterday to say, that I should be *very sorry* that you did not write to me, if you were led to wish to do so at any time

Yrs very affly J H Card. Newman

TO HENRY WILLIAMS MOZLEY

The Oratory Oct 29. 1881

My dear Harry

Private

My question will make you smile. We have lost our birch-maker. Can you tell me of any one we can go to?[2]

Yrs affectly John H Card. Newman

TO MISS M. R. GIBERNE

The Oratory Octr 31. 1881

My dear Sister Pia

Thank you for your remembrance of me on the 9th. This will come to you when the All Saints Octave has begun, when I was confirmed. This year it has a special object of interest, for tomorrow is the last day of a Novena for the Duke's intention who is now at Lourdes with his little boy.[3]

We were glad to see M. Antoine, but some how he did not understand my English, for I took him expressly to my little chapel in order he might

---

[1] See letter of 3 Nov. to Augusta Drane.
[2] H. W. Mozley was a Housemaster at Eton. See letter of 3 Nov. to him.
[3] The mentally retarded Earl of Arundel was now two years old. Newman was confirmed at Oscott College on 1 Nov. 1845.

see and might report to you how nice your life of St Francis looked — but he came into the chapel kept silence, turned round, and went away. Yet *after* that Fr William too spoke to him about the pictures. I think he was in a fit of absence.

It is the same confusion of mind which has made him report to you that I 'complain that you do not tell me about your actual state of health.' I really do think he has fallen back in his knowledge of English, if I have not in mine. I thought you had most kindly told me more about yourself than I could have expected.

I think you must forget, for I have always associated your name Rosina with Rose, and, at least often, have said Mass for you on that day.[1]

Ornsby was a fellow of Trinity, brother in law to Fr Dalgairns, and for nearly 30 years one of my Dublin appointments. He has published a good deal, and was editor after me of the University Gazette. What can you mean by asking whether Hurrell Froude wrote Mr Hope Scott's life? Hurrell died in 1836, Hope Scott in 1873.

You really must not neglect what you say about that local ailment. You really should go by the advice of a good doctor. What you say makes me anxious.

I am grieved at what I hear about a pupil of mine whom I suppose you did not know, Thomas Stevens. He was a man of some landed property, and in a generous way, some 25 or 30 years ago, about the same time as Sewell at Radly[,] founded a school, which seemed to prosper. Various youths we knew were there — as the young Froudes. He has failed, I am told, with a debt of £100,000; and all his property has gone. Is not this melancholy[2]

The youngest Miss Poole, the successor of Mother Margaret has died almost suddenly

Ever Yrs affly J H Card. Newman

TO LOUISA ELIZABETH DEANE

The Oratory, Birm Nov 2. 1881

My dear Louisa

It pleased me very much to get your letter, which was the fulfilment of a sort of promise you made me. You give a very good account of your husband, to whom I send my kindest remembrances. For yourself, I trust your handwriting may be taken as a token how well you are. Generally *I* cannot write at all, because I have not the command of my muscles. For the same reason I find it difficult to go up and down stairs — Also I am weak — but though I fail in strength, I have nothing to complain of in point of health; and

---

[1] Cf. letter of 30 Aug. 1881 to Miss Giberne.
[2] See letter of 17 July 1881 to Anne Mozley.

cannot say I have any thing the matter with me. I say all this because you seem to wish it.

I should think Dr Lee would be much pleased to have your application for a second copy of that pedigree.[1] But, if you wish me, I should have no difficulty in writing to him for you myself — and indeed, should be pleased to have the excuse. I don't know him well, but he has in many ways shown me kindness. Perhaps you know that his wife and son are Catholics.

T. Mozley told me some ten days ago that he was publishing his Reminiscences of Oxford.[2] That it will be a very clever book, very interesting, and very kind to me, as far as I have a place in it, I know well — but it is a bold thing to do. I saw him in London in the summer — and thought he looked older — but his eyes are much better than he feared.

To have charge of the Shah seems to me an important post, and one of great trust, but that, in spite of its anxieties, is just what a professional man likes.[3]

Millais has been exhibiting his picture of me in Bond Street, but now it is with the engraver.

Ever yours affectly J. H. Card Newman

TO AUGUSTA THEODOSIA DRANE

Birmingham Nov. 3. 1881

My dear Mother Prioress

Unless it is foggy, I propose to come to Stone this day week, the 10th, with a father from this place. I understand you to say that the 10th is an open day. I suppose you have *purple* vestments. A Cardinal does not wear black

I mean to arrive at 9.25 and to depart at 2.29 or 3.14[4]

Yours affectly in Xt   J. H. Card. Newman

---

[1] *Pedigrees of the Family of Withie, together with that of Fourdrinier in alliance with Grolleau.* See letter of 4 Aug. 1880 to F. G. Lee.

[2] See letter of 21 Oct. to T. Mozley.

[3] This probably refers to a son or a son-in-law of Mrs Deane. The Shah visited England in 1873 and 1889, but at this period Russian influence was strong in Persia.

[4] Newman went to Stone on 10 Nov. and said Mass for Imelda Poole. An account preserved there describes how, 'After his breakfast, he came to the Community Room, and spoke to us in the most beautiful and touching way, of the *joy* we ought to have in the midst of our bereavement . . .

After dinner the Cardinal asked to be taken to the Choir that he might pray by Mother Margaret's and Mother Imelda's graves — He knelt by them for some time in silent prayer, evidently deeply moved. There was a most wonderful hush and silence all the time: no sound indoors or out, but a profound stillness. It was a dull grey morning; but as we knelt there one clear bright ray of sunshine suddenly darted thro' the casement and fell directly on the grave of our dearest Mother Imelda. The effect of *that silence*, and that sudden *ray of light* was something impossible to describe.

When he came away he said to Mother F. Raphael "I would not have missed this for the world."'

See also *A Memoir of Mother Francis Raphael*, edited by Bertrand Wilberforce, O.P., second edition, London 1897, pp. 111–13, where Newman's Address is given.

TO HENRY WILLIAMS MOZLEY

Bm Nov 3. 1881

My dear Harry

I am very glad to find by your post card that I am not acting improperly in getting you to tamper in my behalf with your Head Master's Servant.

I inclose a P.O.O. [Post Office Order] for £1. and shall be glad to receive from him the precious freight which it purchases[1]

Yours affly J H Card. Newman

Turn over

P.S. The inclosed letter has just come. I suppose it is apropos of my inquiries for a tenant for the Palace at Eccleshall, about which you wrote to me some time back. It comes late in the day. I don't know the writer.[2]

I have had the kind present of a graceful Latin translation of 'Lead Kindly Light' from 'H. Broadbent   Eton' do you know him?[3]

TO JOHN RICKARDS MOZLEY

Bm Nov 3. 1881.

My dear John,

I send you back the Fortnightly. Mr Lathbury's article is a very interesting one.[4] It always makes me wonder that Liberals don't see the contrast of our treatment of Ireland with our treatment of Scotland. I should be indignant did I not suspect they *did* see it, but did not like to confess their *dread* of the *power* of the Catholic Religion. Of the 'power' — we Catholics say of the 'divinity'. Education is the great point. Englishmen allow children to be Anglicans, Baptists, Wesleyans, Presbyterians, Unitarians; not, if they can help it, Catholics.

This is what the Irish Bishops had in mind, when in their late Manifesto they spoke of the Land Act only as an *instalment* of what was due to Ireland.[5]

Yrs afftly J. H. Card. Newman.

Excuse my writing: my fingers are getting so stiff.

[1] See letter of 28 Oct. to H. Mozley.
[2] There is a ruined palace of the bishops of Lichfield at Eccleshall. See letter of 27 Nov. to H. W. Mozley.
[3] Henry Broadbent, Scholar and then Fellow of Exeter College, Oxford, in 1874, when he took a First in Classics, was an assistant master at Eton, 1876–1919.
[4] D. C. Lathbury, in 'Radicals and Irish Ideas', the *Fortnightly Review* (Sept. 1881), pp. 271–83, first pointed out how differently from Scotland England had treated Ireland, but then went on to object to Gladstone's Land Act as interfering with the property rights of landlords.
[5] At a meeting at Maynooth on 28 Sept. the Irish bishops pronounced that the Land Act was 'a great benefit to the tenant class and a large instalment of justice, for which the gratitude of the country is due to Mr. Gladstone . . .'

TO THOMAS ISAAC BALL

Birmingham Nov. 5. 1881
Dear Sir
I have pleasure in giving you permission to insert 'Lead, Kindly Light' in your Hymnal, on condition that you take the text from my own edition of it, as published by Burns and Oates.[1]
I am not the translator of the Collects in the Horæ Canonicæ of 1841[2]
I am, Yours very truly J. H. Card. Newman
The Revd T. I. Ball

TO THE EDITOR OF THE BIRMINGHAM DAILY GAZETTE

Nov. 5. 1881
The Editor of the Bm Gazette
52 High Street Bm
Cardinal Newman presents his compliments to the Editor of the Daily Gazette, and shall be obliged by his inserting in his Paper the enclosed paragraph
The Memoir of Cardinal Newman. — We are authorised to state that Cardinal Newman has not seen any portion whatever of the memoir of him about to be published by Messrs Houghton and Co., not even a single line of it, nor anyone deputed by him; and, when asked to inspect it by them he expressly declined to do so. Neither has he given any photograph of himself, or fac-simile of his handwriting, with a view to any memoir.[3]

TO MATTHEW RUSSELL, S.J.

Birmingham Nov. 6. 1881
Dear Fr Russell
Your letter, as all that you write to me, is full of kind feeling towards me. What you tell me of Mrs O'Hagan is of a like character, and touches me nearly.[4]

[1] Ball was preparing a *Supplement to The Hymnal Noted*, Edinburgh 1882.

[2] A translation of the Roman Breviary was begun by F. S. Wood and Robert Williams in 1838. Part of it was printed, but it was not published, owing to the opposition of some of the Tractarians.

[3] This was printed in the *Birmingham Daily Gazette* (7 Nov.), which on 4 Nov. contained an announcement, sent to the newspapers by Messrs Houghton, that they were about to publish a biography of Newman by H. J. Jennings, which would contain a photo 'for which the Cardinal has recently given a special sitting.' Further 'The Cardinal, having seen early proof sheets of the work, pronounces the memoir to be written in a careful, conscientious, and impartial manner, and at the same time thanks the publishers "for the interest in him which is shown in their proposition to publish a life of him."' See letter of 26 Oct. to Messrs Houghton, and as to the portrait, third note to letter of 5 Oct. to T. A. Pope.
On 4 Nov. Newman received a letter from W. J. Rivington urging the importance of contradicting Messrs Houghton's statement, to which they were giving a wide circulation. See letters of 8 and 12 Nov.

[4] Russell wrote on 4 Nov. that 'Mrs O'Hagan urged me to make any preparation I could for some short memoir of my Uncle [Charles Russell]; and she said I ought to enquire if any extracts could be made for this purpose from his correspondence with the man whom he loved and esteemed the most.'

Of course the Judge is much in my thoughts just now — I hope his health will stand what must be a trial soul and body, but he is in a position as singular and rare, as it is high.[1] All judges are, to use St Paul's word, 'ministers of God,'[2] but he, as being brought forward on so great and critical an occasion, is especially and emphatically the dispenser of at once justice and mercy. I pray God that the measure of which he is the representative, may issue in a large blessing to Ireland.

Dr Russell was never a correspondent of mine — though every now and then letters passed between us. His letters were generally to the effect that he was coming to England, or passing near Birmingham on a certain day, and could I give him a night's lodging? which I was very glad to do. On these occasions we conversed together for long hours — this superseded correspondence.

I send you his three last letters to me; also your own on his death. My eyes are so bad, that I am more surprised that I have been able to put my hands on these, than that I have not yet found Judge O'Hagan's.[3]

Very sincerely Yours John H Card. Newman

The Revd Fr Russell S J

TO PUBLISHERS

[8? November 1881][4]

For publishers
Sir

I think it will be found that Messrs Houghton have published only part

[1] See letter of 26 July to O'Hagan.
[2] *Romans* 13:4.
[3] Charles Russell died on 26 Feb. 1880 in the house of John O'Hagan, who sent Newman a description of his last days.
[4] On 4 Nov. W. J. Rivington, now a partner in the publishers Sampson Low and Co., wrote to Newman: 'In consequence of the long connection that my father and myself have had with yourself in the printing business at St. John's Square I do not hesitate to draw your attention to an announcement which is being sent to various papers and which I feel certain is quite untrue.' This was Houghton's statement about the Newman biography. A few weeks earlier Houghton had told Rivington that Newman had undertaken to revise it, but when challenged admitted that this was not the case. Rivington continued: 'to-day we have received the enclosed MS. announcement for insertion in the Publisher's Circular which we publish, and which I feel certain has no foundation. The printed similar announcement has been sent to a friend of mine Editor of another paper . . . I think if there is no more foundation for Messrs: Houghton's statements than I believe there is, some steps should be taken to stop the wide circulation that they are attempting to give to them.'
Newman replied confirming Rivington's suspicions, and the latter wrote on 7 Nov., 'You ask my opinion as to whether you should write to the London Press. No doubt your feeling would be that it is well to treat such a matter with contempt, and not to allow it to gain an importance which otherwise it would not have by taking notice of it.
But unfortunately if the statement Messrs: Houghton have spread so widely should be uncontradicted, and the Life be received as one revised and acknowledged as authentic by yourself, there may be some serious errors and mis-statements in it that may go down as having your authority.' Rivington recommended that Newman should send two or three lines in contradiction to *The Times*.

of Cardinal Newman's letter to them, and that, as it went to them from him, it ran as follows —

'Cardinal Newman etc' overleaf.[1]

TO JOHN HUNGERFORD POLLEN

Nov. 8 1881

My dear Pollen

As I can't make out how to direct my letter to your friend, I must trouble you to send it on to him. I inclose it.

My love to Antony [Pollen]. I hope he gives satisfaction.

Yrs affly J H Card. Newman

TO THE EDITOR OF THE ACADEMY

Birmingham Nov 12. 1881

for publication

Sir,

With regard to Messrs Houghton's Memoir of me, noticed in yours to-day and Monday, I beg to state that I have not read a line of it, and therefore can 'pronounce' nothing about it. This is not inconsistent with my having spoken kindly of the writer of it.

I am, Sir, Your obedient Servant, John H. Card. Newman[2]

TO THE EDITOR OF THE ATHENAEUM

Birmingham Nov. 12. 1881

Sir[3]

With reference to an announcement in today's *Athenaeum*, I beg to state that I know nothing whatever of Messrs Houghton's biography of me, and that when they asked me to read the proof sheets I refused, saying that the time for a biography of me had not come, though as regards the author, I did not doubt, that he would do his work conscientiously and impartially.

I am your obt Servt[4]

John H. Card. Newman

[1] Overleaf was a copy of Newman's letter of 26 Oct. to Messrs Houghton and Co. The *Birmingham Daily Gazette* (8 Nov.) published two letters, one from H. J. Jennings: 'Permit me to say that I am in no way responsible for the statement contained in your issue of the 4th inst., to the effect that Cardinal Newman had read and approved advance proofs of my forthcoming life of his Eminence.' The other from Houghton and Co. repeating their claim and requoting Newman's letter of 26 Oct., but again omitting its final paragraph.

There exists a letter in Neville's hand, intended for the *Tablet*, and probably drawn up by Newman, calling attention to this omission.

[2] Newman sent a covering note: '*private* Birmingham Nov. 14. 1881

Cardinal Newman presents his compliments to the Editor of the Academy, and begs the favour of the insertion in his columns of the inclosed letter.'

The letter appeared in the *Academy* (19 Nov.), p. 385.

[3] This word is in the draft only.

[4] These five words are in the draft only. Newman's letter appeared in the *Athenaeum* (19 Nov.), p. 666.

TO THE EDITOR OF THE LITERARY WORLD

Birmingham Nov 12 1881

Sir

In respect to your yesterday's announcement, I beg to say, that I have not seen any proof sheets whatever of Messrs Houghton's Memoir of me, and that, when they asked me to inspect them, I refused. I could not, and did not 'pronounce', to use the word of your advertisement, on what I had never seen.

I am Yours etc J H N

TO THE EDITOR OF THE GUARDIAN[1]

I beg to inform you that I have not seen one line of Messrs Houghton's memoir of me, that I refused to see proof-sheets of it when asked by them to do so, and, as to any photographs or fac-simile of my handwriting which they have obtained, I never gave either for the purpose of a memoir.[2]

TO THE EDITOR OF THE MORNING POST[3]

Sir — I beg to state with reference to a late paragraph in your columns, that I have not read a single line of Messrs Houghton's intended memoir of me; that, when asked by them to do so, I met their proposal with a distinct negative, and that I gave neither photograph nor *facsimile* for the purpose of a memoir — Your obedient servant, John H. Card. Newman.

TO MRS ALEXANDER WHYTE

Birmingham Nov. 12. 1881

My dear Madam

You pay me a very kind compliment in selecting my portrait for such a gift, and I gladly send you my autograph.[4]

[1] The *Guardian* (16 Nov.), p. 1644. On 9 Nov., p. 1610, the *Guardian* announced Jennings's biography, 'illustrated by a new cabinet photo portrait, for which the Cardinal has recently given a special sitting, and a fac-simile of the original MS. of "Lead, kindly Light." The Cardinal having seen the early proof-sheets of the work, pronounces the memoirs to be written in a careful, conscientious, and impartial manner . . .'
[2] At the end of this letter there was an editorial note, 'We confess to having inserted the paragraph with some misgivings, and some explanation or apology is due from the publishers. The practice of inserting such paragraphs is becoming a nuisance . . . It appears to give what are in truth mere advertisements, editorial sanction.'
[3] The *Morning Post* (14 Nov.), p. 6.
[4] Mrs Whyte wrote from Edinburgh on 10 Nov., 'I have secured for my husband an early copy of the Etching of Mr Ouless' portrait; you will not blame me that I desire it should have what I know will be to him the great enrichment of your autograph.
He has indeed some true claim that I should ask this for him. Since our marriage three months ago I have heard your name from his lips oftener than that of any other living man,

I have to thank you also for what you say about the interest which Dr Whyte takes in my writings, which suggests the hope and trust, that, in spite of the sad divisions of Christendom, a great work is going on in the hearts of serious men, tending towards a restoration of the scattered members of Christ, even though not in our day, at least in the future, in 'the times and seasons which He has appointed.'[1] Is it not hard and strange that they who have strong religious sympathies in common, should not enjoy that Unity, which He has made the outward token that they are His?

I well recollect the visit of the three gentlemen, though they were not long enough here for me to distinguish one from the other. As to their request, I will gladly remember my dear Scotch friends unknown, when I say my daily Mass.[2]

Thank you for the Year book. It is a very interesting memorial of work.[3] I fancied I found two or three misprints. Is 'Pope' right p 30 line 7? I thought the lines were in Johnson's Imitations of Juvenal.[4]

With my best respects to Dr Whyte I am,
Very truly Yours, John H Card. Newman

John H. Card. Newman
John Henry Newman
J. H. Cardinal Newman[5]

and the shelf which holds your volumes, — they are all there —, is nearest to his study desk and oftenest consulted.'
The etching was Rajon's of the Birmingham Ouless portrait.

[1] *Acts*, 1:7.
[2] Mrs Whyte's letter continued: 'You may not recall the day of Spring five or six years ago when he came with two friends within the Oratory, but it will always be to him a day outstanding in honoured memory and it was only the very greatness of his debt and the presence of his friends which held him back from trying to acknowledge how much he owes to you, how you have moulded his life and thought, how you have been to him a friend and teacher in lonely and difficult days.
May I dare to ask as prime request that when the evening prayer rises to heaven, your thought may gather in the Scotch friends who think of you in love and honour.
With sincere reverence Yours faithfully Jane E. Whyte.'
Alexander Whyte described this his only visit to Newman of 14 March 1876, in his Inaugural Address as Principal of the New College, Edinburgh, on 13 Oct. 1909, *Former Principals*, pp. 24–5, quoted in G. F. Barbour *The Life of Alexander Whyte D.D.*, eighth edition, London 1925, p. 195: 'He received us with all that captivating urbanity which has become proverbial; and though we did not intrude ourselves long on the courteous old man, a good many points were touched on in our short interview — Rome, Oxford, Scotland, Abbotsford, Sir Walter Scott, Matthew Arnold, and so on — the old saint treating us in all that with a frankness and with a confidence as if we were old friends of his, as indeed we were. . . .'
[3] Mrs Whyte enclosed *The Free St George's Year-book for 1881–2*, and wrote in a postscript: 'In the little accompanying year book is given the plan of the winter and the work by which my husband has surrounded himself in this part of our dear ancient city, where he is shepherd of some fifteen hundred souls.'
[4]
'Still raise for good the supplicating voice,
But leave to Heaven the measure and the choice.'
is from Johnson's imitation of Juvenal's tenth *Satire*, 'The Vanity of human Wishes', 349–50. Whyte quoted the lines in the notes prepared for the 'Young Men's Sabbath Morning Fellowship Meeting'. Newman himself had quoted them on 12 May 1880, in his Address to the Catholic Union, *Add.*, p. 268.
[5] Newman sent four autographs. One was cut out and affixed to the etching.

TO JOHN HUNGERFORD POLLEN

Nov 14. 1881

My dear Pollen

I said Mass yesterday for your daughter
And rejoice at your account of Antony.
And condole with Jack. As Louis Bellasis is going up next for his 2nd examination any light you can throw on Jack's most strange failure will be valuable to us[1]

Ever Yrs affly J H N

TO THE EDITOR OF THE ATHENAEUM

Nov. 17 1881

Card N. in answer to the communication which he has this morning received from the Editor of the Athenaeum begs to express his regret that against his intention he should have seemed to imply in the Letter he sent for insertion that the Athenaeum had stated that the biography of the Cardinal in question was approved by him.[2]

Should the Editor consider any notice on the subject unnecessary he is quite content to acquiesce in the Editor's judgment.

TO MRS ALEXANDER WHYTE

Bm. The Oratory Nov 18. 1881

Dear Madam

I ought to have said in my letter to you the other day, that, if I have not, in my autographs, sent you what you wanted, I hope you will tell me. In that case, I will follow your instructions, and send you what is more to the purpose.

Very truly Yours John H. Card. Newman

TO ARTHUR WOLLASTON HUTTON

Nov 21. 1881

Copy
My dear Arthur,

I put this down as a memorandum.[3]

I am extremely afraid lest the Congregation incur expense in this projected addition to the school building even in the initial shape of architect's and builders' plans.

[1] John, Anthony Pollen's elder brother, had evidently failed his London B.A.
[2] The Editor wrote on 16 Nov. to say that the *Athenaeum* had not stated that Newman approved the biography. See letter of 12 Nov.
[3] See also letter or Memorandum of 24 Oct.

I consider we have not in any way made ourselves liable for Naden's plans, or for the tenders of the builders — nor have I, in any thing I said just now, or desired you to get from them any additional plans of any kind J H N I write this for safety sake, lest there should be any mistake. J H N

TO MICHAEL O'SULLIVAN

The Oratory Nov. 21. 1881

My dear Canon

I could not be surprised at your tidings.[1] Your dear Uncle has been in my thoughts, as expecting to hear he was gone, for many days. I had said Mass yesterday before your letter came, but I said Mass for him today, as did others of us. Thank you for what you tell me about his feelings towards me. It is a great pleasure to me to know them

Most truly Yours John H Card. Newman

TO J. SPENCER NORTHCOTE

The Oratory Bm Novr 25. 1881

My dear Canon Northcote

Your inclosure startled me. Such is the penalty of being notorious   How people can like it I can't conceive.[2] It is a wonder how it came into your parts. It was given to a girl long dead, who, I believe never was to the north of Essex   The length of the Sermon, as well as the doctrine, is marvellous. I hope, if it is to be in the Town Library, it will slumber soundly there. I suppose the owner would not let me exchange it for a recent volume, he will prefer the old lamp for the new. And it would encourage him to look for similar specimens, which may be numerous. These finds, to speak seriously, can but remind one of the discoveries destined for the great day.

With all best blessings
Yours very sincerely John H Card. Newman

P.S.   I said Mass for your Sisters' intention this morning.[3]

[1] The death on 19 Nov. of his uncle, Patrick O'Sullivan, aged 88. After working as a priest in South Carolina for eight years, he had been stationed at Wolverhampton and then near Burton-on-Trent.

[2] A man living at Stoke-on-Trent bought at a public auction in Hanley a parcel of books. One of them was Beveridge's *Private Thoughts on Religion*, which Newman had given to his cousin Harriet Fourdrinier on 5 Aug. 1828, with, stuck in it, his letter to her of that date about the book. The book was brought to Northcote at Stoke-on-Trent, to decide whether the letter was a genuine autograph. He obtained leave to copy it, and sent it to Newman. The purchaser of the book was proposing to present it to Stoke Public Library, but eventually Northcote was able to gain possession of it and give it to Newman. See letter to him of 2 Nov. 1885.

[3] i.e. the Dominican nuns of Stone, who also had a convent at Stoke. See letter of 27 Nov. to Mary Gabriel Du Boulay.

Birmingham 25 November 1881

Dear Principal Shairp

Your welcome letter and present have just come, and I thank you sincerely for both, and for the far more than kind chapter about me with which your volume concludes.[1] But it makes me feel very much ashamed, and I do not know how to bear it, from the feeling that it is so far above what I deserve. Yet I cannot but thank God for having put it into your heart to speak so affectionately of me, however partially I can accept your critical judgments.

I wished to have talked to you in Trinity Hall more than I did, from the gratitude towards you (which I have also felt towards Lord Coleridge), for former similar kindnesses, but one cannot always speak because one wishes. And I did not do justice to myself in what I sent [said] to you about Wordsworth.[2] Hurrell Froude somewhat prejudiced me against him, as if he was egotistical, which he thought destructive of all true poetic genius; but no one can delight in his odes and occasional pieces more than I do, and I shall read what you say of him in your present volume, as in a former, with the certainty of rising from it with a fuller sense of his greatness as a poet.[3]

Most truly yours John H. Card. Newman

Birmingham Nov. 26. 1881.

My dear Allies,

I am very glad to hear we are to have another volume of the 'Formation' etc and, if your last work (of Essays etc) succeeded on the plan of subscription, I consider this new volume would.[4]

[1] Shairp sent his *Aspects of Poetry being Lectures delivered at Oxford*, Oxford 1881, the last chapter of which was called 'Prose Poets. Cardinal Newman.' Shairp wrote in the presentation copy 'To Cardinal Newman in reverent admiration of his genius and character, and in grateful remembrance of his Teaching at Oxford.'
Shairp also wrote on 22 Nov., 'Dear Cardinal Newman
When I had the pleasure of meeting you, in the Hall of Trinity College, Oxford, the summer before last, you kindly asked about the subjects and manner of my Lectures in Oxford, and noticed the change that has passed over these and other things, since the days when Keble and Coplestone gave their Lectures in Latin. Remembering this conversation, I have ventured to forward to you, a Volume containing some selections from the Lectures . . . The last Lecture, delivered in Oxford in June last, is meant to draw attention to the essential poetry, which your Prose Works, especially your Sermons, contain. . . . I wrote the Lecture with the single desire of conveying to the younger generation the feeling of profound respect, which I have long had for you and for your teaching.'
[2] In his chapter on Newman, Shairp wrote: 'it was only this time last year that he [Newman] told one in Oxford, that he was quite innocent of any familiarity with Wordsworth. "No! I was never soaked in Wordsworth, as some of my contemporaries were."' *Aspects of Poetry*, pp. 439–40.
[3] Chapter XII of *Aspects of Poetry* was on 'The White Doe of Rystone.' The earlier volume was *The Poetic Interpretation of Nature*, Edinburgh 1877, where chapter XIV was on 'Wordsworth as an interpreter of Nature'.
[4] Allies's fourth volume of *The Formation of Christendom* was published in 1882, *Church and State as seen in the Formation of Christendom*. His essays were *Per Crucem ad Lucem*, two volumes, 1879.

Your 'Life's Decision' is a document, and is not to be measured by a market price.[1]

I know nothing of the Lines you mention. Perhaps they are those which Mr Bickersteth, a clergyman of Hampstead, without my leave added to my 'Lead, kindly Light.'[2]

The volume in which I go farthest as regards doctrinal development is 'Theological Tracts'. I was very anxious about it, and should be so still, had not a friend, whom all acknowledge as an authority in theological questions, spoken in very strong language in its favour.[3]

Yours affly John H. Card. Newman

P.S. Old men live by rule or they die. I *am*, thank God, in good health, but it is because I take no liberties with myself. Bystanders think my good health a token and proof that I *may* take liberties.

TO SISTER MARY GABRIEL DU BOULAY

The Oratory Bm Novr 27. 1881

My dear S.M.G.

I said Mass for your Sisters on the 25, and I congratulate you all on the result of the election. And I congratulate Mother Provincial on being unanimously selected for an office associated with such antecedents.[4]

Strange to say I have just had a telegram about my own dear brother, who I heard was very ill from Samuel Wayte, who most kindly this morning went over from Clifton to Weston to give me tidings of him.[5] I have reason then just now to feel very grateful to him. He gave a good account of my brother.

I felt after I left you the other day, that I had behaved roughly to you in alluding to the 'Three Warnings' in reference to myself; but of course the thought which they suggest is continually before me, and I ought, though it may seem selfish to recollect it in Season, and out of season[6]

It tires my hand to write, so I will say no more.

Yours affectly in Christ   John H. Card: Newman.

[1] *A Life's Decision*, London 1880.
[2] See letter of 20 June 1874 to E. H. Bickersteth.
[3] See letter of 12 April 1874 to Charles Russell and cf. that of 7 Oct. 1874 to H. J. Coleridge
[4] On 25 Nov. Augusta Theodosia Drane was elected Provincial of Mother Margaret Hallahan's Dominican nuns, in succession to Imelda Poole.
[5] Francis William Newman was now living at Weston-super-Mare. S. W. Wayte resigned as President of Trinity College, Oxford, in 1878.
[6] Newman visited Stone on 10 Nov. See letter of 3 Nov. to A. T. Drane, 'The Three Warnings' is Mrs Piozzi's poem. Death promised to give the young man three warnings, and comes when he is 80:
> 'If you are lame, and deaf, and blind,
> You've had your three sufficient warnings.'
Autobiograpy, Letters and Literary Remains of Mrs Piozzi (Thrale), edited by A. Hayward, second edition, London 1861, II, pp. 165–9.

TO HENRY WILLIAMS MOZLEY

Birmingham Nov. 27. 1881

My dear Harry

I would gladly attend to the application of any friend of yours, were it in my power — but Glastone [sic] is unknown to me, except as showing to me some gracious acts since 1864. I hardly was in a room with him three or four times till then — and since, he has shown his friendship to me now and then by calling on me or by asking me to breakfast — but I never could call him my friend.

So I fear you must make my apologies for me to your friend, and explain to her how her wish is beyond me.

I have heard nothing about Eccleshall[1]

Yours affectly John H. Card. Newman

TO BARON DE PENEDO

The Oratory Birmingham Novr 29 1881

Cardinal Newman presents his Compliments to his Excellency the Baron de Penedo and will feel obliged by his forwarding the accompanying letters to their Majesties the Emperor and the Empress of Brazil[2]

TO P. STUDHOLM BRUCE

[End of November 1881]

(sent)

Sir

I do not profess to be a philosopher and my time for correspondence is very limited but, if I must answer your question whether 'it is *probable* that the human soul is immortal,' I should answer it in the affirmative first because the belief has been so long and so widely cherished and next because it is so specially congenial or rather natural to the mind; and these reasons in its behalf seem to me as good as Hegel's against it, derived from the dictum that 'immortality involves the inherent infinitude of spirit', which seems to me a mere assumption. As to Herodotus, he is speaking of the teaching and the doctrine of immortality in Egypt and Greece, sacerdotal or philosophical, not of it as a popular belief or sentiment.[3]

[1] Letter of 3 Nov. to H. W. Mozley.
[2] De Penedo was the Brazilian ambassador. On 25 Nov. Newman sent formal Christmas letters also to the Kings and Queens of Spain, Portugal, Saxony, and the King of Bavaria. Also to all the Cardinals. Cf. the letters of 25 Nov. 1879 and 1880. The forms to be used were sent as before by Achille Liverziani.
[3] Bruce who signed himself LL.D., Ph.D., wrote on 28 Nov. that the immortality of the soul seemed improbable, quoting Herodotus and Hegel. Cf. Hegel, *Lectures on the Philosophy of Religion*, London 1895, III, p. 57 and II, p. 110; Herodotus, II, 123.

But it is a question which is not practical to a Catholic, since it is superseded by revelation. I hope you will excuse so brief an answer.

TO GUGLIELMO SANFELICE, ARCHBISHOP OF NAPLES

[December 1881?]

To the Archbishop of Naples
My Lord Archbishop of [and] dear Brother

We have received a letter from the Provost of the Chiesa Nuova, conveying to us a recommendation ⟨an exhortation⟩ to all Catholics (*from* the Sacred Congregation of Bishops and Regulars) to contribute to a fund for creating pensions for the maintenance of new Fathers of the Oratory of Rome.[1]

I hope I need not say that the Oratory of Birmingham honours and loves the Chiesa Nuova, and sincerely condoles with it on its recent grievous trials — but what can it do in this matter? The fact is that we cannot maintain ourselves? our yearly expenses are not in equilibrium with our income   Our school is not remunerative. We have been obliged to have recourse to loans. How then can we contribute to the needs of Chiesa Nuova when we require pecuniary assistance for ourselves?

Can we help making this plain, however unsatisfactory answer to the Fathers of Chiesa Nuova

MEMORANDUM ON COPYRIGHTS

Dec 4. 1881

My wish is that no copy right of mine should be sold unless all my three executors are unanimous on the point. Indeed, at first sight, and according to my present knowledge a sale *must* be at a disadvantage to the author. Even when the copy right of a book expires there is a sort of prestige goes with an author's executors, which gives *their* editions a sort of precedence or monopoly. Apropos of sales, Pickering have got the copy right of the 'Arians', I don't know when it will run out, but they gave £5 ⟨£4⟩ for it at an auction. (I have just bought back from Pickering the copy right, stereotype and stock of Arians Sepr 26/86, J H N)

The annual income from my books has been on an average between £200 or £300. While an income continues, I wish it devoted (1) to the annual expenses (rates, taxes, repairs etc) of the new dormitory and rooms under, which I built by Castles — (2) an annual £100 for keeping up Rednall, and the rest to the annual repairs of the Edgbaston Oratory House, and of Ambrose's two houses.[2]

J H N.

[1] The Italian government had confiscated most of the house and property of the Roman Oratory. Sanfelice, had, presumably, appealed on its behalf.
[2] These were two houses next to the Oratory and formed part of the Oratory School, as did the dormitory behind them which Newman had built by the contractor Castle, in 1878.

TO LORD EMLY

Birmingham Decr 5. 1881

My dear Emly

Is it true, as the Papers say, that Co Limerick is in such a state of anarchy?[1] How do you fare? How does Fr Flanagan fare? What is to be the end of it? I have long feared that, as Belgium, Lombardy, Hungary, Greece, have got their way, so will Ireland — yet how bettered thereby?

Yours affly J H Card. Newman

TO F. C. PENROSE

[6 December 1881]

Sir

I thank you for your letter and feel great respect for the motives and exertions of the gentlemen who have originated the 'Newdegate Fund' but I know nothing whatever of the letter signed Francatelli of which you inclose a copy in your letter to me, nor have I made any contribution, great or small to it.[2]

TO J. SPENCER NORTHCOTE

Bm Decr 11. 1881

My dear Canon Northcote,

At the end of a week, I write to say, apologising for giving you trouble, that the book has not come to me from Mr Wynne, so I suppose he thinks better of his promise. It is not worth your while to do more than to tell him that the book post or he has failed in what I expected.[3]

It is near enough to Christmas now, to send you and your good nuns my best congratulations and good wishes on the Holy Season. The snow has begun to do its part in fit service to the Bambino Gesù

Most truly Yours John H. Card. Newman

[1] The arrest of Parnell in Oct. increased the unrest in Ireland. The administration of justice had almost broken down, while evictions and agrarian crime continued.

[2] F. C. Penrose wrote on behalf of the Newdegate Fund, of which he was a secretary, about a letter purporting to come from Newman's secretary. This letter read:
'The Palace, Birmingham
Sir   I am desired by His Eminence Cardinal Newman to forward the enclosed small contribution towards the liquidation of the expenses, which he so much regrets you have been put to in the matter of the "Qui tam" action of "Clarke" versus "Bradlaugh" I have the honour to be   Yr Obedient Servant   Francatelli   (Secretary).' The letter had contained 7s.   The Newdegate Fund was being raised 'in token of the admiration of the bold and vigorous part played by the Member for North Warwickshire [C. N. Newdegate] in opposition to the Member for Northampton being allowed to take his seat in the House of Commons'.

[3] This refers to the copy of Beveridge's *Private Thoughts on Religion*. See letter of 25 Nov. to Northcote and first note there.

Hawarden Castle, Chester. Dec. 12. 81

My dear Cardinal Newman

I must write to your Eminence a brief line of apology for my note on your Life by Mr Jennings, which he has put in the newspapers.

It would have been an impertinence in me to have written such a note for publication: and I should not have written it to Mr Jennings had I known he was a journalist for

'tis their nature to.'[1]

This is my excuse, which I hope you will accept.

And I trust also your Eminence is enjoying this mild and beneficient season; as I, now fairly within the precinct of old age, day by day rejoice in it.

Believe me with much respect sincerely yours

W E Gladstone

TO WILLIAM EWART GLADSTONE

Birmingham The Oratory Decr 13. 1881

My dear Mr Gladstone

It is always a pleasure to me to see your handwriting, and, shocked as I am at having been the occasion, however innocent, of your kindness being imposed upon, that pleasure, on reading it, was not diminished.

I could not but be amused at the grand audacity of your correspondents. Two months ago they gave a London firm to understand that they had my sanction for their book. When they were found out, they wrote to ask me to give it; when I answered that I could not do so, for the time was not come for a Memoir of me, they wrote again to press me, and, when upon this I gave a 'distinct negative', they published that I had seen some of the proof sheets and 'pronounced' my approbation on the work. Lastly, when, on the recommendation of a London publisher, I put into the papers a statement that I had never seen one word of the book, they put into the papers that 'perhaps I had had it read to me tho' I had not seen it', and quoted in proof some civil words with which I had accompanied my refusal.[2]

I did not mean to make so long a tale — but I wanted to make a rhetorical $αὔξησις$[3] to this effect, (as is obvious) — that they should bother me, a man with no work on his hands, is no great matter, but that they should persevere beyond me, and lay a trap for a Prime Minister is nothing short of heroic. The only puzzle I have is that they have not sent me your letter, to show their triumph.

May I sign myself without presumption and with great sincerity

Yours affectionately John H. Card. Newman

P.S.   Since writing the above I have seen your letter, which (as is your wont), is kind far above my merits.[4]

[1] Isaac Watts, *Divine Songs for Children*, XVI 'Against Quarrelling'.

[2] See letters of 5 Oct. to T. A. Pope, 26 Oct. to Messrs Houghton, and those in Nov. to periodicals.

[3] 'Amplification.'

[4] On 14 Dec. Messrs. Houghton asked Newman to accept a copy of Jennings' *Life of Cardinal Newman*, and protested at being 'the subjects of a very severe and most undeserved

TO R. W. BLACKMORE

[16 December 1881][1]

Cardinal Newman presents his compliments to Mr Blackmore, and hopes he will excuse him for intruding on him with this letter.

Mr W. Palmer of Magdalen College, who had the advantage at Petersburg of Mr Blackmore's acquaintance has left to the Cardinal all his papers, and the latter intends to publish a volume of notes from the journals of Mr P's visit to Petersburg in 1841 and following years. It would be a great favour, if Mr Blackmore could inform Cardinal Newman whether Count Pratosoff, and M. Mouravich (one of whose works Mr Blackmore translated into English) are alive or dead; officials to whom Mr Palmer everywhere expresses his respectful gratitude. Also he would wish, if it is not unpleasing to Mr B. to record the friendly intercourse which existed between Mr Palmer and Mr Blackmore to whom the former owed so much in the way of information and advice, and to whom he always gives in his journal expression of his sincere attachment

He does not ask of Mr Blackmore [more] than a few words dictated to an amanuensis[2]

TO WILLIAM J. WALSH

Birmingham Dec 19. 1881

Confidential
Dear Dr Walsh

I want to ask you as an Irish theologian, whether you think the following position is tenable. I do not know enough of Irish history or Irish opinion to be able to say that it *is* tenable, but I am not at all sure that it is *not*.[3]

It is a probable opinion and therefore may be acted on by an individual,

rebuke.' They enclosed the leaflet on which they had printed Gladstone's letter: 'Mr Gladstone, in acknowledging a copy of the "Life of Cardinal Newman," by Mr. H. J. Jennings writes as follows to the author: — "In attempting to give an account during his lifetime, of this great and fascinating writer — the most fascinating, I think, of his age — you have undertaken a most difficult task; and you appear to me to have performed it with marked ability, impartiality, and tact. Nor is it your fault, if such an exhibition of such a person should be indirectly favourable to a sectarian interest. The same thing would happen, in another direction, if a portrait equally skilful were to be drawn of [Bishop] Selwyn, or of Pattison, or of Sister Dora [Pattison]. The Cardinal prudently renounced you and your work by anticipation, but I judge from so much as I know of him that he will have accepted it *ex post facto*, in his happy retreat, with a favourable, and even with a grateful feeling.'

[1] Dated from Blackmore's reply on 19 Dec. thanking for Newman's letter of the 16th.
[2] Blackmore replied that Count Pratasoff died in 1847 and 'that Mouravieff the Historian gave up his office in the Synod and retired to his country seat where I believe he died.' Blackmore added: 'As to myself I feel that I may give Carte Blanche to you to transcribe and print any thing my dear friend W. Palmer may have recorded of my intercourse with him.' See letter of 1 Feb. 1882 to Blackmore.
[3] Walsh, who was President of St Patrick's College, Maynooth, had given his support to the Land Act, and was a strong Home Ruler. Newman was preparing his reply to Gladstone's letter of 17 Dec. See letter of 23 Dec. to him.

that the Irish people has never recognized, rather have and continuously since the time of Henry ii protested against and rejected the sovereignty of England, and have seemingly admitted it only when they were too weak to resist; and therefore it is no sin to be what would be commonly called a rebel.

I will beg you to burn this, and, if you are good enough to answer it I will in turn burn your letter[1]

J H N

TO MRS CHRISTIE

Birmingham, Dec 20. 1881

My dear Mrs Christie,

It is very difficult in a few woids to say just what ought to be said in answer to your correspondent, and I have delayed writing, not only from having other letters to answer, but from a wish to say, what it was easy in substance to say, in the best manner.[2]

As to Mr C, and his not having a 'call', in Catholic language he means he has not *faith*. It is not unfrequent for men to be intellectually convinced, and to add that 'they wish they *could* believe, but they can't'. Your friend throws into language which pleases him better the same confession, and says 'I have not a call'. This is just the way men in Calvinistic bodies speak of themselves and others, of their friends, of their children, thinking that they cannot help themselves towards conversion, and thereby excusing themselves or their dear ones in their being still 'in the flesh' and 'unregenerate'.

Mr C. seems to feel that membership with the Catholic Church, *is* the *normal* state of a Christian, and therefore it is his duty to pray earnestly, to pray continually, for that living faith, for that true call, which comes to him indeed from God but which withal comes thro' himself. God gives to all liberally, and it will be a grievous thing to find some day that it is through his own fault that the call has not come to him.

In saying that he must pray for grace, for strength, in order that he may be able to enter the Catholic Church, I imply that the Holy Ghost vouchsafes to act upon the souls of His creatures *externally* to the Catholic Church. Of course I do, and I have written on the subject, when answering myself, in my first volume of 'Difficulties of Anglicans' lecture 3. p. 67, edition 1879 [3] I think I have said in that Lecture all I have to say about the presence of grace external to the Church. However, I have to add, in explanation of one point, that when it is said 'Out of the Church is no salvation' it is meant, there is no religious body but One in which *is* salvation. The contrast is between the

---

[1] Newman presumably burned Walsh's reply. His own letter survives only in a draft.

[2] Mrs Lydia Rose Christie had become a Catholic in 1879, see letters of 5 and 20 Nov. 1879 to her. She was corresponding with a relative as to whether he should follow her example. His initials were E.C., perhaps Edward Richard Christie, who after being at Christ's College, Cambridge, took deacon's orders in 1882 and was curate of St John the Evangelist, Clapham. He was headmaster of Magdalen College School, Oxford, 1886–8, and died in 1889.

[3] *Diff.* I, 'The Life of the Movement of 1833 not derived from the National Church.'

Catholic Church and other bodies. We have grace through her, if we are her members; but we never can receive grace from the Church of England, though she had a dozen sacraments instead of two, any more than an infant could receive nourishment from the breast of its dead mother.

Your correspondent speaks as if 'Out of the Church is no salvation', were peculiar to St Augustine — is not St Cyprian quite as strong in his 'De Unitate'? and a host of other Fathers? Are the Fathers no authority for him? what is the Rule of Faith? common sense? private judgment? Nothing external to him?

Write again if you wish it.[1]

Yours affly John H. Card. Newman

TO R. W. CHURCH

Bm Decr 21. 1881

My dear Dean

Why haven't you written to me for this age? I wanted to hear about Mary, and should have written to you, except that first I did not know where you were, and next because I heard something about her from others.[2]

I now write to wish you and all round you the best blessing of this sacred season.

I am putting together a volume from William Palmer's journals. To me it is very interesting, and, I think, it will be so to his contemporaries — but I much doubt, if I wished it, whether any London publisher would take the edition.

Lest there should be any mistake, I will say I am more than pleased with the result of my drawing attention to the Christian Knowledge Society's shameful circulation of Dr L's book.[3] I say 'shameful' because such a Society should not sanction a controversial work till it has gone through a careful revision. Fifty years ago, when Blanco White's work was on the List, no complaint, as I think, could lie against the Society, because he was a *witness* of what he said, and, if he coloured facts, it was not intentionally;[4] but Dr L's book shocks me. However, for this very reason, because it thus affects me, I am sure that it will also, in the same way, more or less, affect others — and I have quite sufficient proofs that it has. Of course I never for an instant supposed that any one to whom I sent it would acknowledge the receipt, though some did;[5] but I wished to protest against unfair controversy, and thereby to draw attention to it. Even if half of Dr L's book was true, that was no excuse for the other half being untrue

Yours ever affectly John H. Card Newman

[1] See letter of 29 Dec. to Mrs Christie.
[2] Mary Church had been ill. See letter of 8 June 1881 to Church.
[3] R. F. Littledale's *Plain Reasons against joining the Church of Rome*. See letters of 21 April and 13 May 1881 to Church.
[4] See third note to letter of 13 May to Church.
[5] See the last four notes to letter of 13 May to Church.

TO W. J. COPELAND

Bm Dec 21. 1881

My dear Copeland

Your annual remembrance of us has come right — and we all return you our best thanks and kindest greetings on this sacred tide, which is close upon us. They wish me here to sing Mass at 5 a m on Christmas day in full Pontificals, with Mitre and Staff which I have never done and doubt whether I am strong enough to do, though I am very well.

Why have you not written to me this long time? I have supposed you were buried in Cornwall or had been carried off by a balloon, and had no address, or I should have tried to elicit a letter from you.

Myself, I am busy in composing a Volume of William Palmer's Russian etc travels — which will be to his contemporaries, I think, interesting, but I can't answer for the new generation.

Now do give me some sign, over and above the turkey, that you are in rerum natura

I fear your Sister is still very ill

Ever Yours affectly John H Card. Newman

TO THOMAS WOOLNER

Birmingham Dec 21. 1881

Dear Mr Woolner

Your very kind present came to me yesterday. I began to read it directly with much interest. I doubt not that the more I read, the more I shall be struck with its poetic beauty. It is indeed very beautiful, though not so severe perhaps as would suit the taste of the old classics[1]

Thank you very much and believe me to be

Most truly Yours John H Card. Newman

TO JOHN RIVINGTON

Birmingham Decr 22. 1881

Dear Sir

I have to thank you for the kindness which allowed me to take up so much of your time last week, but it has not been thrown away upon me. It has enabled me to see more clearly than before the course I ought to take in publishing the work which I spoke to you about.[2]

[1] Thomas Woolner who made a bust of Newman in 1866, sent a copy of his poem *Pygmalion*, London 1881. He wrote on 20 Dec., 'The story is a very beautiful one, but so far as I have seen it treated or alluded to in literature wholly misunderstood. The Greeks were not so silly as to believe that a woman in marble could change into a woman in flesh. The myth merely indicated that the passion of the sculptor inspired the marble with that vitality for which all true artists strive; and this feeling I have taken great pains to express in the best English that I could command.'

[2] William Palmer's *Notes of a Visit to the Russian Church.*

35

I had proposed to myself to gain for it the wide circulation which a London house secures for its publications, and the additional guarantee for its success which lay in its first edition belonging to the publishers. But I did not properly realize the risk which would be incurred by a volume that related to matters long past and was on subjects less interesting to others than to myself.

Accordingly, I have now determined to keep to my usual mode of publishing, and with sincere thanks and many apologies to withdraw the question and proposals I made to you, when I had the pleasure of conversing with you.[1]

Wishing you a happy Christmas,

I am, Dear Sir Very truly Yours John H Card. Newman

J. Rivington Esqr

P.S.   I fear my address to you is not quite correct

TO WILLIAM EWART GLADSTONE

Birmingham December 23. 1881

My dear Mr Gladstone

You may be sure I feel honoured by your confidence, and should gladly find myself able to be of service, however slight it might be, in a political crisis, which must be felt as of grave anxiety by all who understand the blessing of national unity and peace.[2]

[1] Rivington, who was a partner in the firm of Sampson Low and Co. offered on 23 Dec. to publish on commission, Newman meeting the expenses of production. See letter of 2 Jan. 1882.

[2] Gladstone wrote on 17 Dec.,
'I will begin with defining strictly the limits of this appeal, I ask you to read the inclosed papers; and to consider whether you will write anything to Rome upon them. I do not ask you to write, nor to tell me whether you write, nor to make any reply to this letter, beyond returning the inclosures in an envelope to me in Downing Street. I will state briefly the grounds of my request thus limited. In 1844, when I was young as a cabinet minister, and the government of Sir R. Peel was troubled with the O'Connell manifestations, they made what I think was an appeal to Pope Gregory XVI for his intervention to discourage agitation in Ireland. I should be very loath now to tender such a request at Rome. But now a different case arises. Some members of the Roman catholic priesthood in Ireland deliver certain sermons and otherwise express themselves in a way which my inclosures exhibit. I doubt whether if they were laymen we should not have settled their cases by putting them into gaol. I need not describe the sentiments uttered. Your eminence will feel them and judge them as strongly as I do. But now as to the Supreme Pontiff. You will hardly be surprised when I say that I regard him, if apprised of the facts, as responsible for the conduct of these priests. For I know perfectly well that he has the means of silencing them; and that, if any one of them, were in public to dispute the decrees of the council of 1870 as plainly as he has denounced law and order, he would be silenced.
Mr. Errington, who is at Rome, will I believe have seen these papers, and will I hope have brought the facts as far as he is able to the knowledge of his holiness. But I do not know how far he is able; nor how he may use his discretion. He is not our official servant, but an independent Roman catholic gentleman and a volunteer.
My wish is as regards Ireland, in this hour of her peril and her hope, to leave nothing undone by which to give heart and strength to the hope, and to abate the peril. But my wish as regards the Pope is that he should have the means of bringing those for whom he is responsible to fulfil the elementary duties of citizenship; of Christianity, of priesthood, it is not for me to speak.' John Morley, *The Life of William Edward Gladstone* Book VIII, Chapter IV, Cheap edition III, pp. 48–9.

I think you overate the Pope's power in political and social matters.[1] It is absolute in questions of theology, but not so in practical matters. If the contest in Ireland was whether 'Rebellion', or whether 'Robbery' was a 'sin', we might expect him to anathematize its denial; but his action in concrete matters, as whether a political party is censurable or not, is not direct, and only on the long run effective. Again, local power and influence is often more than a match for Roman right.

I learned this at Rome in 1847, when I was asking the Pope's sanction for introducing the Oratory into England. Besides what we asked for, he gave us the Oratory at Malta with its Church and Library, the Malta community having died out — (what the English Government's rights were, I do not know) Ultimately we declined to accept it; but, when I first talked the proposal over, an ecclesiastical friend at Rome said to me, 'The Pope of course is acting within his right, but don't fancy you have got the House because he has given it. Every thing will depend on the Bishop at Malta. Do you know *him*?'[2] I have had experience, that my friend's words were only true, all through my Catholic life. The Pope's right keeps things together, it checks extravagancies, and at length prevails, but not without a fight. Its exercise is a matter of great prudence, and depends upon times and circumstances.

I observe too that your Papers relate mainly to the intemperate, dangerous words of Priests and Curates. Surely such persons belong to their respective Bishops, and scarcely require the intervention of the Supreme Authority.

I will mind your directions about your Papers[3]   Believe me,

My dear Mr Gladstone Yours affectionately
John H. Card. Newman

The Rt Hon W. E. Gladstone M P

[1] The draft of this letter began:
'I hope you have considered I had some good reason which has led to my delay in acknowledging your confidential papers. They came quite right.
But before I can give them that serious attention which they claim, I am bound to explain what I conceive to be the relation of the Holy See to them, which I cannot accept as you have stated it.
You seem to think that the duty of interference on the part of the Sovereign Pontiff in view of the present open opposition to the imperial Government and indeed to the Royal authority in Ireland, is parallel to what he would certainly feel to be a call upon him in case Catholics, Bishops or others, were to resist a dogmatic statement of the Vatican Council — and therefore that he is inconsistent and worse, in not making himself [obeyed] in the former case as he certainly would in the latter   But the latter is in the province of faith and morals and in this he is undoubtedly directly responsible for what he says and what he allows to be said and there is only one thing that has to be said   there is but a true and a false, but matters of conduct do not resolve themselves into right and wrong with such simplicity and ease. Even were it a question of dogmatic faith in Ireland, years might pass before any decision would come from Rome on the subject, but it is not a parallel. The parallel would be, if Irish priests were from the Altar to announce that rebellion against legitimate authority was right or robbery a virtue.'
[2] See letter of 23 April 1847 to Mrs J. W. Bowden.
[3] George Errington, Home Rule member of Parliament for County Longford, was putting the English government's case in Rome, bearing a private letter of recommendation from Earl Granville, the Foreign Secretary. See Newman's letter of 2 Jan. 1882 to Gladstone.

TO EMILY BOWLES

Christmas Eve 1881

My dear Child

All the best blessings of Christmas be yours and Frederic's. I am glad you are near Frederic, though the want of a common roof is a sad difficulty.[1]

I have been busy with Mr W. Palmer's MSS and hope, if I live, at least to get out one volume — but perhaps I told you. It will be from his Russian journals — perhaps his Greek.

I am quite well, though not strong

Yours affectly J H Card. Newman

TO EDWARD NEWMAN MOZLEY[2]

[Christmas 1881]

1881
To my dear Edward
May the best Christmas blessings
be his
now and for ever.
John H. Card. Newman

TO LOUISA ELIZABETH DEANE

The Oratory Birmingham Decr 27. 1881

My dear Louisa

It was a great pleasure to me to receive your letter and Christmas card. Let me send in turn my best and kindest remembrances to you, Mr Deane, and your Christmas circle.

I thought I told you that I fancied our Grandmother's maiden name was White, and that in some way she was connected with Norwich.[3]

Ever yours affectly J. H. Card Newman

P.S. As to my portrait all persons whom I have heard speak about it, think Millais's the best
Mrs Deane Bath

[1] Frederic Bowles was now at Harrow.
[2] 1875–1950, Newman's great nephew, son of J. R. Mozley.
[3] This was Jemima White, who married Henry Fourdrinier. See letter of 16 April 1881 to Louisa Elizabeth Deane.

TO J. R. BLOXAM

Bm Decr 28. 1881

My dear Bloxam

Your welcome present has come, and I have already read a good deal of it.[1] It is surprising how many of the men recorded in it I more or less knew. I make one criticism. It is provoking you don't put in the running title at the top of the pages, the name of the persons treated of successively, E.g.

p 8	p 9	p 304	p 305
Demies	Routh	Demies	Palmer

I am sorry to say I have mislaid my Photographs — I have written my name on the opposite page

Yrs affectly John H. Card. Newman

P.S.   All kind greetings to you suitable to this sacred Season from all of us

TO JOHN O'HAGAN

Birmingham Decr 28. 1881

My dear John O'Hagan

Your letter has given me very great pleasure, and I return you and Mrs O'Hagan with all my heart my prayers for you that the best blessings of this sacred season may descend upon you both.

You are in the midst of an anxious and absorbing work, which all your friends must follow with prayers for your success. And every one has confidence in you in spite of party criticism, and it is pleasant to find from yourself that you consider the clouds are breaking.[2] What a great work you will have done, if it is God's will you should do it!

Fr Russell lately asked me for any letters which would be useful for dear Dr Russell's life. I sent him some — I have not been able yet to put my hand upon the letter you sent me on his death, though I found Fr Russell's own.[3] I was not much surprised, for I was in bed with broken ribs when he died, and my letters got into confusion — but I know it is in some safe place. I say I was in bed, for my accident happened on the 19th or 20th and he died on the 26th[4]

I am quite well, but in various ways feeble and lose confidence in myself, which is often a trial.

[1] *The Magdalen College Register*, Vol. 4, Oxford and London 1881. Inscribed: 'For His Eminence Cardinal Newman   From an old attached and affectionate friend J R Bloxam Christmas, A.D. 1881.'
[2] O'Hagan, who had been appointed a Commissioner in the new Irish Land Court, wrote from Dublin on 25 Dec., 'As to the general state of the country, hope with me prevails over the temptation to despondency. . . . things are certainly looking better.'
[3] Letter of 6 Nov. to Matthew Russell.
[4] This was in Feb. 1880.

Mind and give your wife a kind message from me and tell her how much I need her prayers.

Yours affectionately John H Card. Newman

P.S.   I have not been able to satisfy myself with my direction to this letter. It concerns me to hear of Mr Mc Carthy's illness[1]

TO H. LA SERRE

Dec 28. 1881

To Henry la Serre

All the blessings of Christmas be upon you,
and all dear to you

J. H. Card. Newman

TO MRS CHRISTIE

Birmingham Decr 29. 1881

My dear Mrs Christie

I can't possibly tell you what you ought to do in regard to a relative of yours whom you know and I do not; but, advising you without advantage of that knowledge I should say you either ought not to answer him at all, or in a few kind words to tell him that it is useless to argue with a man who will not reason.[2] If he said 'I believe *the word of* the English Church that she is God's creation and the ark of salvation', it would be some kind of reasoning; but he seems merely to assert his determination, not a conviction — 'stat pro ratione voluntas'.[3]

I am not sure that it would not do him harm to continue the correspondence. Perhaps he feels the truth of what you *say* more than he shows he does. You must leave him to himself or to God.

Yours most truly John H. Card. Newman

TO ANNE MOZLEY

Bm Decr 29 1881.

My dear Anne Mozley

The week must not pass away without my sending to you my best and most affectionate Christmas greeting — also, through you to your Sisters and

[1] O'Hagan wrote that James J. McCarthy the architect was dying. Newman had appointed him Professor of Architecture at the Catholic University in Dublin, in 1857.

[2] A copy of a letter from her relative to Mrs Christie is at the Birmingham Oratory. He wrote to her, 'As to myself, Cardinal Newman I know would be the last man in the world to wish anyone to act against his conscience: as I should do if I left my present position — it may well be that for my sins my conscience is darkened — or it may be that God has work to be done which can be done more effectually at present without the walls of Jerusalem than within . . .' See letter of 20 Dec. to Mrs Christie.

[3] Juvenal, *Satires*, VI, 223.

Charles, and to Jane.[1] I hope you are all well and that all is well about you.

I have very little to tell you about myself, except that I have a great deal to do and very little time to do it in. A[n] hour does not go near so far with me, as it used years ago — by token, I am obliged to write nearly as slowly as a child does, and, if I attempted to write *running* hand, my strokes would run off towards the four corners of the paper, thus — Miss ? called the other day.[2] This surely is quite enough, a favorable specimen

I am editing a first volume of Mr Palmer's Notes on Russia. To me it is very interesting, but I don't know how it will seem to a new generation

Tom tells me he has written Reminiscences of Oxford. This will be *most* interesting — and he tells me he has so managed as not to give pain to any one[3]

And now the light is going, and I have nothing to say but to repeat my good wishes and to sign myself

Yours affectly ever John H Card. Newman

TO CATHERINE ANNE BATHURST

Bm Decr 30. 1881

My dear Child

The old year shall not go out, without my sending you my thanks for your communion and prayers for me.

I am very well, but somewhat and (I think) increasingly feeble — and therefore have to take care of myself. But on the whole few men of my age have so little to complain of as I.

You must not wonder at your finding the dead weight, the 'vis inertiæ', of so great an Establishment as Harrow an obstacle in the way of conversion, especially so far as it gains some sort of momentum by the action of fear and suspicion.[4] But it is cruel that that defenceless portion of Society should, as at other times, should [sic] suffer it. You recollect, at the time of Hierarchy row, the old Birmingham woman who said 'Heaven alone knew how much she had to suffer along of Mr Wiseman.' I suppose all bodies, like yours, in their beginning must suffer, and their people with them.

I am glad to hear from some one, I think Miss Bowles, that you seem so young and vigorous, in spite of your uphill work. That the best blessings of

---

[1] Charles was Anne Mozley's brother and Jane her and Newman's niece.
[2] These words Newman wrote as a specimen.
[3] See letter of 21 Oct. 1881 to Thomas Mozley.
[4] Miss Bathurst had established a convent of Dominican nuns at Harrow. The 'great Establishment' is Harrow School.

Christmas may be yours, and may continue to you all through the year, is the earnest prayer of

Yours affectly John H. Card. Newman

Sister Catherine O.S.D.

Lake View, Windermere. 28th Decr. 1881.

Dear Cardinal Newman,

You may perhaps remember me calling upon you a few months ago. I at least have a very pleasant remembrance of my visit and the great kindness I received from you on that occasion. I had Mr Fisher of Cockermouth staying here and he was much interested in hearing of you and the account I was then able to give him of your health. Since seeing you too I have had communication with my friend Mrs Harward of Winterfold, near Stourbridge, and she was much touched by your recollection of her departed husband and what you said about him.[1]

My object in writing however is to ask if you have any intention of reprinting your 'Apologia'. Mr Fisher would very much like to possess a copy, as well as myself, but the book is very scarce and difficult to obtain. I am sure many would rejoice if you were led to reprint it, and you might perhaps be led to add some words in the preface or otherwise, on some of the phases of the unbelief of our day, which I doubt not would command great attention. Mr Froude in his last paper in 'Good Words' quoted a beautiful passage from the 'Apologia', which I believe led many to desire to possess the volume.[2]

I was sorry to see that you have been annoyed by some one proposing to write your life, and seeking to carry out the intention in what seemed a very objectionable way, and I think the practice, becoming too common, of writing the biographies of men in their life time, is much to be deprecated.

As I named when I had the pleasure of seeing you, I occasionally see letters of your brother to a friend in County of Durham, though I have not done so very recently — I was concerned to hear of his serious illness some weeks ago, but I trust he is now recovered. In the last letter of his I read, I was glad to read two sentences which struck me — 'I certainly do not myself disbelieve in a future life or in future meetings of those who here have loved and esteemed each other. . . . I do look, as you would wish me I am sure, to a heavenly Guide and Comforter'. I have not forgotten the words I heard you utter, 'he is the subject of many prayers', and may that heavenly guide and comforter answer the petition, 'Lead kindly Light'.

I do not know if you have seen a copy of the inscription he placed on the monument to his dear wife in the Cemetery at Weston, but in case you have not, I enclose a copy, as it may interest you.[3]

[1] For Newman's only meeting with John Cowley Fisher see letter of 29 July 1861 to Bittleston. Newman corresponded occasionally with Fisher, see letters of 19 Aug. and 14 Oct. 1861 and 25 Nov. 1864.
John Harward was the Stourbridge solicitor who in 1870 acted for Newman in the matter of land at Rednal, and refused to take a fee.
[2] J. A. Froude quoted *Apo.*, pp. 241–6 (on the need for an authoritative church), in *Good Words* (June 1881), the sixth and last of his 'Reminiscences of the High Church Revival', reprinted in *Short Studies on Great Subjects*, 'The Oxford Counter Reformation', London 1907, V, pp. 245–50.
[3] 'With no superiority of intellect, yet by the force of love, by sweet piety, by tender compassion, by coming down to the lowly, by unselfishness and simplicity of life, by a constant sense of God's Presence, by devout exercises, private and social, she achieved much of Christian saintliness and much of human happiness.
She has left a large void in her husband's heart.
Obiit, 16th July, 1876.' I. Giberne Sieveking, *Memoir and Letters of Francis W. Newman*, London 1909, p. 59.

I hope your health continues good and pray be assured how much many of your countrymen — will you allow me to say, your fellow Christians, are interested in all that concerns you, and I believe you will not despise the prayers of even the humblest of them — Begging you to excuse my troubling you, with great respect, I remain,

Your faithful and obliged, Geo. T. Edwards.

Soon after seeing you, I met Mr James, brother in law to the late Bishop Wilberforce whom I mentioned to you and he was much gratified at your remembrance of him — He is living in retirement in Gloucestershire.[1]

TO GEORGE T. EDWARDS

Birmingham Decr 30 1881·

Dear Sir

I wish you the best blessings of this sacred season.

It pleased me to find you had an opportunity of mentioning my name to the kind persons whom you speak of.

The Apologia has never been out of print and has ever been on fair sale. I take the liberty of sending you a copy — and an advertisement of it in this envelope

Very truly Yours J. H. Card. Newman[2]

P.S. I have forgotten to thank you for the Epitaph. My brother's illness was exaggerated — nay, he exaggerated it, not in its significance as regards the future, but as regards its present seriousness.

G. T Edwards Esqr

TO MRS SCONCE

The Oratory, December 30th. 1881.

Thank you my dear Mrs. Sconce for your kind Christmas letter and your amusing Alphabet. This joyful week shall not pass without my acknowledging it.

I trust you are quite well again, in spite of the journey which followed so close on your indisposition. It would have been a great pleasure to us to have seen you, as you proposed — but you had quite enough to try you, and, tho' it was our loss that we did not see you I hope it was your gain. A friend called to-day, who had lately been at Friesch[Fiesole?], and he described the weather to be nothing short of summer. I hope you share this wondrous season at Florence.

[1] Barbara Wilberforce married John James in 1831 and died in 1832. He was at Queen's College, Oxford, B.A. 1828, then Rector of Rawmarsh, Yorks, 1831–43, and from 1853 to 1879 Rector of Avington, near Hungerford. He died in 1886 at Lydney, Glos.
[2] Edwards was a devout Evangelical, and this was the beginning of a correspondence which continued until Feb. 1890.

I am attempting to publish a volume from dear William Palmer's M.S on Russia; but am not sure I shall live to do it — from its difficulty.

Excuse this slovenly letter, but to write is not easy to me.

Yours affectionately, John H. Card: Newman.

TO ANNIE GOLIGHTLY POPE

Dec 31 1881

Annie G. Pope[1]

May all best blessings
of Christmas
descend in full measure
upon her
J. H. Card. Newman

TO LORD BLACHFORD

Birmingham, Jan. 2nd. 1882.

My dear Blachford,

Your letter has just come and I return with all my heart your and Lady Blachford's Christmas and New Year's Greetings.

I should have written to you before this, but my hand is so tired and I write so slow, and have so many letters that must be written, that ad libitum letters fare ill — especially when, as in your case, I could make to myself the shabby excuse that I did not know for certain where you were.

As to W. Palmer's Journals I do not know what will come of them. He was paucorum hominum — and perhaps no one could quite understand him; but he had a simplicity, affectionateness, unselfishness, and self sacrifice, which gained him the love of all who knew him. I suppose he had no dislike of shewing himself to disadvantage, or even of misleading as to the estimate to be formed of him, in the case of those he felt were distant and unsympathetic towards him (I don't mean you) He had no dislike in such cases of putting out paradoxes, and (according to our St. Philip's rule) 'despising being despised'[2] What I have put into shape of his Russian Journal I think very interesting, but I am not sure that others will think so.

I am very well — but I can't deny I am feeble, and the line of Sophocles has for years beyond counting been in my mind.

σμικρὰ παλαιὰ σώματ' εὐνάζει ῥοπή[3]

Ever yours affectionately, John H. Card: Newman.

---

[1] This was the younger daughter of R. V. Pope by his first marriage.

[2] P. G. Bacci, *The Life of St Philip Neri*, end of Book II, Chapter XVII, London 1902, I, p. 289.

[3] *Oedipus Tyrannus*, 961. Newman translates it (to Mrs Hawkins, 21 Nov., 1882), 'A light stroke puts to sleep aged men'.

TO WILLIAM EWART GLADSTONE

Birmingham Jany 2. 1882

My dear Mr Gladstone

I have reason to believe that documents have lately reached the Holy See as formal in character and through channels of communication as intimately influential with the Pope, as those which, in observance of your directions, and with much gratitude for the confidence you have placed in me, I hereby return.[1]

I wish I could be sanguine as to their effect. It seems to me very doubtful what the Pope can do at a moment. He is a good and firm friend to the civil power on the whole and on the long run; he educates a people in obedience, and keeps things straight. But on an emergency, when a people are mad, I doubt his available power. A Garibaldi at a crisis is stronger than a Pope; and Leo has no encouragement in the events of the last 50 years that he could interfere now in Ireland with good effect.

I fear I am prosing and preaching — pray forgive me, if so. With my best good wishes and prayers for your health and strength and all blessing upon you for the New Year,

I am, My dear Mr Gladstone, Yours affectionately
John H. Card. Newman

The Rt Hon. Wm E. Gladstone M P &c &c

TO THOMAS WIMBERLEY MOSSMAN

Birmingham Jan 2. 1882

To the Revd T W Mossman
Dear Sir

I am much obliged to you for your letter and its contents; and shall be still more so, if you will be so good as to send the inclosed to the Editor of the Nonconformist for insertion in his paper. If such imputations are not repudiated, they will be believed[2]

J H N

[1] See letter of 23 Dec. 1881 to Gladstone. It does not appear that Newman intervened directly with the Holy See, but Gladstone's letter to him of 17 Dec. is not at the Birmingham Oratory, and was perhaps sent where it might carry weight. The influential channels of communication to which Newman refers, were presumably Lord O'Hagan, who was a personal friend, and who was sent on a secret mission to Rome in the last days of Dec. by the Chief Secretary for Ireland, W. E. Forster, 'who was not satisfied with the results of the Errington Mission.' Stephen Gwynn and Gertrude M. Tuckwell *The Life of Sir Charles Dilke*, London 1917, I, pp. 375–6. See also Lord Edmond Fitzmaurice, *The Life of Granville George Leveson Gower, Second Earl Granville*, London 1906, II, pp. 286–8.

[2] On 31 Dec. Mossman sent Newman a page from the *Nonconformist and Independent* (22 Dec. 1881), containing a long letter by R. Teare of Wesley House, King's Lynn. He objected to a review the previous week of the biography by Jennings, in which the reviewer gave a laudatory account of Newman. Teare made a number of damaging quotations from 'the life of Bishop Bonner, by "A Tractarian British Critic" (Newman).' Mossman wrote at once to the

2 JANUARY 1882

TO THE EDITOR OF THE NONCONFORMIST AND INDEPENDENT

Birmingham Jan 2, 1882.

Sir,

You will be glad to know that I have nothing whatever to do with the 'Life of Bishop Bonner' or its dedication, that I never read the book, and that I do not know who wrote it.

From the specimens which your correspondent gives of it, I believe it to be a ponderous and stupid squib against Tractarians, embodying in its composition several sentences and phrases, apart from their context, from various of their works, such as 'unprotestantising the Church of England' — sentences and phrases which they certainly did adopt, and which they never have been ashamed of.

However, about the origin, author, and composition of the book I know nothing and care nothing; only I am sure that no one who knows me or my writings ever so little will impute to me such vulgar stuff.

I am, your faithful servant, John H. Card. Newman[1]

TO JOHN RIVINGTON

W J Rivington Esqr
Dear Sir

Janry 2. 1882

I have to thank you for the trouble you have taken in answering my inquiry, and the considerateness with which you and the other members of your firm have met it.

They could not do more than what they propose to do, but I am unable to avail myself of it. Catholic works, I see, are not within the ordinary range of their publications; and tho' I have had no intention at all of making my volume subserve any controversial purpose, still I must follow Mr Palmer's lead, and therefore do not like to incur the risk of a condition which may embarrass me. The work of a Catholic may easily become a Catholic work.[2]

Will you convey this answer to your colleagues with my compliments

I am J H N

editor to say that Teare was the victim of a hoax and that Newman 'had never written a line of the so called Life of Bishop Bonner.'

The Editor took no notice of Mossman's letter but on 29 Dec. inserted a leading article which assumed the genuineness of Teare's quotations. Mossman in his letter to Newman of 31 Dec. said: 'It is quite possible you may not think it worth while to disavow what is attributed to you in the *Nonconformist*, though it has a large circulation, and very considerable influence. Perhaps, however you will favour me with a few lines just to say that I am not wrong . . .'

[1] This was published in the *Nonconformist and Independent* on 5 Jan.

[2] On 23 Dec. Rivington replied to Newman's letter of 22 Dec. that his firm, Sampson Low and Co., was prepared to publish Palmer's *Notes of a Visit to the Russian Church*, 'as the book is not distinctly a Catholic one.' 'Had it been decidedly of a Catholic character' a Catholic publisher would have been more advantageous. The book was published by Kegan Paul and Co.

TO ORBY SHIPLEY

[3 January 1882]

answered that I thought Fr Caswall's executors could not give so many as ⅓ of 500! Nor could I give 44, a fourth of my Volume!¹ He ought to [know ?] that for all of mine which are in the Lyra Apostolica Messrs Rivington's leave must be asked. The utmost I had given leave for hitherto was three or four!

TO JAMES FREEMAN

[4 January 1882]²

sent

Cardinal Newman, in answer to Mr Freeman's inquiry, has to inform him that he cannot boast of being of 'pure English race', as he is on one side of a French family.³

TO JOHN WILLIAM OGLE

To Dr Ogle Jany 4. 1882

Design

By Design in creation is generally meant the application of definite means for the attainment of a definite end or the aim at a final cause. I am not able to accept the 'argument from design' in this sense as a strictly logical proof of a creative mind in the universe

But design also means *order* — as when we speak of decorative patterns in architecture, mosaic, needlework and speak of them as beautiful etc *designs*. In this sense of *order* Design is in every part of the Universe, and a proof of an Intelligent Mind.

In 'Arians' p 76, ed. 1876 I have referred to 'final causes' as if not a logical argument. In 'Grammar of Assent' I have spoken of 'Design' in the sense of Order at p. 72 Ed. 1881

I shall take it for granted that you have neither book, unless you say you have, and shall without asking your acceptance send them to you.

J H N

¹ Shipley wrote thus on 29 Dec. about his hymn book 'mainly compiled from the works of the fathers of the Oratory', although there were to be various other contributors.

² Freeman wrote on 3 Jan. from 15 Francis Road, Edgbaston, enquiring whether there was any published record of the family from which Newman was descended. He had found him described in biographical notices as of 'a pure English race and Puritan Family.'

³ Newman drew up another answer: 'Jan. 4. 1882 not sent
Cardinal Newman, in answer to Mr Freeman, begs to say that, feeling the difficulty of tracing up the pedigrees of ordinary men through the disastrous scattering and destruction of documents during the troubles of the 17th century, he has never thought it worth while to set himself to consider the question'

Bm Jan 5/82.

My dear Child

I think those shocking imaginations against every thing supernatural and sacred, are as really diseases of the soul, as complaints of the body are, and become catching and epidemic, by contact or neighbourhood or company.[1] (Of course the will comes in, as a condition of their being caught,) (as, on the other hand in the cures effected by St Paul's handkerchiefs and aprons, faith would be a condition.)[2] But were I, deliberately to frequent the society, the parties of clever infidels, I should expect all sorts of imaginations contrary to Revealed Truth, not based on reason, but fascinating or distressing, unsettling visions, to take possession of me. Recollect, devil's imps come out of their mouth and their breath is poison. This does not apply to intercourse with hereditary and religious Protestants, but to our Heresiarchs, to the preachers of infidel science, and our infidel literati and philosophers. This leads me on to recur in thought to the fierce protests and shuddering aversion with which St John, St Polycarp, and Origen are recorded to have met such as Marcion and his fellows — and, though it may be impossible to take their conduct as a pattern to copy literally, yet I think we should avoid familiar intercourse with infidel poets, essaists, historians, men of science, as much as ever we can lawfully. I am speaking of course as [of] such instruments of evil as really propagate evil.

As to your very distressing intelligence, which has led to the above, I should hope and pray, hoping with great hope and praying with great anxiety, that like a bodily complaint it will at length run its course though the course may be long

It pains my hand to write

Yrs affly J H Card. Newman

The Oratory Bm Jan 5. 1882

My dear Sister Mary Pia

This is the anniversary of my dear Mary's death in 1828, an age ago; but she is as fresh in my memory and as dear to my heart, as if it were yesterday; and often I cannot mention her name without tears coming into my eyes.[3]

I have nothing to say, except to wish you the best blessings on the season. I should have written earlier, were I not half drowned by correspondence, and

[1] Emily Bowles made a note that this 'letter was written after applying to him for certain answers to be given to a friend disturbed with doubts.' Cf. letters of 29 May and 15 June 1882 to Emily Bowles. According to *Ward* II, p. 477, they concerned 'a common friend who lived much in the intellectual life of London and had ceased to be a Catholic or Christian.'
[2] *Acts* 19:12.
[3] See letter of 11 Jan. to Anne Mozley.

find it difficult to handle my pen without pain. My best good wishes of the season to all your community, and to M. Antoine.

I do not like what you say of yourself. If you have not teeth, you *cannot* eat hard substances without danger. Unchewed meat is as dangerous to the stomach as brick and stone, or a bunch of keys. You are not an ostrich. I am *very serious*. As to myself I have for years lived mainly on soup and milk. Any doctor would recommend you such a diet — and peas pudding very well boiled, and eggs in the shape of omelet — but not with the white in lumps. I dare say, you think of all this, but perhaps you don't. Talk to Mgr Place about this — and, when you see him, give him from me a kind and respectful message.

I grieve about your tooth ache, having experience of it, and I wish I was sure that you were attending properly to that more serious complaint

Ever Yrs affly J H Card. Newman

Have you got *spectacles* which suit you?

TO ORBY SHIPLEY

[5 January 1882]

(sent in substance)

Neither I nor the Executors of Fr Caswall contemplated so wide a use of our Hymns as I now understand from you[1]

1. In Fr Caswall's letter I don't think 'any hymns' meant 'all', and your own use ⟨interpretation⟩ of his words goes to this extent

2. 'I said Fr Mills would give you the *same* leave as he has given to others.'[2]

3. Mr Mills gave leave to 'select' — As to mine, I do not call those small poems by the name of Hymns, but the Matins, Vespers etc. translations from the Latin.

4. For I said expressly 'I have *very few* Catholic hymns' and I said expressly you are welcome to the use of *any* if you *name* them to me, which implied conditions which might become a veto   Fr Caswall especially wished his volume to be *kept on sale*. This hinders the executors in allowing so wholesale a surrender of them. I cannot then either for myself or as one of Fr Caswall's executors go the lengths you ask of me

TO ORBY SHIPLEY

Jany 7. 1882

Dear Mr Shipley

Fr Caswall used to be paid considerable sums for permission to use his hymns — his executors have never received or asked any thing, nor have I

[1] Shipley wrote on 4 Jan. that Newman's letter of 3 Jan. 'makes shipwreck of my entire plan' for a hymn book.
[2] See Newman's letter of 16 April 1880 to Shipley for this and what follows.

49

ever for the use of my own. But my real objection to giving a wholesale permission, lies much deeper than any pecuniary question.[1]

J H N

TO ANNE MOZLEY

Jany 11. 1882.

My dear Anne Mozley

You speak with so much interest lately of my dear sister Mary, that I send you what I have just received from Maria Giberne I don't want it back[2]

Yours affectly John H Card. Newman

[1] See letters of 7 and 9 Feb. to the Duke of Norfolk.
[2]   'V + J   De notre Mon. d'Autun Saône et Loire Jany 8 1882
My dearest father
I cannot help writing at once to acknowledge your dear kind note which arrived yesterday, though I never slept all night till 4 this morning and was awake again and up by ½ past 5. This I call one of my worst nights, for though I rarely sleep more than 3 or 4 hours at once I do manage to get 5 hours often which I call a good night.
But I do not wish to talk of myself yet, I want to tell you of my entire sympathy with you in what you say and feel about the anniversary of our dearest Mary's death. This season never comes round without my repassing in my heart of hearts all the circumstances of those few days, my first visit to your dear family.
Who could ever behold that dear sweet face for any length of time, and forget it again [;] and again who could ever have been acquainted with the soul and heart that lent their expression to that face and not love her. My sister Fanny and I arrived at your house on the 3rd and sweet Mary who had drawn figures under my advice when she was staying with us at Wanstead, lent over me at a table in the drawing room and in that sweet voice said "I am so glad you are come, I hope you will help me in my drawing." I forget about the dinner and evening on that day, for I was doubtless under considerable awe of you in those first days — but the next day the 4th M Woodgate and M Williams dined there and dear Mary sat next you and I was on her other side — and while eating a bit of turkey she turned her face towards me her hand on her heart, so pale and a dark ring round her eyes and she said she felt ill and should she go away, I asked you and so she went, I longing to accompany her but dared not, for fear of making a stir. It was the last time I saw her alive. Soon after Jemima went with her and then your Mother who soon returned looking so distressed and she said, "John I never saw Mary so ill before, I think we must send for a doctor —" You answered as if to cheer her "Ah yes Mother and don't forget the fee" How little I thought what the end would be. I suffered all that night with toothache which a little dentist in North St tried to extract the next day but he broke his instrument and raised my tooth without being able to get it out.
Harriet came to walk with us about one o'clock after the doctor had been, I think, but though she said Mary had had a very bad night, she did not seem to apprehend danger — so we went to dine with a friend and only returned to your house about nine. I felt a shock on entering the house seeing no one but you, so pale and so calm and yet so inwardly moved — and how when I asked you to pray with us for her you made a great effort to quiet your voice sitting against the table your eyes on the fire, and you answered "I must tell you the truth she is dead already —" then you went to fetch vinegar which I did not need for I felt turned to stone Fanny cried I envied her her tears.
You told us a little about her with gasping sobs in your voice and then you left us. My tears come now in writing it though they could not then. I never can cry suddenly I must think about it first. Now dearest father I hope while I relieve my own heart by speaking of these sad scenes, I am not selfishly overtaxing your feelings — but I think you will not mind it for you like to go over old times as well as I do I think, and I cannot tell all this to any one but you, you know. Do you recollect that you and I are the only 2 survivors of that event?
And then how can I ever forget all your kindnesses to me because of my toothache, how your mother sent out for soft cakes soaked with wine, the only thing I could manage to eat — you all seemed so unselfish in your grief, forgetting your own trouble to minister to my wants. I was deeply touched and learnt a lesson which though I have not practised as I ought I have always striven to imitate — not to suffer myself to be so absorbed by my own feelings that I could not feel for others.
I meant to tell you about my watch but it is so dark I must wait till tomorrow.'

TO EDWIN PALMER

Birmingham Jany 11. 1882

Dear Archdeacon Palmer

I want to ask you a question, which never mind if you can't answer — but if you can *without trouble*, I shall be glad.

Was William at Moscow *twice*, and if so, was the additional time *before* or *after* his visit in 1841?

The difficulty in determining the point *from his Notes* is as follows:

He speaks of Petersburg in 1840 and of Moscow in 1841, as if he had never seen them before. He pays a visit to two Monasteries, the Holy Trinity, and the New Jerusalem, one immediately after the other, *from Moscow.*

Yet he speaks, in one account of this visit to New Jerusalem, as if he had been there (New Jerusalem) *before*, and had, in the *interval* between his two visits, been to the Holy Land.[1]

I am, Dear Archdeacon Palmer Yours sincerely

John H Card. Newman

1840

August 8 (Old Style) I rose and took my first walk in Petersburg.

1841

May 13 (Old Style) The morning after my arrival, I went for the first time down the street called the Dmitriefka to the Kremlin.

May 17 (Old Style) being the Eve before Pentecost I started at 4 A.M. for Troiza, the great Trinity Lavra of St Sergius.

May 22. I took leave and returned to Moscow.

May 31. started at 9 A.M. to go to New Jerusalem, about 45 versts from hence

(When arrived there and inspecting the Church built after the pattern of the Holy Sepulchre, he says) There is a north door, which *exists not in the true* Jerusalem.

(and speaking of other features of the church, he says) most of these *answer to what exists* in Jerusalem.

(This shows that he had visited Palestine *before* 1841, which may well have been, but the difficulty is to understand it consistently with the following, which occurs in another fragment.)

A few *days after my* expedition to the Trinity Lavra, I set out again from Moscow for the New Jerusalem, *which I had visited once before, but not since I had been in* the East, and I wished to compare our Russian copy of the Church of the Holy Sepulchre etc with my recollections of the original.

---

[1] Palmer replied on 12 Jan. that his brother visited Moscow in 1841, and again at least once (in fact in 1862). In 1850 for the first time in his life he visited the Holy Land.

Bm Jany 12. 1882

My dear Lady Henry

I grieve indeed at your account of the sad illnesses which you and Lord Henry have suffered from these last months. I have not forgotten the trials of health you both lay under, but they have been heavier than I supposed. I return your kind Christmas greetings to you and Lord Henry and to Mamo [Maxwell-Scott] and her husband with all my heart.

I am very glad that you and she are carefully looking over Mr O's M.S. You must not fancy that I favour every sentence or sentiment which I do not set a mark against. My eyes and attention are both bad, and not to be relied upon. I shall send Fr A's criticism, without mentioning his name to Mr O at once.[1]

Did I tell you that dear William Palmer left me all his M SS. and that I am trying to make a volume from his Russian visit? It is not a Catholic work, of course, but to me very interesting, from the witness it really contains against the Russian church and virtually against the Church of England.

It is not at all a controversial work, though he has disputes with the Russian ecclesiastics, but mainly a narration of facts —

With every kind thought and prayer in your behalf and Lord Henry's and Mamo's and all of you.

Yours ever affectionately John H. Card. Newman.

Birmingham. Jany 12. 1882

My dear Pusey,

All kind thoughts to you for the New Year.

Lady Henry Kerr has written to ask me whether you have kept, or can put your hand upon, any letters to you from her brother — as they are publishing a memoir of him.

I am afraid you need a clearer atmosphere than that which we have now but the mildness must suit you.

Yours affectly John H. Card. Newman.

Jany 16. 1882

My dear Ellacombe

I have been thinking of you and was very glad to have your Card. [2]

May God be good to us both. I wish from my heart we were on the same

[1] This refers to the manuscript of Robert Ornsby's Memoir of Hope-Scott. It had been seen by William Amherst, S. J.
[2] Ellacombe sent an undated letter: 'My dear Newman
I pray you send me your Blessing — tho' we are not on the same platform —   Though

platform. Secular matters are worse and worse. It is as if Antichrist were coming

Yours affectionately John H Card. Newman

TO OSWALD JOHN SIMON

Jany 19. 1882

Cardinal Newman presents his compliments to Mr Simon, and begs to say, in answer to Mr Simon's letter that he does not see his way to append his name to the requisition addressed to the Lord Mayor of London on the subject of the Jews in Russia.[1]

O J Simon Esqr   36 Tavistock Square

TO J. R. BLOXAM

Jany 23/82

My dear Bloxam

I take the chance of your caring to have the last letter I had from Dr Routh — the year before his death — and inclose it. It was, I think the year before his death[2]

Yrs affly J H Card. Newman

TO THE DUKE OF NORFOLK

The Oratory Jan. 23. 1882

My dear Duke

Fr John Norris has told me of your cordial, affectionate language about the school and our Fathers.

As to giving up the School, there has never been such an idea in any one of the Fathers. This I am told positively, and on two conversations, by a junior Father, who ought to know.

Englishmen think they have a right to grumble and criticize, and often do so thoughtlessly and unkindly, and particular Fathers, for what I know, though I *don't* know, may have had their own hobbies, and may have said 'Too

surrounded with daily mercies I am very depressed and cast down feeling the penalty of old age in having lost all my Contemporaries — it is very sad — and to think of the coming of Antichrist is one would think beginning beginning — iniquity and infidelity daily increasing.
Your health is I hope good? tho' very feeble in my walking powers — I have great cause to be thankful Misericordias Domini in aeternum cantabo
Ever Yrs εν Χτῶ affectionately H T Ellacombe'

[1] The Requisition asked the Lord Mayor to call a public meeting 'to express the feelings of English Christians upon the barbarities to which the Jews of Russia have been and are still subjected.' The Requisition was signed by Cardinal Manning and Archbishop Tait. cf. letter of 17 Feb. 1882 to an unknown correspondent.
[2] 'Magdalen College Oxford, Feb 18 1853. The President of Magdalen College thanks Dr Newman for his kind remembrance of him in sending him his Discourses on the scope and nature of University Education.' *Newman and Bloxam*, p. 202.

much money has been laid out on the School' or 'it ought never to have begun,' or, 'if it were not for the School we should have money for this or that' — but I am told that *no* Father ever had the idea of the School stopping

Indeed it would be a tremendous blow to us, if it stopped. We have many thousands of our own money laid out upon it. Of much of this it has to pay us the interest. To put an end to the school would be almost to put an end to the Oratory

Again: of our 12 Fathers *seven* have come to the Oratory *through* the School, having been Masters in it, or boys. And there is reason to think it will be as useful to us in the future as in the past.

I could say a great deal on the position of our Oratory; Birmingham seems hardly the best place for St Philip.

I don't like to seem to forget the many calls on your munificence, and how great a sin it would be to squander money. But I don't think it would be thrown away on the School. Perhaps it would be well, if you prescribed definite objects — e.g. the Ravenhurst *playground* costs us about £300 a year, or the *salaries of the masters*, which are too low to get the best heads — or *painting* etc the School.

I don't fear Mr Petre — though for a time he may embarass us.[1]

A question has often occurred to me whether it would be best to raise the pension, or to lower it, or to leave it as it is

(Confidential) I suppose you could not help us in one way — viz. Allequin, who has now been with us twenty years, is getting old for the management of boys. Would it be possible to find a clerkship or the likes for him in London[2]

Yours ever affectly John H Card. Newman

Excuse my bad writing and blunders. It is old age

TO E. B. PUSEY

Birmingham Jan. 27. 1882.

My dear Pusey,

Thank you for your Volume, so valuable in itself and so expressive and touching a memorial of dear Philip.[3]

I have read enough of the Introduction to be much interested in it.

If I have preferred to extol S. Cyril as a great Doctor rather than as a

---

[1] Mgr. Petre opened a school at Woburn Park in 1877. See fifth note to letter of 30 Aug. 1881 to Miss Giberne.

[2] Edmund Henry Alleguen, who came as a master to the Oratory School in 1862, did not retire until 1894.

[3] This was the translation in 'The Library of the Fathers' of *S. Cyril Archbishop of Alexandria, On the Incarnation against Nestorius*, Oxford 1881. The translation and the first part of the preface were by Pusey's only son Philip, who died in Jan. 1880. Pusey wrote in the copy he sent 'John Henry Cardinal Newman with E B P's love'.

man, it has been from my extreme devotion and love for St Chrysostom, than whose wanderings and huntings about in Armenia there is nothing more tragic in the History of the Saints.[1]

But this is his Feast Day, and since he is long since united and at peace with St Cyril in heaven, it is not the time to think of the latter except in his pre-eminence as a theologian.

I am glad to find the un-seasonable mildness of the weather, so seasonable to you.

I dont think Lady H. wishes you to have trouble about the chance of letters. She and her husband are in very weak health.[2]

Ever yours affectly J. H. Card. Newman.

TO AN UNKNOWN CORRESPONDENT

The Oratory Jany 28. 1882

Dear Sir

I fear my answer will not be of a kind to satisfy your friendly wishes.

I never was at Hadleigh. I think I was not in England, when the meeting there, to which you refer, took place. But if I was returned from abroad, I certainly was not there.

The meeting at Hadleigh was at the end of July 1833. As far as I recollect it was composed of Rose, Perceval, Palmer of Worcester, and Hurrell Froude.

The Tracts for the Times I began Septr 9, issuing them from Oxford. Two out of the above four friends, Perceval and Palmer disapproved of them and wished them stopped — and Rose did not like them. They would have stopped, but for Froude and Keble.

I now recollect that I came home from abroad July 9.

Your best published authority for these matters, though I don't at all distrust the accuracy of my memory, is 'Froude's Remains, vol. 1.' A.D. about 1837 or 8.[3]

Very faithfully Yours John H. Card. Newman

TO HENRY BEDFORD

Birmingham. Jan. 29th. 1882.

My dear Professor Bedford,

I thank you very much for your remembrance of me on St. John's Chryosstom's day; I know you pray for me. I am very well, though not strong.

Yours affectionately, John H. Card Newman.

[1] See *H.S.* II, pp. 341–58.
[2] See letter of 12 Jan. to Pusey.
[3] See also *Moz.* I, pp. 431–6, for the meeting, 25–9 July 1833, in Hugh James Rose's rectory at Hadleigh.

TO THE HON. WILLIAM TOWRY LAW

The Oratory January 29, 1882

My Dear Mr Law,

Thank you for your most interesting Memorials of your Son.[1] There is not a word too much in them, as you fear. It is a favour we are not often given to be able to follow year by year the formation of a saintly mind. How God has blessed you in giving you such a Son! It is a consolation for much suffering, and a sort of pledge of other mercies yet to come.

Most truly Yours, John H. Card. Newman

The Honourable W. T. Law

TO R. W. BLACKMORE

The Oratory, Birmingham Feb 1. 1882

Dear Mr Blackmore,

I hope I may be allowed to ask your acceptance of my Volume, as soon as it has passed the Press — but I fear some months must pass first.[2]

I have to thank you for your kind information in answer to my questions; also for the instruction I gain from your translation of Mouravieff with its notes, which form quite a treasure house of facts.[3]

Might I ask you some further questions? Is the Archpriest Koutnevich alive? and Philaret, Bishop of Riga.[4]

Also is the name 'Protosoff' or Pratasoff? You spell it with *a*. Mr Palmer and F. Theiner with *o*. And is it G*a*letsin or G*o*letsin[5]

Pray excuse the trouble I am giving you, and believe me to be

Sincerely Yrs John H. Newman.

TO THE DUKE OF NORFOLK

Febr 9/82

sent

My Dear Duke

If I went into the matter, I think you would see that I was not unreasonable with Mr Shipley[6]

---

[1] This was Volume I of *A Memoir of the Life and Death of the Rev. Father Augustus Law, S.J.*, London 1882. Law was born in 1833 and after being in the Royal Navy, joined the Jesuits in 1854. He became a missionary in Rhodesia and died in 1880. Volume II of *A Memoir* appeared later in 1882 and Volume III in 1883.

[2] Blackmore died on 24 June 1882, before the publication of *Notes of a Visit to the Russian Church*, see p. xvii there.

[3] A. N. Mouravief, *History of the Church of Russia*, Oxford 1842, translated by Blackmore.

[4] Blackmore replied on 11 Feb. that since he left Russia in 1847 he had had no communication with his friends there. The two mentioned were older than he was, and he was in his 92nd year.

[5] Blackmore thought Palmer was correct in spelling with an 'o' in both cases. A. Theiner in *L'Eglise schismatique Russe*, Paris 1846, p. 4, spelt 'Protasow.' In *Notes* Newman spelt 'Pratasoff' and 'Galitsin.'

[6] The Duke of Norfolk wrote on 7 Feb. to ask whether Newman's decision was irrevocable as to the number of his and Caswall's hymns to be included in Orby Shipley's hymn book.

He asked leave to use in his Volume any of my Hymns. I gave him leave, not imagining that 'any' meant 'all'. However, since he is so pressing, he may take them all if he will. They are 37 in number. As each Hymn is marked as a 'Hymn' he cannot mistake which they are. I cannot do more than this. Nearly all the rest of my Verses were written when I was a Protestant and have no place in a Catholic Collection. Indeed the same may be said of most of my Hymns, but they are Translations. I make it a condition, for the same reason, that no where in his book, or Preface, in the Title Page or Advertisement, it should be called an 'Oratorian Collection' or 'Hymns by Oratorians', or the like.

The case of Fr Caswall is more difficult. That Mr S's Collection will damage the sale of Fr Caswall's Poems, I do not at all doubt. He left an injunction on us to keep his books on sale. In his life time he was remunerated by those who asked leave to use them. The £50 which he gave towards building the mission Boys school, I think he gained in this way. Till I know more from Mr. Shipley, I cannot say which and how many Poems he wants — but any how if he made fitting remuneration to Fr Caswall's executors for his use of them, we must spend it in Advertisements for Fr Caswall's Volumes

J H N[1]

The Duke wrote, 'I own I shall be much disappointed if it is as I think such a work as we projected would be a very valuable one.' See letters of 3, 5 and 7 Jan. to Shipley.

[1] Newman has left a first draft of this letter, dated 7 Feb., which he marked 'Not sent': 'My dear Duke,

Mr Shipley asked my leave to make use, in his work of 'any' of my 'Hymns'. I answered that I had written *few* 'Hymns' but he might use 'any' of them, *if he told me first which they were*. I did not by 'any' dream of 'all' — I did not mean any number, but any which he *chose*. Yet instead of confining himself to 'Hymns' and 'any' he wrote to me to say that he proposed to make use of my whole Volume, and to take of my sets and Verses, as many as a fourth of the whole number.

Now I think I shall be able to show you, that I am not *able* to consent to this.

Only last year I laid out above £1000 in reprints of my Volumes. This year already I have paid between £70 and £80 upon reprints. Most of these will not repay me; for instance, the 'Athanasius' which cost me above £160. My Volume of 'Verses' is just one of those which does sell well, and I can't afford to lose what I gain from *it*. Publishers are not agreed whether 'Selections' are of advantage to the works they are taken from. When I had to get leave for Mr Lilly to publish specimens or 'Characteristics' of my prose, some of the publishers gave leave grudgingly. Nor is it easy to say what compensation should be made to me for taking from me a quarter of my Volume, except buying the copyright, which I could not consent to sell.

Then again, if I consent to Mr Shipley's wishes, I am making him the judge which are my best Verses and which are second best. His book will be cheaper and will have a wider circulation than mine, and (without his intending it) will exercise a more than critic's office over mine. I don't feel disposed to depute to him the power of exalting one quarter of my book, throwing the remaining three quarters into the shade, I feel unequal to exercising such an office myself, and leave it to the future.

Further, Mr Shipley's book is to be a *Catholic* Collection. Now, only 19, out of my 176 pieces, were written since I have been a Catholic.

As to Fr Caswall's hymns, I have always understood that he was paid by applicants for the use of them. Since his death we have not asked remuneration, but he left it as a charge upon us, if possible, to keep them on sale, which will not be promoted, if Mr S has the run of them. Perhaps, if remuneration were offered us, we could lay it out in advertisements.

As to myself, I will allow Mr Shipley to use my 'Hymns' and 'Songs' about 50 altogether — but he must be good enough to let me have a veto on each he takes, and to let me see each *in proof*, and to let me see, first of all his *Title page*
Yours affly John H. Card. Newman

TO THE DUKE OF NORFOLK
Bm Febr 10 1882

My dear Duke

I will gladly see the Lady you speak of and her husband, whenever they are good enough to fix a time.[1]

As to the Lecturing in London, I know how kind your wish is to keep me in the eyes of men, but please to recollect I am within a few days of 81.[2] An old man has a number of little ailments, which he must bear as he can, by living by rule.

For myself any public appearance is painful to me, and I rarely leave home without suffering afterwards for it. Then again I could not go to London without agreeing to go to Oxford and Liverpool, and what I have wished to do is to take leave of all friends and prepare for that summons which cannot be far off. Then, my mind works so slowly now; just as I cannot write a letter except letter by letter with an effort, so a Lecture or other composition is a very great trouble to me — And indeed altogether, tho' in good health, I am weaker and weaker. Also, I am full of Work which I cannot put aside. But I won't go on

Yours affectly John H Card. Newman

TO GEORGE T. EDWARDS
Bm. Febr. 15. 1882

Dear Mr Edwards

Your kind present came safely. I know the value of the book, for I have it — as well as Dr Brown's interesting Memoir of Dr Duncan — but that does not lessen your kindness in sending it to me.[3]

Thank you for your very favorable account of my Brother.[4]

Very truly Yours J. H. Card. Newman

TO THE HON. MRS MAXWELL-SCOTT
Birmingham Febr. 15. 1882

My dear Mamo

I think Lord Petre's decision should be taken as final, for there would be great difficulties in saying a little and not all.[5]

[1] The Duke wrote on 9 Feb. that a great friend, Bernard Constable-Maxwell, brother of Lord Herries, had just married a young American. She was much disposed to become a Catholic, and her husband was anxious that she should have a talk with Newman. This was Mathilda, second daughter of Alfred Dupont Jessup of Philadelphia. She was married on 8 Nov. 1881, and died on 13 Nov. 1882, after giving birth to a son.

[2] In another letter of 9 Feb., the Duke asked Newman if he would again address the Catholic Union at its annual meeting in June, suggesting such subjects 'as "the future of Catholicism in England" or the "duty of English Catholics" or "How to spread the Faith in England."'

[3] Edwards's present was John Duncan's Colloquia Peripatetica, of which Newman already had two copies. See letters of 25 May 1870 to David Douglas and 9 Dec. 1871 to William Knight. David Brown sent Newman a copy of his Life of the Late John Duncan. See letter of 26 May 1872 to Brown.

[4] Cf. Edwards's letter of 28 Dec. placed before that of 30 Dec. 1881 to him.

[5] See postscript to letter of 11 Sept. 1881 to Lady Henry Kerr.

As to my writing an introduction, alas, alas, you have touched what is a very sore place with me. I have been obliged to make it a rule to refuse to do what is in so many cases a great pleasure in itself, and honour. And I have done so in the instance of such intimate friends, that I should give great pain both to them and to myself, if I acted otherwise.

And moreover, great as are the necessary defects and shortcomings of my Funeral Sermon,[1] I could not now do any thing so well — for, though I am, thank God, in health, I am weak in mind as well as body, and my brain works slowly and feebly. And really so beautiful a life speaks for itself.

Pray remember me, as warmly as you can, to your husband, and tell him that I hear there are as various pronunciations of Spanish as there are provinces in Spain — so that he and you must not be cast down if you have fallen on a difficult dialect.

Yours affectly John H Card. Newman

TO EDMUND STONOR

Febr. 15. 1882

My dear Monsignor Stonor

Might I ask you to take the trouble to answer the following question?

To whom am I to apply to get permission for our Birmingham Oratory to have as the *fixed place*, in the Ordo, of St Lawrence (Suppl. Nov) the *13*th of February, instead of Febr. *3*, on which day the Oratory always keeps St Martina.[2] Excuse my bad writing — my fingers are in fault

Very truly yours John H Card. Newman

TO J. R. BLOXAM

Bm Febr. 17. 1882

My dear Bloxam

Your splendid book has come quite safely, and I thank you for it — It is too beautiful for such a Library as ours. It is for a nobleman's.[3] And the dictionary is very complete, containing four languages.[4]

---

[1] 'In the World but not of the World', *O.S.*, pp. 263–80.

[2] The feast of St Lawrence, Archbishop of Canterbury, had just been fixed to be kept on 3 Feb. in England. The feast of St Martina was transferred by the Oratory from 30 Jan., which was the feast of the Oratorian Blessed Sebastian Valfrè. Stonor replied on 21 Feb. that he could make the application.

[3] *Bishop Burnet's History of the Reign of King James the Second*, Oxford 1852, 'Presented . . . By his old and affectionate Friend John Rouse Bloxam, Feby 15. 1882.' This was Martin Routh's 1823 edition, enlarged.

[4] On 11 Feb. Neville wrote to Bloxam, 'You will like to know that yesterday evening the Cardinal wanted to know the meaning of a Russian word and said "A Russian Dictionary is what Dr Bloxam should send."'

I am sure I told you I was publishing one of Palmer's theological tours —
Don't you recollect my asking your leave to use your account of him in your
Register?[1]

I do not expect to go from home, except perhaps a day or two at Arundel
Castle.[2] But moving from home is a great difficulty to me now

Ever Yours affectly John H Card. Newman

TO AN UNKNOWN CORRESPONDENT

Febr 17. 1882

I would gladly accede to your request, were you simply asking of me an
act of benevolence towards persons in sore distress — but the subscription
for which you ask my name is so mixed up with matters of opinion and fact,
political and other, of what I have no accurate knowledge or definite view,
and to which in consequence I should not like to commit myself, that I am
obliged to say in answer that I do not see my way to consent to take part in it.

J H N

TO GERARD MANLEY HOPKINS

Feb 22 1882

Thank you sincerely for the kindness of your remembrance and for the
kindness of your letter

J H Card. Newman

TO MR KING

Febr 22. 1882

My dear Mr King

Thank you for so kind a remembrance of me. The flowers have come,
quite well. They are wonderful. Their fragrance quite marvellous.

Most truly yours John H Card. Newman

TO MRS WILSON

The Oratory, Birmm Febr. 22. 1882.

My dear Mrs Wilson

Your remembrance of me is very kind. It will give me much pleasure to
see you here. I have only one engagement and the time of it does not depend
on me. But I trust it will not be fixed so as to interfere with you.

Most truly Yours John H. Card Newman

---

[1] See letter of 28 Sept. 1881 to Bloxam.
[2] cf. letter of 7 Aug. 1881 to the Duke of Norfolk, who on 14 Feb. 1882 wrote that he
hoped Newman would come to Arundel at Easter.

TO LORD BLACHFORD

Birmingham, February 23rd. 1882

My dear Blachford,

Many thanks for your remembrance of my birthday — I did not forget yours — January 31st. — but somehow I let it pass without shewing you my sympathetic feeling.

I began Paget's Address at once because I liked the subject, and it seemed to come with a grace from him as having lately got into trouble for vindicating Vivisection. I have been much interested and pleased with what I have read of it, though my profound ignorance of the scientific terms and the elementary facts of Botany adds a dissatisfaction to the pleasure.[1]

My poor friend Amadeus, if I read you rightly, is on his death bed as it seems.[2] Last Monday he underwent a serious surgical operation, and has, I fear, only the alternative of dying under it, or under the disease, which it was intended to mitigate. The operation seems only to have discounted suffering, not to have paid it off. He is not much past 50, and is popular with Protestants as well as Catholics in the Potteries where he has a Mission.

Does not a *precedent* make a step 'constitutional'? and if there is hitherto no precedent, does not the step itself become and make a precedent? Perhaps the 2 Houses have *no* recognized relation to each other, as when their members speak of what was said 'in another place'. Each House may be counsellors to the Sovereign, yet ignore each other, but, Lord Granville the other day, seemed to drop the circumlocution of 'the other place.'[3] Is it not the fact that the Reform Bills of 1831–2 have opened gates which cannot shut? Did not Canning defend firstly the *principle* of that old world, antediluvian state of things, as Bismark seems now to be doing, on the ground that King, Lords and Commons all had virtual Seats in the People's House.[4]

However, I know nothing at all about it.

[R. F.] Wilson has been ill, ever since he went to Rome, and is now leaving it.

Yours affectionately, John H. Cardinal Newman.

[1] Newman was evidently reading Sir James Paget's Presidential Address at the meeting of the British Medical Association in Aug. 1880 at Cambridge. This was *Elemental Pathology*, on the diseases and injuries of plants and trees, published later in the same year. There are extracts from it in *Memoirs and Letters of Sir James Paget*, edited by Stephen Paget, London, 1901, pp. 299–305. Sir James Paget had been attacked for his article 'The Pains of Vivisection' in the *Nineteenth Century* for Dec. 1881.

[2] Amadeus was the name taken by Charles Meynell in his discussion with Wilfrid Scawen Blunt, *Proteus and Amadeus: A Correspondence*, edited by Aubrey de Vere, London 1878. See letter of 22 July 1878 to Lord Blachford. Meynell, who had read the proofs of *G.A.* for Newman, was the priest at Caverswall, and died on 3 May 1882, aged 53.

[3] On 16 Feb. Lord Granville replied in the House of Lords to an accusation made in the House of Commons that George Errington was being paid for the mission on which he had been sent, in order to put the British Government's case in Ireland before the Holy See.

[4] Gladstone had moved a resolution for an inquiry into the working of the Irish Land Act, which contradicted a decision of the House of Lords. He was accused of passing a vote of censure on the Upper House. In Germany Bismarck had reversed his policy and was trying to win the support of the Catholic Centre deputies for his plans.

Bm Febr. 25. 1882

My dear Mr Plummer

I think it particularly kind of you writing to me on my birthday and shall be much disappointed, if you cease to take that trouble.

In answer to your question I have to say, with thanks to God, that I am very well, having nothing the matter with me; but I cannot deny that I get more and more infirm.

I have not had time to go into the interesting controversy about the Revision of the text and translation of the New Testament, not even have I seen the Article in the Quarterly, which I took for granted was Burgon's, before you told me.[1]

I am busy in passing through the Press a volume containing the Journal of William Palmer's first visit to Russia. To me it is exceedingly interesting — but it may, for what I know, be too ancient for this generation. He left me all his papers — and it is a pleasure to me to do what I so pressed upon him in vain to do himself.[2]

Most truly Yours John H Card. Newman

TO THE HON. MRS MAXWELL-SCOTT

Bm Febr 27. 1882

My dear Mamo

I said Mass for your brother in law yesterday morning and am very sorry to find you have so great a grief.[3]

Since you and your Aunt are disappointed at my stating my difficulties in writing an introduction to the Memoir, I will face those difficulties and write one, if on consideration you and she should wish. But I am obliged to state my conviction that you will be more disappointed by what I write than at my not writing at all. I cannot write any thing to the purpose, imperfect as it is, so apposite as my Funeral Sermon, which is to have a place in the volume. It came from my heart and I cannot write so well now. My brain works slowly, and after all can only produce my second best. All I will ask is, that you will make your decision, with what I have said in view.[4]

Your dear Aunt expects too much. Mr Ornsby cannot do more than use the materials given to him. Your Father, though he wrote long letters on points which interested him, could not be called a good correspondent. Till

---

[1] Burgon had three articles 'New Testament Revision' in the *Quarterly Review*, Oct. 1881, Jan. and April 1882, republished as *The Revision Revised*, 1883. He criticised the *Revised Version* for not following the Textus Receptus. See also letter of 8 Feb. 1884 to Lord Blachford.

[2] Plummer wrote on 10 Nov. 1882 to thank for *Notes of a Visit to the Russian Church*.

[3] This was John Constable-Maxwell, born in 1855, who died on 16 Feb. 1882.

[4] See letter of 15 Feb. to Mrs Maxwell-Scott. Her aunt was Lady Henry Kerr. Newman's funeral sermon was reprinted as the first appendix in *Memoirs of James Robert Hope-Scott* II, London 1884.

1844 Gladstone was his special confidant. From my own conversion till after his, I had very few or rather no letters from him. Afterwards, from the necessities of his professional engagements his letters to me are infrequent and seldom long.

Ever Yours affectly John H Card. Newman

TO ÉDOUARD REFFÉ

[March 1882][1]

but, alas, Parliament has never had the wisdom to grant a whole measure of justice to Ireland — but spoils what it does in the right direction by niggarly [sic] and ungenerous reservations and limitations   I fear I saw in the Papers that the proposition you advocate[2]

TO JANE MOZLEY

Birmingham March 1. 1882

My dear Jane

I ought to have thanked you for your kind birthday letter before this — but I write with difficulty, and almost daily letters come which require an immediate answer, and thus those which admit of delay fare badly. And my brain works so slowly now, that now, when I take up my pen, I can hardly do more than thank you.

Your Aunt Anne asked me lately what literary work I was at, for she was sure I could not do without writing. That was, begging her pardon, a shallow philosophy. In 1874 I said in print, that I had fired my last shot — and in fact I have never written any thing since but letters. And now you may tell her when you see her, that what I am doing now, which she wished to know, is passing thro' the Press a volume of Notes of Mr Palmer's about Russia, he having left me all his Papers

Say every thing kind from me to your Aunts, and believe me

Yours affectly John H. Card Newman

TO ROBERT WHITTY, S.J.

Bm March 2. 1882

My dear Fr Whitty

I was very glad to see your hand, and had been hoping before that some good chance would occasion an interchange of letters between us — And I only wish I could display penmanship equal to yours — but I find it difficult

---

[1] This extract from a letter of March 1882 was published in the *Blackrock College Annual*, 1932, p. 34, but the autograph can no longer be traced. Reffé, a native of Alsace, was a Holy Ghost Father, and Dean of Studies at Blackrock College, County Dublin, 1864–88.

[2] Newman was replying to a letter from Reffé, who sent a copy of his pamphlet *The Royal University Fellowships and the Queen's Colleges*, written under the pseudonym 'Fair Play', at Archbishop McCabe's request.

and irksome to write, which must be my excuse for sending you so shabby a letter as this, I fear, will be.

Of course I was attracted by your friend's Article both for his Father's sake and his own — He, I believe, is one of two, who called on me together in passing through Birmingham some years ago. I thought his subject for discussion a very happy one, as being seasonable and important — and he treated it with marked ability. He made various good suggestions for the settling of it, but, through my own fault, I did not take it in as a whole, and, like the writer in the Spectator, I thought it required some thing more of analysis than he had found room for in the 19th Century.[1]

When I say 'through my own fault,' I am not using words of course. My brain works slowly as well as my hand, and is soon tired.

Your Sister was so kind as to send me a letter about the good Bishop. I was grieved to hear of his death, and from my recollection of him it seemed to me premature. Was he not the youngest of three brothers, all priests?[2]

Yours ever affectionately John H. Card. Newman

TO PIERCE CONNELLY

March [3?] 1882

Dear Sir

I have no recollection of receiving any letter or Sermon from you, as you inform me, a year ago

Nor have I any recollections of writing about the xi Article, or any Article, of the Apostles Creed in my letter to the Duke of Norfolk[3]

But even if I had, I do not feel it to be necessary to answer the criticisms made on any thing I have written. I am willing they should stand for the judgment of the public

J H N[4]

[1] The article in the *Nineteenth Century* (Feb. 1882), pp. 195–216, was 'The Wish to believe: a dialogue in a Catholic college', by Wilfrid Ward, reprinted as a volume and in *Witnesses to the Unseen and other Essays*, London 1893. R. H. Hutton reviewed it in the *Spectator* (4 Feb. 1882), pp. 150–1, and complained that Ward had not analysed 'what the causes are by virtue of which the optimists are made credulous of the things they hope, and pessimists are made credulous of the things they fear.'

Wilfrid Ward, who was born in 1856, paid his second visit to Newman on 30 Jan. 1885.

[2] This refers to James Quinn, Bishop of Brisbane, born in 1820 with brothers priests. Whitty's sister Ellen, became a Sister of Mercy, and went out to Australia at Quinn's request in 1861. Quinn, who had been Dean of St Laurence's House at Newman's University in Dublin, died on 30 Aug. 1881.

[3] Pierce, the husband of Mother Cornelia Connelly, and American Episcopalian chaplain in Florence, wrote on 1 March, 'Dear Lord Cardinal

If, remembering me, you will still allow me to address you so!' and went on to say that in Oct. 1880 he had sent a copy of a sermon he had published to Newman. In it he maintained that in *A Letter to the Duke of Norfolk* Newman had misunderstood the meaning of the XIth article of the Apostles' Creed.

[4] Connelly replied on 14 March that he would send another copy of his sermon. If he did so this did not arrive, for he wrote on 17 May to say that it had not been acknowledged. Newman made a note of his reply: 'May 20/82 answered that a letter came to me from him some weeks ago and that I answered it at once, according to the address which Mr C. gave him and by the international post office.'

TO R. W. CHURCH

Bm Mar. 6. 1882

My dear Dean

Poor Golightly! I half hoped I should have met him in Oxford two years ago. His brother was in confinement when I knew him, and I could fancy he talked to me a great deal about him. I knew his mother almost before he was born and recited to her on Ham Common 'The Butterfly's Ball and the Grasshopper's Feast'.[1]

Yours affly John H. Card. Newman

TO LADY HENRY KERR

Birmingham. March 9. 1882.

My dear Lady Henry

I said Mass for your dear husband this morning, so did Fr Neville.[2] Fr Bellasis as perhaps you know had done so too before us —

I do not know how to use the language of condolement   The thought of him is so happy. For myself I can only recollect the many kindnesses he showed me, and I pray for him from gratitude though I am sure he cannot need my prayers.

You will be supported by our good God — You have an abundance of consolations. May we, when our time comes, be as ready and prepared to go as he was

Yours affectly in Xt   John H. Card. Newman.

TO AUGUSTUS HENRY KEANE

[11 March 1882]

Dear Mr Keane

Of course I cannot but feel interest in the success of those first members of the Catholic University with whom I was connected, and I readily bear the witness of my memory to the fact that you were then a clever and promising young man, and that I looked forward to your doing us credit when you had entered upon the business of life. I shall be glad to hear you have been chosen for the post to which you aspire[3]

I am J H N

---

[1] According to *DNB* notice of C. P. Golightly, who died in 1885, 'For the last three years of his life he was haunted by painful illusions.' Golightly's parents lived at Ham, where he was born in 1807. His mother, Frances Dodd, was of Huguenot descent. The nursery classic, 'The Butterfly's Ball and the Grasshopper's Feast', by William Roscoe appeared in the November 1806 number of the *Gentleman's Magazine*. It was set to music for the royal princesses and published in 1807 as the first in a popular series of children's books.

[2] Lord Henry Kerr died on 7 March.

[3] Keane was applying for one of the thirty-two Fellowships at the Royal University of Ireland, for which appointments were to be made on 18 April. He asked for a recommendation. Cf. letter of 31 Aug. 1858 to him. He eventually became Professor of Hindustani at University College, London.

TO ST GEORGE JACKSON MIVART

Birmingham. March 12. 1882.

My dear Professor Mivart,

Mr Keane has written to me as he has to you. I recollect him when I was in Ireland (1854–58) as a clever young man, especially (I *think*) in his knowledge of languages — but I have no recollections of him after that date, though his name is familiar to me.

I was much attracted by the subject of your article in this month's Month, and read it with great interest and sense of its importance and appositeness; but I was not a little shocked, as well as grateful to you, by the passage which suddenly came upon me at p. 338.[1]

Very sincerely yours John H. Card. Newman

TO F. G. PINCOTT

Birmingham March 13. 1882

Dear Sir

I feel the compliment you pay me in proposing to put my lines to music, and I gladly give you the necessary permission.

Very truly Yours John H Card. Newman

F. G. Pincott Esqre

TO ORBY SHIPLEY

Mar. 13. 1882

Dear Sir

Please be so kind as to give me an answer to the question which both through the Duke of Norfolk and thro' Fr Neville I have already asked you. I cannot consider anything settled till you do.[2]

---

[1] Mivart's article in the *Month* (March 1882), pp. 333–44, was 'A Danger from Diffidence.' On p. 338 Mivart in defending our knowledge of the substantial self, wrote: 'There are some of us who may have known Cardinal Newman for years, now as a most kind and sympathetic friend, now as a leader of thought at Oxford, now as a poet, now as a philosopher, now as a master of style, now as a leader in the defence of truth, now as a devoted son of St Philip, now as a Cardinal of the Holy Roman Church, now as a patient and judicious guide in religious difficulties, now as a man of saintly life, now as a man of commanding genius. But we none of us have ever known him except in some "state" . . . This plain truth, however, in no way prevents our having very truly and really known him, and known him to be the very same person through all these changing states.'

[2] On 29 Dec. 1881 in his first letter about his hymnbook Shipley had written: 'I would ask your Eminence to bear in mind that the Hymn book will be mainly compiled from the works of the fathers of the Oratory; that, if it be successful, a proportion of the results will be given to the Oratory; and that I should wish to make the Oratory benefit by the copyright eventually.' On 4 Jan. Shipley wrote: 'The foundation of the book was laid in the dogmatic translations of Fr Caswall and the more subjective pieces of Fr Faber.'

Newman kept the draft he wrote out for Neville to send: 'March 9. 1882
My dear Sir
Cardinal Newman wishes me to repeat to you what he has already said to the Duke of Norfolk that any permission for you to print any of the Cardinal or Fr Caswall's Hymns

Do you give me an assurance that neither in your title page, nor in your Preface, nor in Advertisements nor in any other way will you call your Volume an Oratorian Hymnal, or Hymns by Fathers of the Oratory, or the like[1]

JHN

Mr Orby Shipley

TO GERALDINE PENROSE FITZGERALD

Birmingham Mar. 17. 1882

My Dear Child

I congratulate you on St Patrick's day, and join all friends of Ireland in an earnest prayer that its present melancholy troubles may be brought to an end.

I have begun your story, and it reads very well, with more ease and natural flow than your earlier Tales. But I dread what is to come. Old men do not like tragedy or sensation.[2]

I would do for your friend what I could, did I do so for any — but I should already have committed myself in behalf of another candidate, if I had found it right to interpose for any one. I know no one, who is more able to exercise his patronage well, than the owner of it in this instance.[3] I am sure you will understand my delicacy and difficulty. I am very sorry.[4]

TO THE HON. MRS MAXWELL-SCOTT

Birmingham 17 Mar. 1882

My dear Mamo,

You have indeed accumulated sorrow.[5] One's consolation under such trials, which are our necessary lot here, is that we have additional friends in heaven to plead and interest themselves for us. This I am confident of — if it is not presumptuous to be confident — but I think, as life goes on, it will be brought home to you, as it has been to me, that there are those who are busied about us, and in various daily matters taking our part.

I trust the blow will not be too great for your Aunt in her weak state of health — that is what I cannot help being anxious about.

I feel the tender consideration for me which has led you and her to give

depends entirely on your abstaining from calling your collection whether in the Title Page or Preface or in Advertisements or in any other way by the title of "the Oratory Hymn Book", or Hymns by Fathers of the Oratory, or Oratory Hymns, or any such name

This he is decided about, and he would take it as a favour if you would send him your acceptance of this condition in writing before printing any of the Hymns. He hopes you will excuse this, on the ground of the grave misunderstanding which has already occurred.

Also he would ask for a sight of the printer's proofs of each of them.'

[1] On 14 March Shipley replied giving the assurance asked, and saying he had never intended to call his book Oratorian.
[2] See letters of 8 and 13 July 1882 to Miss Fitzgerald.
[3] This perhaps refers to the Duke of Norfolk.
[4] The conclusion has been cut out.
[5] See letters of 27 Feb. to Mrs Maxwell-Scott and 9 March to Lady Henry Kerr.

up your wish that I should prefix an Introduction for the Memoir — and I still will attempt it, should you change your minds, but I still think the volume will be better without it.

I forget whether I told you that Mr W. Palmer has to my surprise left me all his Papers, including various valuable Journals of his visits to Russia etc. It is impossible at my time of life, I can use them as they deserve to be used, but I am seeing a first volume of them, which I often pressed him to publish, through the Press

Yours ever affly John H Card. Newman

TO EDWIN PALMER

Birmingham March 18. 1882

Mr dear Archdeacon Palmer

I have sent the first sheets of your brother's Journal to the printer As perhaps you observed, he had prepared a portion of the MS for the Press himself; but still there has been a good deal to do. I have transcribed a great part of it myself, it has besides been all transcribed for the Printer, and I have read most of it several times over, and of course shall see it again in proof

I do not think any part of it can offend any one. All but all the personages who are named in it are dead — and I have excluded any half sentence which I thought would pain any one.

It gives a vivid and I believe a true picture of the Russian Church, and if it has the same effect on others, which it has upon me, it will make them, not only know Russia, but feel love, interest, and tenderness towards it and its people.[1]

As for the author, he is consistent from first to last. Holding as we all did, (and of course as I do still) that the Church is Catholic, and One and Holy, he said 'Oriental' is but a name in Russia for that one Catholic Holy Church, and therefore I as a child of the One Church, claim to be admitted to its Sacraments. The Russian Ecclesiastics refused — and this is the staple of his narrative. He goes to Petersburg, Moscow, and then back to England. I have left untouched his interposition with the Russian converts at Geneva, and his negotiations with the Scotch Episcopalians.

I expect the Volume will run to about 450 pages — duodecimo or small octavo

I have written a preface of a few pages, which I think of sending you.

I got a very kind answer back from Mr Blackmore, who is past 90, and who has allowed me to insert all his conversations etc with your brother, and gave me some useful information[2]

Very truly Yours John H Card. Newman

[1] Palmer replied on 19 March that his brother's Journals had 'produced the same impression upon you that they (and his conversation) produced upon all his brothers and sisters and our parents.'
[2] See letter of 1 Feb. to Blackmore.

TO EDWIN PALMER

Birmingham March 20. 1882

My dear Archdeacon

Your letter was a great satisfaction to me, though I hope you do not expect too much. Thank you for the notice of Mr Kh's book, which I shall try to get.[1] My Preface will be short, and will attempt to explain that the ecclesiastical view which took your brother to Russia, was no fancy of his own, but the teaching of the High Anglican School, which many who might be interested in his name and the matter of his book might not know.

I have introduced nothing of my own, but only here and there, where he or his Russian friends say something to the disadvantage of the Church of Rome, I have explained (in a note), or defended, the latter.

As to my publisher, I have not settled who, and should be glad of advice. My way is to keep a considerable hold on my volumes, publishing them on *commission* — and therefore not deciding by whom till they are printed. I found the great London Houses are shy, except Longmans, of the work of a Catholic[2]

Any suggestions you can make will be very welcome.

Very sincerely Yrs J H Card. Newman

TO HENRY SPENCER KENRICK BELLAIRS

Birmingham March 21. 1882

Dear Sir

I have not answered you sooner, because I was perplexed what to say. And, even if I could say anything, in what way to say it as to keep within the bounds of a letter.

As to the doctrine of eternal punishment, the question was, I think, of prudence in discussing it, and the imprudence of adding to it, as is so commonly done, what is not in Scripture. There was no question whether the doctrine was true or not[3]

But now, in questions of science, if I understand you, the question comes in as to what is true and what is not true, what the Scripture says and what it is silent upon; and how far it admits of interpretations different from those which are traditional; and comparisons and contrasts arise between probable truths in science and probable interpretations of Scripture.

For myself I should lay down as a Catholic, that mere probability of a scientific fact should not be allowed to tell against a received interpretation of Scripture. It ought not to be allowed, it has no right, to be brought into

[1] See letter of 22 March to Palmer.
[2] See letter of 2 Jan. to W. J. Rivington.
[3] Bellairs, who wrote on 9 March, referred to his earlier letter. See that of 27 Nov. 1879 to him. He now asked how to deal with Christians who doubted because of objections against their faith drawn from science.

court. Many things are probable which are eventually proved to be false. Evolution of vegetable and animal life is not proved — but it may be probable, and that, without being in the way to be proved. Dr Pritchard wrote to prove the descent of mankind from one pair. It was, as I recollect, a beautiful instance of close reasoning. It had one defect — it made Adam a negro.[1] This will illustrate what I mean when I say that we have no need, we are not called on, to meet probable cases, which may, as time goes on, be refuted by other probabilities.

Very truly Yours J. H Card Newman

TO WILLIAM PHILIP GORDON

Bm March 21/82

My dear Fr Gordon

I had just said Mass for Fr Knox, when your letter of this morning came to me.[2] Of course we could not be surprised at yesterday's telegram, and we knew well how much you had to console you.

I expect Fr Mills every hour from Rednall — and I am sure he will gladly accept your invitation for Friday.

Yours affectly John H Card. Newman

P.S. Fr Mills will avail himself of your offer and come on Thursday evening

TO LADY SIMEON

Birmingham March 21. 1882

My dear Lady Simeon

Though I had not felt dear C's vocation to be otherwise than uncertain as yet, the failure of it has, on your account, given me very great pain.[3] It is not by any means a common blow, and I grieve for it with all my heart. You have nobly and with great self-denial and silent suffering taken on you a very difficult office and work for the sake of most dear and ever present memories, and it seemed as if your reward had come, and the day of peace had come for you and   .[4] I am saying more perhaps than you will yourself allow — but it is the way I view it for you, though I know full well you will be strengthened and cheered and prospered to do whatever is God's will in respect to you.

May God bless you and guide you and lift up His countenance upon you, and give you peace.

This is the earnest prayer of yours affectionately

John H. Card. Newman.

[1] This was James Cowles Prichard in his *Researches as to the Physical History of Man*, London 1813, second edition in two volumes, 1826. He held that our first parents were black and that white skin was due to the influence of civilisation.

[2] T. F. Knox of the London Oratory died on 20 March.

[3] This refers to Cecilia, Sir John Simeon's youngest daughter by his first wife.

[4] The copyist has left a blank here. Presumably Newman wrote the name of Lady Simeon's own daughter, Catherine, who was not married.

Bm Mar. 22. 82

My dear Sir Henry

I had already seen your name in so prominent a position in the movement in defence of the integrity of the Abbey, that I was led to inquire about it; and now you give me the opportunity of taking part in it[1]

I will tell you why, with much regret, I cannot.

First, because I have never come forward on such an occasion. It is not my line.

Next, because I have no kind of relation or connexion with the Abbey

Thirdly, because, if I took the exceptional step of interposing in any such matter, it would be with the artistic object of rummaging out of the poor old Abbey the ill placed, ugly, tasteless monuments which make it look like a broker's shop, whenever I have been led, from old love, to go through it, and remind me of the necessity of applying to it the remedy which Andrew Fairservice says was successfully used in the instance of Glasgow Cathedral, which was washed and combed as clear of its images, as a cat may be cleared of fleas.[2]

And lastly, I have friends connected with the School, who would be hurt, if, instead of minding my own business, I went out of the way in my old age to do a disservice to them.[3]

Judge me compassionately, and believe me to be, in spite of this discourtesy,[4]

Most truly Yours John H. Card. Newman

Sir H. Cole K C B &c &c

Bm March 22/82

My dear Archdeacon

I thank you for the extract you have taken the trouble to copy, and I have to thank Dr Liddon as well as you for the trouble you both are taking and have taken for me as regards Khomiakoff's book, itself.[5]

[1] Sir Henry Cole wrote on 21 March: 'Would there not be an historical fitness in your name appearing to the Memorial to preserve Westminster Abbey against Elizabethan intruders?' Under the Public Schools Act Westminster School had been separated from Westminster Abbey and from the authority of its Dean and Chapter. A memorial had been sent to the Prime Minister asking for a royal commission to enquire into the state of the School and why the Act contained a clause alienating it from the Abbey. *The Times* (16 Jan. 1882), p. 9.
[2] Sir Walter Scott, *Rob Roy*, end of Chapter 19.
[3] Newman's friends connected with Westminster School welcomed its independence.
[4] Sir Henry Cole replied on 25 March: 'Your letter although conveying a refusal charmed me. Looking with your eyes I agree with its reasons'. This was his last letter to Newman. See letter of 20 April to his son.
[5] Palmer told Newman of a note in which Alexis Stepanovich Khomiakoff had spoken tenderly of his friend William Palmer. Edwin Palmer and Liddon were trying to find the book containing it so that Newman could use it in his preface. It was printed in Khomiakoff's

I do not need to see it, thank you. The note you quote will enable me to use some words in illustration of what I say in my Preface, but as a whole is it written in the author's first burst of anger (1857) on hearing that his friend had joined 'the Latin Church'. There is none of his bitterness in the conversations which your brother had with ecclesiastics at Petersburg, distant as they were from any drawing to Rome; but M. Khomiakoff is so little himself, that he finds fault with his Supreme Synod, because they acted towards William as only they could consistently act. He seems to have made it too much a party question, whether a man joined the Russian Church or the Latin; whereas your brother, whether his decision was right or wrong, had only one thought before him, which was that ecclesiastical communion which our Lord set up in the beginning. But you must not suppose I am going to say any thing of this kind in my Preface.[1]

I had no thought of going to Longmans — though they have heretofore taken volumes of mine. It is my wish to put the book into hands which would give it the widest circulation — but I have failed in the one application which I have made.[2]

How could you fancy that I should allow you to 'order the book,' unless I had no chance of persuading you to accept as many copies as you please from me.[3]

Very sincerely Yours John H. Card Newman

TO SIR HENRY COLE

Bm March 26/82

My Dear Sir Henry

I thank you very much for your Abbey Guide — which, I see at once, is very much superior to what Guides are commonly.[1] The woodcuts make a

L'Eglise Latine et Le Protestantisme, Lausanne 1872, p. 258, but the note first appeared in his *Encore Quelques Mots d'un Chrétien Orthodoxe sur Les Confessions Occidentales*, Leipzig 1858, p. 62. It said:

'Aucun pays n'a montré autant de désir de se rapprocher de l'Eglise que l'Angleterre, et dans ces derniers temps nous avons encore vu un de ses plus dignes enfants, William Palmer travailler avec ardeur à rétablir l'antique unité. Quoique tombé plus tard dans l'erreur Romaine, nous osons espérer que sa faute lui sera pardonnée en faveur de la lutte si longue et si douloureuse qu'il avait soutenue. Quant à ceux (quelque haut placés qu'ils soient) qui lui ont fermé la porte de l'Eglise et ont occasionné sa défection, tout ce que nous pouvons dire d' eux, c'est que nous désirons que Dieu les juge dans sa miséricorde; car ils ont été bien coupables. Cette âme si pure et si avide de vérité, maintenant jetée au centre même du mensonge constant et volontaire, n'a pas de repos à attendre sur la terre à moins d'un retour qu'il est impossible de prévoir. Pauvre Palmer! Si jamais ces lignes tombent sous ses yeux, je voudrais qu'il apprît que sa chute a attristé bien des coeurs amis, et que les souffrances qui l'ont précédée avaient déjà fait verser des larmes amères à des yeux que la mort a fermés à jamais.'

[1] In the preface to *Notes of a Visit to the Russian Church* Newman explains that Palmer's appeal for the recognition of Anglo-Catholicism 'is the main subject of this volume, though not the main object of its publication. It is published for the vivid picture it presents to us, for better or for worse, of the Russian Church . . .' pp. vii–viii.

[2] See letter of 2 Jan. to W. J. Rivington.

[3] Palmer on 21 March said he had only asked about Newman's publisher so that he could order the book in question.

[4] Cole sent a copy of the guide or handbook he brought out in 1842, *Westminster Abbey*.

great impression on even an unartistic person like myself. I see you agree with me mainly as to the monuments. I have added to it the plan of the monastery, which you sent me before

Most Sincerely Yours John H. Card Newman

Sir Henry Cole K C B &c &c

TO BARONESS ANATOLE VON HÜGEL

Bm March 26 82

My dear Isy

Your letter was very welcome to me. I said Mass for dear Agnes just now. I have not been so much shocked, I don't know when, at the accounts about her.[1]

Don't, please, make it a trouble your writing to me. I always like hearing about you, and I am glad that you and your husband have found a home, but I never expect a letter. I know what a job letter writing is

I wish you were stronger than people tell me you are

Ever Yours affectly John H. Card. Newman

TO WILLIAM HOBART KERR, S.J.

Bm March 30/82.

My dear Fr Kerr,

I now thank you for your very kind letter on dear Lord Henry's death because I am going to ask of you another kindness, thinking it not unlikely you may be still at Huntlyburn.[2]

Will you then tell me how Lady Henry is and how she bears her trial. As she was so ill herself several months ago, this is with me a very anxious question, and a few lines from you would be gratefully received by me —

Very truly yours, John H Card Newman

TO LORD BLACHFORD

Birmingham, April 1st. 1882.

My dear Blachford,

I am very much tempted by my own fears and feelings to put my name to the protest made against the Channel Tunnel. But am held back by my utter ignorance of political and military matters, and that in such an act I run the risk of its being refracted, like a stick in water, by being poked into a medium of which I have no experience and which I do not understand e.g., it may be fraternizing with some party or other — or fairly mean something which I have no intention of its meaning.

[1] This refers to Agnes Wilberforce, who had married Richard Hurrell Froude on 25 April 1881. See letter of 26 April to Miss Giberne.
[2] W. H. Kerr had written on 9 March.

73

Among those who have given their names to it are Lord Bath, Lord Lytton, Lord Halifax, Lord Bury, Cardinal Manning, Sir James Paget, Mr. Tennyson, Professor Huxley, Mr. Hutton, Mr. Knowles and Mr. Holyoake.[1]

I suppose *you* have reason against it — or does a Private Bill come before the House of Lords.[2]

A Happy Easter to you and Lady Blachford.

Ever yours affectionately, J. H. Card: Newman.

TO LORD BLACHFORD

Bm April 4. 1882

My dear Blachford

Thank you for your letter, from which I gather, that you do not feel that the names of the Protest are significant of any party movement. In consequence I shall put my own name to it, though it is sore penance to me to let it stand in any soever sort of connection with some of those already attached to it.[3]

With King Leopold, as quoted (I think) in the xix century,[4] I weigh 'a probable advantage against a possible disadvantage' — and the advantage after all being nothing more than the saving travellers from sea sickness and an increase of French visitors, and the disadvantage being the utter ruin of the British Power, I can come to but one conclusion. And even without the real possibility of the evil contemplated, I think the idea of a possibility will act upon the imagination of the nation with results to the national character so serious, that, though they be not unmixed evil, yet involve a great responsibility in those parties who brought them about. I am only expressing the alarm which I suggested 50 years ago, when I compared England to 'haughty Babel, when the huge moat *lay bare*'; and warned her that 'Mad counsel in its hour, or *traitors* will prevail;' viz some Fenian of a Secret Society.[5]

Now I have begun to egotise, I will refer, lest I should seem not to have an ever-present consciousness of it, as an habitual imagination of mine, to a sentiment like Keble's which is remarkable as being independent of Keble. Keble, I fully grant, is the *one* Prophet and Preacher, as he may be called, of

---

[1] The protest against the proposed Channel Tunnel appeared in the *Nineteenth Century* for April. Lord Blachford seems to have written about Newman's feelings to the editor, James Knowles, because on 3 April the latter sent him a copy of the protest, and asked for his signature to it. See next letter.

[2] There were two private bills about the Channel Tunnel before the House of Commons.

[3] Newman's name appeared with many others in the *Nineteenth Century* for May. Six other members of the Birmingham Oratory also signed the protest.

[4] The quotation seems not to be in the *Nineteenth Century*.

[5] 'Dread thine own power! Since haughty Babel's prime,
    High towers have been man's crime,
Since her hoar age, when the huge moat lay bare,
    Strongholds have been man's snare.
Thy nest is in the crags; ah! refuge frail!
Mad counsel in its hour, or traitors, will prevail.'
'England', 2nd stanza, *V.V.*, XLIII p. 89.

the spiritual miseries which now surround us, that is since 1827, when the Christian Year was published — but before that, and before I knew *Froude*, I said something in his ⟨Keble's⟩ tone in 1826, about Freethinkers, in my first University Sermon and continued the theme in others on to 1832.

I say then, 'Although Christianity etc. . . . yet, as the principles of science are, in process of time, more fully developed, and become more independent of the religious system, there is much danger lest the philosophical school should be found to separate from the Christian Church etc etc.'[1]

I am glad at what you say about South Africa. I had not followed the history lately.

Yrs affly J H Card. Newman

TO CARDINAL LAVIGERIE

Birmingham die 4 Aprilis 1882

Eminentissime et Revme Domine mi Observandissime

Gratias Eminentiae Tuae habeo, quod me certiorem fecisti, in acceptissima Tua Epistola, de promotione Eminentiae Tuae meritissima ad Sanctae Rom. Ecclesiae amplissimum Purpuratorum Senatum.[2]

Sic voluit et ordinavit pro perspicaci prudentia sua, Sanctissimus Dominus noster Leo; ego vero S.S. Pontificis servus et creatura ipsemet, quid aliud re cognita Eminentiae Tuae debeo quam Tibi gratulari, quod quidem ex animo facio, de co-optatione Eminentiae Tuae in fraternitatem nostram, et omnia bona, et faustissima quaeque, ad multos annos optare Tibi et augurari dum humillime manus Tuas deosculor?

et me Emae Tuae offero et commendo
Humillimus et devotissimus Servus

Emo ac Revmo Dño
Card. Carolo Lavigerie Archiep. Alger

TO CARDINAL MACCABE

Birmingham, Die 4 Aprilis 1882

Eminentissime et Reve Domine mi Observandissime

Mirum profecto foret, nisi me singulari quodam gaudio afficerent litterae Eminentiae Tuae, in quibus de Tua ad Cardinalatum promotione certior factus sum.

---

[1] 'Although, then, Christianity seems to have been the first to give to the world the pattern of the true spirit of philosophical investigation, yet, as the principles of science are, in process of time, more fully developed, and become more independent of the religious system, there is much danger lest the philosophical school should be found to separate from the Christian Church, and at length to disown the parent to whom it has been so greatly indebted.' 'The Philosophical Temper, first enjoined by the Gospel', preached 2 July 1826, *U.S.*, p. 14.

[2] Charles Lavigerie, Archbishop of Algiers and Edward McCabe, Archbishop of Dublin, were made Cardinals on 27 March.

Quis est enim qui me sibi arctioribus charitatis et gratitudinis vinculis jure devinctum tenet, quam Eminentia Tua?

Quis porro in dilectissimâ sua patriâ, pro bono publico, pro concivium suorum et libertate et felicitate, ut decuit Antistitem, fortiorem, prudentiorem, honestiorem agendi cursum elegit, Eminentissime Praesul, quam Tu?

Ego proinde Deo O. M. gratias habeo qui in mentem Summi Pontificis Leonis, Sanctissimi Domini nostri, injecerit, Eminentiam Tuam in amplissimum nostrum Purpuratorum Senatum introducere, et Tibi, Eminentissime Domine, toto animo et pleno corde gratulor, et manus Tuas simul humillime et peramanter deosculor, et me Tibi offero et trado

Eminentiae Tuae
Humillimus et devotissimus Servus

Emmo ac Revmo Dño
Card. Eduardo MacCabe

TO MRS. F. J. WATT

Rednall April 11. 1882

My dear Eleanor

I am glad you are so prudent, though it is a sad penance, to keep at home these festal days. The weather is very treacherous, and the frosts are very severe.

All our trees here suffer seriously from them, and still more, (mild as the winter has been,) from the blights. It has quite put me out of heart with planting, so many of our shrubs and young trees have come to grief.

It is sad to think how few you now know of our Community. But it is the course of life. Your thoughts are meant to be directed to those who are growing up around you. Tell Daisy that I find that Mama has not managed to leave off the habit of calling her by that name, to judge by Mama's letter to me, though she is now so great a child. I am glad to hear so good an account of you all.

The best Easter blessings be upon all of you.

Yours affectly John H Card. Newman

TO EDWIN PALMER

Bm April 12 1882

Dear Archdeacon Palmer

In a few days I shall trouble you with my short Preface. I hope I have said nothing in it to displease members of the Church of England, but I send it to you mainly for the remarks at the end of it about your brother.

Strike them out without scruple if you wish to do so. I am not sure that

I shall not be better pleased by their being cut out, than kept in. So, I repeat, have no scruple, and believe me

Yours very sincerely John H Card. Newman[1]

A happy Easter to you

TO EMILY BOWLES

Bm April 13. 1882

My dear Child

Thank you for your affectionate Paschal greetings, which I return with all my heart. I send them also to Frederic, since I find you are still with him, and to Miss Bathurst and her community.[2]

I am very glad to know that Cecie is going to Mary; and that they will be somewhere on the south coast of France.[3] It seems to be a very good arrangement. You don't say what has become of Eddy, and I am very sorry to find that Louy is so far from well.[4]

I suppose dear Lord Henry's [Kerr] death has thrown back the printing of the Memoir. The facts, that is, Hope Scott's acts and letters, are so striking, that they carry his wonderful character with them and need no comment. I say 'wonderful', because it is rare to find a man of the world so deeply religious, so holy in the inner man. A man may have many good points, yet have no interior. Hope Scott speaks for himself. I have heard nothing of the alterations you speak of.[5]

I am very well, thank you, though infirm. I wish people would learn the difference between the two words. Then they would not wish me to leave home.

Yours affly J H Card. Newman

TO LOUISA ELIZABETH DEANE

Birmingham Ap 16. 1882

My dear Louisa

I want your daughter who has made me so beautiful a present, (Louisa) to accept from me an Easter gift in turn. I should have written to you a week ago, had I had time.[6]

[1] After reading Newman's preface to *Notes of a Visit to the Russian Church*, Palmer wrote on 15 April: 'I cannot tell you with what pleasure I have read the prefatory words which you have so kindly sent me, and which I now return. I thought it a great, but wholly unnecessary, piece of consideration on your part to show them me before publication. I knew perfectly well that there would not be a syllable that I should wish to see altered, Nor is there one. I am sure that all who loved William will agree with me.'
[2] Frederic Bowles was at Harrow, where also was Catherine Bathurst's convent.
[3] This refers to Cecilia Simeon and her sister Mary, see letter of 21 March to Lady Simeon.
[4] i.e. Edmund Simeon and his sister Louisa Ward.
[5] i.e. alterations in Ornsby's *Memoirs of James Hope-Scott*.
[6] Mrs Deane's daughter Louisa had given Newman her painting of his church of San Giorgio in Velabro. See letter of 8 July 1881 to her.

I believe it to be by Overbeck. So I understood Miss Giberne who gave it me, whose name you may recollect, and who gave it to me, and told me, (as I fully believe) that Overbeck gave it to her.

'As I fully believe', — but a friend here, declares that Miss G. did not say it was by Overbeck, but by a well known artist in Rome, named Soldaties or rather Szoldaties, whom perhaps Louisa knows.[1]

Any how, I hope she will like it, from the sacred subject, suitable to this season, and as an Artist's work, and as coming from me.

My best remembrances to Mr Deane, and to all of you at home

Yours affectly John H. Card. Newman

TO EDMUND STONOR

Birmingham, 16 April 1882

It is very kind in you to let me give you trouble about St George's. In answer to your letter to Fr Pope, about his (St G's) Festival, I inclose a cheque for £20 . . .

I do not forget the good Dean's application about the repairs of the Basilica . . . All I could contemplate doing would be tax my Cardinal's income with a certain percentage . . .[2]

TO A. J. HANMER

Birmingham April 17. 1882

My dear Hanmer

I am much concerned to hear of your great affliction. This morning I said Mass for the soul of your dear sister, and till I had been able to do so, I waited to write to you. I heard from her not so many years ago, and was rejoiced to find she was ending her days so happily.[3]

Looking back to her life, you have nothing but what is consoling and hopeful to think of — and now she has ended it happily. Your sorrow will in a short time pass away, and nothing but soothing reminiscences of her and gratitude to God remain

I am very sorry to hear of your serious accidents. Falls, I suppose, are

[1] Francis Szoldatics was a Hungarian painter of the school of Overbeck. He lived Rome in from 1853 until his death in 1916.
[2] The extract is incomplete. In his letters of 23 Sept. 1882 to an Unknown Correspondent and 27 March 1886 to Renouf, Newman states that he receives no income 'by the rank or office of Cardinal.' Perhaps this state of affairs had not yet become clear.
[3] On 5 April Hanmer wrote to Newman that his sister Sophia Ainsworth had died on 1 April. Newman received her into the Church in 1850. After her husband's death she became in 1875 a Redemptorist nun.

the chief perils of advancing life — and I am wont to speculate when my own turn will come.

Thank you for the promise of your book[1]

Yours most truly John H Card. Newman

P.S.   I thought you were in America.

TO THE HON. MRS PEREIRA

Birmingham April 17, 1882

Dear Mrs Pereira,

I feel with you that it does George much credit to wish to go to Oxford, and that it would be a permanent advantage in many ways to him and especially enable him to enter the army as a man, and not as a mere boy, as many do.

But I have great difficulties in advising you. It is now near 20 years, since the frightful evil of infidelity or agnosticism has been epidemic in Oxford. And about the same time a general feeling arose among our Catholic laity to send their sons to one of the two great seats of education, originally belonging to the Catholic Church.

My own notion was to meet the difficulty, not by forbidding Catholic youths to go to Oxford — but by establishing (by the powers which I possessed from the Holy See) an Oratory there, which might be the protection of the Catholic students from the intellectual dangers of the place.

But the Bishops judged otherwise — and not only brought out a serious warning against Catholic youths going to Oxford, but prevailed at Rome to hinder my beginning an Oratory there. In consequence there has been no effectual safe-guard; for the Jesuits, though they have had very able Fathers there, have not put forth their whole strength, or acted on a plan; and not only this, but what I have called an epidemic has increased in virulence, intensity and extent for the last ten years.

Thus I have two reasons against advising you letting George go to Oxford, first the actual warning of the Bishops, and secondly, the very alarming state of Oxford itself.

I don't like to delay my acknowledgement of your letter — and therefore I write this — but I must think more and inquire more, before I make up my mind what to advise you.[2]

You must excuse my mistakes in writing. It is one way in which old age is telling upon me. I am forgetting how to spell.

Very sincerely Yours John H. Card. Newman

[1] Hanmer was preparing his translation of Jean de Cartigny, *The Voyage of the Wandering Knight*, London 1889.
[2] See letter of 16 May to Mrs Pereira. George Pereira, aged seventeen did not go to a university, but in 1884 became an officer in the Grenadier Guards.

TO A SON OF SIR HENRY COLE

Bm April 20. 1882

Dear Mr Cole

I see in this mornings Paper with great concern the affliction which has fallen on your Mother and all of you,[1] and I write a line, which requires no answer from you, for the purpose of expressing to your whole family circle my sympathy under such a trial, and my own true sorrow at the loss, to me so unexpected, of one who without any claim on my part, was so persistently kind and friendly to me. May you all have that comfort and strength, which God alone can give, and which He gives according to our need so abundantly.

Very faithfully yours John H Cardinal Newman

Excuse the imperfect address on my envelope

TO MRS WILSON

April 20. 1882

Dear Mrs Wilson

Saturday will quite suit me. So as it turns out would Monday.[2]
I should have to ask you to wait a while, if you came at 2.

Very truly Yours John H. Card. Newman

TO DAVID BROWN

Bm April 21. 1882

Dear Dr Brown

It will give me great pleasure to see you on Monday, as you propose.[3]

Very sincerely Yours John H Card. Newman

TO MRS FREDERICK GEORGE LEE

The Oratory April 22. 1882

My dear Mrs Lee

You may be sure I should rejoice to serve you in any way I can, and that I would gladly speak to the Duke about Ambrose, if an opportunity offered. I never have yet taken such a step, and in consequence I am quite ignorant of the particulars or circumstances of his patronage, and of what he can do and what cannot. But I will not forget your wish[4]

Yours most truly John H. Card. Newman

[1] Sir Henry Cole died on 18 April.
[2] 22 and 24 April.
[3] cf. letter of 20 June 1882 to Brown.
[4] Mrs Lee's son George Ambrose, was studying heraldry, and hoped to get a post in the College of Heralds, to which the Duke of Norfolk as Earl Marshal appointed. Lee entered the College in 1889.

TO ROBERT ORNSBY

April 22. 1882

My dear Ornsby

I am glad your suspense is over; tho' for myself I could not doubt that you and Stewart would be appointed.[1]

I have mislaid the extract you took the trouble of writing out for me. Is the inclosed correct?[2]

Yours affectly John H. Card. Newman

TO THE HON. MRS PEREIRA

Birmingham April 25. 1882

Dear Mrs Pereira,

There are certainly reasons, as Fr Norris says, for preferring, of the two Universities, Cambridge to Oxford. I have long heard that Religion is not a popular subject as a matter of party or controversy there, as it is at Oxford, and that young men pass their appointed time there without knowing each others creed. If Catholics are known, they are respected and let alone.

Also Fr Norris tells me that there are two or three youths from here going to Cambridge, who are special friends of George's, and will be useful to each other, whereas those now at Oxford are older than he is, and not intimate with him.

He (George) seems to have no difficulty about Cambridge himself, and I cannot deny that tho' it has not so high a name as Oxford, it is safer for a Catholic.

If it is to be Oxford, I think we must begin with the assumption that there is a religiously dangerous epidemic in the place, and that our first work is to guard against it. As far as I can learn, Worcester College is the safest. I cannot speak of the Fellows or Undergraduates — they doubtless are mixed or unformed in the matter of religious belief; but the head is a very high-churchman, who, I believe, would act fairly and respectfully to the Catholic Church and its members. He is the friend of an intimate friend of mine. I know him a little, and could write to him about George.[3] The Catholic Church is nearer Worcester College than most Colleges, and the Jesuits, I suppose, have a higher name than the secular priests at Cambridge, respectable and active as these are.

---

[1] Ornsby and James Stewart were appointed to Fellowships in the newly established Royal University of Ireland.

[2] This was an extract from a Trinity College, Oxford, testimonial for Orders of 1663, to say that the candidate held that which 'ex doctrina veteris ac Novi Testamenti Catholici patres ac veteres Episcopi collegerunt.'

[3] This was William Inge, who became Provost of Worcester College in 1881, and was a friend of W. J. Copeland. See letter of 22 Feb. 1881 to Copeland.

If you wished me to write to the Head (Provost) of Worcester, I would not commit George, but ask for information.

Very sincerely Yours John H. Card. Newman

TO EDWARD BELLASIS, JUNIOR

Bm April 26 1882

My dear Edward

I have had your music of the Two Worlds in my hands for some days past, lamenting and lamenting that I have no means of hearing it sung, and now I get your letter increasing my lament, inasmuch as my eyes are not strong enough to master its contents.

I make a shot at your difficulties, and, if what I say is nothing to the purpose, you must forgive me, and be so good natured as to take the trouble to set me right[1]

The copyright of my Verses is mine, but I am continually asked by Protestants and Catholics to give permission to them to print in their collections or to set to music particular Poems, and I commonly give leave up to six sets of Verse. I only bargain that they will take the words as they stand in Burns's Edition. As for you, you may use as many sets as you please. Of course, I consider it a compliment to me. I can't let you go to Stationers' Hall and register my words as yours. No one has a right to take your Music, but you have no right to appropriate my words.

By publishing, I understand rightly or wrongly, putting on *sale*.

I hope you had a pleasant trip to Dresden[2]

TO HENRY BITTLESTON

April 26. 1882

My dear Henry

I have just now found the missing letters — And, as I do not recollect Mrs Simpson's direction, must ask you to be so good as to direct and post the inclosed:[3] With my best Easter greetings

Yours affectly John H. Card. Newman

TO J. R. BLOXAM

Bm April 26. 1882

My dear Bloxam

I shall rejoice, if all is well, to see you on May 15
One of Ouless's portraits is in this House, the other in Oriel Hall

[1] Bellasis, who had set to music 'The Two Worlds', *V.V.*, p. 319, wrote on 24 April, asking if he might register for copyright this and other poems by Newman for which he had composed tunes.
[2] The conclusion has been cut out.
[3] Richard Simpson's widow had lent Newman some of his letters to her husband. Bittleston was a friend of the Simpsons, cf. letter of 25 June 1876 to Bittleston.

The final set of my Trinity rooms are known — And my freshman's, except that they have been rebuilt[1]

Yours affectly John H Card. Newman

Bm April 26. 1882

My Dear Sister Pia

A happy Easter to you and all yours

Dear Agnes Froude has had a more dreadful time of it. I suppose six or eight weeks. She is only now out of danger. The child was baptized. It is quite shocking and frightful to think what she has suffered. Even now she is not allowed to see her sister in law, Mrs Clutton. I look to the future with dismay.[2]

Lady Georgiana Fullerton, as perhaps you have heard, is ill of a form of gout, and needs your prayers.

I am relieved to hear what seems to me a fair account of you

My brother Frank had a touch or warning of paralysis in his hand, but it has pretty nearly gone away.

The notion of Priests eating before communicating is impossible, what ever the Papers may say.

By classic writers is meant first class writers — and every nation has its classics. But the Latin and Greek writers have writers, whose standard of classicalness is higher than the standard of classicalness in other languages. Hence they have appropriated the title.

Prince Alphonso Doria, our boy, is about to be married — to one of the daughters of the late Duke of Newcastle.[3]

Hell certainly was believed by pagans — so was the being of a God — so were sacrifices for sin — all of them corrupted, but still held.

Our school is 50; that is not a falling off.

Ever Yours affectly John H Card. Newman

Birmingham, May 2. 1882.

My dear Mrs Pereira

Since I wrote, I have been talking to a Cambridge friend, of the High Church, and he confirms me in my judgment that a young Catholic would be let alone there.

[1] See letter of 22 April 1870 to Alfred Plummer.
[2] See letter of 26 March to Isy Froude. Agnes Froude lost her first child but bore three children to R. H. Froude, before her death in 1890. Mrs Clutton was the sister of R. H. Froude's first wife, Beatrice Ryder, and the first cousin of his second.
[3] Prince Alfonso Doria came to the Oratory School in 1861. He married Lady Emily Pelham-Clinton, daughter of the Duke of Newcastle, on 24 June 1882, and wrote two days before to ask Newman's blessing.

I should then at once say to you that you had better send George to Cambridge, not to Oxford, except for the report, which may be without foundation, that the Bishops are going to bring out some new prohibition of Catholics going to the Universities. You could not act in direct opposition to the Cardinal Archbishop. A little time will make clear if there is any truth in the report.[1]

Most truly Yours John H. Card. Newman

TO ROBERT CHARLES JENKINS

Birmingham May 7. 1882

Dear Canon Jenkins

Thank you for your Tragedy.[2] I almost read it through without stopping which shows how interesting I found it. And its diction is quite worthy of a first class Tragedy. If Roscoe is accurate you seem to have taken some poetical licence, with certain of the facts. I cannot call the history sad or saddening, the conspiracy seems to me atrocious; and the murderous Cardinal, according to Roscoe, as I read him, was not directly stimulated by Leo's acts against himself but against his brother Borghese. Nor was he made Cardinal in order to divert him from seeking to wrest the Lordship of Siena from his brother. But I suppose either if I looked into Guicciardini, I should find he contradicted Roscoe, or else that you did not correct history more than Shakespeare does.[3] Since the Tempus Paschale is not yet over, I may without incorrectness myself wish you the blessing of the Season, which I do most heartily.

Very truly Yours John H. Card. Newman

Canon Jenkins.

TO WILLIAM B. MORRIS

Bm May 7/82

Dear Fr Morris

I thank you for the catalogue of your Lending Library[4]
May God bless so good a work

Yours very sincerely J. H. Card. Newman

[1] See letter of 16 May to Mrs Pereira.
[2] *Alfonso Petrucci Cardinal and Conspirator an Historical Tragedy in Five Acts*, London 1882.
[3] Jenkins replied on 14 May that he thought William Roscoe's *Life of Leo X*, London 1805, and Francesco Guicciardini's *Della Istoria d'Italia*, Friburg 1774, unreliable. He based himself on Palatius, *Fasti Cardinalium Omnium*, five volumes, Venice 1703. This is a work considered to have little value.
[4] Morris was a priest of the London Oratory. His library was prepared to send books to all parts of England.

TO THE DUKE OF NORFOLK

May 13. 1882

My dear Duke,

You may be sure that we shall observe the Novena with all our hearts. We mean to say a Mass or go to communion for your intention every day, and those of us who can will say more than one Mass. For myself, you know I have made it a rule to say a weekly Mass for the Duchess and your child and have for a long time.[1]

As to your question, I answer it thus. If you kindly wish to aid our School, you can do it in one of several ways. For instance

1. In the three years ending April 20, 1880, we lost, by the balance against us in the Debtor and Creditor account on the report of an accountant £749. 15. 2

2. As not every parent pays punctually, we have almost always to pay, the masters, tradesmen etc etc, before we have received all that should come to us — In consequence we cannot pay butcher, baker, etc soon or punctually, and therefore we have no hold on them. The average of these *standing* arrears is £700   At present we have taken a loan of £1,000 from our bank, for which we pay 5 per cent. interest

3. The due painting, papering, carpeting, bedding, linen, etc in the school premises would easily run to £200 a year — at least for some years. An additional Servant, if we could get one, would be a great gain

4 As to masters, one has £300 a year and a house, another £150, a third has £100, two more are wanted at £100 each. The French master has £80, the German £21, Alleguen £100. The board of the masters is an additional expense. Of course I do not mean that the school must not and cannot pay the greater part of this — but something towards it would be a great relief

5 Ravenhurst finds us a play-ground, and milk but we pay £150 for rent and for a man £52 a year and £13 to his wife, to keep the house and place and do the servants work.

The repairs of the house at the renewal of the lease cost us £226.[2]

JHN

May 20

---

[1] The Duke and Duchess of Norfolk were going on pilgrimage to Lourdes, hoping for the cure of their mentally deficient son.
[2] The Duke of Norfolk wrote to Richard Bellasis on 19 Aug. 1882: 'I enclose a cheque for £750 — being half of the sum I promised to pay in three years for purposes connected with the School.

I send half of my next year's donation now as I want to make it possible for you to furnish the library as well as reconstruct it . . .'

Birmingham, May 14th, 1882

Dear Father Casey,

I thank you for your Verses, portions of which I have already read with great pleasure. They have a clear, easy, musical flow, the more welcome, because it is the fashion just now to be obscure and harsh.[1]

Your faithful servant in Christ, John H. Card. Newman.

Rev. James Casey, P.P., Athleague.

TO W. S. LILLY

May 14. 1882

(not sent because Mr L. did not touch upon the professed miracles etc in Buddha's life, but insisted on the beauty of his character)[2]

Dear Mr Lilly

I return your books tomorrow or next day — I have not studied, but I don't find, in such a view as I have taken of them, the satisfaction which at least the Xtian Kn. Soc. [Christian Knowledge Society] proposes to give to souls troubled by the half science of the day. As to Dr Carpenter, it is nothing to him whether the contents of the four gospels are or not legendary. Rather he holds that, since miraculous stories are the natural and necessary issue of religious faith, the closest similarity of the stories of Buddha to the gospel narratives is no proof at all that the Apostles cribbed from Buddha — of which, he says, and shows, there is a [as] little external evidence as there is (he considers)

But to those who believe that the miraculous conception, and birth, and baptism, of our Lord are facts, the question comes to a very serious one, how are we to account for this reproduction, as it is alleged, in Christian history, of statements, which have already been published as belonging to a course of events which took place 500 years [before]? I allow indeed to Dr Carpenter as much as this:— that the moral sense being one of our natural gifts, an ethical code like Christianity and prior to it, need not be the origin, carries with it no proof that it is the origin, of Christian ethics; but, if I find in the

[1] Casey was Parish Priest of Athleague, County Roscommon, and a prolific writer in prose and verse. He used this letter in an advertisement for his *Verses on Doctrinal and Devotional Subjects*.
[2] There exists the second part of a letter from Lilly to Newman, evidently written early in May 1882. It ends: 'That the New Testament is largely indebted to Buddhism has been maintained by certain Rationalists: But Dr Carpenter — a Unitarian of very "Liberal" views — has in a very learned article which I send you refuted their opinion. I send you also Mr Rhys Davids little book on Buddhism, a popular Manual but extremely carefully done. Would you kindly return both? Very truly yours W. S. Lilly.'
Joseph Estlin Carpenter's article was evidently 'The Obligations of the New Testament to Buddhism', the *Nineteenth Century* (Dec. 1880), pp. 971–94, from which Newman quotes in his letter of 12 June to Lilly. Thomas William Rhys Davids' *Buddhism* was published in 1878 by the Society for the Promotion of Christian Knowledge.

books of Buddha a miraculous life and a series of miraculous events almost identical with those recorded in the gospels (I say, if) then I must conclude either that Buddha's biographers copied from the Evangelists, or the Evangelists from the Buddhists, in the case of Christians, and I am at once lead on to ask, since Buddha lived before our Lord what is the proof that the narration of his life was contemporary with him, and was as certainly prior to the gospels as he himself to our Lord.

The question of the date of the gospels has been thoroughly discussed and investigated. To put aside other portions of the inquiry, there has been a rigid scrutiny exercised upon the MSS codices, their antiquity, their trustworthiness — the omission of words or variants, sentences, passages in particular MSS. has been carefully noted and valued. Can this be paralleled as regards the evidence of quasi contemporaneous testimony and authority, for what is told us about Buddha? ⟨I do not here question, for it is not to the purpose Buddha's system of ethics [illegible words]⟩ We are told his religion has its sacred books — true, but is their genuineness guaranteed? ⟨the points of parallelism to the gospel many copies are there [?] of this, with what date, how far perfect etc etc⟩ ⟨I only ask for as — do but wish⟩ Polycarp edited Ignatius's Epistles and Eusebius only [200] years after speaks of them as extant and well known, and quotes passages still it [to] be found in them, yet learned Christian scholars are to be found who think their genuine[ne]ss as Pearson and Bull received them, to be doubtful — what is the evidence in proof that an existing Eastern narrative which professes to belong to a date long before the Christian era is not in whole or part composed after it? If we are to consider the end of St Mark's of doubtful authority because some MSS have it not, are there any MS at all, that tell of Buddha's incarnation, temptation, transfiguration etc as are now set before us?

If there are no MSS possible so far back as 500 before Christ, or copies of such, are there inscriptions in stone etc., not merely stating the fact of sacred Buddhist books parallel to our gospels, but recording contemporarily their contents? Perhaps I have overlooked the mention of them; but I want information on the point.

No one will say that mere oral tradition will be a sufficient warrant for facts occurring in the reign of Darius Hystaspes.

The only sufficient evidence of the truth of a biography of such great antiquity would lie in lives of Buddha in Burmese, Chinese etc etc, that is, in various countries and languages; to this Dr Carpenter points, but he says that 'little has been translated from the Pali Scriptures' and that 'the Chinese must be received with great reserve.'[1]

---

[1] Newman's draft becomes increasingly illegible. He included it in substance in his letter of 12 June to Lilly.

TO THE HON. MRS PEREIRA

Birmingham, May 16. 1882

Dear Mrs Pereira,

The Bishops have issued a circular, quoting a document of the date of 1867 from Propaganda, to the effect that 'except under special circumstances which are next to impossible, no Catholic can attend non-Catholic Universities without sin', that none but the Bishop under whom the parents are, can be the judge of what *are* special circumstances, and that no priest, secular or regular, 'can encourage or permit' such residence at the national Universities without grave sin.[1]

This decides the anxious question on which I have been writing to you.

Very truly Yours John H. Card. Newman

TO EDWARD HEALY THOMPSON

Birmingham May 20. 1882

My dear Thompson

Thank you for your letter and paper. Your account of Mr N. is very pleasant. Both Fr Ryder and myself welcome with great satisfaction the news that your quarrel with him is at an end.[2]

I am sorry you have the trouble of that woman. It is the penalty you pay who live at watering places. People have got wiser here, and have other things to do — but such adventuresses are a great gain, where numbers have time on their hands. Only take care you don't incur an action for libel, as I once did.[3]

I beg to congratulate Mrs Thompson on the conversions you tell me of, & am

Very sincerely Yours John H Card. Newman

[1] The English bishops met in Low Week, 17–21 April 1882, and issued the circular from which Newman quotes. See the *Weekly Register* (20 May 1882), p. 615. The third resolution declared 'That the principles and spirit which animate the national Universities and pervade the Board School system, and the intrinsic dangers which such institutions present to faith and morals, create a proximate occasion of mortal sin.' It then quoted from the Propaganda Letter of 6 Aug. 1867, 'It is next to impossible to discover circumstances in which Catholics could without sin attend non-Catholic Universities'. See fourth note to letter of 23 Oct. 1867 to William Monsell. The fourth resolution laid down that not even 'the Clergy, whether secular or regular' could decide whether in a particular case a parent might send his son to a university. The fifth resolution declared that 'The Bishops have agreed, each in his own diocese, to instruct all members of the Clergy, both secular and regular, that they are bound *sub gravi* not to encourage or to permit Catholics to frequent Board Schools, or to reside at the national Universities for the purposes of education.'
[2] Mr N has not been identified.
[3] The impostor Edith O'Gorman 'the escaped nun' had been invited by the Rector of Cheltenham, an extreme Orangeman, to deliver her immoral anti-Catholic lectures there. Thompson wrote a letter to the *Cheltenham Examiner* (17 May 1882), in proof of her untrustworthiness and liability to stir up religious strife.

TO T. W. ALLIES

Birmingham May 21. 1882.

My dear Allies,

I have been so busy with Palmer's Russian Journal, that I have not been able to do more than to look through your last volume and to see, how comprehensive and how important is the view which it contains.[1] But various of our Fathers have read it whole or part, and they are unanimous in their praise of it. They are all struck with its eloquence, of which our Bishop also spoke.

Nevertheless, we have no 'public', which supplies a market for our books, and none of us have any great encouragement to write, and perhaps there are great people who do not wish to encourage literature. I cannot forget that one of Cardinal Wiseman's questions, in a circular which he sent round to the laity against University education, was, 'Do you wish your children to be better educated than your Priests?' that is, nearly in those very words; — which was, besides, a slander on our clergy as well as a prophecy of evil for the Catholic body generally.[2]

You must excuse my mistakes in writing, for I am getting incapable. I am dimsighted, deaf, and lame, and my brain won't think, nor my throat speak, nor my fingers write. Yet it is all negative for in spite of all, I am, thank God, quite well.

Yours affectly J. H. Card. Newman

MEMORANDUM ON THE TEMPORAL POWER OF THE POPE[3]

[22 May 1882]

3. I detested what I considered an underhand way of pledging English Catholics to views which they had no intention by any act of theirs to favour. E.g. at one time there was to be a lay address to the Pope, and at the proper moment the word 'Infallible' was slipt in and this, I think, was the reason that a lay friend of mine of great influence either would not sign it, or withdrew his name.

And again, as to the case of the Academia, it was started as if intended in the interest of Catholic literature, history etc. I suspected mischief, and sure enough at the right moment a paragraph about the Temporal Power was inserted. This occasioned my letter

4. As an illustration of my point [of] view and feelings, I refer to my

[1] This was the fourth volume of *The Formation of Christendom, Church and State as seen in the Formation of Christendom*. On 16 May Allies thanked Newman for having bought six copies. He went on to complain that the Catholic reading public seemed to be diminishing, and that he had received no judgment from any competent person on his book.
[2] See letter of 14 Dec. 1864 to Lord Charles Tynne, and Volume XXI, Appendix 2.
[3] This is part of the first draft of a Memorandum which is printed in Volume XIX, Appendix 3. See the notes there, p. 561.

sermon on the Pope and the Revolution, in which I speak strongly against the treatment which the Holy Father met both from the Piedmontese and the Roman people — but I will not allow that the Temporal Power is the only way in which the spiritual power can be preserved.

I should say the same now — 1. that we cannot tell what is befoie us 2 that, as far as man can see, an international recognition of the Pope as a Temporal Power, is the natural and normal security for his ecclesiastical freedom. 3 but that [it] would be imprudent to affirm that it is the only way.

Further, I have no reason to suppose that our present Holy Father Leo xiii, differs from such a statement; but at the same time, now, as being a Cardinal, I should think it right to submit to him, and act with him, what[ever] might be his view and his resolve

TO LADY HENRY KERR

Birmingham May 25. 1882

My dear Lady Henry

I thank you for your beautiful cards, and will not forget your wishes. I will place one of them by my altar in my private chapel where I have a portrait of your dear Brother.

James is going on surprisingly well.[1] I say surprisingly because we expected the first term naturally to be a trial to him.

I was startled and much concerned by what you said of your daughter. I never forget her coming here with her dear Father and how surprised I was to find she was to be a nun. She has indeed chosen the better part and what a consolation to think of it —[2]

I wish you had said a word about your own health.

As for me, since you inquire, I can but be thankful that I should be so very well, not even having had a cold these three years since I was so ill at Rome; but I cannot deny I am feeble and infirm, somewhat lame deaf and blind and finding it difficult to think speak or write   But still in a true sense in good health

Yours affectionately in Xt   John H Card. Newman.

[1] Hope-Scott's son, James Fitzalan Hope, had just come to the Oratory School.
[2] This was the Sacred Heart nun, Henrietta Kerr. See letter of 31 Aug. 1863 to Lord Henry Kerr.

TO EDWARD HEALY THOMPSON

Bm. May 25. 1882

My dear Thompson

Your letter is a very powerful one, and must have a great effect upon all but very prejudiced persons, and on men of sober judgment and good sense. I suppose you are quite right about Gavazzi.[1]

I am pleased to see Mr N's letter and return it[2]

Yours most truly John H Card. Newman

TO CATHERINE ANNE BATHURST

The Oratory, May 29/1882.

My dear Child,

Thank you for your affectionate letter. I was glad to hear from a separate source of information that you were getting on well at Harrow, and were well and vigorous yourself.

It pleased me much to hear your account of the Pope, and the more so, because it is not the only witness to the same effect. An Anglican parson friend of mine was received by him at Christmas with his wife, and he was, I may say, quite tender with them, and, as in your case spoke so very kindly of me. It really perplexes and almost frightens me, that he shows such personal and persistent kindness towards me — and I am continually saying to myself, 'How did you come to hear anything of me?' and still more 'what has interested you in me?' Everyone reports him as painfully feeble — this e.g., was the report of the Warden of Keble[3] and his wife, (who by the bye also was much struck by his great grace and cordiality of manner) but those who know him best are so used to his looks as not to be frightened.

I am busy with Mr. Palmer's Journal to Russia. To me it is very interesting — but it is too long ago, and too ecclesiastical to be popular.

Yours affectionately, John H. Card. Newman.

TO EMILY BOWLES

The Oratory May 29. 1882

My dear Child

Thank you for your affectionate greetings on St Philip's day.

I wish I had any news to tell you to repay you for yours in your letter — but I have been confined to the shaping for publication of William Palmer's Journal of his visit to Russia in 1840, 1841 — and have had no time for any

---

[1] Alessandro Gavazzi (1809–89), was an Italian Barnabite, who left the Church and took an active part in the Roman Republic in 1849. He then fled to England, became a Protestant and supported Garibaldi. He returned to Rome in 1870 and tried to organise an Evangelical Church of Italy. In a second letter about the 'Escaped Nun' published in the *Cheltenham Examiner* (24 May 1882), Thompson gave evidence of how discreditable the anti-Catholic champions were, and stated that 'Signor Gavazzi, after his last visit to Cheltenham, got fifteen months' imprisonment in Paris for outraging public morality.'
[2] See letter of 20 May to Thompson.
[3] Edward Stuart Talbot.

thing else. He went in a simple and honest heart, to prove that the Anglican and Russian Churches were integral portions of the One Catholic Church, by finding himself allowed to communicate in the Russian Church. But, as might have been expected, he was refused. He afterwards tried the Greek Church, with still less success. And then since he had a firm faith that our Lord had established a Church upon earth, which was to last to the end of time, he saw that that Church was to be found *there*, where he had hitherto only recognized a 'branch Church,' viz in Rome.

He has left me all his papers. The Volume I am publishing does not go beyond Russia.

I grieve deeply, though I am not surprised, that you have no good news to tell me in that distressing matter you wrote about[1]

Yours affectly John H Card. Newman

TO MRS KEON

May 29. 1882

Dear Mrs Keon,

Thank you for your congratulations on St Philip's Festival

I have your dear husband's name down for June 5 in my obituary — so I shall not forget it

Very truly yours J. H. Card. Newman.

TO CHARLES KEGAN PAUL

Bm May 30. 1882

Dear Mr Kegan Paul

I have been shown your account of me in the New York 'Century', and lose no time in thanking you for the great kindness which has both suggested and dictated it[2]

You will easily understand that such publicity as it involves, or rather presupposes, is somewhat trying to me, but I shall be lucky, if, in time to come, I never fall into the hands of critics whose fault will not be that indulgence, which is the uniform characteristic of your Notice of me

I have discovered no inaccuracy of statement in your pages, except that you ascribe St Bettelin to Mr J. A. Froude. My own memory may be in fault, but I am led to ascribe St B. certainly the verse part, to Mr Dalgairns, and St Neot to Mr Froude[3]

Very truly Yours John H. Card. Newman

C. Kegan Paul Esqr

P.S. This is a singular instance of 'Exceptio probat regulam' — for I have

[1] See letter of 5 Jan. 1882.

[2] Charles Kegan Paul contributed a biographical article 'John Henry, Cardinal Newman', to the *Century Illustrated Monthly Magazine* (June 1882), pp. 273–86. See also letter of 4 Jan. 1885 to R. W. Church.

[3] Art. cit., p. 278. Newman is correct. See first note to letter of 2 Oct. 1881 to Lockhart.

been surprised at the exact knowledge you display throughout [?] of similar little matters; and specially have I cause of gratitude to you for the pains and exactness with which you have read what I have written

TO THOMAS AVERY, MAYOR OF BIRMINGHAM

The Oratory, June 2. 1882

Dear Mr Mayor

I do not think I can be wrong in asking you to be the channel of the contribution which I enclose to the Public Library Fund, but if I am taking an informal step I rely on your known zeal for its interests to excuse me. I have long wished to take a part, however small, in so great a work, but it is only within the last few weeks that to do so has been in my power.[1]

I am, dear Mr Mayor, Your faithful servant John H. Card Newman

TO JOHN THOMAS WALFORD, S.J.

Bm June 3. 1882

My dear Fr Walford

I ought before now to have thanked you for your beautiful verses, especially welcome to me as coming on our Festival day.[2] Pray thank for me also your kind Fathers, who associated themselves with you in the message you sent me

There is one friend of mine, no longer yours, separated from you by a melancholy illness, who I suppose, from his particular case, those of you who knew him must still take an interest in, Father Meyrick; does anyone of you at Stonyhurst know any thing about him, where he is, and in what health? At some time or other you may hear something about him, and if so, I should be glad if you will tell me.[3]

[1] Newman sent £20 to the Free Libraries Restoration Fund, which was setting up the new Reference Library after the fire of 11 Jan. 1879. The new Library was opened on 1 June 1882, with an address by John Bright.
On 5 June the Mayor wrote a grateful acknowledgment and on 12 Sept. wrote again arranging to accompany Newman when he visited the Library on 15 Sept. He was shown round by one of the librarians, Richard W. Mould, who in the *Library World* (Aug. Sept. 1925) quoted in *B P L* [Birmingham Public Libraries] *Bulletin* (May 1968), p. 3, wrote, 'I well remember the benignity of his age-worn face.' See also letter of 11 Dec. 1882 to the Chief Librarian, J. D. Mullins.
[2] Walford had translated 'Lead, kindly Light' into Latin.
[3] Thomas Meyrick had been for a time at Littlemore with Newman, and became a Catholic early in 1845. He joined the Jesuits the following year, but twice left the Society. He was subject to fits of depression. In 1879 he was at the Irish house, Clongowes Wood, and from there was put into an asylum. He secured his release and left not only the Jesuits but, for a while, the Catholic Church, and lived at Bournemouth. Towards the end of the century he was restored to the priesthood. His last years were spent at a convent in Rome, where he was cared for by the nuns, and he died at Brescia in 1903. He published a pamphlet *My imprisonings; or An Apology for Leaving the Jesuits,* privately printed, about 1881.

I have no news to tell you from this place — we are all older, for better or for worse: the younger coming forward, the old are going off, like the slides in a Magic Lantern

Yours affectly in Xt   John H Card. Newman

TO THOMAS MOZLEY

Birmingham, June 9. 1882

My dear Mozley

I have just received your volume, and chapter 2 has so knocked me down, that I shall not have courage to read a line more. It is full of small misstatements and I must take it as a specimen of the whole.[1]

It is not true that my Father was a clerk in Ramsbottom and Co. He was first a Partner in Harrison, Prickett and Newman; the partners of which retiring from business, another firm was formed.[2]

It is not true that my Mother knew any of the authors you mention. She would be called an Arminian and Remonstrant. The only Sermons she seemed to know were 'Tillotson's'.[3]

I never dreamed of being 'converted' and had no lasting religious thoughts till I knew Mr Mayers.

My Father's bank never failed. It stopped — but paid by the end of the month its creditors in full.

Henry Bowden should be John William Bowden.

I could notice other mistakes — but all that you have said is so uncalled for, that I am almost stupefied.[4]

Yours affly J. H. Card. Newman

[1] This was a copy of Mozley's *Reminiscences chiefly of Oriel College and the Oxford Movement*, London 1882, in which he wrote:
'To his Eminence Cardinal Newman from his affectionate friend Thomas Mozley in the confidence that all errors whether of statement, or of spirit, or of tone, will be treated with as much kindness as may be felt compatible with the supreme obligations of piety and of truth June 8. 1882'
[2] Mozley altered the preface to the second edition of his *Reminiscences*, dated July 1882, and added to it that he had availed himself 'of the opportunity to rectify some of my "Reminiscences", and even to surrender them in one or two cases, where they clash with memories entitled to regard. I must leave to others the spiritual *incunabula* of the future Cardinal, as it is plain my own impressions are derived from what I saw and heard long after. John Newman, the father, was partner in two successive banking firms, from the year after the French Revolution to the year after the battle of Waterloo.' This and other mistakes pointed out by Newman were corrected in the second chapter, where they occurred.
[3] Mozley wrote in his first edition, 'The mother was from first to last thoroughly loyal to her family traditions, and all the early teaching of her children was that modified Calvinism which retained the Assembly's Catechism as a text, but put into young hands Watts, Baxter, Scott, Romaine, Newton, Milner — indeed, any writer who seemed to believe what he wrote about.' This passage was entirely omitted in the second edition. See F. W. Newman's comment in note to letter of 13 June to him. John Tillotson, Archbishop of Canterbury, who died in 1694, whose sermons were very popular, was neither a Nonconformist nor an Evangelical. The Catechisms of the Westminster Assembly were completed in 1647.
[4] There was general agreement about Mozley's inaccuracy. See letters of 29 June and 4 Aug. to Pusey and 8 July to Anne Mozley. About the *Reminiscences* Copeland wrote on 21 July, 'I was scarcely prepared for such mistakes and inaccuracies as abound in them.' See also letter of 22 Feb. 1884 to George T. Edwards.

TO WILLIAM PHILIP GORDON

Bm June 9. 1882

Dear Father Superior

The inclosed is addressed to you rather than to me — so I send it to you.

Yours affly J. H. Card. Newman

P.S. I see by the new Gerarchia Catholica that in point of age I come third Cardinal! Four have passed 80; the Archbishops of Bordeaux and Rouen are older than I, and the Archbishop of Paris younger.

TO MARGARET DE LISLE

The Oratory, Bm June 10. 1882

Dear Miss de Lisle

I have meant to send this to thank you for your Volume[1] — but writing is now such a difficulty to me, and even pain, and achieved so slowly, that my thanks have been delayed.

I began to read the book at once — and am very much interested in it, and trust and pray it may do a good deal of service in stirring up the devotional feelings of readers

Yours most truly J. H. Card. Newman

TO JOHN BANNISTER TABB

The Oratory June 11. 1882

Dear Mr Tabb

I thank you very sincerely for the kind present you send me, and I send you back in turn my blessing with all my heart[2]

I feel it to be a great mercy from above, that I should have such good friends in a country so far away

I am Yours very sincerely John H. Card. Newman

---

[1] This was Margaret de Lisle's translation of J. J. Gaume, *Life of the Good Thief*, London 1882.

[2] Tabb was at this time studying for the priesthood at St Mary's Seminary, Baltimore. He wrote on 24 May, 'I beg herewith to lay at your feet the tribute your Eminence deigns to accept from a singer so rude.' This was his first book, *Poems*, privately printed, 1882, with a dedication to Newman, 'These poems are, with his gracious permission, reverently inscribed by his servant, the Author.' There followed a dedicatory sonnet.

June 12. 1882

Private

My dear Mr Lilly,

Many thanks for the letter of Mr R D's, which I herewith return.[1] I have opened so large a question, that it is no wonder that he has not hit the points which constitute my difficulty in the matter.[2]

Dr Carpenter says, 'It is not the Fourth Gospel only which has drawn upon itself the suspicion of not being a native product of the Palestinian soil.'[3] He goes on to say that the resemblance in life and teaching between Buddha and the Galilean Prophet, is at first sight so close as to give rise to 'the crude suggestion' that the later is but the reproduction of the earlier. He says the facts of history do not allow of this explanation of the coincidence, but he allows the coincidence itself and he accounts for it by the 'pious fancy of Buddhist disciples,' leaving it apparently to be inferred that to the 'pious fancies of Christian disciples' was owing the other side of the parallel. But I cannot follow him in this solution of the difficulty. The coincidence of biographical notices in the memoirs severally of our Lord and of Buddha, is so close and so minute, that it seems to me plain that the record of our Lord's life, our written gospel, is taken from biographies of Buddha, or the biographies of Buddha from Christian sources. I am then naturally led to ask what [is] the trustworthiness of the account of the life and actions of Buddha, as contained in Dr Carpenter's article.

Now what is the coincidence which I think so startling? Not the mere claim to a supernatural sanction. A divine birth, a gift of miracles, an heroic life, a great success, are the claim historically of every great moral teacher and social reformer. Nor again is there a difficulty in a close resemblance in the accounts left us of the ethical code promulgated by our Lord and Buddha. There is little in the ethics of Christianity, which the human mind may not reach by its natural powers, and which, here and there, in the instance of individuals, great poets, and great philosophers, has not in fact been anticipated. It is not this, which I want explained, but it is the series of details wrought into the life of Buddha, so parallel to what we find in the Gospels, it is this which leads me to ask for the authority on which it is reported to me, and on first hearing to meet it with deep suspicion of its untrustworthiness,

---

[1] On 30 May Lilly wrote, 'The other day Mr Rhys Davids, the great authority on Buddhism was dining with me and I discussed with him the points raised in your last letter.' This was presumably Newman's letter thanking for the works on Buddhism; see draft of 14 May and first note there. Lilly continued, 'The day afterwards he was so kind as to send me a communication of which I enclose a copy.'
[2] In the draft of this present letter Newman added here: 'for the same reason I dare say I shall not be able to make you feel that difficulty — but I will try. I will tell you how I came to put it before you.'
[3] Newman's quotations are all from the first pages of J. E. Carpenter's article 'The Obligations of the New Testament to Buddhism', the *Nineteenth Century* (Dec. 1880), pp. 971–4 and 977.

and to ask whether it is not posterior to Christianity and referable to its teaching

For instance, I am told that Buddha came on earth with the object of 'redeeming the world;' that he 'voluntarily descended from his high estate'; that his descent was the last of a series of 'incarnations with the one object from first to last of delivering mankind from sin and sorrow'; that he became incarnate in a married woman; that he was born, when his mother was journeying to her paternal home; that on its taking place, the angels in heaven sang, 'This day is one born to give joy and peace to men, to shed light in the dark places, and to give sight to the blind'. When the child was presented to his father, an aged saint wept and predicted his future greatness, saying, 'My time of departure is close at hand. What happiness from the birth of this child shall ensue'. He had the name of the 'Establisher;' he grew in wisdom and stature; he taught his teachers. The Tempter appeared and promised him universal sovereignty; but he replied, 'I want not an earthly Kingdom, depart!' Then he said 'All guilt and sorrow are for ever done away.' On this followed great miracles, the blind saw, the deaf could hear, the lame walked freely, and the captives were restored to liberty, 'he himself was transfigured,' etc. etc.

Now what is the authority, what evidence for all this? Buddha came 'to *redeem* the world'; (we must keep to the very words; else, there will be no difficulty to be solved); then I ask, who told us this? the gospels were written, say, 10, or 20, suppose 50 or 100 [years] after the events which they record, and are separate witnesses for those events; — is the Buddhist gospel as near the time of Buddha as the Christian to Christ? Who tells us that the angels sang on Buddha's birth and proclaimed peace to men? Who were the witnesses or at least the reporters of the fact of the Buddha's fight with the Tempter? To prove the authenticity and the date of one of our gospels, we are plunged into a maze of MSS of various dates and families, of versions and patristic testimonies and quotations, and to satisfy the severity of our critics, there must be an absolute coincidence of text and concordance of statement in these various MSS. put forward as evidence. If a particular passage is not found in all discoverable MSS, it is condemned. There are MS of St John which omit the account of the Angel at Bethesda, as it stands in his 5th chapter; accordingly the exegetical lecturer thinks himself at liberty to disbelieve the narrative. The termination of St Mark is wanting in another MS; in consequence, as if this omission was an actual disproof of its authenticity, a critic expresses his gratification that we are no longer bound by the text 'He that believeth not etc.' And in vain are the 'Three Witnesses' found in the Latin text of St John's first Epistle it is fatal to their reception that they are not found in the Greek. Why are we not to ask for evidence parallel to this before we receive the history of Buddha? Perhaps you will answer, 'But he lived so long ago; how can we expect a contemporary life of one who lived in the days of Darius Hydaspes?[sic]' True but I remark that the mere absence

97

of evidence is not itself evidence; may it not rather be urged, from the parallel of Roman history, that the absence of historical evidence is the sure fore-runner and token of *myths*?

There is nothing producible, as far as has [been] brought home to me to show that the words and deeds and history attributed to Buddha form a whole, such as the gospels, and existed in detail earlier than 1000 years after Buddha; nothing to show, that the passages in the Buddhist books which are now received do not belong to Christian sources; nothing to show that the very best reason for thinking that they were in existence as early as 700, 800 years after Buddha is the fact of Christianity having spread through the East, by that time as the Aristotelian Saracens and Moors in the middle ages influence on the Catholic schoolmen is a proof of them. There is more evidence that Christianity influenced the Buddhist traditions, than that the history of Buddha, as now reported, existed, as it now exists before the Christian era.

I write this as an empirical view, as a case which has to be investigated. I am quite unlearned in the subject, but I want to know whether my question can be satisfactorily answered. I do not of course deny the singular greatness of Buddha: it is the details of his history that I am suspicious about. Meanwhile, in order to prove that my belief in the influence of Christianity in the East in the first centuries is not unwarranted, I quote the following passage of Gibbon about the Nestorians.[1]

TO EDWARD HEALY THOMPSON

The Oratory June 12. 1882

My dear Thompson

I am very glad to hear of your success in your controversy. You are certainly doing a good service to the Catholic cause. All gentlemen, to say nothing of Christians, are with you, and the only fault which I conceive Catholics made was the application to the Mayor to interfere.[2]

Another 'Godfrey Faussett' was at Canterbury. His family, on his death

[1] The draft is occasionally more detailed than the letter as sent, and ends, 'What are the objections for supposing that the Nestorians from AD, 330 seriously influenced the East, recollecting Gibbon's words' Newman's reference is to *The History of the Decline and Fall of the Roman Empire*, chapter XLVII, Bury's edition, V, pp. 148–52, where Gibbon speaks of the Nestorian missions in India and the East.

Lilly sent Newman's letter to T. W. Rhys Davids, who replied on 19 June: '. . . all that exact identity of phraseology which is necessary to support the hypothesis of a borrowing either from one side or the other, seems to me to fade quite away when the supposed resemblances between Christian and Buddhist accounts are examined . . . I have the honour therefore to find myself in agreement with your revered correspondent . . .'

[2] At Cheltenham in the case of Edith O'Gorman, 'the Escaped Nun'. See letters of 20 and 25 May to Thompson. He headed a deputation to the Mayor explaining the danger of rioting and the demoralisation her lectures would cause. The latter was the primary objection of the deputation, but the former was the one emphasised in the *Cheltenham Examiner* (24 May 1882).

sent me his Remains; and I have the pleasantest recollections of them and him.[1]

I can't write me [more], my hand is so stiff

Most truly Yours John H Card. Newman

TO FRANCIS WILLIAM NEWMAN

June 13. 1882

My dear Frank

I have seen Mozley's book so cruel as well as untrue about my Father[2]

I don't mean to utter a word in consequence for he is a wild beast who rends one's hand when put up to defend one's face.

I trust you will not notice his book. I don't suppose you will either. I could show, by letters which I have kept, as well as from personal memory that what he says or implies is untrue[3]

TO HENRY BITTLESTON (1)

June 14. 1882

My dear Henry

Thank you for your letter. I am very glad to make use of it, and will tell you what I am doing

I think the middle portion of your letter very apposite, and, as I have for

[1] One of the sons of Godfrey Faussett, Margaret Professor of Divinity, to whom Newman addressed his *Letter* in defence of Hurrell Froude's statements on the Holy Eucharist, *V.M.* II, 197, also Godfrey Faussett, was living at Cheltenham. He was a Fellow of Magdalen College, Oxford, 1848–53, and Rector of Edgworth, Glos., 1860–4. His brother, Thomas Godfrey Faussett, the Kentish archaeologist died in 1877. Newman was sent one of the 150 copies of *Memorials of T. G. Godfrey-Faussett*, edited by W. J. Loftie, London 1878.

[2] See 9 June to T. Mozley.

[3] The draft is unfinished. On 9 July 1882 F. W. Newman wrote to his friend Mrs Phillipps a letter, now in the possession of J. S. F. Parker of York University, who kindly sent a copy to the editor. In it he wrote 'Now Mr Mozley is a very generous warm-hearted man; and he is incapable of malice or any unkindness. I left Oxford myself in 1830, and ought to have been entirely left out of mention. We did know each other slightly when he was an undergraduate, but he does not refer to that. I am hardly a just critic of any thing to which he can claim *memory*. But I strongly repudiate his mention of things which he cannot pretend to remember, things of which he had no cognizance. My brother the Cardinal writes me words too strong to repeat, as to the impropriety of his lugging in my Father to his narrative; and says he has documents which prove him to be quite incorrect. For my part I strongly complain of his statement concerning my mother, and flatly deny it; both as untrue, and as a most gratuitous aspersion on her good sense. The religious training of us which he ascribes to her and the religious books to which he says she introduced us, — I entirely deny. I suppose he elaborated the fancy, out of the idea that sons who fall into Puritan reading *must* have got it from their mother, if one of her grandfathers fled from French persecution as a Protestant. Not one of the books he names was put into my hands by my mother, and if she ever read even one of them (*which I doubt*) it is likely to have been *our* introducing them to her. As to the Assembly's Catechism, I do not believe I ever set eyes on it, and am as ignorant of it as of the Westminster Confession.'

F. W. Newman went on to complain of Mozley's account of his relations with his eldest brother and spoke of 'how much I owed at that time to his warm affection.' F. W. Newman concluded, 'Mr [James Anthony] Froude tells me that whenever *he* has cognizance, he finds Mr M's *memory* to be at fault.

I feel for my *mother's* sake I ought to protest.'

some days past written a note, I *add* it to yours. I inclose *just what* I have sent to the Paper in William's Transcript of it.[1]

And I have sent it to the Tablet — because they of their own accord put in my 'Letter without date' very complimentarily, whereas the Register, as if it wanted to get up a controversy to sell the Paper, put in Dr Barry without giving me an opportunity of anticipating and superseding it, by seeing.[2]

You will receive your letter with my added note entire, (viz what I am now writing) *before* it is published in the Tablet; so if you don't like it, you can stop it

Yours affly John H Newman

Your letter to the Register was not directed, so, we have sent it to the Tablet.

I am sorry to say I have made your letter sadly abrupt, from being in much haste.

TO HENRY BITTLESTON (II)

[14 June 1882][3]

My dear Henry,

As for the letter:— 1. I have no recollection of writing it.
2. Anyhow I am sure it was before the Vatican Council.[4]

[1] See next letter, and also first note there.

[2] At the end of his article on Newman in the *Illustrated Century Magazine* for June, Kegan Paul published an undated letter, ascribed to Newman, on the inspiration of Scripture. This was reproduced in the *Tablet* (10 June 1882), pp. 883–4. It had already appeared in the *Weekly Register* (3 June), pp. 673–4, followed on 10 June, p. 730, by one from William Barry, a young theologian who had studied in Rome, quoting the decrees of previous councils as though contradicting what Newman said.

[3] Newman's letter as it appeared in the *Tablet* (17 June), p. 937, was headed 'Cardinal Newman and the Inspiration of Scripture', and was preceded by a letter from Henry Bittleston: 'Sir,

Allow me to draw attention to the fact that as to Cardinal Newman's private letter, now first published by Mr. K. Paul, it has no date. I conclude that it was written before the publication of the Vatican decrees, and as at the time of their publication I had the inestimable privilege and happiness of some intimacy with the good Father, then simple Dr. Newman, I think it worth while to bear testimony that in his careful and reverent reading of those decrees, he at once noticed and was struck by the words adduced by Dr. Barry, as *the first formal definition* that the Church had given on the subject.

H

P.S. Since writing the above I have received the following letter from the Cardinal: —'

[4] Newman's letter as printed in the *Illustrated Century Magazine* (June 1882), pp. 285–6, was as follows:

'Very little has been formally determined by the church on the subject of the authority of Scripture further than this, that it is one of the two channels given to us by which the *salutaris veritas* and the *morum disciplina* (in the words of the Council of Trent), which our Lord and his apostles taught, are carried down from age to age to the end of the world. In this sense Scripture is the "word of God", *i.e.*, the written word.

There has been no formal definition on the part of the church that Scripture is inspired.

It is defined that Almighty God is *auctor utriusque Testamenti*. I do not know of any definition that He is *auctor omnium librorum* which belong to each Testament.

But it is not to be supposed that, because there is no definition on the part of the Church that Scripture is inspired, therefore we are at liberty at once to deny it.

1. First, St. Paul's words cannot be passed over *omnis scriptura divinitus inspirata*. [2 *Timothy*, 3:16]

100

3. Also it must have been written in recollection of the words of Bouvier, who, speaking of Scripture, with all its parts, says: 'Quia Sacrum Concilium [Tridentinum] ipsa voce *inspirationis* non utitur propositio nostra, licet certissima, non est de fide Catholicâ.[1]

4. Of course the Vatican Council has distinctly adopted as *de fide* what from the beginning was taught in the Church, though not defined.

Yours affectionately, John H. Card. Newman.

TO HENRY EDWARD WILBERFORCE

The Oratory June 14. 1882.

My dear Harry

Our Fathers beg me to ask, through you, as Secretary, your Oratory Club, one and all, to take part in and to witness the Cricket match which is to be played on Tuesday July 18, to which we shall devote, if necessary, a second day on the 19th[2]

The order of things will be as follows:— We shall be ready for all comers on Monday night, the 17th, and we will give or provide as many beds as we can. Low Mass for the Oratory Visitors at half past eight. Then, after

2. Next, the very strong opinion on the subject of the early fathers must be taken into account.
3. Thirdly, the universal feeling, or φρόνημα, of the Church in every age down to the present time.
4. The consent of all divines, which, whatever their differences on the subject in detail, is clear so far as this, viz., that Scripture is true. This, when analyzed, I consider to signify this, viz, "Truth in the sense in which the inspired writer, or, at least, the Holy Ghost, meant it, and means to convey it to us."
Thus, though it be not proposed to us by the Church *de fide* that we should accept the doctrine of the inspiration of Scripture, only that we must accept all the Church teaches us to be in Scripture and teaches us out of Scripture, yet it is a matter of duty, for the first reasons I have given, not to encourage, to spread, or to defend doubts about its inspiration.
As to the extent of its inspiration, I do not see that the Council of Trent speaks of it as the authoritative channel of doctrine in other matters than faith and morals; but here, besides the four considerations above set down, I would observe that it is often a most hazardous process to attempt to enunciate faith and morals out of the sacred text which contains them. It is not a work for individuals. At last it has been felt and understood that faith and morals are not involved in a doctrine which Scripture seems to teach, that the earth is fixed and the sun moves over it. The time was necessary to ascertain the fact, viz., that the earth *does* move, and therefore that the divine spirit did not dictate these expressions of Scripture which imply that it does not, rather that He did not mean to convey that notion by these expressions.
As to the questions you put to me, I do not see anything in the text of Scripture which obliges us, or even leads us, to consider the six days of Genesis i to be literal days.
The literal accuracy of the history of Jonah, or that of Elisha, rests upon a different principle, viz., whether miracles are possible, and to be expected. I see no difficulty in believing that iron, on a particular occasion, had the lightness of wood, if it is the will of God in any case to work miracles, *i.e.*, to do something contrary to general experience. And while I say the same of Jonah and the whale, I feel the additional grave and awful hazard how to attempt to deny the history without irreverence towards the express teaching of the incarnate God.' [*Matthew*, 12:40]

[1] Jean Baptiste Bouvier, Bishop of Le Mans, *Institutiones Theologicae ad usum Seminariorum*, nona editio, juxta animadversiones a nonnullis theologis Romanis propositas emendata, Paris 1856, II, p. 29. The quotations at the beginning of Newman's letter in the *Illustrated Century Magazine* are from the Council of Trent, *Denzinger-Schönmetzer* 1501.
[2] Wilberforce was the honorary secretary of the Oratory School Society.

breakfast, to Ravenhurst for the cricket. In due time a provisional meal, and then a return home to dinner, and a classical concert.

If the match is not finished, it is resumed on Wednesday the 19th

Let us know, as well as you can, as the time approaches, how many are coming

Yours affectionately John H Card. Newman

TO EMILY BOWLES

Bm June 15. 1882

My dear Child

If all is well, I will say Mass for your intention on Saturday. I do really think it an epidemic, and wonderfully catching. It does not spread by the reason, but by the imagination. The imagination presents a possible, plausible view of things which haunts and at length overcomes the mind. We begin by asking 'How can we be sure that it is not so?' and this thought hides from the mind the real rational grounds, on which our faith is founded. Then our faith goes — and how in the world is it ever to be regained, except by a wonderful grant of God's grace. May God keep us all from this terrible deceit of the latter days. What is coming upon us! I look with keen compassion on the next generation and with, I may say, awe[1]

Yrs affly J H Card. Newman

TO ARTHUR MCKENNA

Birmingham. June 15th. 1828.

Dear Canon Mc Kenna,

I thank sincerely the members of the Roman Association for their very kind invitation of me to their Annual meeting.[2]

But I hope they will allow me to plead my advanced age, as a sufficient reason for being unable to avail myself of it.

Very truly yours, John H. Cardinal Newman.

TO ALEXANDER FULLERTON

Bm June 16. 1882

My dear Mr Fullerton

I thank God for your good news. We are all in His hands, and He knows what is best for all of us.[3] May I ask your and Lady Georgiana's prayers for an intention of mine

Very sincerely Yours John H Card. Newman

[1] See letters of 5 Jan. and 29 May 1882 to Emily Bowles.
[2] cf. letter of 3 Sept. 1881.
[3] Her husband wrote on 15 June to say that Lady Georgiana Fullerton was recovering from a serious illness.

TO JEROME VAUGHAN

The Oratory June 17/82

My dear Fr Prior

Mr Walsh has brought me your very kind and beautiful present. It is most acceptable to me, and I thank you heartily for it. I shall place it in the room into which I have brought together other memorials of the sympathy shown me by my friends, and in particular by the English Benedictines. It will bring, I am sure, the blessing of St Benedict upon this House.[1]

Very truly Yours John H. Card. Newman

TO ARTHUR BERTRAND WILBERFORCE

Bm June 17. 1882

My dear Fr Bertrand

I thank you much for your volume, which I shall read with much interest, and, I am sure, profit.[2] Thank you too for your letter

I am glad of your account of Agnes — it is long since I had heard of her, dear child[3]

Yours affly J. H. Card. Newman

TO EMILY BOWLES

Bm June 20. 1882

My dear Child

I think in *most* cases, which come under the prohibitions, if the parents put their real difficulties before their diocesan, he will give leave. Whether *any* Bishops will be hard in a case of real difficulty is more than I can say[4]

Yours affly John H Card. Newman

TO DAVID BROWN

Rednall June 20. 1882

My dear Dr Brown

I have not been at all neglectful of your wish, and have been ashamed that day has past after day — and I have not been able to send you the letter — but really in spite of all I can do, my letters multiply so much, and each day brings its own duties so urgently, that I cannot sort and put in order my

---

[1] Vaughan, who was Prior of Fort Augustus Monastery, Inverness-shire, sent by William Hussey-Walsh, a gift of a painting of St Benedict.
[2] *Life of St Lewis Bertrand, O.P.*, London 1882.
[3] This was Wilberforce's sister, Mrs R. H. Froude.
[4] See letter of 16 May to Mrs Pereira.

letters as I should like, and cannot at a moment put my hand upon particular ones[1]

This, however, I promise you, and have charged it upon my future Executor who is now sitting in the room with me, Revd W. P. Neville that when I am gone and my letters must all be put to rights, yours shall go to you or to your Executors. But, if I can, I will find them myself. I have always been very careful of my letters, and in earlier days have spent much time in setting them in order — but I work very slowly now, and cannot work for long together

I have ever been touched with your kind regard for me, since you first called here — and have felt much gratitude — and I pray that God may reward you abundantly for your goodness, and bring you to His eternal kingdom

Yours with much affection J. H. Card. Newman

TO DAVID BROWN

The Oratory June 21. 1882

My dear Dr Brown

I have read with much interest your clear and vigorous, rather I should say, your powerful statement; of course it has shocked me much.[2] Not that I did not know substantially the dreadful facts which it details, but I was not aware of the eloquence and force which were at the command of the writers to whom they related. The passage about the 'infinite sea and the silent stars' is as dreadful as it is beautiful[3]

As to your notice of my brother, it was simple news to me, and is horrible[4]

[1] On 24 April Brown had called on Newman and asked to see his letters lest he should have written too freely. He wrote again on 18 June, anxious especially about what he had said in a previous letter about William Robertson Smith, Professor of Old Testament at the Free College, Aberdeen, who was removed from his chair for his critical views, held to undermine belief in the inspiration of the Bible. See Newman's letter of 22 July 1878 to Brown. Brown's letter was found, see at 27 Nov. 1882.

[2] On 18 June Brown sent Newman his article 'The latest Outcome of Free Thought in those who still cling to the name of Christian', the *British and Foreign Evangelical Review* (Jan. 1882), pp. 93–106, 'Being the substance of a Lecture delivered at the opening of the Free Church College, Aberdeen, on 2 November 1881'. Brown replied to James Martineau's lecture 'Loss and Gain in Recent Theology', delivered on 23 June 1881 in Portland Street Chapel, London. Brown summarised Martineau's conclusions: '*First*, all revealed religion is formally renounced, and with it, of course, all external authority in religion; *secondly*, and naturally enough, all faith in a promised Messiah is not only given up, but pronounced to be pure mythology. . . . The prediction of the Church of Rome (he says) has at last come true, that those who threw off the yoke of the Church would never rest till they had thrown off the yoke of the Bible too. Yes, he says, we have cast off the yoke of the Bible.' p. 99.

[3] Martineau described our Lord as 'simply the Divine flower of humanity . . . And to see Him thus we go to His native fields and the village houses of Galilee . . . All that has added to that real historic scene — the angels that hang around His birth, and the fiend that tempts His youth, the dignities that await His future, the throne, the trumpet, the great assize, the bar of judgment, nay, the very boundary walls of the kosmic panorama that contains these things, — have for us utterly melted away, and left us amid the infinite sea and the silent stars.' p. 102.

[4] On p. 104 of his article Brown referred to an earlier lecture in which 'I adverted to the difference between Francis Newman's view of the character of Christ, and that of Dr. Martineau. Mr. Newman maintained that viewing Jesus of Nazareth as a mere man — as both of

104

Gibbon's famous sentence is more than justified — 'The predictions of the Catholics are accomplished; the web of mystery is unravelled etc'[1]

And so in your last sentence you come of necessity and as a duty, to *faith*! Most true; so from the house tops said Catholics, when Protestantism began[2]

Most truly Yours John H Card Newman

TO W. S. LILLY

June 27. 1882.

My dear Lilly,

I return with this letter your proof.[3]

The article is most singularly interesting and arresting.[4]

I think you praise my *Arians* too highly; it was the first book I wrote, and the work of a year, and it is inexact in thought and incorrect in language. When at a comparatively late date I was led to re-publish it, I should have liked to mend it, but I found that if I attempted it would come to pieces, and I should have to write it over again.

In saying this, I have no intention of withdrawing from the substance of what you quote from me; on the contrary, I hold it as strongly as I did fifty years ago when it was written; but I feel the many imperfections of the wording.[5]

Very sincerely yours, John H. Card. Newman.

them did — it was impossible to admire his character; impossible, rather, not to condemn it — marked as it was, by an arrogance intolerable in any mere man, by pretensions which, in a mere man, were simply incredible ... In these dreadful conclusions I was constrained to admit that Mr. Newman was right, following, as it seemed to me, irresistibly from the premises common to both gentlemen.' In a footnote Brown added: 'Since the present Lecture was delivered I have read a pamphlet entitled, *What is Christianity without Christ?*, by Francis W. Newman (1881), — which, though not naming Dr. Martineau, seems plainly to have been written in reply to his Lecture ... The whole object of that pamphlet is (1), to show that the character of the "Christ" of the Gospels is far worse than anything the writer had ever said of him before (and here his language is such that it would defile these pages to quote even a line of it); (2), that when you cut out of the Gospels all that goes to prove what is here affirmed, you leave no Christ at all ...'

[1] 'The predictions of the Catholics are accomplished; the web of mystery is unravelled by the Arminians, Arians, and Socinians, whose numbers must not be computed from their separate congregations; and the pillars of revelation are shaken by those men who preserve the name without the substance of religion, who indulge the licence without the temper of philosophy.' *The Decline and Fall of the Roman Empire*, end of Chapter LIV. Bury's edition, VI, p. 128.

[2] Brown's article concluded: 'May the Spirit of all grace come down in power upon all our Halls of Divinity, upon those of our sister Presbyterian Churches, and upon every such Hall of Divinity, as a quickening, heart-warming power, before which scepticism, whether open or covert, will never stand. For now as ever "this is the victory that overcometh the world, even our *faith*."'

[3] Lilly, who printed this letter in the *Fortnightly Review* (Sept. 1890), could not remember what this proof was.

[4] This was 'The Sacred Books of the East', *DR* (July 1882), pp. 1–32, reprinted in Lilly *Ancient Religion and Modern Thought*, London 1884, Chapter III.

[5] At the end of his article Lilly quoted with high praise from *Ari.*, pp. 81–6.

105

TO AUBREY DE VERE

Rednal, June 28th. 1882.

My dear Aubrey de Vere,

Thank you for your Volume[1] which, judging by what I have read, is very successful, as good in its line, (though a different line) as 'Alexander' and 'the Saxon Saints'.[2] I was especially pleased with the eight line Italian metre in which the children of Lir and another poem is written.[3]

But I have no right to give any opinion, for my brain and my eyes work so slowly that I am good for nothing.

I am seeing through the Press William Palmer's Journal of his visit to Russia.

I hope you will let me ask your acceptance of a copy when it is finished.

Yours affectionately, John H. Cardinal Newman.

TO E. B. PUSEY

Rednall. June 29. 1882.

My dear Pusey,

Your kind and considerate letter has just come here.

I opened Mozley's book, and was so much offended by what I saw in it (offended, because it was so incorrect in what it stated or suggested,) that I put it down, and have not opened it since.[4] What was the use, when I could not condescend to answer it? Some time, if I have leisure, I shall note down its serious mistakes. All that I have seen of it since, has been, when, on looking into newspapers, my eye has been caught by some quotations of it; and every where, in little things as well as great, I find him loose and inaccurate. When a man aims at gossip, he is obliged to dress up facts in order to make his story stand upright.

I did not see what he says about the Oriel election; as usual, from what you say, his story will not run on all fours — nor does any one page, I think, of his book. I recollect your own words in your Sermon perfectly well.[5]

[1] *The Foray of Queen Meave*, London 1882.
[2] *Alexander the Great*, London 1874; *Legends of Saxon Saints*, London 1879.
[3] In Newman's copy only the pages of the preface and of two-thirds of 'The Children of Lir, an ancient Irish Romance', have been cut.
[4] See letter of 9 June to T. Mozley and 8 July to Anne Mozley.
[5] Pusey wrote on 27 June about a passage in T. Mozley's *Reminiscences chiefly of Oriel College and the Oxford Movement*, II, p. 139, stating that Newman was 'much surprised and *concerned* when he read in a sermon preached by P. [Pusey] at the consecration ⟨(opening)⟩ of the chapel at K.C. [Keble College on 25 April 1876] that Newman had lived to regret the part which he had taken in Hawkins' election to the Oriel Provostship.'
After quoting this Pusey added: 'Mozley is not accurate in things which he does not know from his personal knowledge. Of course, I did not name you: my expression was quite vague . . .' Pusey at the end of the account in his sermon of the preference for Edward Hawkins over Keble as Provost of Oriel in 1828, said 'To us it has been a sorrow of our lives.' Pusey explained in his letter, 'I did not mean to include you prominently in what I said.' See letter of 4 Aug. 1882 to Pusey. cf. letter of 3 Aug. 1876 to Anne Mozley, also Liddon's *Pusey* I, p. 139 and R. D. Middleton, *Newman at Oxford*, London 1950, p. 35.

I am at a volume of W. Palmer's Visit to Russia, and meant to send it to you when done. It seems to me exceedingly interesting, as bringing out the genius and position of the Russian Church. He makes the Filioque question somewhat more difficult than I hoped it would have proved.

Ever yours affectionately J. H. N.

P.S.   I ought to have added that though *you* did not in your Sermon say that I was one of Hawkins's advocates, I *was* — and Jenkyns, who at first said he feared Hawkins would not get on with the Fellows, and so was against him, was turned round and voted for Hawkins (so, I think, did Awdry) on finding three residents, Dornford, you and me all for him — I recollect making Jenkyns laugh by saying in defence of my vote 'You know we are not electing an Angel, but a Provost. If we were electing an Angel, I should, of course vote for Keble, but the case is different.' I voted, however, for Hawkins from my great affection for, and admiration of him. I have never ceased to love him to this day.

I certainly was sorry I had helped in electing Hawkins — but I cant say I ever wished the election undone. Without it, there would have been no movement, no Tracts, no Library of the Fathers — I could go on at great length, had I time for it.

TO MRS JOHN RICKARDS MOZLEY

[July ? 1882]

My dear Edith

Unless my brain and my fingers worked so slow, I would say more than I can and shall about John's interesting, original, and suggestive article.[1] Another more immediate difficulty is that I cannot bring to bear such knowledge of the classics as is necessary to criticise a Paper which shows such a mastery of them. All I can do is to set down such remarks upon its various statements and conclusions, as occur to me, with the full consciousness that I have not worked out the subejct as he has.

The sense of the beautiful is part of our nature; our eyes are one special channel by which it is conveyed to us, and not only colour and form, but the combination and contrast of colour and form, and of colours inter se and forms inter se, are, as far as the eyes go, the chief subject matter of the beautiful. Is not scenery one great portion of that subject matter? How then is it possible if the beautiful exists, and if the perception of it is natural, that the cultivated mind, in proportion as the eyes act, unless the sense of sight be more developed now than formerly (e.g. by distinguishing colours from each other, which in Homer's day were not distinguished) must not in all ages enjoy a landscape as being beautiful? Here I agree with John.

---

[1] 'Natural Scenery', the *Quarterly Review* (July 1882), pp. 151–74. Mozley argued that the contemplation of life' is the reason for our delight in scenery, and compared the attitudes of ancient and modern poets.

I know that I am not going to the bottom of the subject: however, in spite of this I will venture to say that I doubt whether the contemplation of life, as such, is, as John considers, 'a refreshment and consolation'. It must be *still* life to be such, or at any rate *harmonious* life. I do not feel a scene of a fox pursued by hounds, or a battlepiece, or a shipwreck, to be soothing; but such is a harvest home — such (if I recollect it rightly) is 'Rubens's farm' in the National Gallery — and that, because such life is harmonious, and harmony is one source of the beautiful. And thus, while life is not essential to the 'refreshing', it is sometimes incompatible with it.

I am disposed moreover to think that mere power or sublimity is not a source of the beautiful, or of the refreshing and soothing. It is the change of scene, the mountain air, the provocation to exert the limbs and to overcome physical difficulties, which is the charm and restorative virtue of Switzerland, in so far forth as its *beauty* of scenery is not the account of it; and John almost allows this. I am perhaps an unfair judge here — for wonderful as the Swiss mountains are, they so little attract me, that in 1833, to the surprise of my friends and almost in spite of their remonstrance, I preferred to go to Sicily by myself to going to Switzerland, on the ground that the former was the more beautiful. The sublime did not attract me as being soothing or refreshing.

John brings together various passages from the ancients showing in them a sensibility to beautiful scenery. To these I will contribute one from St Basil, and as he may not know it, I will send him a volume of mine in which he will find it — at page 59. Basil 'climbed a mountain to see a view'.[1]

I should have added above, that all poetical minds so associate the natural with the moral, that in this is an adventitious source of refreshment and consolation in scenery. Thus Keble,

> How quiet shows the woodland scene!
> Each flower and tree, its duty done,
> Reposing in decay serene,
> Like weary men, when age is won:[2]

and so Virgil, as in the passage John quotes:

> et virginibus bacchata Lacaenis Taygeta.[3]

(vide also John about Wordsworth, on p. 169.)[4] It is not the 'wonderful' which delights Virgil, but the ethical association.

Yrs afftely J.H.N.

---

[1] *H.S.*, II, pp. 59–60, 'Basil and Gregory', where Newman quotes St Basil, *Ep.* 14.
[2] *The Christian Year*, 'All Saints' Day', second stanza.
[3] Art. cit., p. 155. Virgil, *Georgics*, ii, 487–8.
[4] After quoting Milton, *The Hymn*, stanza XX, Mozley said, 'No one could at all events be thought unreasonable, who should prefer the last-quoted stanza to any part of Wordsworth's . . . Tintern Abbey.'

Bm July 3. 1882

My Dear Sister Pia,

I did not forget you on the Visitation, but said Mass for you on two other days instead, because I heard that William George Ward was dying.[1] How it was that his serious state of health was not known generally before, I cannot tell. His principal complaint is that of which Fr Joseph Gordon died, and that was three years upon him.

It will be still some time before Palmer's Journal will issue from the Press. I shall send it to you. It seems to me very interesting — but 40 years is more than a generation, and I can't prophesy how it will strike most people. The Czar does not appear in it, though afterwards he had Palmer to dine with him. I think the book shows the impossibility of the union of Greece with Rome. As for the Russian ecclesiastics, he found that they had all but given up the idea of unity, or of the Catholicity of the Church. So far they were behind the Anglicans, who at least profess belief in One Catholic Church.

I am very well, as far as health goes — but I am more and more infirm. I am dimsighted, deaf, lame, and have a difficulty in talking and writing. And my memory is very bad.

I fear the enemies of the Church are all but effecting its absolute fall in France.[2] The first and second generation after us will have a dreadful time of it. Satan is almost unloosed. May we all be housed safely before that day!

Yours affectly in Xt   J. H. Card. Newman

Are you not 80 now?[3]

The Oratory Birmingham July 6, 1882.

Dear Miss Fortey

Your letter has interested me very much, and has led me to entertain great hopes that God is calling you by His grace into His Church, and of course it is your duty to attend to that call, and that you may duly attend to it, I earnestly pray.[4]

[1] The feast of the Visitation of our Lady was on 2 July. W. G. Ward died on 6 July. Miss Giberne replied in a letter of 4–6 July, 'I hope Mr Ward has asked pardon for all the hard and unjust things he has said and written about you if not — may God have mercy on him.'
[2] This refers to the secularising laws against religion in schools, hospitals, and elsewhere, and the expulsions of religious orders.
[3] Miss Giberne replied that she would be 80 on 13 Aug.
[4] Emily Fortey wrote on 4 July from 7 Vyvyan Terrace, Clifton: 'I do not want to trouble you with my opinions and my affairs, but I do need your help so much and you could give it me by your advice. I am 16 years old and am entirely a Catholic at heart and have been so for about four years. I have lately read the "Characteristics of Your Writings" by Lilly and also "Loss and Gain" which have of course much influenced me. My parents are — nothing in the way of Religion. I have only a step-mother and my father has only been home from India a short time so I do not know either of them well and could certainly never tell them my opinions, or talk at all on the subject. I go to the Clifton High School and one of the mistresses is a

So much I have no difficulty in saying; but, when you come to the question, what your duty is at this time, my answer is not so easy. I consider that a stranger to you cannot give you satisfactory advice. You should have recourse to some priest on the spot, put your whole case before him, and go by his judgment. The Father Jesuits, for instance are sure to be careful and experienced priests, and they would, on talking to you decide whether, young as you are, and dependent, I suppose, on your Father, it would be advisable for you at once to undergo the great trial of breaking with him. Our Lord tells us to 'count the cost'[1] — the change of religion is a most serious step — and must not be taken without great preparation by meditation and prayer. The Jesuit Fathers are to be found at the Catholic Church on the Quay, Bristol.

Do not doubt that our Lord will guide you safely and happily if you place yourself unreservedly into his hands.[2]

Yours sincerely J. H. Card. Newman

TO THOMAS PRETIOUS HESLOP

July 6. 1882

Dear Dr Heslop

I feel the compliment you pay me by your request, and I will send you the two volumes with as little delay as possible.[3]

I have a difficulty in writing my name in them, and thereby making them a direct present from me; for, while I admire and honour the singular munificence which Mr Mason's foundations evidence, I have no sympathy at all with the feelings which, in carrying out that munificence, he manifested towards the Catholic Religion[4]

I am, Dear Dr Heslop Sincerely Yours John H Card. Newman

T. P. Heslop Esqr etc etc

great friend of mine. She is an Anglican and if any thing could keep me from joining the Church it would be love for her. But that seems so wrong. Do you think I ought to join the Church now, or wait till I am of age? I am sure my Father would never give his consent. And if I stay in the Anglican Church ought I to go to Communion? I have always believed in Transubstantiation in the Anglican Church, but after reading your books it seems to me impossible. And then do you think I am wrong in going to Catholic services? That I do without my father's knowledge. I could not tell him. I never talk about these things to him. . . . It is because I feel sure that the Catholic Church is the "Ark of Salvation" that I dare do any thing that may lead me to it.'

[1] Luke, 14:28.
[2] See letters of 18 July to Miss Waring and 21 Dec. 1882 to Francis Loughnan, also that of 3 Oct. 1884 to Emily Fortey.
[3] Heslop, a leading Birmingham physician, was one of the trustees of Mason College. It is not clear which of Newman's volumes he wished to be presented to its library.
[4] Not only did Sir Josiah Mason insist in the trust deed of Mason College, which he founded in 1880, 'that no lectures, or teaching, or examination shall be permitted in the institution upon theology, or any question or subject in its nature purely theological', but he also laid down as fundamental that all trustees of his College must be laymen and Protestants. John Thackray Bunce, *Josiah Mason, A Biography*, Birmingham 1882, pp. 121 and 126. See also p. 163. 'The dogmatic and ecclesiastical aspects of religion were repugnant to him.'

July 8. 1882

Cardinal N. on notice from Messrs G and R sent up, without the delay of a post, fresh copy for Mr Palmer's volume on June 24. It is now a fortnight since he has received any proof from them

He has received from them two sheets of the Via Media — but he has no wish that the Via Media should hinder the printing of Mr Palmer's proofs.

Bm July 8. 1882

My dear Child

Certainly I am sorry that you have brought in Mr Parnell etc — and the more so, that you have given him (and them) satirical names. The Irish matter is so very grave that it does not admit of what looks like a joke.[1]

How am I able to answer your question? You assume that Mr Parnell has murderers at his command; but all I have seen about him leads me to think just the reverse — viz that he is the tool of others. You should not impute a great crime to a man without solid proof and sufficient cause.

Has anyone read your book? I have no doubt at all that it is clever and amusing — but your 'programme' demands for its execution very delicate handling — else, it may make Irishmen angry without pleasing English.

You must not think me severe; is it to be in the Lamp? it would be less criticised there, than if it were a 2 or 3 volumed novel with your name.[2]

You told me there was some criticism of my Verses at the beginning of the year, which you wished me to see; do you recollect the month?[3]

Yours affectly John H Card Newman

Bm July 8. 1882

My dear Anne Mozley

I thought rightly that your brother's volumes might give me the pleasure of a letter from you — and I knew that, if it did, it would be a kind and sympathetic one, and, having said this, I will, please, drop the subject.[4]

---

[1] Miss Fitzgerald in an undated letter asked Newman's advice: 'I am at present engaged in writing a novel in which my design is to bring out the difference between the Irish and English characters the utter absence of all conception of truthfulness in the Irish brought into as sharp relief as I can place it with the sturdy unbending honesty of the English nature. . . .

Well in working out this programme I introduce the Irish members of Parliament and the Land League only under feigned names. Parnell I call Snarlwell, and so on. Now I wanted to know whether you thought this might rouse the vindictiveness of these fiends in human form and that they might order some of their minions to revenge them by murdering either of my two brothers, one of whom is a landlord the other a land agent in Ireland.'

[2] The Lamp was a weekly illustrated Catholic magazine, costing one penny.

[3] For Miss Fitzgerald's reply see letter of 13 July to her.

[4] Anne Mozley in a long letter of 7 July described her brother's Reminiscences as very mixed, some excellent some not. She thought Newman's sister Jemima 'would have differed

I am engaged in passing through the Press a volume of William Palmer's Russian and Eastern Travels, he having left me by will all his papers. To me his narrative is very interesting, and it throws so much light upon the state of religion in Russia, and on the position of the Russo-Greek Church, that I should have no doubt of its interesting the public, except that the innumerable subjects of interest, which the Press now supplies to readers, diminishes the chance of any one of them engaging popular attention.

The Volume begins with his setting out under the sanction of Dr Routh and his difficulties at Magdalen and Lambeth. When he arrives at Petersburg, he at once attacks the Russian language, which is no slight job; meanwhile, he converses with the great ecclesiastics in French and Latin, Latin (to my surprise) being the language (with Russ), which is common to all priests. He visits the two great monasteries one near Petersburgh, the other near Moscow. He lodges with a priest — holds conferences with the Metropolitan of Moscow, and other members of the Holy Synod — and (2) forms the acquaintance of various highly educated princesses, and (1) above all with the members of the Imperial Chancery, which represents the Emperor as head of the Church

His main object is to be recognized as a member of the Holy Catholic Church, and to be admitted to communion as such. In this he his unsuccessful — as for other reasons, so for this, that the Russian Ecclesiastics are not quite sure that any One Catholic Church now remains in the world. There was once, but it has died, and the Russo-Greek Church is all that remains of it — so that Palmer is indeed at liberty to become a Russo-Greek, but not to remain an Anglican. He started August 1840, and got back to Oxford July 1841.

Yours affly J H Card. Newman

TO JOHN BRAMSTON

July 10. 1882.

My dear Dean

Thank you for your most affectionate letter, and I grieve to find you speaking so seriously of yourself.[1]

I am always thinking of you,

Ever Yours John H. Card. Newman.

strongly' from the account of the early religious training in the Newman family. Anne Mozley also said: 'We hear from Oxford that Dr Liddon was reading the Reminiscences to Dr Pusey as soon as they came out   He listened with interest saying now and then "My memory is bad but I think I can contradict that."' For the strength of Pusey's reaction see Liddon's *Pusey* IV, pp. 372–4.

[1] Bramston resigned as Dean of Winchester in April 1883, and died in 1889.

TO MESSRS BURNS AND OATES

July 10. 1882

In answer to Messrs Burns and Oates's letter, Cardinal Newman has to inform them that on their sending him the annual cheque as usual, he will send them the usual receipt. He sees no reason for departing from what has been the rule in their transactions with him for the last 34 years. What possible means has he of pledging himself, as they ask him to do, that 'their statements of account are correct'? He does not doubt it, but they, as ever hitherto, must take that responsibility He expects, as ever hitherto, a cheque at once.[1]

TO GERALDINE PENROSE FITZGERALD

Bm July 13. 1882

My Dear Child,

Your letter has troubled me very much.[2] I grieve over your sufferings and your Mother's from the state of Ireland and I do not wonder at all that it should be a trial and temptation to you, tho' our dear Lord will, I am sure, support you through it and make it all up to you.

As to what you are writing, I spoke merely of the *names* you had given to certain *real* characters. Those names were satirical, and therefore unsuitable to a grave subject — but, though I think you *have* taken a ticklish matter to form a plot out of, I had no intention to criticize, any more than I had the right to do so.

Your account of Ireland is dreadful — but you had no need to tell me that. But as to the future! It seems as if at last a judgment was coming down on England for its centuries of pride and self confidence.

[1] Wilfrid Oates, who had written on 8 July in the first person, replied on 11 July in the same way. He had been sending accounts to other authors 'whose custom it is to look over the statements previous to their receiving cheque', and without thinking did the same to Newman. He did not want Newman to pledge himself as to the accuracy of the account and enclosed a cheque for £282. 2s. 7d.

[2] In an undated letter from London Miss Fitzgerald thanked Newman for his letter of 8 July 'which I received today'. She continued: 'I will at once take Mr Parnell out of my book and all the other Irish members as your least word is law to me . . . and I see myself that it is far wiser to do so. But I hear from my relatives in Ireland that it is well known there that the orders for the murders and mutilations some down from a secret Council of the Land League in Dublin. Did not Mr Parnell say every thing he could to stir up the fury of the people against the land lords and end with "you know how you serve rabbits, eh?". . . . My brothers are getting no rents and their lives are in hourly danger. All last winter my youngest brother never dared to stir out after dark — he has just had a beautiful horse killed in the most cruel manner. The tenants on a neighbouring property who paid their rents have had pins and needles put in their cattles' food so the poor innocent animals died in tortures . . . We cannot help feeling very bitterly just at this moment on this subject, as I see my mother after a long life devoted to visiting the poor and the sick in the village and on our own property at home refused rent from those very people, who are instigated to send the money thus saved to Pat Egan for the Land League funds and to murder either of her sons if they remonstrate. There she is 75 years old and obliged to do without all the comforts she has been accustomed to all her life.' Miss Fitzgerald went on to complain that Cardinal Manning was encouraging the Land Leaguers. In a postscript she apologised if she appeared 'violent and disrespectful', and went on to say what a trial to her as a Catholic the last few years had been, 'when I see the priests about our neighbourhood in Cork stirring up the people to revolution.'

I saw the Article in the Century, and do not therefore want it. Nor do I care for that other article, which you can't recall. I mentioned it, to thank you for the trouble you took about it. Pray take no more.[1]

As to Mr Mozley's article, it is *full* of mistakes. As far as I have looked into it, he is not correct two lines together — and very illnatured.[2]

Yours affectly John H. Card. Newman

TO F. MERCEDES WARING

Birmingham July 18, 1882.

Cardinal Newman thanks Miss Waring for her letter[3]

He will be obliged to her, if she will take a copy of the letter which he wrote to Miss Fortey, and send it to him.[4]

TO ROBERT CHARLES JENKINS

Birmingham, July 21, 1882.

Dear Canon Jenkins

Thank you for your most graceful and musical Poems. As to the conflict, (which you note with such happy point) [between] Cardinal-Archbishops Wiseman and Manning, it is only such as really might take place even between infallible Popes, for it is on a question of expedience, such as varies with times, places, and circumstances.

The Divine law cannot be dispensed from — but the law in question is Ecclesiastical. Cardinal Wiseman had in view the stratum of Society, in which our English Catholics chiefly lie — and thought dispensation from that law advisable. Cardinal Manning, regarding a higher class, consisting indeed chiefly of Protestants, but of Catholics too, felt with Dr. Pusey and the House of Lords that the dispensation was inexpedient.[5]

---

[1] For Kegan Paul's article in the *Century* see letter of 30 May to him. Miss Fitzgerald could not find the article mentioned at the end of Newman's letter of 8 July.

[2] Newman is speaking of T. Mozley's *book*, about which Miss Fitzgerald wrote in her letter, 'We are all just now reading Mozley's Oriel recollections with great interest, and amusement.'

[3] Miss Waring, of 10 St John's Road, Clifton, wrote on 16 July that Emily Fortey, (see letter of 6 July to her), had been forbidden by her father to hold communication with any Catholic priest, and was in great distress at not being able to thank Newman for his letter. Miss Waring said, 'I am a school-fellow of hers, and a Catholic, and, as you had advised her to apply to one of the Jesuit Fathers down at the Quay, I went with her to see Father Hill.' The following day Emily Fortey's father discovered everything and issued his prohibition. She wrote her thanks to Newman on the last page of her friend's letter, and said she supposed she must wait until she was twenty-one before becoming a Catholic.

[4] On 19 July Miss Waring sent Newman a copy of his letter, and she and Emily Fortey apologised for the trouble she had caused him.

[5] This refers to the Marriage with a deceased wife's sister Bill, which would have removed the prohibition existing in English law. It was defeated in the House of Lords on 12 June by three votes, after Manning had successfully urged the Catholic peers to oppose it. Wiseman gave evidence before the Royal Commission of 1847 to enquire into the question

Each Cardinal had a right to his own opinion, and in a matter not of faith, each might differ from each.

Very sincerely yours John H. Card. Newman

TO W. J. COPELAND

Bm. July 22. 1882

My dear Copeland

Thank you for your affectionate letter.[1] I was shocked at T. M.'s wanton mistakes. I call them 'wanton', because a man should not assert things which he does not know. He finds a statement will not go on three legs, so from his imagination he adds a fourth. Whatever I have seen, whatever I have heard of, as to his sayings about me, contains direct or indirect untruths. And it does not become me to set him right by any public statement; so I must bear it.

I have asked various persons about your Sister, but could learn nothing. I grieve to hear your bad account.

I am older than I was — I am dimsighted, deaf, lame — I write, I talk, I think with difficulty. My memory is weak — but I have nothing the matter with me. I fear nothing will bring you this way, and I am not likely to move any way

Yours ever affectly John H Card. Newman

TO MESSRS MACMILLAN

The Oratory, Bm July 28 1882

Cardinal Newman has received this morning from Messrs Macmillan a copy of Mr Hughes's Memoir of Mr David Macmillan, and thanks them for their kindness in sending it to him[2]

of marriages within the prohibited degrees of affinity, and explained that the Catholic Church regarded the marriage with two sisters in succession as prohibited only by positive law, and so within the dispensing power. In his pamphlet, *The Repeal of the Prohibition of the Marriage with a Deceased Wife's Sister Advocated* . . . , London 1883, pp. 19–20, Jenkins wrote: 'A letter of Cardinal Manning, though it admits the right of Papal dispensation, gives no reason for differing from the view adopted by his predecessor in favour of a relaxation of the prohibition except the singular one that it would tend to encourage and multiply such marriages which he would restrict to "a few rare and exceptional cases" . . . At all events the Cardinal advocates two distinct marriage laws, one for the rich and the other for the poor . . .'

[1] Copeland wrote on 21 July: 'You may well believe how I have been haunted by the thought of the pain which T. M.'s [Mozley] volumes might cause you. I had my misgivings beforehand which I could not refrain from expressing but I was scarcely prepared for such mistakes and inaccuracies as abound in them.' See also letter of 9 June to T. Mozley.
[2] This was Thomas Hughes's *Memoir of Daniel Macmillan*, London 1882. On pp. 108–9 two of Macmillan's letters of 1843 were quoted, giving his opinion of *U.S.*

TO FREDERICK K. HARFORD

Aug 4/82

Copy
Dear Sir

I thank you for the very kind spirit in which your private letter to me is written[1]

I inclose the printed letter, which you send, signed, on the understanding, which the list of signatures you inclose, hinders me from questioning, that you have the sanction of the Government of India for the measure you are furthering

J H N

The Revd F. K. Harford

TO MISS MUNRO

Bm Aug. 4. 1882

My Dear Miss Munro

Your beautiful Altar cloth has just come, and I have with many silent thanks put it upon my altar.

I am glad to hear you are better I said Mass for you within the last fortnight

Yours affectly John H Card. Newman

TO EDWIN PALMER

Birmingham. Aug 4/82

My dear Archdeacon Palmer

Some one has suggested to me that the Volume, now nearly through the Press, should have a portrait of your brother, if it can be got. I have no opinion about it. Will you decide the point?[2]

I was exceedingly gratified by your liking my Preface, tho' did not write to say so[3]

Most truly Yours John H. Card. Newman

[1] Harford, who was a Minor Canon of Westminster, sent on 1 Aug. a printed circular concerning a plan to send the National Anthem to India in fifteen languages. He explained in his private letter 'one chief desire we have is to make the multitudes in India understand that there is a kind feeling towards them in Great Britain and that that feeling is shared by persons of various professions and parties in the State.' It was hoped to 'obtain the approval of 500 of those who are most widely known for talent and kindness: — and Your Eminence's most honoured name would shew — like those of Miss Nightingale and Lord Shaftsbury — that this is not a political — but a humanitarian movement.'

Harford added an independent piece of information 'that on Sunday afternoon last "Lead Kindly Light" was beautifully sung by our Abbey Choir at the 3 p m service when the Bishop of Peterborough preached, and the Bishop of London the Dean and almost all the Canons were present.'

[2] Archdeacon Palmer provided a photograph of his brother William, taken two years before his death, which was inserted in *Notes of a Visit to the Russian Church*.

[3] See note to letter of 12 April to Palmer.

Birmingham. Aug. 4. 1882.

My dear Pusey,

If the words you quote in p. 24 of your Sermon are Mozley's, they are in keeping with all other statements which have been reported to me from his book; they contain a reckless untruth.[1]

I never expressed, I never felt any surprise whatever, any concern whatever, at your words about me, including me with yourself in what you said about Hawkins's election.

What I did feel on reading it was, that your saying it on so public an occasion implied that you were not now on such familiar terms with Hawkins as you were up to the time of my leaving Oxford.

That I had any personal feeling about your paragraph is a simple untruth. It is a specimen of all M.'s statements, as far as I know them. To answer him, would require a book as long as his.

I fear that I must have written you a misleading letter the other day from my not having seen M.'s words.[2] It is infamous to make me complain of you, who have always been so careful in your words about me.

Yours affectly J. H. Card. Newman·

P.S.   I hope you will have Palmer's Journal in a few weeks now.

Aug 5 1882

My dear Paul

My bad memory must be the excuse for the following question.

Surely you made a list of Palmer's publications — and I sent it to his brother — and I wrote to Bloxam that *his* list was defective.[3] Now I do not

---

[1] On 31 July Pusey wrote about the reprint of his 1876 sermon at the opening of Keble Chapel (see letter of 29 June 1882): 'I have thought it best to confine myself p 24 to a simple contradiction of poor T. M's [Mozley] statement of what I said. His book is sadly ill-natured gossip, although he has spared me and cannot but respect you: but as Maskell says in the Athenaeum, his stories have mostly about as much to do with the [Oxford] Movement as with the Crimean War.'

In the reprint of his sermon, p. 24, Pusey put his sentence about preferring Hawkins to Keble as Provost of Oriel in the singular: 'To me it became a sorrow of my life', adding a footnote: 'I scarcely know why, as preached, I worded this sentence, "To us it became a sorrow of our lives." One could hardly use so strong an expression except of one's self. In what professes to be an account of "the Oxford movement" it is said, "Newman was much surprised and concerned when he read in the Sermon preached by Pusey at the consecration of the Chapel at Keble College, that Newman had lived to regret the part he had taken in Hawkins's election to the Oriel Provostship," [T. Mozley, *Reminiscences* . . .] T. i. p. 39, I neither said it, nor did I mean to include him in the word "us." Card. Newman writes to me, "I never expressed, I never felt any surprise whatever, any concern whatever, at your words about me including me with yourself in what you said about Hawkins's election. That I had any personal feeling about your paragraph is a simple untruth.' *Blessed are the Meek . . . ,* second edition, Oxford 1882, p. 24.

[2] Letter of 29 June to Pusey.

[3] See letters of 2 Aug. 1881 to Palmer and 28 Sept. and 2 Oct. 1881 to Bloxam.

know where to find a list, for insertion as an advertisement at the end of his volume which I am publishing

Can you help me? and is there any list with publishers' names added?

I hope you are enjoying your holiday

Yours affectly John H. Card. Newman

TO THE SECRETARY OF THE
YOUNG MEN'S SOCIETIES OF GREAT BRITAIN

Birmingham August 7th, 1882.

Dear Mr. Quinn,[1]

I thank you for the notice you have given me of the Annual Meeting of the Catholic Young Men's Societies, in which I take so great an interest. And it mortifies me that I have not been able to say Mass for them yesterday or to-day, but nothing, I trust, will interfere with my so doing to-morrow. I send them my blessing with all my heart, and am,

Very truly yours, John H. Card. Newman.

TO EDWIN PALMER

Bm Aug 8. 1882

Dear Archdeacon Palmer

I should be much obliged by the gift or loan of the Photograph.[2]

What I fear is, that, as you are from home, you cannot send it soon. I ought to have thought of it sooner; but I wrote to you the first post after the thought occurred to me.

I have told the publishers to send the volume to you and to your two brothers — and to the Sister to whom I sent the Nicon, when I know her address from you. And I will send the Nicon to the brother with whom you are, if he has not got it.[3] And I will send more copies of my volume to you, if you would wish it. I am sending it to Magdalen College, to Bishop Charles Wordsworth, to the Bishop of St Alban's,[4] to Sir J. Hoskyns — and will to any one else you will name.[5]

I am rather afraid you will be disappointed with the look of the volume. In dimensions the cover is about the same as my own volumes — but, in order to make it handsome, I have put fewer words in a page; the consequence

[1] cf. letter of 28 July 1881.
[2] See letter of 4 Aug.
[3] Edwin Palmer's two surviving brothers were the Earl of Selborne and George Horsley Palmer, with whom he was staying at East Liss. His only surviving sister Emily was at St Cyprian's Home, Dorset Square, London.
[4] Thomas Legh Claughton.
[5] Palmer named Lady Henry Kerr and Admiral Count Pontiatine at St Petersburg. See also letter of 4 Sept. to Palmer.

is, alas, that it is little short of 600 pages — whereas I meant it to be 400 — and I fear I shall find it fat

Yours very truly John H. Card. Newman

PS. As I am not sure of your Post town, I add Ch Ch[Christ Church] Have I not just seen Mr Blackmore's death in the Papers?[1]

TO A DAUGHTER OF SIR HENRY COLE

Birmingham Aug 11. 1882

My dear Miss Cole

I felt the kindness of your letter, though I have let some days pass before answering it.[2] With you I am deeply convinced that much passes between the soul and its Maker, when the end is coming, which no one else knows; and that you should think that I was of any kind of service to your Father is a most unexpected and great comfort to me. It comforts me the more, because I had felt my debt of gratitude to him, which I owed for the repeated remembrance that he made of me, especially on my birthdays, from the time he knew me.

I am glad to hear so good an account of your Mother, and from my heart send you and her and all of you my blessing

Very sincerely Yours John H. Card. Newman

TO J. M. CAPES

Bm Aug 16. 1882

My dear C.

I was very glad to hear from you, and was struck at your finding Ealing healthy. For, when I went first to school in 1808, I recollect our old nurse speaking of it expressly as healthy, and saying that its name was properly 'Healing.'

I can easily understand how great a gain to poor Catholic children it would be to have another asylum for the blind — but the primâ facie difficulty is the risk of hurting the existing Liverpool Institution. The Catholic body in England is not a large one — and it is so much easier to begin something new, than to consolidate and secure what is already existing, that I should be much afraid that an undertaking such as you have in mind would result in nothing better than a mutually destructive rivalry[3]

[1] Blackmore died on 28 June.
[2] cf. letter of 20 April to a son of Sir Henry Cole.
[3] J. M. Capes was blind in his last years. The Catholic Blind Institute in Liverpool has remained the only one in England to this day.

Like you, it tires my eyes and my hands not to say my brain to write —
and thanking you for your letter and for all you say in it of yourself,

I am, my dear C. Yours affly John H. Card. Newman

TO WILLIAM CHARLES LAKE

My Dear Dean of Durham

The Oratory Birmm Aug. 18. 1882

Thank you for your Sermon, which is very interesting in itself, and is
more than kind to me.[1] It brought to my mind that first act of expressed good
will towards me, when I saw you to my surprise at my door at Littlemore, I
think to call on me.[2] And that other saying which was circulated of yours,
that Golightly had done me as much good as Berkeley had done me [harm].[3]
It was so different from your friend, poor Stanley, who, up to his dying day,
never, as far as I know, said a good word for me.[4]

As to the Sermon itself, it is a most important gain to the E.Ch. Union
to have such an advocacy, and though it may seem inconsistent in me, I
cannot but rejoice in it. I feel great sympathy with the Ritualists because I
know how much high principle goes with their acts, how much successful
work, and again, on the part of their opponents, how much unjust and unworthy treatment of them. For these reasons I am used to think the second
generation of them will triumph, unless indeed, as I hope and am inclined to
believe, that second generation becomes Catholic.[5]

Their want is an intellectual foundation — which, sufficient for practical
purposes, the Evangelicals seem to me to have. The latter say 'This only I
know, that, whereas I was once blind, now I see.' What do Ritualists appeal
to?

Very sincerely Yours John H. Card. Newman

[1] *The Two Religious Movements of our Time, A Sermon preached to the Members of the
English Church Union, in the Church of St. Mary Magdalen Munster Square on June 13, 1882,*
London 1882. Lake defended the faith and practice of the Ritualists. He paid tribute to
Newman's religious influence at Oxford, p. 24, and in the preface called him 'the finest mind
that the English Church has ever produced'.

[2] Lake spent a few days at Littlemore in the summer of 1844, but did not know Newman at
any time intimately. *Memorials of William Charles Lake,* edited by Katharine Lake, London
1901, p. 51.

[3] Newman and the Tractarians were the obsession of C. P. Golightly. George Campion
Berkeley was a tactless supporter of Tractarianism.

[4] Lake replied on 14 Sept. from Wurtemburg:

'I need hardly say with how much pleasure I received your kind acknowledgment of a
Sermon I had ventured to send you, in which I expressed, if I may be allowed to say it, something of the veneration I have ever felt for your character since my early Oxford days. You
may perhaps have hardly realized how deep and warm this was, and is, with many of us who
did not know you intimately; and I will venture to say of dear [A.P.] Stanley, from whom I
was myself much separated latterly, that though in his later life he unhappily fell off from his
allegiance to you, he was certainly not wanting in his feeling towards you in his earlier days.
He had latterly a strong crotchet about your injustice to "Liberals".'

[5] In the draft Newman wrote: 'And I think that on all these accounts they will ultimately
get the better of their enemies — For such initial troubles and such eventual triumph is the
very law of the propagation of truth.

Of course I think the only real success would be, if the movement issued in union with
the old Catholic Church of Rome, but numbers have had that in view, so have I [illegible]
Yet their children and disciples may be led further than themselves, and may follow on their
present conclusion. Do not think me rude in saying so.'

TO ALFRED TENNYSON

Birmingham Aug. 18. 1882

My dear Mr Tennyson

Your and Mrs Tennyson's invitation of me through Aubrey de Vere is very kind, and I account it an honour as well as a kindness.[1]

But, I regret to say, I must decline it. I am of a great age now — and, though in good health, I am so full of the infirmities of old age, in so many respects, that I cannot leave home, unless I am compelled

Beg Mrs Tennyson not to think me ungracious to you, and believe me to be, with kind regards to de Vere,

Sincerely Yours John H Card. Newman

Alfred Tennyson Esqr

TO FRANCIS MORGAN

[22 August 1882][2]

1. If there is money in any of the Letters, it must be given to Fr Austin.
2. If any letter comes from Dr Pusey's friends, you must say I am away for a few days.
3. And you must take the trouble to say the same, should Mr de Vere, write to me to say he is coming here on the days when I am away.[3]

FROM ALFRED TENNYSON

Aldworth, Haslemere, Surrey. Aug 20th —82

My dear Cardinal Newman

I and my wife and my son would have welcomed you to this house with more pleasure than I can well put into words. You and I are both of us old men, and I am the younger, and if you cannot come to me, I feel that some day or other I ought to go to you, for though, I dare say, there are a hundred things on which we might differ, there is no man on this side of the grave, more worthy of honour and affection than yourself; and therefore though I have never shaken you by the hand, let me subscribe myself

Affectly Yours A Tennyson

TO ALFRED TENNYSON

Birmingham Aug. 23, 1882

My dear Mr Tennyson,

You are exceedingly kind in giving me the hope that I may some day have the gratification of seeing you. No time is likely to be inconvenient to

---

[1] Aubrey de Vere, who was staying with the Tennysons at Aldworth, wrote on 17 Aug. how much they wished Newman would pass a few days with them. See also letter of 17 April 1877 to Tennyson.
[2] Dated from postmark.
[3] Aubrey de Vere wrote that he was hoping to come and stay for a night.

me. I am here (I may say) all the year through, unless I run over for a day to a small cottage of ours a few miles off. And, whenever you come this way, on the notice of one post, you would find me here

Very truly and affectly Yours John H. Card. Newman[1]

TO R. H. MILWARD

The Oratory Aug. 24. 1882

Dear Mr Milward

M. Gounod has shown me the great attention of writing to me to express his pleasure that I shall be present at his Oratorio next week.[2]

As he sends his letter through you, and I neither write nor speak French, I hope you will allow me to express my acknowledgments to him by your aid. Especially am I interested by what he tells me of the connexion of his great work with Pope Pius

I am, My dear Mr Milward Very truly Yours John H. Card. Newman[3]
R. Milward Esqr

TO ROBERT COOPER SEATON

Aug. 24. 1882

Sir

I hope in consideration of my age, you will excuse me if I do not answer your theological question

It is, as looked at either a very easy or a very difficult one. In the latter

---

[1] In Nov. 1882 Newman sent Tennyson a copy of William Palmer's *Notes of a Visit to the Russian Church*, and received a letter from Aldworth the same month: 'Dear Cardinal Newman,

I have made a foolish mistake. I acknowledged your volume at once when I had only looked at the back of it: there was the name "Palmer" and I fancied that you had been editing some posthumous work of that Palmer, who was lately murdered by the Bedaweens.' This was Henry Edward Palmer, Professor of Arabic at Cambridge, and interpreter-in-chief to the British forces in Egypt, shot by Bedouins on 11 Aug. 1882. Tennyson's letter continued: 'And I call him "poor" not because he was dead but because he was murdered. I particularly dislike the popular epithet "poor" as applied to the dead for they may be richer in all blessings than ever they were on earth, or than the friends they leave behind them. I write in a great hurry and I beg you to pardon me

Yours ever A Tennyson'

[2] Charles Gounod wrote: 'Mercredi 23 Août/82
Monseigneur,

On m'assure que Votre Eminence est dans l'intention d'assister au festival de Birmingham, pendant lequel doit être exécuté deux fois (le 30 Août et le 1er 7bre) mon nouvel Oratorio "La Rédemption". Je ne veux pas tarder à vous dire, Monseigneur, que je regarderais Votre présence non pas seulement comme un très grand honneur, mais comme une *bénédiction* dont le prix et le souvenir se joindraient dans mon coeur à celle que notre Saint Père le Pape Pie IX a daigné donner au *texte* que j'ai écrit à Rome pendant son auguste Pontificat.

Je suis, Monseigneur, avec le plus profond respect,
De Votre Eminence Le très humble Serviteur Ch. Gounod
Mr Milward's Care
41, Waterloo Street Birmingham.
[3] In fact Newman was unable to attend the performance of 'The Redemption'.

case, it would require many words to answer, in the former, it requires none. I cannot but hope you will not dissent [or] think me unreasonable in taking this view of it[1]

FOR SIMEON WILBERFORCE O'NEILL

[end of August 1882][2]

Utrum opinio illa posset sine temeritate vel periculo teneri, illa refrigeria Petaviana refrigeria [sic] in hoc consistere, in animabus damnatorum suspendi pro tempore sensum illum quo notant temporis lapsum et momentorum successionem, ita ut centum (ut dicunt) anni in unum punctum temporis concentretur.[3]

TO EDWIN PALMER

Bm Sept 4. 1882

My dear Archdeacon

Thank you — I have already got down the names of Allies and Bloxam. Unless some accident prevents me, I will send you a list of the persons to whom I mean to send the volume. You can add to them, if you think best[4]

Yrs most truly J H Card. Newman

[1] Seaton, who was a master at St Paul's School 1876–1905, wrote on 18 Aug. to ask, in connexion with *Apo.*, Note G, 'Lying and Equivocation', '1. How it is possible in practice to separate Lying into a material and formal part . . . 2. Can there ever be a "justa causa" of a lie? . . .'

Seaton wrote again on 14 Sept. 1884, saying he thought Newman's reply two years before 'very kind'. Many moral difficulties in religion which he then felt had since disappeared. He thanked for the 'clearer apprehension' of many things, which he had gained from Newman's writings. This was to be seen in his article 'The Attitude of Carlyle and Emerson towards Christianity', the *National Review* (Aug. 1884).

[2] Simeon Wilberforce O'Neill, who nearly became a Catholic, see letter of 11 Aug. 1865 to him, joined the Cowley Fathers in 1866 and went as a missionary to India. He wrote from Indore on 15 Aug. 1882:

'It was very kind of you to accede to my request with respect to the last chapter of the *Grammar of Assent* and I beg your Eminence to accept my sincere thanks. Of course, we shall take care to observe the condition imposed not to allow the book to be sold in England.

I have not been in any hurry to bring it out because I have been promised the assistance of several friends who have more to do than myself with Hindu students (and one of whom has already made the *Grammar of Assent* a text book) as to the passages which require explanation to natives of this country.

There is now one passage about which I wish to ask you, because it seems to me contrary to S. Thomas. In p. 422, you say that endlessness cannot be a quality of punishment, but S. Thomas in the Summa (2da 2dae q. xviii, a. 3) shews that if the lost are condemned to eternal punishment they must know that it is eternal, since if they were ignorant of its duration, that duration could not be said to be part of their punishment.

Also you go on to specify *continuity* etc as additions to an endless punishment, but are not these involved in the notion of a reasonable human being being the subject of the punishment? If, indeed it be permitted us to believe that the *destruction* spoken of in hell results in such a dissolution of the human mind as reduces man to a state incapable of continuous thought, then punishment might be endless and yet the subject of it might be unconscious of its endlessness. But I have never seen such an opinion stated by any theologian, and I do not know whether it is tenable.' See the explanation Newman now added to *G.A.* at p. 503.

O'Neill also sent Newman 'some lectures which I think will interest you, because they are a detailed proof by a person brought up in the Hindu religion of your assertion that Christianity is the depository of truths beyond human discovery.'

[3] A first draft began 'Utrum opinio illa quam Petavius attribuit S. Chrystostomo et S. Augustino . . .' See *G.A.*, p. 422. O'Neill died at Indore on 31 Aug. 1882, and his edition of the last chapter of *G.A.* seems not to have been published.

[4] See letters of 8 Aug. and 27 Sept.

Birmingham Sept 4, 1882.

Cardinal Newman feels great interest and sympathy in Miss Tucker's case, as she describes it, but not knowing her, finds it very difficult to give her advice.[1]

She is young, and must recollect our Lord's words about 'counting the cost'. It would be better for her not to become a Catholic, than to go back after having joined the Church.

However painful, she ought to tell her parents the state of her mind.

She must not be confirmed, or go to communion, in a Church which she does not believe comes from God.

There is only one Church and that is the Catholic.

The Cardinal earnestly prays God to guide and strengthen her, and to lead her forward, and remove all the difficulties that stand in her way, and in that of others.[2]

TO PATRICK MCLOUGHLIN

The Oratory Sept 7. 1882

Dear Mr McLoughlin

You must not suppose I have not felt the kindness of the present you have made me, because I have not acknowledged it at once.

[1] Miss Tucker wrote on 31 Aug. from 33 Hampton Park, Redland, Bristol: 'My parents are very extreme Protestants, but I am a Catholic at heart, and have been so for some time. I first became unsettled some years [ago] when an aunt of mine, a Miss Butcher, became a Catholic and entered a Convent near here. A short time after my aunt entered this Convent I began to attend the Clifton High School, where I became acquainted with three girls, one of whom was a Catholic, the other two only Catholics at heart, for their parents will not allow them to join the Church. I am a great friend of two of these girls and they have helped me a great deal. My parents know that I am not a Protestant, but they imagine that I am merely a Ritualist, and I have often purposely kept up this delusion, for I have been afraid to let them know the truth, for they are so much opposed to the Catholic Religion, that I do not think my father, if I had joined the Church, would allow me to live any longer under his roof, and yet I am entirely dependent on him. I do not know whether I ought to tell my parents of my opinions or not, I very much dread doing so, and yet I long to be received into the Church. Dear Father, counsel me, I am so young, not seventeen till February, and I dare not act on my own responsibility . . . I have read several of your works, and they have, of course, very much influenced me. I trust you perfectly, and I know that you have found the Truth that I am seeking . . ' Anglican friends wanted her to be confirmed, but she did not feel that it would be right to do so.
See also note to letter of 12 Feb. 1883 to Henry Fortey.
[2] This letter was intercepted and Miss Tucker given a false account of it as though Newman had recommended her to go to some French priest. Her father told her that when her opinions were mature, he would put no obstacle in her way, and anyhow she could become a Catholic at twenty-one. She wrote this on 30 Sept. and on 4 Oct. she wrote again: 'Dear Cardinal Newman
Your most kind letter was not destroyed as I had been told, but at my request was restored to me this morning I now see that the report given to me of its contents was wholly untrue . . .
I feel assured that whether I join the Church now, or five years hence I shall never leave her . . .
Perhaps you will be interested in knowing that Miss Fortey, who once wrote to you and whom you kindly answered, has got her father's permission to join the Church in two years time.' See letters of 6 July to Emily Fortey and 18 July to F. M. Waring, also those of 21 Dec. 1882 to Canon Loughnan.

I have felt it very much, not only as kindness directed towards myself, but as a memento of the many services done me by the good Oxford Jesuits on Trinity Sunday, 1880[1]

My delay has been owing to my wish to ask your acceptance in turn of something which it is not easy to obtain. I have chosen for that purpose the Medal which comes to me as Cardinal from the Holy Father on St Peter's and St Paul's Day[2]

I beg a blessing on you, & am

Very truly Yours in Xt   John H. Card. Newman

TO THOMAS ALDER POPE

Bm Sept 10. 1882

My dear Thomas

I am very glad to find you mean to stay a week longer; you ought to stay, not till you are, not nearly [sic], but quite well. John came back yesterday, looking quite well. Richard and his brother are in Wales — Ignatius comes back next Saturday — Joseph too came back yesterday — Francis is to come back the middle of the month.

I wonder whether we have been civil enough to tell Dr Schobel that we did not feel we could trouble him longer.[3]

The boys' library is finished except as regards plastering, painting, papering, and furnishing. It would be perfect if we could dispense with the stack of chimneys, for strength and warmth.[4] With kind messages from all

Yours affectionately John H Card. Newman

TO FRANCIS BENNOCH

Sept 11. 1882

Cardinal Newman feels the honour done him by the Longfellow Committee, in asking his name through Mr Bennett for the Memorial which they have in view.

[1] McLoughlin presented a drawing of St Aloysius' church, Oxford, in commemoration of Newman's visit in May 1880. Thomas Parkinson, the rector, sent it to Newman on 18 Aug. 1882. He now returned it as a present for the church with the following inscription:
'To the Jesuit Fathers of Oxford
From Cardinal Newman;
In grateful memory
Of the warm welcome,
And the various kind services,
which they showed him,
on Trinity Sunday, 1880
                                                            J H N'
[2] Newman sent the medal he had received in 1882.
[3] Victor Schobel was the professor of dogmatic theology at Olton Seminary, near Birmingham and had perhaps been giving lectures to the young Oratorians.
[4] The Duke of Norfolk provided the means for refurbishing the library of the Oratory School.

He yields to no one in admiration of Mr Longfellow's genius, and of the character and tone of his poems.

But he is obliged with much regret to return a negative answer to Mr Bennett's letter.[1]

TO AN UNKNOWN CORRESPONDENT[2]

Sept 13. 1882

The night is far spent,
The Day is at hand;
For yet a little while,
And He, that shall come will come,
And will not tarry.[3]

J. H. Card. Newman

TO LADY A[?]

Birmingham Sept. 15. 1882

Dear Lady A [?][4]

It is very kind in you sending me Miss Hughes's letter, and in her thinking of me.[5]

Today is the anniversary of the death of two most intimate friends of mine, very dear ones, John Bowden and Charles Marriott; it will be strange if I have to add to them Edward Pusey.[6]

I said Mass for him this morning. I have known him for sixty years; and he has ever been the same, subduing me by his many high virtues, and, amid severe trials of friendship, the most faithful of friends.

I heard last evening of Dr King's visit to him, and that he was hardly able to speak.[7]

Most truly yours John H. Card. Newman

[1] Longfellow died on 24 March 1882. Bennoch, city merchant and writer of poetry, was the treasurer of the Longfellow Memorial Committee for erecting a memorial in Westminster Abbey.

[2] The autograph is now at Georgetown University, Washington. On it is written 'Recd Oct 7/82'.

[3] *Romans*, 13:12; *Hebrews*, 10:37.

[4] Perhaps Lady Acland, the wife of Sir Thomas Acland. The Aclands had close links with Pusey and Sir Thomas was guardian to his children. His brother Henry Acland at Oxford was a lifelong friend of Miss Hughes.

[5] This was Marian Rebecca Hughes (1817–1912), Superior of the Society of the Holy and Undivided Trinity, Woodstock Road, Oxford, and the first woman to take religious vows in the Church of England, which she did in 1841. See letter of 10 Dec. 1851 to Frederick Fortescue Wells. She had evidently mentioned Newman in connection with Pusey's dying.

[6] John William Bowden died in 1844 and Charles Marriott in 1858. Pusey died on 16 Sept. 1882.

[7] Edward King, Regius professor of pastoral theology at Oxford, and in 1885 Bishop of Lincoln, visited Pusey on 13 Sept.

TO GEORGE T. EDWARDS

The Oratory Sept 17th. 1882

My dear Mr Edwards

Your kind present has come, and I thank you for it.[1] I had not heard of the book, nor of the lady who is the subject of it. It is full of matter, and to those who have a curiosity about stars in literature, interesting matter. She has a talent for description of character, and a great sense of humour. What is most remarkable is her union of a taste for society and a deep religious sense. And what is most perplexing to me is her boast and glorying in a Quaker's truthfulness, and her insensibility to truth in matters of faith. Her portrait, which heads the 'memories' is beautiful.

Mr Gutch, Registrar of the University, had a small parish over Magdalen Bridge.[2] He was 80 years old and his Parish, as other suburbs since, suddenly increased. I was just on the point of taking Anglican orders, and I agreed to become his curate. I held the curacy from 1824 to 1826, when I became one of the Tutors at Oriel, I called on his daughter in Oxford, two years since.

Very truly Yours John H. Card. Newman

TO HENRY ACLAND

[21 September 1882]

My dear Dr. Acland

Your and your daughter's kindness to me two years ago will never leave my mind, and your present offer is like it.[3]

I have from the first felt that, as a Cardinal, I represent the Holy See of the Pope so directly, that I had no right to indulge my private feelings by coming to Oxford and taking part in today's solemnities.[4] Nor was I sure that I should be welcome to dear Pusey's immediate relatives; even Mrs Brine, who wrote me a most kind letter, took it for granted that I should not come. No hint came to me, implying such a wish, on occasion of the funerals of Isaac Williams and Keble; and, as regards Williams's, the first of the two, Sir George Prevost wrote to me to say that he was sorry he could *not* ask me. I thought then, and think, that even were I *not* a Cardinal, there would be a

[1] Edwards sent Newman *Memories of Old Friends being extracts from the Journals and Letters of Caroline Fox*, edited by Horace N. Pym, two volumes, London 1882.

[2] Edwards wrote on 13 Sept., 'I saw lately a lady in Carlisle whose maiden name was Gutch, and who asked if you had not once been curate to her grandfather of that name, a clergyman in Oxford, a question I could not answer. One of his daughters, Miss Gutch, is still living in Oxford ...'
Edwards wrote again on 29 Dec. to say that Miss Gutch died on 23 Dec., having reached the age of 90 on 12 Dec.

[3] See letter of 31 May 1880 to Acland, and notes there. Acland had asked Newman to stay at his house in Oxford for Pusey's funeral.

[4] The day of Pusey's funeral at Oxford, during which 'Lead, Kindly Light' was sung.

technical or ecclesiastical difficulty in (say) a Bishop of Oxford receiving me, both on my side and on his, in what *must* be public.

One of our Fathers is going from this place, and, since this house is mainly made up of converts, I and others make him their representative.[1] One thing struck me just now that I might have done. I might have asked to go to see him, before the coffin was closed; but on Monday, I had arranged to go on a matter of private duty to Tenby, returning last night, and my mind was so occupied with the anxieties connected with it, that such a thought did not occur to me.[2]

I have sent your name some weeks ago to my publishers, with the hope you will accept from me William Palmer's *Russian Journal*, but the publication has been unavoidably delayed.

Most truly Yours John H. Card. Newman.

TO J. R. BLOXAM

Sept 21. 1882

My dear Bloxam

Thank you for your commemorative note.[3] I rejoice to have so good an account of you.

As to M's book, I put it away after a very short inspection of it, so full was it of mistakes. He is so incorrect, that I am afraid of publicly noticing any *one* of his delinquences, lest I should seem to be admitting as truths, what I *don't* notice. He cannot speak without a mistake, greater or lesser; and, it is almost more provoking, when the mistake is of lesser consequence, for it seems as if the notice of it comes from touchiness, whereas it is only one of a hundred. E.g. as if I ever spoke a word, good, bad, or indifferent to Braham or he to me! Dr Crotch, who hired Braham, was the man I pitched in to. I should not have deigned to quarrel with a man who was simply following his calling.[4] But, all I saw of the book was true outlines filled up falsely, or half truths leaving false impressions, or whole falsehoods

Yours affly John H Newman

[1] This was A. W. Hutton. See *The Times* (22 Sept. 1882), p. 3.
[2] On Monday 18 Sept. Pusey's body was brought from Ascot, where he died, to Oxford. On that day Newman went to see his brother Charles, now a complete invalid. Dr Chater the local doctor wished him to change his lodgings, where he had lived for years, on grounds of health, but he was unwilling to do so. The Rector of Tenby, George Huntington, thought it wiser to leave him in the surroundings to which he was accustomed, where he was well cared for by the daughter of his former landlady.
[3] The anniversary of the consecration of the church at Littlemore on 22 Sept. 1836.
[4] See T. Mozley, *Reminiscences chiefly of Oriel College and the Oxford Movement*, II, p. 397. Newman was said to have forbidden John Braham the famous Jewish tenor to sing in St Mary's at a service of the benefit of the Radcliffe Infirmary, and then to have demanded an apology when Braham disobeyed him. William Crotch the composer who lectured on Music at Oxford, was organist of St Mary's.

TO GEORGE T. EDWARDS

Bm Septr 23rd. 1882

Dear Mr Edwards

I am very glad to have the volumes you were so good as to send me —[1] still, interesting as I could not help finding them, and instructive, I have a natural dislike of literary and scientific society *as such*, or what Hurrell Froude, (whom I agreed with in this) used to call 'the aristocracy of talent'; and, for this reason perhaps I am not quite fair to the remarkable and beautiful Life which you sent me. I suppose it is a peculiarity common to us two (H F and me) with Keble and Pusey more than any other quality, and has, as much as anything else united us together; and accordingly it is something of a wonder to me, that a mind, so religious as Miss Fox's, should feel pleasure in meeting men who either disbelieved the divine mission or had no love for the person of One *she* calls '*her* God and Saviour'. Our Lord tells that no man can serve two Masters — how can this religious lady be friends at once with Him and with Carlile, Mill, and the like?[2]

I feel with you that the Newspaper you sent me is very unjust in its criticism on Pusey's words — it had, I suspect, nothing to appeal to of his, more to its purpose.[3]

Very truly Yours John H Card. Newman

TO THE HON. MRS MAXWELL-SCOTT

Bm Sept 23. 1882

My dear Mamo

Thank you for your affectionate letter. Pusey had long been so infirm and feeble, as to have prepared his friends for his being taken away. When I last saw him, two years ago, I only wondered he was still alive — but his look would strike me more who saw him seldom, than those who, being near him,

[1] See letter of 17 Sept.

[2] Edwards replied on 5 Oct., that it never seemed to have occurred to Caroline Fox that in making close friends of unbelievers 'she was treading on dangerous or forbidden ground, though she appears to have passed through doubts and struggles of soul as the result of it . . . I quite feel with your Eminence that allegiance to our blessed Lord and Master should keep all who trust and love Him from forming friendships with those who love Him not, whatever be their literary or scientific eminence.'

[3] This was a leading article in the *Christian World* (21 Sept. 1882), p. 623, 'The Late Dr. Pusey', which criticised him severely from the evangelical standpoint, 'A clergyman cannot be at heart a Roman Catholic and still remain in the Church of England.' Referring to *Apo.*, pp. 204–5, the article said: 'So early as 1841 Dr. Newman had taken steps to make Dr. Pusey certain of his state of mind, and yet, in 1845, a few months before Dr. Newman's secession, Dr. Pusey said to a friend, "I trust after all we shall keep him." In his *Apologia* Dr. Newman says he "thinks" Dr. Pusey made this remark, and in the years that have gone by since the *Apologia* was published, Dr. Pusey offered no correction of the statement. That is to say Dr. Pusey was master of some art, or legerdemain, by force of which he could convince himself that the overwhelming reasons which seem to ordinary people to render it impossible for man to be loyally and honestly both a papist and a clergyman of the Church of England, are moonshine.'

got used to it. However, it is said that, if he had kept from his books when the attack came on, he might have rallied.

I hope Mr Palmer's volume will soon be out. I hope to send you a copy It is longer than it should be, to be easy handling. Say every thing kind from me to your husband and believe me to be

Yours affectly John H Card. Newman

TO ROBERT ORNSBY

Bm Sept 23. 1882

My dear Ornsby

Thank you for your considerate letter. Pusey has been so long dying, that his friends must have been prepared for it. For myself, when I last saw him, two years ago, I wondered how he could be alive, he was so unstrung; but his mind was quite his own.

His death is a shock, rather, as being one more of my contemporaries, not to speak of my juniors, who is taken away.

We had an unusual and terrible shock yesterday. Our porter, Michael Doyle, returning to us after a three weeks holiday, was run over and killed with two others by a train at Holyhead. He was a very religious fellow, quite fitted for a porter at the house-door; a great loss to us, but quite prepared for sudden death, which is our consolation.

I am much concerned to hear your account of Mrs Ornsby. What various symptoms weakness of heart takes! I did not know headache was one of them.

What all people say to me is, that the Royal University Act is the thin edge of the wedge. I hope it may be.[1]

Yours affectly John H Card. Newman

TO AN UNKNOWN CORRESPONDENT

Bm Septr 23. 1882

Dear Sir

I truly felt for you in your unexpected difficulties, but you seemed to consider me a well to do man with money at command whereas I have not more than enough for the calls made on me. What could five pounds do to make up a loss of capital, yet it is the utmost I could give. I do not receive a shilling by the rank or office of Cardinal. This so perplexed me that I did not know what to do, nor do I now

Very truly Yours John H. Card. Newman

[1] The establishment of the Royal University of Ireland under the Act of 1879, enabled professors at the Catholic University to be appointed to the thirteen fellowships reserved for Catholics.

Bm Sept. 24 1882

My dear Anne Mozley

Your letter is very welcome. I have so long expected Pusey's death, tha t when it came, it was no shock to me — but it has weighed upon me much as one instance more of the many friends, acquaintances, or opponents, contemporaries or juniors, who have been taken away, and which impress me as mementos that my own turn must soon come. And now you add to them (in like manner not a surprise, but a warning) Hawkins's approaching end.[1]

And I, and all of us here, have *since* Pusey's death, on the eve of his funeral have had something to shock us too. Our hall-porter, who was returning from his holiday, was at Holyhead cut literally to pieces in crossing the line; we do not know yet by whose fault, and wonder we hear nothing of an inquest. He was a singularly religious man, fit to die, if any one was; this is our consolation; but it is very painful thus abruptly to be parted from him, and he is, as a house-guardian, scarcely to be replaced, and is the greatest of losses.

For myself, I have nothing the matter with me but feebleness. That, however, increases slowly, and, even if it did not, leaves me exposed to the serious consequences of a bad cold, or a fall, or any over-exertion, or similar accidents which cannot be guarded against.

Yours affectionately John H. Card. Newman.

Birmingham Sept 25. 1882

My dear Canon Liddon

I shall be glad to see you either Thursday or Friday, the days you name. As I have friends coming to call on Thursday, Friday would be *somewhat* more convenient[2]

Yours very truly John H Card. Newman

[26 September 1882][3]

Emo et Revmo Sig. Mio Ossmo

Ego Eminentiæ Tuæ commendo Virum Spectatissimum, Dominum admodum Honorabilem, Michaelem Morris, in alta Justitiæ Curia Hibernica

---

[1] Edward Hawkins, Provost of Oriel, died on 18 Nov. 1882.

[2] Friday was 29 Sept. On that day Liddon wrote in his diary 'Pretty well made up my mind to resign my Professorship in order to write the "Life." [of Pusey]' On 30 Sept. Liddon sent the Vice-Chancellor his resignation as Ireland Professor of Exegesis. J. O. Johnson, *Life and Letters of Henry Parry Liddon*, London 1904, p. 277.

[3] Dated from next letter.

Michael Morris, puisne judge of the Irish Court of Common Pleas, became chief of his Court in 1876, 'and even at the height of the Land League agitation (1880–3) rarely failed to secure a right verdict.' *D N B*, 1901–11.

Judicem dignitate primarium, Catholicum in temporibus hisce tristibus fidelissimum.

Qui post multos annos Romam visitat, devotionis ergo, et spe, si fieri potest, se praesentandi coram Sanctissimo, et Apostolicam Benedictionem adipiscendi

Osculando peramanter manus Eminentiæ Tuæ, humillimè me profiteor Eminentiæ Tuæ humillimum et dev.m̃um   Servum

Em̃o et Rev. Sig. Mio Ossm̃o Il Cardinale Domenico Bartolini

TO CARDINAL PECCI

Birmingham Sept 26. 1882

Emo e Revmo Sig. Mio Ossmo

Voglia Eminenza Vostra permettermi di presentarle per questa mia lettera un amico. Il Molto Onorevole Sig. Michaele Morris, nell' Alta Curia Giudicatoria Irlandese Guidice Primario; il quale viene a Roma, mosso da devozione in tempi calamitosi al Sommo Pontifice.

Non conosca le regole tenute del Sommo Pontifice nei ricevimenti: me ho creduto di non potere rimetterlo ad una persona più graziosa a stranieri che l'Eminenza Vostra

Le bacio umilissemamente le mani
Di Vostra Eminza Umilissimo Devotissimo Servitore
Giovanni E Card. Newman

All' Emo e Revm̃o Sig. Mio Ossm̃o Il Cardinale Giuseppe Pecci

TO EDWIN PALMER

Bm Sept 27. 1882

My dear Archdeacon Palmer

The engraving is ready, and I expect daily a bound copy of the volume.[1]

I send you a list of the persons to whom I mean to send it. Tell me if you wish any names added to it.[2]

I must give you the trouble of returning it

Very truly Yours J. H. Card. Newman

[1] See letter of 8 Aug. to Palmer.

[2] To the names mentioned in letters of 8 Aug. and 4 Sept., Palmer added on 28 Sept., 'Cardinal Howard, Mrs Foljambe, C Plowden Esq (the Banker) Mr Wegg Prosser, Bishop Wordsworth of *Lincoln*, Rev. F. Meyrick . . . Dean Burgon.' Palmer also wished a copy of his brother's book sent to Fr Pierling, S.J., 'one of the small Jesuit house in Paris (broken up by the French Government) to which William left such of his Russian books as Cardinal Howard did not care to take', but did not know where he was. This was Paul Pierling (1840–1922), who worked all his life to unite the Russian Church with the Papacy. He wrote on 13 Nov. 1882 from 212 rue de Rivoli, Paris, to thank for his copy and said, 'Mr Palmer a laissé en Russie un souvenir impérissable.'

Among those to whom Newman sent copies of Palmer's *Visit* was Friedrich von Hügel, who only found it on moving into a new house, and wrote on 9 Dec., 'I hasten now to thank you very much for your kind thought of me. I am reading the book out to my wife in the evening. It will certainly be — it is already — the most popular perhaps the only popular —

TO CARDINAL CZACKI[1]

Birmingham die Octobris 1882

Eminentissime et Revme Domine mi Observandissime

Gratias Eminentiæ Tuæ habeo, quod me certiorem fecisti, in acceptissima Tua Epistola, de promotione Eminentiæ Tuæ meritissima ad Sanctæ Rom. Ecclesiæ amplissimum Purpuratorum Senatum.

Sic voluit et ordinavit pro perspicaci prudentia sua, Sanctissimus Dominus noster Leo; ego vero S.S. Pontificis servus et creatura ipsemet, quid aliud re cognita Eminentiæ Tuæ debeo quam tibi gratulari, (quod quidem ex animo facio), de co-optatione Eminentiæ Tuæ in fraternitatem nostram, et omnia bona, et faustissima quaeque, ad multos annos optare Tibi et augurari, dum humillime manus Tuas deosculo, et me profiteor,

Eminentiæ Tuæ Humillimum et devotissimum Servum,
Joannem Henricum Card. Newman

Emo ac Rmo Dno
Dno Cardinali Wladimiro Czacki

TO S. B. SMITH

[October 1882]

Card. Newman offers his best thanks to Dr Smith for the gift of his Volumes on the 'Elements of Ecclesiastical Law'. As the Cardinal cannot claim any proficiency in the great subject of Canon Law himself, he is very grateful to a work such as Dr Smith's which tells him so much which is at once important and new to him ⟨to him instructive⟩. He wishes he was better qualified to pass a judgment upon it.[2]

TO JANE MOZLEY

The Oratory Oct. 5. 1882

Private
My dear Jane

Can you tell me whether after all I took away from your Mother the MS memoir of my Life up to 1832 which I lent her. I have a letter from you dated Oct 30 1877, in which you convey her wish that she may keep it a

of Mr Palmer's books, and it is impossible not to think it very fortunate that Mr Palmer did *not* publish it himself, but left the selecting and introducing of his Journal to yourself.

Mrs Francis Ward has been giving us most cheering accounts of the state of your health. We pray and wish for health and long-continued life and vigour to yourself more than for ourselves.'

[1] Cardinal in Curia, created 25 Sept. 1882.

[2] S. B. Smith, writing on 22 Sept. from Paterson, New Jersey, sent his *Elements of Ecclesiastical Law*, volume II, New York 1882, saying 'I would respectfully solicit a kind recommendation from your Eminence', and thanking for Newman's commendation of his first volume, New York 1881.

little longer. If then I took them away, it must have been in 1879, when I was summoned to Rome.

Also can you recollect whether the MS was in my handwriting or of some one's else.[1]

I hope you enjoyed your trip. Weather is always very uncertain in Switzerland — but a little rain or storm adds to the beauty of the scene

With every kind remembrance to your Aunts, I am

My dear Jane, Yours affectly John H. Card. Newman

TO J. R. BLOXAM

Bm Oct 7. 1882

My dear Bloxam

I cannot affirm positively, and it would be rash to rely on my memory; but my impression is that I stood always on the north side of the Altar from the beginning to the end of the service.[2]

Yours affectly J H Card. Newman

P.S.   Could not Whitaker Churton tell you? *Don't* mention my name to him[3]

TO MRS F. R. WARD

Bm Oct. 7. 1882

My dear Mrs Ward,

I have long been wondering where you all were, and resolving to write to you at random. It will give me the greatest pleasure to see you and Maimy [Ward] here on the 20th.

I have preached, I believe, my last Sermon. When you see me, perhaps you will say, with others, 'How well you are looking.' I *am* well, thank God, wonderfully so, but health is not strength. I speak with difficulty; I can hardly walk, never without the chance of tripping up; I with great difficulty go up and down stairs — I read with discomfort. I cannot write except very slowly — and I am deaf.

It is not wonderful then that I have given up preaching, for I never can be sure that I shall not get confused and make mistakes. It is with fear and trembling I say Mass, and cannot anticipate how long I shall be able.

---

[1] See letter of 10 Oct. 1882, and for the Memoir, *A.W.*, pp. 21–107, and *Moz.* I.

[2] Newman's memory was correct. See letter of 24 Dec. 1840 to Bloxam, quoted in *Newman and Bloxam*, p. 16.

[3] Henry Burgess Whitaker Churton, son of the Archdeacon of St David's, went up to Balliol College, Oxford, in 1828, and was a Fellow of Brasenose College from 1833 until 1843, when he became and remained Vicar of Icklesham, Sussex. He was made a Prebendary of Chichester in 1842.

But I have nothing the matter with me, as far as I know. Love to all your party.

Yours affly John H Card. Newman

P.S.   I have taken two rooms for you from the 20 to 22 at the Plough and Harrow.

TO EDWARD BELLASIS, JUNIOR

Bm Oct. 8. 1882

My dear Edward

I am very glad to have your Father's clear and decisive argument, which I had often heard of, but never seen.[1] My only regret is that it should be so well done as to be necessarily[2]

will shirk into some dark corner of my room, and, when I want to refer to it, will be lost to me.

If your Father has written other pamphlets, they should be put together. Answer me on this point

Yours affly

TO ALFRED WYATT EDGELL, LORD BRAYE

Birmingham Oct. 9. 1882

My dear Lord Braye

There is no one whom, if I could follow my wishes, it would please me to visit more than you — but I am too old for moving from home, except when I am compelled.

It is wonderful that I am so well as I am — but I have the infirmities necessary to old age notwithstanding. I cannot walk without the serious risk of tripping and falling — I am deaf, and I cannot converse without soon getting knocked up — I am obliged to lie down several times a day; and as to hours of meals, I am obliged to be particular.

I am obliged then to give up many pleasures, and among them the invitations from friends, which I feel to be as great an honour as they would be a pleasure to me.

I feel grateful to you for every sentence of your letter, for every sentence is a fresh expression of sympathy and kindness towards me. It gives me an assurance that you do not forget how close I am to the end of my life, and to the awful change which is the lot of all of us

Yours most truly John H. Card. Newman

The Lord Braye

[1] *Anglican Orders by an Anglican, since become a Catholic,* 1872, a reprint of four letters written in 1847 and printed several years later, on Bishop Barlow's consecration.
[2] Two or three lines are missing where the signature overleaf has been cut off.

TO BISHOP ULLATHORNE

Oct 9. 1882

My dear Lord

It was very kind in you to send me a message last week about yourself, and I rejoiced to hear you were so much better — and now I am pleased to learn you have got so well to Oscott, which seems always to suit you

Your Lordship's faithful & affte servant J. H. Card. Newman

TO EDWARD BELLASIS, JUNIOR

Bm Oct 10. 1882

My dear Edward

The copies you have already given me of your Father's Tracts are most likely already bound up in our Library Pamphlets.

These new copies shall be bound up at once.[1]

As to the 'Peal of Bells' neither the words nor the idea occur in your Father's pamphlet, and I am sure that I did not take it from him.[2] *My* idea is the *monotonous* repetition in *changed* order of a *few* words, 'atrocious' 'insidious' etc and I got these words not from him, but from episcopal charges, as he did. Moreover, you do not say *when* his pamphlet was published. *My* lecture was delivered, July 5, 1851. and the writing took me some time, especially to get information about bellringers. I ought still to have the MS information from the person whom I got to make inquiries through Birmingham[3]

TO JANE MOZLEY

Bm Oct 10/82

My dear Jane

Your letter is quite satisfactory. My full impression from the first was that I had taken it back.[4] Such too was Fr Neville's impression, who is the only person, besides you and your dear Mother, who has any suspicion that I have written any Memoir at all. He, however, copied it out for me from my MS — and whether it is a second or an *only, fair* copy (of my transcribing), which is missing, is not certain — nay, it is not certain that any copy is

---

[1] For these pamphlets see letter of 19 Oct. to Bellasis.
[2] This refers to the passage in *Prepos.*, p. 77, in which the epithets used by Anglican bishops and clergy about the restoration of the Hierarchy were compared to peals of bells. Newman had Bellasis's pamphlet *The Anglican Bishops versus the Catholic Hierarchy. A Demurrer to Farther Proceedings*, London 1851, see letter of 14 June 1851 to Richard Stanton, but, as he now explains, it was not the source of the passage in *Prepos*. See also letter of 13 Oct. 1882, and Edward Bellasis, *Memorials of Mr. Serjeant Bellasis*, third edition, London 1923, p. 105.
[3] The conclusion has been cut out.
[4] See letter of 5 Oct.

missing, for I cannot be sure, tho' I think, that *I* made a fair copy, and that Fr Neville copied from it and not from a first rough copy.

Yet it is odd that I should have given your Mother my rough copy — and somewhat odd even that I should have let Fr Neville use my rough copy; since the corrections are many, and his copy does not always follow them

Yrs affly J H Card. Newman.

TO SIR ROWLAND BLENNERHASSETT

Bm Oct 12. 1882

My dear Sir Rowland

I have waited to thank you, and to congratulate you and Lady Blenner-hassett, on your news, till I could say that I had said Mass for her and the little child.[1] This I did this morning.

It is a long time since I have heard about you. I suppose you go to Germany for good part of the Summer — Ireland, I suppose, has been hardly possible for the last year or two[2]

My memory is getting so weak, that I can't tell when last I saw you. You will be glad to know that my health is good, but I am very infirm

Yours most sincerely John H. Card. Newman

TO EDWARD BELLASIS

[13 October 1882][3]

My dear Edward

When a new Edition of my volume comes, I will gladly make a reference to your dear Father's forcible pamphlet — nay, I would put the whole of it in my Appendix, if your Mother and brother would like it.[4]

P.S.   His pamphlet is dated March 1851 — but that is when he *wrote* it — I do not know when it was *published*, that is often a later act, and especially in the case of a collection of spicy bits from Episcopal charges etc.

TO GEORGE SLATYER BARRETT

Birmingham Oct 13. 1882

My dear Sir

Thank you much for the present of your Sermon and for your very kind letter.[5] It is a great mystery in Providence how it comes to pass that so many

---

[1] Rowland Lewis William Paul Blennerhassett was born on 6 Oct.

[2] Blennerhassett was a landlord in County Kerry.

[3] Dated by postmark, the date having been cut out for the sake of the signature on the reverse side.

[4] For the pamphlet see letter of 10 Oct. The note in *Prepos.*, p. 77, appears from 1889 onwards, in editions after the fifth.

[5] *The Influence of the late Dr. Pusey, and of the Oxford Movement associated with his Name on the English Nation and the English Church*, Norwich and London 1882. Barrett was pastor of Prince's Street Congregational Church, Norwich, and his sermon was preached on 24 Sept.

minds, all so earnest both in their zeal for God and their good will towards each other, nevertheless, as a matter of strict conscience, keep at a distance from each other.

Whether we in our ignorances of the Protestant denominations, impute to you what is unfounded, let others decide; but what I can affirm and bear witness to is the false conception which the mass of Protestants have of the interior devotion and religiousness of Catholics — as if the love of our Lord was not our first and last, and some created medium admitted between the soul and its God. And this at least I will say, that no mistake which Catholics may make about Protestants can be equal to this grave, awful, because most uncharitable error which Protestants make in their judgment of Catholics.

I hope and am sure you will not be hurt at my saying this, for I am speaking of the mass of Protestants, and have no thought of imputing the error to yourself or to many others of the Congregational communion.

Very truly yours John H. Card. Newman.

TO WILFRID WARD   Bm Oct. 13. 1882

My dear Mr Ward

I shall have no difficulty, I am sure, in complying with your request, tho' in accordance with what I am accustomed to do, I ask you to let me see first my letter to Dr Whitty[1]

I heartily wish you may succeed — I fear, however, that an English candidate may be at disadvantage, and I am half afraid that a testimonial from me on behalf of a second candidate, for I have already given one to Mr Addis, will not go for much.[2]

Very truly yours John H. Card. Newman

TO ROBERT WHITTY, S.J.   Bm Oct 16. 1882

My dear Fr Whitty

I return the letter with thanks to you for sending it. I have told W W for he sent me a copy, that he may make what use of it he likes.[3] But I can't

He spoke appreciatively of the Oxford Movement and of Newman 'the mighty spell of whose character and genius has brought to him love and honour from many in other communions.' p. 9. However, 'the ultimate principle and foundation on which all Romanism rests is the position of the priest, coming between the human soul and the Eternal God.' While 'the ultimate and living foundation of our Protestantism is the blessed truth that now Christ has died for the sins of the world, and has risen . . . all alike . . . have common and immediate access to God Himself through Christ, and . . . may hear, without intervention of Church or priest, from God's own lips the absolution and remission of their sins . . .' pp. 13–14.

[1] Wilfrid Ward was applying for a Fellowship at the Royal University of Ireland, and wished to use part of Newman's letter of 2 March 1882 to Robert Whitty, as a testimonial.
[2] Ward replied on 14 Oct., 'The fellowship I am trying for is the *same* which Father Addis obtained, and afterwards resigned.' Addis was appointed a Fellow in Mental and Moral Philosophy in April 1882, and resigned in Oct.
[3] Letter of 13 Oct. to W. Ward.

think why Addis resigned except that Englishmen at this moment are not personæ gratæ in Ireland — I cannot wonder — but it is very sad. This augurs ill, for Ward's chance.

I am very infirm now — but very well, as far as health goes. I dare say I have said this to you before; for I am often saying it. One reason for saying it is, that I have so little to talk about, except indeed the weather.

You say nothing about your own health

Yours affectionately John H Card. Newman

TO EDWARD BELLASIS

Oct 19. 1882

My dear Edward

I have changed my mind on reading your Father's pamphlets; they are too good and run to too many pages, not to claim a reprint handsomely carried out.

As they now stand, they make 102 pages; in uniform and handsome type they might stretch to 150; they might be made to go further, if the size were small octavo.[1]

The Pamphlets are all valuable. The Vituperations[2] has an historical value. The Barlow Pamphlet[3] has all the conclusive and momentous force (of course) which it had 30 years ago. The Judicial Committee etc deals with the great question still alive and vigorous, the present issue of which is the imprisonment of Mr Green in Lancaster (shame on you!) Jail.[4]

I think I should spoil a good job, if I reprinted in my 'Lectures' one out of so many which ought to be preserved. This would not hinder my referring in a note to Anglican Vituperation. Think of this.[5]

Yours affectly J H Card. Newman

P.S. You must not suppose I think the Volume would by its sale pay its printing — but it would go to the Museum Library etc and you would send it to various institutions and it would be a book of reference for history.

[1] Serjeant Bellasis's pamphlets were: *The Judicial Committee of the Privy Council and the Petition for a Church Tribunal in Lieu of it; Convocations and Synods are they remedies for existing evils; A Remonstrance with the Clergy of Westminster from a Westminster Magistrate,* all London 1850; *Anglican Orders by an Anglican since became a Catholic* (see letter of 8 Oct.); *The Anglican Bishops versus the Catholic Hierarchy* (see letter of 10 Oct.); *Philotheus and Eugenia a Dialogue on the Jesuits* (see letter of 4 Jan. 1875 to Mrs Bellasis).
[2] *The Anglican Bishops versus the Catholic Hierarchy.*
[3] *Anglican Orders by an Anglican* . . .
[4] Bellasis was Lancaster Herald. Sidney Faithorn Green, Vicar of Miles-Platting, was imprisoned under the Public Worship Regulation Act from March 1881 to Nov. 1882.
[5] See letter of 13 Oct.

TO MRS CHRISTIE

Birmingham October 23. 1882

Dear Mrs Christie

I wish I could say more in answer to your difficulty (which I quite feel myself) than what Our Lord and Saint Paul say about the 'wise and prudent' and the 'wisdom of the world'.[1] Not that I would presume to apply the abstract in its full intense meaning to the concrete, or pretend to say that this or that dear friend was to be identified with the type which our Lord and His Apostle have warned us against falling under; but that their words lead us to say that a certain character of mind has, from the beginning to now, been, and ever will be the mark of God's elect, and that the comparative imperfection, that is, that absence of demonstration, in the evidence given us of the divine *origin* of Christianity, is the trial, to us individually, and test, whether we have that character of mind or not. Of course all truth in its *nature* is such as to admit of demonstration; in that case, the reason cannot refuse assent; but in matters of *this* world, social or personal, we allow arguments short of demonstration to be sufficient for absolute belief; why then not in religious matters? Why may not an Almighty Benefactor, addressing rebels, say 'I don't choose to accept from these an act of faith made merely because they cannot help it. They do not demand demonstration in other matters social and personal; if then they let their affections and their interests direct their intellect to an evidence, sufficient, but not formally complete, why am I to be treated with an honour inferior to that which they show to the authorities and the prophets of this world?'

Yours most truly J. H. Card. Newman

TO CHARLES KEGAN PAUL

Birmingham Oct 27. 1882

re-written
My dear Sir

I have just been shown in 'Messrs Kegan Paul, Trench, and Co Announcements', after the notice of Rosmini's Life, 'Rosmini was a loss to the whole Church, for such a man was the property of the whole Church' 'H.E. Cardinal Newman.' added.

I do not recollect ever having said this, as it stands.

And any how, I am sorry to say I can not give any leave to its being put into print, nor will any words from Mr Macwalter, I fear I must say, change my mind.

[1] *Matthew*, 11:25; I *Corinthians*, 3:19.

I make all apologies to him, but I must distinctly request that he withdraws my name from those words

I am sorry to give you this trouble[1]

Very truly Yours John H. Card. Newman

Kegan Paul Esqr

TO LORD BRAYE

Birmingham Oct 29. 1882

My dear Lord Braye

I thank you for your most touching letter which I think I quite understand and in which I deeply sympathise.

First, however, let me say a word about myself, for I think I was not exact in what I said to you, to judge by your letter. I am thankful to say that I am at present quite free from any complaint, as far as I know — but I am over eighty, and it is with difficulty that I walk, eat, read, write or talk — my breath is short and my brain works slow — and, like other old men, I am so much the creature of hours, rooms, and of routine generally, that to go from home is almost like tearing off my skin, and I suffer from it afterwards. On the other hand, except in failure of memory, and continual little mistakes in the use of words, and confusion in the use of names, I am not conscious that my mind is weaker than it was.

Now this is sadly egotistical — but I want you to understand why it is that I do not accept your most kind invitations, any more than I have Lord Denbigh's. I decline both with real pain: and thank you both. But I have real reasons, which friends sometimes will not believe, for they come and see me, and say 'How well you are looking!'

Now what can I say in answer to your letter? First, that your case is mine. It is for years beyond numbering — in one view of the matter for these 50 years — that I have been crying out 'I have laboured in vain, I have spent my strength without cause and in vain: wherefore my judgment is with the Lord, and my work with my God.'[2] Now at the end of my days, when the next world is close upon me, I am recognized at last at Rome. Don't suppose I am dreaming of complaint — just the contrary. The Prophet's

---

[1] The Rosminian Gabriel Stuart Macwalter was about to publish his *Life of Antonio Rosmini*, I, London 1883. Volume II was never published. Kegan Paul sent him Newman's letter, and he wrote on 2 Nov. that the quotation was from the letter of 10 July 1855 to J. B. Pagani, and that it had been used several times in books on Rosmini. This Macwalter discovered by consulting other Rosminians. However, he bowed to Newman's request, and asked to dedicate to him his book. It has no dedication.

Part of Newman's letter of 10 July 1855 to Pagani is given in Italian translation in Volume XVI. The autograph has since been found in the Rosminian Archives at Stresa. Newman wrote: 'The news took me by surprise, and concerned me very deeply, because, though he was so specially connected with your Body, a man like him is the property of the whole Church, while he is allowed to be on earth.'

There was serious controversy within the Catholic Church at this period over Rosmini's teaching. See letter of 29 Feb. 1880 to Bishop Ullathorne.

[2] *Isaiah*, 49:4.

words, which expressed my keen pain, brought, *because* they were his words, my consolation. It is the rule of God's Providence that we should succeed by failure; and my moral is, as addressed to you, Doubt not that He will use you — be brave — have faith in His love for you — His everlasting love — and love Him from the certainty that He loves you.

I cannot write more today .. and, since, it is easier thus to write, than to answer your direct questions, I think it is better to write to you at once, than to keep silence.

May the blessings from above come down upon you — and they will.

I am, my dear Lord Braye Yours, (may I say?) affectionately

John H Card. Newman.

TO THE MARCHIONESS OF LONDONDERRY

[November 1882]

I have received from your Ladyship many kindnesses, and now have a small means of showing my sense of them. May I offer you the late Mr Palmer's volume on the Russian Church, which I am now publishing, by way of expressing my gratitude to you, and also as a token of that respect and honour, which I, with all Catholics, pay to your name . . .[1]

John H. Card. Newman

TO HENRIETTA WOODGATE

Nov 1. 1882

My dear Child

You have not given me your Address. So I direct to Oldbury.

The Volume of Mr Palmer's Journal has been for months out of my hands — and for months have the Publishers had from me directions to send you a copy. I am mortified they have not. I suppose they are keeping it back for the full season. I have written to complain. Thank you for your pleasant account of your brothers

Ever Yours affectly J. H. Card. Newman

TO LORD BRAYE

Nov. 2. 1882

My dear Lord Braye
   Confidential

You have opened a large field of questions indeed! and the difficulty is to select answers or remarks which ought to be made to and upon them. Let me begin abruptly, without considering what should come first and what second.

[1] Lady Londonerry became a Catholic in 1855, and supported many charitable causes until her death in 1884.

The cardinal question for the moment is the Oxford question. Dear Pusey is gone — Canon Liddon has mysteriously given up his Professorship.[1] The Undergraduates and Junior Fellows are sheep without a shepherd. They are sceptics or inquirers, quite open for religious influences. It is a moment for the Catholic Mission in Oxford to seize an opportunity which never may come again. The Jesuits have Oxford men and able men among them. I doubt not that they are doing, (as it is,) great good there; but I suppose they dread the dislike and suspicion which any forward act of theirs would rouse; but is it not heart piercing that such an opportunity should be lost? The Liberals are sweeping along in triumph, without any Catholic or religious influence to stem them now that Pusey and Liddon are gone.

This is what I feel at the moment, but, alas, it is only one out of various manifestations of what may be called Nihilism in the Catholic Body, and in its rulers. They forbid, but they do not direct or create. I should fill many sheets of paper if I continued my exposure of this fact — so I pass on to my second thought.

The Holy Father must be put up to this fact, and must be made to understand the state of things with us.

And I think he ought to do this — he should send here some man of the world, impartial enough to take in two sides of a subject, — not a politician, or one who would be thought to have any thing to do with politics — Such a person should visit (not a 'visitorial' visit) all parts of England, and he should be able to talk English. He should be in England a whole summer.

Next, how is the Pope to be persuaded to this? by some English man in position, if one or two so much the better. They should talk French or Italian — and remain in Rome some months — This would be the first step.

I *would not advise you* to speak to Bishop Ullathorne

Should any thing happen to lead you this way, I should rejoice to have a call

Most sincerely Yours John H. Card Newman[2]

TO RICHARD FREDERICK CLARKE, S.J.

Birmingham Nov 5. 1882

My dear Fr Clarke,

Don't think me lazy, because I feel obliged to decline your suggestion. I have not strength for acting upon it, nor leisure. Nor do I think Canon

[1] Liddon was Ireland Professor of Exegesis at Oxford from 1870 until his resignation took effect on 2 Nov. 1882. He had for many years felt he could not combine it with his work at St Paul's, but Pusey was so distressed at the idea of of Liddon's leaving Oxford, that he decided to wait until his death. Furthermore he had undertaken the biography of Pusey. See letter of 25 Sept. Liddon considered too that the religious basis of the University had gone. See J. O. Johnson, *Life and Letters of Henry Parry Liddon*, London 1904, p. 278.
[2] Lord Braye read this letter in Italian translation to Leo XIII on 13 April 1883. See letter of 2 May 1883 to Lord Braye, also *Ward* II, p. 486 and Thomas Murphy, *The Position of the Catholic Church in England and Wales during the last two centuries*, London 1892, pp. 7–8.

Farrar's paradox worth refuting. See what the Spectator of yesterday says of it.[1] Catholics need not come forward; there is a natural instinct in pious Protestants which the notion in question shocks,[2] as coming from or tending to Socinianism. Even Alford who argues in its favour from Scripture, declines to speak decidedly[3]

There are lectures and books far more dangerous in my opinion than Canon Farrar's. If Atheism at Oxford, with its argumentative methods and assumed first principles, were knocked on the head, we should not have much to fear from the extravagances of broad-church preachers. Don't say I am urging a Tu quoque; but since dear Dr Pusey is gone, and Canon Liddon has resigned his Lectureship in Oxford, I have been saying to myself 'What an opportunity for the Jesuit Fathers!' — an opportunity which may never come again, an opportunity which is almost made for them and for no one else. We know what great things you did in Germany three centuries ago, why should you not do the same in Oxford now? There is a multitude of young men,[4] sheep without a shepherd, sceptics, not willingly, but because they know no better. Two or three priests, zealous and full of work, and successful in their work, as every one says they are, *can* they be sufficient for the occasion of that multitude? You will not think me so untruthful, and so impatient and ill natured, as to be denying their excellence. But you could, if you would, double or triple them. I was bold enough in 1864 to contemplate the mission of Oxford for myself; it is in better hands. The Jesuit Fathers have a teaching, tradition, prestige, all their own. They have the mission of Oxford already, and have long had it; — beati possidentes. My day is past, but the Society is ever new.

Do something for the cause of God in Oxford, you who can.[5]

Very truly Yours John H. Card. Newman.

P.S. Excuse my mistakes in writing. It is old age.

[1] From Clarke's reply on 18 Nov. to this letter it is clear that he asked Newman to write in the *Month* in defence of such doctrines as the Virgin Birth, which had just been denied by F. W. Farrar in *The Early Days of Christianity*, London 1882. The reviewer in the *Spectator* (4 Nov. 1882), pp. 1413–15, dismissed the book as 'of no permanent value', and said, 'Starting with the baseless assumption that the commonly received doctrine that our Lord's mother had no other child originated in a pernicious preference of celibacy over the married state, Dr. Farrar undertakes, with all the unfairness of an ordinary no-Popery fanatic, to prove that the Virgin was the mother of a large family. Whole groups of facts which are inconsistent with his theory are passed by him in silence . . .' Among these the reviewer mentioned one insisted on by J. B. Lightfoot, that our Lord would not in that case have confided the Blessed Virgin to St John.

[2] In the draft Newman wrote 'which shrinks from the notion that the Blessed Virgin had children after the miraculous conception of our Lord.'

[3] Henry Alford in his *The Greek Testament . . . a Critical and Exegetical Commentary*, third edition 1856, maintained the miraculous conception of our Lord, on the strength of the Infancy Narratives, but favoured the view that our Lady had other children later.

[4] The draft begins 'The junior fellows, the undergraduates of that dear place, are sheep without a shepherd.'

[5] Clarke replied that he had laid Newman's views before the Jesuit Provincial, but went on to say 'it would require a phalanx of our best men to make any lasting impression on the University', and these were occupied in the Jesuit colleges and the large cities.

TO BARTHOLOMEW WOODLOCK, BISHOP OF ARDAGH

Birmingham Nov 7. 1882

My dear Bishop of Ardagh

I am very glad to have your Papers and have read them with great interest I wish my brain and my fingers moved quickly enough to master them and report upon them. What the Tablet has been saying I do not know, but, as I understand them, they are excellent[1]

I understand you as follows: that the two houses (i.e. material edifices) in Stephen's Green (Numbers 85 and 86) shall remain the Seat both of the Catholic University and of a Catholic (C. U.) College, other Colleges (C. U.) being added in the City and perhaps beyond to the distance of 5 miles, — as from the beginning, with this difference, that the C. U Professors and Heads of Colleges are more or less connected, nay identified with certain Catholic Fellows of another, new, governmental institution, called the Royal University, whose lectures the Students of the C. U. have a right to attend and by passing whose examinations (excipiendis exceptis in the case of Maynooth) they obtain their degrees.

There may be some difficulty in working such a subtlety as an identification of separate individuals, which can only be resolved by the actual experiment, but, as far as the original object of the Holy See and the Bishops is concerned, the scheme seems to be very satisfactory, and so is what I hear of the temper and spirit of the Protestant members of the Senate, Council, or Committee of the Royal University, who might, if they were hostile do you harm

The primary point was to get rid of Protestant Lectures (except indeed in mathematics) and that you have gained, and unfair Examiners, and that, I suppose you have practically gained too. And the moral unity, yet Collegiate plurality, so necessary for a national institution, you have successfully secured or are securing.[2]

[1] On 5 Nov. Woodlock sent his pastoral letter of 26 Oct. and other papers about the position and prospects of the Catholic University of Ireland. To Newman he wrote, 'Grave misapprehension seems to have arisen — if we are to judge from the "Tablet" — as to the late action of the Bishops of Ireland. For my part, I was never more sanguine of the success of the work.' The *Tablet* (14 Oct. 1882), p. 602, in a leading article said that the Catholic University had ceased to be a national institution, 'this dismal fact is undeniable' and its direction was now in the hands of the Archbishop of Dublin. The *Tablet* (28 Oct.), p. 684, withdrew most of this, said it did not despond, but insisted that the administration of the University was exclusively in the hands of the Archbishop.

In his pastoral Woodlock explained that in the 'Colleges of the Catholic University the Students will be prepared for the Examinations of the Royal University and will receive its Degrees. The chief of these Colleges will be "CATHOLIC UNIVERSITY COLLEGE," Stephensgreen . . . A learned body of Professors, Fellows of the Royal University, assisted by able Tutors, will teach in its Halls, while the Students of the Catholic Colleges in Dublin and the neighbourhood, and others residing with their friends, will frequent their Lectures. In it and the other Colleges of the Catholic University our youth can thus be instructed in every branch of human learning without danger to faith and morals, because under the supreme control of the Pastors of the Church; and at the same time these Students can receive, through the Royal University, Degrees and other rewards of successful studies. It will no longer be necessary to make the Annual Collection for the support of the Catholic University.'

[2] A new paragraph began here of about five lines, which Woodlock has erased, heading it

It was very pleasant to me to find you still remember me   don't forget me in your prayers.

Yours affectly John H. Card. Newman

TO GEORGE T. EDWARDS

Nov. 8. 1882

My dear Sir

I must apologise for keeping your most interesting Memorial so long.[1] I wish at least I could show my sense of its value by remarking about it at length — but it is such a trouble to me to write, and so slow an operation, that I am afraid I shall be so brief as to seem ungrateful to your kindness.

I am very much struck and won as to C. F's [Caroline Fox] inner mind, by this private record of her thoughts and feelings. Don't think me flippant when I say, that she was too good for a Quaker, and that she ought to have been a Catholic

She, as many others, did not understand what Catholics hold.

E.g. her only idea of what we hold about the Sacraments is that they are 'symbols'! Of course they *are* symbols .. but, if we hold them to be nothing more than symbols, we should be like the Jews or Galatians. We believe our Sacraments to be *means* of grace, as well as symbols. Even our pictures are more than symbols, when blessed by the Priest, but Baptism is an ordinance of Christ Himself.

Again — she or some one else in these notices speaks of a dead mother being *present* to her children. It is a soothing and awful thought. Why then do they so little understand the mind of Catholics, who believe that our Lord incarnate is personally present in the Holy Sacrament of the Altar? In one place of this Memorial Paper, the Catholic Rites are said to be a *weight*. Does *any* one say so, who really believes, who vividly holds, that where the Consecrated Host is, there is Christ? Again: *We* have a more wonderful,

'PRIVATE' and writing at the side 'I erased these lines, as they regarded a private matter ✠ B. W.'

Woodlock asked what Newman thought of Thomas Scratton's qualifications for a Fellow-ship in the Royal University, and said that a testimonial from him would strengthen the hands of Cardinal MacCabe and himself, Woodlock, who wanted to make provision for him in this way, at the election of 9 Nov. The erasure must have concerned Scratton. Newman wrote to him at once and received a letter in reply which he sent to Cardinal MacCabe. The latter wrote to Newman on 21 Nov. that it was out of his power to do for Scratton 'what he seems to think I could have done.' Also on 21 Nov. Scratton wrote to Newman: 'I am very grateful to you for your kind letter and thank you heartily for it. In my present gloom and depression, it has given me no little consolation . . .'

Scratton later sued the Irish bishops and obtained £300 in damages from them. See letter of 5 Nov. 1885 and those of beginning of June 1880 and 9 Oct. 1881 to Scratton, also that of 7 Jan. 1883 to Ornsby.

[1] Edwards had already presented Newman with the two volumes of Caroline Fox's *Memories* . . . , which contained extracts from her Journals. See letters of 17 and 23 Sept. Edwards then lent him what both call her 'Memorial', perhaps some part of a journal later burned. See Wilson Harris, *Caroline Fox*, London 1944, pp. 41–5, who confuses this 'Memorial' with her *Memories*.

soothing time of silence than the Quakers. It is the silent half hour, spent, solus cum solo, before the Tabernacle.

No, C. Fox never understood, never realized, what we hold. She might have been a Catholic, if she had.[1]

I send you back the Memorial Papers.

Yours very truly J H Card Newman

TO ANNE MOZLEY

Birmingham Nov. 9. 1882

Dear Anne Mozley

It is very good of you to be thinking of journeying here, and it would be a great pleasure to me. But I have a difficulty over and above that of letting you do so at this time of the year, so dark and cold. It is one of my own. I ought to have change of air just now, and I in vain seek an opportunity of getting to Rednall. Week after week passes, and I cannot get away from this place. And I don't wish to put obstacles

If therefore I think best not to accept your offer now, don't suppose I let you off what I consider to be a *promise*, of which the fulfilment is only postponed.

I am sanguine as to the success of Palmer's Journal, but it is impossible to be sure. Forty years ago is an antediluvian date to the reading public of 1882, and Russia is out of favour, as is theological controversy. Still I hope

Yours affectly John H Card. Newman

TO LORD BRAYE

Birmingham Nov 10. 1882

My dear Lord Braye

It has occurred to me, that I ought to send my letter to Mgr di Rende *before* you go, not *with* you, lest you should find him busy, and he be made uncomfortable at your finding him so.[2]

[1] Edwards replied on 21 Nov., 'Your letter came when I was absent in Cornwall on a visit to C. F's old home, Penjerrick, near Falmouth, where I staid a few days with her sister, also a remarkable and gifted woman, whose life is a continuous ministration to those around her, especially the sick and the suffering. She was much gratified on hearing that you had been interested in the Memorial and expressed a wish that you should know that C. F. had not sought after the friendship of men like Mill and Carlyle — that the Mills were introduced to her parents, and that the whole family always sought to do what they could for the numerous invalids who often came into Cornwall. That J. S. Mill was not then known by the Fox family to be the decided unbeliever that he afterwards proved to be, and that all the visitors to Penjerrick professed so far to admire simple Christian faith, that they never sought to disturb or oppose it. She also said that in the published volumes only such portions of C. F's Journals were given, as the editor thought likely to interest the general public, but that a far larger portion of the Journal than is given to remembrances of celebrities, is devoted to histories of her poor sick people, and her intercourse with them, and to notes of the ministrations she heard in their meetings, or Bible classes.'
[2] Camillo Siciliano di Rende was the zealous Archbishop of Benevento, whom Leo XIII sent in 1882 to the delicate post of Nuncio in Paris. Lord Braye hoped to further in Rome the proposals in Newman's letters of 2 and 15 Nov. See also letters of 9 Feb. 1883 to him and to di Rende.

In consequence I think of sending him the inclosed letter, unless you disapprove.

> Your Lordship's faithful Servt J. H. Card. Newman

TO BERNARD HENNIN

> November 11th. 1882.

My dear Bernard,

I felt your kindness very much in remembering Oct. 9[1] but I am sure you will forgive me for not writing to acknowledge it. I am so tired out with writing, I write so slowly, and with such little time for writing.

God bless you all

> Yours affectionately, J. H. Card Newman.

TO HENRY BEDFORD

> Birmingham. Nov. 13th. 1882

My dear Mr. Bedford,

I have received your gift with much pleasure. What parts I have read of it, were very interesting, and must have been very effective in delivering, for I take it for granted that you read them before printing, or at least portions of them. Thanking you much for your kindness.

> I am, most sincerely yours, J. H. Card. Newman.

TO ANNE MOZLEY

> Bm Nov. 13. 1882

My Dear Anne Mozley,

Thank you for James's review of my 'Grammar of Assent.' It is pleasant to me to find that we agree so well together on an important subject.[2]

I have not read it carefully; but, as regards the only point in which I observe he seems to differ from me, I do not see that he notices that I consider what Aristotle calls 'phronesis' is that habit and act of the mind which leads a man to determine when 'inference' is to pass to 'assent'.[3]

> Yours affectly John H Card. Newman

---

[1] Newman's reception into the Catholic Church in 1845.

[2] Anne Mozley sent Newman the sheets of the reprint of 'Dr. Newman's Grammar of Assent', *Quarterly Review* (July 1870), which was included in J. B. Mozley's *Lectures and other Theological Papers*, London 1883, pp. 275–300. Anne Mozley wrote on 11 Nov. in reference to her brother's article, 'his value for the book he reviews makes me wish you to see it. It was at Worcester that I remember his discussing the Grammar of Assent with Dean Church, and their agreeing on its power.'

[3] Op. cit., p. 277.

TO CHARLES WORDSWORTH, BISHOP OF ST ANDREWS

Birmingham Nov. 13. 1882

My dear Bishop of St Andrew's

Thank you for your beautiful gift. The binding and letter press are worthy of the translations, and the translations (as far as I have read them) are worthy of their originals in the Christian Year.[1]

It is not the first of my books, with your name in it, as the donor. You gave me in 1844 Wetstein's Greek Testament, which has a place in our Oratory Library, as the present gift will have, as lasting memorials of you, when I am gone[2]

I am, My dear Bishop,
Most truly Yours John H. Card. Newman

The Bishop of St Andrew's

TO LOUISA ELIZABETH DEANE

Birmingham Nov. 14, 1882.

My dear Louisa,

It was very pleasant to me to receive your letter, and I congratulate you on your daughter's marriage.

You must not confuse Birmingham with the 'black country' which lies between B. and Wolverhampton. Unfortunately the B. railroad runs through the most dismal part of the town, and creates as unfavourable an impression of the place as can be imagined.[3] I hope, when you next pass through, the time-table will be more kind, and I shall see you here.

Thank you, I am very well, though weak. One of my infirmities is, what I have shown in this letter, misspelling or blotting my words, or leaving words out. In like manner I have a difficulty in talking, walking, hearing and reading, but I have nothing positive the matter with me.

My best remembrances to Mr Deane and to such of your children as are at home and I have seen.

Yours affectionately John H. Card. Newman

---

[1] Newman had sent Charles Wordsworth W. Palmer's *Notes of a Visit to the Russian Church*. In return he sent a copy of his own Latin translations of passages from Keble's *The Christian Year*, relating to the duties of the clergy, *Anni Christiani quae ad Clerum pertinent Latine reddita*, 1880. See *Annals of my Life 1847–1856*, edited by W. Earl Hodgson, London 1893, p. 82.

[2] *Novum Testamentum juxta exemplar Wetstenii, Glasguae, et D. Jo. Jac. Griesbachii, Hallae...*, London 1808. See letter of 2 Sept. 1844 to Wordsworth.

[3] Mrs Deane wrote on 11 Nov., of her railway journey through Birmingham, 'what an immense Town it appears to be, we seemed to encircle it for miles and yet for smoke, could not see 20 yards in; it is too bad that these wealthy manufacturers will not devour their own smoke.'

TO LORD BRAYE

Bm. Nov. 15. 1882

Private

My dear Lord Braye

I heard on very good authority yesterday that important persons at Rome are moving and in correspondence with Englishmen on the subject of the higher education. It is so much better that the initiative should come from Rome than from England, that I think it will be advisable to see what comes of it, before you act yourself.[1]

I had addressed myself to the Nuncio — but luckily on a neutral matter, which was but an introduction to my proposed letter to him and did not refer to the subject we conversed upon here.[2]

Your Lordship's faithful Servt
John H Card. Newman

TO MALACHY O'CALLAGHAN (I)

Birmingham Nov. 15. 1882

Private

Dear Fr O'Callaghan

Excuse me that I have been so slow in sending you the letter I inclose — but I have many letters to answer, and little leisure for them, and my brain works slow, and my hand writes painfully

Very truly yours John H Card. Newman

TO MALACHY O'CALLAGHAN (II)

Birmingham Nov. 15. 1882

Very Rev. Father

If any words of mine can aid in furthering the success of such excellent objects as I learn from your letter you have in view, gladly do I, according to your request, send you these.

I recollect well, how, when I became a Catholic, the first religious body which attracted my reverent notice was yours; and afterwards, when I was resident in Dublin, with what kindness, on my presenting myself at your House at Castleknock, I was received by your Superiour [sic] and Community.[3]

[1] B. F. C. Costelloe was working in conjunction with Thomas Parkinson, Superior of the Jesuit House at Oxford, for the easing of the ban on Catholics attending the universities. Costelloe went to Rome in Dec. 1882 and returned towards the end of Jan. 1883. This effort was independent of Lord Braye's. See the Grissell Papers, St Benet's Hall, Oxford.
[2] See letters of 10 Nov. to Lord Braye and of 9 Feb. 1883 to Archbishop di Rende.
[3] On 9 Sept. 1846 Newman records in his diary his visit to the Lazarists, i.e. Vincentians, in Paris, and in his letter of 18 Oct. 1846 to Dalgairns the impression he received of them.
O'Callaghan was the President of Castleknock College, County Dublin. In 1883 the Vincentians opened a College of Education at Drumcondra.

I am pleased then at the opportunity, which after so many years you give me, of expressing my sympathy and interest in the Congregation of St Vincent, and my sincere hope that your good work, in England as well as Ireland, may extend and prosper.

The Very Rev. Father O'Callaghan.

TO EMILY BOWLES

Bm. Nov. 16. 1882

My dear Child

You gave me various information which I was glad to have; especially about Mr Pusey whom I had not, I think, heard of for 20 years. You did not say whether he had any family[1]

The letters that come to me speak of Palmer's Notes as interesting — but they come from men who were his friends, or were Tractarians

I want to ask you a question. That pamphlet of dear T. Meyrick's about himself which I lent you, did you return it? No matter though you did not, for it is in safe hands — but I am not sure that it ought not to be burned. I read it very hastily.[2]

Also, did I lend you a large quarto MS in loose sheets and in four parts? I think not — but at present it is missing.[3] I don't mean the memoir of Ambrose's last illness. There are various MSS. of importance, which I want to use just now, which I could not at once lay my hand upon, if I wanted

Ever Yours affectly John H. Card. Newman

P.S.   I am sorry I did not give the proper direction to my last letters. I could not find it.

TO LORD BLACHFORD

Birmingham, Nov. 16th. 1882.

My dear Blachford,

I shall rejoice to see you on Dec. 9th. as you propose.[4]

And I am glad of your criticism on Palmer. I wish I had added your word 'generosity' to the traits of his character. It so marked him.[5]

Yours affectionately, John H. Card: Newman.

[1] This was evidently E. B. Pusey's nephew Edward Pusey, Newman's godson. He was married in 1870, and had only a daughter at this time.
[2] See letter of 3 June 1882 to J. T. Walford.
[3] It had not been lent to her. See letter of 10 Oct. to Jane Mozley.
[4] Lord Blachford changed the day of his visit to 11 Dec.
[5] Lord Blachford wrote on 14 Nov. about Newman's account of William Palmer in *Notes of a Visit to the Russian Church*, 'What you say of him is most deeply and touchingly true. His kindness, patience, generosity, industry and singleheartedness besides what lies deeper still, one never can forget.'

TO LORD BRAYE

Bm Nov 17. 1882

My dear Lord Braye

I can see you at any time that suits you except on Tuesday and Thursday next;[1] and at any hour, except between 1½ and 2½

Very sincerely Yours John H. Card. Newman

TO AN UNKNOWN CORRESPONDENT

Bm Nov 17. 1882

Dear Sir

I am afraid you suppose I am more in the practice of giving advice than I am. Indeed, the best advice, in my own judgment, now which I could offer you, is to address yourself to some good priest near you — but I do not of course say this as refusing your request. Only, give a moment's thought to this suggestion.

I could see you on Thursday or Friday next week, at any hour except between 1.30 and 2.30

Very truly Yours John H Card. Newman

TO J. R. BLOXAM

Nov 21/82.

My dear B

You will easily understand I can return no other answer than what I inclose[2]

Yrs ever affly J H N

TO MRS EDWARD HAWKINS

Birmingham Nov. 21. 1882

My dear Mrs Hawkins,

What wonderful kindness it is in you to write to me in your present deep distress; it has touched me greatly.[3]

I thought of writing to *you*, when I heard yesterday of your loss, but on second thoughts I did not dare. Now by your own letter you give me leave, or rather invite me. Your dear husband has never been out my mind of late years. When the first snow came down some weeks back, I thought what the effect of it might be upon him, and only last week, I quoted to a friend with

---

[1] 21 and 23 Nov.
[2] The enclosure ran: 'Nov 21. 1882
Cardinal Newman is obliged to say that he cannot open a letter not directed to him — nor can he read private letters addressed to other persons.'
[3] Edward Hawkins died on 18 Nov.

reference to him (thinking at the same time of my own case) a Greek poet's words, 'A light stroke puts to sleep aged men'[1]

I have followed his life year after year as I have not been able to follow that of others, because I knew just how many years he was older than I am, and how many days his birthday was from mine. These standing reminders of him personally sprang out of the kindness and benefits done to me by him close upon sixty years ago, when he was Vicar of St Mary's and I held my first curacy at St Clement's. Then, during two Long Vacations, we were day after day in the Common Room all by ourselves, and in Ch Ch [Christ Church] meadow.[2] He used then to say that he should not live past forty; and he has reached, in the event, his great age. I never shall forget to pray for him, till I too go, and have mentioned his name in my Obituary book, which dear Mrs Pusey made for me in her last illness.

May God be with you, and make up to you by His grace this supreme desolation

Most truly Yours John H Card. Newman

TO GEORGE TEELING

The Oratory Nov. 22/82

My dear George

I am very glad to hear of your application for the place at Math[?],[3] and willingly bear witness to your possessing those qualities and external recommendations which lead to a man's succeeding with others, whether equals in age or juniors.

According to our experience of you here, I should say you are the man to make friends, wherever you go, and especially that you would know how to gain influence with boys. Our chief trial of you was your taking part in the administration of our school, and next in your working up the boys for the representation of the plays of Terence, a task which required a special command of them, for it involved on their part a great deal of drudgery. No one of our masters, I think, before you was able to get them to know their parts thoroughly by heart till the last moment. I should add that for a work of that kind you are a first rate elocutionist.

⟨Wishing and I almost may dare to say expecting to hear of your success in your application⟩[4]

This indeed does not bear directly on your fitness for the particular province for which you are preparing yourself; but I do not see why you may not in a few months gain such a familiarity with it as will meet the

---

[1] σμικρὰ παλαιὰ σώματ' εὐνάζει ροπή. Sophocles, *Oedipus Tyrannus*, 961.
[2] Cf. *Apo.*, p. 8. The long vacations were those of 1824 and 1825. Hawkins was elected Provost of Oriel on 31 Jan. 1828. He was born on 27 Feb. 1789.
[3] Perhaps 'Malta'. Teeling was at the Priory of Fort Augustus, Inverness-shire.
[4] What follows has been cancelled in the draft.

demands made on a Professor in a place which does not abound, I suppose, with many very advanced scholars in Latin or English literature

Excuse my mistakes in writing. It is old age

Yours affectionately John H. Card. Newman

TO HENRY JAMES COLERIDGE

Bm Nov 24. 1882.

My dear Fr Coleridge

Your silence seems to say to me, Be patient — there is nothing to be anxious about.

And I know how liberal doctors are of their anticipations and promises — so that one ought not to be surprised at delay Still half a line from you would be pleasant[1]

Yrs affectly John H Card. Newman[2]

TO MARIANNE FRANCES BOWDEN

Nov. 26. 1882

My dear Child

I have found the inclosed letters, and think that you and your sisters may wish to have them

Yours affectly John H Card. Newman

Miss Bowden

TO LORD EMLY

Nov 26. 1882

My dear Emly

I have thought you might like to see what your judgement was years ago on the subject of the Catholic oath — Therefore I send you the inclosed. Excuse me if I am officious I don't know whether *now* there is any oath[3]

Yrs affectly John H Card. Newman[4]

[1] This probably refers to the illness of Lord Coleridge.

[2] As in previous years Newman sent on 25 Nov. letters of Christmas greeting to Sovereigns and Cardinals, drafted by Achille Liverziani. He kept a draft of his order: 'Il Cardinale Newman vorrebbe ricevere le lettere Natalizie da Signor Liver stipulato che la carta sia buona, l'inchiostro limpido, la scrittura bella, e l'involto sicuro. Queste condizioni erano mancate nelle copie del' anno passato (1881)'

[3] cf. letter of 28 May 1865 to Lord Emly.

[4] Anthony Trollope had a stroke on 3 Nov. and died on 6 Dec. 1882. On 27 Oct. 1882 he wrote to Newman from the Athenaeum Club:

'My dear Lord Cardinal,

I have received from Lord Emly the specific which you have been kind enough to send me for my asthma, and which he with his usual friendship has been anxious to make known to me. I have told him that I will at once try it and tell him of the effect. I fear that it will not be

Birmingham Nov. 26. 1882

Dear Mrs Whyte

I have to thank you for a very kind letter[1] — also, for Dr Whyte's message through you, for which of course I thank and praise God, not however, if I may presume to use St Paul's words, without 'great sadness and continual sorrow in my heart' that there should not be One Body and One Spirit among those who profess One Lord and One Baptism[2]

I think I shall never preach again, for my voice is gone, and I cannot speak without an effort. This Christmas will be the first, I think, for 35 years that I have not taken the Sermon in the Oratory Church.

I am much concerned to hear of Dr Whyte's bad accident[3]

Very truly Yours John H. Card. Newman

TO DAVID BROWN

Bm Nov. 27/82

My Dear Dr Brown

I am able to send you inclosed the letter (as I trust) which you asked me for. It was safely lodged in its proper place, but my letters are so many, that it took time to find.[4]

Wishing you all blessings of the coming holy season, I am,

Most truly Yours John H Card. Newman

TO MISS M. R. GIBERNE

Nov 29. 1882

My dear Sister Pia

Certainly I never saw a picture with our Lord belonging in one figure to two groups — and for this reason among others, because in the earthly

efficacious, because no smoking, and nothing that touches my throat, is of any avail. But I will nevertheless put the saltpetre and the blotting-paper into requisition at once.

May I be allowed to take this opportunity also of telling your eminence how great has been the pleasure which I have received from understanding that you have occasionally read and been amused by my novels. It is when I hear that such men as yourself have been gratified that I feel that I have not worked altogether in vain; but there is no man as to whom I can say that his good opinion would give me such intense gratification as your own.

I have, the honour to be, My dear Lord Cardinal,
Your most obedient servant, Anthony Trollope'
cf. Trollope's letter of 27 Oct. to Lord Emly in *The Letters of Anthony Trollope*, edited by Bradford Allen Booth, Oxford 1951, pp. 494–5.

[1] Mrs Whyte wrote on 24 Nov. to ask whether Newman ever preached at the Oratory, and whether strangers would be allowed to come. She spoke of 'the extraordinary debt of gratitude' her husband owed Newman 'for intellectual and spiritual quickening and support. . . As I write he says he need not attempt to convey to you what has long been in his heart. 'It cannot be told here.''
[2] *Romans*, 9:2; *Ephesians*, 4:4–5.
[3] a coach accident.
[4] See letter of 20 June 1882 to Brown.

group He is usually the Bambino, which will not represent Him as the second Person in the Blessed Trinity. This is all I can say. I would have a Priest's sanction, if I were you.

One ought not to despair of any one, and some are received on their deathbed. It never can be wrong in telling a Protestant 'how doubts and difficulties vanished' when you were once a Catholic; but whether to say so to the friend you mention will do the friend you mention good, is far too difficult a question to answer.

I grieve at what you tell me about your pain. You say so little about medical advice, that I fear you have not as much as you ought to have. I know your knee is so old an ailment, that doctors cannot do much — but surely they might alleviate pain. I am glad to think, or to see, that your Mother and Sisters seem to take care that your Rule should not press hard upon you.

Dr Pusey's friends are putting on foot a memorial of him in Oxford, which, when carried may serve as a defence of religion there. They contemplate a fund of £50,000. With this they mean to buy ground, to build a Library to receive his books, and to endow two Librarians, who will live on the spot. They don't seem at present to intend to build a church. His books are valued at £2200.[1]

I suppose you have heard of Dr Hawkins's death, aged 93! He was well to the last. Dr Tait too, Archbishop of Canterbury seems to be going[2]

Ever Yours affectly John H Card. Newman

TO BISHOP ULLATHORNE

[December 1882?]

My dear Lord

I have occasion for your advice and assistance in respect to the new Edition of the Raccolta. As time has gone on, fresh prayers (indulgenced) have been included in the translation, and these are now so many that the question has arisen — whether Cardinal Wiseman's original approbation as given to Fr St John can be considered to cover them, or whether rather we should have recourse to some Ordinary, as your Lordship to settle it

Fr Bellasis, the bearer of this and of the New Edition, will give you, better than a letter, all explanations.[3]

J H N

---

[1] Pusey House was opened 9 Oct. 1884.
[2] Archbishop Tait died on 3 Dec.
[3] The *Raccolta* continued to appear with the original approbation and with a new 'imprimatur'.

Bm Dec 1. 1882

My dear Mr Law

I am very glad indeed to have the second part of your dear Son's life. Thank you very much for it[1]

Most truly Yours John H. Card. Newman

The Hon. W. T. Law

TO CHARLES LANCELOT SHADWELL

Birmingham Dec. 5. 1882

My dear Mr Shadwell,

I shall be quite ready to see you here on Thursday, as Dean Church tells me you propose to me, but I shall be ashamed too, that you should have the trouble, conscious, as I am, how little I can serve you in your object of coming.[2]

Unluckily I, as well as Pusey, were suffering in health severely at the time of the vacancy of the Headship in 1827–28; we were away from Oxford during the Christmas vacation; Dornford was the leading actor in the correspondence involved in the prospect of an election.

From the first only two men were thought of as filling Copleston's place, Hawkins and Keble. Dornford was for Hawkins and gained Pusey and me. Awdry and Jenkyns, who had been afraid of Hawkins, as being too severe for a Provost, were gained by the fact that the three first named, who had been years in residence with him, were in his favour. The Fellows were nearly equally divided. But I find the canvass was over before the end of December, and the contest ended by Keble's withdrawing. He wrote to me Dec 28/27 thus: 'I have made up my mind, that it is on the whole unadvisable for me to allow my name to be mentioned on this occasion. It is very kind in you to write to me, but surely your opinion required no explanation or apology.'

The Register Book, I suppose, gives the form, in which the election was conducted. It being unanimous, I suppose it was after the fashion of the Michaelmas elections to offices. 'Magister Decane, quem nominas'. etc.

The election, if I recollect rightly, took place at the end of January. Then the new Provost attended by Dornford (I suppose the new Dean) went up to London to be formally instituted by the Lord Chancellor (Lyndhurst) as the King's representative. They got back to Oxford for the Gaudy Febr. 2

[1] See letter of 29 Jan. 1882 to Law.
[2] Shadwell was a Fellow of Oriel College 1864–98, then an honorary Fellow, and from 1906 to 1914 Provost. He was the College archivist and was seeking information as to the election of Edward Hawkins as Provost in 1828.

I shall be glad if this saves you the trouble of coming — but I shall expect you, if I do not hear to the contrary.

Very truly Yours John H Card. Newman

P S Excuse mistakes in writing — it is old age

TO W. J. COPELAND

Bm Decr 6. 1882

My dear Copeland

Your deep black border prepared me for the contents of your letter. Two such trials as you have had, are indeed, as you say, strange. You say nothing about your health. I trust it has not suffered from so wearisome and exhausting a suspense.[1]

I see Sir W. Palmer's work is to be republished, and have put my name on the subscription list.[2] Palmer can on an occasion be violent, but what a difference in tone, spirit, and statement between him and that strange Highchurchman, Dr Littledale![3]

I am the sole surviving Fellow of Hawkins's election.

Except Bursar Smith, I suppose I am the sole survivor of the Trinity Fellows and Scholars of 1822, when I left for Oriel[4]

Ever Yours affectly John H Card. Newman

TO ELIZA FOURDRINIER

Birmingham Dec 6. 1882

My dear Eliza,

Your letter has made me very sad, especially at the thought of your solitariness, as being the one left of your family.[5] Thank you for writing to me. It recalls so many past days and pleasant meetings, of which you and I are now almost the sole living witnesses. For many years I have had it in mind to attempt to find you out, but I am so little from home, and with so many engagements when I am in London, and felt so uncertain of your abode, that I have never succeeded, and now I am too old to think of it.

I recollect well the last time I saw *you*, I think, *Annie*, and your dear *Mother*, who seemed to me to be looking older than when I had last seen her.

[1] Copeland's sister Mrs Samuel Borlase died on 1 Dec. after a very long illness. He had had a similar trial with his brother George, who died in 1873.
[2] William Palmer of Worcester's *Treatise on the Church of Christ*, two volumes, London 1838, third edition 1842. After his father's death in 1865, he claimed the title of a baronet.
[3] cf. letter of 1881 to R. W. Church.
[4] Joseph Smith, Exhibitioner of Trinity College, Oxford, 1814–24, and Fellow, 1824–52, died in 1886.
[5] Eliza Fourdrinier, born 1812, was the youngest daughter of Newman's uncle Charles. She was the last of his children, her brother John Coles died on 28 Nov.

If I am right, this was July 30, 1844. I believe I know the days of death of all of you.

May God guard and protect you, and be with you now and in the future.

If I can find a photograph of me, since you speak of portraits, I will send you one.

Yours affectionately John H Card. Newman

TO W. S. LILLY

The Oratory, December 7, 1882.

My dear Lilly,

I have read your proof with the greatest pleasure, and with entire assent.[1] Certainly there is no opposition in the respective truths of science and theology, nor do I think that an apparent opposition can be maintained, or is, by the sceptics of the day. It is presumptuous in me to speak on a question of fact, considering I live out of the world, but I will say what strikes me.

First, we must grant — and it is difficult to determine how far we must go in granting — that both the Mosaic and Christian dispensations took the existing state of thought as it was, and only partially innovated on and corrected it. The instance of Divorce makes this plain as regards the Old Testament; as to the New, the first instance that occurs to me is St. Paul's simple recognition of married life in Bishops.

On a far larger scale is the absence of meddling with the social and secular world. God speaks 'for the elect's sake'. He leaves the popular astronomy as it was. Heaven is still above, and the powers of evil below. The sun rises and sets, and at His word stops or goes back, and the firmament opens. And so with social and political science; nothing is told us of economical laws, etc., etc., So from the first there has been a progress with laws of progress, to which theology has contributed little, and which now has a form and substance, powerful in itself, and independent of and far surpassing Christianity in its social aspect; for Christianity (socially considered) has a previous and more elementary office, being the binding principle of society.

This primary and special office of religion men of the world do not see, and they see only its poverty as a principle of secular progress, and, as disciples and upholders and servants of that great scientific progress, they look on religion and despise it. As the scientific parasite says in the play, 'Ego illum contempsi prae me.'[2]

I consider then that it is not reason that is against us, but imagination. The mind, after having, to the utter neglect of the Gospels, lived in science,

---

[1] This was the proof of Lilly's article, 'The Religious Future of the World, Part I', the *Contemporary Review* (Jan. 1883), pp. 100–21, reprinted in his *Ancient Religion and Modern Thought*, chapter IV (first half) as 'Naturalism and Christianity.'
[2] Terence, *Eunuchus*, II, ii, 8.

experiences, on coming back to Scripture, an utter strangeness in what it reads, which seems to it a better argument against Revelation than any formal proof from definite facts or logical statements. 'Christianity is behind the age.'

I have been unable to bring out my meaning as I should like, and am very dissatisfied with myself, but I feel what I have been insisting on very strongly.

Very sincerely yours, John H. Card. Newman.

TO MISS ROBERTS

Immaculate Conception [8 December] 1882

My dear Miss Roberts

I wish you the best blessings of the Day with all my heart — but I cannot prudently answer your welcome visit by coming down stairs to you, as I have a cold which pulls me down enough already

God bless you now and ever

Yours affectly J H Card. Newman

TO JEROME VAUGHAN

Dec. 9. 1882

Dear Fr Prior

I thank you very much for your letter. I am with this sending a Testimonial to Mr Teeling; so the loss of the first is no great matter.[1]

Yours truly John H. Card. Newman

TO J. D. MULLINS

The Oratory Decr 11. 1882

My dear Sir,

I am much grieved that that most acceptable compliment paid me some weeks since by the Committee of the Free Libraries, in giving me your Catalogue of the Shakespeare Memorial Library, has not yet been acknowledged.[2]

[1] See letter of 22 Nov. to Teeling.
[2] This was J. D. Mullins's *Catalogue of the Shakespeare Memorial Library Birmingham*, 'Printed for the Free Libraries Committee' and listing works up to and including 1875. In a covering letter Mullins wrote: 'The Chief Librarian will be greatly obliged if his Eminence Cardinal Newman will accept the enclosed Catalogue as a memorial of his recent visit to the Free Libraries
It is chiefly interesting
1. As a Catalogue of the largest Collection of English Shakespeariana ever made
2. As a Chronological List of the English Editions of Shakespeare's Works.
3. As a chronological and comparative List of the English Editions of the separate plays.'
A dedication signed by Mullins says that the copy was presented by the Committee of the

On hearing yesterday that you had sent it to me, I made a great search for it in my room without success. At length it was found in the room of one of our Fathers, who, from interest in the subject, had taken it and had not returned it.

Pray accept my sincere apology in this untoward occurrence. I am very glad to have the book. It is a beautiful book, worthy in its print and paper, of the great literary labour which it must have involved; and it will remain in our Oratory Library after my day with the Mayor's previous present,[1] as a memorial of the honour which I have received from the Committee of the Free Libraries and their chief Librarian.

I am, My dear Sir Most truly Yours
John H. Card. Newman

J. D. Mullins Esq

TO J. WILLIAMS

Dec. 12. 1882

Cardinal Newman thanks Mr Williams for his wish to promote the circulation of the Cardinal's volumes[2]

He observes on it as follows:

His eleven volumes of Anglican Sermons are not in his own hands, but in those of Messrs Rivington, and their selling price does not seem to him unreasonable. Some 54 of them can be bought ⟨I think⟩ for 5/- that is, at the rate of scarcely more than a penny a sermon.[3]

This is the case of a Protestant publisher. The 'Apologia' and 'Verses' which Mr Williams also mentions are not in Protestant hands and English Catholics cannot afford to sell their books cheaply because being a small body they do not command a wide circulation   The initial expense and the risk in prospect of publication is considerable. The yearly balance of loss and gain in the Cardinal's publications is by no means always on the side of gain[4]

Birmingham Free Library, and is dated 15 Sept., when Newman paid his visit. See letter of 2 June to Thomas Avery.

[1] This has not been traced.
[2] Williams wrote on 6 Dec. from Bank House, Aylesbury to ask 'if there is any probability of your many and useful writings being brought out in a cheap form.
    Your editions of sermons, "Apologia" and hymns especially, would be popular . . .'
[3] This refers to *Selection Adapted to the Seasons . . . from the Parochial and Plain Sermons*, London 1878.
[4] On 7 Dec. Newman began a reply in the first person which ended:
'I will but say that, if after the existing editions have run out, a publisher is willing to undertake a new edition of any one at his own expense at a low price, I am ready to treat with him.
    At the same time it must be recollected that it is a great point for an author to keep the copyright of the text and the power of correcting in my own hands, which is not favorable to an arrangement with a publisher'

TO DAVID BROWN

Birmingham Decr 12. 1882

My dear Dr Brown

I am rather frightened suddenly to recollect that you have not acknowledged the receipt from me of your own letter which you wished to have, which I found and sent you some weeks back

I hope it got safely to you and was the right one[1]

Very truly Yours John H Card. Newman

TO W. S. LILLY

December 13, 1882.

My dear Lilly,

I fear I cannot promise you to get up and remark upon Mills' argument, both because my day is so filled up, and because such subjects try my head now.

As to my *Assent*, I thought and think it to be an erroneous assumption, anything but self-evident, to say that order is causation.[2]

I said too that, if we went by experience, as it is the fashion now to do, our initial and elementary experience would lead us to consider Will the great or only cause. I did not mean to dogmatize, for I am not a metaphysician, but as an inquirer or questioner, I have a right to demand proof from the other side, who *do* dogmatize.

I wrote as I did in my last letter because, though it is of first importance of course to show that there is no contradiction between scientific and religious truth, yet it was not there, I fancied, that the shoe pinched.

Very sincerely yours, John H. Card. Newman.

TO GEORGE T. EDWARDS

Bm Dec 14. 1882

Dear Mr Edwards

My hand has been for many years weak, but that did not excuse the shocking untidiness of my last letter — except so far as this, that, but for that weakness I should have written it again.[3]

I did not mean to speculate on the chance of C. Fox becoming a Catholic, but I was referring to the insufficient grounds on which she put aside th

[1] See letter of 27 Nov. to Brown, who wrote on 17 Dec. that he would not have been anxious about his confidential letter had he remembered that it was headed '*Private*'.
[2] See letter of 7 Dec. to Lilly, who in his article for the *Contemporary Review* (Jan. 1883), p. 116, reprinted in *Ancient Religion and Modern Thought*, p. 226, rejected Mill's assumption that causation is order, and referred to *G.A.*, pp. 66–72. Lilly wrote on 9 Dec. asking for a reply to Mill's argument.
[3] See letter of 8 Nov. to Edwards, and for what follows notes there.

Priest, who never meant, I am sure, to express pain, as she seems to have thought, at her rejecting mere symbols of divine grace, as circumcision might be, but at her making light of those appointed means by which grace is ordinarily given. And the conclusion I tacitly drew was 'She who misunderstood the doctrine of the Catholic Church in one point, perhaps misunderstood it in others', viz in those (if you will) to which you seem to refer as my 'difficulties' at a former time.

Pray thank C. Fox's sister for the kind interest she has taken in removing my criticisms, which sincerely troubled me as made in the case of so excellent and remarkable a person, and with my best Christmas good wishes, which will be very soon in season

Believe me to be

Sincerely yours John H Card. Newman

TO W. S. LILLY

Dec. 18. 1882

My dear Mr Lilly,

Your article, slip 11–18, is full of wide reading and of good argument.[1]

It is not of these that any two opinions can be. I will rather suggest to you what may be criticism of it.

I think you have taken too wide a field of discussion

In consequence your reasoning is not close enough. You pass too quickly from subject to subject with an abrupt logic, which is not intelligible to the casual reader.

For the same reason, admirable in clearness and fairness as is your statement of Pythias's difficulties it is accidentally unfair to Religion, which is not defended with the care and fulness, which his difficulties require.

It is not safe to pass freely from one difficulty to another, lest you should find your fairness towards them tell in favour of the objector rather than of yourself, as if they made up a case

I think you must [be] on your guard against instilling doubts without intending it.

You must know many able orthodox Anglicans. Their cause and ours are one here. Could you not find such a referee, who would tell you whether my fears are well founded or not?

I will send you another note, when I have read the rest

Most truly Yours John H Card. Newman

P.   excuse my bad writing. It is weakness

[1] This was 'The Religious Future of the World, Part II', the *Contemporary Review* (Feb. 1883), pp. 304–39, reprinted in *Ancient Religion and Modern Thought*, chapter IV (second half). It discussed 'the objections to the Christian religion in general, and to the Catholic faith in particular.'

TO MRS EDWARD BELLASIS

Bm Decr 20 1882.

My dear Mrs Bellasis

O those dreadful penny a liners. There is no truth in those reports.[1] Our girls' School was in imminent [danger] of a conflagration — which, thank God, it escaped but it is out upon the ground where once was Bosco, far away from the Oratory.[2]

It gives me the opportunity of wishing you and your daughter a very happy Christmas. I have had the satisfaction of hearing a good account of you from your boys here, and have been deeply rejoiced to find you could be such a blessing to the poor forlorn Australian, to whom, if he is alive say everything kind and considerate from me.

With all kind regards to Clara

I am, Yours affectly John H. Card. Newman

TO FRANCIS LOUGHNAN (I)

Dec 21 1882

private

Dr Canon Loughnan

I thank you for sending me the cutting of the Bath Paper.[3] ⟨I take it for granted that the Bath Chronicle is the same as the Evening Chronicle⟩ Will you kindly get the inclosed inserted in it, as my answer to the charge against me which the cutting contains[4]

J H N

[1] Mrs Bellasis at Hyères had seen a notice in the *Morning Post* about 'a fire at the Oratory'.

[2] 'Bosco' was the name of the first sports ground of the Oratory School, which became and remained the site of the parish schools of the Oratory.

[3] On 19 Dec. Loughnan, one of the priests at Bath, sent Newman a cutting from the *Bath Chronicle*, giving an account of a lecture at the Assembly Rooms by Edith O'Gorman, the 'Escaped Nun'. At the end the chairman, W. Jay Bolton, Vicar of St James's, said 'he was last week in Bristol where a committee meeting was being held in one of the Protestant High Schools, and what was the subject of it? It had been discovered that Cardinal Newman had been writing to young girls of 16 years of age in one of the Protestant schools recommending them to go to the Jesuit fathers in Clifton, and to do so without the knowledge of their parents.'

[4] See next letter on the draft of which Newman wrote 'for publication.' He seems to have thought of writing direct to the Bath paper, since he drafted a different letter to Loughnan:

'Dear Sir, I thank you for your kind letter and its inclosure. I regret I shall disappoint the friendly anticipation about me which it contains. I send you the copy of the answer which I am forwarding to the *Evening* Chronicle J H N'

Loughnan sent Newman's public letter to the *Bath Journal* and another Bath paper, in both of which it was printed on 23 Dec. He did not send it to the *Bath Chronicle* which would only appear on 28 Dec., thinking the matter sufficiently ventilated.

TO FRANCIS LOUGHNAN (II)

December 21, 1882.

Dear Canon Loughnan,

Few days pass without my having letters from strangers, young and old, men and women, on the subject of the Catholic religion.

I answer them that it is the one and only true and safe religion. But as to the personal duty of the particular applicant I decline to determine it at a distance, and advise him to address some one in his own neighbourhood. If I know a priest who has experience of converts, I name him.

This, I have no doubt, is what I wrote in the cases which you bring before me.[1]

As to the Clifton High School, I am not aware that any special religious creed to the exclusion of others is professed in that Institution.[2]

I am, Yours very truly, John H. Card. Newman.

The Very Rev. Canon Loughnan.

TO IGNATIUS GRANT, S.J.

The Oratory, Dec. 23, 1882.

Dear Father Grant,

I owe you and your Fathers at Bristol an apology in neglecting last July, when I advised a young Protestant woman to ask direction of one of your Fathers, to write to you and to tell you what I had done. I can only say in excuse that I had so many letters to write that I got confused, and in this way I forgot to do what was evidently the proper course.

Had I written, I should have said that I was pleased with her letter, but that I had no right to suppose that I could form a judgment so trustworthy as one who had actually seen her, and who had, as your Fathers have, such experience of inquirers and converts.

If I have given you any trouble, I am very sorry and ask your pardon — and, wishing you the best blessings of the Sacred Season, am,

Most truly yours, John H. Card. Newman.[3]

[1] See letters of 6 July to Emily Fortey and 4 Sept. to Marion A. Tucker.
[2] Already in Sept. the *Wiltshire Protestant Beacon* published a letter from 'A Shareholder' of the Clifton High School for Girls, saying that there was a Ritualist influence in the school and that some of the girls had been 'in communication with Cardinal Newman.'
James Wilson, Vice-President of the Clifton High School for Girls replied on 29 Sept. in a letter published in the Bristol *Mercury and Post*. He rebutted the anonymous letter's accusations as to the religious teaching in the school, and admitted that two girls had written to Newman, and that he had answered them.
See also letter of 12 Feb. 1883 to Henry Fortey.
[3] Ignatius Grant, who went up to St John's College, Oxford in 1838 and became a Catholic in 1841, replied on 24 Dec., 'We should have welcomed any one coming to us; with even your Eminence's name, and without an express recommendation in writing.' Grant added, 'the sight of your Eminence's handwriting has given me great joy.
Thrice only since I left Oxford, has it been in my power to express all the gratitude I owe you: once at Littlemore, 1842: once at Edgebaston, — and once, at the funeral of "dear Mr

TO CHARLES BOWDEN

Dec 26. 1882

My dear Charles

I am grieved to see your Aunt's death in the paper.[1] I hope it has not taken your Mother by surprise. Of course one cannot help fearing at first sight, that the fire at Hampton Court, was a shock to her.

Say to your Mother and Emily every thing kind from me. I hope she bears the rough season well and with my best Christmas wishes and prayers for all of you I am

Yours affectionately John H. Card. Newman

TO EDWARD NEWMAN MOZLEY[2]

Dec 27 1882

Christmas Day is past,
and the New Year is coming
God bless you,
My dear Edward N. Mozley,
and Papa and Mama,
at [and] all of you at home,
in the New Year,
and through all years

J. H. Card. Newman

TO RICHARD GRAY

[31 December 1882]

Your very kind letter has touched me very much, and especially your saying that 'hundreds' of your communion are of one mind with you in praying for me[3] No mercy can be shown me from above greater than that of my exciting the religious sympathy of those whom I have not seen, and of so many such. It is a token, most consolatory, that, in spite of our present

Hope Scott:" — but in all those forty years of my life spent, as a son of St Ignatius, in many lands, and various ministries — my heart has "gone forth" at even the mention of your name.
    In France '"Ours" [fellow Jesuits] used to say Père Felix Pere de Pouleroy — and others "Mon Père parlez nous de Lui."'!'

[1] Mrs Bowden's sister, Lady Emily Ward, died on 19 Dec. She lived at Hampton Court, where on 14 Dec. a serious fire destroyed 'grace and favour' apartments at the east end of the Palace.
    [2] Edward (1875–1950) was the fourth child of John Rickards Mozley.
    [3] Richard Gray, Methodist minister at Darlington, wrote on 30 Dec., 'Your presence is a great joy to us in this country; and we are so thankful that, by the books you have written, as well as by the known life which you have lived, you belong to us as a Country and as Christians for all time.
    Believe me, your Excellence, hundreds of Methodists are of one mind in my prayer that the New Year may be to you full of peace and richest blessing.'

warring and our cruel divisions there is a future to the Church when as in the beginning there shall be one fold and one shepherd. May He, Who alone can a second time fulfil his promise to us, hasten the time[1]

TO THOMAS MOZLEY

[End of 1882?]

Dear T. M.

I ought to have reminded myself that before I became a Catholic I hindered you from becoming one. This leads me to say that I think my second judgment in all respects a better than the first[2]

Yours affectionately

TO AN UNKNOWN CORRESPONDENT

[1883]

I thank you for the interest you take in my hymn. I am fully conscious that every part of it admits of improvement, but tastes are so diverse as regards poetical composition that I fear lest, in pleasing one reader, I should displease another.

TO AN UNKNOWN CORRESPONDENT

[1883]

I beg to convey to you our thanks for the great and kind zeal you have shown in the success of the concert lately held in behalf of our Mission Schools. All I hear of it shows that the success would not have been achieved, nay could not have been attempted, without you; and that, not only from an ordinary expression of interest, and an ordinary assistance and support on your part but by real efforts for us which we had no reason to expect, as having no claim on them.

Accept then this acknowledgment from us, poor as it is, and believe —

J H N

TO ALBERT HENRY SMYTH

[1883]

Card N. presents his compliments to Mr Smyth and thanks him for the compliment he has paid him in asking for his literary aid in the Magazine Shakesperiana.

[1] Already on 31 Oct. Gray wrote that for many years he had been wanting to express his gratitude to Newman 'for the good which I have received from the reading of your books, and the singing of your hymns, both in public and private devotion. Your Sermons have helped me to know my heart better than I could have done but for the help from them received . . .'
[2] Tom Mozley wanted to become a Catholic in 1843, after seeing the Catholic Church in Normandy that summer. cf. the later chapters of his *Reminiscences Chiefly of Oriel College and the Oxford Movement*, II.

He is sorry that, considering his advanced age, it is not in his power to avail himself of it.[1]

TO THE MARQUIS OF RIPON

[1883]

My dear Lord Ripon,

I have no special reason for troubling you with this letter, which is only to say that you are very often in my thoughts, and especially of late when I have fancied you had some anxious matters on your hands.[2]

That you are doing a great work in India, none of us doubts, and it is selfish to complain you are not doing work at home, but be sure that Catholics here all feel how much you would be doing for us if your duty did not call you away. Especially do I often think how many young men there are, of position and with a future, who are sadly [deprived] of what only you can do for them.

TO LORD BLACHFORD

Bm January 2. 1883

My dear Blachford,

A happy New Year to you and Lady Blachford.

And to your two Sisters who sent me so kind a message by you, which from some momentary stupidity, I did not return.

The younger Bellasis has written out for you the Numbers and first notes of the two Trios.[3]

I am very much pleased, and they are very proud, that the music was so grateful to you

Yours affly John H. Card. Newman

TO GEORGE T. EDWARDS

Jan 2. 1883

Dear Mr Edwards

Your kind present has come.[4] I knew, when young, Mr Erskine's first publications well. I thought them able and persuasive; but I found the more

---

[1] *Shakespeareana* was a monthly magazine, devoted exclusively to Shakespearean literature, which began in Nov. 1883, published by Leonard Scott and Co., New York and Philadelphia. It lasted until 1893. Smyth, aged twenty, was one of a small group of founders, and edited the magazine until 1886.

[2] Lord Ripon's liberal policy as Viceroy aroused the fierce opposition of most of the English in India. He had written on 12 Dec. 1882 to thank for W. Palmer's *Notes of a Visit to the Russian Church*, 'I feel greatly your kind remembrance of me . . . I trust that you are well and that you sometimes think of me in your prayers.'

[3] H. L. Bellasis copied the Beethoven trios which had been played for Lord Blachford when he visited Newman on 11 Dec.

[4] Edwards wrote on 29 Dec. 1882 that he wished to send Newman *Letters of Thomas Erskine of Linlathen*, Edinburgh 1878. This was the third edition, in one volume. Only a very few pages have been cut, chiefly those about Erskine's last days.

thoughtful Evangelicals of Oxford did not quite trust them. This was about the year 1823 or 1824. A dozen years later I wrote against them or one of them, in the Tracts for the Times, and certainly my impression still is that their tendency is antidogmatic, substituting for faith in mysteries the acceptance of a 'manifestation' of divine attributes which was level to the reason. But I speak from memory.[1]

I have always heard him spoken of with great respect as a man of earnest and original mind.

Thank you for your notice of Miss Gutch's death. I have known her all but about 60 years. She was of great assistance to me in my first curacy[2]

I have left out above my sure anticipation of the pleasure I shall gain, and the profit, by reading Mr Erskine's Letters.

The best wishes of the New Year to you. Thank you for your two beautiful cards.

Sincerely Yours John H Card. Newman

P.S.   I again sincerely apologise for my mistakes in writing, but I cannot help it

FROM WILLIAM EWART GLADSTONE

Hawarden Castle, Chester.
Dec. 31. 1882

My dear Cardinal Newman

Mr MacColl tells me that you intend to have a copy of the New Edition, now in preparation, of Sir W. Palmer's work on the Church.[3] I pray for myself the honour of being allowed to supply your Eminence with one, and I shall infer your consent from a silence, which I hope this note will not cause your Eminence to break.

I read the work of 'Deacon' Palmer, so kindly sent me, with the utmost interest:[4] and with the supposition that a delicate respect for persons may have prevented its publication at the time when it was composed. I remain with deep respect, Your Eminence's

Most faithful & obedient W E Gladstone

---

[1] *Tract 73*, 'On the Introduction of Rationalistic Principles into Religion,' reprinted in *Ess.* I, pp. 30–99.

[2] See letter of 17 Sept. 1882 to Edwards.

[3] See letter of 6 Dec. 1882 to Copeland.

[4] Gladstone had acknowledged this earlier: '10, Downing Street, Whitehall. Nov 9. 1882 My dear Cardinal Newman

Let me thank Your Eminence most warmly for sending me Palmer's Visit to the Russian Church. It is I am certain full of interest in itself, and it is most valuable as a gift from you.

I have stolen a short time from business to-day to read your Preface, for the temptation was irresistible. It leaves upon me an impression, which agrees with the impression left by seeing him in 1866 at Rome, that in the course of his life both character and mind had been considerable modified. I cling to the hope of yet seeing you some day or other, by some happy turn of fortune, and I could then readily explain my meaning. Till then allow me to remain Your Eminence's

Most sincerely & faithfully W E Gladstone'

TO WILLIAM EWART GLADSTONE

Birmingham Jany 3. 1883

My dear Mr Gladstone

I beg to be allowed to offer you and all yours my best wishes for the New Year, and to express my earnest hope that it will not impose on you anxieties and labours so great as you have lately had.

And I accept with great pleasure the present you propose to make me of Sir W. Palmer's work

As to his namesake's Journal, I felt keenly the difficulty you touch upon But on inquiry I found that Count Pratasoph, Mouravieff, Koutnevich, were all dead — also the Metropolitan Philaret.[1] Princess Dolgorouky is still alive — I should have sent her the Volume, if I could make sure of her identity, but I was afraid of a mistake.[2] But since Mr Palmer was quite a stranger to her and the others, I could not think they told him any secrets, and some of them, on his leaving for England, hoped he would publish. I cut out every sentence which had a personal bearing; the only difficulty I had was about Count Pratasoff's dancing;[3] but then I felt that he danced as an Aide-de camp, not as Vice Patriarch; and that the real difficulty was in the Count having duties which were inconsistent with each other. I am glad that you have found the Volume interesting

Most sincerely Yours John H Card. Newman

The Rt Hon. William E. Gladstone M P

TO JOHN HENRY PARKER

Birmingham Jany 3. 1883

Dear Mr Parker

Accept from me my best wishes for the New Year. I hope that this weather suits you, moist as it is

As to your suggestion, I have no books to give.[4] It is now nearer 40 than 30 years since I gave them all to this Oratory, and have no more ownership in them, than I have in one of the Oxford Libraries.

But I doubt whether they would much increase Dr Pusey's collection, even if added — for the greater part would prove to be duplicates of his books.

[1] See letters of 16 Dec. 1881 and 1 Feb. 1882 to R. W. Blackmore.
[2] See *Notes of a Visit to the Russian Church*, Chapters LXXX and LXXXV.
[3] The Russian Church was governed by the Holy Synod, presided over by a lay procurator, appointed by the Emperor. Princess Galitsin 'complained of scandal arising from the present state of things, when the Church is governed by a layman, Count Pratasoff, who (respectable as he may be) dances the Mazurka . . .' Op. cit. p. 392.
[4] J. H. Parker, the Oxford bookseller and from 1870 Keeper of the Ashmolean Museum, wrote from there on 22 Dec., suggesting that Newman should bequeath his library to be united with that of Pusey in the projected Pusey House at Oxford. Parker remarked that 'I could almost make a catalogue of them [the two libraries] by going through my old ledgers of from twenty to fifty years ago.'

The proposed plan of a Memorial seems very good — and if congregational donations can be secured, I suppose, the sum named will not be difficult to raise.

Repeating my good wishes, I am, My dear Mr Parker,

Sincerely Yours John H Card. Newman

TO HENRY WILLIAMS MOZLEY

Jany 5. 1883

My dear Harry

I am too old for controversy, and I cannot write without pain, and I have not seen the Times.[1] But I have spoken to a friend on the subject you wish looked into, and he will, I hope, write something — and I will take your letter of yesterday, as a text for a few remarks.

I want to know if it is 'the Bishops' Catechism.' Some one tells me that it is not. We have many catechisms, e.g. that 'of Perseverance' — again, the Catechism 'of the Council of Trent' addressed 'ad Parochos', i.e. to suggest topics and to be a series of lessons to *preachers*. They are only improprié called catechisms — they are not learned by heart — they are not in the hands of the clergy, but are *books* for the laity. True catechisms are not necessarily addressed to those who *read* — but come to the people thro' the parish priest.

I am told, though I cannot vouch for it, that the catechism quoted in the Papers, is the work of an English priest, published years ago, at a time when Ireland was comparatively quiet;[2] and was after a while circulated in that country, and, since no religious book could be published without the imprimatur of authority, having in its first page the name of the Archbishop.

This may be the case with the catechism in question — *or it may not* — I don't know — but, one thing is certain that, be it a formula from the Bishops or a private publication, it must tell the truth, and the whole truth, and could not as a matter of conscience on the part of its authors, suppress what (if I understand you) you want suppressed.

You want them to say that murder is 'taking away another's life', leaving out 'unjustly'. This is impossible for them to do. The word 'unjustly' is the defence of *legal* executions. Its absence reduces *them* to acts of murder. But you will answer 'Why not say "taking away *illegally*?"' I reply that no word

[1] C. P. Reichel, Rector of Trim and Dean of Clonmacnois complained in *The Times* (2 Jan. 1883), p. 8, of 'a halfpenny manual by the Rev. Father Furniss, which bears Cardinal Cullen's imprimatur,' *What Every Christian must Know and Do*. On p. 23 of the most recent edition, there was a definition, 'Murder, or unjustly taking away another's life.' Reichel complained that therefore 'Justice or injustice are made the measure of the nature and of the guilt of murder,' and that the Irish peasants were being led astray. On 1 Jan. H. W. Mozley had discussed this subject when he visited Newman, who had said 'such things ought to be answered.' Mozley wrote on 3 Jan., 'The word "unjust" raises at once questions which an uneducated population can hardly help perverting.'
[2] John Furniss, born near Sheffield in 1809, died in 1865. His catechism *What Every Christian must Know and Do*, Derby 1856, was published in Dublin in 1857. He was a Redemptorist, renowned for his lurid missions and books for children.

but 'unjustly' covers the large exception which is still to be named. That exception is *war*. The killing in war far surpasses the killing by law — and the question is how far is it sin, how far not. 'Unjustly' is the word absolutely necessary here. A just war is not a succession of murders, an unjust war is. When we think of the first Napoleon's wars what an awful thought is this! But it would [be] a strange manual of Christian doctrine which implied by silence that all wars were unjust. This is but part of [a] large question. As to the Irish, do they know English? can they read? As to the poor Irish of the West I think they have had far too little catechising than too much.

Yrs affly John H Card. Newman

N B There has been a long while a complaint against a certain great man now dead, that he would not have school in the west.[1] It is not catechisms, but the want of catechisms, which has been the evil.

N B The *Standard* this morning talks of 'the *story* of the Deluge'.

TO LORD BRAYE

Jany 7. 1883

My dear Lord Braye

I send you the best wishes of the Sacred Season.

Don't suppose I am forgetting what interests you so much. I am expecting to hear from Rome soon — but, if I do not, I shall write to Paris[2]

Most truly Yours John H Card. Newman

The Lord Braye

TO WILLIAM CLIFFORD, BISHOP OF CLIFTON

Birmingham Jany 7. 1883

My dear Lord

I hope I am giving you the trouble of nothing more than a few lines. The inclosed contains an Article from a man of great consideration, and it seems clear that before long his argument must be met.[3]

Can you tell me, are we bound to the titles of the books of Scripture more than to the notices of time and place at the end of some of St Paul's

---

[1] John MacHale, Archbishop of Tuam, died in 1881. He opposed the 'mixed' National Schools.

[2] See letters of 10 Nov. 1882 and 9 Feb. 1883 to Lord Braye.

[3] J. Derek Holmes and Robert Murray in their edition of Newman's article *On the Inspiration of Scripture*, London 1967, p. 28, explain that it 'was apparently a reply to an article said to be called "History, Criticism and the Roman Catholic Church", which commented on the English edition, just published, of Ernest Renan's *Recollections of my Youth*.' This unidentified article Newman now sent to Bishop Clifford, cf. *Recollections of my Youth*, London 1883, pp. 255–64.

Epistles, which are found in the Protestant version and left out in the Catholic?

I believe we are not bound to consider that St Paul wrote the Epistle to the Hebrews, though of course the writer, whoever he was, was inspired.

The Council of Trent altered, I think, the title 'the Psalms of David' into the vaguer form 'Psalterium Davidicum'.

Is it necessary to hold that Solomon wrote Ecclesiastes?

I am not proposing to you to answer all these questions but can you refer me to any theologian who treats of them?

As you have entered upon this grave subject by the very interesting Paper which appeared lately in the Dublin Review, I am sanguine that you can help me[1]

I am, with all kind wishes to you for the New Year

Your Lordship's very faithful servant John H Card. Newman[2]

The Rt Revd The Bishop of Clifton

TO ROBERT ORNSBY

Jany 7. 1883

My dear Ornsby

I return to you and Mrs Ornsby most heartily your congratulations on the sacred season — and I am sure of your letting me excuse my delay in doing so on the score of my difficulty in writing, which shows itself, first, in my being obliged to write very slowly, and secondly, in my soon tiring.

My head is certainly weaker than it was — for I cannot follow the complications existing between the Catholic University and the Royal. I am speaking seriously in thus speaking, my hope being that what has been gained is to have secured the thin face of the wedge.

I do think Scratton very unfortunate, but what could be done? If I understand the money grant was limited to a certain number of Professors, and they were chosen, if I understand, by what was virtually competition. How could he make a good fight against Testimonials.[3]

I rejoice that Hope Scott's Life is so near publication — you have indeed spent labour upon it. I wonder what *my* letters in it are about.

Yours affly John H. Card. Newman

---

[1] 'The Days of the Week, and the Works of Creation', *D R* (April 1881), pp. 311–332. See letter of 20 Jan. to Clifford.

[2] Bishop Clifford replied on 9 Jan., 'Undoubtedly, as you say, it is clear that before long the argument set forth in the article "History, Criticism and the Roman Catholic Church" must be met. I am not acquainted with any book where it is fully and fairly treated. The points authoritatively decided by the Church regarding the nature and extent of the Inspiration of Scripture are not numerous. . . .' Clifford promised to obtain information from Archbishop Errington. See letter of 20 Jan. to Clifford.

[3] See second note to letter of 7 Nov. 1882 to Bishop Woodlock.

TO MISS M. R. GIBERNE

Jany. 8. 1883

My dear Sister Pia

Of course I grant leave for you to translate the Sermon, and am pleased that your Sisters should wish it.

I said the three Masses on Christmas Day.

It is a great pleasure to find you are so much better — but don't presume

I hope Palmer's book is selling well. With the best New Year's wishes to all your Sisters as well as to you

Yours affecty J. H. Card. Newman

TO JANE MOZLEY

Jany 8. 1883

My dear Jane

Thank you for your good wishes for the new year, which I gladly return to you, and for your Card, which is very pretty, more than most which I have seen, and what an Artist I should think, would call clever, the perspective is so well managed. I inclose a contrast, which, if not clever, seems humourous.

Thank you for your inquiries. I am very well, but very weak. Mr Woodgate, some time before he died, said he had on him the 'Three Warnings' of the Poem — he was deaf, blind, and lame. In some measure I am in his case.[1]

All best wishes of the New year to your Aunts and your Uncle from me

Yours affecty John H. Card. Newman

TO J. P. TAYLOR

Birmingham Jany 8. 1883

Dear Sir

I have not seen your republication of my letter in the Register.[2]

I have no doubt at all how kindly intentioned it is towards me, and I thank you for that intention.

With the best wishes to you of the New Year

I am Very truly Yours John H. Card. Newman[3]

[1] See letter of 27 Nov. 1881 to Du Boulay.
[2] Taylor sent Newman's letter of 19 Nov. 1865 to the Editor of the *Weekly Register*, where it was printed in that same periodical on 6 Jan. 1883, p. 27. This was by way of answer to a sentence of a leading article in the *Standard* a few days earlier. Speaking of the infidelity to come it remarked: 'The Church of England, says Newman, is the only barrier left in Christendom capable of arresting it.'
[3] Newman made a Memorandum:

'January 7 1883

The Anglican Church a "bulwark of Catholic *truth*" No, I did not say this in the first sentence of my "Difficulties" — but the only *political* bulwark of the dogmatic principle.

In the Apologia I was speaking of "Catholic truth", and I called it, not a bulwark but a

TO MARGARET DE LISLE

Jany 12. 1883

Dear Miss de Lisle

I hope I did not misunderstand you. You must allow me to be very stingy of my time. I am so busy, have so few hours in the day, and my brain works so slowly and I am so soon tired, that I am sorry to say that I cannot give more than an hour for the pleasure of seeing you and your young charge.

I say this, because it made me anxious to hear that you had secured a room at the Plough and Harrow

Very truly Yours John H Card. Newman

P S   Fr Ryder wishes me here to send the blessing on 'Alice and her children' which he forgot[1]

TO DR GORDON

Birmingham Jan. 14. 1883

Cardinal Newman begs to assure Dr Gordon that he has not, as Dr Gordon believes, 'a strong opinion' on the Affirmation Bill, and that he should not have written a line about it, unless an appeal had been made to him.[2]

As to the Acts of the Vatican Council he believes that Messrs Burns and Oates could get them for Dr Gordon.

TO WILLIAM CLIFFORD, BISHOP OF CLIFTON

Jany 20. 83

My dear Lord

Thank the Archbishop for me; I sent at once for the book he recommended.[3] It rejoices me to see in the Dublin the account given of the criticisms passed on your late Article on Gen 1 It shows you have succeeded in opening the door, tho' the critics do not like the particular way in which you have

breakwater. I denied that that Church was more [than] a great wall as regards Catholic Truth, a "serviceable breakwater" against errors more fundamental than its own "Letter to Pusey" and "Apologia".
On the other hand enumerating the fair side of Angl. [Anglicanism] I certainly say that its Church is a bulwark, but what kind of bulwark — "A *political* bulwark of the (dogmatic) principle" Difficulties p 1' See also *Apo.* p. 342; *Diff* II, pp. 9–11.

[1] This refers to Margaret de Lisle's sister Alice, wife of the hon. Arthur Strutt.
[2] See letters of 20 Sept. 1881 to the Duke of Norfolk and end of April 1883 to W. M. J. Ring.
[3] See letter of 7 Jan. to Clifford, who wrote on 18 Jan. that Archbishop Errington recommended 'on the question of what Catholics are bound to believe in regard to the inspiration and interpretation of Scripture' T. J. Lamy *Introductio in Sacram Scripturam,* two volumes, third edition, Malines 1877.

opened it. They seem all to imply, some avow, that you *have* opened it. We need not seek to shake ourselves free from science any longer, since you have suggested an interpretation which ignores science altogether[1]

Very sincerely Yours John H. Card. Newman

The Rt Rev the Bp of Clifton

TO MISS CHISHOLM

[27 January ? 1883]

Dear Miss Chisholm

I enclose a cheque for your good works[2]

Yours very truly John H. Card. Newman

TO LORD BLACHFORD

Birmingham, Jan. 29th. 1883.

My dear Blachford,

I think you told me your birthday was the 31st. I daresay I ought to have known it without your telling. If I am now right, I hope this will hit upon the day, tho' I don't know where you are. Yours anticipates mine just by three weeks, and I anticipate yours by 10 years.[3] I wish you many happy returns of yours, as the phrase is — but such bad days seem coming on that it makes one sad to look forward, I suppose the evil which is so threatening, will not move so quick as one fancies.

I have not for a long while heard of my good friend Mr. Bartholomew, I hope he is flourishing.

Yours affectionately, John H. Card: Newman.

[1] Bishop Clifford in 'The Days of the Week, and the Works of Creation,' *D R* (April 1881), urged that the first verses of *Genesis* were a religious hymn not a scientific treatise. John S. Vaughan, younger brother of Herbert Vaughan, published a reply 'Bishop Clifford's Theory of the Days of Creation', *D R* (Jan. 1883), pp. 32–47. He summarised foreign Catholic criticisms, and ended by complaining that Bishop Clifford 'razes the citadel to the ground, and . . . compliments himself on having put it beyond the assaults of the enemy.'
Clifford replied to Newman on 5 Feb., 'What you say about the advantage of having opened the door to discussion regarding the relation of scripture to science is very true. I shall try and force the question on, for there are really a large number of the rising generation to whom this question is the chief difficulty as regards faith . . . Everybody seems afraid to approach it, but it must be approached . . .' See letter of 7 Feb. to Clifford.
[2] Miss Chisholm was a daughter of Caroline Chisholm (1808–77), 'the emigrants' friend,' whose chief charitable undertaking was the provision of homes for emigrants to Australia. She became a Catholic in 1850 and her last years were spent in England. Miss Chisholm also became a Catholic, and her sister married Edmund Dwyer Gray, Irish M.P. and Lord Mayor of Dublin in 1880, when he raised a fund of £180,000 for Irish famine relief. Among Miss Chisholm's good works appears also to have been the relief of distress in Ireland.
[3] Lord Blachford was born on 31 Jan. 1811.

TO W. J. COPELAND

Bm. Jany 31. 1883

My dearest Copeland

They tell me you are not well. I don't want to trouble or teaze you — but tell me in one line that they are wrong[1]

Yours affectly John H Card. Newman

TO ARTHUR SANDES GRIFFIN

Bm Jany 31. 1883

My dear Canon Griffin

I am very glad to hear that the dear Bishop's 'Allocutions' are to be published, as I know how valuable they will be and I feel the honour you intend me in wishing me to introduce them to the public.[2]

The only thought which reconciles me to the seeming ungraciousness of asking you to let me decline, is my perfect knowledge that his addresses do not require it, and that there would be some impertinence, as I feel it, in one who is neither Bishop nor Irishman presuming to ask a hearing for Dr Moriarty.

But my real reason is this — I have been obliged to make and to keep the rule, of abstaining from what in itself would often be so grateful to my feelings, from the impossibility of drawing the line, — and now I cannot accept such invitations without hurting near friends whose kind wishes have not met with a due response.

I hope you will understand and pardon me and believe me to be

Most truly yours John H Card Newman

TO MONSIGNOR MACCHI

Birmingham Jany 31. 1883

My dear Rt Rev Monsignor Macchi

I recommend to your kind attention, of which I have had so many instances, the wife and daughter of the well known Egyptologist M. le Page Renouf, both of them highly educated ladies, Miss Renouf having distinguished herself in Greek and Latin Literature at the University of Cambridge, and Mrs Renouf moreover being a relative of the late Cardinal Reisach

[1] Copeland replied on 1 Feb. that he had been ailing, but was taking care of himself.
[2] On 29 Jan. Griffin sent Newman the proofs of *Allocutions to the Clergy and Pastorals of the Late Right Rev. Dr. Moriarty Bishop of Kerry*, edited by Arthur Sandes Griffin and John Coffey, Dublin 1884. Griffin asked Newman to write a preface, and renewed his request on 3 Feb. See letter of 5 March to him.

Is it possible to obtain for them an audience with the Holy Father before they leave Rome, which will be at an early date?

You will kindly excuse my writing in English, with which, however, I believe you are familiar, but my own poor acquaintance with Italian would cause me to take more days in writing than my friends remain in Rome

I am, My dear Monsignor, Your faithful humble Servant

John H. Card. Newman

The Rt Rev. Monsignor Macchi &c &c

TO MRS WILSON

Febr. 1, 1883

My dear Mrs Wilson,

Let me at the end of the Christmas Season, instead of the beginning, send you my best good wishes and prayers for you.

May God's choicest blessings be upon you, now and ever

Very sincerely Yrs John H. Card. Newman.

TO LORD BRAYE

Febr. 4. 1883

My dear Lord Braye

I have thought of you continually and have been impatient at having nothing to tell you. I wish I could be sure that Mr Grisell's report is later than last autumn.[1]

I have reason to think that a foreign nuntio would feel a delicacy in interfering in the ecclesiastical affairs of another country, and this leads me to say that I had better not go beyond writing a letter of introduction, and you then would naturally converse with him, and be able to get advice without his seeming to be intruding in England.

If you were going to Rome, you would necessarily go through Paris, and when at Paris you would naturally call on the Nuntio. This was my first idea. Since, I have felt or fancied he was too busy to like to contemplate more than a visit from you, which in its form would be casual

Your Lordship's faithful Servt John H. Card. Newman

The Lord Braye

P.S.   I will send you the letter of introduction, whenever you wish to have it. I agree that joint addresses don't answer.

[1] Hartwell de la Garde Grissell, who had been a papal chamberlain since 1869, accompanied Lord Braye and Bishop Hedley on 13 April 1883, when they put to Leo XIII the case for removing the ban on Catholics attending the English universities. See letter of 2 May 1883 to Lord Braye. For the report of the previous autumn see letter of 15 Nov. 1882 to Lord Braye.

TO J. R. BLOXAM

Febr 6. 83

My dear Bloxam

Thank you for your anticipation of my birthday

And for your offer of the Littlemore drawings; I will not accept it, for it would be bringing them into a house, which, when I am gone, has no one who knows Littlemore

I shall rejoice to have your brother's book — pray tell him so.[1]

Yrs affectly J H Card. Newman

Tell Plumer I constantly think of him and wish there was a chance of my seeing him again.[2]

TO WILLIAM CLIFFORD, BISHOP OF CLIFTON

Bm Febr. 7. 1883

My dear Bishop Clifford,

I rejoice to hear that you are turning your thoughts to the question of Inspiration.[3] It leads me to ask whether you would give me your judgment on one or two propositions I have lately been putting down. I have no confidence in myself — and should like to see what a trustworthy theologian, such as you or Dr Errington, would say to them.[4]

A Jesuit work on Judith and Esther has this morning been sent me. It seems to me obscure, but this may be owing to my imperfect reading of French.

He calls Judith a 'tableau', and considers it to have 'scènes' — and to be a lesson on the great war between good and evil — though still historically true. Does he mean 'a narration *founded* on facts?' Would you like to see the book? Perhaps it has been sent to you[5]

---

[1] Matthew Holbeche Bloxam, *The Principles of Gothic Ecclesiastical Architecture . . . ,* eleventh edition, three volumes, London 1882. It was sent accompanied by a note: 'With the respectful Homage of the Author Matthew Holbeche Bloxam F.S.A. and with the affectionate regards of his Brother John Rouse Bloxam These volumes are humbly offered For the acceptance of His Eminence, Cardinal Newman on the anniversary of His Birthday Feb. 21. A.D. 1883.'

[2] Charles John Plumer, Fellow of Oriel College 1821–30, was Vicar of Iford with Kingston, near Lewes, 1868–82. Bloxam wrote on 23 Feb. that he called on him in his retirement at Brighton on 20 Feb., 'by invitation — and was kindly received. He was much gratified by your message. We talked of course much about you . . . His right arm quite paralysed.' See letter of 10 June 1883 to him.

[3] See letter of 5 Feb. from Bishop Clifford, quoted in note to that of 20 Jan. to him.

[4] Bishop Clifford replied on 10 Feb. that he and Archbishop Errington would gladly perform this service. See letter of 25 Sept. 1883 to Bishop Clifford.

[5] Henri Demante, S.J., *Entretiens sur les Livres de Judith et d' Esther,* Paris 1883. Of the *Book of Judith* Demante said, p. 2, 'C'est donc un drame ou tout doit exprimer la guerre, le combat . . .

Empressons-nous de dire que ce drame n'est pas une fiction . . .'

On p. 3 'La première scène' is spoken of, and in the preface, p. x, a 'tableau.'

Bishop Clifford replied on 10 Feb. that the Jesuit censorship having passed Demante's

I have long had your brother on my prayer list. It grieved me very much to hear how serious his illness was. I have not seen him, since I saw yourself and him at Prior Park in 1845[1]

I am sorry to hear your great loss in Mr Leeming[2]

Very sincerely Yours John H Card. Newman

The Bishop of Clifton

TO GEORGE T. EDWARDS

Bm Febr 8. 1883

Dear Mr Edwards

Thank you for Mr Fisher's Pamphlet — and, when you see him, be so kind as to thank him from me for the tone in which he has written about me[3]

If it did not tire my hand and my head to write, I could say much upon what he has said, which is not always correct. The years during which I was much known to Oxford Evangelicals was from 1821 to 1824. I had a great admiration of Missionary exertion, and then I knew (distantly, I forget their names) one or two who were to be sent out by the Church Missionary Society. I recollect meeting them at Dr McBride's or Mr Hill's, I forget which, but I think I was *never* at one of Mr Hill's Edmund Hall parties — I can't be sure. I had no shock to my views, till I became Curate of St Clement's in 1824. Dr Hawkins, the Vicar of St Mary's was good enough to look at my first sermon, and said, 'This is not true — you divide men sharply into converted and unconverted — whereas there are degrees of religion innumerable.' In consequence he gave me Sumner's 'Apostolical Preaching' which had a great effect on me. Then when I became deep in Parish work I made a memorandum in a Private Journal, 'It is true — the Evangelical theory won't work in fact'

From that time I became less and less in concord with Mr Hill and his friends — and without giving up much of their belief, I grew so high church that Samuel Wilberforce who in 1826 heard me preach at St Clement's, went away wondering. And so it was, when I came to St Mary's — but still I was so far evangelical, that several years before 1830 Mr Hill asked me to be joint Secretary with him to the Oxford Church Missionary Association, to which, as well as to the Bible Society, I was a subscriber. I consented, and in

book was a guarantee that its opinions were tenable, and asked to see it. He wrote again on 10 March that Demante seemed to hold *Judith* to be a narrative founded on fact, with invented incidents inserted.

[1] This was the Bishop's only surviving brother, Major General Sir Henry Hugh Clifford, who died on 12 April 1883. See diary for 29 Nov. 1845.

[2] This was Bishop Clifford's friend, John George Leeming 'a great benefactor of the Church' who died in London on 23 Jan.

[3] On 7 Feb. Edwards sent Newman a copy of John Cowley Fisher's Ellerton Prize Essay of fifty years before, privately printed 1882, *The Death of Christ a Propitiatory Sacrifice*, with the addition of an introduction in which he attacked the Tractarians for not preaching sufficiently the doctrine of the Atonement. Edwards sent the pamphlet without Fisher's knowledge. See letter of 10 March to him.

a little while (in 1830) with a sincere wish (among other things) to increase the subscriptions, I circulated in Oxford a pamphlet begging Oxford residents to belong to it, and by belonging *ipso facto* to destroy whatever there was sectarian in its working. On which the Association met, and, Dr Symons in the chair, voted me out of the Secretariship. I still subscribed to it for 4 years.[1]

I have never, thank God, thro' my life for one moment doubted that our Lord died for our sins instead of us; but I thought the *Atonement* was not the instrument of *conversion*, and I could not agree with Mr Erskine that it was a striking *manifestation* of God's justice — but that *how* it satisfied justice was a *mystery*[2]

Very truly Yours J H Card. Newman

P.S. I acted towards that young woman, as I act day after day to man or woman, young or old. I told her she must not change her religion now. She must wait and pray. The time had not come for her to have any thing to tell her father. I believe the Jesuits gave her the same advice. Her father said she might change, when 21.[3]

TO LORD BRAYE

Bm. Febr 9. 1883

Private

My dear Lord Braye

I don't know what is the proper thing to do, to seal a letter of introduction or to leave it open.

I have said in it, what is true, that you wish to employ yourself to serve the Church, if you were told how — for, if you *begin* to speak to great men with bringing forward any scheme, they are likely to shut up. I do not know any one who is likely to assist you at Rome — but (unless I am greatly mis-informed) Mgr di Rende has lived at St Edmunds and speaks English.[4] He too will surely be able to tell you, *who* is most able to assist you at Rome. I am not at all sure that my name will be a service to you in some quarters.

Very sincerely Yours John H Card. Newman

The Lord Braye

P.S. If Mgr di Rende mentioned any names at Rome for you to address, if they were such as I thought would like a letter from me, I would write to

---

[1] *Apo.* pp. 8–10; *V.M.* II, pp. 1–17. John David Macbride, Principal of Magdalen Hall 1813–68, and John Hill, Vice-Principal of St Edmund Hall 1812–51, were leading Oxford Evangelicals, as was Benjamin Parsons Symons, Sub-Warden 1823–31, Warden 1831–71, of Wadham College.

[2] See *Tract* 73, *Ess.* II, pp. 65–7.

[3] Newman's letter of 6 July 1882 to Emily Fortey had been sent to *The Times* and published there on 31 Jan. See letter of 12 Feb. to Henry Fortey. J. C. Fisher had asked Edwards whether he knew any further particulars of the matter.

[4] St Edmund's College, Ware. See next letter.

them. Of course it would be a great gain, if the Nuncio became so far interested in you as to give you a letter himself.

TO ARCHBISHOP SICILIANO DI RENDE

not sent till   [9 February 1883]
Eccelenza
Monseigneur

I had the honour to meet your Eccelenza at Rome three years since, and this it is which makes me venture to address you now on a domestic subject which has long occupied my mind.[1]

For this purpose I wish to introduce to you a zealous Catholic my friend Lord Braye. He has lately spoken to me in confidence on certain matters bearing upon the interests of the Catholic Church in England, which have been a cause of anxiety to him and, as he says, to many others, moreover which ought to be known to the Holy Father. I have felt myself too old, and too little au courant with the affairs of the day to be able to aid him. When I looked round to find some quarter whence he might gain advice on which he might rely, it occurred to me that your Excelency was now so near us that he could without difficulty present himself to you personally, and that on the other hand you knew England well and the English language.[2]

May I ask of you to tell me, whether your time just now, was not too much occupied by your initial duties in France to be able to return a favourable answer to my request, or whether he might call upon your Excellency

TO LORD BRAYE

The Oratory Febr 12. 1883

My dear Lord Braye

I find that Propaganda is moving with reference to the question of the higher education. But I have no reasons for anticipating that much will come of the moving

Very truly Yours John H. Card. Newman

The Lord Braye

TO HENRY FORTEY

(copy)   Febr 12. 1883
Dear Sir

I thank you for your generous letter just arrived, and propose, in a day or two, according to your permission, to send it to the Times[3]

[1] See letters to Lord Braye in Nov. 1882 and Feb. 1883.
[2] The Archbishop, now Nuncio at Paris, had visited England to deal with a dispute about church property, some years earlier.
[3] Fortey wrote on 10 Feb. from 3 Belle Vue Villas, Westbury-on-Trym, near Bristol: 'Sir My daughter has just come to me in some agitation with the enclosed cutting from the

Pray assure your daughter that her distress which you speak of is quite unnecessary. I do not for an instant suppose that the publication of my letter to her was her doing.

As to the letter itself I should have given no sanction whatever to the proposal of her becoming a Catholic without your knowledge — but the question of her conversion was not the question before me. I put it off to a future day. I told her the change of religion was not to be made in a hurry; and I have had reason to think that you did not say much more. Also I believe that the Jesuits would not precipitate conversion more than you or myself

JHN

TO THE EDITOR OF THE TIMES

Febr. 14. 1883

for Publication

Cardinal Newman presents his Compliments to the Editor of the Times and requests of him admission into his columns of a sequel to the letter, written by the Cardinal, to which the Editor gave insertion some days since. It runs as follows:

To Cardinal Newman[1]

TO CARDINAL ALIMONDA

Febr 15. 1883

(copy) sent

Noli mirari, si ad Eminentiam Tuam his litteris confugio, sicut antehac; non enim mihi datum est vetulo et infirmo multos nosse in Româ, et vi benevolentiæ Tuæ ad Te trahor.

Times containing a copy of a letter you addressed to her [see last note to letter of 8 Feb. to G. T. Edwards]
She informs me that at the request of a Miss Tucker a young friend of hers also with Roman Catholic tendencies she gave her a copy of your letter   I know little or nothing of Miss Tucker but my daughter assures me that that young lady is quite incapable of so gross a breach of confidence as would be involved in handing over your letter for publication   I presume therefore that a copy was taken surreptitiously   I am strongly opposed to your creed and have done and will continue to do all I can to dissuade my daughter from joining your Church; but fair play is a jewel and I therefore write to apologise for my daughter's indiscretion in giving a copy of your letter to Miss Tucker and also to express my strong disgust at the conduct of those who have thought fit to publish it without the knowledge or consent either of my daughter or myself   You are at liberty to publish this letter if you please, but should you do so I request in the interest of my daughter that my signature may be suppressed   I am, Sir
Your obedt Servant   Henry Fortey'
cf. letter of 4 Sept. 1882 to Marion A. Tucker. Newman's letter of 6 July 1882 to Emily Fortey was sent to *The Times* by John K. Tucker, who signed himself 'Rector of Pettaugh, Suffolk,' and who dated his letter to *The Times* 'Bristol, Jan. 29.' John Kinsman Tucker had been Rector of Pettaugh since 1844.

[1] Henry Fortey's letter of 10 Feb. followed, with the address and signature omitted. See letter of 16 Feb. to him.

Nec peto ab Eminentia Tuâ quidquam quod Tibi molestum foret; non certè responsum ullum, hoc tantummodo in mente hoc tempore habeo, ut certiorem Te facere possim de re quâdam quæ ad me proxime attinet

Per errorem typographicum in editione cuiusdam libri mei anno 1874, visus sum dicere, contra cursum et scopum argumenti mei, plerosque auctores Antenicenos tenuisse Verbi æterni generationem (quam vocant) Temporalem. Hoc, quod praeposterum est, correxi in editione meâ anni 1881; et infeliciter accidit ut Professor quidam in Franciâ, M. Duchesne, usus sit in opusculo suo, non editione meâ anni 1881, sed anni 1874, in qua error iste locum habet.[1]

At Professeur Duchesne, in versione suâ Gallicâ, graviorem mihi injuriam intulit, ipse marte suo, non consulto quidem, sed imprudenter; nam, cum ego doctrinam S. Phæbadii, S. Ambrosii esse 'sounder' (*saniorem*) quam quorundam aliorum, ille vocem meam 'saniorem' transtulit in opusculo suo, (non 'plus saine', ut debuit, sed) 'nouvelle'.[2]

Profecto ego enixe in hoc opere meo et professus sum et sustinui innatam illam vim traditionis theologicae, ut vere existentis a principio; perfectionem et plenitudinem in hac materia Pontificum Antenicænorum, et integritatem in docendo Episcoporum in Conciliis Antiochenis congregatorum.

Spero, si vixero, in publicum proferre versionem Tractatus mei Latinam.[3]

TO CARDINAL BARTOLINI

[15 February 1883]

no letter was sent to Card Bartolini

Cum memorem servo animum benignitatis erga me Tuæ, credidi licitum esse mihi, bonâ veniâ Eminentiæ Tuæ, paucissimis verbis, rem quæ ad me pertinet, Tibi significare, ne id mihi imputetur, quod ego non merui.

Scripsi antehac de auctoribus Antenicenis, et de opinione quorumdam ex illis de temporali generatione Filii Dei. At M l'Abbé Duchesne scriptum quoddam in publicum edidit, in quo, meâ mente non omnino intellectâ credit me tenuisse Scriptores Antenicænos *omnes* illud praedicare de Filio quod postea judicatum esset hæresis.

Quare volo amicos meos Romæ certiores fieri manu meâ, me ita nec voluisse nec cogitasse.

Hæ lineæ ab Eminentia Tua responsum non exigunt.

[1] In *T.T.*, 1874, p. 181, Newman spoke of 'the early writers' and 'a large proportion of them' holding the doctrine of the Temporal *Gennesis* of the Son. In *T.T.*, second edition, revised, 1881, p. 227, he altered these phrases to 'certain early writers' and 'there are writers.' They had not yet been changed in the unrevised second edition, 1881.
Louis Duchesne quoted the passage where these phrases occur in 'Les Témoins Anténicéens du Dogme de la Trinité,' *Revue des sciences ecclésiastiques* (Dec. 1882), in the off-print of 1883, pp. 25–6.
[2] *T.T.* 1874, p. 251. The passage was omitted in the second edition, revised, p. 296; see also note there, p. 299 of 2 May 1883. The passage was still to be found in the second edition unrevised, p. 297. For Duchesne's quotation see loc. cit. p. 27.
[3] This was never done. Cardinal Alimonda sent a reassuring reply on 2 March.

Febr 15. 1883

Monsieur le Directeur

J'ai l'honneur d'accuser reception de l'essai de M. l'abbé Duchesne, tiré de la Revue des Sciences théologiques, et de vous en remercier.[1]

Dans la citation que M. l'abbé Duchesne m'a fait l'honneur de faire d'un de mes écrits je trouve une inexactitude qui dénature ma pensée. Il me fait dire (page 27) que 'Phæbadius et S. Ambroise en Occident et les deux Grégoire en Orient, inaugurent sur ce point une *nouvelle* littérature théologique.' J'ai écrit 'a s*ounder* theological literature' — *saniorem, plus saine*. Je serais très heureux que cette erreur fût corrigée; ⟨elle me paraît très grave⟩.

Je regrette aussi que M. l'Abbé Duchesne ait cité la première édition de mon livre; car dans la seconde (1881) j'ai fait deux changements dans le passage cité (page 27), afin de corriger deux erreurs typographiques

au lieu de: *les* écrivains de l'Orient etc, j'ai substitué: *various* writers, *diversi* scriptores, et plus bas, au lieu de: la language *des* écrivains antenicéens, j'ai écrit: of *certain quorundam*, de certains, ou de plusieurs écrivains, etc.[2]

Recevez, Monsieur le Directeur, l'assurance de ma haute consideration

John H.[3]

Febr 16. 1883

(copy) To Henry Fortey Esqr
Dear Sir

I have just received the inclosed letter from the Editor of the Times. I hope you will not object to sign your name with date and place on the copy of your own letter which I inclose, as the Editor wishes, and return it to me. If you do this, you will have to cut out your two last lines.

With apology for giving you the trouble

I am J H N

[1] This was an off-print of 'Les Témoins anténicéens du Dogme de la Trinité,' *Revue des sciences ecclésiastiques* (Dec. 1882), pp. 484–547. A letter at the beginning from M. D'Hulst, Rector of the Institut Catholique in Paris where Duchesne was Professor of Church History, explained that the article was a reply to attacks on his orthodoxy by Abbé Rambouillet in the same periodical. On this episode see the article 'Historiens du Christianisme' in *Dictionnaire d'Archéologie Chrétienne et de Liturgie*, VI, 2690–2.
Duchesne began by speaking of the development of doctrine, and went on to quote Petavius and Newman against Bossuet and Bull, on the inadequacy of statements of antenicene writers. He described Newman as 'l'homme de ce siècle qui a le plus étudié les Pères,' and as 'le patrologiste le plus autorisé de notre siècle.'
[2] See letter of this day to Cardinal Alimonda.
[3] This letter was translated into French by T. A. Pope, who ended it thus. For the sequel see letter of 16 April to Duchesne.

The Times's letter

Printing House Square Feb. 15. 1883

(copy)

The Editor of the Times declines to publish this letter, unless the writer signs it with his own name.[1]

TO J. R. BLOXAM

Febr 20. 1883

My dear Bloxam

Thank you for your birthday good wishes. I inclose a letter to your brother. I am much pleased to have his present, which came quite right[2]

Mr Hessey's Appeal is a very striking one, and full of thought.[3] It would seem to show a want of sympathy in what so deserves the respective attention of all religious men, as his Protest does, if I indulged the sad anticipations which I cannot help having. The present evil is a moral epidemic, and is likely to have its course. While it lasts, argument is useless. As he himself says, personal experience of the power of the Gospel is our great, or our only defence from scepticism. Argument is of little use. Beyond this inward evidence, an Infallible Church is the main external safeguard — But, when minds are wilful, there is no safeguard at all. We have a dreadful prospect. I deeply grieve for the young generation, now in arms or going to school. But error cannot last, and light will come after the darkness[4]

Ever Yrs affly J H Card. Newman

TO MRS FREDERIC MILLS RAYMOND-BARKER

Bm Febr 20. 1883

Dear Sir

I am much obliged to you for the gift of your Translation of the work of the Abbe Riche.[5] I am in some perplexity whether I know you personally or

[1] Fortey replied to Newman on 17 Feb., marking his letter 'Private', 'I regret that I am unable to comply with your request My object in writing to you was chiefly to assure you that neither my daughter nor myself were concerned in the publication of your letter to her and I most decidedly object to her name or my own being brought before the public in connection with this matter.'

[2] See letter of 6 Feb. to Bloxam.

[3] Robert Falkner Hessey, *The Twenty Thousand Clergy and the Present Crisis, or, the Pastor in his Parish dealing with Infidelity*, London 1883. Hessey was Vicar of Basing, Hants, and a former Fellow and Tutor of Magdalen College, Oxford.

[4] Bloxam replied on 23 Feb., 'I have copied out and sent to Hessey your painfully just remarks . . .'

[5] This was the work of the Sulpician devotional writer, Auguste Riche, *Agreement of Science and Faith upon the Sacred Heart of Jesus*, translated by Elizabeth Raymond-Barker.

not, and that must be my apology if there is anything in this letter which is out of keeping with the past.[1]

Hoping that your publication may have a full success

I am, very truly yours John H Card. Newman

TO ROBERT J. BLAKE

Feb 21. [1883][2]

My dear Robert

Thank you for your very kind remembrance; and for the newspaper, which was very welcome.

If any thing brings you this way, don't forget to call on us.

Yours affly John H. Card. Newman

TO LOUISA ELIZABETH DEANE

Bm Feb 21. 1883

My dear Louisa

Thank you very much for your birthday present. It is striking as a view of Rome or of Saint Peter's, and beautifully done, though I am no art critic and am quite conscious how little my praise is worth.

Since every one is testifying against the weather as so very prejudicial to health, it must be so, but I am thankful to say that I have not found it bad myself; what I suffer from is extreme weakness which leads to my tumbling about and breaking my shins. Also my age shows itself in my forgetfulness, and my mistakes in writing. I have in no slight degree forgotten how to spell. Another infirmity is my mislaying my letters, and of this, I am sorry to say, I have a case in point; for I have mislaid your letter of to-day, and should delay this except that I did not like to let a post pass without telling you that the picture had come safe.

Yours affectionately John H Card. Newman

---

[1] Mrs Raymond-Barker explained on 22 Feb. that she was the translator of Riche's book, and was 'the wife of one who was your junior at Oriel in past days, Frederic M. Raymond-Barker.

Our four children are, by the grace of God, all Catholics, now that our eldest daughter has lately been received into the Church. One son entered the Society of Jesus four years ago; and the dear young daughter who, two years and a half from now, accompanied me (with Mr Newdigate) to Edgbaston to obtain your Eminence's blessing, is a novice in the English (Augustinian) Convent at Bruges.'

Elizabeth Raymond-Barker went on to say that she and her children had only been back in England for a year, not having been permitted to live at their home at Bisley, for ten years after she had become a Catholic. The Dowager Duchess of Norfolk had ensured the children's education, and Mrs Raymond-Barker begged a remembrance of her husband in the prayers of Newman 'for whom his love and reverence has never wavered,' that he might follow 'his venerated leader.'

[2] Or 1886.

TO SIR WILLIAM HENRY COPE

Febr. 22. 1883

Many and sincere thanks to you, my dear Sir William, for your remembering me and congratulating me on my birthday.

At my age, my birthday is an awful day — and, by my increasing weakness, tho' my health is good, I am reminded that it ought so to be felt.

I half recollected the name of Jephson at Ealing, and since he is so kind to remember me, it seems like ungratitude in me not to be able to return his kindness. I think I must have been older than he was: for young boys look up to elder ones, as the elder do not bear in mind the younger.[1]

Most truly yours John H Card. Newman

TO EDWARD COLERIDGE

Birmingham, February 24th. 1883.

My dear E. Coleridge,

Your letter was very kind and very welcome. There are very few now whom I have known so long as you. The thought of you and your handwriting brings before me those young days, which, I suppose, have a special charm for every one. I did not forget your birthday last year, (May 11 ?) but the day past with my not having an opportunity of writing.[2]

I hope you are well — I feel my age.

Yours affectly John H. Card. Newman.

TO GEORGE T. EDWARDS

Febr. 24. 1883

Dear Mr Edwards

Thank you, and please thank for me Mr Fisher, for your and his kind remembrance of my birthday.

As I am writing, I will observe in explanation of what I said in my reference to Mr Fisher's Introductory Notice,[3] that I thought (and think) that the Evangelical Preaching of the Atonement was irreverent, oratorical, and vulgar. Excuse such hard words, but I use them in self defence. In the sermons of many, the use of our Lord's Name and work was as rude and as mechanical, as the wild idea of some Catholics that Gothic Architecture was the specific for religious conversion. I considered the Atonement was an Object for *devotion*, not for conversion, not denying of course that it was

---

[1] Sir William Cope wrote on 20 Feb. that he had met at Southsea Sir James Jephson, who had been at school with Newman. This was the third Baronet, a Captain R.N. (1802–84). He went from Ealing School to Eton.

[2] Coleridge was born on 11 May 1800.

[3] See letter of 8 Feb. to Edwards.

adapted in itself to convert *religious* minds, but that it was not the instrument, in the case of *irreligious*, as the Evangelicals used it. It was a profanity thus to use it. It was not so used by St Peter at Pentecost, or in the Temple, or before the Council, or by St Stephen, or by St Peter at Joppa, or by St Paul at Antioch, yet they, I presume, believed the Atonement. On the contrary I considered that it was the *Heart*, not the Hand or Arm of the Gospel, as the human heart is hidden, well protected, and the *life* of the whole. vid my Sermons Vol. vi. 7. pp 89, 90.[1] So incorrect then is the statement p 29 that 'the Movement of 1833 would seem to have left altogether out of account (!), not only the *Person* and *work* of Christ, as the Divinely appointed Mediator, but any distinct recognition whatever of the glorious *Plan* etc' that I cannot ask Mr Fisher to alter it for my sake, but only for his.[2] No one who reads my Sermons will attach any weight to his words. My Sermons are a constituent part of the literature of the movement, as much as the Tracts for the Times are. The Tracts are from 1833 to 1841. The Sermons outlapped them, viz they ran from 1825 to 1843.

I began to put down the references distinctly made to the Atonement in my Sermons; (of course they chiefly *take for granted* the doctrine, and treat on points, not on which all Christians *agreed*, but on those on which they *differ*,) and I found them more than I cared to have the trouble to put down. The most explicit in Vol vi 7 pp 89, 90

Very truly Yours J H Card Newman

TO MRS KEON

Feb 24, 1883

You are one of those friends and well wishers, who have so kindly addressed to me letters of congratulation on my birthday, — letters which touched me much, and for your share in which I hereby offer you my sincere thanks.

with my blessing,
J. H. N.

TO MRS FREDERIC MILLS RAYMOND-BARKER

Febr. 24. 1883

Dear Mrs Raymond Barker,

Thank you for taking me out of my confusion. I rejoice at the favourable change you tell me of.[3]

I always think affectionately of F. Barker. Tell him so from me.

Most truly Yours John H. Card. Newman

[1] 'The Cross of Christ the Measure of the World.'
[2] Edwards wrote on 3 April that the passage on p. 29 of the introduction to Fisher's pamphlet was misprinted; it should have read, 'The once famous movement of 1833 would seem to have left altogether out of account, not *indeed* the person and work of Christ...'
[3] See letter of 20 Feb.

Febr. 25. 1883

My dear Dean

Thank you for your affectionate letter. As year goes after year, the steady, irresistible progress of events is awful, and that I think is what a birthday brings home to one, as one gets old. One fears to live into new and unimagined troubles. What is coming on the world? What is coming upon England?

It may be said, 'This is just what you feared from the first reform bill of 1832.' True, but it *was* Act the First and the fear was not vain. We have gone on steadily in the road then entered upon.

But it is absurd to go on with these sad thoughts. One thing I want to know is this — Is Dr Irons alive or dead? I heard from Mrs Irons a year ago to the effect that he was in great danger; and answered her letter, but I have had no news since, and have not liked to write to her. I have thought she was [sic] certainly tell me, if she had lost him[1]

Yours affectionately John H Card. Newman

Febr. 26. 1883

My dear Copeland

My life just now is so uneventful, that I have nothing to say but to thank you for your affectionate letter. What times we have gone through! — there is plenty to think of in the past, as brought out by the departure from us of Pusey and Hawkins, but nothing for a letter. It pleased me to find you could give so good an account of yourself, for I was frightened by what I heard. Do you ever move now? or do you move from Farnham at fixed times? As I write it strikes me that there is a double sense to the word 'move', without my intending it[2]

Ever Yours affectly John H. Card. Newman

Feb. 26. 1883

My dear Anne Mozley

Thank you for your congratulations on the 21st. I have not felt the weather at all, for I keep indoors unless the weather is fine. But March is my trying month; *then* I put on winter things.

I marvel as well as grieve at Alfred's [Mozley] weak health. Every thing had seemed to turn out so happily for him, and this ailment is at once so

[1] William Josiah Irons died on 18 June 1883.
[2] Copeland was one of those Newman thought should move into the Catholic Church.

serious and so unexpected. At least I only thought that he had over-read himself, and that is the lot of so many.

One of his brothers told me that he suffered as the rest of the world from the agricultural distress. This, I suppose, we all feel, more or less; and, as perhaps you have seen, Mr Goschen tells us that at the bottom of the distress is, not the weather, but the scarcity of gold — which is the more frightful, because it is so difficult to comprehend[1]

Yours affectly John H. Card. Newman

TO GERARD MANLEY HOPKINS

Febr. 27. 1883

Dear Fr Hopkins

Thank you very much for your remembrance of my birthday, and also for the complimentary proposal you make in behalf of my Grammar of Assent.[2]

But I cannot accept it, because I do not feel the need of it, and I could not, as a matter of conscience, allow you to undertake a work which I could not but consider at once onerous and unnecessary. The book has succeeded in twelve years far more than I expected. It has reached five full editions. It is being translated in India into some of the native tongues — broken into portions and commented on.[3] It is frequently referred to in periodical home publications — only last Saturday week with considerable praise in the Spectator —[4] Of course those who only read so much of it as they can while cutting open the leaves, will make great mistakes about it, as Dr Stanley has —[5] but, if it is worth anything, it will survive the paper cutters, and if it [be] worthless, a comment, however brilliant, will not do more than gain for it a short galvanic life, which has no charms for me. Therefore, sensible as I am of your kindness, I will not accept it.

Remember me warmly to my friends at Stonyhurst, and believe me,

Very truly yours John H Card. Newman

[1] Alfred Mozley was Rector of Wigginton, Oxford. This was the period of the collapse of English agriculture, under the importation of American wheat. There was also a great demand for gold. George Goschen, statesman and financial expert, explained that its consequent appreciation was the cause of the general fall in prices.

[2] Hopkins wished to bring out a commentary. See letter of 26 April to him. For remarks by Hopkins on the style of *G.A.* cf. *Further Letters of Gerard Manley Hopkins*, edited by C. C. Abbott, second edition, London 1956, p. 58.

[3] See note for Simeon Wilberforce O'Neill, placed at end of Aug. 1882.

[4] In a review of Mivart's *Nature and Thought*, the *Spectator* (17 Feb. 1883), p. 238, said, 'Cardinal Newman, for instance, in his essay on "Assent," . . . makes it plain to his readers that he has thought his subject through and through. No objection can arise in their mind which is not anticipated by him; and . . . it is so clear that all considerations which arise in the minds of his students as difficulties have already been felt by himself, that their trust in him as a teacher is strengthened by the very force of his statement of primâ facie objections.'

[5] In 'Religious Movements of the Nineteenth Century,' the *Edinburgh Review* (April 1881), p. 314. See letter of 21 July 1881 to Miss Giberne.

Bm. March 1, 1883.

My dear Lady Henry

I will most gladly (God willing) say Mass on the 7th for dear Lord Henry whom I always think of with great affection and who, though it is our duty to pray for him here is, I cannot doubt, praying for all his friends in heaven.

You do not say how you are yourself. I trust this strange winter has not been unfavourable to you.

I, I am thankful to say, am very well, though weak and not quite self possessed. This it is which has made me feel perplexed at your speaking of Mamo's being 'forced into print' and of 'her reviews' I hope I have not made some mistake or my memory has not played me tricks; is there any thing which I have been told yet do not know?[1]

I am, My dear Lady Henry Yours affectly in Jesus Xt
John H Card. Newman

TO RICHARD STANTON
March 2. 1883

Dear Fr Stanton

Fr Ryder has shown me your letter, and I thank you for its kindness[2].

The report you mention grew out of another inquiry I made, and has no foundation of its own.

When I was going to Rome to receive the Hat, I thought it just possible that I ought to take with me the certificate of my Father's and Mother's marriage. I knew it took place in 1799, and at Lambeth Church (the parish then extending to Norwood, where my Mother was living). So I went to the Church and found it without any trouble. This is the only search I have made.[3]

I hope Fr Sebastian Bowden is better for his giving up work. He has long looked very ill. *He* should not be reminded, but *you* should know that his Father was the only one for [of] four children who did not die of consumption, besides his two cousins John and Marianne.[4]

Yours affectly John H Card. Newman

TO ARTHUR SANDES GRIFFIN
Bm March 5. 1883

Dear Canon Griffin

I fear you think I put your request as regards dear Dr Moriarty on the level merely of common unknown applicants who ask for a line of recommen-

---

[1] See letter of 9 March to Mrs Maxwell-Scott.
[2] Stanton heard that Newman had been examining registers at Lambeth, and appears to have offered to do any further searching for him.
[3] See letter of 10 April 1879 to F. G. Lee.
[4] Children of J. W. Bowden.

dation for their publications, but it is not so.[1] I have said 'No' to some of my nearest friends, men and women some of whom I have known almost from their birth, and some whom I should pain, if I gave to others what I have refused to them

You must be so kind as to take this into account — and you must recollect too, that it is not an easy thing at my age to write any thing satisfactory when a friend is the object of it. No one who is not old himself can duly estimate this difficulty.

I am sure that in a little while you will let me enjoy my sense of the kindness towards me which your wish betokened, without the sad feeling that I have seriously disappointed you.

Very truly Yours John H Card. Newman[2]

TO MISS M. R. GIBERNE

March 9/83

My dear Sister Pia

Lest you should not have heard, I write a line to say that Mrs Rickards is gone at last, aged 86. She died on Febry 28 — the anniversary of the deaths of Hurrell Froude and Observer Johnson. She is buried beside her husband

I have a good account of you from Mgr Place; I hope it continues.

I suppose the snow has come on you as on us. I trust it won't affect you

Yours affectly John H Card. Newman

TO THE HON. MRS MAXWELL-SCOTT

9 March 1883

My dear Mamo

Your Aunt has sent me your Article in the Scottish Review, and I write to say how pleased I am with it.[3]

The subject is very good, both as interesting, and, to most men, new, and as opened, with such especial success, by Sir Walter in Quentin Durward.

And you have written with far greater command of your pen than young authors commonly show; and in my own opinion, history is not the easiest of subjects to form or to fix a style upon. So I consider your Article a specially good start.

I was grieved to hear of Lord Howard's illness, and said Mass for him this morning[4]

With my best regards to your husband, I am

My dear Mamo Affectionately Yours John H. Card. Newman

[1] After Newman's refusal of 31 Jan. Griffin wrote again on 3 Feb. asking for a preface to Bishop Moriarty's *Allocutions*, 'I should not attempt to intrude on Your Eminence If I was a stranger to the relations that existed between you and the Illustrious dead.'

[2] Moriarty's *Allocutions* contained a long dedication to Newman. See letter of 28 Feb. 1884 to Griffin.

[3] 'The Scots Guards in France,' the *Scottish Review* (Feb. 1883), pp. 286–310.

[4] Lord Howard of Glossop died on 1 Dec. 1883.

The Oratory March 9. 1883

My dear Duke

Many thanks for your thoughtful and affectionate message and present to me through Fr Neville. It has come right, and is very welcome.

You will be glad to know that as yet I have escaped any serious cold this winter, though I am weaker than I was.

I wish you could have seen our improvements in the School buildings, while they had their first gloss upon them. Father Richard B. [Bellasis] has taken great pains to make them smart, and the Library and Lavatory are the admiration of all comers. In any case, however, it is very difficult to make things handsome without cost, and I fear you will think these improvements no exception to the rule.

The accounts which have come in include the brushing up of a portion of the bedrooms, which the ladies who honoured us with their presence in 1879, 1880 spoke of to you at the time, and which we set about without delay

Your Grace's affectionate Servt John H Card. Newman

His Grace The Duke of Norfolk E M

TO EMILY BOWLES

Mar 10. 1883

My dear Child

It grieved me very much to see notice of Mr Eyston's death in the Papers. I can scarcely have seen him, since I made his and his uncle's acquaintance on the top of a mail coach in a heavy downfall of rain; but I have never forgotten him, nor his name Charles, ever since.[1]

How the old generation is fading away, out of sight! What a mystery is life! and how it comes home to such as me to think of old Nestor's melancholy lines, 'as the outburst and fall of leaves, such the generation of men.'[2] How inwardly miserable must the life of man be, without the Gospel! and now men are doing their utmost to destroy our sole solace. My best regards to Lady Downe

Yours affectly J H N.

TO LORD BRAYE

Bm. March 10. 83

My dear Lord Braye

I am too much interested both in your Lordship and in English Catholic Education, not to keep you and its prospects in mind, while you are in Rome.[3]

[1] See end of letter of 11 Aug. 1846 to St John, and diary for 13 Aug. 1846. Charles John Eyston died on 19 Feb. 1883.
[2] *Iliad*, VI, 146.
[3] See letters of 4 and 9 Feb. to Lord Braye.

But you must not be sure that any report I might have to send there on the University question would be pleasing to the good men who feel our present needs as regards it

Twenty years ago, I hoped the Oratory would be established at Oxford; that is, when the residence of Undergraduates in the College was not prohibited to Catholics.

I never advocated a Catholic College there, and, as time has gone on, I have become actually indisposed to the idea, and for three reasons:— 1. the great outlay necessary. 2 the risk by failing to damage the Catholic Name; 3 the probability, that, after all the labour and expense, parents and sons will prefer the old Colleges to the new.

I don't want to discourage you, but you must look at the problem before us all round

Very truly Yours John H Card. Newman

TO JOHN COWLEY FISHER

The Oratory March 10. 1883

My dear Sir

I am still as much pleased by the memory of our meeting at Cambridge, as you are kind enough to be;[1] and I am sure you have intended nothing unfair in your 'Introduction.'[2]

Nevertheless, I feel it so evidently and obviously one sided, that I should never think it necessary to write one word in answer to it. The very fact that it ignores my ten Volumes of Sermons, which had as great run as the Tracts, is sufficient reply to it.

Please to believe me when I say that I have not any sort of unfriendly feeling towards you in consequence

I am, My dear Sir, Very sincerely Yours
John H. Card. Newman

J. Cowley Fisher Esqr

TO MRS EDWARD BELLASIS

The Oratory March 12 1883

My dear Mrs Bellasis

The joy which pervaded this place last week, and especially our group of visitors, has now reached you. Their presence and prayers crowned a good work. And the weather was bright and pleasant as if in sympathy.[3]

[1] See letter of 29 July 1861 to Bittleston.
[2] See letters of 8 and 24 Feb. to G. T. Edwards. Fisher wrote on 9 March to say that his pamphlet on the Atonement had only been printed for private circulation. His criticism of the Tractarian Movement was meant to apply to its history up to the present. He admitted that his library did not contain Newman's sermons.
[3] On 4 March Henry Lewis Bellasis was ordained priest in the church of the Birmingham Oratory.

Nay can we doubt that *he* too had a share in the work and in the joy, who so earnestly desired that God would graciously take to Himself priests from among his sons?

You are indeed favoured; may the best blessings from above be with you to the end

My kindest remembrances to Clara [Bellasis]

Yours ever affectly John H Card. Newman

TO ROBERT ORNSBY

March 18/83

My dear Ornsby

I dare say you have received from Mrs M. S. [Maxwell-Scott] the equivalent to the inclosed, yet I send it from the pleasure it has given me. [Will you tell][1] Stewart, when you see him, that Mrs Rickars [sic] is gone, aged 86, tho' I dare say he has heard it.

With the best wishes of the coming season to you and Mrs Ornsby

TO F. R. WARD

Bm March 20/83

My dear Ward

You are kind enough to say you will give us your advice on a question which makes me anxious.

When I am gone, my executors can swear with a clear conscience that our Library is the Oratorian Fathers' property, and has been theirs ever since the Oratory here was formed But will the official people consider this sufficient? will they appeal to my name being in most of the books, and treating them as a legacy, not as a past donation, charge the Fathers ten per cent upon them?

In addition to the fact of my name being in the greater number, the Officials might argue (and forcibly) '*whose* are they, if not Cardinal Newman's? The Law does not recognize the Oratory, and Card. Newman has not made the Library over to Joint Tenants'

I should say on my part that I have committed no act of ownership for 30 and more years — have never reclaimed a book, though I have often wished I had not included particular books in the gift. Moreover, a considerable number of the books have been given by other Fathers, or by externs.

I wonder whether I have already troubled you with this question — for I know it has teazed me from time to time — but our Fathers have not felt it, as I do.

Is it too late for me by a deed of gift to make it over to trustees, or will it be objected that it would be an evasion of the legacy duty?

[1] Part of a line is missing where conclusion and signature have been cut off overleaf.

The House is, under the sanction of Chan[c]ery, in the hands of Trustees. Does not the House carry the books? would an Appeal to Chancery lie if we attempted to sell the books?[1]

Very truly Yours John H Card Newman

TO LORD BLACHFORD

Birmingham March 24th. 83.

My dear Blachford,

I have read your Pamphlet with great interest. Who could possibly be the Lawyer who inspired the Judicial Committee with the happy idea that the decisions are de fide, a portion of the Anglican Creed or must it be the views of all its Members?

And this too after its decisions, in spite of their being so authoritative turning out inconsistent with each other.

It does not seem to me any scandal as regards the Anglican Church, but a most damaging narrative against the Judicial Committee. Is there no Appeal to the Privy Council itself? A clever Pleader surely might shew up the Committee with an effective force, for which you have supplied the matter, though you have not felt it right to do more.

Lawyers have been so high and mighty in their view of the Clergy's conduct, maintaining that they themselves were the sole calm unbiased judges of the Anglican doctrine, that they deserve to be punished.

I dare say I have not got hold of your narrative as a whole, but I don't see how I can be wrong in the above view of it.[2]

With my best Easter wishes to you and Lady Blachford,

Yours affectionately, John H. Card: Newman.

TO R. W. CHURCH

March 28, 1883.

I said Mass for Helen and her husband elect this morning. So did Fr Neville. Of course it is, however glad an event, a very trying one for all of you, and not least for Mary.[3]

I don't suppose she will find a fiddle make up for Helen, but it has struck me that you and Blachford will let me give the beautiful instrument you and

---

[1] F. R. Ward replied on 21 March from 1, Gray's Inn Square:
'I answer your question about the Books at once because I have no doubt that they would not be liable to duty as your private property on your death — They are not in your exclusive possession or control, any more than is the Library where they are kept. According to the constitution of the Congregation, yours is only a Community interest in these Books . . .
. . . .
The authorities will take the oath of your executors without any enquiry. . . .'
[2] See letters of 14 Aug. 1883 to Lord Blachford and H. P. Liddon.
[3] Helen, twin sister of Mary Church, was married to Francis Paget on 28 March.

he gave me, to Mary. I don't think she will refuse it; I hear much of her proficiency.

You gave it me in 1865 — and I had constant use and pleasure in the use till lately — but I find now I have no command of it; nay, strange to say, I cannot count or keep time. This is a trouble to me; one gets an affection for a fiddle, and I should not like to go without getting it a good master or mistress. My friends in this house have instruments of their own. So has Mary doubtless — but this would come with associations in its history[1]

TO ROBERT CHARLES JENKINS

March 30. 1883.

Dear Canon Jenkins,

I wish you all the blessings of this Easter, and hope you have not suffered from its cold. I was going to write to you to ask whether you had seen the reference to Lyminge in Mr. Rule's St. Anselm, Vol. I. p. 228.[2]

Thank you for your Pamphlet and its Dedication; in consequence of Dr. Holt's enquiry I began it with great interest — but I was so much shocked at what you say about the Athanasian Creed, that I put it down without heart or hope to read more.[3]

Very sincerely yours, John H. Card. Newman.

TO MRS F. R. WARD

March 31. 1883

My dear Mrs Ward,

Will you thank for me Mr Ward for his satisfactory letter. I write to you because I have some fear that I addressed him with a liberty which arises from an infirmity of old age — not absence, but a strange omission of words which I mean to put in. If I have unwittingly done so, you must tell him I am very much shocked

Yours affecty John H Card. Newman

TO WILLIAM BRIGHT

Bm April 1/83

My dear Dr Bright

It is a great satisfaction to me to find that you so nearly agree with me in your view of S. Cyril. You have read the existing documents so much more

[1] cf. letter of 11 July 1865 to R. W. Church, and that of 19 Jan. 1884 to Lord Blachford.
[2] Martin Rule, *The Life and Times of St Anselm*, two volumes London 1883. Jenkyns was Rector of Lyminge and had written on its antiquities.
[3] This was a booklet, dedicated to Newman, *From the Death of St. Athanasius to the Death of St. Basil and the Council of Constantinople, A.D. 373–381, a Chapter of Ecclesiastical History*, London 1883. See letter of 3 April to William Bright.

carefully than I have, that I feel you have a right to be more severe on his acts than I am, supposing you are led to be so.[1]

I am perplexed to understand how S. Cyril could have had so great a part in forming dear Pusey, as he seems to say. When he went abroad in 1827 it was in order to master German and Hebrew. He bought for me some Fathers and for himself doubtless. But Neander was his master at that time, and he was almost a devotee of Luther[2]

Then when he came back in 1828 as Canon [of Christ Church], his great work for years was the finishing Nichol's Catalogue of Arabic MSS. I may be going too far, but, speaking under correction, I should if left to myself say that he did not turn to the Fathers much before he took up the great design of the Translation of the Fathers, that is in 1835, and then St Augustine was his Master, not St Cyril. And I cannot recollect his ever speaking or doing any thing which showed St Cyril was in his thoughts or affection. In the published list in 1838 of 'preparing for publication', it was I who was put down for S. Cyril. Pusey's line of reading was Tertullian, Cyprian, Augustine.[3]

But Dr Liddon will clear up my difficulty.[4] I suppose his Memoir is getting on.

Very sincerely Yours John H Card. Newman

[1] Bright reviewed Philip Pusey's translation of St Cyril of Alexandria's *Five Tomes against Nestorius* and other works for the *Church Quarterly Review* (Jan. 1883), pp. 257–91. He blamed both Puseys for glossing over the various violent acts of St Cyril and in his criticisms sheltered himself behind those of Newman in *H.S.* II, p. 342. Bright replied on 2 April that he had only agreed to write 'with great misgiving and with the fear that I should give dear Dr Pusey some offence. What weighed with me was the conviction that an indiscriminating "éloge" or defence of *all* St Cyril's acts would produce on not a few minds a reaction towards the unsympathetic and inequitable view taken by the Milman and Stanley school. And if I may say so, I felt that in this more delicate portion of my task I was under the protection of your Eminence's judgment as to the natural effect of the vast power of the Alexandrian patriarchate on natures of less "select" mould than was that of St Athanasius.'

[2] At the beginning of his review Bright quoted E. B. Pusey's words at the end of the preface to his son's work, p. civ; 'S. Cyril was my own early teacher on the connection of the doctrine of the Incarnation and the Holy Eucharist.' He also spoke of him as 'My early benefactor, S. Cyril.'

[3] Bright replied on 2 April: 'I always supposed that Dr Pusey's peculiar feeling towards St Cyril grew out of and dated from the use which he made of St Cyril's argument from the Holy Eucharist to the Incarnation, when he was preparing his famous sermon on "The Eucharist a Comfort to the Penitent." [1843]

The particulars which your Eminence is so good as to give me as to the successive stages of Dr Pusey's student life before 1835, that in one sense he looked after 1835, to St Augustine rather than St Cyril, I inferred from some touching words at the end of the last Volume of Parochial and Cathedral Sermons.'

[4] On 4 April Bright transcribed for Newman a letter he had received from Liddon: 'No doubt your account of Dr Pusey's late attachment to St Cyril is the true one. I think I have heard Dr P. connect him especially with the holy Eucharist. And then Philip's work, continued for so many years, and under such difficulties completed the feeling. Still, up to the last, I should have supposed, St Augustine ruled his habits of theological and devotional thought more than any other Father.'

TO WILLIAM BRIGHT

April 3. 1883.

Dear Dr Bright

I have told Canon Jenkins how much his notice of the Athanasian Creed shocked me. It was going out of his way.[1]

Of course you saw Dr Holt's dissertation. Did I mention this in my letter of Sunday? It seemed to me very plausible.

I am glad you come to the conclusion that the Epistle to Caesarius is not St Chrysostom's. An additional argument to the ordinary ones against it, has seemed to me to be the presence of the word πρόσωπον[2]

Very Sincerely Yours John H Newman.

TO HENRY BEDFORD

April 4th. 1883.

Dear Mr. Bedford,

Thank you for your interesting Article on the Relics of St. Ambrose.

My Correspondent whom you quote, was my dearest friend Father Ambrose St. John, and his informant whose account of the find of them you state to be 'quite incorrect' and 'must have been misunderstood by him', I believe to have been Father Secchi with whom he travelled from Milan.[3]

Wishing you all the blessings of Easter Tide.

I am, Very sincerely yours, John H. Card. Newman.

TO FRANCIS WILLIAM NEWMAN

April 8. 1883

My dear Frank

I thank you for your pamphlet just come.[4] I suppose it is an argumentum ad hominem.[5]

It pleased me much to understand that you were publishing your Notes on Aeschylus. For myself I am not able to criticise them. Years back I had a great

[1] Bright wrote on 2 April of R. C. Jenkins's pamphlet, (see letter of 30 March to him), 'There are some strange things in the book, and two offending passages on the Athanasian Creed . . .'

[2] The *Epistle to Caesarius* said that the natural substances remained in the Holy Eucharist. The *Epistle* is not considered to be a work of St John Chrysostom. See third note to letter of 6 March 1867 to Pusey.

[3] Ambrose St John's letter is in *H.S.I.*, pp. 443–4, and confirms that Angelo Secchi, the Jesuit astronomer and scientist, was present. Cf. letter of 23 Sept. 1872 to Anne Mozley.

[4] *A Christian Commonwealth*, London 1883, denounced on Christian principles the injustices committed by England in her foreign and colonial activities during the previous half century.

[5] F. W. Newman replied on 6 April: 'I beg you not to imagine that my tract on a Christian Commonwealth is written as an *argumentum ad hominem* by one who separates his own convictions from those to whom he appeals.

I have never ceased for a day to look up with gratitude for the writings of Paul of Tarsus, and to be thankful that I learned spiritual morals in his school. At no time of my life have I ceased to have sympathy as to practical matters with *Christian* morals as contrasted with those of materialistic philosophy. . . . To *the Churches* I look (and not to the unreligious reformers) as *the main force of goodness* in our future.'

love of Greek plays and have still for the memory of them but they have got beyond me now. I think you may like it back — so I inclose it[1]

Yours affectly John H Card. Newman

Bm April 9. 1883

My dear Emly

I have been full of your letter ever since I got it, but have felt the difficulty of answering so great that I have delayed doing so.[2]

As to books on the subject of it, it is not my forte to have a memory for such, and I can suggest nothing.

My own difficulty in attempting it, is because, as I think, theologians decide many questions about Scripture which the Church has not decided — and the Vatican Council while defining four points hitherto open, has not found it right to pronounce open, by any positive act, points which many writers determine to be shut. Of course I fully acknowledge it to be God's will, and believe that He who has willed our difficulty will sustain us through it and in His own time bring us out of it.

Another great difficulty is the ignorance of our people in the Scriptures. It is to them a terra incognita. The Old Testament especially excites no sentiment of love, reverence, devotion or trust. They hear bold things said against it — or fragments of it quoted detached from the context, and they have no associations with it in their affections. It creates in them no distress or horror to hear it contemptuously treated as a 'venerable book.'

This is not the Holy See's doing for you recollect the Brief of Pius VI, prefixed to our Bibles.[3] In our Bishops' Catechism there is no reference to Scripture as a book given to us by God, inspired, a guide — and a comfort. One such reference is the exception — thus 'We ought frequently to read good books, such as the Holy Gospel, the Lives of the Saints and other spiritual works'[4]

[1] F. W. Newman published his *Comments on the Text of Aeschylus* in 1884.
[2] Lord Emly wrote on 1 April: 'Father Walsh an excellent Jesuit in Dublin has asked me to write to you on the following subject. Until recently he had little difficulty in dealing with those who came to consult him about their religious states. They accepted the Scriptures as inspired.
He had this common ground to meet them upon . . . Now all this is changed. Confessional controversy seems to be at an end. Those who come to him look upon the Scriptures as nothing more than a venerable book. Their faith in revelation is gone or shaken. He knows of no book to put into their hands. He is well acquainted with your writings, and thinks that . . . there is a great deal to suit his purpose — but he wants me to ask you whether you can recommend him any book calculated to be useful to such minds as he has described. . . . Our Lord seems always to appeal to miracles, and to the fulfilment of prophecy, — When I said this to Father Walsh, he answered that the ones he had to deal with would only laugh at miracles, and when the fulfilment of some prophecies was pointed out to them, would point to others such as the glories of the church which have not yet been fulfilled. . . .'
[3] This was Pius VI's Brief of 1 April 1778 to Antonio Martini, Archbishop of Florence, praising him for his Italian translation and saying how important it was that the faithful should read the Bible.
[4] Answer 360 in *The Catechism of Christian Doctrine* authorised by the English bishops.

This is out of 368 questions and answers

I wish I could do more than thus lament — but at present I see nothing better than to pray God to open a way for us

This is hardly a fit letter to go to Fr Walsh[1]

> Yours affectly John H Card. Newman

TO WILLIAM CLIFFORD, BISHOP OF CLIFTON

13 April. 1883

Dear Bishop Clifford

I grieve to see an announcement in the Papers which will be so great a distress to you.[2]

I have not forgotten your brother's state, and hope to say Mass for him in a few days

> Most truly Yours J. H. Card. Newman

TO WILLIAM STANG

The Oratory, Birmingham April 13. 1883

Dear Rev Sir,

I am much touched by your letter and thank you for it with all my heart.[3]

It is a great consolation to me to know that in my declining strength, I have the spiritual aid of your prayers, and, though I should like to know you personally, still there is a special gratification in the circumstance that he who is so charitable to me, is, like the Good Samaritan in the Parable, a stranger to me.[4]

Praying all best blessings upon you,

> I am, Dear Rev Sir, Sincerely Yours John H. Cardl Newman

Rev Wm Stang

The Cathedral, Providence U.S

[1] Newman wrote again to Lord Emly on 17 April.

[2] The bishop's brother, Sir Henry Hugh Clifford, V.C., died on 12 April.

[3] Stang had gone as a priest from Germany to the United States four years earlier, and was Rector of the Cathedral, Providence, Rhode Island. He had to learn English and wrote on 23 March:

'I bought your works and ever since I am a faithful reader of them. Often when I am alone with your books, I feel a desire to express to the author my sincerest thanks and to tell him, how much I honor and love him.' Stang promised to remember Newman each day at Mass, and hoped God would long keep him 'for the good and glory of his Church, of which you are so warm a defender.'

[4] On 28 Sept. Stang sent Newman a copy of his *The Life of Martin Luther*, 'as a slight token of the great veneration and warmest love which I entertain for you, and which was heightened by the kind letter you sent me last April.' Stang became in 1904 the first bishop of Fall River.

TO JOHN THOMAS WALFORD, S.J.

Birmingham, April 13. 1883

My dear Fr Walford,

I congratulate you on your approaching ordination and thank you for telling me of it. If all is well with me, I will say Mass for you on the 21st. Thank you also for your prospective kindness towards me, and your affectionate remembrance of the Oratory. We all thank you.[1]

Yours affectionately John H. Card. Newman

TO JOHN MAYALL

Bm. April 14. 1883

Cardinal Newman, in answer to Mr Mayall's question, incloses a list of his works.[2]

Another list, otherwise drawn up, can be got at Messrs Burns and Oates's Orchard Street, Oxford Street

The Cardinal edited the Catena Aurea, but did not translate, and so of 'Maxims.'[3]

The proposed 'Preliminary Matter' is in 'Theological Tracts' (vid Ed 2 p 142)[4]

TO GEORGE T. EDWARDS

Bm April 15. 1883

My dear Mr Edwards

Thank you for your kindly intended and well argued letter, but I am too old and weary to enter upon a life long controversy.[5]

I will briefly state what I believe to be the main difference between the Evangelical party and myself, and hope you will allow me to do no more.

[1] In his letter of thanks on 29 April, Walford wrote:
'Edgbaston was my only Catholic home — and the happiest of homes too — before I entered our Society.'
[2] Mayall wrote on 13 April from 47 Adelaide Road, London N.W., to say that he was collecting a complete set of Newman's works 'for presentation to a College friend,' and asked about three of them.
[3] Newman wrote the preface to Catena Aurea, three volumes, Oxford 1841–2. Maxims of the Kingdom of Heaven was published by Burns and Lambert, London 1860, second edition 1873. Newman wrote the 'Advertisement:' 'The following Collection of passages from the Holy Evangelists has been put into my hands by the compiler to carry through the press. I could not but gladly avail myself of the opportunity, which a friend thus presented to me, of having a share, however small, in a work directed, in so pious a spirit, towards the promotion among Catholics of an habitual reverent meditation upon the sacred words of Him who spoke as "man never did speak."'
[4] Select Treatises of S. Athanasius in controversy with the Arians II, contained a note 'The Preliminary Matter is unavoidably postponed
                                                    J.H.N.   Dec. 6, 1844.'
The reference to T.T. is to 'Causes of the Rise and Successes of Arianism' written in 1872.
[5] In defence of the evangelical stress on the doctrine of the Atonement in preaching, Edwards, in a letter of 3 April, appealed to John 12:32 and many other New Testament texts.

I conceive that the Atonement is a 'mystery', a glorious 'mystery', to be gloried in *because* it is a mystery, to be received by a pure act of faith, inasmuch as reason does not *see how* the death of God Incarnate can stand instead of, can be a Vicarious Satisfaction for, the eternal death of his sinful brethren. And sad experience of the want of this faith in most men, (for which ordinarily a deep sense of sin is required, which the multitude of sinners have not, not to speak of the need of an initial love of God) was what made St Paul give utterance to his glorying in the Cross, which was to the political Pharisee and Sadducee a stumbling block and to the proud, supercilious Greek foolishness. It was indeed the great proof and instance of God's love to man, but he gloried in it, not on this account, but because it was wisdom and love in a mystery, spoken against by the world, but the life of the believer.

'You, Corinthians,' says St Paul 'must begin by humbling your intellect to a mystery, and your selfishness to mortification of soul and body, for in your pride and sensuality you have forgotten your pattern Christ crucified.'[1] Now, with all that is good and spiritual in the Evangelical party, I think they have forgotten that the Cross of Christ is a 'mystery', and to be treated with deep reverence. Instead of this, they call it a 'manifestation' and flourish it about as a 'plan', a 'scheme', a great argument addressed to the world, and in itself exciting faith, the one instrument of God's grace, convincing, satisfying the reason, and thereby the means of conversion; whereas my great fear has been, as I have said in my Essay on Mr Erskine's work, lest this doctrine of a manifestation, which he took from the Evangelicals, though he gave up the forensic view, should lead to a wish to destroy all mysteries, even to Sabellianism.[2] And I feel this strongly still.

Excuse me if I have said anything unfairly

Yours very truly John H Card. Newman

TO LOUIS DUCHESNE

[16 April] 1883

Monsieur l'abbé

Je regrette infiniment que ma lettre aux redacteurs de vôtre revue vous ait paru si sévère, et je dois vous remercier de la bonté avec laquelle vous avez bien voulu me répondre.[3] J'ai cru devoir écrire comme j'ai écrit parceque

---

[1] I *Corinthians*, 1–2.

[2] *Ess.*, I, p. 57. See letter of 2 Jan. 1883 to Edwards.

[3] In reference to Newman's letter of 15 Feb. to the Editor of *Revue des sciences ecclésiastiques*, Duchesne wrote on 14 April from Paris: 'La Revue des sciences ecclésiastiques publie une lettre de vous, ou je suis accusé d'avoir commis une erreur très grave, dans la traduction d'un passage de vos *Tracts theological and ecclesiastical*. J'ai lu cette lettre avec une douloureuse suprise, car j'étais loin de m'attendre à être traité si durement par Votre Eminence au moment où je suis pris à partie et persécuté pour avoir adopté et cherché à répandre ses idées sur le développement du dogme. Mes adversaires feront grand bruit de cette lettre; aux yeux des gens ignorants elle passera pour un désaveu.

Et pourtant, l'erreur est-elle si grave? Oui si l'on considère la différence qu'il y a entre le mot *sounder*, pris isolément, et le mot *nouvelle*; en réalité elle n'affecte pas le sens de la phrase.

l'expérience m'a montré que, sur un point si capital et si délicat, je ne pouvai pas permettre le moindre doute sur la portée de mes paroles. Je ne me suis pas permis d'apprécier vôtre travail comme j'aurais voulu parceque à mon grand regret, je ne suis pas assez maître de français.

Veuillez, Monsieur l'abbé, agréer les sentiments de respect avec lesquelles j'ai l'honneur d'être,

Vôtre très dévoué serviteur en J.C.[1]

TO MALCOLM MACCOLL

Rednall April 16th/83

Dear Mr MacColl,

I feel some shame in having to say that I have a very vague notion what the Affirmation Bill is, and a simple ignorance what the amendment to it may be.[2] This has led me to read your printed letter over twice or three times and I have come to the conclusion which on the whole I suppose is right that the Government propose to substitute an affirmation for an oath on fresh M P's and that the conservatives prefer a profession of Theism in some shape, with the option of not taking it granted to each member.

You will think my want of interest to be strange; but I think it implies

Du moment où Votre Eminence dit que St Basile, St Ambroise, etc. inaugurent (iniate) [sic] une littérature théologique, c'est que cette littérature n'existait pas encore, et par conséquent qu'elle est *nouvelle*. Quant à la qualification de *plus saine*, elle ressort suffisamment de la manière dont leurs écrits sont comparés avec ceux des anciens auteurs; aucun lecteur n'aura pu se tromper là-dessus.

Il y a donc erreur, mais simplement philologique, sur un mot dont le sens est suffisamment indiqué par le contexte. Je regrette néanmoins cette distraction, causée par la rapidité avec laquelle j'ai du tracer ces pages apologétiques, et je demande pardon à Votre Eminence de l'ennui que je lui ai causé par cette negligence involontaire.

Mais je ne puis lui taire combien il m'est pénible de me voir traité aussi sévèrement, pour une faute légère, en somme, et sans qu'un seul mot d'encouragement vienne tempérer l'amertume des reproches qu'elle a cru devoir m'adresser, "Si inimicus meus maledixisset mihi, sustinuissem utique . . . Tu autem, dux meus!"

Que votre Eminence veuille bien me pardonner la liberté de mon language et croire que malgré la douleur que j'eprouve, je m'incline cependant avec respect sous sa main vénérable.'

Newman wrote in pencil on this letter: 'On so important a point I did not feel I could religiously allow my meaning to be mistaken.'

[1] In July Newman sent M. D'Hulst, the Rector of the Institut Catholique at Paris, in which Duchesne was a Professor of Church History, a copy of the revised second edition of *T.T.* On 28 Aug. 1883 D'Hulst wrote his gratitude, which he said was 'bien vif en moi quand je pense qu'un Prince de l'Eglise qui est une lumière de la Science Sacrée, a daigné s'intéresser aux travaux de notre Institut Catholique et, en attirant notre attention sur les perfectionnements qu'Elle a cru devoir donner à l'expression de la doctrine, nous tracer à nousmêmes la voie que nous devons suivre.

Je prie Votre Eminence de croire qu'un Conseil tombé de si haut ne sera pas perdu. M L'abbé Duchesne, comme l'humble Recteur de notre Institut en fera son profit, et nous demeurons bien honorés d'avoir pu, même par certaines imperfections de langage, obtenir l'honneur de fixer un instant vos regards et de provoquer vos paternels avis.'

[2] MacColl wrote on 15 April that he was a strong advocate of the Government Affirmation Bill: 'The large majority of the English clergy take the other side; but I have an influential minority on my side, including such names as Dean Church, Dr Liddon, and Dr Bright, Regius Professor of Ecclesiastical History at Oxford.' MacColl asked for Newman's opinion and enclosed a long letter of 7 April on the matter, which he had sent to the *Guardian* (11 April), p. 535.

that in the main I agree with you. At least two years ago, when the question of protesting against abolishing the Parliamentary recognition of Almighty God came before me, I felt that since Christianity had ceased to be the religion of Parliament for many years, the God of the Christians was no longer the God of Parliament, and I did not see what was gained by acknowledging any God but Him who in Scripture and the Creed is defined to be 'Maker of Heaven and Earth' and 'Father of our Lord Jesus Christ' I had other reasons for being indisposed to protest but this I believe was the main one. But when you ask me whether you may print my words I do not feel that it is my place to do more than what I did not do two years ago.[1]

Yours very truly John H. Card. Newman[2]

TO LORD EMLY

Rednall April 17. 1883

My dear Emly

I know I sent you a very shabby letter the other day,[3] and I have wished to make up for it, but I am always weary, and my brain and my fingers work very slowly.

Miracles were the proof that Christianity came from heaven *at the date* of its coming; but, if an inquirer fancies that they are now what they were in the beginning I cannot agree with him, and have said otherwise these fifty years.

I am not up to write a good letter, but I will observe that no one has been able to assign a cause for this phenomenon in history except a supernatural. We have recourse to supernatural agency even because we cannot assign natural. Gibbon's attempt at five causes has not lasted a century[4]

If a book was written at this day in defence of Christianity, I think it ought to bring out what in its popular form is called 'the Four Notes of the Church', showing, as Butler does in so many ways, that a positive conclusion may be imperative on the mind, in spite of difficulties in detail which cannot be answered.

I would not urge arguments, however good, as *demonstrations*, which seems to be Paley's fault in his 'Evidences', conclusive as his first volume is. A great deal may be made of Prophecy Another head would be the martyrs,

---

[1] See letters of 3 June 1881 to Lord Blachford, 20 and 25 Sept. 1881 to the Duke of Norfolk and William Lockhart.

[2] MacColl replied on 18 April: 'My printed letter has somewhat misled you. The facts, in brief are as follow: —
The old Parliamentary oath used to be: "On the true faith of a Christian, so help me God." "On the true faith of a Christian" was struck out of the oath for the express purpose of admitting into Parliament men who are not Christians. So that the Oath is now merely a vague profession of a theism, of which all that can be said is that it is not Christian. The Government proposes, in the Affirmation Bill, to give fresh members the option of not taking this oath. The Conservatives propose simply to negative the Bill.' See also letter of 26 April to MacColl.

[3] Letter of 9 April.

[4] *The Decline and Fall of the Roman Empire*, Chapter 15.

and so on. There is nothing new in this, except the suggestion that the book should *profess* to be a cumulative argument, and should [bring] out the wonderful characteristics of the fact of Christianity, the concrete fact[1]

Yours affectly John H Card. Newman

The Lord Emly

TO WILLIAM NEVILLE

Rednall Apr. 21/83

My dear W

You had nothing to tell me about my Fiddle?

Do you know you ran away with my hat and gloves?

Yrs affly J H N

TO GERARD MANLEY HOPKINS

Rednall April 26/83

Dear Fr Hopkins

In spite of your kind denial, I still do and must think that a comment is a compliment, and to say that a comment may be appended to my small book because one may be made on Aristotle ought to make me blush purple! As to India, I suppose all English books, even Goody Two Shoes, are so unlike its literary atmosphere, that a comment is but one aspect of translation[2]

I must still say that you paid me a very kind compliment. You seem to think compliments must be insincere: is it so?

Most truly Yours John H Card. Newman

[1] There exists an earlier draft of this letter:
'The miracles converted those who saw them and this conversion of those first witnesses, and supernatural effect of this conversion was the conversion of those who did not see them. It is the sudden rise and creation of the Church out of nothing, the victory over the Roman power, the triumph of the weak over the strong, is our main proof of the divinity of the gospel now.

No one has been able to assign a cause for this strange success ⟨phenomenon⟩ of a few fishermen of Palestine except a supernatural one. Gibbon's attempt has not lasted 100 years. It is a cumulative argument in its favour. First consider Paley's argument ⟨the weak convincing the strong⟩ for our Lord's Resurrection; then there is the morality so original — then the argument from prophecy and then the history of the martyrs. Then the life and energy which has maintained and extended the Church age after age. Of course I can't go through the combination of marvels which make up the strange history ⟨fact⟩. But the chance is it never occurs to a young man who comes to a priest to consider the history. He has some shallow smart dictum to justify his unbelief such as '*I* never saw a miracle,' or it is easy to fancy or some prophecies have not been fulfilled, and that settles [it]

I think, if a book for the lay was written it ought to bring out, what in its popular form is the same as "the Notes of the Church —" showing, as Butler does in so many ways that a positive conclusion may be imperative though there are many objections in detail which cannot be answered, nothing being easier on any subject than objections, which on that account we brush aside every day'
[2] See letter of 27 Feb. to Hopkins. *The History of Little Goody Two-Shoes* was a nursery tale, first published in 1765.

TO MALCOLM MACCOLL

Rednall April 26, 1883

Dear Mc Mac Coll

There is one consideration which, since I wrote, I learn from the Papers, which I think would weigh with me, if I had to give an opinion, not to take so active a part as you are taking.

Perhaps I am mistaken in my fact, but it is stated that great numbers of Anglican laymen all through the country, as represented by parochial petitions to Parliament, are shocked at what seems to them a sanction of atheism. Perhaps you will say that the petitions are really the work of one or two men, e.g. the Incumbent in each parish; and that the people did not get nearer to the truth than to suppose that Gladstone was an atheist. But, if on the contrary, it is a genuine protest against atheism, and a fear of its spreading have we a right to throw cold water on what we may at a later date seek in vain for in the religious sentiment of the nation.

This consideration would be sufficient to lead me to keep neuter, though one might think the vox populi illogical.[1]

Very truly yours John H. Card Newman

TO J. READER

April 27. 1883

Dear Sir

I thank you for letting me see Fr Caswall's letters, which I hereby return.

I wish I could do more than express the interest I take in the good work in which you are engaged.

Yours truly John H. Card. Newman

JReader Esqr

TO MALCOLM MACCOLL

April 28. 1883

Dear Mr Mac Coll

Don't think me inconsiderate, if I send you a brief letter. Thinking and writing tires me.[2]

---

[1] MacColl in his letter of 18 April, thanking for Newman's of 16 April, wrote, 'what is shocking to me is that pious and good Christians should insist on imposing a non-Christian profession of theism on members of Parliament as "a safeguard of the Christian Character of the Legislature."'

He replied to Newman on 27 April that the opposition to the Affirmation Bill had been artificially organised by the 'Church Defence Institution' whose officers had much greater zeal against Gladstone than for Christianity.

[1] MacColl in his letter of 7 April to the *Guardian* (see first note to that of 16 April to him) had said: 'Suppose the 'Ομοούσιον were struck out of the Nicene Creed for the express purpose of admitting Arians to Church communion, would not the Creed cease to be Christian, and become an Arian symbol? And would not the use of it in its mutilated form be

The logic of the passage you have marked is undeniable, but a case, which is clear in the abstract, does not stand, it may be, with the same sense in the concrete. I suppose this is what is meant by 'Summum jus, summa injuria'.

The Arians had an animus, a directness, and a purpose, which cannot be imputed to the statesmen who in the course of years have altered the Parliamentary Oath.[1]

For myself, I have declined taking part for or against the present bill. It never has been my line to take up political or social questions, unless they came close to me as matters of personal duty, and this Bill by being rejected, would bring so little gain to religion, and by being passed would be so little loss, that I do not see reason for taking a side.

I hope you got my second letter which I posted at Rednall.

Very sincerely yours, John H. Card Newman

TO R. W. CHURCH

April 29. 1883

My dear Dean,

In the 'Contemporary' for next month Sir Wm Palmer says, that Froude asked Dr Wiseman at Rome, on what terms we (i.e. personally) could be admitted to communion at Rome. He adds 'Had I been aware etc I do not know whether I should have co-operated so cordially' etc[2]

This is quite a mistake, but I want you, if you can, to tell me in what way, and where, most naturally and effectively to set it right. It comes from Froude's Remains vol 1 p [306–7][3]

Yrs affly J H Card. Newman

TO W. M. J. RING

[End of April 1883]

My dear Sir

I would gladly respond to the compliment you pay me by your question, by giving it a satisfactory answer.[4]

equivalent to an abjuration of Christianity? How does that differ from the use of an oath from which "the true faith of a Christian" had been expelled?' MacColl asked Newman's opinion of this passage.

[1] In his letter of 5 May to the *Guardian* (9 May), p. 698, MacColl quoted this opinion of Newman whom he described as 'one who would be acknowledged on all hands as the greatest living authority on such a subject.'
[2] For Palmer's article see letter of 5 May to the Editor of the *Spectator*.
[3] Dean Church replied on 30 April: 'It is a very bad misrepresentation.
I cannot think of anything better than the sending the *whole* passage as it stands to the Times with a little note. In the Times, it is sure to be read immediately after the paper itself. If it is sent to any of the monthlies, it will be so long before people see it.' Church concluded, 'It is stupid and cruel of Palmer.'
[4] Ring, who was Superior of the house of the Oblates of Mary Immaculate in Great Prescot Street, Tower Hill, appears to have been promoting opposition to the Affirmation Bill.

As to the Affirmation Bill, it is not correct to say that I am in favour of it.

The truth is, I think so little will be lost to religion by its passing and so little gained by its rejection, that it has not seemed to me one of those political or social questions on which it was a duty to have an opinion

Certainly it never entered into my mind to disapprove of Catholics being prominent in their action regarding it. I know how pure the motives are of those of them who have public duties, and how greatly their Catholic brethren are indebted to their exertions.

I gladly send you my blessing, as you ask on your Pilgrimage, and pray God you may gain the full merit which is due to so pious an undertaking[1]

Revd W M J Ring
Committee Rooms 26 Prescot Street London E

TO WILLIAM HENRY ARCHER

Birmingham May 2. 1883

Dear Sir William

I was glad to receive your letter. Some long time ago I wrote to you directing to you in New S. Wales, and in due time the letter came back to me from the Dead Letter office — so I am glad to receive from you your present address, and am pleased to find it is your old one.[2]

Also I must thank you for your kind congratulations on my birthday. Your letter hit the day as near as possible. I am very well, thank God, though weakness, (in contrast to illness,) grows upon me. Difficulty of writing is an instance of what I mean by weakness.

I forget whether I have ever thanked you for your photograph, it was very kind in you to send it.

You have, I fear, the Fenian question to distract you, as well as us. The prospect of what is to come weighs sadly on the interests of the Catholic Church

May God's blessing rest upon you

Most truly Yours J H Card. Newman

TO LORD BRAYE

Bm. May 2. 1883

My dear Lord Braye

I am afraid from the tone of your letter, you are disappointed in your hopes, but, when the facts of the case are considered, there is not much reason

---

[1] Ring organized many pilgrimages to Lourdes and to Rome.

[2] Letter of 30 June 1880. In his letter of 3 Jan. 1883 Archer explained that he had returned to his old home, Maryvale, Upper Hawthorne, near Melbourne.

to be cast down.[1] Is not the real difficulty in contemplating a Catholic House at the Universities the want of pecuniary means? Such failures as that of the Kensington College, not only are a waste, but deter the donors from the risk of a second waste.

I don't know whether you are still in communication with Mr Costelloe. Some time ago I wrote to him to say that I thought it impossible to do more at present than to attempt a sort of lodging house for unattached students — but even for this money is wanted — and the men who would be wanted to carry it out can hardly sacrifice their prospects which would lead them to the bar, or to the civil services, etc by giving their best years to an experiment which may be a failure.

Do you know where Mr Costelloe is? and whether he continues his attempt? That seems to be the first question to ask[2]

Most truly Yours J. H. Card. Newman

The Lord Braye

TO GEORGE T. EDWARDS

Bm May 2. 1883

Dear Mr Edwards

Number 80 of the Tracts of the Times is written by Mr Isaac Williams — I am responsible for it as Editor — but I had (as I have still) that confidence in him that no part of it (I think) passed under my eyes before publication.[3] 'Reserve' was a very strong point with him and Mr Keble — so it was with me, as specially a pupil of the Ante-nicene Church; but the religious education of my two friends having been so different from my own, I can easily believe that there may be sentences of theirs which I could not myself adopt verbally, as there were, in matter of fact, statements of mine which they criticized.

There is hardly a half sentence in your letter to which I do not subscribe;[4] certainly with all my heart to the doctrine that we are saved solely by the vicarious suffering of our Lord for us. Nor did I dream of saying that men like Mr Erskine were Sabellians or Socinians —[5] but, as I hold still, that, when their views were fully carried out by successive generations, they would end in heresy. You may recollect that Mr Jacob Abbot, on whom I was so

[1] Bishop Hedley, Lord Braye and Grissell had their interview with Leo XIII on 13 April, on the subject of university education for Catholics. Lord Braye read to him in Italian 'a succinct statement of the position', and Newman's letter of 2 Nov. 1882. The Pope said he would consult Cardinal Manning. See Lord Braye, *Fewness of my Days*, London 1927, p. 271, and Thomas Murphy, *The Position of the Catholic Church in England and Wales during the last two centuries*, London 1892, pp. 7–8.
[2] See letter of 15 Nov. 1882 to Lord Braye. B.F.C. Costelloe wished, as a first step, to see the restrictions on Catholics going to Oxford interpreted with less severity. See letter of 20 May to Lord Braye.
[3] John Cowley Fisher had criticised *Tract 80* 'On Reserve in communicating religious knowledge.'
[4] Most of Edwards's letter of 28 April was an explanation of his views on the Atonement.
[5] See end of letter of 15 April to Edwards.

severe, came to me and acknowledged that he might have said some things better than he did.[1] It humbled me to find in him such simple candour; I always felt affectionately towards him afterwards, and I have lately had friendly correspondence with his Sons.

Let me remind you that all this correspondence which I must not call controversial, was from Mr Fisher's outrageous account of the Oxford movement, as being a rally for a mere outside religion![2] He had not read one of my Sermons, though the one which stands first in the first volume was sufficient to confute him.[3] Where have I misrepresented the Evangelicals by saying their religion was nothing but sentiment, emotion, self contemplation, and false spirituality?[4] though I *have* spoken of *such* a religion and condemned it.

But enough. Thank you, I don't care to see the article in the Record. The life of St Wilfrid was written by Faber. I don't suppose I ever saw it, till it was published[5]

Very truly Yours John H Card. Newman

G. T. Edwards Esq

TO MALCOLM MACCOLL

May 3. 1883

Dear Mr MacColl,

Thank you for your kind interposition.[6] To suppose that H. Froude and I had contemplated even the bare idea of being admitted to communion at Rome is monstrous, too monstrous to gain credit, and I think every reader of Sir W.P. will think with you. The Spectator will insert a letter of mine[7]

Most truly yours, J. H. Card. Newman.

TO AUGUSTA THEODOSIA DRANE

Bm May 4. 1883

Dear Mother Provincial

I much fear that I have been faulty in not answering your letter of last year, and leaving you in suspense whether we accepted the offer so kind in you, and so valuable to us, of renewing with you and yours the interchange of Masses and Communions. We accepted it joyfully as soon as your letter

---

[1] See *Ess.* I pp. 100–1, and *Moz.* II, pp. 416–17. Edwards wrote on 12 May, agreeing that Broad Church theology must end by destroying the integrity of the faith.

[2] See letters of 24 Feb. to Edwards and 10 March to Fisher.

[3] 'Holiness Necessary for Future Blessedness,' *P.S.* I.

[4] Edwards replied on 12 May, 'I am not aware that you have ever done so, though of course you have given the Evangelical view of the Gospel the most solemn condemnation by abandoning it.' See also letter of 2 June to him.

[5] Edwards reported that a correspondent in the current *Record* quoted at length from *St Wilfrid* in *The Lives of the English Saints*, and attributed it to Newman.

[6] On 1 May MacColl told Newman about William Palmer's article in the *Contemporary Review* for May, and said he was writing to him that he had entirely misunderstood the passage in Froude's *Remains*. On 4 May MacColl wrote that he and Gladstone agreed as to Palmer.

[7] That of 5 May.

came but there was a technical reason, which made me delay writing at once and then, pardon an old man, I forgot it.

Now I hope you continue in the same mind towards us as when you wrote last year, and, relying on it, we mean to say Mass for you tomorrow.[1] We are now in all eleven Priests, but we cannot anticipate that that full number will continue long — but we shall give the Masses with much Christian love and gratitude to you all, while God keeps us here, and for ten years What will be the state of our Community, who will represent it when that decade is fulfilled which now begins?

We are all, you and we, in God's hands.

Quid enim mihi est in cælo? et a Te quid volui super terram? Defecit caro mea et cor meum, Deus cordis mei, et pars mea Deus in æternum[2]

Yours affectly in Christ John H. Card. Newman

TO ROBERT ORNSBY

May 4. 1883

My dear Ornsby

Will you direct and post the inclosed for me?[3]

I have been some time going to write to you on one point.

In your new Edition of Hope Scott's Life, do you bring in the sudden journey to the continent for some unknown purpose?[4] I did not see any reason against it, your impression was otherwise; but the feeling has never left me that when there was a difference of opinion, it was safer to omit. Hence I shall be sorry if it stands.[5]

I have nothing to tell you. This cold wind I suppose is very trying to Mrs Ornsby. Perhaps it is not so bad in Dublin as here

Yours affectly John H Card. Newman

TO WILLIAM ROBERT BROWNLOW

Bm May 5. 1883

My dear Canon Brownlow

Mr Kegan Paul says that Palmer's drawings etc have been returned to you.

I fear I must ask you to return them to me. I gave them to Lord Selbourne as soon as I received them — and I don't like to risk the chance of my not putting him into possession of them in my lifetime[6]

Very sincerely yours John H. Card. Newman

The Very Rev Canon Brownlow

[1] The feast of St Catherine of Siena.
[2] *Psalm* 72 (73): 25–6.
[3] This sentence has been erased, almost certainly not by Newman.
[4] The manuscript of Ornsby's *Memoirs of James Robert Hope-Scott* was not sent to the printer until Aug. 1883.
[5] This journey seems to have been omitted.
[6] See letters of 1 April, 28 Aug. and 11 Sept. 1881 to Brownlow. Also those of 21 July 1883 to Northcote and 13 Aug. 1883 to Edwin Palmer.

TO JAMES DONNET

Birmingham. May 5th. 1883.

Sir,

I am not well read in Medieval history, and in consequence cannot, I am sorry to say, solve your difficulty.[1]

But I had thought, that unbelievers generally take wider grounds against Revelation than the medieval belief merely in witchcraft will furnish. Nor can I, with the account of the Witch of Endor in mind, absolutely deny the existence of witchcraft, confirmed as it is by the injunction, Thou shalt not suffer a witch to live.[2] This Scripture testimony has overcome Protestants as well as Catholics, and great men as little.

I am sorry that I have neither the learning nor the leisure to say more.

Your faithful Servant, John H. Card. Newman.

James Donnet Esq M.D

P.S.   Since writing the above I am told that the great opponents of witch burning were two German Jesuits, who succeeded in the work of Charity to which they gave themselves, Father Spee and Father Tanner.[3]

TO THE EDITOR OF THE SPECTATOR

May 5. 1883[4]

Sir

You have for many years taken so kind an interest in me, that I venture to hope you will let me publish in your columns a few lines on a personal matter, which in no sense concerns the *Spectator*.[5]

Sir William Palmer, with whom I was very intimate fifty years since, and who had so much to do with the start of what was called the 'Oxford Movement,' in an account of it which he has given in the May number of the *Contemporary Review*, writes about me as follows: — '(Hurrell) Froude had, with Newman, while travelling in Italy, been anxious to ascertain the terms upon which they could be admitted to communion by the Roman Church, supposing that some dispensation might be granted which would enable them to communicate with Rome without violation of conscience.' (p. 647). Again, after saying that I considered myself 'predestined,' etc, he proceeds: —

---

[1] James Donnet, Inspector-General of Hospitals and Fleets, wrote on 3 May that he found rationalists assigning as the chief cause of hostility towards the Catholic Church 'the encouragement it gave — during the mediaeval ages — to the belief in the existence of demons, Sorcerers, Witches etc' and the consequent torture of the innocent.

[2] *Exodus* 22:18.

[3] Friedrich von Spee, 1591–1635; Adam Tanner, 1572–1632.

[4] Newman wrote this date beside a copy of his letter as it appeared in the *Spectator* (5 May 1883), p. 576.

[5] R. H. Hutton was editor of the *Spectator* 1861–97.

'Those who conversed with him were not aware of this; nor did they know that while in Italy he had sought, in company with Froude, to ascertain the terms on which they might be admitted to communion with Rome, and had been surprised on learning that an acceptance of the decrees of the Council of Trent was a necessary preliminary. Had I been aware of these circumstances, I do not know whether I should have been able to co-operate so cordially as I did with this great man.' (p. 654).

To this statement, namely, that I was party to an inquiry as to the terms on which, by dispensation or otherwise, Hurrell Froude and I might be admitted to communion with Rome, I give an absolute and emphatic denial. The passage in Froude's 'Remains,' on which Sir William founds it, with the note appended by me as editor on its publication, runs as follows: — Froude says, in a letter to a friend, 'The only thing I can put my hand on as an acqui-sition is having formed an acquaintance with a man of some influence at Rome, Monsignor (Wiseman), the head of the (English) College, who has enlightened (Newman) and me on the subject of our relations to the Church of Rome. We got introduced to him, to find out whether they would take us in on any terms to which we could twist our consciences, and we found to our dismay that not one step could be gained without swallowing the Council of Trent as a whole.' (pp. 306–7.)

I added this note in protest: — 'All this must not be taken literally, being a jesting way of stating to a friend what really was the fact, viz., that he and another availed themselves of the opportunity of meeting a learned Romanist to ascertain the ultimate points at issue between the Churches.' (*Ibid.*)

As on the publication of the 'Remains' I disclaimed by anticipation Sir William Palmer's present misstatement, so I repudiate it again now. One thing I thank him for, that, by publishing it in my lifetime, he has given me the opportunity of denying it.

I am, Sir, &c., John H. Cardinal Newman.

TO LORD BRAYE

May 6. 1883

My dear Lord Braye

Any day will suit me for your call, and any hour except between half past 1 and half past two. To save you the trouble of a letter, I will say Tuesday. On Monday I am engaged as well as your Lordship

Yours very truly J H Card. Newman

The Lord Braye

P.S.   I send the Pamphlet.

Bm May 8. 1883

Dear Sir

I do not know how to answer your question without using more words than I like to trouble you with[1]

I feel myself to be so little of a judge on political and even social questions, and religious questions so seldom come before us, that I rarely feel it a duty to form and to express an opinion on any subject of a public nature.

I cannot consider the Affirmation Bill involves a religious principle; for, as I had occasion to observe in print more than thirty years ago, what the political and social world means by the word 'God' is too often not the Christian God, the Jewish, or the Mahometan, not a Personal God, but an unknown God, as little what Christians mean by God as the Fate, or Chance, or Anima Mundi of a Greek Philosopher.[2]

Hence it as little concerns Religion whether Mr Bradlaugh swears by no God with the Government or swears by an Impersonal, or Material, or abstract Ideal Something or other, which is all that is secured to us by the opposition. Neither Mr Gladstone nor Sir Stafford Northcote excluded from Parliament what Religion means by an 'Atheist.'[3]

Accordingly it is only half my meaning, if I am made to say that I 'do not approve, in any sense of the word, of the Affirmation Bill.' I neither approve nor disapprove. I express no opinion upon it; and that first because I do not commonly enter upon political questions, and next, because, looking at the Bill on its own merits, I think nothing is lost to Religion by its passing and nothing is gained by its being rejected.[4]

I am, Dear Sir, Your Faithful Servant

John H Card. Newman[5]

[1] On 26 April the *Daily News* stated, 'We hear that Cardinal Newman has declined to join in any action against the Affirmation Bill,' and a few days later the *Morning Post* said that it was 'authorised' to state that Newman did not approve 'in any sense of the word' of the Affirmation Bill. On 5 May the journalist F. W. Chesson wrote to Newman 'as the announcement in the "Post" directly commits you to a side in the controversy, it has occurred to me that perhaps you would be willing to inform me whether you really authorised the statement referred to, or whether your views have been misunderstood by the writer.'

[2] *Idea*, p. 57.

[3] The Affirmation Bill was rejected in the House of Commons on 3 May by 292 votes to 289, although Gladstone's government had a large majority. Sir Stafford Northcote, leader of the Conservative opposition, allowed the initiative to a small group round Lord Randolph Churchill, 'who first saw the political possibilities lurking in the religious issue. Not only might they rally their own benches against the "Radical atheist", but a great many nonconformist radicals and the whole Irish party (under Cardinal Manning's direct instigation) could be brought into the same lobby. Gladstone, than whom no more devout Churchman lived, pleaded finely for tolerance. But he could not command a majority.' R. C. K. Ensor, *England 1870–1914*, Oxford 1936, p. 68.

[4] In his draft Newman began and rejected here a paragraph saying that if it could be shown that in practice the Affirmation Bill was a betrayal of religion 'of course I side with the opposition.'

[5] Chesson sent this letter to the *Daily News*, where it was published on 14 May, p. 5, with an explanation: 'During the last few weeks several irreconcilable statements concerning the views of Cardinal Newman on the subject of the Affirmation Bill have been published in the

TO EDWARD HAYES PLUMPTRE

Bm May 8. 1883

Dear Dean of Wells,

Your gift came quite punctually.[1] I wish my knowledge of Italian enabled me fully to appreciate and enjoy it; but Dante is a language in himself. This, however, I am able to say: in spite of my deficiencies in Italian scholarship, I may have a right to a taste and a judgment in English, and I think your translation has a merit which cannot be claimed by such other English Dantes as I have come across. It is very few men who can write good blank verse, at least in Translations. How inferior is Cowper's Iliad compared with his Task! I have attempted Cary's Dante times beyond counting, but I have always failed to get to the end of the page. On the other hand, your lines being in rhyme were to my taste so flowing and musical that I found myself far into the Fourth Canto, before I was well aware that I had begun. I doubt not I shall find the rest equally attractive[2]

Very truly Yours John H. Card. Newman

The Very Rev. the Dean of Wells.

TO WILLIAM ROBERT BROWNLOW

May 10. 1883

My dear Canon Brownlow

I fear I have seemed to you unreasonable — but I did not know how matters stood. I was frightened lest the drawings should have been lost in the fire — and when Mr Kegan Paul told me he had sent them back to you, I was not sure he had not been asked by you, and had declined to publish them. And thus it seemed that there was no future for them. I am very much surprised to find from you that I did not tell you I had given them to Lord Selborne. This I did, as soon as they came into my possession.[3]

Pray don't hurry the engraving improperly. September or October, which you mention, will quite do.[4]

newspapers. . . . I wrote to the Cardinal . . . The answer which his Eminence has been good enough to make to me is so interesting, and at the same time so important, that I beg to send you a copy of it in the hope that you will publish it for the information of your readers.' Newman's letter was reprinted generally in the newspapers. See also letter of 23 May to the Editor of the *Manchester Examiner*.

[1] Plumptre sent a sample of his translation of Dante, later published as *The Commedia and Canzoniere of Dante Alighieri*, two volumes, London 1886–7, asking for Newman's criticisms.
[2] In his letter of 29 March announcing his gift, Plumptre also asked if he might republish, with Newman's name, their correspondence about probation after death. See letter of 13 April 1878 to Plumptre. They were reprinted in his *The Spirits in Prison*, London 1884, as 'Correspondence with a Roman Catholic Priest.'
[3] See letter of 5 May 1883.
[4] Brownlow wrote on 7 May that eight of William Palmer's plates remained to be engraved. The two years Newman had allowed for this purpose would not end until Sept. or Oct.

Sir W Palmer has for years and years been at war all' outrance with Mr C. Weld[1]

> Very sincerely yours John H. Card. Newman

The Very Rev Canon Brownlow

TO LORD BRAYE

> Bm. May 11. 1883

My dear Lord Braye

I very much fear you will think I am treating you rudely. The thought has troubled me ever since you were here, and at last I have made up my mind to write to you.[2]

I should like to come to you on your Feast day very much, but it comes upon me more and more strongly, that, if I go to you, I must go to other kind friends, who have asked me, and to whom it would hurt me much to seem disrespectful and ungrateful. A necessity sometimes calls me to London; otherwise, I do not go from home. Indeed, I could not without my health suffering, and I must plead my age; — but that does not excuse my having said I could come to you and then retracting

I hope that, in spite of this mistake of mine, you will let me be au courant of the proceedings of men in whom I take so great an interest

I am, My dear Lord Braye

> Your Lordship's faithful servant John H Card. Newman

The Lord Braye

P.S.   I am not unwilling to write a letter on the subject, if you thought my views about Oxford went *far enough* for your purpose.[3]

TO PERCY WILLIAM BUNTING

> May 14. 1883

My dear Sir

I feel much obliged by the opportunity you offer me of writing on the subject of the Oxford movement in the Contemporary Review — but I do not avail myself of it, because at present my Apologia sells very fairly and in it I have said all I had to say on the ecclesiastical theory, on which, as far as I am concerned that movement was founded.[4]

---

[1] Brownlow wrote about William Palmer (of Worcester College), 'I hear of him at Chidiock, where he is a disagreeable neighbour to Charles Weld. I suppose he thinks it his duty to withstand popery everywhere.'

[2] When Lord Braye called earlier in the month he had invited Newman to the celebration of the patronal feast of his chapel at Stanford, near Rugby, on 7 July, the Translation of St Thomas of Canterbury.

[3] See letter of 20 May to Lord Braye

[4] Bunting, who became editor of the *Contemporary Review* in 1882, wrote on 12 May to ask whether, following on William Palmer's article on the Oxford Movement, Newman would write on the same subject. See letter of 5 May to the Editor of the *Spectator*.

Sir W Palmer, who is a more thoroughly well read man than I am, wrote a work in two volumes on Anglicanism about the year 1839 — which is now in course of republication, which, agreeing with me in the main, goes nearer, as *I* think, to the Church of Rome than I did. I was glad to hear of its republication for this reason.[1]

I take this opportunity of saying, what I forgot to say when you were so good as to call on me here, that for some past years I have felt myself engaged, if I did write any thing more, I should ask its acceptance from the conductor of the Nineteenth Century Review.[2] It is so little probable, considering my age, and so much against any expectation of mine, that I should be carrying such a purpose out, that it did not come across my mind during our conversation.

I am, Dear Sir, Very truly Yours

John H Card. Newman

TO MISS M. R. GIBERNE

May 14. 1883

My dear Sister M. Pia

I grieve to hear of your bad nights, though on the whole your account of yourself is good. I inclose a memorial for your little novice. And I shall be much honoured by your Bishop's gift.

Those lines on your Feast Day are pretty and touching, and especially precious as showing the feelings towards you of your Sisters.

Your ever affectte John H. Card. Newman

TO MISS BAINES

The Oratory, Hagley Road   May 15 1883

Cardinal Newman will be very glad to see Miss Baines, if she will favour him with a call at any hour and day which she will name to him.

TO MICHAEL FROST

Birmingham May 17, 1883.

Dear Sir,

I must decline the honor and the responsibility you are so good as to attribute to me, and must beg you to believe that in what I say in answer to your question I am representing no one but myself.[3]

---

[1] See letter of 6 Dec. 1882 to W. J. Copeland. Palmer's *Treatise on the Church of Christ* was not republished.

[2] The editor of the *Nineteenth Century* was James Knowles, who founded it in 1877 on ceasing to be editor of the *Contemporary Review*, owing to a disagreement with its proprietors.

[3] Frost wrote on 16 May from Dunlemey, Plymouth, to ask whether Newman thought Christianity would suffer from the passing of the Affirmation Bill. Frost expected a tide of atheism to sweep over the Church, 'Is the Holy Church capable of offering a resistance? If so, what stand will she take, and in what way will she view the "rejected measure"?'

Nor have I much to say even in the way of private opinion, and very little beyond what I have said these forty or fifty years.

I have ever anticipated a great battle between good and evil, and have ever been led to think the duty of the champions of truth, when the conflict came, was anticipated for them in the words of Moses, 'Fear ye not, *stand still and see* magnalia Domini. He shall fight for you, and ye *shall hold your peace*'.[1]

And so in the Psalm, '*Be still,* and know that I am God.'[2]

And the past history of the Church enforces the same great lesson. How was it that the poor weak Christian body overturned the Roman Empire? *Who* did it? was it some great converts? was it some great Pope? We are driven to call it the work of God, because it was no one's else.

So, when the innumerable tribes came down from the North, not pagan, open to conversion, but bitter Arians, enemies of the Church, who was it changed them into Catholics, as if in one day? 'The earth opened her mouth and swallowed up the flood.'[3] It was not man that saved us.

So again three centuries ago. So completely was Christendom deluged by Protestant teaching, that ambassadors, writing to their courts, spoke as if the Church was simply gone. Man's instrumentality had indeed a larger part here in the revival than in the former instan[c]es, but on the whole the same rule holds.

And again at the end of last century, the entire structure of civil and religious polity went — but as regards the Church, only for a time. But we did not accomplish our own resurrection. God wrought.

So I think it will be now. We shall have a bad time of it, but 'be still and see the salvation of God.'[4]

Yours very truly J. H. Card. Newman

TO LORD BRAYE

May 20. 1883

My dear Lord Braye

I have today seen a letter from Mr Wood, and in case you have not seen it, I will tell you what it says as to the first step in any movement to be made towards gaining for Catholics a hearing at Rome in behalf of a house of studies at Oxford for Catholics.

If I have carried off rightly the words of his letter, it agrees with what you told me, but is more definite. The question to be asked on the part of Catholic parents is whether it is possible, with the regard that they are bound to pay to the words of their Bishops for them to send their sons to an Oxford house of studies. I cannot answer for the fidelity of my report of his words — but I

[1] *Exodus* 14:13–14.
[2] *Ps.* 45 (46):10.
[3] *Apoc.* 12:16.
[4] *Exod.* 14:13.

think, if I give it correctly, the advice is very practical and diminishes the difficulty of getting signatures to an application on the subject to Propaganda[1]
Your Lordship's Very faithful Servant

John H Card. Newman

TO TIMOTHY BROSNAN

Bm May 22. 1883

Dear Canon Brosnan,

I hope you will not think me insensible to the great name of O'Connell or wanting in due honour to his name, if I ask you to let me decline writing the letter, which you propose to me in behalf of the Church which is to be built in his memory.[2]

My reason is simply this. I have found it so difficult to supply the many notices of this kind which have been asked of me by friends, that I found it necessary to make a rule against writing any.

Please to consider too how advanced my age is, and what little leisure I have for the duties which have a direct claim upon me. Thank you for the cuttings and other papers.

Very truly yours — John H Card Newman

P.S.   I beg to enclose a cheque for £5 for your religious undertaking.

TO H. P. LIDDON

May 22. 1883

My dear Canon Liddon

I, like you, am engaged on the 29 and 30 — but I am sorry to say I shall be engaged on the 31st too — This week too is a very busy week with us. But I have no engagement after the 31st and shall be glad to see you any day you name.

Very truly Yours John H Card. Newman

[1] Alexander Wood, a convert from Trinity College, Oxford, now in Rome, was one of those, who, with the approval of Bishops Clifford of Clifton and Hedley of Newport, was planning an approach to Propaganda on the subject of allowing Catholics to attend the English universities. It was proposed to ask the opinion of a canonist as to the force of the existing prohibition. See the printed letter of 5 March 1885, from Carlo Menghini to H. de la Garde Grissell, *Catholics at the Universities, An Opinion upon certain instructions addressed to the English Bishops by the Sacred Congregation of Propaganda.*
  Eaglesim, who was in correspondence with Wood, had presumably shown Newman one of Wood's letters.
[2] Brosnan, parish priest of Cahirciveen, County Kerry, from 1879 until his death in 1898, was collecting funds for the O'Connell Memorial church there. Its foundation stone was laid on 1 Aug. 1888.

TO THE EDITOR OF THE MANCHESTER EXAMINER

May 23. 1883

To Editor of Manchester Examiner

Card.   Newman presents his compliments to the Editor of the Manchester Examiner, and begs to thank him for the courtesy and considerateness shown him in the able article which he has inserted in the columns of his Journal.[1]

TO WILFRID MEYNELL

May 23. 1883

To W. Meynell Esq Editor of Weekly Register
Dear Sir

I thank you for the considerateness which has prompted your question. I beg you, however, to allow me to say that I am not prepared to give any answer to it[2]

J H N

[1] The article in the *Manchester Examiner* (21 May 1883), p. 6, which also appeared in the *Manchester Weekly Times*, was a warm defence of Newman's attitude over the Affirmation Bill, as expounded in his letter of 8 May to F. W. Chesson, which *The Times* published on 14 May, p. 6, headed 'An Ambiguous Cardinal.' The *Manchester Examiner* said: 'A protest against the Affirmation Bill, declaring that it tended to "dispense with the recognition by Parliament of the supreme authority of God," had been signed by the two Archbishops and twenty Bishops of the Church of England, by the Cardinal Archbishops of Westminster and Dublin, and twenty-three other Catholic prelates, by two Archbishops and nine other prelates of the Protestant Church in Ireland, and 763 Wesleyan Methodist ministers.' But, as for Newman he 'looked at the Bill only from a religious point of view, and having satisfied himself that it involved no religious principle he did not care to go further. . . . The *Times*, in publishing Cardinal Newman's letter in reply to Mr. Chesson's inquiries, thought fit to describe him as "an ambiguous Cardinal." This is just what happens when people do not take the trouble to appreciate positions and ways of thinking with which they are unfamiliar. There is nothing ambiguous in what Cardinal Newman says about the Affirmation Bill. He says explicitly that in his view it does not involve any religious principle . . . He expresses no opinion upon it as a political measure, because he is not a politician, and does not know enough of politics to enable him to form an opinion. . . . Mr. Bradlaugh's affirmation is as religious as the oaths taken by most of our legislators, with the recommendation perhaps that it contains no formal impiety. In his views regarding the Affirmation Bill Cardinal Newman shines far apart from the other great ecclesiastical luminaries, and offers especially a striking contrast to his English colleague of the Sacred College. Cardinal Manning has had his eye fixed on Mr. Bradlaugh ever since Northampton sent him to Parliament, and has two or three times made him the subject of a solemn appeal to the nation. In Cardinal Manning's eyes . . . we still have one virtue left. The oath still keeps out the atheist, or obliges him to pay toll in the shape of a hollow and worthless profession. Cardinal Manning has besought us again and again . . . to maintain intact this last bulwark of religion. Cardinal Newman on the other hand, sees nothing in it. He regards the oath as useless for religious purposes, and cannot admit that the Affirmation Bill, against which the other Cardinal has been declaiming, involves any religious principle at all. The divergence could not well be wider, and it is agreeable to know that such diversities of opinion on great questions exist within the Catholic pale.'
[2] The *Weekly Register*, which had questioned the *Daily News* report of Newman's views on the Affirmation Bill, and also criticised them, the *Weekly Register* (April 28), p. 530, (May 5), p. 563, printed (19 May), p. 617, his letter of 8 May to F. W. Chesson. Meynell, editor of the *Weekly Register*, wrote on 22 May that he had 'received one or two letters in defence of the Affirmation Bill, and containing strong expressions of approval' of Newman's letter to F. W. Chesson. He asked whether he should publish these letters which might intensify the controversy, and said he intended to publish no letters on the other side.

24 MAY 1883

TO JOSEPH PIERSE DEVINE

[24 May 1883]

Card N etc. — and assures him that he has not [sic] knowledge of Mr Bradlaugh and never thought of him when he wrote the letter to which Mr Devine refers.[1]

TO H. P. LIDDON

Bm May 24. 1883

My dear Canon Liddon

Tuesday, June 5, will suit me very well. As you speak of coming in the *afternoon*, I am led to say that we can give you a bed, if you like. I should add that on every day I am generally engaged from half past one to two or a little past two

Very sincerely Yours John H Card. Newman

TO THOMAS ALDER POPE

May 24 [1883?]

My dear Thomas

I must ask you to take the trouble to put the inclosed into Italian for me and am

Yours ever affectly J. H. Card. Newman

TO MARGARET DE LISLE

May 27. 1883

Dear Miss de Lisle

I do not like to lose a post, before thanking you for your affectionate letter — May God bless you and keep you from all harm, and increase in you the knowledge and love of Himself and of His Son our Saviour[2]

Most truly Yours John H Card. Newman

[1] Devine wrote on 23 May, in reference to Newman's published letter of 8 May to F. W. Chesson, that Bradlaugh was a much maligned man:
'I as a Catholic cannot avoid thinking that both our Catholic Newspapers aristocracy and even our hierarchy and priests are unconsciously guilty of great injustice in joining in the hue and cry after Mr Bradlaugh.'
[2] Margaret de Lisle had perhaps written about her vocation. She became a Franciscan nun two years after this.

TO MRS KEON

May 27. 1883

My dear Mrs Keon,

Thank you for your remembrance of yesterday.[1] I have had your dear husband's name against June 5 in my Obituary List ever since 1875.

Excuse a short letter, as I have a difficulty in writing.

Most sincerely yours John H. Card. Newman.

TO SIR CHARLES WOLSELEY

Birmingham   May 27. 1883.

My dear Sir Charles

I am very glad to have your letter, and congratulate you on the tidings which it contains, with all my heart.[2]

Also I feel grateful to you for your affectionate wish that I should marry you and Miss Murphy, and am most reluctant to decline so true a pleasure.

My difficulty is my increasing infirmities. Recollect how old I am. Only a few days ago I had what might have been a serious accident; it was a fall; and I consider it hardly safe to go any where by myself.

And I doubt about my being able to pay Bride and Bridegroom the due courtesy of appearing at the wedding breakfast.

Take all this into your consideration. Be sure I love you too well, not to wish to avail myself of your kindness.[3]

Yours affectionately John H. Card. Newman

Sir C. M. Wolseley, Bart

TO GEORGE T. EDWARDS

Bm. June 2. 1883

Dear Mr Edwards

Thank you for your letter of last month. I do not wish to have *the* last word, but *my* last word shall be what follows.[4]

1.   My own contention, to use the fashionable word, is just this, as I have said before: — viz that our Lord's Atonement for sin is not the ordinary instrument of conversion, but the supreme object of devotion.

2.   I fully allow and believe that in particular cases the preaching of the

---

[1] The feast of St Philip.

[2] Wolseley wrote from Paris on 25 May to announce his engagement to Anita Theresa daughter of D. T. Murphy of San Francisco. He said, 'I cannot help hoping from the interest you always seemed to take in me both when I was at School at the Oratory, and afterwards when my poor Mother consulted you about sending me to Oxford, that you will be pleased to hear of my present happiness . . .'

[3] This letter seems to have miscarried. See letters of 7 and 11 June to Wolseley.

[4] Edwards replied on 12 May to Newman's letter of 2 May, and continued his criticism of the place assigned to the doctrine of the Atonement in the *Tracts for the Times*.

Atonement is the means of conversion. What manifestation of Divine mercy has not this power? and that conversion in such cases may be a formal process such as you describe; but I consider that the faint initial stirrings of religion in the heart, the darkness, the sense of sin, the fear of God's judgment, the contrition, the faith, hope and love, need not be a conscious, clearly defined, experience, but may be, and commonly is, a slow and silent growth, not broken into separate and successive stages, but as regards these spiritual acts composite, and almost simultaneous, strengthening with the soul's strength, advancing with advancing years, till (after whatever relapses and returns, or whatever unswerving fidelity) death comes at length, and seals and crowns with perseverance and salvation what from first to last is a work of grace. Grace is the beginning and the end of it.

3.   I should add that the imagination that the Atonement is the necessary instrument of conversion, results in what seems to me a superstition, viz the fancied obligation of introducing the whole gospel into every Sermon. Thus all Sermons are repetitions of each other. Robert Wilberforce used to call them '180-degrees Sermons'. You heard the same thing, the 'Scheme', 'Plan' etc, every Sunday, and nothing else.

4.   I take for granted that, in speaking against the Tract on Reserve, you quote from its *text*. I say this because Bishop Sumner, in a charge, denounced it as if speaking against the 'distribution of the Scriptures', whereas Mr Williams's words were 'the *indiscriminate* distribution of the Scriptures'. This I was told a few days ago by [a] man who is in high position, who wrote to the Bishop on the point[1]

Very sincerely Yours John H Card. Newman

TO GEORGE RICHMOND

George Richmond Esqr R.A.   June 3. 1883

I am ashamed of having come away from London without having secured your precious gift. My excuse is the great spaces which separate London homes and the whirl of the metropolis[2]

If you will allow me, I will send a friend to receive and send me what I value to [so] very highly

I want your signature on the back as one link in the chain of transmission, as I think after my time of what I may call its sacred frame going to persons

---

[1] This was probably Dean Church, who visited Newman in April. C. R. Sumner, Bishop of Winchester, in his *Charge* of Sept. 1841, p. 63 described *Tract 80* as objecting 'to the distribution of bibles.' Edwards sent Newman part of an article by Henry Rogers in the *Edinburgh Review* of 1843, which gave, he thought, support to J. C. Fisher's criticism of that Tract.

[2] The gift was a portrait of Keble framed in oak from a tree said to be the one tied to which St Edmund was shot to death with arrows. Newman sent it eventually to Charles Gore, as Warden of Pusey House. See letter of 14[?] Nov. 1888 to him and G. L. Prestige, *The Life of Charles Gore*, London 1935, p. 80.

who will be sure to value it for the sake of a great English Martyr, and for your sake, for Keble's sake, and, I trust I may say, my own.[1]

Also, may I ask your acceptance of a book or two of mine, all I have to give, as a sort of memorial of my gratitude to you.[2]

TO LORD BRAYE

Bm. June 6, 1883

My dear Lord Braye

I cannot resist your kind importunity and will come to your festival on July 7 – but I am obliged to state a difficulty.

Some months ago I engaged to marry a friend of mine 'in July', he wrote from abroad, and never answered my letter, accepting or declining the conditions which I was obliged to make — so I don't know how I stand with him.[3]

Also, I must ask you what your function on the 7th is. Fr Coleridge preaches, but who sings Mass? and for myself, I suppose it will be enough if I assist as a layman. If I had to appear in the Sanctuary, I should have to bring a lot of vestments etc which I don't like to move about.

And I shall have to ask you what the station is called, which is near your house[4]

Very sincerely Yours

John H Card. Newman

The Lord Braye

TO SIR CHARLES WOLSELEY

Birmingham June 7, 1883.

My dear Sir Charles

I am sorry my letter has not reached you. I wrote by the first post, directing to the 'Grand Hotel de Louvre, Paris.'[5]

I congratulated you, as I do now again, on your prospective marriage, thanked you for thinking so kindly of me, and expressed the gratification I should have in performing the sacred ceremony.

[1] Richmond replied on 9 June: 'Your visit was a great delight to me — and your most gracious and kind letter, is a crown to that visit, which I shall always treasure, and deposit among my most precious possessions.

I have obeyed the request of your Eminence and signed my name on the print of Mr Keble — and the word "gratitudo" used there is no empty form, but a true expression of what I feel, for in sorrow and in joy I have for nearly half a century, fed upon your published works — which have been to me a rich treasury of instruction and ennobling thought.'

[2] Richmond chose the three volumes of *H.S.* and wrote his thanks on 25 Sept.

[3] This obviously refers to Sir Charles Wolseley.

[4] Lord Braye replied on 8 June that the mass in his chapel would be sung by the Bishop of the diocese, Bagshawe of Nottingham, who in the end did not come. See letter of 26 June to Lord Braye. The station for Lord Braye's house, Stanford Hall, Rugby, was Stanford Park.

[5] See letters of 27 May and 11 June to Wolseley.

I added that, considering my age and infirmity consequent upon it, I hoped you would allow me to absent myself from the wedding breakfast.

May I venture through you to convey my congratulations to Miss Murphy.

Yours very sincerely John H. Card. Newman

Sir C. M. Wolseley Bart

TO GEORGE T. EDWARDS

Bm June 9. 1883

Dear Mr Edwards

Thank you for Professor Naville's work on Modern Atheism.[1] I beg your acceptance of one of my own books, tho' it is not a systematic treatise on the subject, as his is.

Your anecdote from Mr Moffat puts me in mind of a passage in one of my own volumes, written from what a Missionary Bishop told me. I have transcribed it and inclose it[2]

Very truly Yours John H Card. Newman

Set up a large Crucifix at Charing Cross; the police would think you simply mad. Yet, that awful, touching winning form has before now converted the very savage who gazed upon it; he has wondered, has asked what it meant, has broken into tears and been converted ere he knew that he believed. The manifestation of love has been the incentive to faith.

TO CHARLES JOHN PLUMER

Bm June 10. 1883

My dear Plumer

I am pleased to hear you wish to have my photograph, and gladly send it to you.[3]

You have never been out of my memory, and I have often tried to get some

[1] Edwards presented the Swiss evangelical pastor Ernest Naville's *Modern Atheism; or, The Heavenly Father*, translated from the French by Henry Downton, second edition, London 1882.

[2] On 8 June Edwards wrote how much he agreed with Newman's letter of 2 June, and went on to illustrate how God's love as shown in the Cross was the only thing likely to move hard hearts: 'Mr Moffat, the African missionary, father in law to Livingstone, told me that when he went among the Bechuanas, a fierce and savage tribe of people, he was one day told by a native, "You'll never see a Bechuana man *weep*." He said he found on observation that it was true . . . centuries of cruelty and paganism had dried up the fountain within, so that nothing could flow. When however, having mastered their language, he began to tell them of the great God in the Spirit land . . . in his love and pity sending his Son to become man and die for them — as he spoke of Gethsemane and Calvary, and the agony and bloody sweat, he discerned the first tears in the eyes of Bechuana savages, and he told me, how in later days, he has seen groups of the converted savages gathered round the Lord's table, with the tears streaming down their cheeks as they celebrated the dying love of Him who had bought them with his blood.'

The passage Newman now transcribes is from *Diff*. I, p. 283, abbreviated and slightly altered in wording.

[3] Newman heard this from Bloxam. See letter of 6 Feb. 1883 to him. Plumer wrote on 14 June that his intercourse with Bloxam had led to 'the renewal of my communications with you.'

tidings of you. I have your look and your mode of conversing as vividly before my mind as I had 50 years ago, and your playful notice of 'Ingulphus' is quite fresh.[1]

Oh what a pleasant past! and were you present in October in the term when Jelf was chosen Prefect of Sermons and when after Copleston had asked 'Magister Decane quem nominas Censorem theologicum tuum?' or words to that effect, and the answer went round, as we stood at the table, 'Dominum Jelf', 'Dominum Jelf', and Jelf looked so solemn, how when it came to my turn, after in vain trying to master myself, at length I broke silence by a dreadful burst and explosion of laughter through my eyes nose and mouth which evoked a corresponding laugh to my great relief from Copleston. And then again I recollect always that sad time when you came up to Littlemore to wish me good bye, and how Jack Morris told me that in your way back you sat down in Iffley Church-yard and cried.

May God bless you and keep you and bring you into all truth is the affectionate prayer for you of your old friend

John Henry Newman[2]

TO H. P. LIDDON

Bm June 11. 1883

Dear Canon Liddon

Thank you for the Sermons and Pamphlets;[3] I have read the 'Unlaw' with great interest, and think it a powerful Statement — but I wish you had not had to tell me that the Court of Delegates, of which the present Court of Appeal is successor and heir, was framed on the unecclesiastical principle, which Pusey has been all along resisting. If lawyers are to be on the board, of course their influence will tend in a secular direction. When I say 'I wish', I mean 'for Pusey's sake', not that I am surprised.[4]

---

[1] Plumer was elected a Fellow of Oriel College in 1821, a year before Newman.

[2] Plumer replied on 14 June, thanking Newman for 'Your admirable photograph, and still more for your kindly words and pleasing allusions to persons and times in which we both were formerly interested. Sixty years is a long time to look back to; I quite agree with you in saying it was a pleaant time. I well remember, I think it was in 1823, entering the Oriel porters lodge, and saying "well porter, who is elected," and he said, "Mr Newman of Trinity sir," upon which I said in surprise, "Newman of Trinity? I never heard the name mentioned as having a chance". . . . Well do I remember that mournful visit to Littlemore; but if what caused it, was so sad to me, how bitter must it have been to Pusey, whom I met shortly after in the streets of Leeds, at the Consecration of St Saviour's Church, when he seemed overwhelmed with grief.'
Plumer also said he wished he had known beforehand of Newman's revisiting Trinity College, 'for I certainly would have made an effort to clasp your hand once more.'

[3] Liddon, who came to visit Newman on 5 June, wrote from Christ Church, Oxford, on 7 June, 'to thank you for the two very pleasant days which I have spent at the Oratory, and for all your kindness in entrusting me with Dr Pusey's letters.' He also sent Pusey's *Parochial and Cathedral Sermons*, Oxford 1882, inscribed: 'H.E. Cardinal Newman in grateful remembrance of much kindness: on June 6. 1883 from H. P. Liddon.'

[4] Liddon also sent Pusey's *Unlaw in Judgements of the Judicial Committee and its Remedies. A letter to the Rev. H.P. Liddon*, second edition, Oxford 1881, which protested against a civil court, the Judicial Committee of the Privy Council, being the Court of Appeal in Church

Thank you also for Rosmini's 'Five Wounds'.[1] I have read various parts of it, and, though profiting from its learning, cannot say I like the tone of it, and think he undertook a problem to which he was unequal. The book seems to me theoretical — and, I may say, revolutionary — for he almost condemns the principles on which the Church has acted since the days of Constantine. If the Church is to rule in the Orbis terrarum, it must be a secular power as well as a religious, certain as its secularity is to bring spiritual evils with it.

I am sorry so to speak, for I have ever felt kindly disposed to him and his people.[2]

Very sincerely Yours John H Card. Newman

TO SIR CHARLES WOLSELEY

Birmingham June 11. 1883

My dear Sir Charles,

This is a misfortune to both of us; but, never mind, it is the fault of neither of us. You showed your affectionate remembrance of me by asking. I my affection for you by at once accepting it. Father Neville is my witness how I made a point of writing to you without any delay. Yet what could you do in your perplexity at not receiving an answer from me? If there be a case, in which on both sides the will can be taken for the deed, this is such.[3]

I shall at any time be rejoiced to see you; but don't go out of your way to come to morrow. Come some day with your bride.

When the wedding day is fixed, let me know, and I shall say Mass for you and her upon it.[4]

Yours affectionately John H. Card. Newman

Sir C. M. Wolseley Bart

TO HENRY BELLINGHAM

H Bellingham Esq M P   June 12/83
My dear Sir

Thank you for the sight of your very important Letter, which I hereby return.

Certainly I wish that a way should be found, by which Catholic youth might be able to go to the Universities without danger to their faith — while matters. The High Court of Delegates was set up by Henry VIII for this purpose, when he forbad appeals to Rome. Liddon replied on 12 June: 'In *25. Hen. VIII cap 19. § 4.4.* nothing is said about the Delegates being clerical or lay. . . . Dr Pusey used to say that, in this matter, the Church trusted the Sovereign.' The Act of 1833 which set up, in place of the Delegates, the Judicial Committee of the Privy Council, made it legally impossible for all the members of the Committee to be ecclesiastics.

[1] Antonio Rosmini, *Of the Five Wounds of the Holy Church*, edited with an introduction by H. P. Liddon, London 1883. See letters of 23 June and 29 Nov. 1849 to F. W. Faber, and 28 Nov. 1849 to J. M. Capes.

[2] Liddon replied on 12 June: 'What your Eminence says about the Book makes me anxious lest I should in any way compromise Fr Lockhart and the English Rosminians . . .'

[3] See letter of 7 June.

[4] Wolseley was married on 17 July in London.

I cannot deny that at present that danger is real; and that there is a real danger gives force to the judgment of the Bishops, delivered at two several times.[1]

But since the idea of a College cannot be brought into effect for a long time, certainly it is well to begin to agitate the question without delay but something must be done first by the Oxford Jesuits without a College, before a College is possible. They ought to be able by their visible exertions and success to convince Catholics, as they have had the opportunity of making it clear to yourself, that they are doing a work which has a claim upon the support of the laity

June 12.1883

To H Bellingham Esqr

P.S. I am sorry not to be able to acquiesce at the publication of any additional letter of mine on the Affirmation question. Most unwillingly have I written a word of the subject and I have been forced to do so from my opinion being, as I considered, misrepresented. And the appearance of a second letter would, I much fear, lead to my having to write more.[2]

J H N

TO LORD BRAYE

Bm June 12. [1883]

My dear Lord Braye

As you seem to wish a definitive answer from me as to the trains I propose to come by to Rugby, I write to say I propose to start on the 7th July by the Bm [Birmingham] train at 8 A M which arrives at Rugby at 9.15, and to leave you so as to go back by the Rugby 6.26 P M train to Birmingham.

I will avail myself of your leave to bring a Father with me.

Should I assist at high mass in the Sanctuary, I should require a Prie-Dieu on the gospel side. If I am not in the Sanctuary, but in the Church, I ought to be either in a gallery, or with a prie-Dieu separate from the congregation. Will you tell me, if a Bishop celebrates?[3]

Very sincerely Yours John H Card. Newman

The Lord Braye

[1] In March 1865 and April 1882. See letters of 31 March 1865 to Emily Bowles and 16 May 1882 to Mrs Pereira. See also letter of 13 June 1883 to Liddon.
In his draft Newman erased after this paragraph two further ones:
'Also, while I never advocated a Catholic Church [College], I am rather less disposed to the idea of one than I was.
First because of the expense of building, which will be even more difficult to meet than it was, since the failure of Kensington'
[2] When the *Daily News* reported on 26 April that Newman was in favour of the Affirmation Bill, Bellingham, who was M.P. for County Louth, wrote at once to say he had been opposing it strongly and was now quite taken aback. He asked whether Newman 'disapproved of Catholics as Catholics acting prominently in the matter.' At the end of his letter of 11 June about Catholics at the universities, Bellingham asked whether, if the Affirmation Bill came up for further discussion, he might publish Newman's reply to his April letter, as being 'somewhat less pronounced in tone' than that of 8 May to F. W. Chesson.
[3] See letter of 6 June to Lord Braye.

TO H. P. LIDDON

Bm June 13. 1883

Dear Canon Liddon

We were all very glad to see you here; and thank you for the offer of any books of Pusey's which we have not got.[1] I fear we cannot ascertain this at once, as our Librarian is away and our Catalogue has been sadly disarranged in re-making

I have been wishing to say to you what was told me under secrecy, though the secrecy was not directed against the Anglican Church. I now hear that the secret is out, and I dare say you know it already.

Of course, you know that our Bishops have on two separate occasions put out a strong dissuasive against our youths going to the English Universities. A great and successful effort has been made at Rome lately to advocate a contrary course, and, I suppose, out of policy, it has been done without any co-operation of mine[2]

For myself for many reasons I have never advocated a College, nor do I think there is any chance of one, at least during the present generation; but I should be surprised if nothing came of the present agitation. Cardinal Manning, I suppose, will be against it.

I have only this morning heard that the secret has got out, if it has not been an open secret already, and, as I do not yet know how much is known I must ask you not without some real reason to repeat what I have said[3]

Very sincerely Yours John H. Card Newman

TO THE EDITOR OF THE FORTNIGHTLY REVIEW [?]

June 14th. 1883

I smile at the suggestion that I do not recollect perfectly well and in detail the incident of the picture in 1824. I can say much more of it than my brother can.[4]

[1] Liddon on 7 June offered to present to the library of the Birmingham Oratory any works of Pusey which were not already there, besides those mentioned in Newman's letter of 11 June.
[2] See letter of 20 May to Lord Braye
[3] Liddon who had not heard the information which Newman sent him, replied on 14 June: 'For myself, looking to the general interests of Religion in Oxford, — so far as it is possible to forecast them, — I should not now regret the foundation of a Roman Catholic college in Oxford. The risks which are inseparable from controversy are less considerable than the more immediate and pressing danger of our all agreeing to settle down in our almost secularized colleges into a practical indifference to religious truth altogether. Three or four "denominational" colleges would at any rate keep the importance of religious truth before the eyes of residents here, — even if their inmates should not be agreed as to its substance, or rather its frontiers.
The pass undergraduate, as far as I can see, often gets through Oxford, much as he did thirty or forty years ago. But the Classman runs all sorts of risks between moderations and the Final Examination, even if the mischief has not begun earlier. The materialism of some of the Physical Science teachers is less dangerous than the lectures in Mental Philosophy, and Logic, or than some of them . . .'
[4] After reading W. S. Lilly's article 'Cardinal Newman' in the *Fortnightly Review* (July

The circumstances were these: When he took possession of his rooms in Worcester [College], I thought it would be kind to give him a picture to cover the walls. I had not any religious intention in doing so, when I went down to Smith and Parker's, the print-sellers, at the corner of High Street and Long Wall, and asked to look at some engravings. They put before me several full portfolios, which I turned over, and, what so often happens in attempts of this kind, I found nothing that pleased me. At last I chose a Wilkie, I think the 'Rent Day,' and a Corregio, — very different subjects on purpose. The subject of the Correggio was called 'La Madonna col Divoto;' St Jerome and another Saint were sitting at a table, and the latter was presenting a monk to the Blessed Virgin, who with the Divine Child was at the top of the picture in clouds. It was not as my brother says, 'a portrait;' it was in no sense a devotional picture, such as is used by Catholics at prayer. It took my fancy as an artistic work; and I recollect feeling some scruples on the score of its subject.

When my brother refused it, I took it myself: it hung up in my rooms at Oriel till I left Oxford; after that it came with me here, and has been on the wall of my room ever since. Every now and then I have pointed it out to a friend, and told its history. There it hangs now, keeping up its story in my memory.[1]

If his other instances of my invoking the Blessed Virgin are no better than this, they do not go for much. For myself, I utterly disbelieve that any can be produced. That there were disputes between us on the subject of her invocation is an hallucination. I never invoked the Blessed Virgin, as I think — nay, or advocated her intercession, till I was a Catholic. My belief in her gifts and prerogatives grew, but were the growth of a course of years. As far as I can speak from memory, as I think I can, I held that, while I was an Anglican, I was bound by the Anglican prohibition of invocation; and accordingly I said in a letter to a friend, under the date of January, 1845, 'Somehow I do not like using Invocations except under the sanction of the Church.' Apologia, p. 231.

1879), Francis Newman wrote on 13 July 1879 to the editor, John Morley, a letter marked 'Private.' By way of correction Francis Newman said:
'I believe Cardinal N himself does not know certain matters of the past as accurately as I do, to whom his changes of doctrine were a sore distress. He supposes that the Invocation of the Virgin was long a difficulty to him and an objection to the Roman Church; but I remember that in the spring of 1824, when I had my first permanent rooms in College, he sent as a gift to me a portrait of the Virgin, to be hung on my walls; *which I sent back*: and a painful controversy concerning her Invocation, resumed again and again, showed me how widely he had left the Evangelical Creed, of which at that time I was a warm devotee. Numerous small events followed which showed me to demonstration a vast and impassable religious chasm between us in that year ⟨1824⟩, in which he was ordained Deacon.'
Newman's present letter in reply to this was presumably addressed either to John Morley or to Thomas Hay Sweet Escott, who succeeded him as editor of the *Fortnightly Review* in July 1882.

[1] Newman preserved the bill for the two framed prints, dated 17 October 1825, and amounting to £8.6.0., from William Parker, Oxford. His note on it shows a lapse of memory: 'These are the two pictures, which I gave my brother Frank for his rooms when he came into residence at Worcester. Years after, perhaps when he went abroad, he gave them me back.
One I have had ever since, and it hangs in the room next to mine, the "Madonna col Divoto"
J H N Aug. 1. 1874'

Of course there was a 'vast chasm' in religion between my brother and me; but neither his memory nor his insight into my mind was such as to enable him to say what that chasm was. My own testimony is that it lay in such questions as Baptismal Regeneration, Infant Baptism, and a Divinely-appointed Church, its privileges and gifts. E.g. I defended Infant Baptism against him in writing. Again, he once said to me that he would rather say that the Apostles were mistaken than that Baptism conveyed Regeneration. That is a chasm indeed. He has, contemporaneously with the above letter, shown his want of memory in another matter. He has maintained peremptorily that I was Secretary of the Oxford Bible Society; he contended that I was mistaken in denying it, but at last he found that he had no clear view on the subject himself, and he candidly wrote to his correspondent in these words, 'I am sure that his' (that is, my), 'memory is likely to be better than mine.'[1]

As to his insight into my habitual state of mind, nothing shows better his inability to enter into it than that in 1845 he thought it worth while to advise me not to join the Catholic Church, but to set up a denomination of my own. I believe that in 1824 he knew just as much about my mind as in 1845.

I will add that not in the instance of other Anglicans more than in my own has a high exaltation of the Blessed Virgin necessarily involved an invocation of her; as is plain from Keble's 'Thou whose name all but adoring love may claim,' and Wordworth's 'Our tainted nature's solitary boast.'[2] As to myself, I should have certainly recollected my invoking her, had I done so, as I recollected crossing myself at school.[3] I know well that I used to consider the invocation of the Saints and Angels one of the unscriptural additions of the Roman Church, and to be eschewed.[4]

TO MRS EDWARD BELLASIS

June 17. 1883

My dear Mrs Bellasis

We shall be honoured and pleased to have a visit from the Countess Stadnicka, though I fear her son is too old to allow of our being of service to him. Else, we have three countrymen of his with us already, and should welcome a fourth heartily[5]

[1] See *V.M.* II, pp. 1–7, where 'Mr. L' is W. S. Lilly, and the correspondent of the editor (of the *Fortnightly Review*) is Francis Newman.
[2] *The Christian Year,* 'The Annunciation of the Blessed Virgin Mary', ninth stanza; *Ecclesiastical Sonnets*, II, xxv, 'The Virgin Mother.'
[3] *Apo.*, p. 2.
[4] A month later Newman wrote this note on the first page of his 'Sermon No 137 Lecture 3 — on the faith of Mary. Luke i, 26–56 St Clements S.A. [Sunday Afternoon] Febr 19. 1826':
'I put this sermon into the packet [of Francis Newman's letters] as showing how I spoke of the Blessed Virgin two years after the time when F W N accuses me of arguing in defence of her invocation   J H N   July 10. 1883'
[5] Prince Constantine Lubomirski and Counts Stanislas and Ladislas Zamoyski were boys at the Oratory School at this time.

We heard from Richard lately; they were making for the Bel Alp — I could not help wishing they had been during the last fortnight at a higher level — but change of air is itself a medicine, independently of mountain or plain.

Richard has never been properly well, since his pleurisy four years ago. I have been very anxious at his looks being so worn — but travelling generally sets him right.

I am sorry to hear of Mr Bowring's illness, which from your account, must be unusually serious[1]

Very truly Yours John H Card. Newman

TO MRS EDWARD BELLASIS

Bm June 22/83

My dear Mrs Bellasis

I am much concerned at what you tell me, but am not quite unprepared for it. R's [Richard] looks distressed me very much before his leaving us, and I had hoped his plan was to go to some one high spot such as the Bel Alp and to *remain* there. His moving about seems to me a mistake.

He has never been well, since his pleurisy four years ago, and I think will get over it only slowly.

I am not aware of anything which obliges him to be back by July 1. He will tell you himself. I think Henry, now a Priest, could take his place. If he comes to you, you must employ his mind — for he will weary of doing nothing.

I shall look out with anxiety for the next letter.[2]

Very sincerely Yours John H. Card. Newman

TO MISS M. R. GIBERNE

June 22. 1883

My dear Sister Pia

As the 24th is the day on which the Achilli trial ended 31 years ago, I mean to say Mass for you in grateful remembrance of the part you had in it.[3]

As to the Affirmation Bill, I tried to sign my name against it, but had no opportunity, so far was I from refusing. The only opportunity I had was from an anonymous Birmingham Petition to Parliament — but, when I had almost got my pen in my hand, I felt that a Cardinal had no right to put down his name amid a mixed multitude. And then I thought 'have any clergy signed a

---

[1] This was Levin Bentham Bowring, who married as his second wife Mrs Bellasis's daughter Katherine.
[2] Mrs Bellasis wrote on 28 June that Richard Bellasis reported 'I feel much better.'
[3] Miss Giberne secured in Italy and brought back to England some of the witnesses against Achilli.

petition?' and 'would not the Bishop have told me?' So having no hint and no means, I did not express an opinion. At the same time, if you ask my real thoughts, I should say that, tho' I wished to sign, I should merely have done so because others did, not to be singular. For I think it a piece of humbug, and no good will become of the bill being rejected and no harm by its passing. No atheist is kept out as it is, and within the last fortnight a daily paper has in earnest said that atheism ought to be considered one form of *theism*! (look at pp 36–8 of my Idea of a University.) When it was all over, some one wrote to a Paper to say he had *authority* from me to state that I disapproved in every way of the Bill. This was not true, and I was obliged to write a letter to say that I neither approved of it nor disapproved — that it was a mere political bill with which I had nothing to do.[1]

I am sorry to hear your account of the Princess Borghese and of the Duchess of Sora[2]

Yours ever affecty John H Card. Newman

TO LORD BRAYE

Bm June 23. 1883

My dear Lord Braye

I am greatly shocked to see in today's Paper a statement of a serious accident as having happened to Lady Braye. I trust it is exaggerated, as those accounts often are. I hope you will be able, (in two lines,) to tell me so[3]

Very sincerely Yours John H Card. Newman

TO LORD BRAYE

Bm June 26. 1883

My dear Lord Braye

I rejoice to read your favorable account of Lady Braye.

I waited to answer you, till I could know whether any Bishop was coming to you. In that case I felt I ought to come for the High Mass; but, since none can come, I gladly accept your proposal of my starting from Birmingham at 11.30[4]

Very sincerely Yours John H. Card. Newman

[1] Letter of 8 May 1883 to F. W. Chesson.
[2] The Duchess of Sora was Agnes only surviving child of Lady Gwendolen Talbot, daughter of the sixteenth Earl of Shrewsbury, and of the eighth Prince Borghese. She married the Duke of Sora in 1854. Princess Borghese was her stepmother, second wife of the Prince, Thérèse de la Rochefoucauld.
[3] Lady Braye had been in a carriage accident, but was not seriously hurt.
[4] See letters of 6 and 12 June to Lord Braye.

June 26. 1883

My dear Frank

This, I hope, will be in time for your birthday tomorrow, of which I wish you many happy returns.

You, I suppose, for the same reason wrote to me on May 18 for Jemima's birthday, which was on the 19th — June now is the real 'May' month

Yours affectly J. H. Newman

TO LORD BRAYE

June 29. 1883

My dear Lord Braye

I will ask leave to bring with me Fr Eaglesim, a friend of Mr Costello's.

And I will start at 11.30 to arrive at Stanford at 1.11.

And will leave you by the train at 6–14 — which gets to Birmingham at 7.47

This will allow my being present at Vespers and at Fr Coleridge's Sermon, if the Vespers being [begin] at 2.30 as you propose

One point remains to settle — should I be in the sanctuary at Vespers or in the nave. The decision rests with the celebrant. Some ceremonies are required in the former case — none in the latter. If the former, I should have to bring a Cardinal's cassock etc. The celebrant must decide

Very sincerely Yours John H Card. Newman

TO CHARLES LANCELOT SHADWELL

[30 June 1883][1]

Cardinal Newman begs to acknowledge the invitation[2] which he has received from the Provost and Fellows of Oriel to their dinner on Thursday Oct 11th, and is sorry to say that by reason of his advanced age and the infirmities attendant on it, it is not in his power to avail himself of their kindness.

My dear Mr Shadwell,

I hope you will not think it any want of respect to the College, or of insensibility to the friendly feeling towards me of the Provost and Fellows and

[1] Shadwell wrote on 29 June from Oriel College: 'It is proposed on the occasion of the election of a new Provost in succession to the late Dr Hawkins who had presided over the Society for upwards of fifty years, to invite old members of the College to a dinner in the College Hall on Thursday October 11.

I enclose a card of invitation: and I am directed by the College to express the great pleasure it would give us if your Eminence should find yourself able to promise us your company on the day fixed.'

[2] Newman first wrote 'kind' then 'friendly' invitation, but erased both adjectives, evidently satisfied that the word 'kindness' at the end of the sentence conveyed his meaning.

especially yourself, that I do not accept your invitation for Oct 11. No one but an old man can know an old man's various inabilities social as well as physical; not that I will trouble you with them,[1] it is more to the purpose to express my best wishes that tho' your life be long, you may be long too in knowing by experience its usual accompaniment

TO LORD BRAYE

Tuesday July 3. 1883

My dear Lord Braye

I fear a letter of mine to you has miscarried. I wrote to you last week, I think on Friday, directing 'Grosvenor Street' to answer the very questions which you now ask Fr Eaglesim.[2]

I said 1 that I should start from Birmingham by the 11.30 train which would arrive at Stanford station at 1. 11. I said this not knowing you had taken actually the trouble of arranging a through carriage, in order to prevent your doing so. It is very kind of you, but, unless it takes only additional trouble perhaps, I assure you that I shall be pleased at your counter ordering it.

Also, I said in my letter that I thought the priest who officiated ought to decide whether I should be in the sanctuary or not — for, though the ceremonies might be light which the presence of a Cardinal would involve, he might have a preference. As to my own wish, if you ask it, I should say, if Fr Coleridge preaches, it would be more respectful to him for me to be in the Sanctuary — else, I would rather be in the body of the church.

Lastly I said in my letter, that I proposed to leave you by the train which passed Stanford at 6.14.

Your Lordship's faithful Servt John H Card. Newman
The Lord Braye

TO SHAKESPERE WOOD

Birmingham July 3. 1883

My dear Mr Wood

I trust you will not think I have been wanting in sympathy with you in your late trial, though till now I have not written to you.[3]

I deeply felt your kindness in sending me the sad notice, but I was afraid of being rude to you in the beginning of so great a grief. How could I be indifferent to it, while I have in memory your kindness to me at Rome? Not the least touching instance of it was your bringing your children to me; and I

[1] These eight words are hardly decipherable.
[2] Letter of Friday 29 June to Lord Braye.
[3] The death of a daughter. Wood was a sculptor who lived in Rome. See letter of 1 June 1879 to him.

am surely right in my memory that the dear child whom you have lost was one of those who, when I left Rome, saw me off. I have said Mass for her.

May God's mercy come down upon her abundantly — and upon you, in your trial and Mrs Wood and all yours

Yours very truly John H Card. Newman

Shakspere Wood Esqr

TO H. P. LIDDON

Bm July 5. 1883

My dear Dr Liddon

Thank you for your kindness in getting me the two letters, but I feel ashamed of giving you and Mrs Wilberforce so much trouble. If any more turned up, it would be well — but hunting for letters is endless work[1]

Very sincerely Yours John H. Card. Newman

TO JOHN HART

[15 July 1883]

Card. Newman begs to thank Mr Hart for his letter on the subject of the Church Congress at Reading and is sorry to have to disappoint him on the points which led to his writing as he either has no knowledge of the owners of the portraits which have been taken of him, or no influence on the view they would take of his request[2]

TO MESSRS HALL AND ENGLISH

The Oratory July 17. 1883

Cardinal Newman begs Messrs Hall and English to make a lithograph (not a fac simile) of the inclosed — and to send him a proof of it[3]

TO JANE MOZLEY

July 21. 1883

My dear Jane

I am very sorry to hear of your Aunt's illness, and thank you for writing to me.[4] What a great distress it must be to her sisters — especially to Aunt Anne. Say to them how much I feel for them and believe me

Yrs affly John H Card. Newman.

[1] This refers perhaps to letters from Newman to Samuel Wilberforce.
[2] Hart wrote on 14 July that it was proposed to exhibit during the Church Congress a collection of portraits of those who took part in the Oxford Movement. 'Such a collection would, of course, be singularly incomplete without a portrait of your Eminence'. Hart, who was secretary to the exhibition, asked for the loan of an oil painting.
[3] Hall and English were wholesale stationers at 71 High Street, Birmingham.
[4] Elizabeth Mozley died at the end of Aug. See letter of 3 Sept. to Anne Mozley.

TO J. SPENCER NORTHCOTE

July 21. 1883

My dear Canon Northcote

The plates have come all right. You relieve me by saying they were packed up before Canon Brownlow came here, for it shows I have not hurried you. He surprised by not knowing I had given them all to Lord Selbourne — I had meant to have told you of him, and thought I had[1]

Very sincerely Yours John H Card. Newman

TO T. W. ALLIES

Bm. July 22. 1883.

My dear Allies,

Your daughter's article is well written and interesting, and I agree with her in the conclusion at which she arrives.

But you seem to ask me for criticism, so I suggest those points, in which I think, not that she will necessarily offend, certain readers, but as to the risk of which, I think you should get an opinion from some one who lives in the world more than I do.

1. She says p. 386 'the State could afford to be generous.' I said in one of my volumes something like this, and was reminded that Emancipation did not rise from contempt, but, as the Duke of Wellington confessed, from fear of an Irish Rebellion. In consequence I put in my next Edition an explanatory note.[2]

2. Would old Catholics like her saying (ibid) that they were 'uncombed, unkempt, covered with dust and mud.' I have known those who prided themselves on their gentility, and not without reason.

3. 'The Pope will by no means win back his own again.' (p. 391). Is not this a point, on which they are very sensitive at Rome?

I do not rule any thing, but think it worth while your having another opinion.

Yours affecty John H. Card. Newman

TO WILLIAM BRIGHT

Bm July 25. 1883

Dear Dr Bright

Thank you for the sight of your Article in the Church Quarterly. Also for the very friendly spirit in which you have taken the part of my 'Arians'

---

[1] See letter of 5 May 1883 to W. R. Brownlow. Lord Selborne wrote his warm thanks for these Catacomb pictures of William Palmer's on 27 Aug., 'They will be a memorial, in my family, at once of him and of yourself.'

[2] This note has not been traced, nor has the article by Mary Allies.

in it. As most things here below, it has two aspects, it may be praised or it may be blamed, and you have been generous in taking the laudatory side.[1]

For myself, considering it was my first work, that my reading up to then had not got as far as the Nicene Council and that I had but a year to do it in, and that I was in weak health, I do but wonder that it is not worse, and I submit to any adverse criticism which may be made upon it with equanimity. Yet with all its defects I think it has good points in it, and in parts some originality. Years ago I was so discouraged by the coldness with which it was received that I parted with the copyright, which afterwards was sold for £4. I know it is not a first rate book, but I think it is worth more than that.[2]

Very sincerely Yours John H Card Newman

[1] Bright in his long review of H. M. Gwatkin's *Studies of Arianism*, the *Quarterly Review* (July 1883), pp. 375–402, spoke of *Ari.* 'Mr. Gwatkin does not seem to appreciate a work which ... to us appears to be one of the great productions of a wonderful mind.' Bright went on to say that 'Mr. Gwatkin might have learned much from the *Arians of the Fourth Century*, if he had been more truly in sympathy with its interior spirit. It is no discredit to him that his work is inferior to that of a supreme master of English in grace of composition and concentrated force of statement; that, for instance, it contains nothing like the fervid vindication of Origen from the charge of anticipated Arianism in *Arians* (p. 99 [97] ff.), or the bold recognition of a "dispensation of natural religion or Paganism, running side by side with the patriarchal" (*ib.* p. 83 [81]); or the luminous exposition of the necessary upgrowth of theological formulas (however imperfect they may and must be considered as representations of infinite truths), and of their positively beneficial effect in "assisting the acts of religious worship and obedience" (p. 148 [146] ff.) ... or the explanation of the superficial attractiveness of the "Homoion" as "shutting up the subject in Scripture terms," and thus "seeming to be a peaceful doctrine" (p. 317 [304]) ... or, again, that it falls below the high level of the *Arians* in theological depth, keenness, and richness, such as appears so wonderfully in Newman's sections on the "Scriptural" and the "ecclesiastical" doctrine of the Trinity, and on "variations of ante-Nicene theological statements": — but besides this it seems to us that, while Mr. Gwatkin ... has a very real sense of the religious importance of the question, he would hardly assimilate the peculiar combination of awe and tenderness which appears so characteristically in such a passage as the following: —
"More than enough has now been said in explanation of a controversy the very sound of which must be painful to anyone who has a loving faith in the Divinity of the Son. Yet so it has been ordered, that He who once was lifted up to the gaze of the world, and hid not His face from contumely, has again been subjected to rude scrutiny and dishonour in the promulgation of His religion to the world. And His true followers have been themselves obliged in His defence to raise and fix their eyes boldly on Him, as if He were one of themselves, dismissing the natural reverence which would keep them ever at His feet" (*Arians*, p. 225 [219]).
How characteristic are these words! how well we know the thrill of their solemn music! how they illustrate what was said in the *Christian Remembrancer* for July 1864, of one who "at favoured moments half lifted the veil of the unseen, ..." Nothing could be more pitiable than for a person to adopt such a tone as breathes through the above extract, unless it were natural to him . . . this tone, where it exists, does give to a book or speech a special and indescribable charm . . .' Bright went on to say that the lack of it led, in Gwatkin's book, to 'a tendency now to off-hand peremptoriness, now to jerky smartness, and now to grandiose declamation.' pp. 380–2.
[2] Bright replied on 20 Aug. from the Windsor Hotel, New York, that Newman's *Arians* 'lay, years ago, at the foundation of my earliest studies of that period; and my sense of obligation to it is as keen and vivid as when I first read it through.' He added that he was glad also of the opportunity 'of quoting one passage, which teaches one so much *more* than the history of a doctrinal movement, and lifts the whole question into a still "diviner air."'

TO THE HON. MRS MAXWELL-SCOTT

Bm July 25. 1883

My dear Mamo

I grieve at your little child's illness, and for the anxiety which arises from its being catching.[1] I know from experience how very insidious it is. It came down upon my house in Dublin years ago, I had the rooms new painted and papered. This was in June .. but it broke out again in November.

I am glad you have settled with Murray for the Life.[2] I have written to a friend to sound Dollinger. If his answer is promising, I shall ask you to send me a copy of the letter to him to see.[3]

Let me ask. You have omitted all the private journals except the beautiful one on his leaving Chelsea, have you not? That, if I recollect rightly, seemed to me also best.[4]

Yours affectionately John H Card. Newman

P.S.   Will it be in two volumes or one?

TO LORD EMLY

July 29. 1883

My dear Emly

I have anticipated your wish, I am glad to say, by promising £20 to the Dupanloup Memorial[5]

I hope Dr Sullivan will be able to give me notice before he comes. I should be very sorry to miss him — but I am watching the weather to get some days at Rednall, where I have hardly been for a year.

I suppose the state of the Church must be worse before it is better —[6]

Yrs affectionately J. H. Card. Newman

TO LORD BRAYE

Bm. July 31. 1883

My dear Lord Braye

Thank you for the Pamphlet. I think it would be neither prudent nor right for me to take any part in the project of Lectures; — not right, because

---

[1] Mrs Maxwell-Scott's youngest child, Alice, born in 1881, had scarlet fever.
[2] Mrs Maxwell-Scott wrote on 24 July that John Murray held it to be 'an honour' to publish *Memoirs of James Robert Hope-Scott*: 'I am very glad, as he is an old family friend as you know, and I had not hoped he *would* publish anything so Catholic.'
[3] Mrs Maxwell-Scott wanted the permission of Döllinger to publish the letter he wrote to her father on his conversion, *Memoirs* II, pp. 89–90.
[4] The passage from Hope-Scott's diary to which Newman refers is in *Memoirs* I, pp. 100–3. There is a further passage, a year later, ibid. pp. 124–6.
[5] Lord Emly wrote on 28 July asking Newman to give £5 towards the memorial of Felix Dupanloup to be erected in Orléans Cathedral. Dupanloup's successor wrote on 30 June to ask for a subscription, and Newman replied at once.
[6] Lord Emly wrote that William Kirby Sullivan intended to pay Newman a visit. 'He will give you a gloomy account of the moral and religious prospects of Ireland
The priests give pap instead of strong meat to grown up men and they reject it.'

I ought to have some direct call or duty to go so much out of my way — and not prudent, because it is a mere experiment, and for me to take part in it would be to call attention to it, whereas in order to succeed it must begin and and grow 'without observation.'[1]

The Pincerna or Cupbearer is Terence's 'Eunuchus', expurgated or made available for school boys.[2]

If I can put my hand on the English explanations commonly attached to the text of the Play, I will venture to send it to you.

Most truly Yours John H Card. Newman

TO THE SECRETARY OF THE CATHOLIC YOUNG MEN'S SOCIETY OF GREAT BRITAIN

Birmingham, July 31st, 1883.

My dear Sir,

I cannot promise myself the pleasure of attending the annual Conference of the Catholic Young Men's Society, but, as taking the greatest interest in its welfare, I beg God's blessing upon it, and promise if all is well to say Mass for all its members on August 5th.[3]

Most truly yours, John H. Cardinal Newman.

TO BISHOP ULLATHORNE [?]

Bm July 31. 1883

My dear Lord

I know nothing of the parties who have sent me the inclosed. Of course I would do them a kindness, if I could. I should write to Warley, except that I suspect that Mr Smythe is dead. May I ask your advice, if you can give it me without trouble?

My Lord, Your faithful Servt J. H. Card. Newman

TO ANNE MOZLEY

Bm Aug 7. 1883

My dear Anne Mozley

I little thought I should have, when I last wrote to you, so sad a letter to write as I have now. You were then passing from under the shadow of a great anxiety, and now you are under the shock of what is real and irreversible.[4]

I feel very much for you and your sisters, especially Elizabeth in her weak

---

[1] *Luke*, 17:20. There was a plan for some Catholic lectures during term at Oxford. Thomas Parkinson, the Jesuit at St Aloysius's church, Oxford, collected speakers during the autumn of 1883, in preparation for Hilary Term 1884. cf. letter of 24 Dec. 1883 to Miss Giberne.

[2] *Pincerna ex Terentio with English notes to assist the representation*, 'Cardinal Newman's edition', London 1883.

[3] cf. letters of 28 July 1881 and 7 Aug. 1882.

[4] Cf. letter of 26 Feb. 1883. Anne Mozley's brother Charles died on 5 Aug.

state. You are all bound so singularly together as a family — and no one could know Charles ever so little without loving him.

May God comfort you all is the sincere prayer of

Yours affectionately John H. Card. Newman

TO HENRY DE COLYAR

Bm Aug 9. 1883

My dear de Colyar

Thank you for your book. It is a great pleasure to us to find you so steadily rising in your profession.

As I knew nothing about County Courts, your Preface, as you anticipated, interested me a good deal, and I have seen enough of the 'cases' to understand that a large number of them are far from dull reading.[1]

It pleased me of course to find you had been reading my Grammar of Assent, and that you speak so well of it

Yours affectionately John H Card. Newman

P.S. Thank you for letting me see the very favorable judgment on your work of the Law Times. I send it back to you, lest you should want it.

TO ROBERT ORNSBY

Bm Aug 8. 1883

My dear Ornsby

Mrs Maxwell Scott has a letter of Döllinger's to her Father, and D. has several letters of her Father to D. which perhaps ought to come in. But no hurry.[2]

It will quite do if I see my letters in proof.

I congratulate you on its coming to an end. Alas! we have had no 'splendid weather' here

Yrs affly J H Card. Newman

TO THE HON. MRS PEREIRA

Birmingham Aug. 9. 1883

My dear Mrs Pereira,

Your letter gave me the greatest pleasure. I sincerely thank you for it. Of course I was glad to find that George had succeeded in his examination, and I trust and pray and believe that this may be only the beginning of the satisfaction and comfort he will give you, as life opens upon him. It will be our pleasure and satisfaction as well as yours, for we know well and ever bear

[1] De Colyar had evidently sent the new edition of *A Complete Practice of the County Courts*, by George Pitt-Lewis, assisted by Henry Anselm de Colyar, London 1883.
[2] See letter of 25 July to Mrs Maxwell-Scott. Ornsby wrote on 25 Aug. that he thought it better not to introduce more of the correspondence with Döllinger into *Memoirs of Hope-Scott*.

in mind what a great confidence it is which Fathers and Mothers place in us, in committing their children to our care, and it makes us very anxious.[1]

I am sure you will say a prayer for the School now and then, for it has its troubles, and not slight ones.[2]

Very sincerely Yours John H. Card. Newman

P.S.   I beg to present through you my best respects to those of your family who are with you.

The Hon Mrs Pereira

TO JOHN O'HAGAN

Bm Aug 10. 1883

My dear John O'Hagan[3]

I had been thinking of you a great deal lately, and your letter and your Observations on the Report came very opportunely.[4]

I have read the Observation with great interest, but with much sadness, that there should be so much party spirit in so august an Assembly. I have a great admiration of the House of Lords and should protest against any attempt to weaken its authority, but it is sad indeed, if it weakens its authority itself, and though I know nothing of legal matters or of the Irish agrarian question, that does not equitably deprive me of having an opinion at all on the points at issue between you and the House of Lords.

For instance — it is a matter of principle that the Judicial Bench should be treated with a respect and consideration which the Committee has not shown towards you. And there is an animosity all through their charges and criticisms, which surprises me in the otium cum dignitate of such highly placed persons. I say this, not knowing who constitute the Committee

You must have had tremendous work. With kindest remembrance to Mrs O'Hagan when you write to her

I am, affectly Yours John H Cardinal Newman

[1] Mrs Pereira wrote on 3 Aug. that her son George had just passed into Sandhurst. She sent her thanks to all who had brought this about at the Oratory School and 'for all the care and pains that have been lavished on George.' Also for the advantages that had come to her sons 'from having been educated at Edgbaston.'

[2] cf. letter of 19 Sept. to Richard Pope.

[3] The word 'Private' at the head of this letter has been cancelled.

[4] On 27 July O'Hagan sent a copy of the newly published Observations of the Irish Land Commissioners, of whom he was one, on the accusations made against them in the Fourth Report of the Select Committee of the House of Lords on Land Law (Ireland); together with the Proceedings of the Committee, Minutes of Evidence, ordered to be printed July 1883. This was really an attack on the Commissioners and Sub-Commissioners who were implementing Gladstone's Land Act of 1881, and fixing 'judicial rents'. They had the status of judges. The House of Lords represented the landlords, and its Committee's Report accused the Sub-Commissioners of fixing rents that were unfair to them, and of corruption. These attacks were repeated in a debate in the Lords on 27 July. Observations of the Irish Land Commissioners on the Fourth Report . . . Dublin 1883, was signed by the four Commissioners, John O'Hagan's being the first name. It ended as follows: — 'It appears to the Commissioners that the Committee have departed from the constitutional principle which protects the grounds of judicial decisions from being investigated by such a body as the Committee; and that, where the rule does not apply, they have lost sight of a principle quite as sacred by condemning absent men without calling on them for their defence.'

Aug 12. 1883

I have great dread of making any engagement about 'copyrights.' What I have been used to is to let a publisher have an *'edition'* — say of 1000 or 1500 copies at such or such a price. It has been so before with Messrs Kegan Paul Why not now?[1]

J H N

TO EDWIN PALMER

Bm Aug. 13. 1883

My dear Archdeacon Palmer,

The Plates of the Catacombs have been returned to me, and I will send them whenever you tell me.[2] After some thought I have decided to send them mainly as they have come to me in their portfolios. In a matter of taste, convenience, and private choice, I feel they should go to you and Lord Selbourne as they have come to me from William [Palmer], without my attempting to sort or arrange them, except that the originals are separate from the others

How many copies shall I send you of the Symbolism? I have nearly 150.

I hope to send you soon, all the private letters.[3]

About 60 (I think) copies of the Russian Journal were burned in Messrs Kegan Paul's fire. It is the fifth fire in which my books have suffered.[4]

You drew up for me an elaborate notice of the books and quires in stock, for which I have never properly thanked you. I have to make use of it now, and wish you could advise me. Robson tells me he wants me to relieve his premises of 'the Patriarch and the Tsar'. What am I to do? There are, besides 142 bound volumes at Trubner's, 41 volumes (not sets, I suppose) at Robson's and 2238 in quires; altogether 2421 volumes.[5]

I thought of offering a set to various libraries — but room is so scanty in many libraries, and many only admit particular subjects; this perplexes me.

[1] Cf. the correspondence with Lilly in 1878 about Lilly's anthology, *Characteristics from the Writings of Cardinal Newman*. It was arranged in Aug. 1883 that Kegan Paul, Trench and Co. should pay Newman £30 for the 650 copies in stock at the beginning of 1883. He sent the £30 at once to Lilly.

[2] These were William Palmer's plates used to illustrate the new edition of his *An Introduction to Early Christian Symbolism*, London 1885. See letter of 5 May 1883 to W. R. Brownlow and references there.

[3] Edwin Palmer asked on 15 Aug. that these letters of his brother William should be sent to him at Christ Church, and the plates to Lord Selborne in London. See letter of 21 July to Northcote. Edwin Palmer agreed to take six copies of the unillustrated 1859 edition of *Early Christian Symbolism*.

[4] Edwin Palmer once more thanked Newman for publishing *Notes of a Visit to the Russian Church*, 'which has done so much to make William's life and aims intelligible to those who knew his name.'

[5] This refers to the six volumes of William Palmer's *The Patriarch Nicon and the Tsar*, six volumes, London 1871–6.

Then as to the quires — Trubner values the whole 2421 volumes at 6/6 a volume, i.e. at £60. 10. 6. This, I suppose, is if sold at the value of the paper.

Any suggestion you can make me I shall gratefully receive[1]

Most truly Yours John H. Card. Newman

The Ven. Archdeacon Palmer

TO LORD BLACHFORD

Birmingham, August 14th. 1883.

My dear Blachford,

I hope, as I conclude, that you have got over your work in the Ecclesiastical Commission.

I have read the account of your report in the Spectator and wonder whether I read it rightly.[2]

You had two antagonist principles to reconcile, and you seem to have managed to do so very cleverly.

You had to maintain the ecclesiastical supremacy of the Queen, yet to avoid its being felt in definite acts such as her proceeding in the Gorham case.

Accordingly, though she speaks absolutely, by 5 lawyers who need not even be Members of the Church, and without even any necessity of calling in ecclesiastics as consultors, the real work of hearing, arguing and giving judgment is so fully thrown upon the inferior courts, Episcopal and Archiepiscopal, that the high lay Tribunal will either never be brought into play, or will be able reasonably to follow, on an appeal to it, the decisions already made by the inferior Court. And there is hope that, with the threat of 5 laymen looming in the distance, there are not likely to be appeals from the Archbishop.

Another great gain is that Parliament no longer interferes.

I wonder whether this is all fancy of mine. Then as to its answering, I do not know why it should not. All litigants are likely to submit to the Archbishop's Court, if it does not inflict a raw —[3] and it will be too wise to do that.

I suppose the Evangelicals will give the most trouble — for they, as a matter of conscience, are opposed to the Vestments as practically antichristian.

I have more to write about, but my hand is so tired, I must give over.

Yours affectionately, John H. Card: Newman.

[1] Edwin Palmer agreed that the bound volumes should be kept and offered to libraries and the rest sold as waste paper. On 3 Oct. the printers Robson and Sons, 20 Pancras Road sent Newman £17. 17s for the sale of the quires for waste paper. As to Messrs Trübner, see letter of 27 Aug. to them.
[2] The Report of the Ecclesiastical Courts Commission, of which Lord Blachford was a member, was about to be published, cf. letter of 24 March 1883 to Lord Blachford, and *The Letters of Lord Blachford*, edited by G. E. Marindin, pp. 420-1. Newman summarised the article in the *Spectator* (11 Aug.), pp. 1018-19. It was hoped to bring about the practical repeal of the Public Worship Regulation Act of 1874, but this remained on the Statute Book until 1963.
[3] i.e. a 'raw wound', 'raw place'. (*O.E.D.*)

TO H. P. LIDDON

Bm Aug. 14. 1883

Dear Canon Liddon

I wonder what you think of the Ecclesiastical Report. It affirms the Queen's Supremacy masterfully by making the highest Court consist of five Lawyers — but then it seems to throw all *cases* and their treatment and decision to the Archbishops, Bishops and divines. May not the Five Lawyers be like the gods of Epicurus?[1] if the Bishops are prudent.

Also, Parliament, if the Act is passed, can no longer interfere

Will not the danger come from such men as Bishop Ryle?[2]

Very truly Yours John H Card. Newman

FOR HERBERT NEWMAN MOZLEY[3]

Aug 14. 1883

Dear Sir

I make this offer to you —

On condition (1) of your giving a promissory note to the Hotel Keeper at Rawlings's, counter-signed by some responsible friend of yours, that you will repay him the £20 by Christmas Day on his then returning to you my cheque (2) and of your completing by that date the Library Catalogue which has already been commenced by others

I will engage to take off by Christmas Day the suspension of payment of that cheque at present in force as regards my cheque of £20[4]

TO DR HUGHES

Bm Aug 15. 1883

Cardinal Newman has great pleasure in giving permisson to Dr Hughes to use his Hymn 'Lead Kindly Light' as the subject of Dr Hughes's 'Sacred Song'

Dr Hughes must gain Messrs Rivingtons' leave also

[1] Who took no interest in human affairs.

[2] Liddon replied on 15 Aug. welcoming much in the *Report*, as undoing 'the mischief of the Public Worship Regulation Act', but regretting the independence of the lay judges in the proposed final Court of Appeal. 'The Great Lawyers will not easily let go their grip on the Church. They retain and intensify the old Tudor tradition of jealousy of a self-governing Church'. Lord Coleridge had made a reservation at the end of the *Report* 'which lays down the doctrine that we must pay for Establishment by letting the State do what is properly the work of the Bishops, in terms which astonish me as coming from him.'

John Charles Ryle was the staunchly evangelical Bishop of Liverpool. Liddon replied that 'there would be great practical difficulties in the case of such Bishops', and that 'people of Bishop Ryle's mind are more likely to find what they want in the Dissenting bodies.'

[3] Newman sent a copy of this letter with the proper name 'Rawlings' omitted, to his nephew, who was a law coach, for his comment.

[4] Herbert Mozley replied that if the hotel keeper gave a quid pro quo for Newman's cheque, he would be able to claim payment from Newman. Mozley thought the hotel keeper would require a sum larger than £20 for parting with Newman's cheque, and that the borrower might not work conscientiously, since he would not be interested in whether the cheque was stopped or not.

TO J. R. BLOXAM

Bm Aug. 16. 1883

My dear (Dr)[1] Bloxam

I wonder whether you would care to have a set of William Palmer's Nicon. If so, I will readily send you one and am very sorry that it did not occur to me to ask you sooner.[2] I am glad you were able to explain my disinclination to Dr Hessy[3]

Yours affecty J H Card Newman

TO MESSRS TRÜBNER AND CO.

Birmingham Aug. 16. 1883

Cardinal Newman believes he is right in saying that in 1879 Messrs Trubner and Co had on sale 142 bound volumes or sets of Mr Palmer's 'The Patriarch and the Tsar'.

He will be obliged by their telling him, whether they are single volumes or sets, whether any sets or volumes have sold since 1879 (besides those which the Cardinal has sent for,) whether the stock in quires should be kept, or sold as paper.[4]

TO ST GEORGE JACKSON MIVART

Birmingham. Aug. 17. 1883.

Dear Professor Mivart,

I have wished to thank you from the time you were so good as to send me your Article on Catholic Politics,[5] but have been hindered by having a great deal of writing which I could not put off, and by the slowness and effort with which I am obliged to write.

I read the Article with great interest, and think it very valuable. I was particularly pleased with what you said about the limitation of the rights of a national body by the respective qualifications of its separate classes.[6]

I am not sure of the sufficiency of your arguments against the expediency of a Catholic party in England, but I think it *impossible* from our very Catholicity. Catholics come of *all* parties, classes, ranks, professions, schools, orders, ages: how can they combine in any secular object? how in any thing *but*

[1] The brackets were probably inserted by Bloxam.
[2] i.e. *The Patriarch Nicon and the Tsar*. See letter of 13 Aug. to Edwin Palmer.
[3] See letter of 20 Feb. 1883 to Bloxam.
[4] See letter of 27 Aug. to Messrs Trübner.
[5] 'On Catholic Politics', *D R* (July 1883), pp. 1–25.
[6] Mivart argued that 'A community consisting of equal units is not a nation but a horde: a "nation" consists of an orderly conjunction of classes, diverse in their importance and attributes.' p. 6.

religion? What politics will join together the Duke of Norfolk with Lord Ripon? The late Mr Lucas with the late Sir George Bowyer?

I feel the extreme kindness towards me of your last sentence, while I feel that it will not stand criticism.[1]

> Very sincerely Yours, John H. Card. Newman.

Professor Mivart Etc., etc,

TO RICHARD POPE

Aug. 20. 1883

My dear Mr Pope

I hope I shall not inconvenience you, if I say that I wish to reserve the staircase of Number 22 for ourselves. I know perfectly well that the upstairs rooms of Number 22 are in your occupation, but I never fancied that the staircase in question was used as a thoroughfare to Number 21. I have a very strong objection to maidservants coming into our premises, and this being my motive, I hope you will not wonder at what some people would think a piece of needless precision[2]

> Very sincerely Yours John H Card. Newman

TO H. P. LIDDON

Aug. 21. 1883

My dear Canon Liddon

I send you the copies of Pusey's early letters to me on the eve of his birth-day.

I have inquired and find the charge to be £1. 6. 0

> Very truly Yours John H Card Newman

TO WILLIAM AMHERST, S. J.

Rednall, August 23, 1883.

Dear Father Amherst

I cannot call your letter a sad one. Thank you for sending it. While saying 'God's will be done,' I have desired the tidings which you give me, that at length your dear brother has been called away. May we be as well prepared when our time comes.[3]

---

[1] The last sentence said: 'It should never be forgotten that it was one of the greatest of Catholic Englishmen who first proclaimed and demonstrated both the necessary existence, and the laws, of the great process of evolution, in his immortal work on the "Development of Doctrine."' p. 25.

[2] This refers to houses beside the Oratory School in Plough and Harrow Road, Edgbaston. Pope lived at Number 21.

[3] Francis Kerril Amherst, Bishop of Northampton, died on 21 Aug. 1883 after a protracted illness. He had resigned his See in 1879.

TO ARTHUR RIDDELL, BISHOP OF NORTHAMPTON

August 25, 1883

My Dear Lord

I thank you for your kindness in writing to me. The long suspense is ended, and the dear Bishop is taken to his rest. I have thought of him with interest and affection since I heard him sing the 'Exultet' in Oscott Chapel in 1846.[1]

TO THE SECRETARY OF ST GEORGE'S CLUB

[26 August 1883]

I feel the honour which the Management Committee of St George's Club does me in proposing to elect me one of its Honorary members. I accept the offer with much pleasure[2]

J H N

TO WILFRID OATES

Aug. 27. 1883

The books have come and I thank you and your partner for them

By your sending them, I understand you to think, as I do myself, that, as Catholic Publishers, you are neither able effectually, nor ought, to put them on sale.[3]

I am very anxious to know what stock you have of Fr Caswall's books, as he left particular directions about them.[4]

I know nothing of the terms on which your firm took the Masque of Mary. Spottiswood was one of the printers. Could not this be a clue? I should have thought you sold them on commission[5]

J H N

TO MESSRS TRÜBNER AND CO.

Bm August 27. 1883

Cardinal Newman is obliged by Messrs Trubner and Co.'s sending him the account of sales of Mr Palmer's work. He will thank them to send him the balance in his favour £11. 4. 3 as they propose[6]

[1] Holy Saturday, 11 April.
[2] The secretary of St George's Club, Savile Row, V. J. Lewis, wrote on 25 Aug. enclosing a list of members of this Catholic club.
[3] Oates sent Newman the few remaining copies of Edward Caswall's *Sermons on the Seen and Unseen*, London 1846, and *Verba Verbi*, London 1855. Only the first book was written while he was an Anglican.
[4] Oates wrote on 4 Oct. that there was no stock left of Caswall's *Poems*.
[5] Oates wrote on 25 Aug. that he had 300 copies of Caswall's *The Masque of Mary*, London 1857, and asked what were the terms of its publication.
[6] cf. letter of 16 Aug. to Messrs Trübner, who since 1879 had sold seven sets of *The Patriarch Nicon and the Tsar*.

He believes there are 41 bound volumes at Messrs Robson's and will be obliged by Messrs Trubner's recommending him what course to pursue concerning them. He has determined to sell the quires, but is there any use in his sending the 41 volumes to the Messrs Trubner? and in advertising the work?[1]

TO EDWARD THOMAS VAUGHAN

Birmingham Aug 27. 1883

My dear Canon Vaughan,

Thank you very much for your Volume. I know how high a place the Hulsean Lectures hold at Cambridge, and I see you have chosen a subject of all others apposite, considering the needs of the moment.[2]

I wish you had been longer — of course it is safer to be short — yet I think your readers will regret that a Sermon or Lecture does not allow of that fulness of treatment of your interesting subjects which they would otherwise ask of you. But you have said enough, to do, as I trust, much good.

Very truly Yours John H. Card. Newman

TO JOHN HARDMAN POWELL

Aug. 28. 1883

Dear Mr Powell

It would please me much to have your son with us; but you must be so kind as to let my answer to your proposal wait till we are all together here.[3]

Very truly Yours John H Card. Newman

TO THE SECRETARY OF THE SYDNEY LITERARY SOCIETY

[September? 1883]

I thank you heartily for your letter so kind and so gratifying to me. Already I owe much to the Sydney Catholics, and this wish to connect my name with their Literary Society is a fresh favour.[4]

All I should ask before definitely accepting the honour, would be to have

[1] Messrs Trübner replied on 28 Aug. that they did not recommend advertising, but they would take the 41 volumes and allow the sale to go on gradually. This was provided that the quires were not likely to be resold as books. Newman has left the draft of his reply: 'Cardinal Newman has received Messrs Trübner's cheque and incloses a receipt. He will direct Messrs Robson to send the 41 bound volumes to Messrs Trübner. Unless he was incorrect in the transcription, he stated that he was selling the quires *as paper.* He meant "waste paper." Messrs Robson are corresponding with him on the subject.' See letter of 13 Aug. to Edwin Palmer.
[2] *Some Reasons of our Christian Hope, being the Hulsean lectures for 1875,* London 1876.
[3] Kenelm Powell came to the Oratory School on 18 Sept. 1883.
[4] T. A. Coghlan, secretary 'of a Society formed for the promotion of literature among the Catholics' of Sydney wrote on 6 Aug. asking permission to call it the 'Newman Literary Society.'

the approbation of the Archbishop, that is, alas, his representative, lest I should be intrude [sic] into a portion of the divine vineyard where I had no business[1]

J H N

TO ANNE MOZLEY

Sept 3. 1883

My dear Anne Mozley

I was so shocked at your tidings that I took advantage of your leave to wait before I answered. What a succession of trials you have had! alas, the necessary consequence of a large family whose members are so dear to each other. With what pain I turn to the contrast of this time fifty years.[2]

You especially in this last bereavement are left desolate; and here I can especially sympathise with you. I indeed have not a brother or a sister so near to me, as Elizabeth was to you, but in losing Ambrose St John I lost one who was more to me than a brother, and there was in the circumstances of my affliction a likeness to yours thus far, that he, after lying for a month in almost a desperate state, suddenly had a change for the better, and after some days seemed safe, when suddenly, while we were rejoicing, I was roused from my sleep at night, and had to go up to Ravenshurst to find him gone.

May you have all the support and comfort in your trial which the Merciful God can give

Yours affectly John H Card. Newman

Say something of the great sorrow I feel for their loss to your Sisters and Jane [Mozley].

TO ULRIC CHARLTON

Bm Sept 4. 1883

My dear Ulric

I shall not answer your question satisfactorily, but as to the point on which your correspondence with your friend turns, it is clearly in your favour.[3]

He does not dispute your fact, but says that other religions besides the

---

[1] Roger Bede Vaughan, Archbishop of Sydney, died on 18 Aug. at Ince Blundell Hall, near Liverpool.

[2] The death of Elizabeth Mozley came within a month of that of her brother. See letter of 7 Aug. to Anne Mozley.

[3] Charlton wrote on 31 Aug. that he had been an eye-witness of what he took to be an instantaneous cure at Lourdes. A correspondent had objected that 'it is absurd of Christians to point to their Saints as being different *in kind* or superior in degree to the saints of any other creed which accepts the principles of Ascetism [sic] — wherever you find that element you will find the same sentiments, the same visions, the same extasies [sic], the same miracles. The idea of Christianity monopolizing the *supernatural* is one which no educated person at the present day can hold for a moment.'

Catholic have like miracles to show — but you were an eyewitness, and his report is second or third hand, from books or from travelled men.

However this does not settle the matter, which requires careful investigation, more than has yet been given to it.

The great writer on one part is Görres whom Cardinal Wiseman used to talk of and knew.[1]

I do not know whether you read German, or if his book is translated, but I have always heard speak of it with great praise. Perhaps it has been translated in America. His work, I suppose, would proceed on the admission that there were extraordinary phenomena of a religious character, and such as Catholics claim as proper to themselves, outside the Church as well as within. Here then two questions arise. 1. is this really the fact? 2. how are we to account for it?

Neither question can be answered hastily and the second depends of course on the first. For myself I should expect there *is* a difficulty to be met, but I suspect it is greatly exaggerated, and just now a movement has set in against Christianity, and sweeping assertions are made and large generalizations are taken for granted. A appeals to B, and B to C, and C to A, that what they hold and pronounce is too clear, too certain to need proof, and that the whole world thinks as they do.

Now as I have said, the answer to question 2, depends on the true answer to question 1, but before we are able to determine question 1, we may say something towards answering question 2, and, speaking for myself it is this — I say then speaking under correction, as any individual Catholic must speak, that we ought to be cautious about using the article of miracles as an argument for Catholicity. Of course true miracles *are* wrought and I firmly believe and have in print affirmed them.[2]

But I think they are given, as answers to prayers are, far more commonly for the support and encouragement of believers, than for the conversion of unbelievers, and for personal eyewitnesses far more than for the general public. They are not put first by the Church even in her canonization of Saints, for, unless my memory is at fault the supereminent virtues of the person whose process is in question must be proved on good evidence, before the account of his miracles is brought forward[3] — None but God can work a real miracle, but there are extraordinary phenomena which sometimes are miracles sometimes not. Moreover, we must remember our Lord's words (Mark ix, Luke ix)[4] who, when St John said to him 'Master we saw one casting out devils in Thy name and we forbad him, because he followeth not with us'

[1] Johann Joseph von Görres, 1776–1848, *Die christliche Mystik*, four volumes, Ratisbon and Landshut 1836–40, second edition 1879, French translation 1854–5. See also W. Ward, *The Life and Times of Cardinal Wiseman*, London 1897, I, p. 270.
[2] See *Prepos.*, pp. 312–13, 333 and Note II, pp. 407–16; *Apo.*, Note B., pp. 298–309.
[3] Benedict XIV (Prospero Lambertini), *De Servorum Dei Beatificatione et Beatorum Canonizatione*, Romae 1787, Lib. I, cap. xxii, §10.
[4] *Mark*, 9:38–40; *Luke* 9: 49–50.

answered 'Forbid him not for there is no man that doth a miracle in my name and can soon speak ill of me, for he that is not against you is for you' of course 'in Thy name' has special force, still the words give us a lesson.[1]

Write again.[2]

Yrs affect. J. H. Card. Newman

TO LADY WOLSELEY

Sept. 6. 1883

My dear Lady Wolseley

The cake came quite safe, and I thank you for it. I have reserved it for the 8th and shall share it first with those Fathers who recollect Sir Charles at school, then for the rest. We wish you and him a prosperous voyage — and I will not forget you at Mass[3]

Your faithful Sert John H Card. Newman

TO LORD BRAYE

Sept 8. 1883

My dear Lord Braye

I thank you for the venison. This gives me an opportunity of sending you the English additions to the Pincerna, which will show you how we have adapted Terence's Play to a Catholic representation.[4]

Very sincerely Yours John H. Card. Newman

[1] Newman's draft of this letter ran:
'Your correspondent was not eye witness of a like miracle in a Mahometan or Buddhist place of worship which he could set against yours.

But I believe this is the key to the whole difficulty, when it is properly investigated. Facts very like Christian miracles are reported in heathen countries, but the account of them is too recent, too sudden, and too multiform to know their worth. The flood of historical knowledge or at least of alleged facts has poured in, and it requires one or two generations to sift them, and to know what is true, and what is only plausible. I am quite prepared to believe that Christians have something to learn, and that their case is not so exactly such as they have been accustomed to think, and that their side in the argument [is] not such easy sailing. They will have to give up generalizations, and rely on particulars, and then they will find that what they lose is little to what they have gained.

In this spirit of cautious exception the Church, I believe, in processes of Canonization does not say all that looks miraculous is divine, but postpones the inquiry into miracles till it has ascertained the moral eminence of the subject of the process; and I should require a sort of photograph instead of a vague sketch of the Mahometan mystic who is to be compared to one of our Saints before I could acquiesce in allowing the parallel.

You may say that an opponent would make the same remark about Catholic saints. He must know more about them of course. This has made me unwilling to rely on miracles as *evidence* to unbelievers. Miracles are for the comfort of believers, as answers to prayer are, but, like answers to prayer these answers won't convince unbelievers. Görres is the great writer on the subject if you read German.'

[2] See letter of 20 Oct. to Charlton.
[3] See letter of 11 June to Sir Charles Wolseley.
[4] See letter of 31 July to Lord Braye.

TO WILLIAM CLIFFORD, BISHOP OF CLIFTON

Bm. Sept 10. 1883

My dear Lord

You were so good as to say you would look through some notes of mine on Inspiration, if I sent them to you. Do you persevere, in spite of the trouble it will give you, in this kind purpose?[1]

Your faithful Servant John H Card. Newman

TO H. P. LIDDON

Bm Sept 10. 1883

My dear Canon Liddon

I am much ashamed of myself at not having acknowledged your cheque, which came all right.[2]

I take this opportunity of asking whether I can be of any further use in your work as to dates, occurrences etc. I shall be too happy if I can. The Hampden matter (1836) I recollect very little about — and I fear Pusey kept no copies of important letters. What was done by the Hebdomadal Board (e.g. the calling Convocation to censure Hampden) was not done with his (P's) concurrence[3]

Very truly Yours John H. Card. Newman

The Revd Canon Liddon

TO MISS M. R. GIBERNE

Rednall 17 Sept. 1883

My dear Sister

I cannot let the pictures of the witnesses go.[4] They are historical, and are placed for ever in our Congregation Room.

As to the elastic stockings, I have used them these 29 years — ever since I broke a tendon at Dorkey by running up hill.[5]

So the Holy Father has called on all his children to unite their prayers for

---

[1] See letter of 7 Feb. 1883 to Bishop Clifford, who on 12 Sept. again expressed his willingness to read Newman's article on the Inspiration of Scripture.

[2] See letter of 21 Aug.

[3] Liddon replied on 14 Sept. that he would be very grateful for Newman's assistance. 'Dr Pusey kept no diary; and, until quite lately, no copies of important letters, and very few letters of importance addressed to himself. He used to speak of having had letters from Sir W. Scott and Montalembert; but of these I have found no trace. He also had some interesting letters from Archbishop Darboy, which I read at the time. But of these I can find only one.'

[4] These were Miss Giberne's portraits of witnesses for the Achilli trial. See letter of 24 Feb. 1852 to Miss Giberne.

[5] This was at Dalkey. See diary for 14 Sept. 1854.

the deliverance of the Church from her enemies. I wonder what was the last time such an exhortation came from the Holy See. The bicentenary of the victory of John Sobieski over the Turks seems to have suggested it to him. I trust it will be a great demonstration.[1]

Fr William showed me one of your last letters to him, and I am obliged to say that it was so intolerable in its skits and jibes, as almost to make me start as if a gnat stung me, and I saw it was impossible he could do more than he actually did, that is, attend to all your wants, as far as he knew them[2]

Yrs ever affectly J H Card Newman

TO AUSTIN MILLS

Sept 18/83

My dear Austin

My loan to the School Bank was due to me yesterday

I want £50 of it lent to Fr Louis. Will you then draw and sign a cheque for £50 on the Bm and Midland adding 'for Cardinal Newman'? in favour of Lewis

Yrs affectly J H N

TO RICHARD POPE

[19 September 1883]

My dear Richard Pope

I have to write to you on an unpleasant subject, and knowing, as I do, the fellow feeling and gentleness with which you will receive what is a real pain to me to say, only makes my saying it a harder task. It is about your salary. You have had the kindness to mention the subject to me yourself, several years ago, but nothing would induce me to listen to the delicacy towards us of a friend who has been so long with us, and has been so loyal to St Philip but a necessity, such as is just now upon us. By way of excusing ourselves, let me tell you in confidence that during the year 1882–3 we lost by the School about or above £1,000.

We have been for some weeks trying to find some mistake in the accounts

---

[1] Leo XIII's Encyclical Letter on the Rosary, urging that it should be said for the deliverance of the Church, was issued on 1 Sept. This was to be done publicly each day during the month of October. Sobieski relieved the Turkish siege of Vienna on 12 Sept. 1683.

[2] Miss Giberne wrote on this letter, 'I cannot think what he means   I wrote an easy friendly letter and nothing more   How wonderful dear Father you never understand me now — Is it Fr Willm who has changed your ideas about me?'   See letters of 10 Feb., 7 April and 1 Nov. 1880 to Miss Giberne.

but we can find none. Also we find that our *average* loss since we began the School is £100 a year. It is impossible we can go on with the School unless we materially bring down the cost of it.[1]

J H N

P.S.   I hope I shall not inconvenience you, if I ask you to close up the wooden door which is between the two courts of Numbers 21 and 22[2]

TO WILLIAM CLIFFORD, BISHOP OF CLIFTON

The Oratory Bm Sept 25. 1883

My dear Lord

Thank you sincerely for the trouble you have taken with my pages. I need not say how I feel pleased that you have been able to let me off so easily.[3]

Of course I will leave out the paragraph about which you have a difficulty. First, however, as I am not sure that I have quite understood your objection, I will on the opposite page propose an emendation, which leaves out the greater part of it. But believe me to be *quite prepared* to leave out the *whole* paragraph, and have no wish at all to say anything novel.

Most truly yours, My dear Lord, John H. Card. Newman

'This being considered, it follows that a book may be accepted and held as inspired, though not a word of it is an original document. Such is the case of St Matthew's Gospel. The Fathers agree that St Matthew wrote in Hebrew, and the Hebrew is lost.[4] We have it in Greek; yet the Greek, by the Tridentine decree, is canonical, and, as the Vatican has decided, is inspired.

The book of Ecclesiasticus, again, is a simple translation, and etc'

[1] Pope wrote on 20 Sept. suggesting that his salary should be reduced by £100 after the end of the autumn term.

[2] See letter of 20 Aug. to Pope.

[3] On 20 Sept. Bishop Clifford sent his remarks about Newman's article 'On the Inspiration of Scripture'. Neither he nor Bishop Hedley to whom he had shown it, thought it 'open to any censure'.

[4] The paragraph as sent to Bishop Clifford continued: 'We have it in Greek, and the Greek is inspired. But why? Not merely because it is the translation of an inspired work; for a translation of such is not necessarily inspired itself, else the Vulgate would be inspired. The reason why the translated Gospel of St. Matthew is inspired must be, because not only St. Matthew himself but his translator was also inspired, viz., in order to translate infallibly. Even if the Evangelist saw and approved the translation, this would not be enough to make it canonical, as the Vatican Council distinctly pronounces.

The Book of Ecclesiasticus is another instance; it is a simple translation, and is inspired, not because the original compiler, but because his grandson the translator, was inspired.'

This explanation did not seem correct to Bishop Clifford. The view that the translators of the Septuagint were inspired was not the common one. Bishop Hedley agreed that it was not correct to say that the Greek translation of St Matthew was inspired. 'The explanation seems moreover to be unnecessary — You have yourself (page 6.) called attention to the distinction that must be drawn between the Author of Scripture and the Writer. God has inspired the writer i.e. has moved him to write certain things . . . but the actual wording and style and language are not inspired . . .'

See letter of 3 Oct. to Bishop Clifford.

TO EDWIN PALMER

Bm Sept 27. 1883

My dear Archdeacon Palmer

I propose to send you your brother's private and family letters.[1] And I must ask you to recollect that, from the nature of the case, they come to you in a very disorderly state. Of course I did not feel it right to open them, except so far as to see to whom they were addressed — so they go from me pretty much in the shape in which they came to me. And I feel I need not have kept them so long as I have. This arose from my not having to [a] clear view before me, what I should have to do

I write this, as being dissatisfied with myself

Very sincerely Yours John H Card. Newman

TO ANNE MOZLEY

Bm Sept 28. 1883

My dear Anne Mozley

You have done me a great kindness in writing to me your last letter, and I wish I had some way of repaying you.

I can but pray that He who has so keenly smitten you, may give you grace, strength and consolation, in proportion to your sufferings

Yrs ever affectly John H Card. Newman

TO THE PROVOST OF THE BOLOGNA ORATORY

Birmingham England Sept 28. 1883

Very Rev. Father,

I had it in my intention to write to you the sincere thanks of the Fathers of the Oratory on receiving the precious gift of a relic of our Holy Father, St Philip, which you made us through our two fathers Riccardo and Aloysio Bellasis.[2]

We value the gift very much, but we fear that, after the accidental omission of acknowledging it to you, immediately on our reception of it, we have never repaired our negligence, or made to you and to your Fathers an apology for it.

This I wish to do by this letter, and, praying you to accept this tardy recognition of your generous kindness to us, and with my best prayers that all blessings from above may rest upon your Paternity and your community, I am,

My dear Very Rev. Father Your faithful servant John H. Cardinal Newman[3]
The very Rev. the Preposto of the House of Filippini Bologna

[1] See letter of 13 Aug. to Edwin Palmer.
[2] This relic had been given to Richard and Lewis Bellasis, when they visited the Bologna Oratory in May 1881.
[3] Catherine Anne Bathurst spent 27 and 28 Sept. in Birmingham. She wrote to Newman from Harrow on 30 Sept., 'I don't know how to thank you as I desire to do for your kindness to me, on Thursday and Friday, in letting me enjoy two delightful Conversations with you. It cheered me so to find you so well . . .'

TO JAMES H. WALDRON

Oct 1. 1883

To J. H. Augustine Waldron

May the Blessing of God, Father, Son, and Holy Ghost be with you always, through life and unto death[1]

John H. Card, Newman

TO ULRIC CHARLTON

Bm Oct 2. 1883

My dear Ulric

Mind, I have never seen Görres's book: and therefore cannot tell whether it is quite on your subject[2] — The best book on the Resurrection which I know is Paley's evidences, volume 1.[3]

Dr Westcott of Cambridge has so high a name, that I am led to refer you to his 'The Gospel of the Resurrection', though I have not read it, and, on looking into it I thought more discursive than was suited to my own mind.[4]

For myself the conversion of the orbis terrarum, the first overthrow of paganism, is to me the most supernatural event in the history of Christianity.

I have very faintly sketched it in my Grammar of Assent, but it demands a treatise.[5] If you have not seen my book I will send it you.

Very truly yours John H. Card. Newman

TO WILLIAM CLIFFORD, BISHOP OF CLIFTON

Bm Oct 3. 1883

My dear Lord

Thank you for taking the trouble so fully to answer my question. I have no doubt at all that I ought to omit the passage you remarked upon. It would never do to throw down for discussion a debatable proposition.[6]

---

[1] This correspondent, who signed himself James H. 'Augustine' Waldron was 28 years old and wrote on 30 Sept. to thank Newman 'very much for the grand works you have written,' of which he had bought seventeen, as and when he could afford them. 'I have derived a great benefit from reading them and by so doing has passed many a pleasant hour away.' He had been lent *The Dream of Gerontius* by a High Church curate at Banbury where he was a shop assistant and a Sunday School teacher, and became a Catholic at Easter 1879.

[2] See letter of 4 Sept. to Charlton who wrote on 30 Sept. that he would get Görres's *Christliche Mystik*, and thought he could read it in German.

[3] William Paley, *A View of the Evidences of Christianity*, London 1794. Charlton wrote: '. . . am I not right in stating that upon that great event the whole truth of Christianity depends.'

[4] Brooke Foss Westcott, *The Gospel of the Resurrection*, London 1866.

[5] *G.A.* pp. 452 to end.

[6] See letter of 25 Sept. to Clifford, who wrote on 30 Sept., 'When you say "a book may be accepted and held as inspired though not a word of it is an original document," you mean (if I understand you rightly) that the *matter* is not original but copied or abridged from some other book as is the case with the 2nd book of Machabees — When you speak of St Mathew's [sic]

Certainly I do think that often the *words* of Scripture are suggested or inspired from above, and this I fancied was implied when it was said that the 'sententiæ' were inspired as well as the 'res'.[1] It has ever seemed to me that the Scripture text has often various meanings, over and above that first and direct sense which may be dogmatic, ethical or historical; and that the Hebrew or Greek words may have in certain passages a depth (mystical, philosophical, or theological) which is supernatural, which one language may admit and another may not, and which therefore a translation cannot preserve. This defect incident to a translation need not interfere with its authenticity in matters of faith and morals; certainly not in the case of the Vulgate, as a practical standard; but it would suggest a sacredness in the original which no mere version can claim.

Thus considered, the gift of inspiration raises the Greek of St Matthew above the necessity of being a word-for-word translation, such as the Douay, and places it on a level with the other evangelical narratives.

And I thought I was borne out in this view by such passages of theologians as this of Lamy. 'Poterit interpres, si quando auctor Vulgatæ, *ob penuriam latini sermonis*, non expresserit *totam vim* textus primogenii, istius textûs rationem habere.' i. p 198.[2] Here the Vulgate, though authentic, is spoken of as inferior to the inspired original. Could we call the Vulgate 'the sacred text'? At least could we the Douay? But could we not, do we not, call the Greek St Matthew 'the sacred text'?

I did not overlook the passage in the Tridentine decree, 'prout in Ecclesiâ' etc which you quote, but I thought *both* clauses referred in the Vulgate, as the standard regulator of the original text, and its representative.

As I have not treated, in what I have written, of the *senses* of Scripture,[3]

Gospel as not being original, you mean that we do not possess the original *language*. . . . The example you adduce from St Mathews gospel does not prove your statement; the 2d book of Machabees does.'

For the altered passage, where Newman adopts this example, see *S. E.* p. 22, and J. D. Holmes and R. Murray's edition of *On the Inspiration of Scripture*, pp. 29 and 120.

[1] Clifford wrote: 'When you say "St Mathew [sic] wrote in Hebrew and the hebrew is lost, we have it in greek; yet *the Greek*, by the Tridentine decree, is canonical, and, as the Vatican has decided, is inspired," you seem to say that the language is inspired, whereas it is the matter, the res et sententiae that are inspired. They are inspired because St Mathew was inspired to write them, and for this reason the Gospel of St Mathew is canonical and inspired in whatever language we read it, provided the translation truly represents the meaning of the Evangelist. It is not required that the translation be inspired, but that it be *authentic*. The inspiration of the original covers the translation. The decree of the Council of Trent condemns all those who refuse to accept as sacred and *canonical* the books "prout in ecclesia catholica legi consueverunt (v.g. the greek version of St Mathew) et in veteri latina vulgata latina [sic] editione habentur." [*Denzinger-Schönmetzer*, 1504] The books are recognized as *canonical* and *inspired* prout habentur in their authentic translations, but neither the translators nor the translations are declared to be inspired.'

[2] T. J. Lamy, *Introductio in Sacram Scripturam*. cf. letter of 20 Jan. 1883 to Clifford, who quoted this text of Lamy in his letter of 22 Oct. to Newman. There he said, 'I fully admit that the *actual words* of scripture are at times inspired as well as *the sentence* which results from their combination.'

[3] In his first draft Newman wrote: 'I was not unaware that I had altogether passed over the question of the *Sense* of Scripture, but it is a large subject, and would require a treatise to treat of properly.'

I can leave out the paragraph about St Matthew's Greek without any difficulty.

With many thanks I am, My dear Lord Bishop

Your faithful Servant John H Cardinal Newman

TO J. FAWCETT

on cheapening my volumes   Oct 4. 1883

Dear Sir

I rejoice to be told that my publications would prove of use to other classes of the community besides those for which they were intended, and would gladly avail myself of the opening you propose to me, provided serious difficulties could be got over, which at present stand in the way.[1]

I have lately completed a uniform and revised edition of what I have written, (of which I inclose a list). The printing has cost me far more than I can comfortably bear, and, though in time it may be repaid by the sale, hitherto the yearly balance between the printing and the sales has been against me.

I felt it a duty to incur an expense which there was no one to take off my hands; but I am still ready to listen to any offer which will relieve me of it[2]

J H N

TO RICHARD HOLT HUTTON

Bm Oct 8. 1883

Dear Mr Hutton

You so kindly answered my request to know the difficulties you felt in accepting the Medicean MS of St Ignatius's Epistles after the discovery of the Nitrian, that I ought to have thanked you for it long ago.[3]

If now I add to my thanks some of my reasons for not being myself moved by them, it is because you may like to know what I should say to those difficulties, just as I was interested to be told from you what they were.

I have written nothing on the subject since 1871, and just now cannot unluckily lay my hand upon Mr Cureton's volume,[4] nor do I know of any

[1] Fawcett, a convert of Newman's and President of the Islington Conference of St Vincent de Paul, wrote on 2 Oct., 'For many years past, I have often wondered, whether your Eminence would leave as a legacy to the Catholic poor of this, and other English speaking Countries, the inestimable treasure of your Eminences works in a cheap form, say in penny numbers . . .'

[2] On 21 Oct. Fawcett wrote to thank for ten copies of *The Church of the Fathers*, ten of the sermon *The Pope and the Revolution*, seven of *Letter to Pusey*, six of *D.A.* and six of *H.S.* III. He went on to speak of the work of Canon Oakeley for the poor in Islington, 'whom he laboured amongst so long and whom he loved so much.'

[3] Hutton wrote on 7 May giving his reasons for preferring the Syriac text of the Epistles of St Ignatius in the Nitrian MS. to the generally accepted Greek one in the Medicean and other MSS. Newman defended the latter in 'On the text of the Seven Epistles of St Ignatius', first published in *Ess.* I in 1871, now in *T.T.*, pp. 95–135.

[4] Hutton was influenced by the arguments of William Cureton's *The Antient Syriac Version of the Epistles of St. Ignatius*, London 1845.

remarks later than Bishop Hefele's, except indeed an *obiter* passage of Professor Sanday's in his Lecture at the Reading Congress, (Guardian Oct 3. p 1464) where, speaking of the text of the New Testament and of the fourth Gospel, he observes of the Armenian translation of the Epistles of St Ignatius, which I have noticed (vid my Tract p 135) after Hefele[1] 'The Armenian Translations seem to me to be the turning point in the controversy as to their genuineness, and so to decide in favour of the evidence which they contribute.'[2]

Coming, however, to your difficulties, it is remarkable that one of Hefele's arguments in favour of the Medicean is the closer connection between the sentences in that MS than is found in the Nitrian. As I have said, Tract p 135 'in direct opposition to Dr Cureton, Hefele insists that the continuity of context is less close in the Syriac than in the Greek, referring in proof to as many as thirteen passages in the three Epistles' For myself the Epistles, all of them, have ever seemed to me wanting in logical connexion, as being written, or dictated by fits and starts, from the circumstances of the hour, but it struck me as specially curious that among the thirteen passages of Hefele in favour of the superior logic of the Medicean should be the very sentence (unless my old eyes take me in, as they often do) which you think is better placed in ad Romanos with the Nitrian than with the Medicean ad Trallianos, 4 and 5. Hefele says 'Initium capitis quarti (ad Trall) quod in versione Syriacâ Epistolæ ad Romanos adjuncta est, *arctissimo nexu cohæret* cum fine Capitis tertii;' and he proceeds to show this by offering a paraphrase.[3]

As to Athanasius's de Synodis, I cannot imagine it of 'doubtful' genuineness but it would be a long matter to go into. It is Athanasius all over from beginning to end. Few could write like Athanasius. Photius and Erasmus single him out from among the Fathers for special remark; and Gibbon, tho' talking of his 'rude eloquence' speaks of him as 'clear, forcible and persuasive'.[4] As to the 'de Synodis' you may recollect that two thirds of it is a collection of documents made while the composition of documents was in progress and it is like Athanasius to give as many such as he can. Confusion in chronology is no proof of spuriousness. It is not an assumption to say that he puts some of them in a second edition. In this very treatise he has a P.S. in which he says 'After I had written my account . . . I took pains to get copies of etc'[5] This is a specimen of his way. I don't think any one except, like Cureton, with a purpose, would dispute its genuineness.[6]

---

[1] C. J. Hefele, *Patrum Apostolicorum Opera*, fourth edition, Tübingen 1855, pp. lx–lxvi. *T.T.*, p. 135.

[2] Sanday made this remark towards the end of a lecture at the 1883 Church Congress held in Reading. The Armenian MS. agreed on the whole with the Medicean.

[3] Hefele, op. cit., p. 189, note 6.

[4] *The Decline and Fall of the Roman Empire*, chapter 21, Bury's edition, London 1896, II, p. 362.

[5] *Epistola de Synodis Arimini et Seleuciae*, final paragraph.

[6] Cureton was a Broad Churchman and the text he favoured omitted dogmatic passages and those in favour of episcopacy. His opinion as to the text is no longer held.

However, as to the *value* of testimony in the controversy before us, it seems to me very slight, compared with the strong witnesses in favour of the Medicean text derived from the longer Arianizing Epistles[1]

Very sincerely yours J. H. Card. Newman

P.S. I feel my age especially in not being able to write or speak without mistakes of words, as here.

TO BERNARD HENNIN

Oct. 9th. 1883.

My dear Bernard,

You are a very affectionate and mindful fellow — and, though I seldom return answers to you, as I should like and ought to do, you bear no malice, but go on scoring down memorable days, as if I deserved it from you.

May God bless you for this kindness to me, and your wife, and children and all yours.

Yours affectionately, John H. Card. Newman.

TO J. R. BLOXAM

Thursday Oct 11. 1883

My dear Bloxam

Very unluckily I have an engagement with a stranger, of long standing, on Saturday, and shall not be at liberty between 12.30 and 2.30. It is my only engagement

Yrs affly J. H Card. Newman

TO RICHARD HOLT HUTTON

Oct 12. 1883.

My dear Mr Hutton

I don't want to trouble you with a long letter, and I have no wish to write one, but since, when one begins, one finds it difficult to predict the end, I take a large bit of paper.

As to your question, I have written very little certainly of the shocking spectacle the Popes presented to the world in the times introductory to the Reformation, and I don't know the history well.[2]

[1] *T.T.*, pp. 109-15.
[2] Hutton, who was preparing a popular lecture on Newman's writings for the Ormond Street Working Men's College, see letter of 14 Jan., 1884, wrote: '. . . in looking over your more popular writings again I am much struck by . . . the apparent absence of any difficulty as to the moral degeneracy of the Papacy in the time preceding the reformation. To the ordinary Protestant mind it seems the most paradoxical of all assumptions that the centre of unity, doctrine, and even moral faith should be assumed to be in an office liable to be filled by absolutely wicked men, so that the Holy Spirit should have to overrule as it were, for the bene-fit of the Church, the words and acts of a Judas Iscariot almost — indeed of a Judas Iscariot without his remorse . . .'

1. In my letter to the D of N [Duke of Norfolk] p 254, Ed. 1876 I have said 'For a while the Papal chair was filled by men who gave themselves up to luxury, security and a pagan kind of Christianity; and we all know what a moral earthquake was the consequence, and how the Church lost thereby and has lost to this day, one half of Europe etc' 2.   Also in Sermon on St Philip, Occasional Sermons p 202 Ed. 1881.[1]

But I am far from wishing to shirk the argument against us — just the reverse. I think 1. that nothing would do more good than a candid confession, — and that nothing is more stupid than to attempt to disguise facts. 2.   I think that it would bring out much high religious excellence in the worst times, and how many powerful protests and denunciations there were on the part of holy men. And 3. it sets off the wonderful recovery which followed the bad time. Think of the life of St Philip, what he found in Rome and what he did there, so that his great title is '*Apostolo* di Roma.' The recent life of him by Archbishop Capecelatro brings out this vividly.[2] Indeed the outburst of Saints in 1500–1600 after the monstrous corruption seems to me one of the great arguments for Christianity. It is the third marvellous phenomenon in its history; the conversion of the Roman Empire, the reaction under Hildebrand, the resurrection under Ignatius, Teresa, Vincent and a host of others. Think of the contrast between Alexander VI and Pius V, think of the Cardinals of the beginning, and then those of the end of the 16th century. One must not wish evil that good may come, but I am reminded of the Church's words on Holy Saturday, 'O certe necessarium Adæ peccatum, quod Christi morte deletum est! O felix culpa, quae talem et tantum meruit habere Redemptorem![3]

(As to Ignatius's Epistles I know you will sympathise with me and condone me if I do not pursue the subject. Your arguments require an answer, but I so soon get tired, that I cannot do justice to what I would say. Why should not Ignatius repeat his sentences in two Epistles, as St Paul does in his, e.g. in Ephesians and Colossians [;][4] about the σιγή, it would trouble me to master the case).[5]

As to your difficulty about Popes being bad men is not Caiaphas a better parallel than Judas. And is it not *commonly* received in the words of the 26th Anglican article, that 'the unworthiness of the Minister hinders not the effect of the Sacrament'?

Does not our Lord foretell it, when he speaks of the wicked servant who says in his heart 'My Lord delayeth his coming' etc.[6]

I never pursued the matter myself but Cardinal Wiseman used to say that some of the best and most important Papal dicta came from bad Popes. I saw

[1] *Diff.* II and *O.S.*
[2] Alfonso Capecelatro, *La Vita di S. Filippo Neri*, two volumes, Naples 1879, English translation by T. A. Pope, London 1882.
[3] In the *Exultet.*
[4] See letter of 8 Oct. and fifth note there.
[5] See *T.T.*, pp. 121–2.
[6] *Matthew*, 24:48; *Luke*, 12:45.

(truly or not) the other day that when Tetzel raised the row in Germany, Leo brought out an admirable Catholic statement of what the true doctrine was.[1]

> Very sincerely Yours John H. Card. Newman

TO WILLIAM CLIFFORD, BISHOP OF CLIFTON

Bm Oct 13. 1883

My dear Lord

Please do not suppose I write from impatience — but it strikes me that perhaps I did not distinctly accept your welcome proposal to let the Archbishop see my pages — I meant to do so certainly — and I write now only to make it clear to you that I did[2]

> Your faithful Servant John H. Card. Newman

TO H. P. LIDDON

Bm Oct 15. 1883

My dear Canon Liddon

I have just met with a confirmation of what I said to you and you seemed to be ignorant of, Pusey's early efforts for the Soc. of the Prop. Gosp. I said to you I think 'Soon after 1824' — in the proof, which I am reading, of Hope Scott's Life, the writer says 'The beginning of its renewed energy dated from a *pamphlet of Dr Pusey's in 1825*'[3]

> Yours very truly J H Card. Newman

TO ROBERT ORNSBY

Bm Oct 16. 1883

My dear Ornsby

I send you back by this post the Proof.[4] It has heightened in me the reverence for JRH which the reading of your work in MS created. His natural exhibition of his religious devotedness, his living to God's glory, must be a most effective preaching to all readers, and, if you had done no other good thing in your life time, your pains and anxieties in this memoir, have the claim of an emphatically meritorious work.

There is only one consideration which frightens me in the anticipation of the service your work may do — Is it possible that it runs to six volumes! Does his daughter know this? Of course I am thinking of its circulation, when

---

[1] This was the Decree *Cum postquam*, 9 Nov. 1518. *Denzinger-Schönmetzer*, 1447–8.

[2] In his letters of 12 and 20 Sept. Bishop Clifford spoke of discussing Newman's article on Inspiration with Archbishop Errington, who lived at Prior Park, Bath. Bishop Clifford wrote on 14 Oct. that he had sent it to him. See letter of 25 Oct.

[3] This reference to the Society for the Propagation of the Gospel is in Ornsby's *Memoirs of James Robert Hope-Scott*, I, p. 117.

[4] Of the *Memoirs of James Robert Hope-Scott*, two volumes.

I am troubled at its possible lengthiness, but, to take the lowest view of it, it would cost, if six volumes, £600 or £700 — are his relatives prepared for that?

I have made some notes which I inclose

Yours affecty John H. Newman

P.S. Thank you for your notice of me in p. 172[1]

I suppose the references to Gladstone's work 'Sect. 1. Sect 10' etc etc. p. 150 correspond to the book.[2]

TO MESSRS BATH AND STEWART

[17 October 1883][3]

I was very much concerned to hear of Mr Kemp's death, a gentleman for whom I had so great a respect and esteem, though I was not personally acquainted with him.

Pray convey my best thanks to his sisters who have led you to send me a present so sacred from its subject, and presenting so beautiful an appearance. The continuous gospel narrative is to me a novelty and a very interesting one.

It must have caused him much trouble, labour and anxiety as well as enjoyment, and I pray and am sure that so religious a work will not be forgotten by Him for whose glory it was executed.

TO MISS FREER

Oct. 17. 1883

Cardinal Newman glady grants Miss Freer's request to insert his Hymn 'Lead etc' in the compilation she mentions. She will have also to ask Messrs Rivingtons' permission.

TO WILLIAM PHILIP GORDON

Oct 17. 1883

My dear Fr Superior

It is not for want of thinking of you and want of hearty acknowledgment of your letter, that I have not answered it sooner.[4] But I am so busy just now, have many letters to write, and now write so slowly and painfully.

---

[1] Of the second volume. This notice ended: 'Even late in life, when Father Newman's name was mentioned his whole countenance would brighten, as if a chord in his heart were touched which belonged to Newman alone. It seems necessary to use this emphasis here, since the very extent of the confidence shown in their correspondence would prevent an unreserved communication to the world of letters that would prove it the most strongly.'

[2] i.e. Gladstone's *The State in its Relations with the Church*.

[3] On 16 Oct. Messrs Bath and Stewart wrote from 2 Edmund Street, Birmingham that Newman had corresponded with Robert Albion Kemp, who was their friend and worked with them, and who lived at King's Heath. He took a very great interest in Catholic activities and institutions and for three years before his death had prepared a harmony of the Gospels in the Rheims version. His two sisters had had it privately printed and Newman was asked to accept a copy.

[4] Gordon had been re-elected Superior of the London Oratory on 12 Oct.

And I have intended to give you a mass before now, but my intentions are engaged till the end of the week.

I am very well, but my weakness is, I think, increasing

Yours affectly John H Card. Newman

TO MRS KEON

Oct 21. 1883

Dear Mrs Keon,

The old woman you speak of, depend upon it, will be able to do more by her prayers than I can for her — but I will not forget her wish.

I pray God that all blessing may come upon you.

Yours very sincerely, John H. Card. Newman.

TO ROBERT ORNSBY

Octr 22. 1883

My dear Ornsby

Is it not an error of the Press that *your own words* twice in p. 255 are placed in brackets?[1]

I don't think it possible to leave out Hope's passage in p. 255, not even 'the exterior is most repulsive.'[2]

Overleaf, I suggest an alteration at the expense of some insertion and transference of type, in *addition* to your own remarks, on pp 244, 253, which are very good[3]

Let me see the revise

Yrs affly J H Card. Newman

P.S.   Can you tell me the *page* in which in a note you refer to my Pamphlet of 1830 on the Church Missionary Society.[4]

Of the ecclesiastical *exterior* he judges unfavorably, but he may be well excused when we recollect the words of a well known Catholic controversialist, who, even while writing in defence of the Church, allows himself to say, 'The Rock of St Peter on its summit enjoys a pure and serene atmosphere,

---

[1] The references are to the *Memoirs of Hope-Scott* I. This error was corrected.

[2] Ornsby introduced a quotation from one of Hope-Scott's letters from Rome on 18 Jan. 1841: 'Of the ecclesiastical *exterior* he judges unfavourably, but adds: —
On this point, however, my judgment is still suspended, and I am conscious that, without having far more ample means of knowledge than have yet come within my reach, I cannot form a just opinion. Still, the exterior is most repulsive; and the good opinion with which the R. Catholics have elsewhere inspired me, has been considerably lowered in Rome. . . .'

[3] See the paragraph after the postscript. In the *Memoirs* I, p. 244, Ornsby commented on Hope-Scott's remark that Manzoni's ultramontanism was a result of his former utter unbelief, 'And what more natural than for a stray sheep to be attracted by the voice of the shepherd?' At p. 253 before giving Hope-Scott's criticisms of Romans and Rome, Ornsby remarked that 'they prove that his subsequent conversion was not due to any of those enthusiastic emotions to which such a step is often attributed.'

[4] *Memoirs* I, p. 120.

but there is a great deal of Roman *malaria* at the foot of it.'[1] And this very contrast between what was external and what was interior, Mr Hope himself, on his return home, insisted on to an intimate friend, who is my informant

TO ROBERT ORNSBY

Oct. 24. 1883

My dear Ornsby

Thank you for your extracting the Note, in spite of your heavy engagements.

I am very sorry I was putting words of my own into your mouth. While Hope Scott was a *Protestant,* he said to me 'Ah Newman, there may be abuses and scandals at Rome, but there is a higher region and wider views in the governing part.' I had meant only that you should state this *fact* of his so speaking on the authority of a *friend,* I being that informant witnessing to the *fact.* I beg your pardon if my sentence said more than that.

Also, I had no thought at all of making you *agree* with my sentence quoted from my letter to the Duke of N. any more than you agreed with Hope Scott's sentence which I was sheltering under my own.

And I must add that I pointed out my own words at a real self-sacrifice, and therefore it was that I did not put in my *name,* for I thought it did not quite become a Cardinal to have said what I did

Yrs affly J H Card. Newman

P.S.   My argument which I put into your mouth was, 'if even a Father of the Oratory could so speak, much more a Protestant'; but, since there is a chance of others misunderstanding my argument as you have, I for *my own sake* simply withdraw my sentence

TO WILLIAM CLIFFORD, BISHOP OF CLIFTON

Oct. 25. 1883

My dear Lord

I prefer sending my best thanks to the Archbishop through you, instead of writing to him myself, lest I should seem to adopt the tone of a controversialist, though, as you will see I have in fact altered every passage to which he kindly has called my attention.[2] I feel a great relief now that it has been under

---

[1] *Diff.* II, p. 297. The insertion proposed for p. 253 was not made. See next letter.

[2] Archbishop Errington wrote on 19 Oct. to Bishop Clifford: 'I return you the Inspiration Pamphlet with comments — 1st on what appears to me a flaw in the substance of the argument — and 2nd on some accidental expressions that might be changed — 1st The drift of the argument, especially shown in Numbers 4 (last paragraph) 5 and 6. seems to suppose no danger of sin against Faith (though there may be against Charity) except when an opinion is maintained opposed to a formal definition of the Church that such opinion is *heretical*; now I should imagine that opinions condemned under some of the other terms used in qualifying opinions could not be maintained without sin against faith.

Moreover the *formal definition* of a Pope or Council is not the only *Rule of Faith,* (though

268

your and his eyes, though of course I have not and shall not make this known[1]

I have overleaf set down my alterations

Your Lordship's faithful servant John H Card. Newman

The Hon & Rt Rev
The Bp of Clifton

1. The Archbishop says, 'Opinions condemned under some other terms used in qualifying opinions could not be *maintained* without a sin against faith.' Certainly, but I have not said '*maintained*'. (I have spoken of a Catholic investigator's *private* opinions (e.g. whether Adam lived 930 years which is not, I suppose 'dogma') Hence I say 'the internal assent' § 7 and §4. §5. A man may be doubtful what the Church has pronounced, whenever it is not actual dogma, and have haunting suspicions that perhaps he is opening his heart to unbelief, when the magisterium has not in fact settled a host of

necessary to make error *heresy*) — as shown from Number 17. of the Pamphlet — especially considering the *Magisterium* which is far from being so cut and dry as formal definition. By the way I don't like the last sentence of Number 17; if the last clause of that sentence is correct, the Council of Trent made a very useless decree, contrary to its custom.

2d   Remarks on the accidental expressions. Number 13. last sentence. Do *res et sententiae* in theologians use, mean what is there said?

18 *how* the "*Sacredness of a Sacrament*" etc?

20. "never certain that there is not a double sense" — very strong expression.

22. Spiritualized?

23. Par 3d. St Mathew's Gospel — *translation inspired*   What need?

25. "Authorship" . . . "an acquiescence"

You see the 2nd head has nothing of much moment, but if as I understood you the copy is a proof sheet, it might be considered.'

Errington's references are to the paragraphs of Newman's article 'On the Inspiration of Scripture'. See also J. D. Holmes and R. Murray, op. cit. pp. 31–5, for an analysis of the correspondence.

[1] When forwarding Errington's letter on 22 Oct. Clifford commented: 'What the Archbishop describes as having to him the appearance of a flaw in the argument, seems to me to amount simply to this, that he thinks that while in § 4. 5. 6 you lay full stress on "a formal definition of Pope or Council" as establishing what is and what is not de fide in the matter of scriptural interpretation, you do not (in those paragraphs) sufficiently put forward the "ordinarium et universale magisterium" of the Church as having the same effect. It is true you do this in § 17. but he thinks that the former paragraphs give the impression that if the meaning of any given text of Scripture has not been actually defined by Pope or Council, it may be rejected "salva fide", (though *charity* may counsel silence) whereas the meaning may have been settled by the ordinary and universal teaching of the Church.

I do not agree with the Archbishop's remark about the last sentence of Number 17. The words of the Council of Trent "contra unanimem conscnsum patrum" are of great importance for settling the meaning of a particular text in controversy with protestants. v.g. the meaning of the words of consecration. As far as Catholics are concerned it seems to me that all texts, for the interpretation of which a clear consensus of the fathers can be adduced, have already been definitely interpreted in that sense by the voice of the Church, and on the other hand, in those cases where the Church has not spoken, the consensus of the Fathers is also wanting, so that practically (as you say) the rule of duty is obedience to the Church.

The Archbishop's remarks under the 2d head are not of much importance as he himself remarks.

He must have misunderstood your meaning somehow when he says — 20 "never certain that there is not a double sense" "*very strong expression.*" But you must be right because many persons hold that there is a literal and spiritual meaning to *every portion of Scripture* . . .'

At the end of a draft of his present letter of 25 Oct. Newman wrote and then cancelled 'The only criticism which I cannot as a matter of *conscience* accept and acted [sic] upon is upon the statement "that we are never certain that there is not a double meaning"' physical questions now any more than it had settled the question of the Solar System in the time of Galileo. I mean, while most priests could tell a man what interpretations of Scripture were dogmatically forbidden, few could pronounce what interpretations were forbidden by the magisterium — and perhaps, as in the case of the Fathers, few interpretations by the magisterium are practically available for internal faith, unless singled out and confirmed by dogma.) In Scripture interpretation the magisterium is infallible — is uninterrupted tradition identical with the magisterium? if so, it is infallible too. *Is* it?

To make it clearer that I have not meant 'maintained', I now add in § 7 'I do but contemplate the inward peace of religious Catholics in their own persons.'

2. And, to make it clear that I have not forgotten the magisterium, I shall not only in § 4 refer to § 17, but I shall erase in § 4 'or what is called dogma' and in § 5 insert 'dogma or the equivalent of dogma'.[1] And in § 18, instead of 'to submit himself internally to the *judgment* of the Church', I shall put 'the definite teaching.'[2]

3 I have altered the sentence at the end of § 17 thus, 'Though the Fathers were not inspired, their united testimony is of supreme authority,' etc[3]

4 for 'or in respect to res et sententias' § 13 fin I put 'being matters of fact'[4]

5 I say 'informed and *quickened*' instead of 'spiritualized.'[5]

6 In § 20 'never certain λ there is not a double sense' I insert 'with obvious exceptions'[6]

7. St Matthew's gospel inspired. — I have omitted it.

8. § 25 for *acquiescence* in St Paul's authorship of the Hebrews I have put 'acceptance of'[7]

[1] His unrevised sentence ran: 'The question then which I have to answer is, *What*, in matter of fact, has the Church (or the Pope), as the representative of God, said about Scripture, which as being Apostolic, unerring truth, or what is called dogma, is obligatory on our faith, that is, is *de fide*' And 'We are not bound to accept with an absolute faith what is not a dogma, what is not de fide . . .'
[2] The unrevised sentence said that the Catholic scholar 'is bound to submit himself internally, and to profess to submit himself, in all that relates to faith and morals, to the judgment of Holy Church.'
[3] The unrevised sentence said, 'though the Fathers were not inspired, yet it is forbidden "contra unanimem consensum Patrum ipsam Scripturam Sacram interpretari"; at the same time, since no Canon or List has been determined of the Fathers, the practical rule of duty is obedience to the voice of the Church.'
[4] The unrevised sentence ran: 'In this point of view, Scripture is inspired, not only in faith and morals, but in all its parts which bear on faith, or, as theologians say, in respect to "*res et sententias*."'
[5] The unrevised sentence said that the Scriptures, 'if they are man's writing, informed and spiritualized by the presence of the Holy Ghost, they admit . . . of being composed of outlying materials which come from editors who were inspired.'
[6] Unrevised: 'If there be at once a divine and a human mind co-operating in the formation of the sacred text, it is not surprising if there often be a double sense in that text, and never certain that there is not.'
[7] The unrevised sentence said that the authorship of *Hebrews* 'is not a matter of faith as its inspiration is, but an acquiescence in received opinion.'

TO W. J. LINTON

Oct 30. 1883

Cardinal Newman will be glad to give permission to Mr Linton to insert in his volume the Cardinal's two poems, on condition he prints the text from the last edition published by Burns and Oates, Orchard Street W

Mr Linton must also obtain Messrs Rivingtons's permission[1]

TO ST GEORGE JACKSON MIVART

Birmingham. Oct. 30. 1883.

My dear Professor Mivart,

I thank you for your interesting letter, and rejoice to be told that the old Benedictine Abbey is to revive.[2]

I gladly would give my name to your Committee of restoration at once, but for the want of information of the relation of the French Benedictines to other houses in this country already. If the Bishop of Birmingham associated himself with the exertions of the Committee, that would remove my difficulty.

Also I should say that, my means not being very ample, what I have to give away I feel to be best expended upon objects, Catholic or Local, of first importance; and this leads me to ask myself whether there would not be an inconsistency in me in giving my name to an object calling on the public for contributions, and not furthering it by my example.[3]

I am, My dear Professor Mivart, Yours most truly

John H. Card. Newman.

Professor Mivart etc., etc.

TO HENRY IGNATIUS DUDLEY RYDER

Nov 4. 1883

My dear Ignatius

Any course which gives a chance of averting so dismal a calamity should be tried. I little thought that the pestilence, which threatened the next generation, was to show itself now in St Philip's household, and I do trust still that he will protect us from it[4]

[1] The two poems included in W. J. Linton and R. H. Stoddard's collection *Lyrics of the XIXth Century*, New York 1883, pp. 127-9, were 'The Elements' and 'A Voice from Afar', *V.V.*, pp. 188-9 and 40-1.

[2] This refers to the restoration of Buckfast Abbey, Devon, which had been purchased by exiled French Benedictines from La Pierre-qui-vire.

[3] Mivart replied on 10 Nov. that Bishop Ullathorne 'in spite of his general objection to give his name to works outside his Diocese, thinks the reestablishment of Buckfast Abbey a matter warranting him to make "one exception" in its favour.' Mivart added that Newman would not be expected to make a large contribution. See his letter of 11 Nov.

[4] At the end of Oct. Arthur Hutton began to tell several of his fellow members of the Oratory that he had lost all belief in the existence of a personal God, and then gave Newman a long statement of his all-embracing doubts. On 1 Nov. Ignatius Ryder wrote to Newman from

But first A. must be pretty confident of the truth of his views, to have written so exact and logically arranged a statement as he has put into my hands. Next, such a statement must re-act upon him, as putting his ideas into shape, and, by systematizing them, recommending them to his mind. Thirdly, he seems to have no devotional feelings, impulses or habits, nothing to appeal to, nothing in his heart or intellect to act as a remonstrance and protest against unbelief, as if he had neither love nor fear of God, no remembrance of mercies, no misgiving about the future. Hence fourthly, tho' he feels it a *duty* not to be a hypocrite, he has no tenderness, no dread as to acts wrong in their religious aspect, acts which are sacrilegious as well as hypocritical; and this deadness would grow on him, if he continued in the practice of those ecclesiastical actions which form his daily routine. Nor am I sure that temptations quite foreign to his present state (for I have not the shadow of a suspicion about his strict purity now) would, as time went on, and he encountered the various accidents of a priest's life, be successfully resisted, by the mere sense of honour and hatred of hypocrisy. But this is travelling beyond my subject.[1]
Lastly then, I observe his avowal — 'When a boy at school, *from ten to eighteen*, I doubted the existence of a Personal God, and was almost ready to express my disbelief in miracles.' Thus in the depth of his heart, to use his own phrase, he has been without faith all his life.

I fear his remaining here, as I should fear a patient in an Epidemic. His going to the Jesuits would at least indirectly give us advice how to act — but I like Paul's idea, if it is possible, better[2]

Yrs affly J H Card. Newman[3]

Bath: 'Paul has just told me that Arthur has spoken to you. I wish to say that though I agree with Paul in his estimate of Arthur's state of mind I cannot — perhaps unreasonably — but I cannot assure myself that there is nothing of the past for him to appeal to, no point which he may not possibly recover. Therefore I should be inclined to urge him to make a retreat with the Jesuits to begin with.'

[1] On 6 Nov. Hutton left the Oratory for good. He had been in charge of the parish school. In Dec. at the end of the autumn term one of the teachers, Edith Bowerman, also left Birmingham. They were married in 1884.

[2] In his draft, instead of this last sentence Newman wrote, 'I should prefer Addis to the Jesuits.' Paul Eaglesim evidently suggested that Hutton should stay with W. E. Addis, parish priest of Sydenham 1878–88, who had been a member of the London Oratory 1868–78. In fact Hutton left at once. He wrote from the Oratory on 5 Nov. to Ignatius Ryder: 'Many thanks for your kind letter. Yes, I am going this week; probably tomorrow. It is painful to leave, but painful to remain. The Father [Newman] talked to me this morning kindly but plainly. It grieves me most of all to be a trouble to him in his old age. And to you I must say good bye too, whom of all Catholics I have known I have most admired and I may say loved. You must forget my faults, and give me as far as may be a pleasant place in your memory. I cannot write more.'

[3] At a Chapter Meeting, probably on 5 Nov. Hutton announced with tears to his fellow Oratorians that he had lost belief even in the existence of a personal God. This is recorded in Ullathorne's *Relatio Status Diocesis Birminghamiensis 1884* to Propaganda. *S R C Anglia*, 1883–4, f. 988. Hutton left the Oratory on 6 Nov. and on 12 Nov. wrote to Newman from Edinburgh, 'I am happy now in the consciousness that I have done my duty, and have done it also I hope without injuring others, so far at least as was possible; though I must add that I suffer at times from a depressing sense of loneliness; which however is inevitable after having enjoyed for nearly eight years the society of the Fathers, who have one and all been so good to me. But most of all I am pained by the thought of the pain I have given you, who have been so generous to me in my faults. Yet somehow I feel as if I could not have avoided it.'
See also Newman's letter to Hutton placed at 15 Nov.

TO R. W. CHURCH

Nov. 5. 1883

My dear Dean

Thank you for your thoughtfulness about me. I had been made anxious about Copeland for a year past, and then the Bishop of St Albans and Mr Borelase wrote to me.[1]

Also thanks for your asking after my health — I am overwhelmed with letters (which must be my excuse for this shabby one) and teased with calls, kind in intent as the callers are.

Yours affly, J. H. Card. Newman.

TO ST GEORGE JACKSON MIVART

Nov. 11. 1883.

My dear Professor Mivart,

Thank you for the trouble you have taken. I shall be happy to have my name placed upon the Committee for the restoration of the Abbey.[2]

Most truly yours, John H. Card. Newman.

TO MRS EDWARD BELLASIS

Nov. 13. 1883

My dear Mrs Bellasis

What a time this has been, and especially for you.

We have great cause to be thankful and to be hopeful — but still there is a very anxious time to come, and St Philip especially warns us of, in such cases, leaving off prayers too soon.[3]

Yours affectly J H Card. Newman

TO ROBERT CHARLES JENKINS

November 13. 1883.

My dear Canon Jenkins,

I thank you for your learned Pamphlet, which is as interesting as it is learned.[4] I am no judge of the controversy of which it treats. The only view I feel myself able to hold is that, considered in its social aspect, the law ought to

[1] W. J. Copeland's nephew, William Borlase, wrote to Newman on 2 Nov. that his uncle was seriously ill, although not in immediate danger of death. Thomas Legh Claughton was Copeland's diocesan and friend.

[2] See letter of 30 Oct. to Mivart. On 29 Nov. Newman was elected a member of the committee for the restoration of Buckfast Abbey.

[3] This seems to refer to the illness of William Bellasis. See letter of 24 Jan. 1884 to Mrs Bellasis.

[4] *The Repeal of the Prohibition of the Marriage of a Deceased Wife's Sister Advocated . . .* , London 1883. See letter of 21 July 1882 to Jenkins.

stand as it is, if the educated classes are the objects of legislation — and to be repealed, if the interest is to be consulted of the lower classes.

To this must be added, in favour of the law standing, the danger of its repeal acting and having a place in the serious movement now working all over Christendom to relax the sanctity of marriage.

I think you told me that Luther was your ancestor. Have you taken any part in the Festival in his honour?[1]

Very truly yours, John H. Card. Newman.

TO ARTHUR WOLLASTON HUTTON

[15 November? 1883]

My Dear Arthur

Francis has shown me the last page of your letter to him. I will not allow that you are, as you say, 'irrevocably cut off' from your friends ⟨all that is dear to you⟩, — and since your letter to me came, I have wished to say so. I treasure the words in that letter in which you almost anticipate (may I not use the term?) that the time will come, when you will 'make a sincere act of faith in Catholicism.'[2] That will be a joyful day, and I assure you of our united prayers that God will hasten its coming. You believe more than you think you do, and God loves you better than, in your dishonouring thought of Him, you allow yourself to fancy. He will overcome you in spite of yourself

J H N

[Another draft of the letter]
My dear A

Francis has shown me the last page of your letter to him.

I will not allow that you are, as you *say* 'irrevocably cut off from those who are so dear to you.' If you thought I meant it in what I said to you when you came to me, you quite mistook me. Two thoughts filled my mind, the thought of Almighty God, and the thought of you. I could not mean that you had committed an irrevocable act in the sight of God; and so far from my saying that there was anything irrevocable on your part, I earnestly pleaded against you 'how can you be so cruel to yourself.'[3]

[1] Jenkins replied on 15 Nov. that he had not attended the celebrations for the fourth centenary of Luther's birth. 'His youngest but one sister married the Chancellor of the Cardinal Elector of Mayntz, (the Duke Albrecht of Saxony) — Dr Rühl . . . from him my grandmother Fr. Johanna Regina Rühl was descended.'

[2] This was Hutton's letter of 12 Nov. from Edinburgh, part of which is quoted in last note to letter of 4 Nov. to Ignatius Ryder. In it Hutton wrote that 'even if you were willing to receive me back, I could not honestly return to my work as a priest. I can only say that I believe I am acting rightly in coming to this decision; and I will add that if at any future time I can see my way to make a sincere act of faith in Catholicism, wherever I am I will seek to be reconciled to the Church, and will accept any penance that may be laid upon me.'

[3] Neither of these drafts was sent as Newman explained shortly afterwards. He copied and commented on part of another letter from Hutton: 'Extract from Fr Hutton's letter to Fr Paul dated Nov 22, 1883
"I was touched by your account of the Father's *words promising* to welcome me back should I be able to qualify myself to ask for *readmission* by an act of faith. But it *would be*

TO ROBERT ORNSBY

Nov. 23. 83

My dear Ornsby

I have made one or two corrections in the Table of Letters

I dare say it is my own fault, but I do not recollect seeing in your copy, a number of the Letters of mine to Hope Scott now in type.[1]

Yours affly J. H. Card. Newman

TO POPE LEO XIII

[25 November? 1883]

In mediis negotiis et solicitudinibus quæ Sanctitatem Vestram occupant, datur mihi saltem hæc venia, ut S.S. Redemptoris Nataliciis appropinquantibus festis, offeram Beatitudini Vestræ meipsum, et devotionem meam et amorem.

Quinimmo a Sanctissimo Benedictionem humillime posco, ego qui omnium quotquot nunc in vivis sunt Purpuratorum, annis, etsi non meritis, jam sum provectissimus.[2]

Et liceat mihi, Beatissime Pater, consuetum obolum meum, pro modulo meo, £20 sterling (500 franc.) per manus Revmi Stonor, hoc tempore ad pedes Apostolorum ponere.

affectation in me to say that I see any near prospect of my being able to do this. All I can say is that I will do it when I feel I honestly can, and that it would be a happiness to call myself again a son of St Philip who is indeed often in my thoughts."   I observe

1 I did not give any Father authority to give a message to him from me.

2 It was settled that *I* should write to him

3 And that, in order to deny I had implied that his act was irrevocable

4 When I attempted to do this, I found I could not do so, without much more than a mere denial of the word ⟨"irrevocable."⟩ — to say it was not irrevocable was suggesting that it would be in his power at any time to return to us. Accordingly I told the Fathers I could not write to him.

5. His words in the letter I have just read, show how wellfounded was my fear. He spoke of my "promising to welcome him back" if he makes an act of faith, of which, however, he sees no "near prospect"

6 I had absolutely no power to promise him a welcome back, or what he calls "re-admission"

7 That word implies that the option of belonging to the Oratory or not for any time to come lies with him and him only

8. On the contrary, I believe any Father might appeal to Rome against such a promise or understanding proceeding from me or others.

J H N   Nov 25. 1883'

Hutton had renounced his membership of the Oratory. For readmission, as for admission, election by a majority of voting members was necessary.

Towards the end of Nov. Ignatius Ryder wrote to Hutton that he ought to send Newman a formal resignation from membership of the Oratory. This he did on 1 Dec.

[1] Ornsby had acted on Newman's permission in his letter of 9 Aug. He replied on 25 Nov. that he would send the proofs in due course.

[2] After the death of Cardinal Bonnechose on 29 Oct. 1883 Newman became the oldest Cardinal.

TO ARTHUR WOLLASTON HUTTON

Nov 27. 1883

My dear Arthur

There are two pictures which Pope Pius and John Bowden gave me and which you accepted from me

Would you not give them to one or other of the Fathers? I should be sorry if they left the Oratory[1]

Yours affly J H Card. Newman

TO FRAÜLEIN M

Novr. 27. 1883

Cardinal Newman would gladly serve Fraülein M. if it were in his power.

But he feels, as far as his eyes will allow him to read her letter, that what she needs is a good Priest to direct her.

She ought to do what he tells her to do.

As far as he can judge from her letter, she has no real doubts about Christianity, but suggestions from the evil spirit, which dart into her mind and which will do her no harm if she turns away from them.

She ought to cherish a deep conviction that God loves her and desires her salvation. She must not despond, but put herself into God's Hands and say: 'O Lord guide me'. The more we trust Him the more He will do for us. May the Blessing of Almighty God, Father, Son, and Holy Ghost be upon her ever.

TO H. P. LIDDON

Bm Nov 29. 1883

Dear Dr Liddon

I am very much ashamed of myself. Your packet of Athan. [Athanasius] came quite right. My memory is bad — Generally I am very anxious about such matters.[2]

(Private) How strange you should address me thro' Hutton. He is just the Father I have been least intimate with. Tho' you are not the only person who mistook. He has left us. It must be soon known, but I had rather it should not be told from this place

Very truly Yours John H Card. Newman[3]

[1] Hutton replied on 1 Dec. from the Imperial Hotel, St Andrews, that he would be glad for Paul Eaglesim to have the pictures. 'But under the circumstances I hardly like to give them to him myself. Would you therefore consent, (still remembering as I trust the kindly feeling towards me which prompted you to give them to me) to take them back again, and then yourself give them to him or to whomsoever you will?'
[2] Liddon had sent some collations of variants on the text of St Anthanasius, once Pusey's, which Newman had forgotten to acknowledge. On 25 Nov. Liddon wrote to A. W. Hutton asking whether they had arrived.
[3] A letter from the Duke of Norfolk shows that Newman visited London on 30 Nov., when he consulted his doctor.

Dec. 1. 1883

My dear Mrs Ward

I fear I have not had the gratitude to thank you for Mr Devas's book which came to me quite punctually.[1]

I have read enough to understand how large and interesting a subject he has chosen, but it is not mastered in a hurry.

And there is such a prejudice against Catholic works, that any one who publishes must write for the future rather than for the present, and must be content that fairness and sympathy should be denied him, in spite of his obvious claims.

Anyhow I congratulate him on a great subject, carefully thought through, and illustrated with abundant learning

Yours affectly J. H. Card. Newman

TO MARGARET DE LISLE

Decemb. 6, 1883

Dear Miss de Lisle

I was very much concerned to hear of the great loss your family had sustained, and felt especially how grievously it would affect your Mother.[2]

It is very wonderful that she should be visited so heavily, and leads one to expect with greater earnestness the time, when all mysteries will be cleared up.

Only let us keep up our courage, and trust him who never fails his own, however he may try them.

Of course I do not forget yourself or your nephew,[3] tho' I have referred especially to your Mother

I said Mass this morning for your brother, and delayed writing till I could say I had done so

Most truly Yours John H Card. Newman

TO ORBY SHIPLEY

[9 December 1883]

My dear Sir

I thank you for calling my attention to a line in my Hymn.

However, I prefer the reading as it stands. By 'would' I meant 'si vellet'

---

[1] This was *Groundwork of Economics*, London 1883, by C. S. Devas, Mrs Ward's son-in-law. Newman wrote on the fly leaf 'J H N from the Author.'

[2] Margaret's eldest brother Ambrose Charles Lisle March Phillipps de Lisle died on 27 Nov.

[3] Edward Lisle Strutt. See letter of 26 Oct. 1880 to Margaret de Lisle.

si aggrederetur as 'If thou wouldest be perfect,' If thou wouldest enter into life 'Should' is more logical, but somewhat prosaic.[1]

TO LORD BRAYE

Dec 14. 1883

My dear Lord Braye,

Thank you for your eloquent thoughts, which we [sic] have kindly inscribed with my name.[2]

I understood you to write by way of relieving your mind — and you relieve it with words full of poetry and earnestness. It is in some sort a soliloquy, not an Address.

I think I have expressed your feeling, and in a certain sense answered it, in various Verses of my own. Perhaps you have seen these. They record my thoughts towards the Anglican Church, and first appeared with Poems of Keble etc.

I am tempted to send to you the Stanzas which rose in my mind especially as suggested by your 'Paragraphs' in 'Opportunities' at p 83 Also p 235[3]

Very sincerely Yours John H Card. Newman

TO ALEXANDER WHYTE

Decr 15. 1883

My dear Dr Whyte

I thank you for your Commentary which you have sent me.[4] It has interested me greatly; it rejoices me to meet with so much in it, which I can sympathise and concur in — and I thank you heartily for the kind references you make to me in the course of it, and for the words you have written in its first page.

But it pains me that so large a heart as yours should so little enter into the teaching of the Catholic Church, let alone agreeing to it. Thus you say that we consider that we *physically* eat our Lord's flesh and drink His blood in the

---

[1] On 8 Dec. Shipley drew Newman's attention to what he thought was a misprint in one of the hymns from *V.V.* which he was reprinting. See letter of 9 Feb. 1882 to the Duke of Norfolk. The reference was probably to the second line of the third verse of the hymn for 'Matins — Friday', *V.V.*, p. 222:

'If e'er by night our envious foe
With guilt our souls would stain,
May the deep streams of mercy flow,
And make us white again;'

[2] This was Lord Braye's *The Present State of the Church in England, Seventeen Paragraphs*, London 1884. It had a long dedication to Newman, and spoke of the divisions among English Catholics and the opportunities of spreading the truth which they failed to use.
[3] 'A Word in Season', *V.V.*, p. 87; 'Lauds — Friday', *V.V.*, p. 239. See also letter of 30 May 1884 to Lord Braye.
[4] *A Commentary on the Shorter Catechism*, Edinburgh, n.d., [1879?]. Whyte inserted frequent quotations from *G.A.*, *P.S.*, and other works of Newman, specially in connection with the Blessed Trinity and the Incarnation.

Holy Eucharist.[1] It might be quite as truly said that in John vi our Lord speaks of 'eating His flesh and drinking His blood' physically as that we so speak. We consider the *substance* of His body and blood to be in the Sacrament, and thereby to be given to us — and you truly say p 17, speaking of the Holy Trinity, that the 'substance' is that 'awful, mysterious essence of which the qualities are *not* extension, or colour or figure' etc that is, *not* the 'phenomena' which we call physis or nature, and which we could only receive 'physically,' but that unknown reality to which sensible qualities attach themselves and belong, without being *it*.[2]

Excuse this outbreak of controversy, and believe me to be

Most truly Yours, John H Card. Newman.

The Rev. A. Whyte DD

TO ROBERT CHARLES JENKINS

Dec 16. 1883.

Dear Canon Jenkins,

I am confined to my rooms with a troublesome cough — which causes lassitude — else, I should before this have thanked you for the very great kindness you shew me in taking up in your own sympathetic words, and transcribing in your beautiful handwriting the theme of and a response to my verses.

The illustrated card which you send with it is one of the most perfect as a work of art, which I have met with,

I beg to send you my best Christmas greetings. When you get this, we shall be close on O. Sapientia.[3]

Thank you for your antiquarian investigation. It should have been printed in a more permanent shape. By the bye, M. Bunsen[4]

TO W. J. COPELAND

Dec. 18. 1883

My dear Copeland

We are very much touched by your remembrance of us just come. Also it seems to show us that you are better, especially as I wish to persuade myself that the handwriting of the direction is yours. It is very like yours[5]

We have had you in mind since Nov 1. Bishop Claughton and your nephew were kind enough to write to me.[6] We shall go on thinking of you

Ever Yrs most affectly J. H. Card. Newman

[1] *A Commentary*, pp. 184–5. See postscript to letter of 21 Dec. to Whyte.
[2] cf. *V.M.* II, p. 228.
[3] The antiphon for the Magnificat on 17 Dec.
[4] The rest is missing.
[5] The address of Copeland's Christmas turkey was in the hand of his niece by marriage, Mrs Borlase. William Borlase wrote on 21 Dec. to say that Copeland was weaker and 'quite childish' but happy.
[6] See letter of 5 Nov. to R. W. Church.

TO ALEXANDER WHYTE

Dec 21. 1883

My dear Dr Whyte

It is very kind in you to ask me to suggest an emendation in the passage I pointed out to you, now that a second edition is called for.[1] I hope I shall propose nothing that you cannot accept. Any how, I shall quite understand any difficulty which may arise, and shall be sure that you grant me as much as you can. I quote some sentences from our authoritative documents as *references*, but of course only in justification of any changes in your text *not* as if I wanted them introduced into it

Very sincerely Yours John H Card Newman

P.S. I ought in my first letter to have expressed my sense of the service you are doing to the cause of Christian charity by your quotations from authors external to your own communion.

Edition I. p 184, 5.

This is directed against the Popish doctrine of Transubstantiation. According to that doctrine the bread and wine are changed into the very flesh and blood of Christ, so that all communicants literally and physically eat the flesh and drink the blood of Christ.

Proposed correction

This is directed against the Popish doctrine of Transubstantiation. According to this doctrine the substance of the bread and wine is converted into the substance of the very flesh and blood of Christ, so that all communicants literally and substantially partake His flesh and blood. (vid supr. pp 17, 18)

Concilium Tridentinum

Sess. xiii c.4 Persuasum semper in Ecclesia Dei fuit, per consecrationem, panis et vini conversionem fieri totius substantiæ panis in substantiam corporis Christi Domini nostri, et totius substantiæ vini in substantiam sanguinis ejus, quæ conversio convenienter et propriè à Sancta Catholica Ecclesia Transubstantiatio est appellata.[2]

Catechismus ad Parochos.

Part. ii qu.41 Illud saepissimè a Sanctis Patribus repetitum fideles admonendi sunt, ne curiosius inquirant quo pacto ea mutatio fieri possit . . . 'Non est impossibile apud Deum omne verbum'

[1] Whyte wrote on 20 Dec. that a second edition of his *A Commentary on the Shorter Catechism* was about to be printed, and asked if he might insert Newman's criticism of his use of the word 'physically' on p. 85. See letter of 15 Dec. Whyte said, 'I believe it would supply matter for thought to many of my Clerical readers, who, like myself, may have been accustomed to think and speak somewhat too roughly and polemically on this profound subject.'

[2] *Denzinger-Schönmetzer*, 1642.

qu. 42. Doceant (Parochi) Christum Dominum in hoc Sacramento, ut in loco, non esse. Etenim locus res ipsas consequitur, ut magnitudine aliquâ praeditae sunt; Christum vero Dominum eâ ratione in Sacramento esse non dicimus, ut magnus et parvus est. Substantia enim panis in Christi substantiam, non in magnitudinem aut quantitatem convertitur. . . . Nam et aeris substantia, totaque ejus natura, sic in parvâ, ut in magna aeris parte, itemque tota aquae natura, non minus in urnulâ quam in flumine insit necesse est.

TO MISS M. R. GIBERNE

Dec 24. 1883

My Dear Sister M. Pia

All best Christmas greetings to you. I wish you were stronger, and I know from old times how long the night is, when it is sleepless.

As to my book on the Cult of Mary, it is my 'Letter to Dr Pusey' with (I suppose) all that relates to Pusey cut out.[1]

I have not gone to Oxford, nor am going. But I am publishing some notes on Inspiration apropos of words used by M. Renan — and I got Fr William to deliver them at the meeting of the Jesuit Guild at Oxford.[2] As to London, I went for a few hours to consult medical men, who, I am thankful to say, gave a good account of me.

It was the common opinion in early times that Enoch and Elias were the two witnesses in Apoc. xi, who would herald in the end of the world; but I doubt whether in such matters the Fathers are authoritative.

Miss Wood fell backwards down a staircase, (as Mrs Wootten did, shortly before her death) and the fall hurt her spine. Her brain became affected, and after a long illness, or rather a long death in bed, she was (perhaps suddenly) taken away.[3]

William Copeland is dying now, not from an accident, but by a slow death from paralysis. His mind is gone. He is one of my truest, most faithful friends. You will, I know, say some prayers for him

Ever Yours affectly John H Card. Newman

---

[1] *Diff.* II, pp. 1–170.

[2] *S.E.*, Essay I. Neville read the Article on Inspiration on 21 Nov. before a small group collected at the Jesuit house in Oxford by Thomas Parkinson, who wrote next day that it 'seemed to me admirably adapted to its purpose' of keeping the question open.

On 27 Nov. James Knowles accepted it for the *Nineteenth Century*, where it appeared in Feb. 1884. Newman required that it should not appear with 'any downright unchristian articles', and an article by Herbert Spencer was due to appear in Jan. On 3 Dec. Knowles wrote: 'Of course I do not agree, but granting the Premisses — I am frankly amazed — and so I think will the public be — to see how open a man's mind may be under the Catholic System upon matters which I had supposed were close shut up against all liberty of thought.'

[3] Charlotte Wood died on 16 Aug.

TO MARK PATTISON

Bm Dec 25. 1883

My very dear Pattison

I grieve to hear that you are anxiously unwell. How is it that I, who am so old, am carried on beyond my juniors?[1]

This turns me back in thought forty years, when you, with Dalgairns and so many others now gone, were entering into life.

For the sake of those dear old times, I can't help writing to you. Is there any way in which I can serve you. At least I can give you my prayers, poor as they are[2]

Yrs affectionately J. H. Card. Newman

TO JANE MOZLEY

Dec 26. 1883

My dear Jane

Thank you for your Christmas good wishes, which I return warmly. I hardly expected a Derby letter from you, for, unless I misunderstood Aunt Anne, I thought you would by this time be with your brother Frank. It seemed to me a good arrangement and a great gain to your brother.

I feel what pain must lie at the hearts of your Christmas party, however bright the fireside, and festive the meal, and, how in outward seeming all things look the same. I send by you my warmest good wishes to your Aunts and, [from] what you say, I think Aunt Anne will still be with you at Derby, when you receive this. She was so kind lately as to call on me on her way to Leamington.

Since you ask after my health, she would be better to answer you than I can be. I am indeed very well — but she must have seen I was very infirm

Yours affecty John H Card. Newman

[1] On 23 Dec. the Duke of Norfolk sent Newman a letter from Mrs Christie which explained that Mark Pattison was in his last illness. As to religious belief he was in a desolate state, and no one would be likely to have a good effect upon him except Newman himself.

[2] Newman sent this letter to Frances de Paravicini, wife of Baron Francis de Paravicini, Fellow of Balliol College. She was the daughter of W. W. Williams of Oxford, and a niece of Robert Williams, Newman's friend in Tractarian days. (*Apo.*, p. 116). She had become a devoted Catholic convert. (*Further Letters of Gerard Manley Hopkins*, edited by C. C. Abbott, second edition, London 1956, p. 242).

Frances de Paravicini knew Pattison slightly and on inquiring found that he would not recover, but was not immediately dying. His wife was away and he was being nursed by his niece. Frances de Paravicini wrote to Newman on 26 Dec. that he saw a very few friends, and only by appointment. To her inquiry, 'Does he receive letters, and can he read much or interest himself in things?' she received the answer, 'O *Yes*. And he is writing (dictating) some account of his early life, and much about the High Church movement in Oxford of some years ago, and his own connection with it. It (the writing all this) is a great interest for him, and he is very anxious over it.'

Frances de Paravicini then returned Newman's letter to Pattison, and on 27 Dec. he sent him a slightly altered copy of it.

Pattison's niece, Gertrude Tuckwell (1861–1951), niece of his wife, was acting as his housekeeper. See John Sparrow *Mark Pattison and the Idea of a University*, Cambridge 1967, pp. 48 and 60.

Bm. Dec 26. 1883

Dear Dr Whyte

I am sorry to have given you the trouble of a correspondence, and feel I have to ask your pardon.

As to your kind proposal to insert my letter in your second Edition, I will not dream of consenting to it.

It would be a poor return on my part to your courteous treatment of me in your book, to turn your catechism into a controversy. Nor will I do it. The two ideas are quite distinct. Nor would it be fair to myself, as if I felt sore *personally* when my faith was misconceived. What claim have I to introduce myself into your volume? My only possible claim would be your thinking that I had made *a case*. To consider that I had *not*, yet to insert my letter, would be granting more than you have a right to grant, in justice to yourself.

Nothing then can make me approve a course which, though generous in you, does you harm without doing me good.[1]

Your faithful Servant John H Card. Newman

TO CATHERINE BOWDEN, SISTER MARY ALBAN

St John's day [27 December] 1883

My dear Child

Many thanks for your remembrance. It is very pleasant to me to have such — and I have them from both Bow and Stone[2]

Still pray for me

Yours affectly J H Card. Newman

TO MARK PATTISON

Bm Dec 27. 1883

My very dear Pattison,

I grieve to hear that you are very unwell. How is it that I, who am so old am carried on in years beyond my juniors?

This makes me look back in my thoughts forty years, when you, with Dalgairns and so many others now gone, were entering into life.

For the sake of those dear old days, I cannot help writing to you. Is there any way in which I can serve you? At least I can give you my prayers, such as they are,

Yours affectionately John H Card. Newman

[1] Whyte replied on 28 Dec. 'I have inserted your kind correction in the second impression of my commentary within inverted commas, as the best way, as it seemed to me, of making emphatic use of your help, as well as, at the same time, keeping your honoured name out of all connection with such a publication.'
[2] Mother Margaret Hallahan's nuns had convents in both places.

FROM MARK PATTISON

Lincoln College, Oxford 28 Decemb./83

When your letter, my dear Master was brought to my bedside this morning, and I saw your well-known handwriting, my eyes filled so with tears that I could not at first see to read what you had said.

When I found in what affectionate terms you addressed me, I felt guilty, for I thought, would he do so, if he knew how far I have travelled on the path, which leads quite away from those ideas which I once — about 1845–46 — shared with him.

Or is your toleration so large, that though you knew me to be in grievous error, you could still embrace me as a son?

If I have not dared to approach you in any way of recent years, it has been only from the fear that you might be regarding me as coming to you under false colours. The veneration and affection which I felt for you at the time you left us, are in no way diminished and however remote my intellectual standpoint may now be from that which I may presume to be your own, I can still truly say that I have learnt more from you than from any one else with whom I have ever been in contact.

Let me subscribe myself for the last time

Your affectionate son & pupil Mark Pattison.

(Per J.S)[1]

TO MRS WILLIAM BORLASE

Bm Dec 31. 1883

Dear Mrs Borlase

I am told by Mr Borlase that I am indebted to you for sending me dear Mr Copeland's usual Christmas Turkey.[2] My dear friend has sent it to us for at least twenty years past, and it has been a record year by year, and a symbol, of that loyalty to friends, which was one of his characteristic traits.

I have had, through a kind Providence, many friends, but few can be put in comparison of him for faithfulness.

Wishing you all best blessings in the New Year

I am, Very truly Yours, John H Card. Newman

P S.   I have forgotten to say that my purpose in writing to you has been to thank you for Mr Copeland's present.

TO EMILY BOWLES

Bm. Dec 31. 1883

My dear Child

I have mislaid your address, so I write to you thro' Lady Simeon. If you live with Frederic [Bowles], give him my love, and best wishes, (and to you,) for the New Year.

I write to ask about St Philip's picture. How could so large a one? and on what did it fall?[3]

Yours affecty J. H. Card. Newman

[1] The letter was written by an amanuensis, presumably his niece Jeannie Stirke, daughter of his sister Mary.

[2] See letter of 18 Dec. to Copeland.

[3] Emily Bowles had mentioned to Newman an incident of St Philip's picture falling down in the church while A. W. Hutton was saying his first Mass. See letter of 5 Jan. 1884 to her.

TO IDA AND EDWARD MOZLEY

Dec 31. 1883.

Cardinal Newman sends to his dear Ida and Edward his love and his bless-ing[1]

TO MRS JOHN HUNGERFORD POLLEN

Bm Dec. 31. 1883

My dear Mrs Pollen

A happy new year to you, Mr. Pollen, and all yours.

I dare say Antony told you how pleased he was to have got ahead of John in the matter of Orders.[2] Thank you for the poem, which came all right. About Arabi I know nothing, and have no right to have an opinion. Perhaps I am prejudiced but I don't expect heroism from the Egyptians[3]

Very sincerely yours John H. Card. Newman

TO ALEXANDER WHYTE

Bm. Dec 31, 1883

My dear Dr Whyte

You are treating me with extreme kindness, and if any word of mine to you implies annoyance in me, I assure you it misrepresents me, and the nearest approach I have had to any feeling of pain, has been a great anxiety lest I should have quoted our profession of doctrine incompletely, and that I had left out any authoritative testimonies or popular beliefs which would give to our tenet a different aspect.

But indeed I sincerely think such a different aspect cannot be found. Not the most ignorant or stupid Catholic thinks that he eats physically the body of our Lord. What we all believe is that we partake the Body and Blood that hung upon the Cross, and that, in the words of the Anglican service 'that our sinful bodies may be made clean by his Body, and our souls washed through His most precious Blood,'[4] but as to the *how* He brings this to pass, it is a mystery.

To strengthen my feeling that I had acted quite fairly by you, I put my hands on a copy of our authoritative 'Penny Catechism' taught in our schools,

---

[1] These were two of John Rickards Mozley's children, aged thirteen and eight respec-tively.

[2] Anthony Pollen had received Minor Orders early in Dec., long before his Jesuit elder brother.

[3] Arabi Pasha was the nationalist leader in Egypt, now facing the revolt of the Mahdi in the Sudan. An Egyptian army sent against them was destroyed on 5 Nov. 1883, and in Jan. General Gordon was sent to Khartoum as Governor-General.

[4] From the Prayer of Humble Access.

and I now send it, if you will kindly accept it. You will find the passages bearing on the point at pp 42–44

Inverted commas are all that can be needed, and are a happy thought[1]

Most truly Yrs J. H. Card. Newman

TO HENRY IGNATIUS DUDLEY RYDER

[January 1884]

I have read your Paper with the greatest interest.[2] The passages you quote from a friend's letter are beautiful, though there is something of composition in them. On the main question of 'Apostasy', I am able to say nothing. I can only say to myself 'Judge not' 'Judge not before the time.'[3]

As to the condemned Proposition,[4] I don't know if the following will hold, but I should say

1. 'The reasons impelling' are subjective to the individual, and vary with each mind. Now the will determines the selection of reasons, the grouping, the relative disposition

2. And next I question whether the large, subtle and influential antecedent probabilities which vary so much with the individual are included directly in the motive.

J H N

TO CATHERINE ANNE BATHURST

New Year's Day 1884

My dear Child

A happy New Year to you and yours. I congratulate you on your literary success, but I cannot but be anxious about the issues of this tip top education of girls.[5] Of course, as you are used to say, that high education excludes a number of evils, which else abound, but we may find ourselves out of the frying pan into the fire.

St Philip has never, since the congregation began, shown us so great a mercy as he has lately — as strange, as sudden, as unexpected, as awful, as it was great, and in its nature and consequences as marvellous. When I am drawing near my end, it is like an assurance from him how securely I may leave the

---

[1] See note to letter of 26 Dec. to Whyte.
[2] This was a paper by Ryder on 'The moral and intellectual conditions of Apostasy'. It is no longer to be found.
[3] *Matthew*, 7: 1; I *Corinthians*, 4:5.
[4] Innocent XI condemned the proposition: 'Voluntas non potest efficere, ut assensus fidei in se ipso sit magis firmus, quam mereatur pondus rationum ad assensum impellentium'. *Denzinger-Schönmetzer*, 2119.
[5] This must refer to Catherine Bathurst's convent school at Harrow.

future of this House in his hands. In spite of all our errors and omissions, he will not forsake us.[1]

Yours affectionately John H Cardinal Newman

P.S.   Perhaps you had better *burn* this letter.

TO GEORGE T. EDWARDS

New Year's Day *1884*[2]

Dear Mr Edwards

Thank you for your kind wishes to me for the New Year which I gladly and gratefully return. Every day indeed is the beginning of a New Year, but it is well to have a fixed time, and it is natural too, for looking backwards and forwards.

I am still confined to my room by a cold worse than I have had for many years, which I mention as an excuse for sending so stupid a letter

Most truly Yours John H. Card. Newman

TO ROBERT CHARLES JENKINS

New Year's Day 1884.

Dear Canon Jenkins,

Accept my best wishes and congratulations which the beginning of a New Year suggests. I suppose it is not customary to think of the poor old fellow who has just departed, because he can neither do us good nor harm. This leads me to think of your verses, so flowing, musical and amusing. They were read to our Fathers yesterday at Recreation, and heard with much interest and pleasure, as they wished me to report to you.[3]

I say, 'were read' not 'I read', because alas, for a month past I have been confined to my room, or even my bed, by a worse cold than I have had for many years, but I think it is going now. I think I caught it from a damp four wheeler.

I fear your indisposition has been of a more serious kind.

Very sincerely yours, John H. Card. Newman.

TO MARK PATTISON

Jany 2. 1884

My dear Pattison

This requires no answer.

On consideration I find it a duty to answer your question to me about toleration.

[1] This is a reference to the loss of faith and departure of A. W. Hutton.
[2] The year has been added in another hand.
[3] This appears to have been a humorous poem, mostly in Latin, about a Ritualist clergyman. It is in the handwriting of Jenkins.

I am then obliged to say that what Catholics hold upon it, I hold with them[1]

That God, who knows the heart, may bless you now and ever   is the fervent prayer

of your most affectionate friend,

John H Card. Newman

Bm Jany 2. 1884

Dear Dr Whyte

Since I sent to you my letter, agreeing to your printing 'substance' etc in inverted commas, I have been teazed with the thought I have not been fair to you, as I will explain —

You say 'this is directed against the Popish doctrine'. I am right in saying that the 'Popish doctrine' is *not* what you have stated it to be, but I am *not* fair to yourself when I allow you to propose to say that 'the shorter catechism' directs its words against the doctrine, (*really* ours,) of 'the change of *substance*'. Is it not more likely that its writers knew little, or thought little, of the decrees of the Council of Trent and were aiming at the extreme notions of the *multitude* who were in many places superstitious and sadly in want of instruction?

This doubt has made me quite miserable, since you have been so very kind to me; and I so confide in that kindness, that I would rather put the matter entirely into your hands without me.[2]

Excuse this bad writing, but the power to hold a pen is going from me.

Very sincerely Yours John H Card. Newman

Bm Jany 4. 1884

My dear Pattison

I am now well enough, after a cold which has kept me to my room or my bed for a month, to ask you whether you are strong enough to see me, did I call on you?[3]

[1] This refers to Pattison's letter of 28 Dec. placed after that of 27 Dec. to him. Among the Pattison Papers at the Bodleian Library is a letter of 8 Jan. 1884 to Meta Bradley, in which Pattison wrote: 'He [Newman] took my letter in an excellent spirit repeated his offer to come to me should I get stronger, but guarded himself from the sort of suggestion my words had conveyed that his toleration as a Catholic was exceptional and individual to himself.'

[2] 'Dr. Whyte did not apparently feel that the point raised by the Cardinal's sensitive regard for his correspondent was a serious one, since the passage finally stood as had been arranged in the previous letters.' G. F. Barbour *The Life of Alexander Whyte D.D.*, eighth edition, London 1925, p. 247.

[3] Neville in his account of this episode wrote: 'The Cardinal was rather seriously ill in bed with bronchitis when this sad news [about Pattison] came, but, at once he determined to do what he felt would be best — to go himself to the sick man. The doctors gave their forebodings of what would be the result to himself if he went, but he would not be deterred. "Is the little life left me," he said, "to be weighed against the chance of good in a case such as this? Let the doctors say what they will, I shall go!"'

If you tell me *yes*, or at least do not say *no*, I am strongly moved to come to you next Monday, between 11.58 and 2.48.[1]

I hope this abrupt letter will not try you.

Yours affectionately J. H. Newman

TO HENRY MATTHEWS

[5 January 1884]

My dear Sir

I am honoured by Count d' Aglie's proposal to publish a translation in Italian of my Letter to the Duke of Norfolk and readily give my consent, tho' I wish I could belief [sic] my English turn of thought and style would suit Italian readers.[2]

I accept with thanks his proposal to send me a copy of the Translation's proof, before publication

And I should be obliged also to be told what are the passages which he proposes to omit. It seems to me to be desirable that there should be a footnote in loco stating the fact of an omission[3]

J H N

TO EMILY BOWLES

Bm Jany 5, 1884

My dear Child

Many thanks for your answer to my questions — but will you let me ask you two or three more.[4]

1. You say 'it was the *day* of Fr H's first Mass' — yes — but was it *in* his Mass?

2. *Where* was the Mass? the picture of St Philip is in St Philip's chapel.

3   You looked *round* at St Ph's picture. Which way, towards what, were you looking *before*?

---

[1] The draft shows that these were the times of arrival and departure of the trains at Oxford.

[2] Count D'Aglié of Turin had translated *A Letter to the Duke of Norfolk* into Italian and asked for permission to publish it. He proposed to omit some passages about the Irish bishops and Catholic emancipation, because they would require so much explanation, to be made intelligible to Italians. Henry Matthews wrote on 4 Jan: 'Count d'Aglie is one of the few Catholic Conservatives I have met among Italian laymen. He is also one of those who desire to see Catholics in Italy take more active part in public affairs, and endeavour to influence the government of their country. He knows English perfectly: for he was partly educated in England while his father was Sardinian envoy here, and his mother was an English woman.'

[3] The first Italian translation of *A Letter to the Duke of Norfolk* was that by Domenico Battaini, *Il Papa il Sillabo e l' Infallibilità Papale*, Turin 1909.

[4] This refers to the picture which fell during A. W. Hutton's first Mass in Oct. 1879.

Don't think me rude in asking these questions; but the occurrence is so remarkable, that I want to embrace all the facts[1]

Yours affectly J. H. Card. Newman

FROM MARK PATTISON

My dear Master,   Lincoln College, Oxford 4. Jan/84.

Is it possible that you at eighty three can be proposing to make the journey to Oxford and back only for the sake of visiting me?

Were you coming to this place on any other errand of your own, I could not but humbly petition you to let me look on you once more. But to come so far on purpose, that must not be. I could only see you for 3/4 hour and I should be so upset — more by the anticipation than by the visit, that I should not be able to collect my thoughts, to say one of the many things, or to ask one of the questions, which I would fain say, and ask.

I am a little stronger than I was 3 weeks ago, but only a little, and still in a very precarious and feeble state.

I do not think I could bear, what I should feel all the while was a final farewell.

You cannot tell what it costs me to be declining such an offer from you, an offer which thousands would esteem the highest honour that could be done them. Believe me, my dear Master, that I do not esteem it less, but it is too overwhelming and I shrink from it in terror. If I was looking forward to your coming on Monday, I should be in a state of nervous agitation from now till then.

I know if I live that I shall regret what I am now foregoing, but as I am at present, I dare not face it.

I am sure you will not misinterpret my motives and feelings in this letter, and will continue to believe that I am

Yours ever affectionately Mark Pattison[2]

TO MARK PATTISON

Jany 5. 1884

My dear Pattison

I thank you for your touching letter.

Of course I will be guided by your wish.

As time goes on, if you find that can be, which is too trying for you at present, say the word, and I will come (if I can speak of the future)

Yours affectionately John H. Card. Newman

[1] Emily Bowles replied on 6 Jan: 'Your Eminence and my dearest Father,
I see now for the first time how difficult it must have been for you to have understood the occurrence. St Philip's *Chapel* has nothing to do with it. I have made a rude sketch, which though very incorrect may serve to show the positions.
1. Fr Hutton was saying Mass — his first Mass — at the high Altar.   A.
2. The picture hung over the altar in the Sacred Heart transept where the Novena to St Philip is said.   B.
3. During the offertory I *think*, certainly when there was silence, I heard a noise towards B, and looked up. I was looking at my missal, following the Mass. I looked then to the left to B, (it was more behind me than I have drawn it) and saw the picture of St Philip fallen upon the Altar. I half got up, but seeing several men hastening to the place I did not leave my bench.'
See letter of 8 Jan. to Emily Bowles.
[2] Only the signature is in Pattison's hand.

Bm Jany 6. 1884

My dear Sir

I thank you for your learned work on Queen Mary. And I congratulate you on the singular success of the defence of the unhappy Lady whose cause is of such historical interest.[1]

With many thanks for your kind wishes in my behalf, I am, my dear Sir,

Your faithful Servant John H. Card. Newman

The Hon Colin Lindsay

TO ANNE MOZLEY

Jany 7. 1884

My dear Anne Mozley

Thank you for your thoughtful present. I have been for the last five weeks confined to my room or even to my bed, with a cold

I proposed to Pattison to call on him this very day, but he has refused to see me on the plea of his extreme weakness, and its being too much for him. I am intending to go tomorrow without leave; but what a work it is to implant faith! what human power can do it? I may only make him medically worse

Don't tell this — I am burning your slip.

I am better than I was

Yours affectly J H Card. Newman

TO JOHN THOMAS WALFORD, S.J.

Bm Jany 7. 1884

My dear Fr Walford

Thanks for your congratulations and your beautiful memorial.

As to your question, such fatigue my head and hand, especially just now, when for five weeks I have been confined to my room, sometimes to my bed, with a bad cold. And it is a question which cannot be answered in a few words.

I began and wrote a good deal in answer a fortnight ago, but it would not come to an end, and now on looking at it again I see I have not written it in such necessary luminous fulness to make it worth sending you.

So you must pardon me, and pray for me, for I am very feeble

Yrs affectly John H Card. Newman

[1] *Mary Queen of Scots and her Marriage with Bothwell*, London 1883, reprinted from the *Tablet*. Lindsay regarded her as a saint and martyr.

TO EMILY BOWLES

Jany 8. 1884

My dear Child

Thank you for your clear explanation[1]

The only question is Was it St *Philip's* picture which fell.

The only picture of St Philip is in his Chapel over his altar.

The only exception to this is during the Novena before his Feast, May 17 to 25. Then a picture of him which hangs up in the Sacristy is placed in the Transept where commonly a picture of the Agony is placed.

The question then is, was that Sacristy picture, by carelessness, suffered to remain in the Transept till *October*, the month when Fr A [Hutton] was ordained Priest, or was it the *Agony* which fell? This we are trying to find out

Yrs affly J H Card Newman

TO MARK PATTISON

Jany 8. 1884[2]

My dear Pattison

As you only said 'no' to my coming to see you on *Monday*, but implied I might come to you some other day, I will make a call tomorrow, Wednesday.

You need not see me, if it is too much for you — but my coming will not be *sudden* now, as it would have been then.[3]

Yrs affectly J. H. Card Newman

[1] See letter of 5 Jan. to Emily Bowles.

[2] On 7 Jan. Newman wrote a first draft of this letter, on which he wrote [sent] 'in substance': 'My dear Pattison

As you only said No to my calling on you *to-day*, but did not forbid my coming any day whatever, and since the suddenness of my appearance was the danger to you, and the danger does not exist now, I will ask to see you *tomorrow* at about *noon*.

If you can't see me, well and good — no matter — I will not press.

Yours affly   J.H. Card. Newman'

[3] Pattison wrote at once to Newman after his visit, a letter which Neville acknowledged on 10 Jan., saying that Newman had borne the journey well. He also said that he had accompanied Newman, and that 'Yesterday I just saw you at your library door,' as he was saying goodbye to his visitor. Neville's account says that Newman and Pattison 'passed some hours together alone', and that he 'allowed Cardinal Newman before leaving to send for and to introduce to him a priest of the place, expressly for the purpose of thus forwarding a priest's services to him at call.' See also *Ward* II, p. 483.

On 28 Jan. Pattison wrote his account to Meta Bradley, in the last volume of his letters to her, among the Pattison Papers at the Bodleian Library: 'Surely I told you all the particulars of Newman's visit, if I did not it was a strange omission, as it was the most remarkable event of this winter's illness, and has been the object of general wonder and curiosity here. After he had accepted, or acquiesced in my put off for the reasons I gave, on the Wednesday morning I got a note saying he would be here at 12. o'clock. I need not say how flurried I was by this, for other reasons, but also now my invalid routine of hours was upset. He came at 12 and left at 2.15 to return to Birmingham and out of that short time had to be taken lunch. The interview was most affecting. I was dreadfully agitated, distressed even. On the one hand I felt what a proof of affection he was giving, to one who had travelled so far, from what he regarded as important — On the other, I felt that it was not all personal regard which had brought him, but the hope, however slight, that I might still be got over in my last moments. And I could not tell in what proportion these two motives might have influenced N. to undertake a fatiguing journey. The conversation at first turned on old times and recollections. It gradually slid into religious discourse, when I found as I expected, that he had not realized the enormous distance at which I had left behind the stand-point of 1845. More than this he did not seem to appre-

Jany 9. 1884

My dear Duke

Your munificent present of wine has come, and I thank you for it
Also your gift of pheasants.

I went to Oxford today and saw Mr Pattison who is much better and did
not contemplate as I was told, being worse. I had been in correspondence with
him some days[1]

Your affecte Servant John H Card. Newman

His Grace The Duke of Norfolk E M

TO ROBERT J. BLAKE

Jany 10. 1884

Dear Mr Blake

I shall be very glad to see you, as you propose[2]

Very truly Yours John H Card. Newman

hend more than any ordinary Catholic would have done, that there is such a space to travel, or
that one can look back upon the ideas of those days as the ideas of childish ignorance. Of
course I could not set about trying to put things in this light to a man of 84, let alone a
Cardinal. On the other hand I did not feel it right to leave him under the illusion in which he
evidently was that I was still hesitating about my road and doubting as we were in 1845 as to
where the true church was to be found. In this dilemma having to be true and on the other
hand having to avoid the futile attempt to explain to him, what it was evident could not
be explained, I was in great embarrassment as to how to express myself. N. did not of course
attempt the vulgar arts of conversion, nor was there anything like clerical cant, or affectation
of unction like a parson's talk by a deathbed. He dwelt upon his own personal experiences
since he had been reconciled to the Church, the secret comfort and support which had been
given him in the way of supernatural grace under many great trials; that he had never been
deserted by such help for a moment; that his soul had found sweet peace and rest in the bosom
of the Church. Then we got for a moment, but only for a moment, on more controversial
matter. Here he had nothing to say, but the old argument of the Apologia which I need not
repeat to you. I said in answer three hypotheses each less probable than the one before it.
After I had said this I regretted it, but was relieved to find that he had not taken the scope of
the remark, so it passed harmless. We very soon changed the conversation; he allowing me to
ask him several questions about Oriel before I became a member of it. This last conversation
I should have liked to have prolonged as it interested me much more than the other, but I felt
that that was not what he had come for and was therefore shy of pursuing it

There I have given you an outline of what took place; considering the busy life you are
now leading it is probably more than you will care for. But it is the fullest account I have yet
written and as you are so careful to keep my letters I consider that I have placed it upon record
in as permanent a way as I could.' Pattison died on 30 July, and on 20 Sept. 1884 his widow
wrote from Lincoln College:

'Mrs Mark Pattison sends to Cardinal Newman by the same post as this letter a copy of the
Vie de Monseigneur Sibour which she has found among the Rector's books and begs that H.E.
[His Eminence] will permit her to offer it to his acceptance in memory of him to whom it so
recently belonged.

She also encloses several letters of Cardinal Newman's which were preserved with the
Rector's other correspondence and which she thinks the Cardinal may like to have returned to
him.

The Rector spoke to Mrs Pattison in terms of strong feeling of Cardinal Newman's visit to
him last January: he recapitulated every little incident of the meeting and turn of the conversation with a keen sense of the real meaning of the effort and deep gratitude for the affection
which had prompted it.'

[1] See first note to letter of 25 Dec. to Pattison.
[2] On 13 Jan.

TO WILFRID OATES

Jany 12. 1884

Dear Mr Oates

I thank you for your letter.[1] I do not know enough of the business questions connected with the sale of my volumes to do more at present than to state my own difficulties about them. I will only say what I am told by a friend, that, on my publishing my Apologia in 1864, the American Society you mention brought out an American Edition by which, to use the words which the American Priest used to my friend, it gained 'a pot of gold.'

My present state is this — I have spent a great sum lately in making a uniform edition of the 36 volumes. One year the printers bills ran higher than £1000 — and two successive years the balance of account was against me. Before then I have any thing further to say, the above must be taken into consideration. And I will add that, to judge of the instance of my book which has sold best, if I print an edition of 1000 copies, two thirds of them must be sold before the balance turns in my favour.

If an American publisher took an edition any arrangement I made should involve the condition that his edition did not come to Great Britain.

I begin then my answer to you by saying that I cannot afford to be generous to foreign publishers to my own loss[2]

J H N

FROM RICHARD HOLT HUTTON

Englefield Green, Staines. 13 January 1884

My dear Lord Cardinal

I cannot resist the pleasure of telling you how warmly the working men received my lecture on you yesterday, and as the whole charm consisted in my quotations of your own words, of which I gave a long string threaded together by a very slender thread of narrative and criticism, you would have seen at once how heartily you are admired and loved and reverenced even among the Protestants of the working class.[3] When I referred to the lines by which, among Protestants, you are best known, ('Lead kindly Light') there was a perfect thunder of applause, if so large a word be applicable at all to a meeting in which probably the total number was not 300, as the room would hardly hold more though it was full to overflowing.[4]

Knowing how sincerely you love your own countrymen, — especially I think those

[1] Oates wrote on 11 Jan. that the Catholic Publication Society of America said the sale of Newman's works there would be much improved if they were cheaper, and he suggested that it should be given a discount of 50 per cent off the English price.
[2] Oates sent to the Catholic Publication Society the substance of Newman's letter. See letter of 8 Feb. to Lawrence Kehoe.
[3] On 12 Jan. Hutton gave a lecture, 'Cardinal Newman', to the students at the London Men's College, which was published in the Contemporary Review (May 1884), pp. 642–65, in a revised form. See letter of 6 May to Hutton.
[4] In his lecture Hutton gave an account of how Newman's ship was becalmed on his return from the Mediterranean, in the straits between Corsica and Sardinia, 'there it was that he wrote the famous lines, best known of all his poems: — "Lead, kindly light, amid the encircling gloom, lead thou me on."' Op. cit., p. 649.

of the working class, — I think it would have been a great gratification to you if you could have been present without being seen last night. To me it was really a vivid delight to see how they entered into the beauty of every passage I read.

Believe me my dear Lord Cardinal

Ever most truly your's Richard H Hutton

His Eminence Cardinal Newman

TO RICHARD HOLT HUTTON

Bm Jany 14. 1884

My dear Mr Hutton

I feel your great kindness in your late pains to introduce what I have written to a class of men to whom I am not known. The prejudice against Catholics is so great in England that to get thoughtful men to think well of an individual Catholic is to do a service to the Catholic Religion. But, apart from this, as I have felt pain at the false reports, which have been spread about concerning me, so I cannot but be relieved, when I am placed in a favourable light, and feel grateful to those who have so placed me.

You will not refuse the only return I can make you, a Cardinal's blessing.

Yours affectionately John H Card. Newman[1]

TO ALFRED PLUMMER

Bm Jany 15. 1884

My dear Dr Plummer

Thank you for your new Volume, which I doubt not I shall find as useful as your former one.[2]

Were not my fingers so stiff, I should like to ask you a question, but to do justice to it, I should have to use more words than my brain and hand can give to it.

You speak of the argument, that the style of the Apocalypse shows that it was written before the Gospel;[3] — this leads me to ask you whether the style of the gospel itself is not an evidence (putting aside the question of the Apocalypse) of an imperfect command of Greek. I think so, and I would from this I would go on to *account* for the difference of our Lord's discourses as found in St John and in the three former Evangelists.

I am not a Hebrew scholar, but Hebrew seems to me a language which is not flexible enough to admit of clauses and sentences enabling it to be argumentative. I will give one instance (tho a bad one) of what I mean. Uneducated people, as you see in Dickens's novels, cannot use the relative rightly to expand their sentences. Instead of saying 'There are many situations in life, in which it is very difficult to know how to act rightly', they say '. . . many

---

[1] For Hutton's reply see letter of 6 May to him.
[2] Plummer had sent his *The Gospel of St John*, see letter of 24 Feb. 1881 to him. He now sent *The Epistles of St John*, Cambridge 1884, in the same series of 'The Cambridge Greek Testament for Schools and Colleges.'
[3] 'The writer of the Apocalypse has not yet learned to write Greek.' *The Epistles of St. John*, p. xxxvi.

situations . . which . . . . to act rightly in them.' This is like the Vulgate rendering of the 'Cœli enarrant', 'sermones, *quorum* (i.e. qui would be the *exact* illustration) non audiuntur voces *eorum*'.[1]

I do not know an instance like this in St John, but is there not the evidence of his writing with his writing powers in a parallel way tied? does he not write Greek, as I should write or speak Italian? Short sentences, the absence of pronouns, repetition in consequence of substantives, (vid too St John's use of of ἵνα) tautology, these would be my characteristics, if I attempted to report in a journal a sermon or speech. All the flow of the speaker's eloquence would be lost.

This hypothesis doubtless has been considered and has grave objections, but it has interested me sufficiently to lead me to ask where it is to be found[2]

Very sincerely Yours John H Card. Newman

TO THE HON. MRS MAXWELL-SCOTT

18 January 1884

My dear Mamo

I grieve deeply at the news of your Aunt's illness, and will say Mass for her without loss of time.[3] And also I am very sorry you should be unwell.

For myself I have had a bad cold, but am well, tho' feeble

Yours affectly John H Card. Newman

TO LORD BLACHFORD

Jany 19. 1884

My dear Blachford

Thank you for your affectionate inquiries. The papers have much exaggerated about me.[4] What I confess to, is a loss of strength — of course such a loss opens the door to worse ailments — the medical advisers feared my cold settling on my lungs, and my own chronic fear is lest I should break a limb — for I tumble about a great deal.

I am very sorry to find you are still on your sofa — it must be very wearisome. What could I say about Palermo? that fifty years ago there was scarcely one hotel there?[5] I suppose, as you must know as well as I can, it is quite unique in its architectural remains, and the bay is to my taste the most beautiful sight I ever saw, except Taormini.

---

[1] *Psalms*, 18 (19):3.

[2] Plummer replied on 18 Jan. that he knew of no one who suggested that St John's imperfect command of Greek explained the unique character of our Lord's discourses in his Gospel. He thought the difference between them and those in the Synoptists 'is less one of language than of tone.'

[3] This was Lady Henry Kerr, who died on 18 Jan.

[4] Lord Blachford wrote to William Neville on 17 Jan., having seen in the papers reports that Newman was unwell.

[5] Lord Blachford wrote that he was planning to go to Palermo and that Newman had lately protested against it.

I am much pleased at the sympathy shown towards the violin which will vibrate so touchingly at the mention of friends[1]

This leads me to say something else. I have never forgotten that you expressed a special love for those views of S. Marco at Venice which you gave me.[2] Hence I have been led, while disposing of my surrenderings, to reflect that such a rough and ready place as this is no domicile for a work of art — and I have thought of asking you whether you will receive them back, or whether there is any one to whom you would like them given. I took them to London at the beginning of December for binding and why they are not yet returned I cannot tell. But I have written to hasten them, and there they shall wait your instructions, if you will give them.

It is quite true that writing fatigues both my brain and my fingers — but I have more pleasure when it is a friend I write to than pain from the fatigue. What I feel is, what is the staple of my writing, correspondence, important or unimportant (!) with strangers, and the more because I leave out words and am forgetting how to spell, which does not trouble me when I write to friends

Yours affectly J H Card. Newman

TO THE HON. MRS MAXWELL-SCOTT

Bm 20 January 1884

My dear Mamo

I have been saying Mass this morning for your dear Aunt. So I did yesterday, and Fr William Neville too. It was very kind in her to have such thoughts of me, and, though far more than I could claim, they are very welcome to me, as making me anticipate that now, when she is near God, I shall be one of those whom she will remember for good. May my last end be like hers.

She has not seen *the book*, as published, though so near seeing it![3]

I rejoice to hear you are better

Yours affectly J. H Card. Newman

TO HENRY BEDFORD

January 23rd. 1884.

My dear Mr. Bedford,

May I give you some trouble in a matter which somewhat presses.

A good Irish youth, who was one of our servants, has been sent home by

---

[1] In his letter to Neville, Lord Blachford said that Newman 'wrote me a letter some weeks ago — partly about a violin which he had given to one of the Dean of St Paul's daughters. Tell him, if he cares to hear, that I sent his letter to Mary Church, in order to inform her of her duties in keeping up a traditional history of it. It was received with great enthusiasm and I doubt not will form part of the title deeds of the instrument when it passes to other hands.' Cf. letter of 28 March 1883 to Dean Church.

[2] See letter of 16 July 1864 to Frederic Rogers.

[3] Lady Henry Kerr failed to see *Memoirs of James Robert Hope-Scott*, published on 24 Jan.

the doctors here (at his own desire) for immediate care in a Dublin Hospital. He is about 18 miles from Dublin.

How can I get him in? It is an internal complaint which wants immediate attention. Will subscription do?[1]

Very truly yours, John H. Card. Newman.

P.S. I wrote to Stewart some days ago on this matter, and as he has not written, I conclude he is on his holiday.

The boy's address is: —

James Daly, Maudlands,
Naas.

TO WILFRID MEYNELL

Jany 23. 1884

Dear Sir

I have no reason to think that Mr Hutton used the words of me attributed to him in the Guardian, and I have now for 20 years held him, as a journalist, to be a good friend of mine[2]

J H N

TO LORD CHARLES THYNNE

Jan 23. 1884

My dear Lord Charles

It was a great pleasure to me to hear from you, and to be told of Charlie and his belongings.[3] Thank you, I am fairly well — quite well in health, as far as I know, though infirm

One of the things I cannot do easily is to write. I wish I could write like you; but not only do I form letters with difficulty, but I leave out words and

---

[1] W. P. Neville made a note:
'Mr Bedford got the boy taken into the Mater Misericordiæ Hospital, Dublin where he received great kindness and attention from the Sisters. After being there for six weeks, the doctors not being able to hold out any hope of permanent good, he went home and there died about a fortnight later. The Cardinal sent a cheque for £10 to the Revd Mother of the Hospital in return for her great kindness to the youth.' See letter of 1 April to Bedford.
[2] In an article 'A Last Midunderstanding', the *Weekly Register* (19 Jan. 1884), p. 82, complained that R. H. Hutton, in his lecture to the students at the Working Men's College in London on 12 Jan. had said of Newman, 'Since the Cardinal had been a member of the Roman Church, he had used his influence against the late Pope. All his efforts had, however, been directed to support the present Pope.' See the *Guardian* (16 Jan.), p. 79. The sentence is not to be found in the published version of Hutton's lecture in the *Contemporary Review* (May 1884). The *Weekly Register* thought this 'may lead unwary persons to suppose that Cardinal Newman was ever in opposition to Pius IX. Against this supposition it is unnecessary to warn readers who are acquainted with Cardinal Newman's life . . .'
Meynell, who was the editor of the *Weekly Register*, wrote on 22 Jan. that he proposed to reprint passages from Newman's 'The Pope and the Revolution', *O.S.*, by way of disproving Hutton's statement. This was done in 'Cardinal Newman and Pius IX', the *Weekly Register* (26 Jan.), p. 117.
[3] This was Lord Charles Thynne's younger son, who had been at the Oratory School, was married in 1880, and so far had one child.

have forgotten how to spell. This must be my excuse, if I make any mistakes in transcribing the lines which your friend so kindly asks of me.

Most truly Yours John H. Card. Newman

TO MRS EDWARD BELLASIS

Jany 24. 1884

My dear Mrs Bellasis

I send you a few lines to assure you that I have not forgotten this day especially at Mass.[1]

I hope you excused my not answering your letter about William, but I was not well. Also I owe him thanks for *his* letter. I was very glad and thankful about him, and trust he is regaining his strength. It has been a severe time of trial for you.

With my kindest remembrances and prayers for all blessings upon you I am,

Dear Mrs Bellasis Affectly Yours

John H Card. Newman

Mr Hope Scott's Life is published this day. Murray is the publisher

TO THE HON. MRS MAXWELL-SCOTT

Jany 24. 1884

My dear Mamo

Your kind remembrance has come to me from Murray today,[2] Serjeant Bellasis's anniversary.

It has been a very difficult task to do, and Mr Ornsby has taken great pains with it. He has done good part of it, or great part, twice, and has improved it considerably. But it requires, and claims, to be done half a dozen times over, in order to be worthy of its subject — and few literary men could do this.

It must do a great work in the souls of those who read it, but, like his Divine Pattern, he will not 'strive or cry,' nor lift up 'his voice in the streets' but it will be a secret preaching 'without observation.'[3]

Affectly Yours John H Card Newman

TO ROBERT ORNSBY

Jany 24. 84

My dear Ornsby

Your work has come to me today. I congratulate you on having so well executed so anxious a labour. It may not circulate widely, and may be sub-

[1] Serjeant Bellasis died on 24 Jan. 1873. What follows refers to his son.
[2] *Memoirs of James Robert Hope-Scott.*
[3] *Isaich,* 42:2; *Matthew,* 12:19; *Lukè,* 17:20.

jected to irreligious criticism — but it must do extensive good in a bad time still

> Yrs affectly J. H. Card. Newman

TO LOUISA ELIZABETH DEANE

> Bm January 26. 1884.

My dear Louisa,

If I had been quite well, I should not have let Christmas pass without sending a kind word to you and yours. Now, though January is all but over, accept from me an affectionate wish for the New Year.

I have no news to tell, and nothing to say besides expressing this, and signing myself

> Ever Yours affy John H. Card. Newman

TO LADY HERBERT OF LEA

> Jany 26 1884

My dear Lady Herbert,

I have had Lord Pembroke very much on my mind lately, and now I am grieved to find that he has had an accident and is otherwise unwell. The Papers I know, are not to be trusted in such matters, yet I think it well to assure you that I am not forgetful of him, and of your anxieties. This requires no answer.[1]

God bless you and him

> Your faithful Servant John H Card. Newman

TO JAMES STEWART

> Jan 26/1884.

My dear Stewart

Thank [you] for your letter. I directed to you as Professor Stewart, Catholic University College, St Stephen's Green, Dublin. Was 'Catholic' a mistake?[2]

> Yrs affly J. H. Card Newman.

TO ROBERT WHITTY, S.J.

> The Ory Jany 26. 84

My dear Fr Whitty

Thank you for your affectionate and welcome letter, and for your Mass. I hope to show my gratitude by at least remembering you in turn at sacred times.

[1] The Earl of Pembroke was ill with pleurisy. Cf. letters of 19 and 31 Aug. 1879 to Lady Herbert.
[2] Cf. letter of 23 Jan. to Henry Bedford.

It is difficult for others to know one's trials, and their kindness often mistakes where the sharpness of them really lies. We certainly have some great anxieties, but they are not easy to guess; and, as to the one to which you seem to refer, what to the many friends would seem the trial is to me the greatest relief and compensation of it. But God who knows all secrets answers their kind prayers for us by a true interpretation of them.[1]

I am far older than you and have more reason to think it wonderful that I am still alive; and the succession and continual loss of dear friends, which I now suffer, makes me feel that wonder will soon come to an end.

Yours ever affectionately John H Card. Newman

TO MRS F. J. WATT

Private   January 27, 1884
My dear Child,

It is a most cruel disappointment, but what can be done does not at once appear.[1]

First, you must be sure of the fact — You can't go by the Papers. When once the will is proved, I believe any one may claim to see it, but not till then, and the legal forms take time.

Then I doubt whether a bequest would stand in law, if made to the Holy Father. Probably it would be made to English Trustees, and the Pope would not have the direct possession of it. The purposes for which it is left might be determined by secret instructions, which could not be disregarded (in conscience) at the Pope's will and pleasure.

The property might be left to the Holy See, not to the Pope himself; and, even had he the power abstractedly of changing the purposes, these might be so important, urgent, and imperative that he could not alter them without precedents or perplexities.

And further, I suspect every penny that the Holy Father receives is *necessary* to him. For instance, I should not wish it repeated but I heard on good authority that he had to look about him to find means of discharging his monthly expenses at the Vatican — The need of Peter's pence is no matter of words. *Your* need is *one*, his is a hundred fold.

It is impossible then for you to apply to the Holy Father, till you know what is the state of things, and I believe that it is not very unlike what I have been imagining.

---

[1] Whitty in his letter of 25 Jan. wrote, 'I am glad to hear that you keep well in the midst of trials which it has pleased God to permit.' cf. letter of 1 Jan. to Catherine Anne Bathurst.

[1] Mrs Stapleton-Bretherton died on 22 Dec. 1883. She was Mary, the only daughter and heiress of Bartholomew Bretherton, of Rainhill, Lancs. She had been twice married, in 1829 to William Gerard, brother of Lord Gerard, and in 1848 to Miles Stapleton, brother of Lord Beaumont, but left no heir. She had been made a Marchesa by the Pope, and a month after her death there were rumours in the papers that she had left an enormous sum to the Holy See. Newman consoled Mrs Watt, née Eleanor Bretherton, who hoped to benefit under the will.

301

Another very important question is, what was the relationship between Mrs B and you — for the nearer it was, the greater the claim. The *estates*, they say, are left, not to the Holy See, but to some relative.[1]

If anything else strikes me, I will write again

Yours affectly John H. Card. Newman

TO JAMES ST LAWRENCE WHEBLE

Jany 29. 1884

My dear James

I write a line to assure you and your Mother and all of you of my grief and sympathy on this sudden and dreadful blow. I have said Mass for your dear Father on the two days that have passed since I heard of his illness, and I was bound to do so, for he has been persistently a kind and faithful friend to us.[2]

I will not cease to pray for him and for you all

Affectly Yours John H Card. Newman

TO LORD EMLY

Jany 29. 1884

My dear Emly

Our engagements on Saturday and Monday are most unlucky. The Purification is our foundation day, the yearly audit, and this year the triennial election of officials, and a very serious overha[u]ling of the School accounts.[3] Our work will certainly last over Monday, but Sunday will be a free day. Don't let me lose you. Of course too we shall be free at dinner on Saturday, tho' I shall be engaged after dinner.

I have had a sad letter from Aubrey de Vere with his brother's anticipations about Ireland. But for myself I look with quite as much trouble to the consequences to England which Ireland will create. How can we hold Ireland by force, and what other way is there of holding it? I hope you will come here to show me the prospect of things is better than I think

Yours affectly John H Card. Newman

[1] When the will of Mrs Stapleton-Bretherton was published it was stated that she had given a large sum to the Holy See in her lifetime. Her property was held by trustees, and there were various legacies, but none to Eleanor Watt. See letters of 8 July to her and 12 Sept. 1884 to Miss Giberne, also the *Weekly Register* (23 Feb. 1884), p. 248.

On 18 Feb. her mother, Mary Bretherton said in a letter to Newman:

'Eleanor wrote to me saying how kind you had been about the money we thought had been left to the Holy Father. Alas! that it should have been a mistake. The will has been a dreadful disappointment to me I had felt so sure my children would have been provided for and that having promised my dear husband it was so, that Mrs Stapleton was too just a woman to change. If only my poor girls had been remembered I should have been reconciled.'

[2] Wheble's father, James Joseph Wheble of Bulmershe Court, Reading, was seized with apoplexy on 26 Jan. and died two days later.

[3] Saturday 2 Feb. was the feast of the Purification.

TO AUBREY DE VERE

Febr 1. 1884

My dear Aubrey de Vere

Thank you for your brother's 'Letter' and Poem. I gave the last, as you wished, to Fr Ryder

Of course it distressed me that he thought so ill of the prospects of Ireland, having so plain a right to have an opinion on the matter. This such a one as myself cannot have, right or opinion — but what afflicts me is the hopelessness of a modus vivendi between the two countries, and therefore the alternative before us of the break up of our civil status, or a civil war. If the demagogues are able to keep up the cry of national independence and nothing short of it, what else remains?[1]

I am expecting Emly here tomorrow, and I hope he will make our prospects brighter for me.

Yours affectionately, John H. Card. Newman

TO EDWARD BELLASIS, JUNIOR

Private   Birmingham February 4. 1884.

My dear Edward,

Thank you for the letters. The chief thwarters I had at Rome were Ward and Vaughan — and Manning did his part. I tell you this in confidence. I never intended this to be known, and at least of all *now*, when my Cardinalate, so wonderfully conferred on me washes me quite clean. I have carefully kept all the documents, *meaning never to use them* or *letting them* be used except in a case of necessity.

To use them would be a great scandal which I never would bring about, except it was a duty. That is, I cannot be quite sure that, after I am gone, false statements may not be confidently put forward against me (e.g. as maintained at Rome in 1867 that I had set up the Oratory School to feed Oxford, a simple falsehood)[2] and in that case from my papers a brief answer might be given, reaching no further than the occasion required.

Hence I have thought and think that no account of my *Catholic* life can ever be given, for it would involve the saying things which would be disadvantageous to the reputation of men who for their writings (and or) their works are in merited esteem.[3]

---

[1] Sir Stephen de Vere, who was renowned for his kindness to his tenants, was a liberal, and though opposed to home rule, approved of Gladstone's Land Act.
[2] See letter of 21 March 1867 to Cardinal Barnabò and Memorandum on the Oratory School of 30 March 1867. This particular accusation was still being made a century later.
[3] See letter of 31 March 1884 to Edward Bellasis, and see also Memorandum as to a biography at 24 July 1876.

Bm Febr. 4. 1884

My dear Fr Delany

I feel the great kindness of the message which you and the other members of the Catholic University College send me, and you are right in thinking that the Great Feast of the Purification has special claims on my devotion.[1] For 60 years and more I have kept it, since it was founder's day in the 14th century, when Oriel College was established in Oxford in Catholic times, and also the foundation day of the Oratory in 1848 under the brief of Pope Pius. It has thus been in a certain sense twice my birthday, my sponsor I may say, being twice over our Lady.

My literal birthday is February 21 — and I accept with many thanks your letter as an anticipation of it

I am, (wishing you and your College all blessing from above)

Most truly Yours John H. Card. Newman

The Very Rev. Fr Delany

Birmingham Febr 6. 1884

My Lord Duke

I have this morning received a copy of your Grace's new volume, with your autograph on the first page, and I offer to your Grace without delay my best thanks for so welcome a gift.

It treats of a great subject, and I anticipate much instruction from the perusal.[2]

I am flattered by the notice I find of myself at p 512[3]

Your Grace's humble Servant John H. Card. Newman

His Grace The Duke of Argyll M M.

[1] In 1882, after the establishment of the Royal University of Ireland, the Catholic University was divided up, and the chief part of it became University College. In Nov. 1883 the management of University College was entrusted to the Jesuits, and Delany became its President. He wrote to Newman on 29 Nov., 'It is not many days since it pleased God to place on me in obedience the heavy burden of taking charge of this College, the one bright spot in whose history owes its brightness to your Eminence's name.'
[2] The Unity of Nature, London 1884, dealt with the reign of law in nature, inorganic, organic, and human, leading on to conscience and religion.
[3] After speaking of the inadequacy of the abstract definitions which theology gave of God, the Duke said: 'A great master of the English tongue has given another definition in which, among other things, it is affirmed that the attributes of God are "incommunicable." Yet, at least, all the good attributes of all creatures must be conceived as communicated to them by their Creator, in whom all fulness dwells.' A note gave the reference 'J.H. Newman, "Idea of a University," p. 60 [62].'

Birmingham, February 6. 1884

My dear Mr MacColl,

I recollect nothing of the occurence you relate, and cannot fancy my having a view of Mr Gladstone so precise and confident as that you report.[1] I much doubt whether I ever formulated in my mind a view of him, though I always should have spoken of him with friendly feeling and interest, and of course admiration of his gifts moral and intellectual.

I am too near dear Hope Scott to write of him, also, I am not up to any serious exercise of mind now.[2]

My brain works slow, and gets soon tired.

Yours very truly, John H. Card. Newman.

TO WILLIAM J. WALSH

[6 February 1884][3]

answered that the first question is too grave for me to speak of without knowing more that has been said on it. As to the second, I did not see clearly

[1] In a letter of 5 Feb. MacColl, who was writing an article on Gladstone for the *Encyclopaedia Americana*, had received from a friend what purported to be an estimate of Gladstone given by Newman at a conversazione in Dublin in 1854, and taken down at the time by one who was present: 'Mr Gladstone's genius is of a most distinct and special type; ever ready to adopt new impressions, provided they approve themselves to his understanding and conscience, however contrary they may be to his former opinions; but also most tenacious of his old opinions, and clinging to them desperately till he has convinced himself of their unsoundness. He unites in an unusual degree reverence for the past, and candid appreciation of new ideas, and may thus be regarded as a bigoted Conservative by some and an advanced Liberal by others . . .'

[2] MacColl wrote: 'I have read with intense interest the Life of Mr Hope Scott. I learnt from Mr Gladstone long ago, what a remarkable man Mr Hope Scott was. Mr Gladstone thinks him far superior to himself intellectually, though the career of a parliamentary barrister gave no scope for the exhibition of his gifts . . .

I remember Mr Gladstone saying to me three years ago, in the course of a walk at Hawarden: — "Hope Scott could always twist me round his finger. He was the only man who ever could."'

MacColl suggested that Newman should review *Memoirs of James Robert Hope-Scott* for the *Fortnightly Review*.

[3] On 5 Feb. Walsh, who was President of St Patrick's College, Maynooth, wrote that Newman's 'On the Inspiration of Scripture', the *Nineteenth Century* (Feb. 1884), pp. 185–97, 'will give rise to some controversy', and sent three questions that had arisen out of discussion at Maynooth. Against Newman's attempt to limit the scope of Inspiration, Walsh first asked, 'But is it at variance with Catholic doctrine to say that possibly an inspired writer may have erred in his opinion, just as the writers of many passages in the Old Testament undoubtedly held erroneous views as to many matters of fact [also in the New, Walsh instanced 'the nearness of the Day of Judgment'] . . . whereas what they have *written* may be regarded as true, if understood in a certain not unnatural sense?'

Walsh's second question again concerned Newman's wish to limit what had been defined by Councils as to Inspiration and asked, 'is it in any way implied that the *inspiration* is, or may be, confined to matters regarding faith or morals? Or may it not be that, while the *Inspiration of everything in Scripture* is defined, our liberty of *interpretation* is curtailed only as to matters regarding faith and morals?'

The third question was, 'As to the expression "Deus *Auctor*" etc is not its meaning (outside the *classical* sense) defined by the invariable modus loquendi of the Fathers etc — "Epistola Dei ad creaturas"; "S. Spiritu conscripta" etc. etc. etc.'

In §10 of his article, *S.E.*, pp. 8–9, Newman explained that 'Auctor' properly meant 'originator', 'primary cause.'

enough see its bearings; as to the third I inclosed my printed paper about the Auctor Testamentorum.[1]

J H N

TO MRS F. J. WATT

Birmingham Febr 7/84

My dear Child

You have a brave heart, and God will reward you. You have great trials and anxieties, but you will in time to come look back on them, and thank Him for them. Recollect *every one* has his trials, if God loves him.[2]

I have not time for more.

yours affectly J. H. Card. Newman

TO WILLIAM CLIFFORD, BISHOP OF CLIFTON

Bm Febr 8. 84

My dear Lord

It is an extreme pleasure to me to receive your letter of this morning.[3] I knew that, in consequence of your kind revision, I had nothing to fear as to the substantial truth of what I had written — but the further and important questions whether I had said what was called for, what was expedient, what was enough and no more, could not be decided till after publication — and yours is one of the letters which in the course of the last few days have been a great encouragement to me

Your faithful & affectte Servt John H Card. Newman

The Hon & Rt Rev the Bp of Clifton

[1] This was the Note 'On the Phrase "Auctor utriusque Testamenti" in the Councils', which was not in the article in the *Nineteenth Century*, but was included in later printings of the article as a pamphlet, and in *S.E.*, pp. 33–6. Newman held that the phrase in the Councils meant 'Author of the two Dispensations or Covenants.' See J. D. Holmes and R. Murray's edition of *On the Inspiration of Scripture*, pp. 35–6.

[2] See letter of 27 Jan.

[3] In thanking on 7 Feb. for a copy of Newman's article in the *Nineteenth Century* Bishop Clifford said it would 'be highly appreciated by all catholics, but will in a special manner be an immense boon to that daily increasing number of catholics who love and appreciate scientific research, and who are on the other hand puzzled by the difficulties constantly brought forward from Scripture, and the utter disregard, and even contempt for scientific discoveries which is so frequently shown by men who undertake the defence of religion and the inspired word of God.

It is in the peace which you have thus brought to many minds that your Eminence will find the chief reward of your labour.'

On 19 Feb. John Baptist Hogan wrote from Saint Sulpice, Paris, that the article on Inspiration 'will give relief to hundreds — aye thousands of troubled minds. Thoughts accumulated for years will flow freely and gladly into the course you have opened for them. Of course they will not do so without opposition. . . . Cardinal Franzelin will be made to do service in support of the narrow, traditional conception. But what is written will remain written, and, with perhaps some slight qualifications, unassailable.

My University friends here are delighted and will have the article brought before the French public very soon.'

Hogan enclosed a letter of 13 Feb. he had received from Henri Fouard: "Quelle lumière que ces pages du Cardinal Newman, quelle grace et quelle force! . . . . Les *obiter dicta* sont une trouvaille merveilleuse.'

Febr 8. 1884

My dear Blachford

Thanks for your prompt response. I rejoice to know that Music is an open subject. I will explain, that I am in *no* special *hurry*, if waiting insures a better item, and am ready for *immediate* decision, if decision will secure what else would slip through one's fingers.

Again it may be *choice*, as some *old* copy of Palestrina etc etc — or *perfect* as some *new* Edition of Purcell etc etc, or Beethoven etc

I hope I did not speak of Sir J. P. in a way inconsistent with the gratitude and (I may say) affection I feel towards him.[1]

I hope the Dean likes this weather. Give my love to him and his. How sad is Ogle's bereavement![2]

I have been reading some pages of that elephantine work — Burgon's articles in the Quarterly against the N.T. revisers.[3] It shocked me, for to speak so irreverently, as he does, of the well known MSS of the 4th century is to throw suspicion upon *all* MSS. since in no place of his articles (as far as I read) does he show that other MSS are more trustworthy. This does not matter for a Catholic, for he believes the text of Scripture to be genuine on the word of the Church, but it seems to me it must be most unsettling to Protestants who receive St Matthew, St Mark etc. on the mere credit of transcribers to be told that such important specimens of transcription are so miserably incorrect as he maintains they are. Do I speak intelligibly?

Yours affly J H Card Newman

Feby 8. 1884

Copy

To Mr Kehoe of the Cath: Publishing Society. U. States

Dear Sir

Messrs Burns and Oates have sent me your letter to Mr Oates of January 28 last, and in consequence of it I withdraw at once my belief in the report which came to me about the Catholic Publication Society's use of my 'Apologia', and am sorry I gave ear to it.[4]

---

[1] Newman wanted to give a present to Sir James Paget. Lord Blachford on 11 Feb. recommended books, and suggested 'La Renaissance (price 16. 16 in morocco) — 2 folio volumes — large margin magnificent print — altogether "de luxe" — and plenty of etchings of buildings — altogether a beautiful book —' which Newman chose. See also *Letters of Frederic Lord Blachford*, edited by G. E. Marindin, London 1896, pp. 421–2.

[2] Dr Ogle's wife died on 4 Feb.

[3] Burgon's articles in the *Quarterly Review*, attacking *RSV* for its reliance on the great fourth century manuscripts of the New Testament. cf. letter of 25 Feb. 1882 to Plummer.

[4] See letter of 12 Jan. to Oates. Kehoe, in his letter to Oates, denied that the Catholic Publication Society, of which he was manager, had pirated the *Apologia*, and suggested that if he could offer Newman's works at half price, or at $50 the set, he could greatly increase their sale in America.

Of course I should be glad for my volumes to circulate in so wide a field as the United States open upon them, but I have no right to outstrip my means with this object. I have laid out large sums upon the printing, and I cannot dispense with the liquidation of the debt thereby incurred, for which I depend on the sale. I have stereotyped not more than 13 volumes — about 10 are not. — Eleven (Protestant Sermons) are in Messrs Rivingtons' hands, who already I believe have correspondents in the United States

My simple question then to you is whether you will pay me a definite sum for every copy which you sell and what will the sum be.[1]

This question comes more naturally to me than your proposal that I should sell copies at half price

J H N

TO WILFRID OATES

Febr 8/84

Dear Mr Oates

I do not know why I should trouble you to correspond with Mr Keoh [sic][2] The only question that occurs to me on which you can speak is whether I gave the leave about the Grammar of Assent to which he refers.[3]

I have no stereotype plates of Sermons to Mixed Congregations, Occasional Sermons, Doctrine of Assent, Difficulties 2 volumes, Position of Catholics, Verses, Loss and Gain, Callista.

My Protestant Sermons and Lectures are in Messrs Rivingtons' hands. I send you a copy of my letter to Mr Kehoe[4]

J H N

TO JAMES LEONARD FISH [?][5]

Feb. 12. 1884

My dear Mr Fish

I heard with much sorrow of the heavy loss, which had from a Good Providence come on you and Mrs Fish, and feel the kindness of the memorial of your Son, which you have sent me now.

May all our sorrows great and light bring us nearer God.

Most truly Yours John H. Card. Newman.

[1] Newman noted on the copy made by Neville of the draft: 'Sept 18. 1884 This letter was not answered by Mr Kehoe.' See also letter of 19 Feb. to Denny.
[2] See letter of 8 Feb. to Kehoe.
[3] Kehoe had said in his letter to Oates, 'We did publish, and do publish yet "Grammar of Assent" for the right to publish which we paid Burns and Oates 50£. We have sold only about 1,200 copies.'
[4] Oates replied on 11 Feb. that he had posted on Newman's letter to Kehoe 'seeing in it nothing which I should notice to you first.'
[5] James Leonard Fish, at Exeter College, Oxford, held various curacies from 1853 until 1866, when he became Rector of St Margaret Pattens with St Gabriel Fenchurch, London. His wife and children became Catholics in 1880.

TO CATHERINE BOWDEN, SISTER MARY ALBAN

Febr. 13. 1884

My dear Child

I know how much I need, and how much gain from, the remembrance which would follow in my behalf, if my photograph were placed in your Community Room, but I have hardly such an article in my possession. I readily send you two of those which remain, one taken at Rome, one here. The rest I have are some years earlier, but I doubt whether you would care for them, were I to send them

The older I am, the more anxieties surround me, and the more I am weighed down and need help from above.

Yours affectly John H Card. Newman

TO MRS JOHN KENYON

Bm Febr 13 1884.

Dear Mrs Kenyon

How could I help saying prayers and Masses for your dear Mother?[1] so good as she always was to me, and now in her death reminding me that the time must soon come, when I must need from others what I give to her.

Most truly Yours John H Card. Newman

P.S. I am sorry at Mamo [Maxwell-Scott] being forced to travel —

TO LADY HERBERT OF LEA

Bm Febr 14. 1884

My dear Lady Herbert

This requires no answer. I only write in order to assure you again how deeply I sympathise in your distress. I have had Lord Pembroke constantly in my thoughts, saying Mass for him twice a week, since I heard of his illness[2]

Yours most truly affectly, J. H. Card. Newman

TO WILFRID OATES

Febr 16/84

in substance
Dear Mr Oates

It seems to me that the Editor of the Nineteenth Century should be consulted before you ask me your question about a separate publication of my

[1] Lady Henry Kerr.
[2] See letter of 26 Jan. to Lady Herbert.

Paper on Inspiration.[1] But I should be sorry that you gave my name to him as sanctioning or taking part in your application

J H N

P.S.   I think, without bringing me in, you might ask the Editor what the rule of the Review is; whether the Editor chose a Printer or Publisher when one of his Articles was to be reprinted or whether he left it to others. Else it might be ungracious.[2]

TO HENRY MATTHEWS

Febr 16. 1884

Dear Sir

I am obliged to trouble you with an additional suggestion as to what I wrote to you last month about the Count Aglié proposal to translate my Pamphlet, if he still thinks of it

I spoke then with great doubt whether our English mode of writing, or at least mine, would interest an Italian public.

The Count himself feels the desirableness of leaving out in the translation what I said about Irish Catholics; let me now ask him to consider whether there is not serious objection to his putting into Italian what I have said about the Vatican Council?[3]

Pray excuse me and believe me to be

Dear [Sir] Your faithful Servant J H N

Henry Matthews Esq Q C

TO ALEXANDER DENNY

[19 February 1884]

Dear Mr Denny

Thank you for the trouble you have taken about my question —[4] the additional I am going to ask I trust will to a man of business be so plain tho' not to me, that you will perhaps wonder at my asking it.

[1] Oates wrote on 15 Feb. asking for permission to reprint Newman's article 'On the Inspiration of Scripture', and offering an honorarium of £10 for the permission.

[2] Newman received some days later 'With Mr James Knowles's Compliments and best thanks', as he noted 'cheque for £30 which I returned Febr 21/84   He returned it back to me and I found myself obliged to keep it'   Knowles wrote on 25 Feb., 'You could not possibly — I think — "commit an offence" against me — by act of yours — most certainly not — by such a kindly prompted one as led you to return my cheque.'

On 26 Feb. Oates wrote that Knowles 'does not see his way to consent to the republication of your paper.' See letter of 2 April to Knowles.

[3] Matthews replied on 21 Feb. that Count d'Aglié had left London, but had received Newman's first letter and so would be sure to send his translation in proof, and comply with any wishes of Newman's. Meanwhile Matthews would try to pass on the contents of Newman's letter of 16 Feb.

[4] This was in connexion with L. Kehoe's offer; see letter of 8 Feb. to him. Denny on 18 Feb. advised Newman that there was no objection to letting American booksellers have books at half the English selling price, provided they were willing to take at least 100 copies of each.

If I understand you, you say that if a volume costs not quite 2/ per copy, a considerable margin is left for profit — that is, comparing cost with the price — but what is meant by the price? does it mean trade price or the selling price.[1] It cannot mean the cost. This makes me say that I prefer selling to the American bookseller at so much per copy, or (as you say) per 100 copies, to saying 'half price' which I do not understand.

I suppose from what you say there may be this objection to my coming to terms with the American firm, that they, getting the copies cheaper may lower the price to American purchasers, as not depending for their profit on the per centages. Is this so?

The question to me is whether I can get a larger return for my serious expenses on printing than I am getting. Nothing is more capricious than the public taste and interest in Literature. After my death my volumes perhaps will hardly sell; if a really good offer for copies were made to me now, not for copyright, but for copies, it would be an inducement to me to listen to it.

Yrs J H N

P.S.   If a volume sold to the public for 5/ 'half' the (selling) price would be per copy 2/6 and the gain per 1000 copies £25. I suppose I have made some mistake here.[2]

TO BARONESS ANATOLE VON HÜGEL

Bm Feb 20. 1884

My dear Isy

Many thanks for your remembering my birthday. I am walking upon ice which is safe at present, but may suddenly give way without warning.

Canon Brownlow was here when your letter came — and I have just said to him, 'She does not write often but, when she does, she sends a famous long letter', . . .

One thing I might have told you, my true rejoicing at hearing that your husband has got his appointment at Cambridge. Congratulate him for me upon it. It is so difficult, so forlorn, (at least so I feel it,) to cultivate knowledge for its own sake, and apart from duty, that I was delighted to hear the good news.[3]

. . . .

J H N

---

[1] It meant the selling or retail price.
[2] Denny replied that the gain would be £35, i.e. £125 given by the American bookseller, less £90 cost of production.
[3] Anatole von Hügel was appointed Curator of the University Museum of Archaeology and of Ethnology at Cambridge in the latter part of 1883.

TO GEORGE T. EDWARDS

Febr 22. 1884

Dear Mr Edwards

Thank you for your translations, though, since I am not a linguist, I cannot do justice to them.[1]

As to Mr Mozley's volumes, I was so offended at the inaccuracies which met my eye when I first took it up, that I threw it down.[2] I feel that his inaccuracies cannot be all set right without almost my writing a book, which I cannot do. And what right had he to put in a letter of mine without asking my leave?[3] It is one of those incidents which are intended I believe by a good Providence to deepen one's indifference as to what the world thinks of one

Very truly Yours John H Card. Newman

P.S.   Thank you for the Psalter[4]

TO SIR WILLIAM HENRY COPE

Febr. 23. 1884

My dear Sir William

It is very welcome to me to receive such kind letters as yours on my birthday, and I thank you for it. The newspapers exaggerated my illness, but I cannot deny that, though I have no illness, I am very weak

Most truly yours John H Card. Newman

TO BISHOP ULLATHORNE

Bm Febr. 23. 1884

My dear Lord

Will you give me your judgment? In a formal letter 'the Senate of the University of Edinburgh' ask me to receive 'the honorary degree of *Doctor of Divinity*' on April 17 at the '*Festival* of the Tercentenary of the *Foundation* of the University.'

Am I not right in thinking I cannot accept it 1. because it is the doctorate in *Divinity* — and 2 because it is on a *Festival* commemorative of a Reformation or Protestant Foundation

---

[1] These have not been traced.

[2] *Reminiscences chiefly of Oriel and the Oxford Movement*. See letter of 9 June, 1882 to T. Mozley, also that of 3 March 1885 to Anne Mozley.

[3] Edwards on 21 Feb. mentioned and quoted from Newman's long letter of 13 May, 1832, printed by T. Mozley, op. cit. II, pp. 447–50, on God's cutting off those He 'loves, and who really are His, as a judgment.'

[4] Edwards sent a copy of *The Book of Psalms* in large print.

At Oxford honorary degrees are in civil law, not divinity — and again there is no commemoration of a Protestant event[1]

Your affecte Servt J. H. Card Newman

TO T. W. ALLIES

Feb. 24. 1884.

My dear Allies,

I thank you for your affectionate letter.[2] Of course I am not worthy of all you say, but if you had not a love of me, it would not come into your mind to speak of me as you do, and it is a token, which comforts me, that you do not forget me in your prayers. It is indeed a precious birthday letter and I shall carefully and reverently keep it as such.

As to poor Hutton, certainly we should every one of us recollect 'He who thinketh he standeth, etc',[3] but, if you had lived with him, perhaps you would feel more awe than disturbance, though amazed and shocked who could help being? He is of an affectionate disposition, and suffered much. It is a tragedy. We were quite unsuspicious of his state of mind.

Yours affectly John H. Card. Newman.

TO MRS T. W. ALLIES

Feb. 24. 1884

My dear Mrs. Allies,

It is very kind in you, sending your congratulations on my birthday, and I thank you for doing so.

I am very well but weak, and thereby run the risk of not being able to repel an accidental attack, whether it be a sudden illness or a fall or blow. Thus I am in the hands of God.

Most truly yours J. H. Card. Newman

[1] Ullathorne replied on 24 Feb. that 'as a Catholic and a Cardinal of the Roman Church' Newman was debarred from accepting the proposed honour, '1⁰ because you already possess the degree of Doctor in Theology; 2⁰ because as a Catholic, a priest and a Cardinal you can only hold degrees in Catholic Theology, even though the title be but honorary.' See letter of 25 Feb. to Sir Alexander Grant.
[2] Allies wrote on 20 Feb., '. . . I have been accustomed to put you in my thoughts with St Augustine and St Thomas: because I seem to be more indebted to those three than to any other . . . and it is through you that I came to appreciate them. For when I had no guide as an Anglican, and though in orders looked all around in vain for coherent theological instruction, you nursed me, as it were a child, full of errors and false conceptions, and brought me to a better mind — And it was through testing a page of 'Development' that I came to the final enfranchisement of the Faith . . .'
[3] 1 Corinthians, 10:12. Allies wrote of A. W. Hutton, 'The last time I saw him at Whitsuntide, 1882, he seemed so full of zeal.'

TO ROBERT CHARLES JENKINS

[24 February 1884]

My dear Canon Jenkins

Alas, in your criticism you have not borne in view the object of my Paper on Inspiration. It was not written to meet controversial attacks of clever men like you, but to easy the conscience of religious Catholics, who wished to be sure they were not acting inconsistently with what, as Catholics they were bound to hold[1]

JHN

TO H. P. LIDDON

Febr. 24. 1884

Dear Canon Liddon

I cannot answer you satisfactorily. The incident was one of those matters, which in the course of years had simply dropped out of my memory, and, on being led to think of Pusey's early years, had revived partially.

I think Jelf told me about it, from whom too I got the idea that Mr Pusey, the Father, did not like Edward's passion, and created a sadness in his son, which had led me to feel anxiety about him. I recollect some time after telling it to Hurrell Froude, thinking it would interest him, he being not over fond of Pusey — but it had not that effect. It was that P. had walked all through the night to Tintern Abbey, to see the spot where Miss B. had been.

I very much doubt whether you can record such an imperfect report in his life, except as vaguely saying that his attachment to her was romantic He married soon after his father's death in 1828 — the Christian Year had come out in 1827 — and I recollect his observing to me how remarkable Keble should have hit on this idea, viz. 'There is an *awe* in mortals' joy, A deep mysterious *fear* etc.'[2]

I suppose, you have his brother on your side, in whatever you may say. I ask this, for I fancy, perhaps without reason, he has not carried himself quite kindly to me.[3]

If I began to speak about poor Hutton, I should never end. You know him for many years — it requires a man to know him well, to be able to anticipate his future

Very truly Yours John H. Card. Newman

P.S. Thank you for the very interesting Sermon, and for your remembrance of my birthday[4]

[1] Jenkins on 8 Feb. criticised Newman's article as though it was directed against Anglicanism. He wrote again on 23 Feb. in a similar strain.
[2] *The Christian Year*, 'Matrimony', first verse. For Pusey's long engagement to Maria Catherine Raymond-Barker see Liddon's *Pusey*, I, p. 115.
[3] William Pusey, Rector of Langley, Kent.
[4] On 23 Feb. Liddon sent his *Edward Bouverie Pusey* 'A sermon preached in St Margaret's Church Princes Road, Liverpool, in aid of the Pusey Memorial Fund, on Sunday Jan. 20, 1884', London 1884.

TO HENRY DE COLYAR

Febr 25. 1884

My dear de Colyar

I take great interest in your personal doings, and am rejoiced to hear from various quarters so good an account of you in your profession. I heartily wish you success in your present object[1]

Yours affectionately John H Card. Newman

TO SIR ALEXANDER GRANT

Bm Febr. 25. 1884

Private

Dear Sir Alexander

Though I have not the honour of your acquaintance, yet when a letter comes to me, as now, with your signature, I hope I may refer to our common interest and fellowship in Oriel College, as a ground for writing to you in language less formal than I can use in answering the gracious invitation to which you have signed your name.[2]

It is quite true then, as I have said in my answer to the Senatus Academicus, that my state of health is a real and adequate reason for declining the honour you offer me; but I should add to you what I do not wish to state publicly, that I find that it is not consistent with my status as a Doctor in the Catholic Church to hold a like degree from another authority, even though it be honorary, not to speak of those more formal conditions which attach to my being a Cardinal.

These serious difficulties do but increase and deepen my gratitude to those who have shown such good will and such kind regard to one who is a stranger to them[3]

I am, Dear Sir Alexander,

Your faithful Servant John H. Card. Newman

Sir A. Grant Bart etc etc

[1] De Colyar was to stand for election to the Athenaeum Club on 3 March. He asked Newman to ask Lord Coleridge to support him. De Colyar was elected and wrote on 4 March to thank Newman for his intervention.

[2] Newman had been obliged to refuse the offer of an Edinburgh D.D. See letter of 23 Feb. to Ullathorne. Grant had been a Fellow of Oriel College, 1849–60, and was Principal of Edinburgh University from 1868 until his death on 30 Nov. 1884.

[3] Grant replied on 27 Feb.: 'I think that the Senatus Academicus of this University were conscious that there might be many difficulties in the way of your Eminence accepting a degree at their hands, — though indeed they were far from wishing to make a journey to Edinburgh a condition for such a degree. In the case of your Eminence, they would gladly have conferred it by diploma, *in absentia*.

But when, on the occasion of their Tercentenary, they were seeking out those of all living men most worthy of reverence and honour, they could not pass over the name of your Eminence, dear in a more special way to some of us who have been connected with Oxford, but dear also to all who with any fineness of mind read what has been written in the English language. So the vote to offer this little tribute to your Eminence was spontaneous and unanimous. It will gratify the Senatus that, while unable to accept from them the only mark of honour which they had to offer, your Eminence should have so kindly expressed yourself with regard to their intentions.'

Febr 25. 1884

My dear Mrs Wilson,

It is very kind of you to remember my birthday. I have been wishing to know how you were, knowing your trials and anxieties, and am thankful to hear so good an account of you.

Most truly Yours John H. Card. Newman

TO GEORGE T. EDWARDS

Febr. 26. 1884

Dear Mr Edwards

Nothing you quoted from my letter in Mr M's book could pain me — but it did startle me to find it had been published without my knowing any thing about it.[1] Indeed Mr Mozley has acted *strangely*. He has set down things as facts which were not only not facts, but about which he could know nothing, as having happened before he knew me, before he was born — many things trifling — many not trifling because they are parts of a whole, and so many, that they would need a volume almost to set right; and, if I noticed some of them and not others, I should seem to admit those which I did not notice

This is what makes me feel keenly, that one must look out for what God thinks of one, and care nothing for the judgment or the testimony about one of man. Mr Mozley means to be kind to me, but what is the good of being kind, if it is not true? There is One Judge

Yours most truly John H Card. Newman

TO JANE MOZLEY

Febr 26. 1884

My dear Jane

It is a great thing to have an object in life, and I congratulate you on having got one. I trust and pray it may be a success. It is one of the best points of this unhappy age, that it has made so many openings for the activity of women.[2]

I don't understand quite Frank's position, and what 'four boys' means — but I suppose it is a good beginning

Love to him

Yours affly John H Card. Newman

[1] See letter of 22 Feb. to Edwards.
[2] Francis Woodgate Mozley had become a master at Bedford School, and took pupils as boarders. His sister Jane kept house for him.

Bm Febr. 28 [1884]

Dear Canon Griffin

I cannot have a greater favour or a greater pleasure done me than you so kindly propose by dedicating to me the volume of Dr Moriarty's Allocutions. I have ever felt the truest love and gratitude towards him. He was indeed a rare friend, one of ten thousand. He is in heaven doubtless — but I mention him always in Mass, from the good which I am sure I can get from him.[1]

The volume came quite right and I shall read with interest the seven additional Allocutions

Most truly Yours John H Card Newman

The Very Rev. Canon Griffin

FROM GERARD MANLEY HOPKINS

University College, 85 & 86, Stephens Green. Dublin. Feb. 20 1884. YOUR EMINENCE and Dearest Father, Pax Christi — I wish you a very bright tomorrow and health and happiness and the abundance of God's grace for the ensuing year.

I am writing from where I never thought to be, in a University for Catholic Ireland begun under your leadership, which has since those days indeed long and unhappily languished, but for which we now with God's help hope a continuation or restoration of success. In the events which have brought me here I recognise the hand of providence, but nevertheless have felt and feel an unfitness which led me at first to try to decline the offer made me and now does not yet allow my spirits to rise to the level of the position and its duties. But perhaps the things of most promise with God begin with weakness and fear.[2]

These buildings since you knew them have fallen into a deep dilapidation. They were a sort of wreck or ruin when our Fathers some months since came in and the costly last century ornamentation of flutes and festoons and Muses on the walls is still much in contrast with the dinginess and dismantlement all round. Only one thing looks bright, and that no longer belongs to the College, the little Church of your building, the Byzantine style of which reminds me of the Oratory and bears your impress clearly enough.

I should have said in the beginning that I am to convey from Fr. Delany the best wishes of all the College together with my own.

I remain your Eminence's affectionate son in Christ

Gerard M. Hopkins S.J.

TO GERARD MANLEY HOPKINS

Febr 29. 1884

Dear Fr Hopkins

Thank you for your remembering my birthday and for your kind thought upon it. I hope you find at Dublin an opening for work such as you desire and which suits you. I am sorry you can speak of dilapidation,

Most truly Yours J. H. Card. Newman

[1] See letters of 5 March 1883 and 21 May 1884 to Griffin.
[2] Hopkins had just been appointed Professor of Greek at the Royal University of Ireland. See also letter of 4 Feb. to William Delany, S.J.

March 2. 1884

My dear Dr Ogle

I have not written to you, because I don't like to go on troubling you with my trifling ailments — and yet I wish very much to hear about you.[1] Perhaps your daughter or your son would have the kindness to tell me. But, as I am writing, I inclose a report

Very truly Yours John H Card. Newman

TO CHARLES VOYSEY

March 4. 1884

Rev Sir

I thank you for your letters and Sermon — and am glad to learn thence that when you said it was generally admitted that conduct was three parts of life, you did not mean by 'conduct' a man's bearing and behaviour towards and in the events of life, as I misunderstood you to say but something far more intimately inward and personal.[2]

J H N

TO J. SPENCER NORTHCOTE

March 5. 1884

Dear Provost Northcote

I live so much out of the world that I have only today learned that, you have not only been named Provost of our Chapter by the Holy See, but have actually been installed in the Cathedral.

I come then to congratulate the diocese and you *late*, in any attempts I may make to express my great pleasure at your elevation; but I congratulate you first on the Pope's act itself, which must be so gratifying to you, and next on your suceeding to a dignity with predecessors so holy and venerable as the two Provosts who have gone before you. Nor could they be succeeded by one more worthy of their place than yourself.[3]

I wish I could write in a way more expressive of the sense I have of the claim you have created by a long laborious priesthood upon the Church for such a recognition of faithful service — but I am too old and too unstrung to write as I should like

Most truly Yours John H Card. Newman

[1] Ogle, whose wife died on 4 Feb., sent birthday wishes on 20 Feb., and hoped 'that you may experience less discomfort in the present than in the past year.'

[2] Voysey had written several letters and apparently wished to engage in controversy. He had been deprived of his benefice, Healaugh, near Tadcaster, in 1871, for his unorthodox views. He came to reject Christianity and founded the 'Theistic Church' in London.

[3] The first Provost of the Birmingham Chapter was Henry Weedall, 1852–9, the second Rodolph Bagnall, 1859–83.

TO ST GEORGE JACKSON MIVART

Bm March 6. 1884

My dear Professor Mivart

Private Thank you for the confidence you show me in your letter; I wish I could suitably answer it.[1]

For myself, I think the social interests of Catholics in England have been mismanaged the last 25 years, and they are now in such a tangle that it is difficult to understand where we are, much more where we ought to be. Hence it is easy to deny any alleged grievance such as yours as to State Prayers, Trusteeship etc while allowing there *are* grievances, and there I sympathise with your dissatisfaction, while I cannot follow you in your proposed reforms and remedies.

And first I think we ought to realize what a small body we are. You compare and contrast us with the Church of England; but think of the numbers, the wealth, the prestige, the popularity, the political weight of that communion; of the knowledge of the world, the learning, the traditions of its three centuries. Think of its place in English history, its biographies, ecclesiastical and lay, its noble buildings, memorials often of the Catholic past but in the occupation of Protestantism — what have we to show per contra? the Gunpowder Plot, and the blundering Stuarts! 'Sume superbiam Quaesitam meritis.'[2]

Catholics then in England have been cowed, and beaten down by centuries of misfortune. I don't pretend to be able to put out a consistent view on this point but, in a fight of life and death, the party that lost the day must have been flung beyond imagination. Can any but a tradition of the gravest danger and consequent terror account for the abstinence of our Peers from the exercise of their rights in the House of Lords? Recollect too it is but 20 years before my time that Dr Chaloner [sic] died of fright in the Gordon riots. Your complaint virtually in your letter to me is the incapacity of our laity, and does not their past history account for it?

While then I feel as keenly as you do the state of English Catholics socially and think it our duty to improve it, I doubt whether insisting on small grievances is the way to raise it. I more than fear that little can be done in our (or rather your) day, but suffer me to say, while I keenly sympathise with yourself and others, you must go deeper than you do in your letter to me[3]

Very sincerely Yours J. H. Card. Newman

P.S.   This is not written to hinder you writing again.

---

[1] Only part of Mivart's letter is to be found. He regretted that in Catholic services there were not more prayers for the State, considering 'how blessed has been for so many years our political condition compared with that of other nations.'

[2] Horace, *Odes*, III, xxx, 14–15.

[3] Mivart replied on 8 March, 'My desire is to be useful, and therefore to be well guided,' and he asked Newman to explain the words, 'you must go deeper than you do in your letter to me.' See next letters to Mivart.

March 8. 84

sent

Dear Mr Denny

I think it most unlikely that I should close with any offer for the purchase of my copyrights — but considering the fickleness of the public taste and the rise and fall in value of books, I don't think you can be surprised that, in the interest of my heirs, I should think it right not to refuse an advantageous offer.

I have let you know all I had to tell, directly it came to me; and one of my reasons for this was the thought that you ought to have the first refusal, if I took up the idea of disposing of the volumes which you publish.[1] It may be a mere fancy, but I should not wonder if the offer came from America

J H N

TO ST GEORGE JACKSON MIVART

March 9. 1884

Dear Professor Mivart

My brain and fingers get so soon tired by letter writing, that I am as short as I *can* be. Perhaps if I had taken up a second sheet of paper, I should not have seemed mysterious, and I beg you to pardon the appearance.

I will plunge in medias res. Twenty years ago I was desirous that Catholic youths should be allowed to continue at the Protestant Colleges, the Bishop of Birmingham wishing, as he said, an Oratory to be established in Oxford. Now the peril of infidelity is so great that I dare not undertake the responsibility of recommending it.

However, the Jesuits who have the Mission are bound by the Apostolic precept Praedica verbum, insta etc etc,[2] but their mission is large and they have not hands enough. Would they allow a Guild to be set up under their patronage in Oxford, with members all over England, with some blessing or indulgence of the Pope with the express object and duty of opposing the infidelity of the day, Oxford being taken as being a focus, and a special focus, of the evil?

It would be something more than an Academia, but it would involve

---

[1] Newman had written on 6 March, a letter to which Denny replied on 7 March, 'I suppose it must be some one in the trade who has offered to purchase the copyright of your Eminence's works; and, if that be so, I do not think it is in keeping with professional etiquette for one publisher to interfere with the works issued by another . . .'

In the first draft of his reply Newman wrote: 'All that I felt due to you, whom as publishing them, I had been so satisfied with, was to let you know at once that the proposal had been made to me . . .' Newman also said, 'You have frightened me by what implies, (though I doubt that you can mean it), a startling claim upon my management of my own property.'

cf. letter of 10 March to Oates.

[2] 2 *Timothy*, 4:2.

Lectures; and I think would succeed at Rome when other plans would not. Protestants (if they are what is called orthodox,) Anglicans, Ritualists, might be eligible as members. Unattached houses of *converts* might grow out of it.

The great difficulty would be, how to find able and well informed men for the purpose at starting.

Perhaps Fr Parkinson has written to you on this subject

Very truly Yours John H. Card. Newman

TO WILFRID OATES

sent in substance   March 10. 1884
Dear Mr Oates

It seems to me that it is so difficult to ascertain the real prospective value of my copyrights that a sale and purchase must be a speculation on both sides.[1] The taste of the public and external circumstances are ever changing and of this I have had many instances, as others have. A second edition of a book once was called for, the first not being large enough for the demand — it was at once sent to press — but, from a press of work, the printing took six weeks, by which time the sale had died away, and consequently an edition of 2000 was left on my hands for 20 years. This of course is of common occurrence. And so my being raised to the Cardinalate almost doubled the sale of some of my books.

I am not, however, averse to the idea of a sale of my books, if I was sure of an adequate offer Nor should I speculate on getting the largest possible sum. There are offers which could satisfy me in themselves, but not all would

I think of my 36 volumes only one is not my property, the Arians. Messrs Rivington pay me a royalty on eleven volumes, viz Sermons and (say) 10 others are stereotyped. If you would give me some vague idea of what an offer would be like, I could give you an answer at once.

J H N

TO ST GEORGE JACKSON MIVART

March 11. 1884
Dear Professor Mivart

Had I recollected that you had been one of those who did all that could be done to support the Kensington University, I should not have recommended a new scheme to your notice, which promises so little.[2]

[1] Oates asked on 5 March whether Newman was prepared to sell the copyrights of his works. See letters of 14 March and 18 Sept. 1884 to Oates.
[2] Mivart wrote on 10 March: 'I have heard from Fr Parkinson and he has, of course, my thorough sympathy and good will but I very much doubt if we have got the men and I do not want to join in a second fiasco.' On 12 March Mivart added, 'I should be sorry for your Eminence to think that my connexion with the College at Kensington arose from any wavering of my views about the need of University education. I accepted my post there very reluctantly and only in obedience to the express desire of the Archbishop of Westminster.'

Therefore I comply with your suggestion, and should be pleased to have my letters back, (or else burn them.)[1]

I shall not forget what you have told me, but whether I can be of any use in respect to it is another question.

I gladly send you my Letter to the Duke of Norfolk, and am writing to the Publishers for that purpose.[2]

Very truly Yours John H. Card. Newman

P.S. I fully think as I said, that, unless I misunderstood you, I could not feel it fair to contrast us with the Established Church

TO EMILY BOWLES

[12 March 1884]

My dear Child

We are under a great disadvantage. We kept Fr Hutton's reason for leaving us a secret, but he let it out.

And now, we could show it has had nothing to do (by reaction) with his being a Catholic — but we do not know what he would consider telling secrets *It is his duty to clear* the Catholic Religion, *as he can do*[3]

Yrs affly J H Card. Newman

P.S. So much I can say, for it does not come from him. The Bishop of Lincoln[4] sent me a letter to stop our receiving him. I answered, as was the fact, that he was received already. I am told now, by one of our Fathers, that the Bishop in his letter said that 'Fr Hutton was of a sceptical turn.' However, he showed no signs of it up to the day when he suddenly told us he did not believe in a personal God, and forthwith left the house in great distress. He *would not* delay going.

TO THE BOYS OF THE ORATORY SCHOOL

March 12. 1884

My dear Boys[5]

You could not have made me a more opportune present than you have made me on my birthday, since hitherto my altar candlesticks have been borrowed from the Sacristy.

[1] Mivart on 8 March offered to keep his correspondence with Newman a secret, and to return his letters.

[2] Mivart had lost his copy of the *Letter to the Duke of Norfolk* and found the work unobtainable.

[3] See letter of 4 Nov. 1883 to Ryder, and notes there.

[4] Christopher Wordsworth.

[5] A note accompanied the gift: 'St Valentine's [21 Feb] 1884

Dear Father

We wish you, in the name of the School, many happy returns of this day, and hope you will accept these candlesticks for your altar

We are, dear Father

Your affectionate children in S. Philip

T. Mathew	R. O. Eaton
D. Sheil	E. Pereira
R. S. Lamb	G. Shillingford'
A. H. Pollen	

One or two of you should come and see how well they look in their place.

And I want in turn to make your Library a present of some of my books, when I learn what you have already.

And now I give you my blessing; it is the blessing of an old man who is soon to go. Your life is opening; — May God be with you, as He has been with me! and He will be with all who seek Him

Yours affectionately John H. Card. Newman

TO HENRY WILLIAMS MOZLEY

March 14. 1884

My dear Harry

I thought your letter very kind, but could not answer it at the time, as I think you were already in motion.[1] I heard more fully from others the forced march you had to make from Barrow; and hope your journey to Rome had less of effort.

I have had your letter on my table ever since it came, intending to answer it on your return to Eton, and now when I look for it, though I saw it only yesterday, it has vanished.

This mischance happens to me so often, that I suppose it is one of the infirmities of old age — though how it is brought about I cannot analize.

I should be curious to know what impression Rome made on you.[2] Most men are struck favorably. I never have been, and, unless it is too long for any one to rely on his memory, I think Archdeacon Denison wrote me a letter from Rome expressing the same want of sympathy which I felt myself.[3] I recollect he especially criticized the ruins, as being so sadly disappointing; as being mere shapeless masses of brickwork, or solitary columns or huge structures, like the Coliseum, remarkable only from their size.

I hope you had fine weather there, for it is in that respect that I have been specially unlucky myself

Yours affectionately John H. Card. Newman

TO JOHN RICKARDS MOZLEY

March 14. 1884

My dear John

You are quite right in thinking I should be deeply interested in your letter, and grateful to you for writing it. It is that which all these scientific men need, and which is hid from them, the experience of the religious soul. . . .[4] Of

[1] On 6 Jan. H. W. Mozley wrote from Rome his impressions, during his first visit there.

[2] Mozley, in a letter of 18 March from Eton, about the antiquities of Rome, wrote that he had enjoyed his visit extremely.

[3] George Anthony Denison visited Rome in 1829–30.

[4] J. R. Mozley made this omission when copying. He prefaced his copy: 'The following letter was in answer to one in which I had expressed my belief in that doctrine which, as I suppose, is the primary addition which Christianity makes to simple Theism; the indispensability, namely, of the personal help of Jesus Christ for our permanent welfare; and I had said that I judged so by my own experience.'

course what are called 'experiences' involve often much that is enthusiastic and wild, but usum non tollit abusus.

For myself, now at the end of a long life I say from a full heart that God has never failed me — never disappoint me — has ever turned evil into good for me. When I was young, I used to say (and I trust it was not presumptuous to say it) that our Lord ever answered my prayers. And what He has been to me, who have deserved His love so little, such He will be, I believe and know, He will be to every one who does not repel Him and turn from His pleading.

And now I believe He is visiting you, and it rejoices me to think He will gain you.

Yours very affectionately John H. Card. Newman

TO WILFRID OATES

March 14/84

In substance
Dear Mr Oates

I do not think it worth for you to take the trouble of any calculation upon the present circumstances of my books with a view to the value of their copyright; certainly not of your coming down here.[1]

I know what their average return of sale is at present — and I am sure nothing to equal it could be given by a purchaser

What I thought possible, without trouble was to select one book, say the Sermons to Mixed Congregations, or the State of English Catholicism, and see what the market price would [be] for it. I should not wonder if it was more than £20 — whereas at present it more than pays for the printing.[2]

Yrs very truly J H N

P.S. I have another difficulty. I feel I ought to give the refusal in each case to the present publisher.

TO HENRY DE COLYAR

March 15. 1884

My dear de Colyar

I congratulate you on your election, being quite ignorant of the difficulty of securing it, till now.

Since then, something has occurred which makes me wish to ask you as a friend a legal question, if you can do it without any trouble to yourself.

Years ago at Oxford there was a great alarm in the Debating Society which rented for its Library a Bookseller's first floor, lest, if he failed, the

[1] Oates wrote on 12 March proposing to make an offer for the purchase of the copyright of all Newman's works.
[2] Oates replied on 14 March tentatively suggesting the purchase of the copyright for £1000 and an annual sum of £100. See letter of 18 March to Lord Coleridge.

Society's books would be claimed, as part of his assets, at least in payment of the Queen's Taxes, if not by his creditors.

How does the law stand now? I only want a yes or no answer.[1]

Very sincerely Yours John H Card. Newman

TO MESSRS GILBERT AND RIVINGTON

[15 March ? 1884]

Cardinal Newman received from Messrs Gilbert and Rivington under date of February 14 [1884] a statement of account by which he found that he was indebted to them the sum of £188. 14. 3 for reprinting 500 copies of each of two volumes of his and stereotyping 'Difficulties vol II' and 'Via Media vol II.'

He has usually of late paid such an account at once — but he had found from Messrs Pickerings the publishers on March 11 that they had not yet received copies of either volume, and though copies of one of the volumes came to him a few days back, the other has not come yet

TO ADAM HAMILTON, O.S.B.

March 15 1884.

My dear Fr Hamilton.

I congratulate you on the step you are making towards the restoration of the Abbey and thank you for your invitation of me to be present on the happy occasion.[2]

I am obliged to decline but I beg God to bless your commencement with an abundant blessing.

Your faithful servt John Henry Card. Newman.

TO LORD O'HAGAN

March 15. 1884

My dear Lord O'Hagan

I am very glad to possess, especially as your gift, your interesting and important volume. It gives me various information in matters in which I am not well versed.[3]

[1] De Colyar replied on 17 March that 'a simple "yes or no" reply would not be satisfactory —

Originally, lodger's goods were liable to distress in respect of rent due from *their* immediate landlord to *his* superior landlord. This hardship has been removed by "The Lodgers' Goods Protection Act 1871".

As regards Queens Taxes, however, I am of opinion that a distress in respect of them might be satisfied by taking the goods of a lodger. . . .'

cf. letter of 17 March to Denny.

[2] Hamilton wrote on 14 March: 'On the twenty-fifth of this month we shall open a little temporary church built of stone at Buckfast Abbey. In the meanwhile we have brought to light by excavations the whole plan of the old Cistercian Abbey . . .'

[3] Lord O'Hagan, K.P., *Occasional Papers and Addresses*, London 1884, inscribed 'To His Eminence Cardinal Newman, with reverence and affection, O'Hagan, Biarritz, 19th Feb: '84'

Of course I am touched at your kindness in inserting in the volume your Edgbaston Address, and, though I am ashamed of the warmth of your language, I am very grateful for the friendliness which inspired it.[1]

I hope the account, which I have heard, is accurate, that you are gaining health and strength for the climate of Biarritz

With my best respects to Lady O'Hagan, I am My dear Lord,

Your faithful & Affectte Servt John H Card. Newman

TO ALEXANDER DENNY

March 17. 1884

Dear Mr Denny

I am quite sure it must be very painful to you to write the letter I have received[2] Also I doubt not that your difficulty arises from the zeal for an increased sale of my books which has led to some imprudence in sending out copies — but I am obliged to say in answer that I quite reckoned upon the notice which you sent me last December, that the full sum (220 I think) has been disposed of by me by anticipation, so it is a great disappointment to me; and of course I am glad to hear that you will pay me in April the balance due; but I ought to be sure that such an occurrence will not happen again. But it unsettles my views when I look on to the future; one thing I must say at once, and I hope you will not think me hard, that I must name shorter intervals than a year for the settlement of accounts. Also it weighs in favour of my selling the copyrights

TO EDWARD BELLASIS, JUNIOR

March 18. 1884

My dear Edward

Thank you for your Life of Gen. Gordon — and pray express to Mr (I can't recollect his name) my acknowledgments for his courtesy in sending me the translation of the 'Lead,' etc. Both writer and sender do me honour[3]

Yrs affly J H Card Newman

[1] This was the Address 'Cardinal Newman', op. cit. pp. 243–5, presented on 10 April 1880. See also *Add.* pp. 249–55.
[2] Denny wrote on 15 March: 'I herewith send a cheque for £100/–/– on account. — I have to express my extreme regret that I am not sending the whole amount due, but trade has been so unprecedently bad, and I have experienced such difficulty in collecting the money owing me, that I have found myself, unexpectedly, very short at my banker's. — I shall, however, settle the balance, during the course of next month . . .'
[3] Bellasis sent Archibald Forbes, *Chinese Gordon, A Succint Record of his Life*, London 1884, and a Latin translation of 'Lead kindly Light.' See also Edward Bellasis, *Coram Cardinali*, London 1917, p. 123.

March 18. 1884

My dear Lord Bishop

A Professor at Maynooth, in criticizing my Article on Inspiration, says, if I understand him rightly, that, though to believe that Nebuchodonossor was King of Nineveh is not de fide, still not to believe it is inconsistent with accepting Scripture as the Word of God.[1]

And I understand him to hold that 'Nebuchodonosor is King of Nineveh' is a certain proposition because it is an indisputable conclusion from a revealed premiss.

I have no difficulty in answering him if the point between us is a matter of reasoning and logic, but has it been *ruled in the schools*, that the conclusion *'this proposition about Nebuchodonosor is true,'* is an indisputable conclusion from *'Scripture is the Word of God?' Is* it necessarily inconsistent to believe that Scripture is *wholly* God's word, yet that He has not always spoken in that Word in the case of secular facts.

If the weight of authority in this particular case is so strong as to be decisive, I shall not appeal to logic.[2]

Most truly Yours J H. Card. Newman

[1] This was John Healy, a professor of theology at Maynooth, editor of the periodical in which his article appeared 'Cardinal Newman on the Inspiration of Scripture', the *Irish Ecclesiastical Record* (March 1884), pp. 137–49, reprinted in Healy's *Papers and Addresses*, Dublin 1909, pp. 404–17. See J. D. Holmes and R. Murray's edition of *On the Inspiration of Scripture*, pp. 37–41, who write 'he does not seem to have seen the problem. He showed no historical sense at all.'

[2] Clifford replied: 'The question you have put to me . . . lies at the root of the controversy we have to carry on with the opponents of Inspiration at the present day. I believe that it *is not* inconsistent. At the same time the contrary opinion seems most common. Archbishop Errington does not hold with me on this point. . . . St Thomas Summa. Pars I. Q. cii, art. 1 says — In omnibus quae *sic* (i.e. per modum narrationis historicae) Scriptura tradit, est pro fundamento tenenda veritas historiae. — This is true, but it is fair to ask 1st are all secular facts recorded in Scripture, narrated per modum narrationis historiae? are they not at times merely incidentally referred to? and 2dly Does Scripture always *teach* a fact or supposed fact because it refers to it? The incident related in the book of Judith (per modum narrationis historicae) is, that the King of Nineveh vanquished the King of the Medes. — It is incidentally mentioned that the name of the King of Nineveh was Babuchodonosor [sic]: but there seems no reason for holding that the name is more than incidentally given, as the name perhaps by which he was commonly spoken of by the Jews at the time when the Book of Judith was written, when the name of the more famous enemy of the Jews may have superseded that of the less known one. —

At the same time I must say the common opinion on the subject is stronger on the other side.'

Clifford asked for a copy of the 'Maynooth Professor's' words, if printed, and spoke of giving his own view and the reasons for it, in reply.

March 18 1884

My dear Lord Coleridge

Your letter was so complete and satisfactory that for that very reason I give you further trouble, as you encourage me to do. It is not a fancy that I am so weak in brain and fingers that I cannot write a sentence without a chance of mistake.[1]

Yes, I suppose for a year or two after my death my books might increase in circulation, but I have a profound impression that the age is as fickle in its literature as in its fashions. Every season brings its changes: books die yearly as leaves in October. Walter Scott is getting a mere name — it is enough to read a mere skeleton in the place of his novels. The competitive examinations here breathe a galvanic life into Addison, Pope, Johnson, etc. And consider this, my own writings are 'occasional' even in their titles. They are the record of accidental controversies, they are full of allusions which in little time it will require a commentary to explain. But I need not go on. What have you to put against this, but the partial judgment of a friend?

As to your question, of course [I] would gladly accept your offer of making inquiries for me — suppose you *can* have any leisure to use for that purpose even in the most leisurely way.

I will ask your confidence in naming the parties offering — Messrs Burns and Oates Granville Mansions, Oxford Street. Mr Oates is the acting man. He is young, his father having died prematurely. He is *said* to be less well off. He has just now offered £1000 for Formby's library.[2] I am told he is establishing a house in New York, where, I suppose, he would sell my books at half the English price. (An American publisher offered also to take a good number at half price.)[3]

It would not be fair to Oates to say simply 'he offered me £1000 down and £100 a year.' I pressed him to give me some vague idea of what the copyright would fetch when he first suggested purchasing — and he answered 'What should you say to £1000 down and £100 per ann.?'

Yours affectionately John H Card. Newman.

[1] After receiving Oates's letter of 14 March, Newman asked Lord Coleridge whether he should sell his copyrights and what he thought of the price offered. See letter of 14 March to Oates. Newman estimated that his books brought in about £200 a year. Coleridge replied on 17 March: 'The price offered you is altogether inadequate. Take £200 a year as the datum. I have to say £3500 or £4000 was nearer the mark than what is offered. *All* your works you know have 8 (or is it 6?) years after your death however long a time you may have published them. Many of them must have 20 — 30 — 35 years to run; and I think you must be conscious that yours is not a decaying reputation either as a Divine or as a literary man in general. . . . *many* years cannot in the nature of things be expected; but when it pleases God to leave us without you there will certainly be an immense interest for a time at least in your writings. . . . So that I do not think I overrate the value of your whole copyrights.' Lord Coleridge offered to make further enquiries. See letter of 29 April to him.
[2] Henry Formby died on 12 March.
[3] See letter of 8 Feb. to Kehoe.

March 19. 1884

My dear de Colyar

Thank you for your information, so prompt and complete. I take the up-shot to be, that the Oxford Society would not, in the present state of the Law, risk much more than the House tax if their landlord failed.[1]

Yours affectionately John H Card. Newman

P.S.   Are you not a great man to be in Paper Buildings? I have always looked up to them with great reverence from a boy.[2]

TO WILLIAM PHILIP GORDON

March 19. 1884

Dear Father Superior

What a pity I should be asked for more than I can possibly grant![3]

Three years ago, I was the first to move towards you, before any one had said a word to me, in order that we might end well with acts of grace on both sides; and, in the first page of the memorial which your Community accepted from me, I spoke of myself solely as a Cardinal.[4]

Both then, and the year before, I was indebted to you for acts of hospitality.[5]

Thus things seemed well settled: now all is reversed. I am appealed to in the name of St Philip to renew a tie which he broke thirty years ago; and am

---

[1] See letter of 15 March to de Colyar, who replied that Newman had understood him correctly. But later, on 21 July, he cited a more recent decision which changed the state of the case by defining 'lodger'.

[2] Paper Buildings in the Temple have retained their prestige.

[3] The Duke of Norfolk wrote to Newman on 18 March:
'Father Gordon is I believe writing to you to ask you to come to the opening of their new Church. He is in a state of great anxiety on the subject and I see that it will be a most bitter disappointment to them all if you are not able to come. I think it possible you may feel it easier to do so if you have a choice of houses to go to and I write therefore to say how very glad we shall be to see you here if such an arrangement should suit you better than going to the Oratory. . . .
I hope you will not think I am urging this in preference to your going to the Oratory. On the contrary I think you would find the Oratory the simplest and best plan and it would of course give much more pleasure to them but if you should prefer coming here I need not say how glad we shall be to see you.
It would be a terrible blow not only to the Fathers but to all of us who have any right to call St Philip our Father if you were not present at the opening and able to crown the work you set on foot.'
[4] See at 2 July 1881 the dedication in the first volume of the set of Newman's works, which he presented to the Fathers of the London Oratory. Also second note to letter of 23 March 1884 to the Duke of Norfolk.
[5] See letter of 18 June 1879 to the Duke of Norfolk, Appendix III to Volume 29, and letter of 14 April 1881 to Gordon.

asked to take part in an act, which concerns intimately and solely the London Oratory. Thus we shall end with a recognized disruption.[1]

Why could you not have sounded me, before you let the Duke write to me? Why did you so little consult for me as not to hinder his making a request to me, which I am obliged for so many reasons not to entertain? Have I shown anything but kindness to you personally?

I have delayed my answer to the Duke for several days. If you wish to be kind to me, prepare him in the interval for what that answer will be. It will, alas, be a disappointment to him, and to the kind hearts which surround him. But that is all you can do now.

God bless you

Yours affectionately John H Card. Newman

The Very Rev. Fr Gordon

TO H. P. LIDDON

March 19. 1884

My dear Canon Liddon

It is a pleasure to me to exercise my memory on dear Pusey, especially in relation to those early times, when he struck me so much as being the first good man I had come very near who was not an Evangelical

I wish I knew more on the point you mention. I recollect his interest in Dupuis and his theory, and that he was writing against it. I recollect even now what he told me about some of its ingenious absurdities and I bought the work of Dupuis in consequence, and it is now to be found in our Library here.[2]

---

[1] Had relations between Newman and the London Oratorians been normal, their invitation to him as founder would have been quite in order. The actual state of affairs was this: a false report had been spread by the London house in 1855–6 and later that Newman claimed formal power over them. See Newman's letter of 14 June 1856 to the Fathers of the Birmingham Oratory, and the correspondence between Birmingham and London early in July 1856; also notes at 27 and 28 Dec. 1855, and third note to letter of 17 Jan. 1856 to Caswall. This charge had been very damaging, a grave injustice, though initially based on a complete misunderstanding of Newman's representations to them; and it had been given wide publicity in London, in Rome, and among the Oratories of Italy. The charge had never been withdrawn. Newman's initiative in 'acts of grace', contained in his letter of 18 June 1879 to the Duke of Norfolk, was the courtesy of a Cardinal; the London house apparently read it as a condoning of the past. But the injustice remained, and with it the need to make public reparation, at least by some letter that could become part of history. 'St Philip' had 'broken a tie' in the sense that under his providence the situation had arisen, and had remained unrepaired; and Newman could only accept it, preserving as it did the legal and social separation normal between Oratories, but also involving the impossibility of completing his role as founder as if nothing had happened. See first draft of letter of 21 March 1884 to the Duke of Norfolk. The 'recognised disruption' was the impairing of pacific relations by recalling the past, which moreover could hardly be done without the reasons for it becoming to some extent public.

The responsibility of the London house in the matter was corporate; there were sixteen or seventeen priests there in 1884, of whom six or seven were already there in 1855–6, though only Stanton had taken a prominent part. See Volume 17.

[2] Charles François Dupuis (1742–1809), was a French infidel whose *Origine de tous les cultes, ou la religion universelle* was published in 1795. Newman's edition in ten volumes was that of Paris 1835–6.

As I knew he was writing against Dupuis, I must have known it was in behalf of someone, but I have no recollection of his speaking of anyone definitely, and I don't believe he ever mentioned the name of any one.

I believe, as you say, he was taken off his work by being sent to Germany by Lloyd.

Is Mr Hibbert alive? Does any thing come of mentioning his name? Has he relations who might be hurt? You alone can answer such questions?[1]

Very sincerely Yours John H Card. Newman

The Rev Canon Liddon &c &c

TO THE DUKE OF NORFOLK

March 19. 1884

My dear Duke

I am obliged to ask your leave to wait a day or two, before I answer your letter of yesterday[2]

Yours affectionately John H Card. Newman

His Grace The Duke of Norfolk E.M

TO MICHAEL FROST

March 20 1884

Sir,

I am not able to answer your question; of this only I am fairly sure that were the Established Church to lose its present high political and social position, this event would not be for the advantage of religion.[3] I consider Unbelief a worse evil than Protestantism, and the Protestant Establishment is, at least at present the most capable opponent in England of Unbelief. If the Establishment were removed a powerful obstacle to the spread of Unbelief would be removed at the same time; and while this is the case I do not see how its removal could be a benefit to Catholics[4]

J H N

[1] In 1823 Pusey was trying to convert an Eton school friend, Julian Hibbert, who had renounced Christianity and begun to associate with Richard Carlile and other freethinkers and extreme radicals. Pusey wrote long letters to Hibbert, began a refutation of Dupuis, and one of the reasons for his second visit to Germany in 1826 was to study the conflict between faith and rationalism at universities where it had long existed. See Liddon's *Pusey*, I, pp. 44–9 and 88–9. The above information is derived from the Oxford thesis of 1967 by D. W. F. Forrester, *The Intellectual Development of E. B. Pusey 1800–1850*, who writes, p. 43, Note 1, 'H. P. Liddon's account of this episode is inadequate and misleading. Though he recognized the significance of the event, Liddon concealed Hibbert's identity under the letter 'Z', gave the false impression that Hibbert was resident in France, referred to Pusey's brother's loss of faith as having occurred to an 'intimate friend' of Pusey's, and made no mention of Hibbert's radical activities.'

[2] Quoted in note to letter of 19 March to Gordon.

[3] In view of the controversy over the disestablishment of the Church of England, Frost asked on 14 March: 'Would the Catholic Church benefit by disestablishment of the English Church? if so, in what way?'

[4] See also letter of 23 March to Frost.

March 20. 1884

My dear Mr Fullerton

I grieve indeed at your account of dear Lady Georgiana's state of health. You speak of the prospect of her rallying to a certain point. Will you say to her, that, till this improvement takes place, it is my purpose, please God, to say Mass for her once a week.[1] Thank you, I am very well, but feeble

Most truly Yours John H. Card. Newman

A. G. Fullerton Esqr

TO JOHN P. MCINCROW

March 20. 1884.

Dear Rev. Sir[2]

I thank you for your publication and for the compliment you pay me in wishing me to send some lines to you for insertion — but, if you knew how it fatigued a man of my age to get through the ordinary duties of the day, you would excuse him for saying that he cannot go beyond them, and would not be surprised though he said that even a letter like this is too much for him. With my hearty blessing on your good work, sincerely Yours

J. H. Card. Newman

TO WILLIAM PHILIP GORDON

March 21. 1884

My dear Fr Superior

I am shocked to find I have said something in my letter to you, which seems to accuse you of 'presumption' I grieve this should be so, which is quite foreign to my intention; and I at once withdraw the phrase or sentence which is so unworthy of my writing and you receiving[3]

I am this evening writing to the Duke in great pain at the refusal I *must* give him

Yours affectly John H Card. Newman

[1] Lady Georgiana Fullerton died on 19 Jan. 1885.
[2] McIncrow was the priest at Amsterdam, in the diocese of Albany.
[3] In his letter of 20 March to which Newman is replying Gordon wrote: 'I cannot say how keen and how unexpected was the mortification I felt on reading your Eminence's letter this morning. An impression the very contrary of my intention has been given and I know how difficult it is to efface an impression once made.
Every act of kindness on the part of your Eminence to myself or to any member of our Congregation has been welcomed by me with joy and gratitude but I have never for a moment presumed on it, or have I ever put any interpretation on your Eminence's acts and words of kindness more than they most strictly expressed, and I am sure, if the Duke in his eager kindness had not written off at once, your Eminence would not have thought my invitation when it came, in any way presuming. What happened was this. Some of the Bishops had expressed a wish that our opening should take place in Low Week, that they might assist at it while they were in London. I went to Norfolk House for two purposes — one was to ask the

TO THE DUKE OF NORFOLK(DRAFT)[1]

Mar 21/84

My dear Duke

There are few wishes of yours to which I should not at once accede; and when I make your present proposal one of those exceptions my only consolation in my real pain in not complying with it is that the very earnestness with which you urge it upon me shows that you are partly prepared for its being very difficult for me to grant.

And indeed it is impossible for many and various reasons, among which I will only note this that I have been represented, at Rome and elsewhere as well as at home to my great disadvantage, as claiming formal power over the London Oratory, and that to participate in an act so simply internal to it as that to which you invite me ⟨under past circumstances⟩ would seem to justify ⟨countenance⟩ a charge as injurious to me as unfounded. This is not said in the spirit of controversy but because I was bound out of respect and love towards Your Grace not to send ⟨leave⟩ you a blank or a bald refusal You must kindly believe that my words mean more than they say.

I am sure you will trust me as writing seriously and deliberately, as being Your Grace's affectionate Servant

J H N

P S   Thank you kindly[?] for your offer, had I come to London to take me in at N. [Norfolk] House.

TO THE DUKE OF NORFOLK[2]

March 21. 1884

My dear Duke

There are few wishes of yours to which I should not at once acceed [sic]; and, when I make your present wish one of those exceptions my only

Duke whether Low Week would suit him and the other was to ask him whether if your Eminence honoured us with your presence he would be able to receive your Eminence in case you wished for greater quiet than we could promise in the bustle and confusion of such an occasion. The Duke said he would be most glad but I did not for a moment think he would write till I told him that your Eminence had consented to come. I went to him for my own information that I might, when the time came for writing to your Eminence not seem to be asking too much in the way of exposing you to fatigue.

I can now only leave myself in your Eminence's hands. Of the many Prelates who have kindly intimated their willingness to honour our opening, the presence of none would give us so much pleasure at that of your Eminence. To ask the favour is surely not presumption. We do it in all simplicity and if your Eminence cannot grant it, our great regret will not in any way lessen our gratitude for your Eminence's former condescension.

I beg to remain my dear Lord Cardinal with great respect
Yours most obediently & affectionately
William P. Gordon'

[1] This is the draft of Newman's reply to the Duke of Norfolk's letter of 18 March quoted in note to that of 19 March to W. P. Gordon. It is given in full for the sake of the explicit second paragraph, which Newman omitted in the letter as sent.
[2] This is the letter Newman actually sent in reply to that of 18 March from the Duke of Norfolk.

consolation in my real pain at not complying with it, is that the very earnestness with which you urge it upon me, shows that you are partly prepared for my finding it very difficult.

And indeed it is impossible, for many and various reasons. I will not say more, lest I should say too much; and, though I should say too little, this is the safer mistake. I am sure you will believe that I write seriously as well as deliberately

As to the world, every one who thinks about it at all, will impute my absence to old age, and with sufficient reason.

I am, My dear Duke, Your Grace's faithfully & afft Servt

John H Card. Newman

His Grace The Duke of Norfolk E.M.

TO EDWIN TREVELYAN

March 21   1884

Dear Mr Trevelyan

I am very glad to hear from you, and thank you for your letter, which I answer at once.[1]

I do not believe *any* statement of fact made about me by Bishop Wilberforce, because, from passages in his Life, which have already come before me, I know how little, in his statements about me, does he care about their accuracy.[2]

If any one really wishes to know what I said about the Anglican Church to Mr Isaac Williams in December, 1863, about which of course I cannot profess to make an act of memory at the distance of 21 years, he cannot do better than refer to my actually *published* words a few months later, in my Apologia as found in [Appendix] § 3 pp 23–30 in the Edition of 1864, and in Note E pp 339–342 in the edition of 1881

What I ever have said and do say now, is, that, if the Established Church was removed, a powerful obstacle to the spread of Unbelief in England

---

[1] Trevelyan, who had been living for six years at Combe Down, Bath, wrote on 20 March: 'You may remember me at the Oratory as a master for about a year, a Friend of Fr: Henry Bittlestone and late Vicar of Cannock; my name then was Edwin Trevelyan Smith; I have now for some time dropped by Deed Poll the last name . . .' Trevelyan then explained that 'just lately there has been a great Meeting of the Bath Church Defence Association at which a Mr Robinson lectured and a Mr Minchin in seconding a vote of thanks said "A combat was coming on not between Roman Catholic and Anglican etc but between the cross and the forces of agnosticism; what Church was capable of carrying on the warfare? Cardinal Newman had said 'Our Church cannot do it; the Church of England must do it.'"'

Trevelyan then wrote to ask C. H. Minchin where Newman's words were to be found, and sent his reply to Newman, who copied it out: 'In the third Volume [1882] of Bishop Wilberforce's Life p 100 the Bishop in a letter to Mr A. Gordon, dated Dec. 10. 1863 quotes from a then recent letter from Dr Newman to Isaac Williams the words I repeated the other day, "We can do nothing against it (i.e. the decay of faith) it all rests with your Church."'

[2] See letter of 26 Sept. 1880 to Bloxam.

would be removed with it. This I said in a letter, as it happens, only last night.[1]

You may make what use you please of this — I return your inclosure.

Very truly Yours John H Card Newman

March 23. 1884

Dear Sir,

I cannot give you my permission to publish my letter to you, because I have already published my opinion at *great length* is my Apologia to which I refer you. You will find the passage at Appendix 3, pp 23–28 of Edition 1864 and at Note E pp 339–342 of Edition 1881. This of course you may quote publicly.

Your faithful Servant J. H. Card. Newman

March 23. 1884

My dear Anne Mozley

I write a line to tell you that my poor brother Charles died yesterday. He must have had some curious natural gifts, for eccentric, violent and self-willed as he was, he attached to him the mother and daughter with whom he lodged and, the mother having died, the daughter has refused a nurse and has nurst him day and night through his last illness.

It is more than sixty years that he embraced and acted on the principles of Owen the Socialist.

He was past 80. I believe you just saw him once.[2]

Yours affecty John H. Card. Newman

[1] Letter of 20 March to Michael Frost.

[2] George Huntington, the Rector of Tenby, wrote on 23 March that Charles Robert Newman died 'without a struggle and apparently without pain.

I saw him several times and last on Thursday afternoon [20 March]. He had been very patient and gentle and I was much struck with the cleanliness and air of comfort in his person and surroundings   He had loving attention from Amy Griffiths, his waiting maid and every nourishment he could desire.

In my last interview I told him of the death of a young man here from cancer. I remarked that I was deeply thankful that this young man died "trusting in the mercy of God." "Of course you may well be Sir" was your Brother's reply. I then said "Are you afraid to die? Sir," to which with energy he replied, "Not in the least." I could not find him open to anything more directly on the Christian faith but his attendants say that he was patient gentle and resigned'

Huntington wrote again on 26 March to describe the funeral, which was taken by him and one of his curates. Newman arranged for the inscription on the tombstone, which had on one side 'Charles Robert Newman second son of John and Jemima Newman born June 16 1802. Died March 22 1884' and on the other the last verse of Psalm 137,

'Domine misericordia tua in seculum
Opera manuum tuarum ne despicias.'

TO THE DUKE OF NORFOLK   March 23. 1884

My dear Duke

I am quite distressed and ashamed that your kindness of heart has led you to so much annoyance and trouble.[1]

I assure you at once, in answer to your letter of the 21st that Fr Gordon's fear is quite unfounded, viz that you 'had said something in your letter to me, which I thought implied a wish on the part of the London Fathers to connect me with their undertakings in a way which they had never for a moment contemplated.'

Nor again did I think, or dream of thinking that any act of his was 'presumption', as in my letter to me he said that he feared.

No — but it is quite true that I was disturbed that he should have let you write to me, or have contemplated doing so himself and have told you he so contemplated. I thought he would have had such a vivid and delicate sense of the indelible relations which had been created years ago between the London Oratory and me, as would have warned him against an act which could only bring trouble to me and to him, and the like of which I had been very cautious myself not to commit.

Certainly Father Knox seemed to me not to forget those relations, on occasion of my offering my volumes to the Brompton Library, though I don't at all mean that he was uncivil.[2]

I end by thanking you and the Duchess, as I had intended to do in my first letter, for so kindly asking me to Norfolk House, had I gone after Easter to Town

My dear Duke of Norfolk
    Your affectionate friend & servant   John H. Card. Newman[3]

[1] The Duke of Norfolk wrote on 21 March a long letter which crossed that of Newman: 'Father Gordon told me yesterday that he had heard from you and that he feared you would not see your way to coming to the opening of their church. But he also said he feared I had said something in my letter to you which you thought implied a wish on their part to connect you with their undertakings in a way they would not be justified in doing and which they had never for a moment contemplated. I did not intend anything of the kind either but any impression I may have given you arose entirely from myself and not in the smallest way from the Oratory.' Towards the end the Duke said: 'I cannot but think too that if Father Gordon's fears are well founded you must have read my hurried letter in a sense I had not in my own mind. I have no copy of it but I think I said something of the grief all connected with St Philip would feel if you were not present at the opening and I spoke of it as the crowning of a work set on foot by you. I suppose I am right in believing that the Oratory in London would never have existed but for you and as they have been all this while in a temporary church I think their getting into their first permanent church is the crowning of their work. I am sure you will feel that when several of the Bishops have expressed a wish to be present if you an Oratorian Cardinal were not there it could not but be a source of great sorrow to us all.'
[2] At the end of his visit to the London Oratory in June 1881 Newman offered to present a set of his works to the library. See at 2 July 1881. Knox had taken a prominent part in the London house, acting as secretary in 1856. See also notes to letter of 15 Aug. 1856 to Cardinal Barnabò. The 'indelible relations' were created by the unjust accusations of those years, which had never been withdrawn then or since. The London Oratorians, for their part, could not or would not explain this aspect of the matter to the Duke.
[3] Newman's unexplicit letter of 21 March to the Duke of Norfolk meant that he indulged in speculation of his own. On 25 March he forwarded Newman's letters of 21 and 23 March

March 25. 1884

My dear Fr Superior

I thank you for your letter received yesterday, and in turn I sincerely withdraw any thing I have said which was unnecessary and inconsiderate towards you, for which I am very sorry, but it is most difficult to say just what one means, and nothing else.[1]

No one here, as far as I know, had, or has, any thought of my being asked to the opening of your Church, (so no harm is done,) or, as far as I have heard, has wished it. Rather, they have thought that a building on so grand a scale implied that *they* at Birmingham were very rich, and that impression in various ways has been a disadvantage to us.

I have for 30 years enlarged to every one who asked, what little intimacy, according to my experience, there is between the Italian Oratories: and kept a strict silence about any deeper cause in our case. I don't think then any remark will be made, especially considering my age, on my absence from your opening

Yours affectly John H Card. Newman

March 25. 1884.

Dear Professor Mivart,

Thank you for your kind notice of the loss of my brother. One thing I will take the opportunity of saying upon your letter of last week.[2] When I said to

to Gordon, with a covering one of his own, now at the London Oratory: 'I fear it looks as if it was not my letter but the mere fact of his being intended to receive an invitation to the opening which has affronted him.

Is it not likely that the two Novices having chosen London instead of Birmingham has re-opened all his old feelings. From what one knows of him is it not of all things the one most likely to work such an effect. Would it not seem to his mind almost as if the past were being acted over again. One of his consolations about the School was that it had at least brought Novices to the Oratory, yet here are two who though they join the Oratory will not stay with him. Again he may think that the glory and glamour of the new church may have had something to do with "drawing the young hearts from him". I cannot help thinking this must be the explanation and that he may really when he came to the Oratory have had more of a reconciliation in his mind but that he repents of it now.

I do not know what he alludes to about Father Knox but it cannot be a very recent occurrence and it looks therefore as if he were looking back in his mind for reasons to support his position. It is very sad. What can one do with such an extraordinary mind.'

Since the Oratory School had recently provided the Birmingham Oratory with five new members, the hypothesis about the two old boys who had joined the London Oratory was an unlikely one.

[1] Gordon wrote on 23 March: 'I can only again express my great sorrow at having most unintentionally displeased your Eminence. I regret very much having spoken to the Duke before I had written to your Eminence but it was in my mind a very preliminary step and I had no idea that the Duke would act upon it.

I could hardly have had a greater mortification than to have seemed wanting in appreciation of your Eminence's past kindness, and to have actually caused you annoyance by my want of tact and judgment.'

[2] See letter of 11 March to Mivart and notes there.

you that I should not have asked you to take part in Fr Parkinson's proposal, had I recollected that you were engaged in Mgr Capel's University College, I think you hardly understood my reason for saying so. My sole reason was that I should not have had the courage to ask you to take part in another forlorn hope, after you had already taken part in a first.

And now I should like to have said a good deal about your letter of yesterday, were it not that I am just now full of anxious business, and that, unless I husband my strength carefully, I shall be unable to meet what I feel is required of me. This has been the case with me in a measure all my life — but it is especially so now.

All I can say is in answer to your question, whether thirty years ago I realized the amount of good there was in the members of the Anglican Church. I think *I did*; I think my writings as an Anglican show it. I think the third Lecture, which you have been reading of my Catholic volume on the Difficulties of Anglicans shows it, to refer to nothing else.[1] If you say that that Lecture speaks of a good *set* of Anglicans, not of the Anglican Body, you must recollect that, both as an Anglican and as a Catholic, I have felt and professed distinctly 'Many are called, few are chosen.' Had I not a vivid sense of this, I could not have become a Catholic, for there are plenty of bad Catholics. My main argument for becoming a Catholic was that Anglicans themselves professed to believe that our Lord had set up a *Church*. Had He or had [He] not? If He had, then it was a teaching Church. What could it be else? Now the Church of England was not a teaching body — it was a house divided against itself.

This I say now. An experiment is going on; whether a Christian Church can be without a definite, recognized Creed. It is a problem which cannot be worked out in a generation. Nothing has happened to change the view I held 30 to 40 years ago. The Church of England has the 7000 in Israel which St Paul speaks of as being in the time of Elias. Still it was true that 'salvation was of the Jews.'[2]

Yours sincerely J. H. Card. Newman.[3]

[1] 'The Life of the Movement of 1833 not derived from the National Church', *Diff.* I, pp. 67–95.

[2] *Romans,* 11: 2–5; *John,* 4:22.

[3] F. Baelemanns wrote from Trinity College, Louvain, on 28 March: 'In May next, on the occasion of the 50th year of its foundation, the University of Louvain, in a solemn assembly presided by the Belgian Episcopate, will give degrees of honour to some of the learned men of the Catholic body.

The name of St George Mivart has been proposed.

Would your Eminence have no objection to say confidentially whether this name would likely be favourably received amongst the English Catholics.'

Newman wrote on this letter the summary of his reply: 'March 30/84 answered praising Professor Mivart but saying there was no Catholic "public opinion" in England.'

TO EDWARD BELLASIS, JUNIOR

Private   March 31. 1884.

My dear Edward,

I said to you in a recent letter something which from what has lately happened, I wish not to have said, about Ward and Vaughan.[1] I think I never wrote the words to any one else. I cannot withdraw them, for they are true — but I would thank you much *to burn them*.

Yours affectionately, John H. Newman

TO JOSEPH MONTEITH

March 31. 1884

My dear Joseph

I grieve to have your letter. I have been thinking about your dear Father lately wondering I have heard so little of him lately.[2] Say every thing most kind to him from me. I have put his name on our prayer list, and, please God, will lose no time to say Mass for him — With the kindest remembrances of your Mother and all of you, I am

Yours affectionately John H Card. Newman

P S   Fr Richard Bellasis sends you his kind remembrances

TO THE HON. FRANCES CHARLOTTE MONTGOMERY

[End of March 1884]

Thank you for your new volume.[3] It is full of beautiful thoughts — but I am too old to be able to read it as a whole and to do justice to it. And this I am sure you will make allowance for.

TO HENRY BEDFORD

April 1st. 1884.

My dear Mr. Bedford,

Perhaps you have heard that James Daly is gone. He died very happily receiving all the sacraments, looking death in the face, and waiting for it.[4]

I write to thank you for the trouble you took about him — and to ask you what I can do to show my gratitude to the Hospital. What are the rules of subscription etc.?[5]

Very sincerely yours, John H. Card. Newman

[1] Letter of 4 Feb. What had recently happened was evidently the invitation to the opening of the London Oratory church. Newman could not explain his inability to accept the invitation without recalling the actions of Faber and others in 1855–6. This, too, as the omitted paragraph in his letter of 21 March to the Duke of Norfolk shows, he was unwilling to do.

[2] Robert Monteith died in the evening of 31 March, after a short illness.

[3] *The Divine Ideal*, London 1884.

[4] See letter of 23 Jan. to Bedford.

[5] See end of letter of 5 June to Bedford.

TO JOHN HUNGERFORD POLLEN

April 1. 1884

My dear Pollen

I want to write you a *confidential* letter.

Perhaps I may want to make a present of Church Plate and can you take the trouble of going to the tip top goldsmiths, and looking at their wares. I don't wish to give more than £20. But I would go up to £50 for a really good thing.

I write on the supposition of your being allowed at such shops to inspect things and give trouble without opposition or grumbling.

The difficulty is what to look for, not an ordinary chalice — and I suppose a high Mass chalice would cost too much. Four candlesticks would need to suit an altar. A monstrance seems to me most likely. Is a crucifix suitable likely to be found?[1]

Yours affectly John H. Card. Newman

TO JAMES KNOWLES

To James Knowles Esqr Queen Anne's Lodge
St James's Park S W

April 2. 1884

My dear Mr Knowles

Your letter is a great blow to me, tho' I confess it is my own fault.[2] The notion of copyright did not come into my mind. The Rivingtons let me publish my articles in the British Critic as 'Essays' without disputing, rather with allowance the copyright was mine.

It is a matter of extreme consequence to me. Already the Article has been reviewed in a Catholic quarter with strange misquotations, and, to wait a year, to wait two months may inflict upon me very great harm — as to a year, shall I then be alive?

Would the following plan do? ⟨it has the advantage for you as well as for me⟩ I would purchase of your publishers a number of copies of your February number at the selling price — I would separate my article there from the other articles — I would add to each as an appendix a series of the Notes which I mean to add in explanation of the Essay; and I would sell the pamph-

---

[1] Pollen replied on 2 April, 'I will go and look out to-day at Messrs Lamberts (where I can rummage unchided)' Newman presented a chalice to the London Oratory. See letters of 6, 9 and 25 April to Pollen.

[2] Newman wished to republish his article 'On the Inspiration of Scripture' with a 'Postscript' in reply to John Healy. See letter of 18 March to Bishop Clifford and cf. that of 16 Feb. to Oates. Knowles, editor of the *Nineteenth Century* replied on 1 April to a request from Newman: 'I scarcely ever agree to reprints from "the XIX Centy" (unless by some special previous arrangement) until after a full year has elapsed from the date of an article's first appearance in the Review. This is taking one year's lease of my legal term instead of 28.' Knowles, who wanted his review to have 'the character of permanence', suggested he might publish a 'second edition' of part of the February number.

let thus formed at Messrs Burns's for a shilling — stating in a title page that it comes from the Nineteenth Review.

I have no time to lose. I am already having it translated into Italian, and if it be necessary must ask your leave.[1] You have no idea how important it is to me

JHN

April 3. 1884

My dear Father Superior

I suppose some of our party here will be going up to the opening of your new Church. I want your Fathers to accept from me an offering for one of its altars or devotions, which I should send up to you with a letter by them.

I write to you now, knowing how many precious gifts you have, in order to ascertain in what special department[2]

April 3. 1884

(answer of a letter from the Duke to Fr John Norris)[3]

Alas, alas, why did I not confine myself to the true and sufficient reason that I was too old, too infirm, too worn in mind to leave home? That, my dear Duke, would have been my proper answer to you and there would have been an end of it — but, wishing to be frank with one whom I so greatly respect and love I said more ⟨too much⟩ and have involved myself in a correspondence which I cannot carry through; for the weariness, which unfits me for going to London, unfits me for letter writing.

[1] Knowles replied on 3 April, 'I have not the very least objection to an Italian translation being made — provided it states that it is "translated by permission from the Nineteenth Century"'

[2] The letter as sent ended thus. The draft continued, 'it would be most welcome to you JHN'.

Gordon replied on 5 April, 'Your Eminence's kind letter was a great consolation to me and our Fathers are most grateful for your promised present to our church.

Your Eminence bids me tell you "in what special department a gift would be most welcome". I venture therefore to say that its great value in our eyes would be its being a memorial of your Eminence and we should therefore like some object that would endure and could be preserved in our sacristy with other gifts that have a special value on account of their donors.'

[3] On 25 March Norris replied to a letter from Gordon about Newman's declining to be present for the opening of the London Oratory church. Norris said that if the Duke of Norfolk wrote to him, he could approach Newman with his letter, in the hope that he might alter his decision, 'it is too sad!' Norris had joined the Birmingham Oratory nine years after the breach, from which time Newman had enjoined silence on its members. He can have known little of the circumstances. Norris continued, 'As to inviting the Fathers generally — do so by all means — we should not like to be left out — we want to share your joy — perhaps the best way would be to send the invitation to us as a body.' Norris concluded, 'Be sure that I am ready to do any thing and everything I possibly can to put this dreadfully crooked matter straight.' On 30 March Norris wrote again to Gordon, 'The Cardinal will make no objection to our coming — so send your invitations as soon as you like'. The Duke, who quite misunderstood Newman's reasons, wrote to Norris on 31 March a letter no longer to be found. This is the draft of Newman's reply.

Oratories were never meant to be intimate. I have done what I could. I have written to Fr Gordon to ask if [of] his Fathers to accept from me, an offering for their New Church. This I should send with a kind letter to him.[1]

I know how good you are. Do you think it does not annoy me to vex you; but be sure, the less said, the soonest mended.

J H N

TO JAMES KNOWLES

April 4. 1884

Dear Mr Knowles

Thank you for your letter, and its offer.[2] At first sight, your proposal is one which ought to satisfy me, but I am not quite clear on one or two points. First, would the second edition of my Essay (with its Postscript) be published by itself or with others in the same fasciculus? I doubt whether my essay would sell at all among Catholics unless it was published by itself.[3] On the other hand, I think you are hardly aware how few I expect will be wanted in any case. I very much doubt whether your publishers would find a second edition pay the printing. This difficulty I suppose you obviate by my being answerable for the expense, which I suppose could be done in some way that would not interfere with your copyright. I doubt whether even 50 copies would sell. What I want is a reprint with the Postscript for those whom it concerns, and for those who have been misinformed about it. Further, I should wish to put a title page to this effect 'Inquiry into what must be internally accepted by Catholics as of *de fide* obligation about Scripture and its interpetation,' reprinted *verbatim* from the Nineteenth Century.

Of course I should like to write the Postscript off for publication in May, if I could, but I work slowly now both in brain and fingers.

J H N

James Knowles Esqr

TO JAMES KNOWLES

April 6. 1884

Dear Mr Knowles

My head gets confused. If I am making any mistake, pardon me — but I consider I accept what you offer.

I put aside the notion of the 50 copies of edition 1, which you considerately offer me at a wholesale price, and shall send them back to Messrs Kegan Paul and Co, when they arrive.

---

[1] Three of the Birmingham Oratorians went to London for the opening of the London Oratory church on 25 April.

[2] Knowles wrote on 3 April that he had no objection to Newman's proposal of 2 April, but thought it would be cheaper to issue a second edition of the article itself with the Postscript and that this could be done immediately.

[3] Knowles replied on 5 April that his proposal had been for a second edition of the article, with Postscript, by itself.

I accept your offer of a second edition, you choosing size, type etc and naming on starting number of my copies, and I guaranteeing to make up any deficiency in the sale as set against the cost of printing my copies

And I don't see a difficulty in your making my Article one of a set, that is, selling it bound up with other articles of the Nineteenth century, so that it is professedly your doing (as owning the copyright) without my having part in it, and if my copies are separated from yours.

I should wish to print my Article *verbatim*, saying so on the Title page. The Postscript would not be (I expect) as long as it.

I should like the (1. 2. 3. 4. etc) Paragraphs divided from each other, the numeral being in the middle of the line, both in essay and Postscript (thus:
1
It has been lately said etc)

As to what I consider the number of copies likely to be sold, I was only thinking of Catholics. Whether there would be a Protestant sale of an Essay of mine on Inspiration, I cannot tell. Perhaps, if the type might be kept standing for a month, one should be able to see.

Very truly yours John H. Card. Newman

P.S.   The Essay might be printed (the second edition) at once. As far as I am concerned, the Postscript would follow it very soon — but I can't be sure of the Revisors to whom I should think it prudent to send it.

April 7.   There is one other point which I am not clear about. Whose business is it to circulate and to advertise my copies? Will Messrs Kegan Paul do it for the xixth Cent. or do I get Messrs Burns to do it? I have very little idea, that my Essay now will carry its own sale, tho' it might in February[1]

TO JOHN HUNGERFORD POLLEN

April 6. 1884

Private

My dear Pollen

I won't say a word about Hope Scott to-day, as I wish to be brief.[2]

Thanks for your promptness. It is to be a present to the London Oratory on the opening of their Church.[3]

After writing to you it struck me to write to Fr Gordon, lest I should be merely adding to their overabundant treasures. I am glad I did so for they want *nothing*. Only they would like much some *memorial* of me to be put up in the sacristy.

---

[1] Knowles replied on 10 April that Kegan Paul and Trench would advertise and circulate.
[2] Pollen wrote on 2 April: 'I am reading the life of Hope Scott. It is very well done. Curiously enough I was myself asked to do it and began some preliminary M.S. for it. Lord H. Kerr promised to send me the correspondence in his possession. But this never came — nor could I get any answer to a letter of enquiry. I thought the proposal was dropped.
I could have filled up the picture had I known it was fairly in other hands with extracts from diaries at Abbotsford and Merton College and elsewhere.' Pollen added that it was 'a faithful sketch of the noble and beautiful subject of it.' See letter of 25 April to Pollen.
[3] See letter of 1 April to Pollen.

As I am rather hard up for money just now, this is a relief to me — for a mere memorial need not be splendid.

Consequently, I should not wish to go beyond £20.

What I would ask you to do, if there is no reason against it, would be for you to call on Fr Gordon and settle with him about it   Excuse me

Yours affectly John H Card. Newman

TO JOHN HUNGERFORD POLLEN

April 9. 1884

My dear Pollen

Many thanks for your great despatch. I choose the chalice £23. (I don't want to see it) and   [1] to send you back your letters with the chalice in red ink.

One condition I make, which I suppose is of very possible performance, [1]try room for an inscription. Could the inscription be engraved by the proper day April 25? I suppose I must not make this a *condition*, as it may be impossible. In great haste

Ever yrs affectly J H Card Newman

INSCRIPTION   Te judice, for I have forgotten my Latin

Fratribus Londoniensibus suis
Templum novum et splendidissimum
Jam nunc introeuntibus
    in memoriam rei
       Joan H. Card Newman

N.B.   I am very diffident about the Latinity, I suppose I ought to see a *proof*.[2]

TO EDMUND STONOR

April 10. 1884

My dear Monsignor Stonor

I thank you much for reminding me, and inclose a cheque for £20[3]

Make my condolements to the Priests at S. Giorgio at their loss.[4]

I am told you have had a beautiful season at Rome this winter — but the experience of individuals varies so much in such matters.

Our Fathers send you their kindest remembrances and I am, My dear Monsignor Stonor

Sincerely Yours John H Card. Newman

---

[1] Words omitted by the copyist as illegible.
[2] Pollen replied on 10 April, 'what fetches me quite unmistakeably is my being tutor to Yr E. in the Latin Language.' The inscription on the chalice is as Newman here wrote it.
[3] This was a payment for Newman's titular church of S. Giorgio in Velabro.
[4] Stonor wrote on 24 Jan. that one of the Canons of S. Giorgio had died.

TO W. H. KEATING

April 23. 1884

My dear Sir

I thank you heartily for the very kindly worded letter, which I received from you with your book.[1]

I never have been a politician, and do not pretend to have an opinion how best wrong may be set right. But I know that a Catholic University is Ireland's due, and I cannot understand why she has been so long refused it   It is then most welcome news to me to hear from you, if I understand you, that there is a fresh prospect of a supply of this great need

Very truly Yours John H. Card. Newman

W. H. Keating Esqr

TO JAMES KNOWLES

April 23. 1884

in substance

Dear Mr Knowles

My copy of Postscript is ready for the Press. It is about ⅔ rds of the Essay itself. I shall send it to a friend to read which will take a day or two — I cannot, however, put in the references in it to the Essay till I see the new Edition of the Essay — I should like it advertised as soon as possible, that Professor Healy may know I am not going to leave him alone. My best chance of its finding readers is the United States — the next Ireland — the worst England. I send the Title page over leaf

Very truly Yrs J H N

Title Page
What is of obligation for a Catholic to believe
concerning the inspiration of Canonical Scripture
reprinted *verbatim* from the xix Century Review
with a Postscript
in answer to Professor Healy
by
John H. Card. Newman[2]

[1] Keating, who wrote from 10 Lower Sherrard Street, Dublin, sent a small book he had written concerning the Catholic University of Ireland.

[2] On 26 April Knowles sent a proof of the reprint, but advised against the use of the word 'verbatim', since it implied a doubt which the word 'reprint' should prevent. See letter of 30 April to Knowles.

TO ROBERT ORNSBY

April 23. 1884

My dear Ornsby

All the blessings of Easter to you and Mrs Ornsby. I was glad to hear from Mrs M. Scott that the Memoir has already [come] to a second Edition. There seems a general opinion that your part is well done. I got home with Fr St John Dec 24. 1847, making a great effort to get home for our Christmas dinner, and finding every one engaged, so that we dined tête a tête at Hatchetts White Horse cellar Coffee Rooms[1]

Yours very truly J. H. Card Newman

TO JOHN T. SECCOMBE

April 23. 1884

Dear Sir

I thank you for naming to me the Duke of Argyll's recent work. His Grace had the goodness to send it to me. And I have read quite enough to understand how fully it deserves your eulogy[2]

Your faithful Servant John H. Card. Newman

TO HENRY JAMES COLERIDGE

April 24. 1884

My dear Fr Coleridge

I opened your letter in great discouragement which turned at once to great joy You are sure of course, there are no *other* promises. This thought has been teazing me. I have burnt your letter[3]

Yrs affly J hon [sic] Card. Newman

TO ROBERT CHARLES JENKINS

April 24. 1884

My dear Canon Jenkins

I smile at your fancying I could do you good in an Inscription. Yours is grammatically and classically perfect. Of course I could not expect you to write 'Orate pro anima'.[4]

---

[1] Ornsby had stated in the first edition of his *Memoirs of James Robert Hope-Scott*, II, p. 64, that Newman was in Rome 'to the beginning of 1848'.
[2] See letter of 6 Feb. to the Duke of Argyll, whose *The Unity of Nature* Seccombe on 5 April recommended as congenial to Newman's own line of thought.
[3] The reference has not been traced.
[4] On 31 March Jenkins sent his proposed inscription in memory of Thomas Duffyn, Vicar of Lyminge 1480–1508, who built the tower of the church, 'D. Thomae Duffyn, Presb.
  Hujus Eccles . . . Vicar.
  Campanilis ejusdem Fundatori
  Juxta Altare . . . sepulto.'

I ought to have answered you sooner — but my fingers move slowly, and I cannot write without pain.

Very sincerely yours John H. Card. Newman

TO JOHN HUNGERFORD POLLEN

April 25. 1884

My dear Pollen

Thanks for your trouble, considerable as it was and for your success You have done me a great service. Three of our Fathers were bearers of the gift to London; so, unless it falls between them according to the proverb of the two stools, I suppose it is sure to arrive at its destination.[1]

I want to write to you about Hope Scott's Life, if I can say all I want to say. I never heard your name mentioned for the purpose, and was surprised on reading your late letter that, when asked by the family I had never thought of you — My heart and judgment would have leapt at the notion.

I can only say in explanation that my memory is bad now, and I did not recollect, or did not know, your relation with Hope. Of course, I knew you had been a fellow of Merton but you were not so when I was in Oxford — I did not know you till I was a Catholic, nor Hope as an Oxford man after 1844.[2]

Soon after Hope's death the family asked me, if I could recommend some-one for a Memoir, I could think of no one but Ornsby — and I at once named him. My reasons were that he knew Hope Scott — Hope had asked him to meet me at Abbotsford the summer before his death, so that he naturally came into my head — he was Librarian at Arundel — and he travelled with the present Duke into the East. And I know he was very painstaking, a par excellence littérateur, and versed in biography — I think he had given lectures on the Life and writing of Seneca, perhaps of others, so I named him. But I heard nothing more about the Memoirs for years, when suddenly I found Ornsby was upon it. He took great pains with it — came here with his manu-script and made me read it. After that he almost re-wrote it — and I think I have read it twice before publication since it has been in type I never heard a single word about you from first to last — and am quite puzzled. Most critics have as you been pleased with Ornsby's work — but you would have entered into Hope's character in a far deeper way — He is a literary man, but not a man of the world — still his praise is that he has let Hope speak for himself

Yours affectly John H. Card Newman[3]

[1] This refers to Newman's present of a chalice on occasion of the opening on 25 April of the church of the London Oratory. See letters of 6 and 9 April to Pollen. W. P. Gordon wrote on 28 April: 'The very handsome present by which your Eminence conveyed your congratula-tions to us on the opening of our church gave us all great pleasure and with this kind thought of your Eminence nothing seemed wanting to our joy. . . . It was very kind of your Fathers to come in such force it was difficult for me with so many guests to say all that I felt to indi-viduals.'

[2] Hope-Scott was a Fellow of Merton College, 1833–47, and Pollen 1842–52.

[3] Pollen on 26 April described at length Hope-Scott's character and the worldly pro-mises before him: yet he kept steadily to the confession of the truth 'through all consequences'.

347

TO LADY SIMEON

My dear Lady Simeon

April 25. 1884

I hope you will not think me ungrateful of the great kindness and considerateness you always show to me who so little deserve it, if I say simply that to write verses is simply out of my *power*.

I rejoice to be told of your own purpose of making a collection, and earnestly trust you will carry it out, but I have no [more] power whatever in taking part in it myself, than in riding a bicycle.

It seems very unkind in me, and I cannot explain it, but I cannot write prose or verse, because I will to write it, nor, if I do it to-day, can I therefore do it to-morrow.

Fr Caswall had the gift that, if a stranger wrote to him saying 'Will you write me a poem on the Pope's white skull cap', he could sit down and write it off. *I* cannot for a *friend*.

And now especially my brain works slow, and I cannot tell whether I am not getting much weaker than I was, but I suspect it.

Thank you from my heart for your thoughtful and sympathetic words about my brother, but to thank you is all I can do.

I have just had a new Edition printed of Fr. Caswall's Lyra Catholica. He apparently wished to publish a standard Edition of all his Poems in one volume. This led to his correcting the Lyra Catholica, destroying its identity, and throwing it out of print. His Executors have now published it by itself with his last corrections, and I hope it will sell.[1] Thank you for thinking of his memorial — there is, I suppose, no hurry.

I never saw an instance so like what one gathers from the gospels and from history, of a possession, as what has lately come before me. One time the poor subject speaking in the tone and with the feeling and the faith of a good religious priest — and then as distinctly and determinately denying the existence of God and opening the way to an all miserable future. God keep us all.[2]

Yours affectionately, John H. Card. Newman.

The Honble. Lady Simeon

TO THE HON. MRS MAXWELL-SCOTT

My dear Mamo

April 26. 1884

Thank you for your good news about the Memoir.[3] It has excited great interest. Thanks too for your promise of your own Article. And especially for your promised prayer in my behalf in St Ignatius's room.[4]

[1] Edward Caswall, *Lyra Catholica*, London 1884, first published 1849.
[2] cf. letter of 4 Nov. 1883 to Ignatius Ryder.
[3] This refers to the second edition of the *Memoirs of James Robert Hope-Scott*.
[4] Mrs Maxwell-Scott wrote from Biarritz, en route for Rome.

I am sorry to hear of your husband's troublesome companion — but it can't last in so young a man.

My difficulty about a portrait of your dear Father is that none is good enough to please me, though not from fault of the artists, but from the necessity of the case.

Thank you for inquiring after my health. I am very well, but am very weak. I cannot well walk, or talk or hear or write or read or see, but have no ailment.

My kindest regards to Mr Maxwell Scott

Yours affectly John H Card. Newman

TO ROBERT ORNSBY

April 28. 1884

My dear Professor Ornsby

Thank you for your notice. I should like to see the new letters or parts of letters of mine which are to come into the Second Edition of the Memoir.[1] I will return them at once.

The parcel has just come.[2] As to the passage in 1852, I read it thus,

'by rest I understand and suspect your doctor *means* total' etc.[3]

I am sure of it, and not only as a question of penmanship but because a verb is wanting, and because J.R.II.S. would not have written Dr as 'Doctor' in the Irish way, and because my Advisers were Dr Evans of Birmingham and Sir Benjamin Brodie, perhaps Mr Babington.

Yrs affly J H Card. Newman

Fr Bellasis is surprised his father's name does not occur more in the Memoir — at least that it is not mentioned as being that of one of the 'Parliamentary bar.'[4]

TO LORD COLERIDGE

April 29. 1884

My dear Lord Coleridge

Thank you for applying for me to Longman and sending me his satisfactory answer.[5] I have been trying to get together the facts necessary for him to have before him before he can form a judgment on which to act; But am I bound to accept his offer? I suppose not.

---

[1] Newman was told of these letters by Ornsby on 26 April, but see letter of 30 April to him.

[2] Ornsby was returning the letters Hope-Scott wrote to Newman.

[3] Newman so read the passage which Ornsby had printed in his first edition of *Memoirs*, I, p. 142, thus: 'by rest I understand, and I suspect from Dr. Murray (?), total'.

[4] See letter of 2 May to Ornsby.

[5] See letter of 18 March to Lord Coleridge, who on 16 April sent Newman letters he had received from John Murray and Charles James Longman. The former did not feel able to purchase the copyrights of Newman's works, the latter said on 14 April, 'We should have much pleasure in becoming the purchasers of these copy-rights, on suitable terms.'

There is another question which you can answer for me. What my publications have brought in the last 20 years. I attempted to tell you, but made a hideous mistake. The gain has been far more than an average £200 a year which I told you: in fact it is in the course of 20 years £7731. 5. 8. which gives an average per annum of a little more than £380   Ought I in the details I put before him, number of volumes, date, stock, etc mention this average gain? No hurry for an answer[1]

J H N

TO ANNE MOZLEY

April 29. 1884

My dear Anne Mozley

I suppose from your letter I did not answer your last. I meant to do so, but a day or two ago, I began to ask myself whether I had.

Of course I cannot but be pleased with what James says of me — but I am in a most sensitive state as to what your collection of Letters is likely to say about my belongings.[2] About me and in my lifetime things are said, which about Keble, and I may say Pusey, are not said after their death. As your Collection is now in print, of course I must bear it (don't take this as said harshly). Your brother Tom knocked me down.[3] I have not got on my legs again yet, nor am I likely. I take it as a penance from above, a penance of ill-speaking about me, so full of untruths that it is safe from having an answer. It has set the fashion. Just now my poor brother Charles finds matter for the Athenaeum and Catholic papers.[4] The account, whatever it may be, is taken

___

[1] Lord Coleridge replied on 30 April: 'Certainly you are in no way at all bound to accept Longman's offer. The Statement you are preparing I should submit to one or two other men and compare their offers; so it is well worth having it done.
I don't think the gain on the publications at all signifies in the first instance. The publisher will make his offer from his knowledge of the bookmarket and his general skill in foretelling what will and will not sell in years to come. Of course if Longman asks you might think it right *in confidence* to tell him'

[2] Anne Mozley, at the suggestion of Dean Church, was preparing her *Letters of the Rev. J. B. Mozley, D.D., edited by his Sister*, London 1885. She wrote to Newman on 24 March: 'Now I am aware it is impossible to omit your name even if I wished it which I am very far from doing. Your influence, for all that has passed, has been a mighty one; *intellectually*, I may at any rate say on both my brothers   Of course I would not consciously [?] put in any thing you would not like, and remembering how vexed you might reasonably be with parts of Tom's book [T. Mozley, *Reminiscences chiefly of Oriel College and the Oxford Movement*] I am nervous and feel as if approaching a most tender subject, but really I do little more than illustrate by passages of letters of James what you say in the Apologia'

[3] See letter of 22 Feb. 1884 to G. T. Edwards.

[4] The *Weekly Register* (26 April 1884), p. 531 had a notice: 'A singularly unfortunate and misleading paragraph about the late Mr. Charles Newman has been communicated to the Athenaeum by Precentor Venables. To drag before the public doubtful but not easily refuted statements of events happening forty or fifty years ago, and concerning a person who has just been carried to the grave, but who had no claim to public attention other than that he bore a name which two of his brothers have made famous, is a proceeding which seems strange on the part of a clergyman who has, presumably, the feelings of a just and gentle man. But Precentor Venables has not been content merely to make use of the names of Cardinal Newman and of Mr. F. W. Newman to give some sort of point to his singularly ill-conceived narrative;

for gospel, because it ministers to a thirst. Why is 'Harriett' brought in? If on account of her clever books, well and good. So Mr Kegan Paul brought her in in a short memoir of me —[1] but is this so in other cases? And what have 'the Newmans' to do with public talk?[2]

TO WILFRID OATES

April 29 1884

sent

Dear Mr Oates

I shall not give up my proposal to sell my copyrights, but the sum you threw out for purchase does not at all correspond to what the sale of the last 20 years would justify me in anticipating in the next 20.[3]

J H N

P.S. My Article on Inspiration will be sold by Messrs Kegan Paul and Co for /6

TO JAMES KNOWLES

April 30. 1884

Dear Mr Knowles

You have no time for writing any more than I, but I must apologise for what I would gladly spare you.[4]

If the copyright of my Postscript becomes yours by your printing it in one

he charges them with having, in their Evangelical days, "cast off" their brother because he was an infidel; and implies that they left him in a position of some pecuniary need when they might have relieved him. This at least, among all the statements made by the Precentor, is one of which the truth can be easily ascertained; and we are able to say on the authority of one who cannot be in error, that there is not the very slightest foundation for the statement or the implication so recklessly made . . .'

The *Athenaeum* (19 April 1884), p. 475, published a letter from Edmund Venables, who became a curate under J. C. Hare at Hurstmonceaux in 1844. From Archdeacon Hare he heard an account of Charles Newman, who had been an usher in a school there at some time in the previous decade. He was said to have been dismissed for biting one of a number of boys who set upon him. Venables concluded: 'Hare, I remember, used to make excuses for Newman's religious and moral obliquities on the ground of partial insanity. "There was a screw loose somewhere."'

[1] This was in Kegan Paul's article 'John Henry Cardinal Newman', the *Century Illustrated Monthly Magazine* (June 1882), p. 274, where Harriett Newman's novels were mentioned.

[2] Anne Mozley began her reply of 30 April 'I have been exceedingly touched by your letter, both by the trouble the thought [?] of the coming volume has caused you and the confidence you have placed in me. The page you wish me to burn shall be burnt before the day ends.' This evidently explains why Newman's letter is incomplete.

Anne Mozley added 'By this post you will receive all the proofs that have come to me so far.' See letter of 4 May to her.

[3] See letter of 14 March to Oates. Newman noted at the bottom of his present draft, 'N B he offered £1000 and £100 a year, that is £150 yearly — but the average of 20 years by return of the Income Tax Office is £380 per annum' See letter of 9 June to Oates.

[4] This letter crossed with Knowles's of the same date, in which he reaffirmed that the copyright of the reprint would be his, and offered to print Newman's Postscript in the June number of the *Nineteenth Century* before it appeared with the reprint. On the same day Newman made a memorandum:

'1 to publish only my postscript 2 to prefix a resume or table of contents of the original article, and of the points which Professor Healy has urged against it and heads of the Postscript.'

351

pamphlet with the original Article, the xixth Century will gain nothing by it, for you cannot use the memorandum rising out of a past article and a private quarrel, such as the Postscript is. On the other hand, if the copyright of it is not mine, it may be of serious consequence to me since I have a personal antagonist.

This obliges me to ascertain whether the new Pamphlet is yours, you issuing, selling and paying for it, or whether it is, from first to last, mine, with a notice on the Title page that the original Article is re-printed etc by me by your express permission.

We must recollect that the future is concerned, in which we do not decide merely for ourselves, but for representatives.

Excuse my weak memory and confusion of head.

Yours very truly John H. Card. Newman

P.S.   Since writing the above, Mr Lilly's volume has come to me. I see that one of his chapters *appeared in the xixth century*[1]

TO ROBERT ORNSBY

Dear Ornsby

April 30. 1884

Since you tell me the sheets are printed off, and the additions are immaterial, I am writing to the Printers not to send me the sheets, nor do I wish any from you[2]

Yrs affly John H Card. Newman

TO THE MAYOR AND MAYORESS OF WOLVERHAMPTON

[May 1884]

Cardinal Newman feels the honour done him by the Mayor and M [Mayoress] of [Wolverhampton] in the invitation of him to the opening of the Art Gallery and to the luncheon thereupon on Friday May 30 and regrets that his advanced age deprives him of the pleasure of accepting it.[3]

TO JOHN PERCIVAL

[May 1884]

Cardinal Newman begs to express to the President and Bursar of Trinity College his warm sense of their invitation to dinner on Trinity Monday June 9 and his regret, that, as before, his advanced age prevents him from the pleasure of avail[ing] himself of it

[1] The first chapter of W. S. Lilly's *Ancient Religion and Modern Thought*, London 1884, was a version of an article in the *Ninteenth Century* and was inserted with the editor's permission. Knowles agreed that this was so, but he felt obliged to alter a custom which had become too frequent.
[2] See letter of 28 April to Ornsby.
[3] The Art Gallery at Wolverhampton was opened on 30 May 1884 by Lord Wrottesley, the Lord Lieutenant of Staffordshire, after which the Mayor and Mayoress entertained a large party to lunch.

May 1. 1884

Dear Mr Knowles

Thank you for your letter of last night which has decided my course.[1] I will not attempt impossibilities. I give up the idea of a separate edition of my February Article and am writing to Messrs Paul and Co to be so good as to send me a statement of every expense I may have incurred by my attempt.[2]

I shall publish my Postscript by itself in my own type and size, at my own publishers — they have correspondents in Ireland and America

Yours etc   J H N

I shall put the following title page
('What is of obligation for a Catholic to believe
about the inspiration of the Canonical Scripture
an answer to Professor Healy's criticism
to an article in the Febr. number of the Nineteenth Century Review
by
Cardinal Newman'
and to introduce this Postscript I shall prefix a few lines, or a table of contents, stating the subject discussed in the Article of February.)

TO ROBERT ORNSBY

May 2. 1884

Dear Ornsby

I could not, thank you, write any thing myself at the end of your second volume — but Fr Bellasis would be pleased, if you could add the inclosed at the end as a notice of his Father[3]

TO MESSRS KEGAN PAUL, TRENCH AND CO.

May 3. 1884

Messrs Kegan Paul and Co

Cardinal Newman begs to apologize to Messrs Kegan Paul and Co for asking them to advertise a pamphlet for him and then withdrawing the order.

As far as he can anticipate, his purpose as regards his Article in the xix century continues as it was, and is only postponed, and that in consequence of the difficulty of putting it under one copy with the Postscript, without thereby losing the copyright of the latter

[1]What decided Newman is clear from a crossed-out draft of this letter: 'I never could have precluded myself from using my own work, as I thought of it and I fancied I was so doing. I did not expect a battle, but I cannot fight with my arms and legs shackled. I cannot part with the copyright of the Postscript.
I think I must return to my original idea, into which you so kindly entered . . .' namely to buy copies of the *Nineteenth Century* for Feb. and append the *Postscript* to his article there.
[2] See letter of 3 May to Knowles.
[3] See postscript to letter of 28 April to Ornsby.

May 3. 1884

Dear Mr Knowles

I thank you for your considered offer, but I am distinctly of opinion that it will be best for me not to accept it just now.[1]

I think it best to publish now my Postscript separate from the Article, and I hope the Notice the first lines of which I inclose will remove your disappointment at my doing so. I therein profess publicly my loyalty to your Rules, yet do not deny that at a later date I shall be pleased at your relaxing them, and in the sequel of the Notice I give some short account of my February Article[2]

TO ANNE MOZLEY

May 4. 1884

My dear Anne Mozley

I know how much I must try you, and will say as little as I can. My eyes don't read writing well now, — but I did find from you that your brother Tom was bringing out, as I feared, fresh volumes, with no assurance that I did not directly or indirectly, come in.[3] As your today's columns are about Number XC, I ask your acceptance of my Via Media Vol ii which will remind you how I defended *then*, and tell you how I defend *now*, that Tract.

My short letter to the Vice Chancellor was as simple and sincere a letter as I ever wrote.[4]

---

[1] Having heard that Kegan Paul had incurred advertising expenses which would fall on Newman, Knowles wrote on 2 May that if he would 'let the matter go through', he would give up his own rights in the article at the end of the year.

[2] '*Notice.* In the February Number of the *Nineteenth Century*, an article of mine appeared, which has elicited a criticism from a Catholic Professor of name. As I acquiesce neither in his statements nor his reasonings, I am led to put on paper a Postscript in answer to him; and that without availing myself of the offer made to me by the Editor of the Review to re-publish, together with this Postscript, my Article itself: an indulgence beyond its rules, which I feel I have no right to accept, unless the Article shall be expressly called for by the public.' See *S.E.*, p. 39.

There is also a note by Newman of 19 May, on which he wrote 'not sent Confidential': 'A great objection was made by the xixth to my publishing the Article. I found I could not obtain this without losing also the copy right of the Appendix.

At last I gained it, but felt I had done as much as I ought in the "Notice".'

[3] Besides sending the proofs of her *Letters of the Rev. J. B. Mozley*, see letter of 29 April, Anne Mozley wrote, almost certainly on 30 April, about her brother Tom, 'He has told me the title of his forth coming Reminiscences. It seems to keep perfectly clear of Oxford and all connected with it, but of course one cant rely on this . . .' The reference is to his *Reminiscences, chiefly of Towns, Villages and Schools*, two volumes, London 1885.

[4] See *Letters of the Rev. J. B. Mozley*, pp. 111–15. He wrote on the latter page 'J.H.N. has written a very polite answer to the Vice-Chancellor. But whether they will be provoked to think it humbug and concealed triumph, or be softened by it, I hardly know. Though admiring the letter, I confess, for my own part, I think a general confession of humility was irrelevant to the present occasion . . .' This refers to Newman's letter of 16 March 1841, acknowledging the authorship of Tract *XC, V.M.* II, p. 363.

Also you ought to look into Hope Scott's Memoir lately published by Murray   He knew and liked your brother James, but he does not appear in the Memoir

As to dear James, in my own defence I must say one thing. So little did he understand me, that, in order to stop my becoming a Catholic, he offered ⟨*proposed*⟩ to me personally 'to make me the head of the Movement *instead of Pusey*.' His words to me were to this effect (vid. Apologia pp. 232, 3 also p. 390 for the *date* and *occasion*) And some years afterwards, a Catholic pressing a *friend of James's* to join the Catholic Church as I had, that friend replied 'O, Mr Newman was fond of power and left us from disappointment.' All this is to corroborate what I have ever held that he treated me as 'having betrayed my *party*.' I have ever felt it, though I can't at a moment determine whether it was a private letter, or an Article in the B.C. [British Critic] or other means by which the impression was conveyed to me.[1] N.B. the Article in the B.C. of April 1845 was his, and goes the same way.[2]

Had you not better insert Faber's name (Francis) — *Frederic* Faber his younger brother was at University[3]

I have nothing more to say

Yours affectionately John H Card. Newman[4]

May 6. 1884

My dear Fr Coleridge

I was glad to have your letter. Of course I readily consent to her printing the lines. You don't say if she suffers much[5]

Of course I am very anxious about your other subject[6]

Yours affectly John H Card. Newman

---

[1] It was an article in the *Christian Remembrancer* (Jan. 1846). See letters of 8 Jan. 1846 to Ambrose St John and 27 Jan. 1846 to Henry Wilberforce.

[2] 'Recent Proceedings at Oxford', the *Christian Remembrancer* (April 1845), pp. 517–71; see pp. 549–52, and *Apo.* p. 232.

[3] cf. *Letters of the Rev. J. B. Mozley*, p. 148.

[4] Anne Mozley replied on 5 May, 'my feeling is that I had better leave the subject of Number XC. to James's own letters . . . I don't think there is any one who doubts the absolute purity of motive of your action in it. . . . His letters indeed all along at this time are a running note, as it were on your narrative in the Apologia. As time goes on and the divergence of view widens I can imagine vexation on James's part but I can't fancy him really using the words *fond of power* in earnest. . . .'

[5] See letter of 25 April to Lady Simeon.

[6] cf. letter of 24 April to H. J. Coleridge.

TO RICHARD HOLT HUTTON

May 6 1884

My dear Mr Hutton

You have anticipated my letter which was going to you today.[1]

I should have written to thank you sooner, but I was like a man out of breath from the action of a plunging or shower bath, or rather like a baby in Martha Gunn's hands, who begins to cry.[2] Not that I did not feel your extreme kindness, or rather indulgence, as well as the depth and force of your criticism. But I am necessarily suffering from having lived too long.

I can't expect that affectionate friends such as you (for the words 'affectionately yours' were in my own heart and at the end of my pen before I found them in your letter) that such can wait till my full years on earth have run out, before they speak of me; nor that the purveyors of gossip of the past should refrain from tearing off my morbidly sensitive skin, while they can with public interest; but turning from what is accidental, I am obliged to look higher — but I am too tired to bring out here my meaning.[3] Don't suppose I am strong, because my writing is clear — unless I write very slowly letter by letter, my writing would be unreadable.

Here I am but writing a letter of thanks. It is about 20 years since I wrote to thank you for your Notice in the Spectator of my Apologia on its first publication. I dare say it was against the etiquette of the literary world, for no one was kind enough to answer me but you. In consequence I called on you at your Office. I have never seen you since, have I? but whenever in London, from the gratitude I left [felt] for the continuance of the kindness you first showed in 1864, I have wished to do so.[4] Now I suppose there is no chance of my ever going to London, at least for many hours. You will accept instead, I am sure, the blessing of a Cardinal of Holy Church, even though you cannot accept that title of 'Holy' as given her in the Creed

Yours affectionately John H Card. Newman

P.S   Your article brought home to me a curious misprint in your copy of the Apologia or the text of the Contemporary. At p 650 it reads 'to the *apparent*

[1] In answer to Newman's letter of 14 Jan. 1884 Hutton wrote on 5 May:
   'I never thanked you for a very kind note received in reply to the report I sent you of the enthusiasm with which the working men received my reading from your works. But I do so now most heartily. In the Contemporary Review for this month I have adapted some few parts of that reading, but having a different audience and a different grade of culture in view I have altered it very materially and indeed rewritten the greater part of it.'
   [2] Martha Gunn was the fat bathing woman at Brighton, one of the original dippers there. When the sea was too rough to push the bathing machines into it, she took her clients and dipped them in the waves.
   [3] See Newman's mention of Tom Mozley and the newspaper gossip about C. R. Newman in letter of 29 April to Anne Mozley.
   [4] See letters of 22 and 26 Feb. 1864. Hutton wrote on 10 May, 'I have seen you since that memorable call upon me which I treasure as one of the white days of my life. I was present at your address to the Catholic Union in Willis's rooms [12 May 1880] and tried to see you after it . . .'

charge of fierceness'[1] My copy (edition 1881 p 46) reads 'to the *opposite* charge'

Have you yourself written or can you recommend to me any *reliable* Catholic or Anglican statement of the real undeniable instances in which the *facts* of science are inconsistent with the text of Scripture.[2]

TO P. SPRAGUE ORAM

May 6. 1884

Dear Sir

We are so far apart, that I do not see how I can be of use to you. Apart, I mean in belief.[3]

You have been moved by two or three of the great doctrines of the Gospel which are surely fitted wonderfully to affect the best emotions of our nature, even separate from the grace of God.

But, though they *affect* powerfully, they cannot *effect* much without the grace of God.

And the grace is lodged in the Sacraments of the Holy Church

And that Holy Church is the Catholic Apostolic Church of Rome

And you have not gone to her and to her sacraments for that grace, which alone will enable you to do great things.

Great things are done through grace, and one attribute of the great things which grace enables the soul to do is their *lastingness*, their continuance, their permanent life and strength, as years roll past. I say, the works of grace are *permanent*.

But if you, Sir, went to India, even if you did do a work, it would not be a permanent work, because you would not go with the grace and the blessing of God

Alas! I honour your zeal and earnestness. I pray God to enlighten you. But you want a Teacher. You cannot teach yourself.

Yours truly J. H. Card. Newman

[1] In the *Contemporary Review* (May 1884), p. 650, Hutton misquoted from *Apo.* p. 46, which reads, 'This absolute confidence in my cause . . . also laid me open, not unfairly, to the opposite charge of fierceness . . .'

[2] Hutton replied on 10 May 'I know no trustworthy book of the kind you mention . . . But is not the inconsistency between St John and two or three verses in the first three evangelists as to the passover . . . . as strong an instance of inaccuracy in an important point in Scripture as could be required?' Newman's question was perhaps prompted by a letter from Mivart, see letters of 8, 9 and 11 May to him.

[3] Oram wrote from Edinburgh on 27 April that his heart had been often drawn towards Newman. He was a Salvationist, who had been a doctor, whom 'God called one night to give up all and follow Him. He promised me then, as well as in His book, if I did so to fill me with a happiness and peace and joy indescribable.' This had been Oram's experience, he had received 'the baptism of the Spirit' and he was about to proceed as a missionary to India. There he hoped to preach by example and to tell men that Christ died for them,

357

TO LOUISA ELIZABETH DEANE

May 7. 1884

My dear Louisa,

I was very glad to hear from you, and congratulate you and your husband on what I believe is called your Golden Wedding. I did not recollect how many daughters you had — they are just enough to have a Muse's name apiece, which some of them at least can fairly claim, if my S. Georgio speaks for Louisa, whose gift I never tire of looking at.[1]

For me, after whom you inquire, I am very well, but very weak — this without doubt I have said to you before. I am weak in seeing, in hearing, in speaking, in walking, in writing, for I write at a snail's pace, but as far as I know, I have nothing the matter with me. What most threatens me is the chance of accidents. I ought to be very thankful at having gone through so long a life with so little pain, so little discomfort.

Yours affectionately John H. Card. Newman.

P.S. It is very good in you and in Emmeline [Deane] thinking of my Portrait. But the idea is difficult when looked at closely — the how and the when and the where and many other questions rise up in opposition. And then they say that no one ever succeeded in taking me, which makes it quite unkind to let any one try.[2]

TO ST GEORGE JACKSON MIVART

May 8. 1884

not sent

Dear Professor Mivart

The weakness and stiffness of my fingers react upon my brain. I have thoughts and forget them, and lose my thread of argument and any vivid impression, before I can write it down. I never could think, never profitably meditate, without my pen, and now that I cannot use it freely, I cannot use my mind.

I pity and sympathize with the poor priests whom you animadvert on.[3] Three centuries ago they would hear about the earth going round the sun, an idea so simple, so beautiful, so antecedently probable, but so utterly opposed to tradition, to the word of Scripture, and to the apparent necessity of Christian doctrine. What a threatening difficulty to faith and to catechetical teaching!, but what evidence, what scientific proof had they that the new doctrine was true?

---

[1] See letter of 8 July 1881 to Louisa Deane.
[2] See letter of 1 Aug. 1884 to Mrs Deane.
[3] According to Jacob W. Gruber *A Conscience in Conflict The Life of St. George Jackson Mivart*, New York 1960, p. 243, 'This refers to the scientific ignorance of the clergy which forms the central theme of his article entitled "The Conversion of England,"' *D R* (July 1884), pp. 65–86. This subject is only discussed in two or three pages. On pp. 81–2 Mivart said, 'We are strongly impressed with the absolute necessity of our clergy being so far instructed in physical science as to be able to intelligently discuss the religious difficulties which are so often supposed to be therewith connected.' See letters of 9 and 11 May to Mivart.

Far more difficult is the position of priests and confessors now. They are in the front of a battle with unbelief, not merely against a school here or there of scientific research, and they have no time to get up a knowledge of physics, of biology so broad, so deep, as to have a right to judge of the strength and cogency of the views which at first sight are so difficult to harmonize with Scripture. How can they give up what is received by Catholic tradition without some better grounds for surrendering it than they have?

What increases their difficulty, and what supports them in their scepticism, their dislike, of the whole scientific movement is the sudden disappearance perhaps of supposed facts, which have been confidently urged against Scripture, and which at length are found by scientific men not to hold water, after some Catholic has elaborated an answer to them; — and they are naturally led to think that, as in other cases, error will eat up error, if they are but patient, without their trouble.

For myself, I confess I share these views to a great extent, and the more so because I am impressed especially by a fact which I have not yet noticed. What is the good of argument, unless opponents can join issue on some certain general principle? how can a priest combat a man of science, when the latter virtually denies the possibility of miracles, and the former holds that the most stupendous have actually occurred? The man of science ought to know that he has not proved that miracles are impossible; yet he uses that assumption as confidently against the Catholic, as if it was the most necessary of truths. Why am I to deny that our Lord rose again the third day because Professor A or B says it is impossible? He brings no facts.

Before I can fairly be called upon to enter upon difficult questions which involve great study and research for the answering I have a right to make two conditions before I have that responsibility; first, does the inquirer allow the possibility of a miraculous revelation, and next, what are the *facts*, and what the *proof* of the alledged facts, which are supposed to interfere with the belief that such a revelation is to be found in Scripture

Very truly Yours J. H. Card. Newman

P.S.   I send you back (except your A and B) your letters, and should like this back myself; but don't scruple, if you wish, to write again.

TO CARDINAL MANNING

May 9. 1884

My dear Cardinal

I am sorry you should be troubled with superfluous letters.[1] The Oceanus dissociabilis does but add to their throng[2]

Yours affecty John H. Card. Newman

[1] Manning wrote on 8 May: 'The inclosed, though directed to me, is clearly for you; as I found by reading my own name in it.'
[2] Horace *Odes* I, iii, 22, — presumably the letter was from abroad.

TO ST GEORGE JACKSON MIVART

not sent[1]   May 9. 1884

Dear Professor Mivart

I return the rest of your letter, having to apologize for the difficulty I find in reading running hand

I can fancy a really Catholic, really scientific Article doing much good, but it strikes me that the first step which an author ought to take, before he asks for information from the Church on additional points, is to show that he believes what is propounded already. Most writers ignore the question whether miracles are possible, are admissible in argument. What is the good of the Church breaking silence on the question of the Deluge, if it only leads to men of science questioning the fact of the Resurrection? The primary point is does the writer believe that the Resurrection is a fact? and the second, is therefore the Deluge possible? He may have many good reasons for thinking so strange an event improbable, or not to be taken literally — but if he begins with the avowal that it is too great a matter to accept on faith, I don't see how good can come from arguing.

I said something of this kind in yesterday's letter, but I am afraid not distinctly

Yours very truly John H Card. Newman

TO RICHARD HOLT HUTTON

May 11. 1884

My dear Mr Hutton

I am very ungrateful to you, if I have given you serious pain, but I do not understand you so, and I feel that really you understand me[2]

The shock of a shower bath turns into a feeling both pleasurable and permanent, and it was a great omission in me if I did not make this clear to you.

Yours affectly John H. Card. Newman

Thanks too for your postscript[3]

[1] This is in pencil, apparently in another hand.
[2] Hutton wrote on 10 May: 'Your letter gave me pain as well as pleasure, I hardly know which most. I enter so heartily and entirely into the feeling you have of dislike to read about yourself, that I wish with all my heart I had refused to write anything for publication about you — And yet it was a pleasure to me, while you are still with us, to let my Protestant friends know what a mine of wealth I have found in your writings. Nevertheless I bitterly regretted it when I read your note, for . . . I have felt in my small way exactly what you feel at being the subject of that kind of attention at all.' See letter of 6 May to Hutton.
[3] In the postscript Hutton wrote '. . . may I say that I hope it is some alleviation to you of the burdens of life, to know how it lightens the world to many of us, that you are still with us, and to know what a passionate grief it will cause to your most intimate friends, and how keen a pang to all who love you, when you leave us.'

May 11. 1884.

Dear Professor Mivart,

It seems to me that a Pamphlet or Essay or Letter calling the attention of Bishops and other prominent ecclesiastics to the present relations in which revelation and science stand to each other, as a *Fact*, would be very desirable — but it must come from a Catholic and must be logical, — and it must be persuasive.[1]

Among the facts, I should state, if they *be* facts, that (e.g.) the scientific world accepts a body of facts or phenomena as true which are inconsistent with the received teaching of Scripture;

that it has good reason for *so thinking*

as facts stand at present

or good reason for *anticipating*

or *plausible* reason

or (say) two or three perplexing facts

or its reasons are *good, supposing* certain antecedent, unproved *principles* are true

or its reasons are mainly the effect of imaginations created out of the phenomena with which its researches are most conversant with e.g. the effect of the daily contemplation of *law* creates an inability to accept in the *imagination* the idea of a *transgression* of law.

This would be one heading for discussion, which should be perfectly impartial, viz., the *fact* of the testimony, and the *value* of the testimony of the scientific world. On the other hand should of course be considered whether the non-scientific world is a sufficient judge of scientific argument, any more than a man of science is a judge of theology.

After this, a second heading would come of the physical facts, whatever they are, which are a difficulty in accepting the Scripture doctrines or facts.

And thus the way would be opened for other headings, such the course of thought would supply. But of course, if it is to do good, it must be accompanied with a profession of Catholic doctrine, and, whatever anticipation the writer may have that it will be found true ultimately that Eve was not taken from Adam's side, if a writer began by saying (as excuse me, you did) by saying that such a statement was against all biological laws, he would be stating as an objection what would provoke the answer, 'No body said it was'nt'.

Very sincerely yours John H. Card. Newman.

---

[1] This paragraph suggests that Mivart was writing about some other article than that in *D R* for July. See letters of 8 and 9 May 'not sent.'

TO EMILY BOWLES

May 12. 1884

My dear Child

I was made a Cardinal five years today — how time goes! You must not come for St Philip's day. The Bishop and priests dine with us and no one else but I know of no other difficulty on your coming here these weeks, and shall rejoice to see you[1]

Yrs affectly J H Card. Newman

TO JOSEPH WHITAKER

(copy) J Whitaker Esqr
Dear Sir

May 15 1884

You have acted a very kind part by me.[2] Of course I know well my poor brother's absence of religious belief — nor, as the world goes now, would [it] be any great pain for the world to know it. But there are two questions which I could solve only by the sight of the letters, and these are, first whether I am right in the suspicion he may have had very free ideas on fundamental morals, as he was (I believe) all thro' his life an advanced Socialist and secondly whether he may not in his letters speak of members of his family in terms as cruel as they would be untrue

Therefore, I should be obliged to you to lend me the packet   I suppose the letters are numbered or dated. Of course I will carefully keep them, and, if I do not buy them will return them safely to you without delay. I suppose it will be best to register them by post.

One question has struck me to ask you. You call the owner of the letters 'an old acquaintance.' This is not enough to show you have confidence in him. Is it possible that, if I bought them, a second batch might come from (say) a new quarter?[3]

J H N

[1] Emily Bowles noted, 'It was my last visit to him at Edgbaston.'
[2] Whitaker, the founder in 1868 of *Whitaker's Almanack*, wrote on 14 May: 'An old acquaintance of your deceased brother is in possession of some seventy letters written by your brother. They are described as wonderfully clever pieces of Criticism on books and authors, on philosophy, and on events. Some as being very free in their religious notions and some as very questionable indeed.'
Whitaker added that he had been consulted about their publication, 'but it occurred to me that if published they might cause your Eminence much pain, and would create a good deal of unpleasant criticism. As my friend is in needy circumstances I gave — nominally lent — him £5. on the security of the packet of letters which he left in my hands . . .' Whitaker thought they might be purchased for £15 or £20.
Whitaker's acquaintance was Thomas Purnell, who had been born in Tenby in 1834, and became a journalist and author. He was of a bohemian temperament, and a friend of Swinburne and Mazzini. Purnell wrote a notice of Charles Newman, whom he visited during 1859 and 1860, for the *Athenaeum* (29 March 1884), p. 408, which announced (12 April), p. 475, 'It is not improbable that Mr. Purnell will publish a volume of correspondence with Newman entitled "Letters of a Recluse."'
[3] See letter of 6 June to Whitaker.

May 16. 1884.

My dear Lady Simeon

I have behaved unkindly to Mary Simeon in not answering her letter weeks ago, and, since I don't know her address, I must ask you to set me right with her.[1]

I believe I wanted to offer her some trifle towards her object, which of course pleased me much, and then I found I could not do so just now — and after a delay thus caused, I forgot to write.

Pray tell her I thought it very kind in her to write to me[2]

Yours affectly John H. Card. Newman

(Copy)   May 17/84

Dear Lord Coleridge

My tables of books, prices, date, stock etc are now ready, and I think of sending them, in accordance with your introduction to the Longmans — but there is one point on which I want your opinion first.[3]

Unless you are against it, I should like at present to confine my negociation to Longmans. I take it for granted from their high position, that they are fair and upright, as well as experienced traders, with whom I should be safe; whereas I don't like a competition with other firms, which would involve the principle of speculation   Of course, if I did not like Mr Longman's offer, I might *then* open the subject with another publisher.

I should be obliged as a matter of courtesy to my two publishers, Burns and Pickering to say I was contemplating the sale; indeed I have done so already, (except Longmans' name), but not as if I supposed any practical offer from them

J H N

Birmingham May 21. 1884

My dear Dr Griffin

I have been long expecting to see some notice of the publication of Dr Moriarty's Volume, — I may say, looking out for it with the greatest interest.[4]

---

[1] In the draft Newman wrote a long explanation about the difficulties of old age.

[2] On 8 Feb. Lady Simeon's step-daughter, Mary, wrote to ask Newman's blessing on a girls' orphanage, St Mary's Home, Eastleigh, which she was about to found, and where she intended to live. She wrote from there on 19 Aug. to thank Newman for a cheque. Six month. later she had moved into a larger house and had fifteen children, with room for fifteen mores After her death in 1905, the Home was carried on for another twenty years by Maimy, daughter of F. R. Ward.

[3] See letter of 29 April to Lord Coleridge, who on 19 May approved of all that Newman proposed in this present letter.

[4] For this and what follows see letter of 28 Feb. 1884 to Griffin.

It seems to me from the portions which I have read in the Volume which you kindly sent me, to be one of the most instructive and edifying volumes I have read, and, wishing much that others besides myself might have so great a benefit, I wanted to order at the Publishers a dozen copies to be sent to me with this purpose. Will you kindly inform me, I have lost your address and you must pardon what is, I fear, not sure to get to you at once

Believe me to be,

Most truly Yours John H. Card. Newman

TO CHARLES JAMES LONGMAN

Charles Longman Esqr   May 21. 1884
Dear Sir

I feel it a compliment to me that you have expressed to my friend Lord Coleridge a willingness to purchase ⟨contemplate⟩ the copyright of my writings, supposing it could be so arranged. And I write to say that I have nearly prepared for you a table of my volumes, giving date, price, stock etc etc of each, and I inclose herein a list of the works themselves, as an introduction to the tables.

There is one question on a point of law which affects the determination of the dates, as they affect copyright; I do not know how the law stands on several points in the case of suppose a dozen pamphlets which were published at different dates, even though corrected, arranged and new-edited when afterwards published together, will begin to date their copyright from the time of their original and separate publication; but what is the case supposing in a second edition have been made various and serious transformations and substitutions but in no respect a separate work? or supposing 90 pages (bodily) are new and 350 old? How stands the law then? In consequence I have introduced into the tables a double list of dates.

I have told no one that I am in correspondence with you. If you should still think it well to make me an offer, my final ⟨sole⟩ feeling will be one of assurance that it accurately represents the market value of what I have written if there is possible such a value — and if I decline it, it will be because the result does not fulfil the personal object which I have in wishing to part with the volumes[1]

I had the pleasure of knowing personally William Longman and was grieved when some time since I heard of his death. He did me good service on the publication of my Apologia in 1864.[2]

J H N

[1] Longman replied that his firm would give the matter their best consideration. They asked to know the annual sale for the previous four years and also for a copy of each book.
[2] C. J. Longman and his brother became heads of the firm on the death of their father William in 1877.

TO MICHAEL HIGGINS

Bm May 24, 1884.

Dear Rev. Sir

You were so kind some time since to suggest to me a passage in my Lectures on Anglicans which must have given occasion to a report that I had called the Anglican Church a bulwark to the Catholic Roman Church. I hope you got my answer to you. It was to the effect that another correspondent, as well as you, had been kind enough to notice it, and a note upon the point has been inserted in a new Edition which was passing through the press.[1]

I will ask your acceptance of a copy of it, if you will give me your address[2]

Yours truly John H. Card. Newman

P.S.   You will find the correction in a note at p 11.

TO WILLIAM NEVILLE

Thursday [29?] May 1884

My dear W

I never saw anything so splendid as the red rhododendrons
You *must* come out next Monday

Yrs affly J H N

TO LORD BRAYE

Rednal May 30. 1884

My dear Lord Braye

You have a claim on me to write to you, from the very earnestness of your wishing it. But, besides the difficulties of subject itself, the stiffness of my fingers is one impediment and the hoarseness of my voice would, if I saw you, be another; and these two so act upon my brain as to confuse and distress me.

When you ask me what line of life you should, as a matter of duty pursue, my first and fundamental difficulty is my seclusion from the world and my ignorance of Catholic matters

I see just enough to be very much pained I don't see more

Some time ago I referred you for an expression of my own opinion to some verses of mine, which I cannot quote from memory, but, which were to the effect that, if we did not see our way, we ought to wait for opportunities, and to 'use them as they rise —'

---

[1] Higgins, who was a curate at Queenstown, Ireland, wrote on 4 May and had not received Newman's reply. See *Diff.* II, p. 11.
[2] This Higgins did on 26 May.

With this on my mind, it is plain I could not like the 'paragraph' which you first printed and then *published* with a dedication to me.[1]

I have heard that a young man gets on in Parliament by humdrum diligence, which is like serving an apprenticeship — but I think this is the path of duty (mutatis mutandis) for prominent persons such as your Lordship.

Are there not institutions which deserve and require the aid of men in station as you, which you can protect and aid? But I cannot go on for very weakness

May God bless you and guide you. If any thing occurs to me I will write again[2]

Most truly Yours J. H. Card. Newman

P.S.   I am certainly very weak, and tho' I write this before noon, very sleepy.

TO LORD EMLY

Bm May 30. 1884

My dear Emly

I am much relieved on reading your letter a second time. I thought it was Lady Emly's health you wrote about — and said Mass for her this morning. I see you speak of a 'relation' of hers. I will not forget your wish

It is very kind of you to send me the remarks made to you on my Article and Postscript.[3] Of course the subject has made me very anxious, both as to *what* I should say and *how* I should say it   Any how my manner is open to criticism, and a real fault in it might damage my cause. However, I have taken very great pains, and I trust (if the look of things is to be trusted) successfully

I have had it translated into Italian — and perhaps shall have it at once printed[4]

I have lost the easy use of my fingers, and write this with difficulty

Yours affectly J. H. Card. Newman

June 1. By mistake this has not gone to the post

[1] See letter of 14 Dec. 1883 to Lord Braye.
[2] See letter of 4 June to Lord Braye.
[3] In the letter of 27 May asking prayers for his wife's relation Lord Emly wrote: 'It may interest you to hear that a very able French Jesuit, Pere René, in talking to me yesterday on the inspiration of Scripture, expressed his opinion that it was limited to matters bearing on faith and morals. He never had heard of your article, but with clearness and confidence, he expressed his entire concurrence with the principles it contains. He hardly would have done so if the schools in which he was brought up had not taught the same doctrine. An Irish Jesuit, who dined with me, also a clever man, had read your article, and your reply to Father Healy, with which he was delighted, and entirely agreed with you.' Jean Baptiste René (1841–1916) was the Superior of a school in Limerick 1880–8. He was then for eight years Prefect Apostolic of Alaska, and later Professor of Scripture and of Hebrew at Spokane.

On 9 May Bishop Clifford wrote to Newman about the *Postscript*: 'Of its thorough orthodoxy there can be no doubt. Besides being a called for vindication of yourself and your article on Inspiration, it is a very important and useful complement to that article, and it will help still further to quiet the minds and consciences of many good and thoughtful men . . .'

[4] This was privately printed. cf. letter of 29 July to Bishop Clifford.

TO LAUNCELOT JOHN POPE

June 2. 1884

My dear Launcy

Your good choir master does me a compliment, but makes me smile, when he asks me to write a hymn to St Ignatius I should get more than a complimentary return, I know, from a Saint, but whether St Ignatius or a good religious asked me, I should know well that it was a thing which a poet could do, and I could not.

I am sure, in spite of this refusal, you will do me a kindness. The two boys, F. P. and J. H. Watt have sent me congratulations on St Philip's Feast. Will you thank them for me?[1]

Yours affectly John H. Card. Newman

TO LORD BRAYE

The Oratory June 4. 1884

My dear Lord Braye

I wrote you a poor letter the other day —[2] yet the sense of it was what really I meant to express, tho' I was too weak to bring it out.

Very keenly do I feel the thought that troubles you. You wish to do something for God, and there is no opening. Well then I say, though I seem hard in saying it, you cannot force an opening; you can but wait for *his* time and call. We are all mere instruments in His hands. He can do without us. He uses us when He pleases. We must be patient — if we are not, we suffer for it.

Next, I wanted to say, what seems to be our duty, what we *can* do, at once, and before He assigns us our proper work. I think the usual way which leads to opportunities being thrown open to us is to serve an apprenticeship. How was it that any one *could* do a dis-service towards you with the Nunzio?[3] I consider it was because he had nothing to set against what might be said to your disadvantage. I know you have felt this duty; therefore it was that you had let yourself be a supporter of the Catholic Union Society, nor can I say you were wrong when you ceased to take part in it. But is it impossible to find existing objects for religious or moral undertakings, which are hopeful, such as the Society of St Vincent etc.[4]

I am perfectly aware I may be suggesting what it is impossible to comply with — *that* only would show that I am not the fit person to consult; but I

[1] Pope was at Stonyhurst College. The two Watt boys were sons of Mrs F. J. Watt.
[2] On 30 May.
[3] See letter of 9 Feb. 1883 to Archbishop Siciliano di Rende.
[4] The Catholic Union of Great Britain existed to protect the public interests of Catholics, the Society of St Vincent de Paul cared for the poor.

should still hold to my principle that, till a man has done something in which he has not originated, he will find it difficult to promote good objects which are more intimately his own.

There is another very serious condition of success in good objects — it is the command of money, a condition which I fear is most formidable and very plain

Very sincerly Yours John H Card. Newman

P.S.   *Since* I have written the above, I have seen your letter to Fr Eaglesim. It is very kind and considerate, and I thank you for it with all my heart; I showed at the worst in my Rednall letter, but certainly I find a difficulty in reading, writing, and speaking[1]

TO ALEXANDER FULLERTON

Bm June 4 1884

My dear Mr Fullerton

I thank God for your good news about Lady Georgiana [Fullerton]. Assure her how pleased and thankful I am. Also, that I do not forget St Philip's warning not to give over praying because the subject of the prayer is better, for all may be lost by over confidence

Most truly Yours John H Card. Newman

TO HENRY BEDFORD

June 5th. 1884.

My dear Professor Bedford,

Last month I had a letter dated Allhallows which I did not answer as not knowing whether it was from one of your Professors, from a Priest, or like yourself a layman.[2] Another difficulty was my inability just then to answer it favourably. It was on the subject of the funds required for the increasing demand for missionaries for foreign Catholics.

These two reasons have delayed my answer, and I see no other means of expediting it, than that of giving you the trouble of a letter to me.

I have not been able yet to fulfil my wish as regards the Mater Misericordiae Hospital, but I hope to do so soon.[3]

Very sincerely yours, John H. Card. Newman.

[1] Lord Braye had written to Eaglesim offering to make a present to Newman. See letter of 13 June.
[2] This was the Rev. Dr McDevett. See letter of 9 June to Bedford.
[3] See letter of 1 April to Bedford. Newman sent his cheque on 9 July.

TO JOSEPH WHITAKER

June 6. 1884

Dear Mr Whitaker

In your letter of May you gave me hopes that in the course of the following week you would be able to give me a satisfactory account of the matter on which you have been so good as to take an interest in my behalf. I write to you, not as if forgetting that such settlements as you aimed at are [not] to be made in a day, but as thinking that you may have directed to me at Oscott College, which is some miles from Birmingham and from which the Oratory in Bm is quite distinct. It is not wonderful that I have not heard from you, but it would not be wonderful that your address of a letter had carried it in a wrong direction[1]

J H N

TO CHARLES JAMES LONGMAN

Saturday June 7. 1884

sent in substance

Dear Sir

I hope by Monday night's post to send you the details necessary for judgment about my volumes. They are appended to each in ten columns under the heads of Title, length, contents, original date, date when brought together, Publisher, selling price, stock, stereotyped, remarks.

Also I send the amount of sales in the course of the last six years. And the neat gain, after all expenses paid, in the course of the last 20 years

When you have no further use of their various memoranda, I should be glad to have them returned to me[2]

Dear Sir etc J H N

Charles Longman Esqr

TO HENRY BEDFORD

June 9th. 1884.

My dear Professor,

Thank you for your letter, and for the pleasant and instructive reading furnished by your Articles.[3]

---

[1] This letter crossed one from Whitaker of 6 June, in which he wrote that he had negotiated the purchase of the letters of Charles Newman, would bring them to Birmingham the next week, and felt 'morally certain there are no other letters.' See letters of 15 May and 23 June to Whitaker, who wrote on 7 June that delay was partly because he thought it unwise to exhibit any undue anxiety in dealing with Purnell.

[2] Longman asked further questions. See letter of 11 June to him.

[3] Bedford sent reprints of recent articles of his in the *Irish Ecclesiastical Record*.

Also, for your remarks about Professor H. I thought correctly then when I said that 'If he had not been so hasty he would have made a better article'.[1]

Pray let me ask you to thank for me Dr. Mc Devett for his letter, and explain to him my regret that just now I am unable to show my interest in his good work.[2]

Very truly yours, John H. Card. Newman.

TO ALEXANDER DENNY

June 9/84

Dear Mr Denny

I inclose a statement of details, in order to help the determination whether I should dispose of my copyrights or not

Very truly yours J. H. Card. Newman

TO WILFRID OATES

June 9/84

Copy in substance
Dear Mr Oates

Not certain whether I shall dispose of copyrights.

I inclose a list of details. The *neat* gain in 20 years is an average of £330 per annum.[3]

I cannot tell you name of my friend who helps me

TO CHARLES JAMES LONGMAN

June 11. 1884

Dear Sir

I have to acknowledge the receipt of your letter of yesterday.

With a little delay I think I can answer your three questions myself.[4] In that case, as Lord Coleridge who wrote to you, is the only person who knows I am in negociation with you, I prefer to answer them myself if I find I can.

You will be able to judge when you see them whether my returns [?] are sufficient for your purpose

J H N

[1] Newman made this remark about John Healy's article in the *Irish Ecclesiastical Record* when replying to it in his *Postscript* to *On the Inspiration of Scripture*, S.E., p. 41. Bedford wrote on 7 June: 'You must kindly remember that the Record is Irish and Ecclesiastical both which imply, pugnacity and haste, and very Irish is the Editor — hot headed in truth but also warm hearted, with the "pen of a ready writer" he rushes into the fray, and is carried away by his own excitement and blinded by the dust he himself kicks up . . .'

[2] See letter of 5 June to Bedford.

[3] Newman perhaps meant to write '£380.' See letter of 29 April to Oates, who told Neville on 18 June that he now thought Newman's copyrights worth £2500.

[4] For the three questions in Longman's letter of 10 June see letter of 16 June to him.

TO RICHARD STANTON

Bm June 12. 1884

My dear Fr Stanton

I am told you are Superior, but, as I am not certain, I only *direct* my letter so to you.[1]

to have your Catalogue, and I thank you for it

Yes, thank God, I am not aware I have any serious ailment, but I am in a certain sense dim-sighted, deaf and lame, and write with great difficulty.

This must be my excuse, if my letter seems abrupt

Yours affectly

TO MISS E. SPOONER

June 13 1884

Answered I had been advised not to grant her request.[2] A series of extracts was made from my Anglican works some time since which was not sent ⟨shown⟩ me and did not answer to my conception of it under which I gave leave ⟨when [?] at length I saw it⟩[3]

J H N

TO LORD BRAYE

June 13. 1884

My dear Lord Braye

I meant to have written to you before this — and to thank you more distinctly for your kindness.[4] What I have meant Fr Eaglesim to say is — that a case might arise when such a present, such as you propose would be most acceptable — For instance, had I suddenly a call to go to Rome — but that I would rather reserve the acceptance of such to some critical occasion, as indeed you meant yourself.[5]

Most truly Yours John H. Card. Newman

The Lord Braye

---

[1] A line is missing where the signature has been cut out.

[2] Miss Spooner, of 41 Upperton Gardens, Eastbourne, asked Newman's permission 'to place about 20 short passages from your Parochial Sermons in a book of extracts'. Newman sent her letter on to Rivington and Co., who agreed that it would be better to refuse permission.

[3] This was *Miscellanies from the Oxford Sermons and other Writings of J. H. Newman*, London 1870. See letters of 29 March 1873 to W. S. Lilly, and 28 Dec. 1873 to Emily Bowles.

[4] See postscript to letter of 4 June to Lord Braye.

[5] Lord Braye replied on 14 June 'pray command me and my purse.'

TO CHARLES JAMES LONGMAN

in substance sent   June 16. 1884
Dear Sir

I hope the following will sufficiently answer your questions[1]

The first is What is the sale of *each* volume for the last 3 or 4 years? I am sending you in a registered letter by this evening's post statements of account drawn up from yours for the five years 1879–1883, from Messrs Rivingtons for the same five years, from Messrs Burns and Oates for 4½ years and half years, and from Messrs Pickering 5 years and half years. Also I send you the *original* accounts of these four publishers.

Your second remark I am not sure I follow. It says 'No doubt your books are published on different terms with the different publishers.' Since the Autumn of 1845, I have always had my volumes published on commission — and have paid for the printing etc etc myself as in the case of the Apologia. The only exception I can recollect is that Messrs Burns and Co engaged to pay me £10 for every 1000 copies of a small edition of Loss and Gain, while the stereotype lasted, and for the later thousand copies, a larger sum. Perhaps there was a like engagement for Callista. This payment ceased many years ago — but I believe I am write [sic] in saying that some hundreds of this edition of Callista was lately found at Messrs Burns, and they are just now selling it. Also, most of the Articles which make up the two volumes of Essays are reprints from the 'British Critic'. Mr Rivington says of them in a letter to me Dec 5. 1870 'We have no objection to your reprinting them with Mr Pickering. The Act gives you the copyright, though we paid for them at the time of their appearing.' To which I have appended this Note 'This is hardly the case — vid Rivington's letter to me of Novr 2. 1840.'[2]

Lastly, as to the question about the royalty, which is 'whether your Firm would have to buy the publisher's interest or leave you the power of terminating etc' I think it best to send you the five engagements themselves, in the registered Packet above spoken of, as you can understand the wording and drift of such documents better than I do.

I fear I must give you the trouble of returning these various papers to me when you have done with them.

J H N

TO AUGUSTINE FRANCIS HEWIT

Rednall, June 19, 1884

Dear Fr Hewit

Thank you for forwarding my letter to Fr Hecker I had not fancied he was the Editor of the C. W. Burns and Oates, I thought would send it to you as

---

[1] In the letter of 10 June from Longman.
[2] cf. letter of 2 April 1884 to Knowles.

editor.[1] I should be very wrong if I interfered with a Catholic's holding as high a doctrine about the Inspiration of Scripture as is left by the Church open to him — but for the same reason I think he may be allowed to hold as little as the Church insists upon; and the great evil the history of Galileo does us by prejudicing Protestants against us, warns me not to commit myself to more than the Church really teaches in matters of faith and morals by means of inspired Scripture. St Paul tells us that omnis Scriptura divinitus inspirata is useful ad docendum, ad arguendum, ad corripiendum, ad erudiendum.[2]

I hope Fr Hecker's absence does not imply that health is the cause of it.[3]

TO JOSEPH WHITAKER

Rednall June 23. 1884

sent in substance

Dear Mr Whitaker

I have read through the letters, as well as my eyes allow me to read writing, and am agreeably surprised to find so little in them to offend me personally. Of me he scarcely speaks at all. More than once he even speaks well of me, as of my brother Francis, of whom indeed he has in truth good reason to speak well. In one letter he speaks rudely of the whole family, but not in a way which, if published, would gratify a reader's curiosity. I cannot fancy the collection answering as a publisher's speculation for, whether its philosophy and its literary criticism be able or not, it is too much mere 'Table Talk' to gain toleration or attention except as coming from a man of recognized reputation

I am, however, quite satisfied in paying twenty Pounds as the price of possession and propose to send you that sum at the beginning of next month. I think the owner is a lucky man to get it — but one must pay for chances, just as one insures one's life without expecting to die immaturely and I thank you heartily for the friendly part towards me you have taken in the matter. It would have been a continual distress, if I had known there were such letters in existence without knowing what was contained in them.[4]

JHN

[1] Newman sent Isaac Thomas Hecker his *Postscript* on the Inspiration of Scripture, and Hewit acknowledged it in his absence. Hecker was editor of the *Catholic World* and Hewit managing editor.

Hewit sent a notice of Newman's pamphlet to the *Catholic World* for July. See letters of 26 June and 22 Oct. 1884 to Hewit who wrote on 30 May: 'I have expressed myself with reserve for reasons of prudence in regard to the only real point of controversy the *obiter dicta* . . .

I am inclined to accept the view which you have suggested, although it has always been my way to hold to the stricter and more common teaching in respect to the extent of inspiration until there appears to be a very strong reason for relaxing somewhat of its tension. The Protestant defenders of Holy Scripture in this country against extreme rationalism and neologism are going in a way of concession which seems to be hazardous . . .'

[2] II *Timothy* 3:16.

[3] The conclusion has been cut out

[4] Whitaker decided that £20 was too much to give Thomas Purnell for Charles Newman's letters, and sent him £15, the sum he had been led to expect.

As I am writing, I will repeat with reference to the question you asked me viz 'whether I became a Catholic because I was dissatisfied with the Church of England, and, on looking about I could find nothing better, if I must leave it, than the Church of Rome', that I joined the Catholic Church for *its own* sake and that no one can have read my Essay on 'the Development of Christian doctrine' without seeing this.[1]

J H N

TO HENRY JAMES COLERIDGE

Bm June 24/84

My dear Fr Coleridge

I am made extremely anxious by a notice in today's paper to the effect that your brother,[2] though able to take out door exercise, is unable to go into Court. Another account is that it is lumbago; what does this mean?

Your present silence is my only relief

Yours affectly J H Card. Newman

TO MARGARET DE LISLE

Bm June 25. 1884

Dear Miss de Lisle

I will gladly say Mass for your nephew, and trust his pilgrimage will be blest.[3]

I could not name a time to see him — as I have long wished to retreat to our place at Rednall and wished first to celebrate here the great feasts. If he has been an Oscott boy, perhaps I shall meet him at the annual meeting there, should I have the favour of an invitation there and be strong enough to accept it

May God's best blessings rest on you and your nephew

Very sincerely Yours John H Card. Newman

P.S. I am getting so deaf and difficult of speech, that I fear I should much disappoint you, if you took the trouble, as you throw out, of coming here yourself. You must not forget my age.

[1] This paragraph is deleted in the draft, but Newman must have sent its equivalent, for Whitaker replied on 24 June in regard to his visit: 'I hope you did not think me impertinent in speaking so freely and unreservedly. In some way you had been more or less in my mind for forty years, and I had accustomed myself to think of your Eminence almost historically — almost in the same manner as I would of Andrewes or Laud: but I hope you will believe me when I say that during the whole time I do not remember to have had one single disrespectful or unkind thought respecting you. The speculation I mention afforded my mind a solution for your leaving the English Church, but I now fully and unreservedly accept and believe your statement to the contrary'

In a letter of 8 July Whitaker wrote: 'The interview I had with your Eminence is one of my red letter days and will not soon be forgotten, you cannot conceive what a gratification it has been . . .'

[2] Lord Coleridge.
[3] This probably refers to Edward Lisle Strutt.

TO P. J. HUGHES.

[25 June 1884]

Cardinal Newman begs to acknowledge Mr Hughes's letter, and to refer him on the subject of Freemasonry to the recent Encyclical Letter on it, which, after the precedent of former Pontiffs in 1738, 1751, 1821, 1825, 1829, 1832, 1846, 1865, the present Pope Leo has issued. It is translated into English and he believes can easily be procured.[1]

TO AUGUSTINE FRANCIS HEWIT

June 26, 1884

My dear Fr Hewit

Excuse a short letter, but my fingers are so stiff now, that I write with difficulty. I write to express the pleasure I have received from your notice of me in your July Number. It is every thing that I could wish. You would have been wrong to take a side: and it certainly would have been imprudent to do more than to give a hearing to that laxer [?] side which I wish to take myself. I wish to take it from the difficulties I see ahead, and for the sake of younger men who are very sensitive.[2]

But I can't use my fingers, so I sign myself,

Most truly yours J. H. Card Newman

TO ARTHUR SANDES GRIFFIN

Bm July 1. 1884

My dear Canon Griffin

Thank you for your having written for me to Messrs Browne and Nolan. I am very glad to have the twelve copies and have given most of them away already.[3] But I have some fear that my letter was badly worded, for I did not mean to give you the trouble of sending them

[1] P. J. Hughes wrote from Pontypridd in connexion with a reported condemnation of Freemasonry by Cardinal McCabe (see letter of 12 July 1884 to the Hibernian Bank) to ask whether Newman disapproved of Freemasonry, and if so on what grounds. Leo XIII's Encyclical condemning freemasonry was *Humanum Genus* of 21 April 1884.

[2] This was Hewit's review in the *Catholic World* (July 1884), pp. 565–6, of Newman's article *On the Inspiration of Scripture* and *Postscript*. Hewit said: 'Their whole intent and scope is to defend the majesty and authority of the Divine Scriptures, to corroborate the faith of Christians in God's word, and to alleviate the difficulty, created for some minds by certain tendencies of modern speculation, in regard to the harmony between rational knowledge and faith in the divine revelation. We would glady see these two productions . . . published together in a form convenient for general circulation.' In reference to what Newman had written about *obiter dicta* not relating to faith or morals, Hewit said, 'On this controverted question we express no opinion except so far as this, that it is a question open to discussion.'
See also letter of 19 June to Hewit.

[3] This refers to *Allocutions and Pastorals of the late Right Rev. Dr. Moriarty*, published by Browne and Nolan, Dublin. See letter of 21 May to Griffin.

I hope to order more from Browne and Nolan. It is a book which must be welcome to every priest.

Most truly Yours John H. Card. Newman

Excuse my bad writing. I have lost the use of my fingers

TO JOHN HEALY

Birmingham, July 3rd, 1884

My Dear Lord Bishop Elect

I thank you for your kind message through Dr Walsh, and for your acceptance from me of the offering which I proposed to make to you.[1]

That long life and a career of usefulness and happy service in the Church of God may be granted to you from above is the sincere prayer of

Your faithful servant, J. H. Card. Newman

P.S.   This requires no immediate answer; you may be going on Retreat, and must have many occupations besides.[2]

TO GEORGE ANTHONY DENISON

(In substance)   July 4. 1884
My dear Archdeacon,

Excuse me if I write at no great length — it is my fingers that are stiff and feeble, not my mind which is unsympathic [sic].[3]

I greatly rejoice at such a creation material and moral as Keble College

[1] William Walsh, who was President of Maynooth, where Healy was a Professor, wrote on 27 May to thank for the *Postscript* replying to the latter. He said 'From the tone of the "Postscript" it is plain to all that anything now written by Dr Healy to clear himself of the grave charges your Eminence has brought against him could not fail to make matters much worse than they are. I trust Dr Healy will take this view of the case . . .'
Walsh wrote again from Maynooth on 2 July: 'Many thanks for your Eminence's kind letter. Our Bishops are here just now and I ventured to take the liberty of letting several of them see it. As to Dr Healy he is profoundly grateful to your Eminence. I happen indeed to know that he had made up his mind some time before to write to your Eminence asking your forgiveness for anything said in his Paper that offended or annoyed you.'
Newman gave Healy a Canon of the Mass as used by bishops.
[2] Healy thanked Newman for the promised present on 17 July, describing it as 'a striking proof of the nobility and generosity of your own heart.' He continued: 'It is fitting that I should take this opportunity of expressing my regret for any words that have escaped me during the late controversy, and which were calculated to cause the least pain or annoyance to your Eminence.
In any case I had intended to say this much to your Eminence. I must add, however, that I certainly never had intended to make use of any uncourteous expressions, but we do not always succeed in carrying out our good resolutions.'
Healy wrote again on 1 Sept. after the Canon had arrived, saying that the bishops assembled for his consecration 'greatly admired the gift, but still more the nobility of heart of the giver.'
Walsh himself gave Healy a complete set of Newman's works as a consecration present.
[3] Denison wrote on 3 July suggesting that Newman might be willing to put in a word with Gladstone in furtherance of a plan to obtain a peerage for Antony Gibbs, in recognition of his gift of £135,000 for the chapel and other buildings of Keble College. Denison replied: 'I owe you an apology for my request or rather suggestion.
I doubted the fitness of it when I made it — your kindness will not remember this weakness'.

under the present state of Oxford, but can I, as a Cardinal of the Holy Roman Church, allow myself to give a public sanction to a religious system, which in spite of the claims which many of its adherents have upon my love and esteem, does not, as I believe, come from God? I have alas, but one answer to this question, and in consequence to your proposal

Yrs affly J H N

TO CHARLES JAMES LONGMAN

Copy   July 4. 1884
Dear Sir

I thank you for your letter of yesterday, which I [is] just what I wanted.[1] I should be sorry to cause unnecessary trouble, and the sum you name, as expressing the probable result of further examination into the value of my copyrights quite enables me to give you the answer you desire

I do not wish you then to continue the calculation, because I feel I should not see my way to accept it, if carried on to the end, though I am sure that, as a valuation, it is scientific and accurate

I have no intention of pursuing the inquiry elsewhere, and, if I have caused expense, I will ask you to let me know the amount.[2]

Also I will ask you for the various documents which went to you, and, thanking you for your courtesy

I am, Dear Sir, Your faithful Servant

John H. Card. Newman[3]

TO ARTHUR SANDES GRIFFIN

The Oratory July 5. 1884

My dear Canon Griffin

I thank you and Dean Coffey for the beautifully bound copy of the Allocutions etc which you have sent me. It came quite safe.

When I first read the volume, I thought that in many ways it would do good to Anglican friends of mine. So I think it would, and I should send it, but for a fear that you might be afraid that it might do harm as well as good.

Have you and Dean Coffin [sic] an opinion on this point? For instance, a Catholic Priest, to whom I gave the Volume, in my admiration of it, disappointed me by criticizing the Allocution on Avarice.[4] I don't agree with him

---

[1] C. J. Longman's rough estimate of the price he could pay for the copyright of Newman's works was £2500—£3000, but he did not wish to be bound by these sums, without further enquiries.

[2] Longman replied on 5 July, regretting the end of the negotiation but saying no expense had been incurred.

[3] Early in 1885 negotiations were renewed with Longman and successfully concluded.

[4] Bishop Moriary's *Allocutions to the Clergy*, pp. 53–72, contained a forthright one on the avarice of his clergy, delivered at a diocesan synod in 1861.

at all — but it makes me ask you, what you would think and wish about it. I am sure it would in many good Protestants raise their opinion of the Catholic Church and of its authorities; but we have fierce enemies.[1]

Excuse bad writing, but I cannot use my fingers

Very truly Yours John H. Card. Newman[2]

TO JOSEPH WHITAKER

July 5. 1884

(in substance)

Dear Mr Whitaker

Without having gone so far on my side as to receive an offer for my copyrights I see clearly that they cannot reach such a value in the market, as to make it worth while my selling them. As you may easily understand, I do not want a high price for myself. I should not know what to do with it, if I possessed it, but I am contemplating the future and others in it; and, in the interest of others, I do not think it right to acquiesce in a valuation, which experience may ultimately verify, but not at first.

I quite understand that your feeling about my volumes is not marketable — but I cannot sell at a fancy[3]

J H N

TO EMILY BOWLES

July 7. 84

My dear Child

Thanks for your letter, but I write to ask you to you read your direction. *I* have signed myself so before now[4]

Yrs affly J H Card. Newman

[1] Griffin replied on 8 July that he and others he consulted thought the Allocution on Avarice would do much good: 'Is it not better to make known to all that Bishops warn their Clergy against possible vices and denounce them when they exist? This very sin of Avarice dragged Judas down to hell, and his crime is published to the entire world in the Sacred Volume and stands as a warning to all priests.

An old avaricious parish priest died lately in this diocese and left all his money, some thousands of pounds to his relatives, and a ruin of a Church to his people and successor. Our revered Bishop would not attend his burial — his fellow priests remained away in disgust, and the few who did go to the place, not having heard of the facts, would not chant the office or join the Curate of the Parish in reading the short service when they heard of his will. This emphatic condemnation of his sin, edified the people of the entire diocese.'

[2] There exists a later note to Griffin, written on a card: 'I thanked you in my heart for your Congratulations, knowing that I had them

J H N'

[3] Whitaker had written on 28 June: 'With regard to your Copyrights. I have been thinking the matter over and would very much like to become the publisher. When you have obtained a bona fide offer from any respectable publisher for them will you give me the refusal of them at an advance of ten per cent upon the very highest price you can obtain from any one else. . . . . I can hardly hope to make much money but other feelings prompt me to make the offer.'

[4] Emily Bowles wrote on the autograph: 'He sent the cover. I had written "Wiseman".'

July 7. 1884

My dear Lord Braye

I did not forget your feast day this morning, and said Mass for you

Have you heard the report that the Pope contemplates publishing a letter on the University question?[1]

Yours most truly John H Card. Newman

TO MRS F. J. WATT

July 8. 1884

My dear Child

I have for many weeks been very anxious about you. And I write, lest you should wonder at my silence.

I do not write now to get a letter from you, for I think and thought that your Mother alone could give an account which would satisfy me, and, to my great disappointment, she has again and again put off her return.

I know it is your sister that has kept her. When she returns, ask her to write to me.

Yours ever affectly John H Card. Newman

P.S. Mrs. Stapleton's will has been in the Papers — and is the legal testimony how her money went.[2]

TO ANNE MOZLEY

July 10. 1884

My dear Anne Mozley

I congratulate you on being near the end of your anxious work, tho' it surprised and disappointed me to find that you have not before this been released from it.[3] I don't think you need fear it is not exciting interest, and I do not expect there will be any thing in it which ought to hurt me. In expectation of its coming here, I have got ready a small copperplate engraving by an amateur, which every one who has seen it admires; and this, though it has no worthier subject than myself, I shall ask you to accept. It has its history written on the back.[4]

I am glad to have your home news, for Frank, Jane, and Alfred are still

---

[1] On 30 Jan. 1885 Cardinal Simeoni at Propaganda wrote to Cardinal Manning reaffirming the ban on Catholics attending the universities.

[2] See letters of 27 Jan. 1884 to Mrs F. J. Watt and 12 Sept. 1884 to Miss Giberne.

[3] This was *Letters of the Rev. J. B. Mozley, D.D.*

[4] This appears to be the engraving of a sketch by J. Robertson, frequently reproduced. On it is written 'from life May 12, 83'.

part of home, and will be coming to you as John's party now.[1] Say every thing to them affectionate from me. You will be sad when you have finished your work, and their coming will be very opportune.

I have tried in vain to recollect what book I can have offered you. I will send you any number you may name. I suppose by the turn of your sentence, it was one of my writing. Well, there are 36 which have that peculiarity[2]

Yours affectly John H Card. Newman

TO LORD EMLY

July 11. 1884

My dear Emly

You wrote to me last year wishing me to put my name to a few pounds subscription for the Bishop of Orleans Monument.

I had already been applied to, and, as I felt that, as a Cardinal I ought not to give a small sum, I named as my contribution £20, as I think I told you.[3]

I wrote word, at the time I subscribed, that I could not pay up till 1884

Wishing to do so now, I wrote, as you had last year suggested to me, to M. Cochin. I inclose his answer. He says that the subscription is nearly sufficient for its purpose already, and that no difficulty is anticipated in what is still wanting

Is not this like saying, I am sorry you have felt it necessary to subscribe? Of course it would be a great gain to be let off the giving so great a sum. I have many large sums to meet.

Please, let me have back M. Cochin's letter

Yours affly John H Card. Newman

P.S You will see that M. Cochin gives no encouragement, such as, 'It is a great pleasure to find etc' and no compliment. etc etc[4]

TO JOHN HUNGERFORD POLLEN

July 11. 1884

My dear Pollen

Some day, as you pass Lambert's Shop, will you ask him to be so good as to send in the bill for the chalice

Yours affectly[5]

---

[1] All these were children of Newman's sister, Mrs John Mozley.
[2] The book Newman offered was *V.M.* II. See first paragraph of letter of 4 May to Anne Mozley. She now asked for a copy of *Apo.*
[3] Letter of 29 July 1883 to Lord Emly.
[4] Lord Emly showed Henri Cochin's letter to his French wife and gave her verdict 'that, according to French ideas, he could not have written otherwise to a Cardinal.'
[5] The signature is missing. See letter of 9 April to Pollen.

TO THE HIBERNIAN BANK

July 12. 1884

NB   The £32. 14. 7 remained to my credit in the BBCL[1] till this date, when I wrote to Cardinal MacCabe, telling him I was paying it to the credit of 'MacCabe and Neville' in the Hibernian Bank I said (I think) that I should interpret his *silence* as *consent*

July 14. But eventually I thought I had better not pay it into the Hibernian Bank till I heard from him, and just now I have received a letter from him all about *Freemasons*, apropos of my having in my letter to him sympathised with him about his late trouble with them, and containing *not one word* about Captain Robins's money.[2] He has *not* been silent. To write about Freemasons (!) when I wrote about Captain Robins, is a positive, not a negative silence, and I asked for a negative.

July 14   I wrote to the Hibernian Bank thus. Cardinal Newman will be much obliged to be informed by the Manager of the Hibernian Bank, whether the account of the Bank under the names of 'MacCabe and Neville' is still open and whether the Bank receives deposits in its behalf.[3]

TO ALEXANDER DENNY

(a letter I sent to him to this *effect*)   July 16. 1884

Dear Mr Denny

In reference to what I wrote to you in (I think) March,[4] I now say that I wish the agreement between us still to hold by which every Christmas you send me, up to that date an account of sales of my publications, settling with me, according to it, in the middle of the following March. But I ask in addition and in consequence I should wish you every 15th of July to inform me how my account stands as the result of the just finished half year. And as a beginning, if it would not give much trouble, I should like you tell me how it stands between last Christmas and the 15th of July, 1884, that is, yesterday.

I am vexed to find that the Title Pages and the lettering on the back of vol 1 and 2 of 'Difficulties' are not uniform. I have written to Messrs Gilbert and Rivington to print cancels. And

J H N

---

[1] This was a sum received from the executors of Captain Robbins for Irish University purposes, and held by Newman at the Birmingham Banking Company Limited.

[2] At the end of June Cardinal McCabe had defended two members of the Dublin town council who had been censured for voting against a candidate for the Civic Chair because he was a freemason. cf. letter of 25 June to P. J. Hughes.

[3] The account was still open in the name of 'McCabe and Molloy'. On 16 July Newman transferred the money to this account.

[4] Letter of 17 March to Denny.

July 16. 1884

Cardinal Newman wishes the Title Pages of volume 1 and volume 2 of 'Difficulties of Anglicans' to be uniform, and in consequence he thinks it necessary to have cancels of them, for which he incloses copy[1]

TO WILFRID OATES

July 16. 1884

Dear Mr Oates

I have received your Advertisement for Prize Books, and, after reading it, I am not surprised that my own volumes are accused of being dear and do not sell.

The Dream of Gerontius is not mentioned, even once, I think, thro your Twenty Four Pages, not even among the shilling books, though Catholic Legends, Conversion of Ratisbonne, French Revolution, Saints of the working classes, William of Wykeham etc are found there.

In the books high priced because well bound my Essay on Miracles price 6 shillings is there [?] 12 shillings that is, six shillings for the binding, and my 'Tracts' the same

Among the well bound prizes priced from 6/ to 12, ought to come my Apologia (6s) Callista, 5/6 — Verses 5/6 — Discussions, 6/ Sketches 6/ Loss and Gain 6/ Occ Serm. 6/ Discourses to Mixed C 6/ Position of C 7/ But none of these are found, tho' you have the works of Lady G Fullerton, Cardinal Manning (and Wiseman) Fr Coleridge.

And in the list of my volumes which comes (together with those of Cardinal Manning and Fr Faber) comes distinct after the Prize List 'The Essays' are priced at 12/ and the Historical Sketches at 18/ whereas they are 6/ a volume[2]

FROM BARON FRIEDRICH VON HÜGEL

St Valéry-sur-Somme. July 1st. 84.

My dear Cardinal Newman,

It is now so long since I last ventured to trouble you with a note, that I feel more than usually diffident as to my right, or indeed permission, to take up some of your most valuable time with the reading of what necessarily concerns and interests almost exclusively myself alone. —

It is the repeated reading and study of your article with 'Postscript' on the Inspiration of Scripture which, following upon a five years study and consideration of the Greek New Testament text and modern commentaries of various German schools upon it, leads me to wish to thank you, — small as I know the value of such thanks to be, — for the profound interest and subtle help your papers have been to me personally. — It is now some time since I have thought that, for the New Testament at

[1] As it appears in *Diff.* I and II.
[2] Oates's explanation on 18 July was that *The Dream of Gerontius* was being reprinted, and the high priced books represented copies expensively bound, which they were trying to dispose of.

least, (the Old I cannot hope ever to know otherwise than at second-hand), the position of a critic such as Wendt, the editor of the new (1880) edition of Meyer's Commentary on Acts, is stronger against the Tübingen critics by all its difference from the ordinary ultra-conservative line of defense. Now Wendt gives up just those points of detail, — such as the correctness of the mention of Theudas in the speech of Gamaliel; the reconcilableness of every detail in the three accounts of S. Paul's conversion; and even (and this is of course much the most important) the complete reconcilableness of St Luke's accounts of the resurrection period in the Gospel and Acts respectively, — which I understand you to allow the Catholic student to wave [sic]. — I think one of the first circumstances which rendered me thoroughly suspicious of the reconciliation-at-any-price system was finding that Fr Coleridge in his 'Life of Our Life' had, by some mistake, attributed only one of the two miracles of Our Lord (the healing of the deaf man and the blind man, both with spittle) to S. Mark, and found excellent reasons why they were distributed among two, and exactly those particular two Evangelists; whereas these miracles really both belong to S. Mark's narrative.[1] — Now it seemed to me in its way very ominous for his degree of conservatism that the very best system a man of Fr Coleridge's delicacy of perception could discover to account for the differences in the parallel narratives of the Evangelists should be so utterly subjective as this little incident proved it to be. —

I am also very grateful for your remarks about the two passages in St John and the last 12 verses of St Mark.[2] — At present I am inclined to abandon as glosses John V 4; the suspected [sic] parallel passages in the last chapter of St Luke, and (above all) the '3 heavenly witnesses' in 1 John; to maintain the authenticity of the 'Adulterous Woman' in S. John, and the last 12 verses of St Mark, but to admit that the former (historically) certainly, the latter possibly do not form part of the original edition of the Gospels in which we now find them; and to maintain the authenticity *in situ* of the suspected unique passages in the Passion of St Luke. —

I was much interested the other day in Paris to hear myself (at a soirée given by the Rector of the Institut Catholique as such) the Rector, (Mgr d'Hulst), the Professor of Apologetics (the Abbé de Broglie), and the Professor of Ecclesiastical History (the Abbé L. Duchêsne), all three, while discussing your papers, agree to their conclusions and maintain that their subject was the burning religious question of the hour, and that our Apologetics would cease to fail of their due effect only when the concessions you would allow can be fully applied and explicitly proclaimed. —

When, some months ago, Mr Wilfrid Ward asked me to be allowed to dedicate to me the posthumous collection of his father's published Philosophical Essays, I was flattered but also somewhat surprised and certainly a little embarassed;[3] for much as I always appreciated Mr Ward's dialectical vigour and personal kindness, and fully as I agreed with his general philosophical principles (to which I was first won by the 'Grammar of Assent'), there was yet as complete a difference of temperament and of conclusion in such subjects as the Church's Infallibility, and indeed historico-critical questions generally as could well obtain between faithful Catholics, and at the end of nine years intercourse such subjects were all but altogether tabood, and quite absolutely disagreed upon between us. — It was only the consideration of the marked difference in his treatment of philosophical and of historico-theological subjects, and his general coincidence with the tone and conclusions of the 'Grammar' in the former which overcame my fear that the few who care about my views at all might misinterpret them by my acceptance, and allowed me to accept the honour of some association with a work in its chief features so much your own.

I hope your Eminence will be so good as very kindly to forgive this somewha shameless letter.

[1] Henry James Coleridge, *The Life of our Life*, London 1876, p. 213. The mistake is not made in the harmony later in the book.
[2] *S.E.*, p. 26.
[3] W. G. Ward, *Essays on the Philosophy of Theism*, two volumes, London 1884, edited with an introduction by Wilfrid Ward.
In the letter, dated March 1884, dedicating the Essays, Wilfrid Ward explained that many of them treated of subjects his father frequently discussed with von Hügel, and spoke of the great esteem in which he held his friendship.

My wife begs to be very respectfully remembered to you. We continue to receive good news of and from her brother Pembroke who must, however, be very long before he can hope to be quite his old self again. Lady Herbert is well and as active as ever.

I am, my dear Cardinal Newman,

Yours very respectfully and grateful Friedrich von Hügel.

We return on the 3rd inst. to 4 Holford Road Hampstead London N W.

TO BARON FRIEDRICH VON HÜGEL

July 21. 1884

My dear Baron Von Hugel

You must have thought it quite unkind in me not to answer your welcome letter sooner — but just now I have been very much occupied and I get through much less work, especially in the use of my fingers, than I used to do. It pleased me to think that my Article in the xixth century had been acceptable to you. Of course it is an anxious subject. It is easy to begin a controversy — and difficult to end it. And often one does not wish to say, what logically one is obliged to say. If indeed I knew exactly where to draw the line in such questions, I should not have had the anxiety which I cannot even now get rid of. I knew from the first that it is easier to open a controversy than to close it, and it has been a relief to my mind to find what I have written approved of by those whose judgments I respect.

I am surprised at some of the statements in Scripture which you consider to need reconciliation — but, I suppose, every one has his own difficulties. And the fact, that the private judgment of one man comes into collision with the judgment of another, leads one to be suspicious of one's private views altogether.

I have been interrupted in writing this, and am sorry I see I have had the same thing twice over.

Every one speaks well of young Mr Ward, and I hope he will do much service to the philosophical side of religion in our English controversies.

Pray remember me most kindly to Baroness von Hugel, and excuse what I feel to be a very stupid letter; but I do not like to delay my answer to you.

I was glad to find your brother had succeeded in his Cambridge object[1]

Most truly Yours John H Card. Newman

TO MARGARET DE LISLE

July 22. 1884

My dear Miss de Lisle

You must not think it unkind in me to wish to limit my intercourse with friends.[2] No one but an old man can know an old man's difficulties, and he can

---

[1] See letter of 20 Feb. 1884 to Baroness Anatole von Hügel.

[2] See letter of 25 June 1884.

not attempt to state them without talking of himself more than he would like. I will but say that, in consequence of the slowness with which I get through the imperative duties of the day, I find it difficult to find time for saying office, and am obliged to let the letters sent to me accumulate unanswered, and often, after any unusual exertion, I am often obliged to lie down. Though I am well in health, I am far from strong.

I am sure you will take this into account, and believe me to be

Most truly Yours John H Card Newman

TO ROBERT WHITTY, S.J.

July 23/84

My dear Fr Whitty

Will you read and send on to Fr Lucas the inclosed.[1] His uncle's Life would be to *me* very interesting, and, I should think, to the public, but I can not rely on any anticipation I might form

I have had a disappointment lately which has discouraged me, tho, I confess, the cases are not parallel. Neither among Catholics nor Protestants, has my publication of W. Palmer's Russian Journal sold — On the other hand, there is nothing of *politics* in them, while Lucas was a *politician*

I rejoice to hear of the chance of your coming this way, and shall be glad to make your friend's acquaintance[2]

Yours affectly J. H. Card. Newman

TO THOMAS WOOLNER

July 24. 1884

Dear Mr Woolner

I thank you for your new Poem.[3] You have the gift of writing what is *music*, and it is kind in you to send it to me. In some respects I am little fitted to be your critic; for (tho' I am not sure,) you seem to me to have some deeper meaning than the smooth and calm tenor of your versification makes necessary, but what this is, I cannot determine.

You illustrate by your subject what Gibbon, I think, calls the 'clegant mythology' of Greece and Rome —[4] but, as found in the great classic poets, it is severe as well as graceful, and, putting aside other considerations, I prefer, as a matter of critical rule, the severe school.

[1] On 17 July Herbert Lucas, then a Jesuit Scholastic, wrote to ask whether a life of his uncle Frederick Lucas, which he proposed to write, 'would be of real service to the Catholic cause in this country?' Whitty sent his letter to Newman and explained that Sir Charles Gavan Duffy, proposed to publish Frederick Lucas's long Memorial on Irish Politics, written in 1855 for the Pope.
Newman sent his reply through Whitty. The life was written not by the nephew, but by the brother, Edward Lucas *The Life of Frederick Lucas, M.P.*, two volumes, London 1886, and included the Memorial.
[2] Whitty proposed to bring Herbert Lucas to see Newman, in the autumn.
[3] On 13 July Woolner wrote that he was sending Newman a copy of *Silenus*, London 1884.
[4] 'The elegant mythology of Homer gave a beautiful and almost a regular form to the polytheism of the ancient world.' *Decline and Fall of the Roman Empire*, chapter ii, J. B. Bury's edition, London 1896, I, p. 29.

Excuse a short acknowledgment from an old man, whose brain and fingers move slower than they once did

Very truly Yours John H. Card. Newman

Thomas Woolner Esqr

TO THE SECRETARY OF THE CATHOLIC YOUNG MEN'S SOCIETY OF GREAT BRITAIN

July 26th, 1884.

Dear Mr Quinn,

I congratulate you and the members of your Society generally on the coming of your anniversary, and gladly send you my blessing upon it. I trust I shall say Mass for you all on Sunday, August the 3rd.

Very truly yours, John H. Card. Newman.

TO MESSRS KEGAN PAUL, TRENCH & CO

July 26. 1884

Dear Sirs

In answer to your letter of this morning I observe as follows.[1]

I have been engaged for almost fourteen years in making a uniform edition of my writings, and have completed it in *36 volumes*. I inclose a list. I have the copyright of all of them but one. Twelve (my Anglican Sermons) are under a royalty.[2] Perhaps half are stereotyped.

The printing has cost me a large sum, and I have about 10,000 copies in stock. I look to the sale of this stock for the payment of my outlay

These facts will show you that your question does not admit of a direct answer. Whether it could take a shape which I could entertain, you will now be able to see[3]

I am, Dear Sirs Yours faithfully

John H Card. Newman

Messrs Kegan Paul, Trench and Co

TO THOMAS HARPER, S.J.

July 28 1884

My dear Fr Harper

I thank you for your new Volume — as magnificent in its exterior, as valuable in its contents.[4]

[1] Kegan Paul, Trench and Co., wrote that they had heard that Newman might be contemplating a new uniform edition of his works, and expressed readiness to offer terms for its publication.

[2] i.e. *P.S., S.D., U.S., Jfc.*, and *Selections for the Seasons*. Newman had not recovered the copyright of *Ari.*

[3] See letter of 30 July.

[4] *The Metaphysics of the School*, vol. iii, London 1884. The presentation copy is bound in red leather with Newman's arms stamped on the cover. The subject of the volume is 'The Efficient Cause'.

And I thank you for the kind wish you express about me, but what is the good of living when work seems too much for one?[1]

Yours affectly John H. Card. Newman

P.S.   I hope you have not found your own work too much for you.

TO WILLIAM CLIFFORD, BISHOP OF CLIFTON

July 29 1884

My dear Lord

The translation has come back safe.[2] I feel very grateful to you for the pains you have taken with it, and the great value of your corrections.

You will be glad to hear that pleasant letters have passed between Dr Healy and me — and that the immediate controversy is at an end[3]

Most truly Yours J H Card Newman

TO THE CHIEF INSPECTOR OF THE GENERAL POST OFFICE, BIRMINGHAM

The Oratory Hagley Road July 30. 1884

Cardinal Newman has been asked to recommend Mr William Louch for the office of letter carrier. He has much pleasure in doing so, inasmuch as he has known him from being in the choir since 1863, and he can certify that he has always been a most respectable, trustworthy, useful and punctual man.

John H. Card. Newman

TO LORD RONALD GOWER

July 30 1884

Dear Lord Ronald

I think of venturing to ask your acceptance of the Volume of Verses in which the lines occur (p 152) 'Lead Kindly Light.' May I?[4]

I am, Your Lordship's faithful Servant John H. Card. Newman

Lord Ronald Gower

[1] Harper, who had been abroad for his health, wrote on 26 July of his 'undying gratitude for all that you have done for England and for me,' and hoped to be able to send Newman all the projected eight volumes of his work.
[2] The Italian translation of the article and Postscript on Inspiration. cf. letter of 30 May to Lord Emly.
[3] See letter of 3 July to Healy.
[4] Lord Ronald Gower wrote on 12 July quoting a letter he had received from Queen Victoria: '. . . referring to her son, (Duke of Albany) H.M. writes — "This is but a pilgrimage — a great struggle, and not our real home — and we may say with those beautiful Lines
'So long thy power has blessed me —'"
and the Queen — (not quite correctly, bless her) — quotes till the end of that hymn which has given comfort to thousands.' This was the last verse of 'Lead Kindly Light'. The Duke of Albany died on 21 March.
Lord Ronald Gower, who was the youngest son of the second Duke of Sutherland asked for a signed photograph of Newman. He thanked for it on 17 July, and asked if he might call, when staying at Trentham. This he did on 29 July.

TO MESSRS KEGAN PAUL, TRENCH & CO

July 30. 1884

Dear Sirs

I thank you for your letter.[1] I have no particular view, nor any definite wish, as regards the copyrights or editions of my volumes. My letter to you was written almost with the feeling that nothing would come of it. I thought and think it discouraging, but I did not like to shut up abruptly the prospect which you have opened

J H N

TO LOUISA ELIZABETH DEANE

Aug 1. 1884.

My dear Louisa,

I am shocked at what you tell me. Your writing is most clear and good, but my eyes are very bad, and my power of attention. I can't otherwise explain my great unkindness and rudeness to your and Emmeline's proposal.[2] But really I am deaf and blind and lame — and my brain and my fingers move very slow.

I shall be rejoiced to receive the compliment which you and Emmeline intend for me — and the only difficulty is the when and how long.

We have a nice little quiet hotel next door to us — as being small it requires bespeaking rooms.

Would the 1st of September, Monday, suit you? or September 8th?

The only difficulty on my part, a serious one, is my difficulty in keeping awake. Recollect, I am 83.[3]

Yours affectionately John H. Card. Newman

TO MRS JOHN HUNGERFORD POLLEN

Aug 1 1884

My dear Mrs Pollen

Your photographs are splendid. They could not be better. Thank you. The poor Duchess! But what can we wish for better than what she naturally shrinks from?[4]

Yours most truly J H Card. Newman

[1] Messrs Kegan Paul wished to postpone until autumn any offer for a uniform edition of Newman's works.

[2] Mrs Deane reminded Newman on 31 July that she had asked in the spring that her daughter Emmeline might make a sketch of Newman. See postscript to letter of 7 May to Mrs Deane.

[3] Mrs Deane replied that she and her daughter would come on 1 Sept.

[4] The Duchess of Norfolk's son, the feeble-minded Earl of Arundel, was seriously ill.

Aug. 3. 1884

My dear Wilfrid Ward

Thank you for your letter which was very acceptable to me. I have read your article with great interest and like it much —[1] but my brain works so slowly and my fingers are so stiff, that writing is a difficulty and a trial to me.

I should say that the theories of Mr Spencer and Mr Harrison have that hearing and acceptance from the public, as to need an answer, and, that your answer to them is unanswerable, but in saying this, I am not paying you so great a compliment as it appears to be at first sight; for I say so from the impatience I feel at able men daring to put out for our acceptance theories so hollow and absurd. I do not know how to believe that they are in earnest, or that they preach the Unknowable and Humanity except as stop gaps, while they are in suspence and on the look out for the new objects of worship which Sir James Stephen thinks unnecessary as well as impossible.[2]

I then am too impatient to refute carefully such theorists; if it was to be done, it required to be done with both good humour and humour, as you have done it. You have been especially happy in your use of Mr Pickwick;[3] but this is only one specimen of what is so excellent in your Article.[4]

It tires me to write more

Very sincerely Yours John H. Card. Newman

Rednall Aug. 13. 1884

Dear Sir

I would gladly answer your question at length, had I time and were I strong enough.[5]

---

[1] 'The Clothes of Religion', the *National Review* (June 1884), pp. 554–73, reprinted in W. Ward's *The Clothes of Religion*, London 1886 and in *Witnesses to the Unseen*, London 1893. Herbert Spencer wished to make the 'Unknowable' and Frederic Harrison 'Humanity' wear the clothes of religion, writing in the *Nineteenth Century* for Jan. and March.

[2] Sir James Fitzjames Stephen in 'The Unknowable and the Unknown', the *Nineteenth Century* (June 1884), pp. 905–19, attacked both Spencer and Harrison, declaring that the 'Unknowable' and 'Humanity' were mere shadowy figments.

[3] 'That a man should refrain from beating his wife because he believes in God . . . is reasonable and natural. But that love for the human race should make him refrain when love for his wife is an insufficient motive, is hardly to be expected. "Keep yourself up for my sake," said Winkle to Mr. Pickwick, who was in the water. The author remarks that he was probably yet more effectively moved to do so for his own sake. And to tell a man to be good to his wife for the sake of the human race has in it a considerable element of similar bathos.' Art. cit. p. 567, *The Clothes of Religion*, p. 60, *Witnesses to the Unseen*, p. 55.

[4] On 4 Aug. W. Ward thanked Newman for his 'encouragement of a peculiar kind which nothing else could be to me.' For his publication of Newman's letter see those of 20 and 21 June 1886 to Allies and W. Ward.

[5] Goodwin, a solicitor, wrote from Hastings on 11 Aug. that he had been brought up a Methodist but for twenty years had had 'little or no dogmatic faith but my religious *feelings* are unaltered.' He felt the need of certainty in religious belief and asked Newman for 'the secret . . . of combining real religious spirituality with perfect freedom to accept all knowledge.'

It seems to me that the great differences in religion between man and man arise from their difference from each other in first principles, so that according to their first principles such is the religion which they severally adopt.

For instance — one man thinks sin to be so great an evil, as not to be named in the same breath with any other evil, but to stand simply by itself. Another thinks it nothing but a coming short of ethical perfection, more or less, not involving any sense of guilt.

And first principles *hold together* so that these imply those.

I fear I may seem running very far back for a beginning, but I now come to my answer to what you seem to ask of me. What you, as all men, need, is *true* first principles, and who can give them to you, but He who made you?

I say then to every one who feels the pain and unnaturalness of scepticism, it may be a hard matter for a man to *detect* and recognize his own first principles, and you may *never* know them, nor is it necessary that you *should* know them, but it *is* necessary that they should be true — and, I repeat, who can give you them but God?

It is usual to say that the choice of a religion is an intellectual work and matter of reasoning — it may be an object of the *intellect* but as a work of reasoning, it is subordinate to first principles, which is that very intellectual gift, which God alone can give us, and from which reasonings follow.

You ask me for a 'secret'. The secret is prayer. 'Ask ⟨for true first principles⟩ and it shall be given you; seek and you shall find.' It is a slow process. The same scene looks very different when viewed from various stand points. Pray God to give the true stand point.

Excuse a letter which it would be easy to criticize for it is the writing of an old man. But it is my *answer* to your question.

Your faithful Servt J H Card. Newman

TO W. S. LILLY

August 17, 1884.

My dear Lilly,

I rejoice to be told that your book has in so very short a time come to a second edition,[1] and I would send you a long letter about it were it not that I am obliged to write very slowly, which has this among other evils, that before I come to the second half of my sentence, I forget what I was going to say. I have always held that thought was instantaneous — that it takes no time — and now that doctrine is confirmed to me, when I want a subtle shorthand to record what otherwise, like a flash of lightning, goes as rapidly as it comes.

Your first chapter[2] is as startling as it is new to me — and, unless you

---

[1] *Ancient Religion and Modern Thought*, London 1884.
[2] 'The Message of Modern Thought', on Schopenhauer.

make too much of the man, gives rise to dismal apprehensions, but I think nature and reason, to say nothing of grace, will prove too strong for his theories.

I have already spoken to you about Chapter II.[1] By cutting a little here and there, and piecing them together, you have ingeniously made me write a sort of philosophical theory. I shall only be deeply rejoiced, if your attempt succeeds, of course, but time is the test of truth.[2]

As a personal matter I must quite negative having been indebted to Kant or Coleridge. I never read a word of Kant. I never read a word of Coleridge. I was not even in possession of a single work of Coleridge's. I could say the same of Hurrell Froude, and also of Pusey and Keble, as far as I have a right to speak of others.[3]

As to the three or four great Oriental religions, you have not satisfied me as to their transmission by trustworthy tradition from their founders.

What can be the instrument, what the guarantee, of trustworthy tradition, but a promise from above of infallibility? Would not, for instance, the Christian teaching of the first half of the Fifth Century have broken down but for the providential stumbling (vide Gibbon) of Theodosius's horse?[4]

I did not observe you mentioned M.S.S., except in the case of Zoroaster. How far go they back? As to Mahomet, what I think a real omission (and your *first*) — perhaps the fault is in my eyes — is, your not giving authorities for Mahomet's amiableness. Your account of his private life reminded me of Luther also. I think that not only should good authorities be given for the fact of the Mahometan ascetics and saints (lest weaker brethren should be scandalised), but two points should be considered; first, whether there is anything in the Koran to countenance such saintship (as there *is* in the Gospels and the Epistles of the New Testament), and secondly, whether the existing recognised and sanctioned *developments* of Mahomedism, especially its sensuality, were compatible with such teaching of the duty of purity, as to make a

[1] 'The Claim of Ancient Religion', about Newman and Tractarianism. See letter of 8 July 1879 to Lilly.
[2] The next paragraph appears word for word in Newman's letter of 7 Jan. 1885 to Lilly, of which the autograph is extant. Lilly probably inserted it in this present letter, which only exists as he printed it in the *Fortnightly Review* (Sept. 1890).
[3] In this paragraph Newman refers to the origins of Tractarianism. Lilly wrote in his Preface, p. ii: 'As the founder of a religious movement, the philosophical basis of which was indirectly derived from Kant, John Henry Newman's spiritual history is peculiarly worthy of attention in view of the great question which Modern Thought so imperiously raises.' On pages 59–61 Lilly said: 'Samuel Taylor Coleridge was the first among English thinkers to study and understand Kant, to assimilate his teaching, and to reproduce it in a new form. . . . I am, however, immediately concerned with his [Coleridge] effect upon that particular intellectual and spiritual phase represented by the Tractarian Movement. Cardinal Newman, in a paper published in the *British Critic* in 1839, reckons him one of its precursors . . .' See the *British Critic* (April 1839), p. 400; *Ess.* I, p. 269; *Moz.* II, p. 39; *Apo.*, p. 97. Also H. F. Davis, 'Was Newman a disciple of Coleridge?', *DR* (Oct. 1945), pp. 165–73, Edward Sillem, *The Philosophical Notebook of John Henry Newman*, Louvain 1969, I, pp. 227–9, and John Coulson, *Newman and the Common Tradition*, Oxford 1970, pp. 254–5.
[4] *The Decline and Fall of the Roman Empire*, chapter xxxiv, edited by J. B. Bury, London 1897, III, p. 444.

high standard of saintship congenial and possible to the genius of the religion.

If I did not know you were doing a good work I should not be so critical

Very truly yours, J. H. Card. Newman.

As *you* led me to write on Inspiration, I send you a copy of my *Postscript*.[1]

TO THOMAS FISHER UNWIN

Copy   Rednall Aug 19. 1884
Sir

I thank you for your letter and what you say of the MS in question[2] However, I think I am right in saying it could not have been given to the public without leave of the writer's family ⟨heirs⟩, according to the legal decision in the case of Lord Ward's representatives v. Bishop Copleston.[3]

I thank you for your offer and wish to publish it for me — however, I have no intention to make use of it, as I agree with you in considering that when looked at carefully it would be found to have little claim for public notice

J H N

TO MRS J. W. BOWDEN

Birmingham Aug. 24. 1884

My dear Mrs Bowden

I grieve indeed at my missing you and Emily. I have hardly slept a night at Rednall since last October, and now, the weather being so wonderfully fine, I was driven there by Medical pressure! I return here in order to be *sketched* next week — I suppose continuously, but I don't know.

Where are you? at Malvern? do you stay there?

Love to Emily

Yours affectly John H Card. Newman

[1] cf. letter of 7 Dec. 1882 to Lilly.
[2] Unwin, the publisher at 26 Paternoster Square wrote on 9 Aug. to say that he had been offered the letters of Charles Newman but had decided that there was little in them worth publishing. But if Newman proposed to print literary remains of his brother, he would be glad to publish them. See also letters of 15 May, 6 and 23 June to Whitaker.
[3] Edward Copleston published in 1841, when Bishop of Llandaff, the letters he had received from John William Ward, first Earl of Dudley. The volume was suppressed and is very scarce. See Samuel Smiles *Memoir and Correspondence of John Murray*, London 1891, II, p. 443. That the copyright of letters lay with their writer and his heirs was decided a hundred years earlier than the Ward-Copleston case, which appears to have been settled out of court.

Aug. 24. 1884

My dear Mr Powell

I congratulate you and Mrs Powell on your daughter's marriage. Tell her so, and that I send her my blessing, praying Him from whom all blessing comes, to fulfil abundantly what I ask of him

I have said Mass for her and her husband this morning, and waited to write to you till I had done so

Yours most truly John H Card. Newman

TO PETER LE PAGE RENOUF

The Oratory August 24. 1884

My dear Renouf

I am mortified that I cannot say at once 'Come'. At medical pressure, I am out (except to-day) at our country cottage now for several weeks. Also tomorrow week I have to sit for my picture, I suppose continuously. But I should be glad to see you. What do you mean by a 'convenient' time? Come if you can. Direct to me 'Rednall, Bromsgrove'. Rednall is 8 miles from Edgbaston.[1]

Yrs affectly J H Card Newman

TO GEORGE T. EDWARDS

Rednall Aug 29. 1884

Dear Mr Edwardes

Thank you for your friend's Address.[2] Of course I am pleased at any kind word said of Catholics by those external to the Church, for it seems to mark them as included in the number of the 'men of good will' to whom the Angel at the Nativity sent 'peace' — but I mourn over the hindrance to the cause of Missions, which, from the time they woke up to the thought that if they were Christians they must be Missionaries, Protestants have effected.

Happy Henry Martin, who, as far as I recollect, never thwarted a Catholic Missioner, and who was rewarded by dying on the spot where Chrysostom

---

[1] Renouf was retiring from the post of a Chief Inspector of Schools, and in 1885 became the Keeper of Egyptian and Assyrian antiquities at the British Museum.

[2] On 20 Aug. Edwards sent an Address given at a missionary conference, by a friend of his. It spoke 'of a member of the Committee of the Bible Society, and the Church Missionary Society, calling on a Cardinal Archbishop at Tunis [Lavigerie] for friendly Conference as to locating missionaries in Africa', and gave the testimony of 'a very decided Protestant to the Christian heroism of a Jesuit priest' who died at the mouth of the Zambesi river. cf. letter of 29 Jan. 1882 to W. T. Law. Edwards thought Newman had set an influential example of irenicism.

consummated his slow martyrdom.[1] But as to the Missions in general of English Protestants, they were a new idea to them in 1800, two centuries after their Lutheranism, or Calvinism began, and then, judging by Dr Macbride's article in the British Review in 1821 they seem never to have heard of Catholic Missionaries existing in heathen countries, as a fact.[2]

Thank you for referring to my friend Mr Pattison.[3] Forty years ago he was on the point of becoming a Catholic. Stopping short of it, his mind was too logical to have faith in any other Creed. I fear nothing from his Reminiscences;[4] he was an accurately minded man — and never would pretend to know things about me before he ever saw or heard of me — or rather, before he himself was born. My fear is that his book will subserve the cause of infidelity, which is a dreadful thought

Very truly Yours John H Card. Newman

TO CHRISTOPHER SCOTT (1)

Rednall Aug 29. 1884

Dear Dr Scott

I rejoice to hear from you that the work which your Bishop has committed to you, of providing for Cambridge a larger Church than the present has had so favorable and promising a commencement.

In an evil day, such as this, when a new and plausible form of infidelity is in our midst, the Catholic faith and worship is the only availing refuge of religion, and our Universities are the natural seat of that conflict, which now, as at other times, is the condition of victory.

The Cambridge Catholics have a great mission before them, and I pray with all my heart that the fulness of the Divine Blessing may be with them for the fulfilment of it

I am, dear Dr Scott

Your faithful Servant John H. Card. Newman

[1] Henry Martyn, evangelical and pioneer Anglican missionary, went out as a chaplain to the East India Company in 1805. He did missionary work in India and also in Persia, dying on his way home at Tokat in the north of Asia Minor. The final stage of St John Chrysostom's journey into exile was from Tokat to Comana in Pontus, five miles distant.

[2] The reference is evidently to the article 'The Unitarian Controversy', the British Review, XVII, (March 1821), pp. 154–5, where it is stated: 'The whole Christian world is now intent upon the great work of evangelizing the heathen. England in particular, is pouring forth her wealth, and sending forth her sons, to aid the cause.'

[3] Edwards wrote: 'I fear the death of Mr Mark Pattison, the late Rector of Lincoln [on 30 July], has removed almost the last of your early Oxford friends. I heard with much interest of your visit to him shortly before the end, and I trust that "at Evening time it was light". Since the publication of the notorious "Essays and Reviews", he seems to have taken little part in matters theological, though I hear he has left ready for publication some account of the Oxford Movement. I have no doubt he will be more accurate in his statement of facts than Mr Mozley, whose book I fear gave your Eminence pain, as it did indeed to many others.'

[4] Memoirs, London 1885. In the letter of 8 Jan. 1884 from Pattison to Meta Bradley, quoted in note to that of 2 Jan. to him, Pattison wrote: 'Nothing that has happened to me during my illness has moved me so much as this renewal of correspondence with my old Master after a very long interval. . . . And I had just been giving an account in my Memoirs of the steps by which I had passed beyond him leaving him as it were, wallowing in his fanaticism. I feel it hard-hearted now to let that page stand and yet it is the simple truth.'

TO CHRISTOPHER SCOTT (II)

Private   Rednall, Aug.29. 1884

Dear Dr Scott

I wrote the above in compliance with the wishes you have expressed to me but, on reading it over, feel a great difficulty in it.[1]

Two reasons can be given to external readers for asking for aid in the Cambridge undertaking; to provide for the religious necessities of the Catholic Undergraduates, and to convert the Protestant Undergraduates. If I understand you, the Cardinal Archbishop will not countenance your assigning the first reason, and how can you put forth in public your second, as I have done in the above letter without rousing a strong feeling against you all thro England?

It is a difficulty I found years ago as regards Oxford — and now it presents itself to me, as it did then, with great force. Perhaps you have already felt it, and spoken about it to the Bishop. I am inclined to ask you to do so, and[2]

---

[1] Scott wrote on 19 July that he had been appointed to the Cambridge mission the previous November. It was essential to build a proper Catholic church on a prominent site since 'the present Church is small, dark, almost suffocating in summer, and so badly situated that many who come to the University go away ignorant of its existence, and others who come (and they are many, including earnest enquirers) are so greatly inconvenienced by the crowd and heated atmosphere, that it is a matter of astonishment they ever pay a second visit . . .'

Scott pointed 'to the interest many protestant undergraduates manifest even in our difficult circumstances, and to the need of the Faith being well represented for the sake of our own Catholic students of whom there are always few in residence.' He asked Newman for 'a letter of approbation and an expression of your opinion of the importance of this mission.'

The prohibition against Catholics frequenting the universities was still in force, and Newman delayed his reply. On 25 Aug. Scott wrote again: 'Since applying to your Eminence for a recommendation of this mission, an absolute promise has been made to me to build a good Church worthy of the site.

I attribute this in a great measure to a letter I was able to show to my munificent Benefactor from the Cardinal Archbishop in which, while condemning Catholic students coming up to the University, with equal earnestness he urged the importance of a Church at Cambridge of the highest order of excellence.'

Scott wanted a letter from Newman to include in a circular to raise money to pay off the mortgage on the site. The benefactress who would pay for the church, Mrs Lyne Stephens, was old, and the work had to be done in her lifetime.

[2] The draft ends thus. Scott replied on 1 Sept., 'Your Eminence's very kind letter makes me reproach myself for giving so much trouble.

As to the difficulty arising from the prohibition by the Bishops of Catholic students coming to Cambridge my answer is that Cardinal Manning has given me a letter in which he earnestly presses the need of a church here of the highest order of excellence attainable. This letter is for publication and I enclose a copy, as also of my Bishop's letter, who is one of the Bishops most opposed to our students coming here.' This was Arthur Riddell, Bishop of Northampton.

Scott went on to say he did not think the University would regard the new church as 'the inauguration of an aggressive movement.'

Newman did not send his first letter of 29 Aug. but in a cancelled draft wrote 'answered Sept 9/84 that before writing to him a letter for publication I should feel obliged to him if he thought he could tell me the amount of the mortgage, and any at present promised list of subscriptions. JHN' Newman wrote at the end of his draft:

'I am glad to find that the attractiveness of the proposed Church is not considered an objection to the work. In 1867 I was forbidden by Propaganda to go to Oxford on the express ground that I should be attractive.' See letter of 12 Sept. to Scott.

TO MISS LOUISA DEANE

Sept 1. 1884

My dear Louisa

The bearer of this is my friend, Father Neville.

He will provide you with a conveyance, and will take you to the Hotel.

I shall be ready for Emmeline at 3 o'clock, and will send some one to bring you both over. If you prefer to get over your dinner first, I shall be ready for her at 4 or later, quite as well.[1]

Yours affecty John H Card Newman

TO MESSRS KEGAN PAUL, TRENCH & CO

Sept 5. 1884

Dear Sirs

In answer to your enquiry I beg to say, that it is my practice to note the day on which I send cheques to my Birmingham Bank here, and that as to the cheque you write about, in my Banker's book as also in my own private account I find only from you 'Sept 26, 1883, £15.13.11' and March 18. 1884 £1.15.11

I am very careful to send at once receipts due for cheques which come to me. Have you any from me besides the above two cheques?

I do not think any cheques have come in [to] me from you besides the above two.[2]

I am &c J H N

TO LOUISA ELIZABETH DEANE

Septr 8. 1884

My dear Louisa

Thank you for your letter.[3] It was a great pleasure to me to see your daughters. It was a renewal of the affectionate interest which I felt in you, when you were young, and which I have never lost. What a time ago! and none remain![4]

[1] Mrs Deane was too ill to come to Birmingham, and so Louisa Deane accompanied her sister Emmeline, who was to sketch Newman. Neville met them at New Street Station at 1.30 p.m. on 1 Sept.
[2] Kegan Paul mistakenly supposed Newman had failed to pay in a cheque.
[3] Mrs Deane wrote on 6 Sept., 'Louisa and Emmeline returned yesterday evening, deeply impressed by your goodness to them. . . . I am delighted with the Portrait.' Newman insisted that they were his guests at the Plough and Harrow hotel.
[4] At Christmas 1884 Baroness Isy von Hügel wrote to Newman: 'We were very grateful to 1884, which brought us to you, and gave us those happy days at Edgbaston, of watching Emmeline Deane drawing you and feeling that we might see you, and talk to you all the time without fear that we were taking up too much of your time.
And for me in another way, I could not ever say what it was to me to feel that my husband had seen you, — and that you had given him your blessing and that I might hope you liked him. Both of us feel that to have been with you those days, has made life very different to us, —

Should you come this way together with the summer, I should rejoice —
but the weather must be fine to allow of it.

With all kind remembrances

Yours affly J. H. Card. Newman

TO BISHOP ULLATHORNE

The Oratory Sept. 10. 1884

My dear Lord

Thank you for your impressive sermon. I have fastened to it your accompanying letter as giving it an additional interest over and above its power[1]

Your Lordship's affecte Servant[2]

TO MISS M. R. GIBERNE

The Oratory Sept 12. 1884

My dear Sister Pia

I have had so many letters which required an answer, and find it so difficult to use my fingers, that I have delayed this letter.

I was confirmed in Oscott Chapel, I think on November 1, 1845.[3] I made my first communion October 10, 1845 in our little Oratory in our house at Littlemore — no strangers were there

Neve is alive, but past all work.[4]

Lady Georgiana was better when last I heard from her husband but the terrible pain may come suddenly at any time, I believe.[5]

Our Bishop is wonderfully well — though his state seemed so serious a year on two ago. I think the prayers of his religious houses have kept him alive.

I am sorry to hear from you that Mgr Place feels his age. What an escape he

and when we came away, Anatole said "It makes one feel how it is worth while to be a saint."' After apologising for saying so much Baroness Anatole went on to say how she had seen the portrait at Mrs Deane's house in Bath, 'on an easel in the drawing room, — and I was indeed rejoiced to see how perfect and how beautiful it was. Mrs Deane said, it sometimes "held large receptions," — and that it had gone to Eton too, and had there "received" through all a Sunday afternoon.' See also letter of 2 Sept. 1885 to Lord Blachford.

[1] This was a copy of Ullathorne's sermon *The Drunkard*, the first he published in Australia, in 1834. A new edition had just been brought out by Burns and Oates. When sending it on 10 Sept. Ullathorne wrote: 'It was preached in a Court house at Sydney, in a public house at Appin, and in a ball room over the stables of the Crown Hotel at Bathurst, beyond the Blue Mountains. Such were our chapels in those primitive days. The Colonial Secretary, the celebrated naturalist Mac Leay told me that he read it once a fortnight to his convict servants, and asked me to write a similar one against profane swearing, which I did. And [sic] old military pensioner told an Australia [sic] friend of mine, after reading it: "The gentleman who wrote this must have drunk very hard at some time of his life." Father Matthews [sic] told me in 1839, that he had printed 20,000 copies of it. There have been many editions since, so I suppose it is found useful, though savage.' See also *Butler* I, pp. 87–9.

[2] The signature has been cut out.

[3] See diary.

[4] cf. letter of 27 Oct. 1881 to Augusta Theodosia Drane.

[5] See letter of 4 June to Alexander Fullerton.

has had in not being now at Marseilles![1] It must have been a great disappointment to you not to have had his visit.

We have nine new boys in the school — not all a *gain*, for many old ones
are leaving. We recommence next week

Eleanor Bretherton is, I fear, in a serious way at last She has winter after
winter been confined to her bed — and has not been to Mass for many
months together. At last she seemed getting better, and the wounds in her
lungs healed. Lately came the news that old Mrs Stapleton had left the family
nothing.[2] The shock has opened the wounds. You may recollect her as a little
child. She has 7 or 8 children. I ask a prayer for her.

I have nothing to tell you. Dr Northcote has a chronic cramp in his hands
and, I fear, cannot say Mass. Escourt, you know, is dead.[3]

Ever Yours affectly John H. Card. Newman

TO CHRISTOPHER SCOTT

Sept 12. 1884

Cambridge, as being the seat of a great University, has a hold on the
hearts and minds of Catholics in all parts of England.

This is why I feel a special satisfaction in learning from you that with
your Bishop's sanction you are receiving subscriptions with a view to building
there a new Church on a new site, an undertaking, which, though local in its
purpose, is not local in the interest which attaches to it, nor in the call which
it makes on our co-operation.

I pray God to bless so important a work, and I beg of you to accept from
me in aid of it the inclosed offering[4]

J H N

TO WILFRID OATES

not sent?[5]   Sept 13. 1884
Dear Mr Oates

As a Publishing firm has without any initiative of mine expressed a wish to
correspond with me on the subject of my Volume,[6] I find I cannot at present
answer any question from you. But it has concurred [sic] to me to ask you
what you would think of an arrangement such as the follows: —

[1] Charles Place, Bishop of Marseilles in 1866, became Archbishop of Rennes in 1878.
There had just been a severe outbreak of cholera at Marseilles.
[2] See letter of 27 Jan. to Mrs F. J. Watt.
[3] E. E. Estcourt died on 16 April 1884.
[4] See end of last note to letter of 29 Aug. to Scott, who wrote on 10 Sept. to say that a
mortgage of £1910 must be paid off before the church at Cambridge could be built, and giving
the short list of subscriptions received. In a note on this letter Newman explained that he
wrote his present letter for publication, and that he enclosed a cheque for £20.
[5] See letter of 13 Oct. 1884 to Oates.
[6] Probably a slip for 'volumes'. See letter of 26 July to Messrs Kegan Paul, Trench and
Co.

viz for a publisher to *buy of me the liberty* of printing and selling a *large* edition of my writings say 2000 of all, or of some volumes only 1000 copies, of some 3000 volumes, or again some volumes to omit, but in all cases at a small and uniform size and at a *low price* and to let this cheap, small edition to run against my present uniform high-priced edition.

Or say again you bought a cheap edition of a few volumes, 2 volumes Sermons, Catholicism [*Prepos.*], Verses, Callista, Apologia, or you might make the experiment with one book, say the Apologia.

Even, if you thought such a plan possible yourself, I on the other hand might at first sight have this difficulty that, without any unfairness on your part, my own edition would be at a disadvantage with your customers, if you had a rival edition to set against it

TO MRS F. J. WATT

September 13th. 1884.

My dear Eleanor,

I enclose a cheque for the boys' clothes, not *excluding* poor Daisy — but coats I suspect are dearer than frocks.

Yours affectionately, John H. Card: Newman.

TO EDWARD HAYES PLUMPTRE

Sept. 14. 1884.

My dear Dean of Wells

After you were gone, it struck me that, since I asked you to omit words of mine which you had referred to in the first edition of your Sermon, I ought to have told you in what respect those words come short, as well as Pusey's, of what I wished to say by way of facing the difficulty of a doctrine which by many good men is thought to be so terrible.[1] Now my own answer to myself, is that we know too little about the necessary bearings and issues of the Divine Rule of Justice as regards the moral creation to be judges what is and what is not consistent with the idea which nature teaches us of a good God. This thought has ever kept me effectually from any disturbance of mind on the subject, or any need of hypotheses or explanations. You will say, 'But you ought for the sake of others to be furnished with some explanation.' 'Well, I *am*.' I reply. I maintain, that objectors take for granted certain conditions of the punishment as existing, which are not necessary and which change its character, and which are not revealed as elements in it. Now since the

[1] This was the doctrine of eternal punishment. Plumptre had arranged to visit Newman on 11 Sept. He was about to republish his sermon *The Spirits in Prison* in a volume, *The Spirits in Prison and other Studies in Life after Death*, London 1884. See note to letter of 26 July 1871, where Plumptre's quotation from *The Dream of Gerontius* will be found. He applied what Newman said of purgatory to eternal punishment, and retained the quotation in his republication, p. 24.
For Pusey, see letter of 4 Aug. 1880 to him.

difficulty admits of a certain explanation, whether in whole or in part, it also suggests that there may be other explanations, though we do not know them. Let us have a little faith; which ought to be no great hardship to those, who starting with the profession that there *is* a God, ought not to be surprised that we cannot always understand him, who is infinite. The assumption on the part of objectors to which I refer I have spoken of in my 'Grammar of Assent' — not explicitly in the First Edition, for it is too awful a subject easily to dwell upon without 'fear and trembling', but in Edition Five, *p 501. note iii.* If you cannot find the Edition in Wells, I will ask your permission to send it you. Excuse my handwriting — for I cannot form my letters without pain and slowly

Very sincerely yours John H. Card. Newman

The Very Rev. Dean Plumptre.

TO JOHN HUNGERFORD POLLEN (I)

Sept 15 1884

My dear Pollen

Judge Mathew is in a difficulty at the moment to know what to do with his son, who like Arthur [Pollen] is leaving us. We have suggested to him to let him be at Richard Pope's, whose house opens upon our playground. He and Arthur being great friends would it not be a gain for Arthur as well as for young Mathew if A went there too? They would have the same lectures as if within the House. You know best. I hope Mrs Pollen is getting over her accident

Yours affly J. H. N.

TO JOHN HUNGERFORD POLLEN (II)

Monday Sept 15/84

My dear Pollen

Pardon me — I have since my letter of today seen your letter to Fr Norris and heard his remarks on it — and this makes me feel that I had no business to interfere in Arthur's matter[1]

Yours affly J H Card. Newman

TO THE COUNTESS OF DENBIGH

Bm Sept 16. 1884

My dear Lady Denbigh

I shall not forget the 24th   I congratulate you and Lord Denbigh on the happy event. Nor must I forget to congratulate Lord Feilding himself who

[1] Norris had written to Pollen on 14 Sept. that his son Arthur needed more emulation. He was head and shoulders above the rest. He and his friend Theobold Mathew were matriculated together at Trinity College, Oxford, on 17 Jan. 1885.

is the chief person concerned, and who has favored me with a visit here more than once[1]

I am, My dear Lady Denbigh

Most truly Yours J. H. Card. Newman

The Countess of Denbigh

TO WILFRID OATES

Sept. 18. 1884

Copy

Dear Mr Oates

I certainly shall not sell my copyrights. What I am thinking of is publishing a cheap edition of some of my volumes, if I can do so without materially hurting the sale of them in their present shape

Will you send me 4 copies of fifth edition of Grammar of Assent, *which runs to 503 pages*

Yours very truly J H Card. Newman

TO THE HON. MRS MAXWELL-SCOTT

Sept 20./84

My dear Mamo

It pleases me so much that you and your husband like the engraving.[2] I did not write my name, when it came to the point of sending it, for several reasons. Ink would spread, and pencil would not mark. Now I send two specimens. Of course it will be no trouble to me to send you any other which you might prefer.

Fr Bellasis is enjoying himself. To me it excites a painful pleasure, from my thoughts of your dear Father. His excessive kindness illuminates all my reminiscences of Abbotsford, but I feel deeply my unworthiness of them. But his kindness and considerateness was for all about him; that took him a last visit to Traquair.[3] My best remembrances to Mr Maxwell Scott

Yours affectly J H Card Newman

TO ANNE MOZLEY

Sept 22. 1884

My dear Anne Mozley

I am glad you like the engraving. It pleased very much all who saw it here[4]

As you mention the 'Family Picture' T. Mozley never asked my consent.

---

[1] Viscount Feilding, eldest son of the Earl of Denbigh, married on 23 Sept. 1884, Cecilia Mary, daughter of the eighth Lord Clifford.

[2] cf. letter of 10 July to Anne Mozley.

[3] See diary for 18 July 1872. Richard Bellasis was visiting the Maxwell-Scotts at Abbotsford, and went over to Traquair House.

[4] See letter of 10 July to Anne Mozley.

Harriett is represented so unlike the rest that strangers must think that she is a young lady I am sweet upon[1]

Yours affly J H Newman

TO EDWARD HAYES PLUMPTRE

Sept 22 1884.

My dear Dean of Wells

I have read to my profit your Article on Dante's great Poem.[2] I will explain what I mean by profit. I am not enough of an Italian scholar to read the original, and I have many times taken up Cary with an earnest wish to master it, and have been forced to lay the book down again as being intolerably dry. Also, I have not a sufficient knowledge of Italian history to understand the allusions, and I have been perplexed to make out as a whole the idea and conception of the Poem, for instance whether Virgil, Cato, Statius etc. were in heaven, purgatory, or hell, or in some fourth state which the Church knows nothing of. Now I think your Article has made me feel, apart from my difficulties, the special ethical and personal beauty of the Poem, which must exert a powerful influence on every one who knows it well. Your extracts, though in translation, have brought this home to me. You have had a difficult task, but you have in no slight measure surmounted it, if you have done as much as this for me, for what I feel, others may feel too. At the same time I doubt whether the Divina Commedia can ever be popular in England. I have sent you my volume;[3] vid pp 501–503 not as if I could hope that you would concur in what I have said, but as my own answer to an objection, and moreover to poor Dean Stanley's great misinterpretation of what I hold.[4]

Very truly yours John H. Card. Newman

The Dean of Wells.

TO J. R. BLOXAM

Sept 27. 1884

My dear Bloxam

Fr Neville has just returned from Rednall and has shown me your letter. I am simply aghast at it and do not know how to answer you. It must be some mistake between him and me that you had no acknowledgement of your

---

[1] This was the sketch of 1829 done by Miss Giberne, and mentioned by T. Mozley in his *Reminiscences chiefly of Oriel College* . . . I, p. 28. He appears to have had it reproduced in a periodical, it was in *Merry England* (Oct. 1885), p. 364 and it has several times since appeared as an illustration in books. See also letter of 28 Oct. 1885 to Wilfrid Meynell.

[2] 'The *Purgatorio* of Dante: a study in autobiography', the *Contemporary Review* (Sept. 1884), pp. 322–42. There was a passing reference to Newman. Speaking, p. 335, of 'the music of the Church', Plumptre said that Dante 'had known, as Milton, Hooker, Newman knew how it could soothe the troubles and attune the discords of the soul . . .'

[3] See letter of 14 Sept.

[4] See letter of 21 July 1881 to Miss Giberne.

beautiful present.[1] I fancied I had told you that I could not write without pain and very slowly — and, considering there are so many letters I am obliged to answer *myself* I thought I had asked you to let Fr Neville write to you in my name. I know something of the kind was said, though I forget particulars. Nothing is left to me but to express my extreme sorrow, and to apologize to you for seeming to behave to you unkindly

Yours affectly John H Card. Newman

TO SHIRLEY DAY

Bm Sept 27. 1884

Dear Sir

I left the Anglican Church because I could not believe it was a portion of that Catholic Body which the Apostles founded and to which the promises are made. I felt I could not be saved, if I remained where I was.

In my Apologia I think I have brought this out; that the bad reception by Anglicans of Number 90 increased that conviction, and that the present improved state of the Anglican Church would have been a temptation adverse to that conviction, I do not of course deny — but from first to last I have had the clear conviction, independent of all such accidents, that the Church of England is a Parliamentary Church

May God bless you and lead you into the Truth[2]

Your faithful Servant John H Card. Newman

TO MESSRS RIVINGTON

To Messrs Rivington
Sept 29. 1884

I did not send you the letter overleaf (written in June last)[3] because I was in doubt how to answer it.

Now I write to say that I am willing to accept the terms you propose for the Latin Plays which as I understand them are as follows: viz that you will print on commission terms the plays uniformly in size and type, the printing being ultimately paid by me.

As to stereotyping the plays, I have too little confidence in their sale, to be able to contemplate such a step.

You must judge what plays must be reprinted in order that they may have

[1] On 19 Feb. 1884 Bloxam wrote that he was sending Newman a birthday present. He sent *The Catholic Church in Scotland, from the Suppression of the Hierarchy till the present time*, edited by J. F. S. Gordon, Glasgow 1869, inscribing 'One more Token of reverential regard and affection.'
Bloxam wrote to Neville on 21 Sept. to say that his letter and present had never been acknowledged. It was Neville who undertook to do this and forgot.
[2] Within a few weeks of receiving this letter Shirley Day moved from Water Orton to Edgbaston, and was there received into the Catholic Church together with his wife.
[3] The bracketed words are in square brackets as if not part of what was sent. Rivington wrote on 7 June about the republication of Newman's adaptions of Plautus and Terence.

403

the uniformity necessary for binding together It will be my business to find you pattern copies for the printer

I suppose your binding them together will not hinder you selling them separately if required

I am &c. J H N

TO EMILY FORTEY

Birmingham Oct 3. 1884

My dear Child

I thank God with my whole heart for His goodness to you, and gladly send you my blessing. I will not forget you on Saturday.[1]

I think your Father has been very good to you. It was right you should have a trial, but he has not opposed your convictions, as some parents have in their dealings with their children.

You must not suppose your present state of peace and joy will always continue. It is God's mercy to bring us over difficulties. As time goes on, you may be cast down to find that your warmth of feeling does not last as it once was, and instead of it you may have trials of various kinds. Never mind; be brave; make acts of faith, hope, and charity; put yourself into God's hands, and thank Him for all that he sends you, pleasant or painful. The Psalms and Saint Paul's Epistles will be your great and abiding consolation.

'Rejoice with trembling'.[2] I say all this, not as dissuading you from enjoying your present joy and peace, but that you may enjoy them religiously.

I repeat, God bless you, keep you, and direct you. Through His grace you have begun life well. May he give you perseverance.[3]

Yours most sincerely John H. Card. Newman

TO THOMAS JEFFERSON JENKINS

Oct 3. 1884

Dear Revd Sir

It is very kind in you to send me your Volumes and I thank you for them They are in very different ways interesting to read, and especially the

---

[1] On 2 Oct. 1884 Emily Fortey wrote: 'Nearly two and a half years ago, when I was feeling rather in a muddle, I wrote to you and you were kind enough to write a very beautiful letter to me. [That of 6 July 1882]. Then, following your advice, I went to see a Priest, and I have never been in a muddle since. All this time I have not been allowed to go to a Catholic Church or see Priests, but my father found that it made no difference to me; I was still at heart a Catholic, so lately he has given me permission to do as I like. So I have been instructed and on Saturday, the Feast of S. Francis, a day specially chosen by me, I am going to be received into the Church. And now I am writing to thank you *very* much for your kindness to me more than two years ago. Perhaps if you had not written to me I might never have become a Catholic . . .' See also letter of 12 Feb. 1883 to Henry Fortey.

[2] *Psalm* 2:11.

[3] See letter of 4 Aug. 1887. When Newman died Emily Fortey wrote from 11 Orchard Gardens Teignmouth 'Dear Father Ryder, May my flowers be put somewhere near his feet?'

Volume on Secular Schools is as seasonable here and important as it can be in America[1]

Very truly Yours John H Card Newman

The Rev T. J. Jenkins

TO JOSEPH F. X. O'CONOR, S.J.

Oct 3. 1884

Dear Rev. Father

I thank you cordially for your letter and your pamphlet.[2] It is of course very pleasant to receive such testimony in my favour from one who is so far removed from me, as to be able to claim impartiality. And I have that great opinion and respect for the Society of Jesus, that the good word of a member of it is most acceptable to me.

Our respective countries so differ from each other, that what I am going to say is perhaps out of place, but in England I should have some misgiving lest the generous praise you bestow on what I have written should lead in some quarters of the literary world to a re-action against it. In my past life I have found that some of my best benefactors were those who abused me, and by abusing raised a feeling in my favour, while those who spoke out boldly their liking for what I was saying or doing raised a contrary feeling which was adverse to me. I should not be surprised to be told, that this is *not* the case of America, but I have thought it worth while to mention it to you.

Excuse my stiff writing, which is the trouble of old age.

Begging your good prayers for a very old man I am

Your faithful servant John H Card. Newman

TO MRS F. R. WARD

Oct 3. 1884

My dear Mrs Ward

I shall be very glad to see you and Mr Ward on the 11th and 12th, as you propose. It is very kind in you.

---

[1] Jenkins was a priest of the diocese of Louisville and a writer in defence of Catholic schools. One of the books he sent to Newman was *The Judges of Faith and Godless Schools. A compilation of evidence against secular schools the world over, especially against common state schools in the United States of America, wherever entirely withdrawn from the influence of the authority of the Catholic Church*, New York 1882. See also letter of 14 Nov. to Jenkins.

[2] O'Conor wrote on 20 Sept. from Woodstock College, Maryland, his gratitude and that of the young Jesuits he taught, for Newman's writings. He enclosed what seems to have been a collection of extracts from Newman's works, perhaps *Something to Read*, a course of English reading, first published in 1881 for the students at Georgetown University.

O'Conor contributed to *Donahoe's Magazine* (June 1882), pp. 481–5, 'Cardinal Newman as a literary study.'

You had better write at once to the Plough and Harrow, as they are sometimes full

Yours affly John H. Card. Newman

TO THE HON. CHARLES LINDLEY WOOD

Bm Oct 3. 1884

My dear Mr Wood

I shall be rejoiced to see you, as you propose, on Thursday or Friday next. You have a claim on my affection, not only from what I know of you personally, but from the deep and undying love I have for your uncle[1]

I know you will take us as you find us, and make allowances when necessary[2]

Most truly Yours John H. Card. Newman

TO HELEN P. WILLIS

copy
Oct. 4. 1884

Cardinal Newman begs to return Mrs Willis's inclosure, as being addressed, not to him, but to a London Priest[3]

TO JOHN PYM YEATMAN

Oct 5/84

Copy
Dear Mr Yeatman

As my letters were private and addressed personally to yourself, I gladly accept your acquiescence in their not appearing in your volume. Perhaps you will feel it enough if I consent to the insertion of the one I herewith send back to you[4]

J H N

[1] Relying on Newman's invitation at his previous visit, 4 Nov. 1878, Wood wrote on 2 Oct. from Hickleton to ask whether he might stay the night. Referring to his mother's illness and death, he said, 'We have been in great trouble all this year, and it has led to reading over many old letters, among them those you gave me of my uncle's. I was looking at them again last night, and my heart so went out towards you, that I felt, at the risk of seeming a great intruder in your eyes, and altogether presuming upon your goodness, that I must ask you to let me see you again —' Wood added that he was going to the opening of Pusey House on Thursday 9 Oct., and would be able to give news of that event.

Wood wrote to his wife at this time of the interest with which he had read the letters of his uncle Samuel Francis Wood in 1837-8 to Newman, which the latter had already given him. J. G. Lockhart, *Charles Lindley Viscount Halifax*, London 1935, I, p. 260.

[2] See letter of 7 Oct. to Wood.

[3] Helen P. Willis wrote an agitated letter asking for an interview, enclosing what was apparently a letter of introduction to a London priest. She said she was a convert of a year, and now in a state of uncertainty.

[4] Yeatman wrote on 29 Sept., 'I am publishing a kind of Apologia for my life', and asked if he might publish the letters Newman had written to him. Newman gave permission for the publication of the last, that of 10 July 1871. See notes there.

TO J. R. BLOXAM

[Oct. 7. 1884][1]

My dear Dr Bloxam

I shall be glad to see you any time on Friday

Yours affectly J. H. Card. Newman

Wednesday

P.S.   I dine in the middle of the day; but I am at liberty at 2½

TO AN UNKNOWN CORRESPONDENT

Birmingham Oct 7/84

Dear Sir

Your letter is as considerate as it is candid. I wish especially to answer it fully, but my fingers are weak and stiff and I write slowly.

I never in arguing should think of entering upon your question whether or not the Anglican Church was 'in schism' or whether or not it was in possession of an 'Apostolical Succession'. These questions seem to me beside the point in dispute. I never indeed, as I think, have said, that its orders were certainly invalid; what I have said, if I have spoken against them is that their validity was doubtful, and that doubtful orders were unsafe, following the rule ordinarily laid down, as by St Alfonso Ligori: 'In Sacramentorum collatione *non potest* minister uti opinione *probabili* aut probabiliore de Sacramenti valore, sed *tutiores* sequendæ sunt, aut moraliter certæ.' Newman's Essays vol 2 p 81[2]

Even then allowing a *probability* to the Engling [sic] orders, I cannot call them, especially after considering Serjeant Bellasis's pamphlet, *safe*.[3]

But my direct and patent reason against the Catholicity of the Anglican communion is quite clear of the question of orders. Anglicans consider the Church to be only a *family*; but it is more than that, it is a state, a polity, a *kingdom*, a visible kingdom. Daniel spoke of it as a kingdom parallel to the pagan monarchies which preceded it[4] — Our Lord announced that the kingdom of heaven was come, St Paul speaks of the one body with many members, (not branches, a body has not branches.)[5] If then the Church is a kingdom, and the one predicted Kingdom, the communion of Rome and the Anglican communion cannot *both* be that Kingdom, any more than King James and King William could each at the same time be King of England.

[1] Date added by Bloxam.
[2] *Ess.* II, p. 81; St Alphonsus, *Homo Apostolicus* I, iii, Malines 1842, pp. 11–12.
[3] *Anglican Orders, by an Anglican, since become a Catholic*, London 1872, consisting of letters sent to a newspaper in 1847.
[4] *Daniel*, 2:44.
[5] *Matthew*, 4:17; 10:7. 1 *Corinthians*, 12:12–27.

On this subject I will quote my Essay on Development of Doctrine p. 265

It may be possibly suggested that this universality which the Fathers ascribe to the Catholic Church lay in its Apostolical descent, or again in its Episcopacy; and that it was one, not as being one kingdom or civitas 'at unity with itself', with one and the same intelligence in every part, one sympathy, one ruling principle, one organization, one communion, but because, though consisting of a number of independent communities, at variance (if so be) with each other even to the extent of[1] a breach of communion, nevertheless all these were possessed of a legitimate succession of clergy, or all governed by Bishops, Priests, and Deacons. But who will in seriousness maintain that relationship, or that sameness of structure, make two bodies one? England and Prussia are both of them monarchies; are they therefore one kingdom? England and the United States are from one stock; can they therefore be called one state? England and Ireland are peopled by different races; yet are they not one kingdom still? If unity lies in the Apostolical succession, an act of schism is from the nature of the case impossible; for as no one can reverse his parentage, so no Church can undo the fact that its clergy have come by lineal descent from the Apostles. Either there is no such sin as schism, or unity does not lie in the Episcopal form or in the Episcopal ordination. And this is felt by the controversialists of this day; who in consequence are obliged to invent a sin, and to consider, not division of Church from Church, but interference of Church with Church to be the sin of schism, as if local dioceses and bishops with restraint were more than ecclesiastical arrangements and by-laws of the Church, however sacred, while schism is a sin against her essence. Thus they strain at a gnat, and swallow a camel. *Division* is the schism, if schism there be, not *interference*. If interference is a sin, division, which is the cause of it, is a greater; but where division is a duty, there can be no sin in interference.'

I will in a few words refer you to some of the places of my writings, in which I have treated of the objections with which you end your letter.

1. Papal Supremacy — vid Development pp 148–165
2 Purgatory — Vid Via Media vol 2 p 110 note (or 102)[2]
3 Cultus of Bl. Virgin — letter to Pusey, in Difficulties of Anglicans vol 2

I am, Dear Sir Yours very truly J. H. Card. Newman

THE HON. CHARLES LINDLEY WOOD

Bm Oct 7. 1884

My dear Mr Wood

We shall be very glad to see you on Thursday. As you come at 6, you will be in good time for dinner at 7. I wish to introduce to you some of our Fathers before dinner. I have to go into Church at half past 8. But perhaps

[1] This paragraph is in William Neville's hand; the words 'the extent of' were added by Newman, who also probably underlined the two words lower down.
[2] This is the page number in the first edition of *V.M.* II.

you may like to go too. We are sadly anticipating our Bishop's death, but we always have Benediction on Thursday[1]

Very sincerely Yours John H Card. Newman

The Hon C. Wood

P S   One of our Fathers was a godson of your Uncle, Henry Ryder[2]

TO LORD BLACHFORD

Bm Oct 8. 1884

My dear Blachford

I have for some time wished to find some excuse for writing to you, and now I have found one.

I inclose a passage from Lord Malmesbury's Autobiography — and I want to know, if I should take notice of it.[3] Lord Granville on what seems a less matter about himself, has published a letter.[4] He writes to Lord M. directly — but, as I deny Lord M's *facts*, which he says he *witnessed*, I could not ask him to withdraw them, and could not deny them without personal offence to him.

My own preference would lead me to take no notice of them now, but to leave a memorandum behind me — but I don't see I can do this in questions of fact on the authority of eye-witnesses — it would be leaving till the narrator of them was dead, what he ought to have opportunity of meeting.

However, I want your judgment on the case

[1] Bishop Ullathorne was seriously ill. Wood wrote to his wife from the Oratory about this visit on 9 Oct., 'I got here about half past five . . . The Cardinal came into my room for a minute before dinner, and at ¼ to 6 we went down stairs.

Someone read during dinner, and afterwards each of the Fathers including the Cardinal delivered *a few thoughts* upon a text . . .

After dinner we went to the recreation room where there was fruit, wine, etc. We all sat in a circle round the fire, I next the Cardinal, and conversed. I thought it rather a shy proceeding, but on the whole it did very well. At ½ past 8 there was Benediction in Church, and after that the Cardinal came to my room and we had a very pleasant talk. He was really delightful, and I cannot tell you how drawn I felt towards him. I think I never met anyone who so realised the ideal I had formed of him.' J. G. Lockhart, *Charles Lindley Viscount Halifax*, I, p. 259. The 'fruit, wine, etc', were provided by Newman on 9 Oct. each year, to celebrate the anniversary of his reception into the Catholic Church.

[2] Henry Ignatius Dudley Ryder was a godson of Samuel Francis Wood.

[3] The passage concerning Newman in *Memoirs of an Ex-Minister, an Autobiography*, two volumes, London 1884, I, p. 18, stated:

'Of this celebrated writer and divine, and now a cardinal, no one at that time would have predicted the future career. He used to allow his class to torment him with the most helpless resignation; every kind of mischievous trick was, to our shame, played upon him — such as cutting his bell-rope, and at lectures making the table advance gradually till he was jammed into a corner. He remained quite impassive, and painfully tolerant. I once saw him nearly driven from Copleston's table, when the Provost, who was an epicure, upbraided him for what he called 'mutilating' a fine haunch of venison, and shouting out, "Mr. Newman, you are unconscious of the mischief you have done."'

The passage was quoted by the *Daily News* and other newspapers, when they reviewed Lord Malmesbury's *Memoirs*.

[4] Lord Granville sent to *The Times* (7 Oct.), p. 5, a copy of a letter of 27 Sept. which he had written to Lord Malmesbury, correcting a story in *Memoirs of an Ex-Minister*, reproduced in *The Times* of 26 Sept., that Lord Granville had once been personally discourteous to the Austrian ambassador in London.

409

Even if I am right in thinking I ought to notice it, the question comes, how can I get it published — a newspaper will only insert what it has itself already given occasion for; but, even if the Times had quoted Lord M's I have no reason to think it would admit my answer, for it refused a letter I sent to it in parallel circumstances, within the year.[1]

I heard of you from de Vere lately. A very good account

Yours ever affecty John H Card. Newman

TO MRS DAVIES-COOKE

Bm. Oct 9. 1884

Dear Mrs Cooke

Your anxious difficulty does not admit of a satisfactory solution. For myself I have a difficulty of my own, as I do not know the received rules on such matters in the Westminster diocese. It would hardly be right in me, to propound a rule of duty different from what was customary with you, in London.

Left to myself, I should say that your question is one, which must be determined by expedience. There are cases in which you are obliged to allow, or to suffer, what is short of being the best course, to avoid greater evils.

[1] cf. letter of 14 Feb. 1883 to the Editor of *The Times*. Lord Blachford sent Newman a copy of his letter of 9 Oct. to the Editor of the *Daily News*, where it appeared on 13 Oct. It began: 'Sir, The following extract from Lord Malmesbury's reminiscences respecting Cardinal Newman has appeared in some newspapers, and in one is characterised as "not without its pathos".' This was the *Weekly Register*. See letter of 4 Nov. to Lord Blachford.

After giving the passage quoted in the first note, Lord Blachford continued: 'As this passage was quoted some days since in the *Daily News*, perhaps you will allow me — an old friend and pupil of the Cardinal's — to question its accuracy. I went up to Oriel in October, 1828, a few months after Lord Malmesbury (then Lord Fitzharris) left; and I then attended Mr. Newman's lectures for three years. I am quite sure my contemporaries will agree with me in saying that during that time Mr. Newman's conduct to the undergraduates and theirs to him was absolutely the reverse of what Lord Malmesbury describes. He was very kind and retiring, but perfectly determined (as might be expected from his subsequent history) — a tutor with whom men did not venture to take a liberty, and who was master of a formidable and speaking silence calculated to quell any ordinary impertinence. I can scarcely imagine a revolution in his character such as Lord Malmesbury's description would imply to have taken place during the Long Vacation of 1828. But further. Among the tutors of Lord Fitzharris's time was a gentleman of the name of James. He was a kind, joyous, and overflowingly good-natured person, full of quips and puns, whom it was impossible not to like, but who could not pronounce his r's, and left behind him precisely the reputation ascribed by Lord Malmesbury to Mr. Newman. I did not know him as a tutor, but I knew him well enough as a brother fellow, and I was familiar with the legends of him with which Oriel was alive when I joined it . . .

This is given to introduce a legend more to the present purpose. It was that Mr. James's class, by gradual and combined pushing of the lecture table, contrived (in the manner described by Lord Malmesbury) to make Mr. James recede before it as far as he could go. . . . Whether the legend as received in 1828 was accurate or embroidered, Lord Malmesbury best knows. But I cannot myself doubt that after half a century of active life he has fastened on Mr. Newman his recollections of Mr. James. To those who have known both men well, it is difficult to imagine a confusion more surprisingly whimsical. If what I have said, in the interest of future history, is insufficient for its purpose, I cannot help hoping that the Cardinal (if not unbecoming the purple) will be induced to come into the field on his own behalf and mine. — I am, Sir, your obedient servant,

Blachford.'

For a confirmation of the attribution to William James see letters of 14 Nov. 1884 and 23 April 1885 to Lord Blachford.

Your daughter may be repelled from the Catholic Church, if you forbid her a step which she desires from good motives, though mistaken in her act. You cannot indeed sanction her, but you can suffer her, she knowing that it is contrary to what you have recommended to her.[1]

We are very glad to have your boy with us, I hear a good account of him I am,

My dear Mrs Cooke Your faithful Servant
John H. Card. Newman

TO ALEXANDER DENNY

Oct 9. 1884

private
Dear Mr Denny

I have received from a publishing firm a proposal to take the sale of all my books on a royalty. I wish to tell you at once, though I am not well disposed to royalties and think it unlikely any thing will come of it. Have you any thing to say about royalties, or about the terms of per centage which they offer[2]

J H N

TO WILFRID OATES

Oct 9. 1884

in substance
Dear Mr Oates

It must have got about that I have been thinking of selling my copyrights — In consequence I suppose I have had an offer to take the editions on a royalty. I lost no time in telling you this

Very truly yours J H N

P.S. I was much concerned to hear just now, that Mr Cornish the Oscott bookseller here, had written to you for a book ⟨publication⟩ of your house without getting an answer. Oct 10[3]

---

[1] Mrs Davies-Cooke, widow of Major James Robert Davies-Cooke, who died in 1883, was a convert. She had a daughter, Beatrice, who spent her life in Catholic good works, and is probably the one mentioned here. Mrs Davies-Cooke died in 1929. One of her sons, Aubrey, came to the Oratory School on 21 April 1884, another, Arthur, became an officer in the 10th Hussars.

[2] Kegan Paul, Trench and Co. wrote on 7 Oct. offering to bring all Newman's works out in a uniform edition, paying him a royalty, which would eventually amount to two thirds of the profit on each volume. See letter of 23 Oct. to Denny.

[3] Cornish was the bookseller, 39 New Street, Birmingham.

Oct 10. 1884

My dear Mr Lilly

I have attempted the sort of substitution which you could admit, but I feel it almost a liberty to do so. What I have written overleaf is only a suggestion[1]

Yours very truly John H. Card. Newman

p 328 As to the origin of the soul — On this point the church has decided nothing; and her silence is a *prima facie* reason for thinking it is a question which is beyond us. There are writers indeed who have proposed an hypothesis which will supersede your conclusion, but our theologians do not consider it successful. If you prefer to follow St Augustine, you will say etc[2]

October 12. 1884

My dear Blachford

You have done me a great service and given me a great relief. It has touched me very much. It is not pleasant to be always writing about oneself, or against other people; but if Lord M's [Malmesbury] friends cannot persuade him to be wise enough to accept your gentle letter as an opportunity of getting out of a scrape, I shall be obliged to show that he is in one. If so, I shall do my best to say little, but I am very sanguine that your letter will end the matter.

If he is a gentleman, if he has not committed himself too deeply, as if witnessing what he states (e.g. the venison?) he will withdraw it. I have always thought Kingsley made a great tactical mistake. After I had finished the publication of the Apologia week by week, I left a *fortnight* before publishing my Appendix with the 39 'Blots'. If he had been wise enough to cut in with some lines of apology in the Papers, saying that he was very sorry for having made his charges, for my history of myself had shown him, (which the evidence as yet before him had not sufficed to show him,) that I had been

---

[1] The review of Lilly's *Ancient Religion and Modern Thought*, London 1887, in *D R* (July 1884), p. 212 remarked, 'We think Mr. Lilly ill-advised in revising or countenancing the view of Traducianism. Even if no formal condemnation of that view can be pointed to, yet the consensus of theological teaching would surely make it rash to hold it.' Lilly wrote on p. 328: 'First, as to the origin of the soul. No doubt many considerable authorities have held, and still hold, that when a man chances to beget a child a soul is immediately created to animate it. But this Creationist doctrine is not of faith. The Traducian view — that the soul like the body is derived from the parent — has been held by theologians of much repute, and, although fallen into discredit, has never been condemned. Or if you elect to say, with St. Augustine, I do not like to dogmatise about a matter of which I know nothing . . . you would be quite at liberty as a Catholic Christian to do so.' Newman's suggestion overleaf follows as a postscript.

[2] Lilly replied on 14 Oct. that he would be only too glad to avail himself of Newman's suggestion.

unfair to myself in what was hitherto but a partial revelation of me, he could have stopped my 'Blots' which are said to have stung him so much, and I should have been cut off from that portion of my defence which the treatment of the Blots involved

I am not going to be *fierce* with Lord M. but, if I have to clear myself from the charge of cowardice, I must explain how the charge came

Yours affectly J H. Card. Newman

P.S. I trust you will get into no trouble by mentioning James by *name* He was Mrs W. G. Ward's uncle — and left her money. I suppose Ward's sons never saw him.[1]

Excuse small writing — my fingers are so stiff

TO WILFRID OATES

Oct 13. 1884

sent

Dear Mr Oates

I corresponded with you many months ago about the sale of my publications, you spoke of my copyrights, but made no acceptable offer for them.[2] Time went on, and then I wrote to you my intention of publishing cheap editions, but again you had nothing at all to say.[3] It is in these circumstances, without any application on my part, that a publishing firm has made me a proposal of taking my volumes on a royalty. (It was no thought of mine, and I am not at all sure I shall accept the offer — but,) if you wish to make an offer for your house, I fear I must ask you not to delay.[4]

J H N

TO MESSRS RIVINGTON

October 13. 1884
To Messrs Rivington and Co

copied and sent

Dear Sirs

I beg to inform you that I have had an offer of taking all my publications off my hands. I would gladly have interested you in them, but, considering most of them as written since I have become a Catholic, that I felt was impossible. This will involve, should I accept what has been proposed to me, a

---

[1] See last note to letter of 8 Oct. to Lord Blachford. William James, son of a Scottish doctor who settled at Rugby, was at school there before going up to Oriel College, where he was elected a Fellow in 1809. He became Vicar of Cobham, Surrey, in 1823, and then Rector of Bilton, Warwickshire from 1853 until death in 1861.

[2] See letters of 10 and 14 March and 29 April to Oates.

[3] See letters of 13 and 18 Sept. 1884 to Oates.

[4] Kegan Paul made an offer on 7 Oct. Oates replied on 14 Oct. that he would make an offer within a week. See letters of 25 Oct. and 11 Nov. to Oates.

14 OCTOBER 1884

relinquishment of the royalty which for many years I have received from you for 11 or rather 12 of them.[1]

J H N

TO LORD BLACHFORD

Oct 14. 1884

My dear Blachford

I think your letter reads very well in print.[2] It *must* be successful. Should it not, I must write — but you have most skifully [sic] prepared the way Can it be possible that *another* Oriel contemporary can be found, some friend of Lord M's [Malmesbury] to say 'Now he thinks about it, he recollects he *had* heard of or *had* witnessed some insulting acts done towards me!'

But this is my constitutional fidget, as what I said to you about James's name.[3] I said it, because I was not sure that your letter had actually been posted; but since, I have felt that you could not help giving the name, if you wanted utterly to demolish its application to me.

I am disgusted at the bullying line taken by the Liberals in the Franchise question, and cannot understand how Gladstone can sanction it.[4]

I am interrupted by the going off of the morning post

Yours affectly John H. Card. Newman

TO LOUISA ELIZABETH DEANE

October 14. 1884

My dear Louisa,

Your letter was a very gratifying one, and I am more than sanguine that our original judgment of the portrait will be the general one. It is a great success.[5]

I was rejoiced to become acquainted with your daughters

Yours affectly J. H. Card. Newman

P.S. Excuse a short letter.

[1] Rivington and Co. replied on 15 Oct. 'The royalties are only terminable by mutual consent. As the Publishers, we have the sole right of publication during the legal term of copyright; but as the Author, you have the right of incorporating in any new editions alterations and corrections. May we ask whether you propose to transfer this right?' Against the last sentence Newman has written, 'I don't understand the question'. Rivington were unwilling to surrender their copyright, and this brought Kegan Paul's plan to an end.
[2] In the *Daily News*, 13 Oct. See letter of 8 Oct. to Lord Blachford.
[3] See letter of 12 Oct. to Lord Blachford.
[4] Gladstone's bill for extending the franchise was opposed by the Lords unless accompanied by a bill for the redistribution of seats. Many Liberals were for forcing the first bill through, but in the end Gladstone effected a compromise by which both bills were passed. Lord Blachford replied on 15 Oct. agreeing with Newman's criticism.
[5] Mrs Deane wrote on 7 Oct. that her daughter Emmeline's sketch of Newman was much admired. It was sent to H. W. Mozley at Eton, where 'there was quite a Levée to see it.' See also letter of 8 Sept. to Mrs Deane.

414

TO W. S. LILLY

The Oratory, Birmingham Oct 15. 1884

Dear Mr Lilly

Thank you for your proposal to speak to Messrs C. and H. [Chapman and Hall] Be quite sure that it is not unusual to take the advice of one publisher against another. How could you avoid giving my name? and, tho' that would not matter to me it would suggest perhaps Messrs K. P.'s [Kegan Paul] name. The two great questions are the amount and the time of paying the royalty or percentage. Two thirds as the average royalty for 36 vols seems fair. And so I think is the lumping all the volumes together, tho' to pay for (say) 20 stereotypes as first cost before the percentage in my favour is struck would delay much return to me in my life time. At present the 36 vols bring me in perhaps £350 per ann on an average of years. The stereotypes would cost £400. If they were made only when they were actually wanted, their cost would be only for 2 or 3 a year

I want the letter I sent back please[1]   J H N

P.S.   As to the question of probability I think you have said somewhere(?) that you follow Butler in considering probability to be the guide of life.[2] This has a good sense and a bad. I think Anglicans, even Keble(?) mean by probability a mere *practical* probability i.e. what is safe to act upon, whether true or not; whereas Catholics hold that it is a real speculative assent (or certitude) to a truth, to which I add 'speculative, true, but arising, not from demonstration, but from the result of a combination and joint force, equivalent to demonstration, of many separate probabilities, how many and how strong in order to such an equivalence, being left to the judgment, ⟨an act of φρόνησις⟩[3] which goes by rules to[o] subtle for analysis. I quote in the Grammar of Assent a passage from Amort p 412 who says that there is a natural reason principle that God intends that in religion moral arguments and moral certitude should be made to take the place of metaphysical.

TO LORD BLACHFORD

Octb. 16. 1884

My dear Blachford

I suppose my referring to Kingsley's case, is why you think I contemplate answering Lord M. if he writes. *You* set me on thinking of writing by your last words about the 'purple.' I have no wish at all to do so. Both my brain

---

[1] Newman had evidently sent Kegan Paul's letter of 7 Oct. about royalties to Lilly, and was asking him to negotiate.
[2] *Ancient Religion and Modern Thought*, pp. 55–6. The review of Lilly's book in *DR* (see letter of 10 Oct. to Lilly) objected to his saying that Newman's 'main principle' for attaining religious truth was 'that *probability* is the guide of life.' Lilly wrote on 14 Oct., 'You say nothing of the Dublin Review's remarks about my statement of your doctrine of probability: whence I infer that you attach no more importance to them than I do.'
[3] 'practical wisdom'.

and my fingers move very slowly now, and I have enough to do without adding controversy to my necessary work.

I shall not write unless you tell me I ought.

Yrs affectly J. H. Card. Newman

TO MESSRS RIVINGTON

Oct 16. 1884

Copy

My dear Sir

I thank you for your letter

I am asking my friend Mr Lilly to act for me in the disposal of my Volumes. If you can give him half an hour, it will be more satisfactory than correspondence.

As to Terence etc when the four are bound together in one volume, they must stand in the following order — Phormio, Pincerna, Aulularia, (Andria.) And they must have a common title page, in addition to that of each play.

Phormio — to be reprinted with the corrections on the patern [sic] copy

Pincerna to be reprinted from the patern copy

Aulularia, to be reprinted from the pattern copy

These three are all those at present can be bound together As to the Andria it must wait — but it (the Andria) can be sold separately, as well as the other three

My chief reason for thus determining is the expense. Four plays would come to £50.

TO MESSRS BULL AND AUVACHE

Birmingham Oct 17. 1884

Cardinal Newman has been shown a Catalogue of books on sale at Messrs Bull and Auvache's, in which is found the following

'847. Newman (John Henry) Anselmo, a Tale with other poems (pp 31) etc etc.' He begs to inform them that Anselmo is no book of his writing, as they advertise it to be, and therefore he is obliged to ask them to withdraw at once from their list this notice ascribing it to him.[1]

TO LORD BLACHFORD

Oct 19. 1884

My dear Blachford

I keep to my purpose of silence as regards Lord M [Malmesbury], if you still advise it, because your judgment in the matter is better than mine.[2]

---

[1] On 15 Oct. Dean Church sent Newman the page from the catalogue containing this entry. He had bought the pamphlet and asked the booksellers their grounds for attributing it to Newman, but had received no answer. See letters of 29 Oct. to R. W. Church and to the Editor of the *Academy*.

[2] This was Lord Blachford's advice in his letter of 15 Oct., also in that of 18 Oct., which crossed Newman's of 19 Oct.

My reason for writing would be, not as if your letter already published had not done for me what I could not do for myself, but because Lord M may plausibly say that he was [had] no call to write till I came forward who alone can contradict him, and because lookers-on may suspect, if I keep silent, that I am conscious of something in the back ground, which Lord M. may bring out if I provoke him. Also, if a year hence some writer assumed Lord M's account to be true, and I remonstrated, he might retort 'Why did you not tell us at the time?'

To give you matter for your decision, I send you the following

To the Editor of the Daily News. Sir[1]

Yours affectly John H Card Newman

TO LORD BLACHFORD

Bm Oct 20. 1884

My dear Blachford

I should be as great a donkey as another person in this matter, if I did not go by your deliberate judgment just received.[2]

At bottom, my only wish to write now is the reluctance to write about a man not till he is dead†

Yours affectly J. H. Card. Newman

† Ten years ago I made a sketch of my life up to 1833

TO ANNE MOZLEY

Bm Octr 20. 1884

Confidential

My dear Anne Mozley

I think your volume, not only singularly interesting and valuable, for so it must be to *me*, but well done as a sample of clear and careful putting together and of good judgment in literary work.[3] James [Mozley] would have reason to say with Queen Catharine, 'After my death I wish no other herald, But such an honest chronicler as Griffith',[4] and that, because you have let him speak for himself.

This leads me to speak of myself. Many years ago, at two separate independent times, I came to the conclusion, that, if a memoir was to be published of me, a Protestant Editor must take the Protestant part, and a Catholic

---

[1] This was a draft of letter of 24 Oct. to the Editor of the *Daily News*.

[2] This refers to Lord Blachford's letter of 18 Oct. in which he says: 'I really think you may absolutely dismiss Lord Malmesbury from your mind — unless he repeats his story.
My last sentence [at end of his letter to the *Daily News*, see final note to Newman's letter of 8 Oct. to him] was only intended to save your dignity whether you wished to be silent or whether you wished to speak'

[3] *Letters of J. B. Mozley*, London 1885, 'edited by his sister.' Anne Mozley's Advertisement at the beginning is dated 'September 1884'.

[4] Shakespeare, *King Henry the Eighth*, IV, ii.

the Catholic. When I went down at a later date, 1876 to Blachford, I was struck by Lord B. volunteering the same judgment   As to the Catholic part, it does not concern me. It cannot be written for many years. I never could take part in it myself; it would involve a criticism on various persons. My representatives have instructions only to answer misrepresentations to my disadvantage from curious persons wishing to elicit secret history, if they can

What I thought could be done, and what only, was a sketch of my life up to 1833, which with the Apologia from 1833 to 1845 would finish my Protestant years. With this view in 1874 I wrote a brief memoir of my life up to 1833.[1] This, I think, of printing so as to have it ready almost upon my death in order to break, as much as I can, the sale and the gossip of catch penny publications.[2]

Though I am open to the criticism and advice of friends, that is not my special desideratum just now — but the following. I have a number of letters of my own, and of my mother and sisters, and memoranda, and while I know they afford illustrations of my Memoir, yet in a matter so personal I cannot go by my own judgment.

The only persons (besides Fr Neville) who have seen the Memoir are Jemima and Jane [Mozley].

What I venture to ask of you is to read the Memoir, when I have got it copied, and to say whether it needs illustration and where[3]

Yours affectly John H Card. Newman

TO LORD BLACHFORD

Oct 22. 1884

My dear Blachford

I am sorry for all this trouble has caused you. I know it by what I experience myself. I had quite [made] up my mind the whole matter was at an end. As far as I have said [made] you change your mind, it is my doing. This you would see, if our letters had not crossed.[4]

[1] *A.W.*, pp. 29–107. See also *Moz.* I, between pp. 26 and 160.
[2] In the draft Newman added, 'and any interference on the part of injudicious Catholic friends.' The next paragraph ran:
'The work would if I pursued this plan be short, consisting of the sketch which I have spoken of above, and letters and memoranda of my own, of my Mother and Sisters to illustrate it. And what I should ask of you is to receive from me the Sketch and letters, in order to give a fair judgment upon the expedience of publishing them.'
[3] Anne Mozley thanked Newman on 21 Oct., 'Your most kind judgment of the work as a whole has set up my spirits' and added, 'the book has already brought a lasting satisfaction — your entrusting me with the MS. you tell me of. I have been feeling that my work of this sort was quite over and here comes a task of all others most interesting to me.'
[4] i.e. Lord Blachford's of 18 and Newman's of 19 Oct. On 21 Oct. Lord Blachford replied to Newman's of 19 Oct. which enclosed his proposed letter of 24 Oct. [see there] to the Editor of the *Daily News*:
'My dear Cardinal
I had almost written to you, before receiving your letter, to recall my recommendation not to speak, — and that almost exactly on the grounds which you give.
The state of the case, which you disclose, makes it quite clear that your letter is wanted. I

I dare say you will after all think the alteration you have led me here to make has taken the sting out of the whole, and that I had better be silent. I did not mean to say more than that a lax *traditional* party was in the College. Colquhoun Gent. Commoners published his pamphlet in 1822 and took his first class Michaelmas 1823[1]   I cannot prove the tradition between him and Lord M's [Malmesbury] day, but, if a man protested in 1822 and was set upon, it is not likely that the state of things would be bettered thereby. However, I say truly that it will be a great relief, if after all you pluck the letter.

C's [Colquhoun] pamphlet is addressed to the *Heads of Houses* — but he could not address it to Oriel authorities without its getting out who he was. But it was understood and therefore Hawkins answered him.

When in 1826–7 I said to Copleston 'Are the men *expected* to take the Sacrament?' He answered me abruptly ⟨sharply⟩, 'I beg you will not put such an idea into their minds. I am persuaded the idea never occurs to them.' When I said to Tyler, 'Your men had a champayne breakfast the other day after the Sacrament', he answered, 'I don't believe it, and if it were *true* I don't wish to know it.'

I am sorry you dislike 'high and mighty'.[2] I could find nothing else to intimate that from the first they thought me 'only a Tutor' and that 'of *course*' their conduct 'cowed me.'

Ever Yrs affly J H Card. Newman

do not exactly know what is your idea of not being fierce. It seems to me you give Lord M. [Malmesbury] such a shaking as few men have to endure. It is like the spring of a lion. But you are *dans votre droit* — and, under the circumstances, I do not wish it less severe.

There are however one or two expressions — or rather epithets which might be taken to indicate a surviving soreness. "*High and mighty* youths" and "*gallant* feat" have a little of this ring. Though I admit that some thing is in place to show that the insult was not an open one, but under cover of night.

Then, if I may be so audacious as to criticize your composition —

1. "Memory of many *men* [word added by Blachford]" I suppose you mean undergraduates of Lord M's standing. But is this sufficiently expressed.

2. I suppose that the undergraduates' protest against compulsory reception of the Sacrament was *expressly grounded*, on the misbehaviour of Lord M's set. But this is not said, and unless it is said the argument seems to me to halt.

Yours affly   Blachford'

Newman who had referred to the cutting of his bell wire as 'the gallant feat at midnight' now omitted the adjective.

[1] John Campbell Colquhoun's pamphlet *An Appeal to the Heads of the Oxford University*, by an Under-graduate, London 1822, was answered by Edward Hawkins in *A Letter to the Author of "An Appeal to the Heads of the University of Oxford" upon compulsory attendance at the Communion*, by a Graduate, Oxford 1822, defending the practice.

Colquhoun was a Gentleman Commoner of Oriel College, and a staunch Evangelical.

See also fourth note to letter of 14 Jan. 1885 to Anne Mozley.

[2] See third paragraph of letter of 24 Oct. to the Editor of the *Daily News*.

Lord Blachford replied on 24 Oct., 'By all means publish your letter as it stands.

I feel the want of something (as you imply) to suggest what is suggested by "high and mighty" — i.e. the empty insolence of station. But I am sure I am right in objecting to the *words*.

I think I should have liked it better if you had merely struck out "high and mighty" so that it would stand "youths who relying on the claims of birth and station."

How would "accustomed to rely" do instead of "relying"

I shall look forward with amusement (I confess) to seeing it in Tuesdays (?) Daily News. See letter of 26 Oct. to Lord Blachford, and *A.W.* p. 89.

TO AUGUSTINE FRANCIS HEWIT

Bm Oct 22, 1884

Dear Fr Hewitt,

Every day since your most acceptable Article on Inspiration came out, I have wished to write to you and to Fr. Walworth, to whom pray give my sincere thanks, as well as accept them for yourself.[1]

Really I am overpowered with letter writing — my brain and my fingers suffer from it, and it tells upon my health. The great trouble however is that I cannot address myself to those letters which would be really pleasant to me, or excite from their importance a real interest, but the way is blocked up by a set of missives from strangers, of very little importance, but which must be answered: so that at the end of three or four hours I find myself tired out and with no time left for friends. And my fingers won't write fast, which increases the labour, and the waste of time.

I have been made very anxious on the subject of Inspiration. On a parallel subject there is a remarkable article in the Month. It is apropos of Fr Curci. Both arise out of the question of the relation of Science to Dogma.[2] And that is the question of the day. The Holy See acts always with great deliberation. If it is not moved to make a decision on certain questions, perhaps by its very silence it may decide that certain questions are to be kept open.

Most truly Yours, John H. Card. Newman.

TO FRANCIS WILLIAM NEWMAN

Oct. 22. 1884

My dear Frank

I have not another or better copy to send you just now. They have never yet been put together. The Pincerna has some bad mistakes and the Andria and Aulularia some corrections in ink.[3]

J.H.N.

[1] For Hewit's article see letter of 26 June 1884 to him. C. A. Walworth wrote on 'The Nature and Extent of Inspiration', the *Catholic World* (Oct. 1884), pp. 1–13, full of praise for Newman for holding a liberal view and keeping the question open. Walworth himself preferred not to use the principle of *obiter dicta*.

[2] 'Father Curci and the Roman Congregations', the *Month* (Oct. 1884), pp. 171–81, discussed the submission and assent required to dogmatic and disciplinary decisions of the Roman Congregations. It said that Carlo Curci was only obliged to keep silent in his views on the temporal power, not to give internal assent to rulings on the subject.

[3] This letter was written on the flyleaf of a copy of Newman's *Pincerna ex Terentio*, London 1883.

TO LADY WOLSELEY

Oct 22. 1884

Dear Lady Wolseley

If you will send me the portrait, I will do my best to comply with your friendly wish — but recollect that the paper used for Etchings does not bear printer's ink.

With my kindest remembrances to Sir Charles, I am,

My dear Lady Wolseley Sincerely Yours

John H Card. Newman

TO ALEXANDER DENNY

Oct 23/84

copy in substance

Dear Mr Pickering ⟨Denny⟩

I have had a definite offer made me, and it is one which I consider a fair one, as far as I can see at present. All depends on the per centage offered

Before I make up my mind, I shall of course hear from you what you propose[1]

J H N

N.B.   Before I make an agreement with a new publisher I shall have to purchase from you the copyright of the Arians.

TO HERBERT JAMES SHAW

Bm Oct 23. 1884.

Dear Sir

I have not preached for two years. My preaching days are past.

If anything brings you at any time this way, I shall be pleased by your calling on me.[2]

Yours very truly John H. Card. Newman.

P.S.   You should give me notice, lest I be away.

[1] In reply to Newman's letter of 9 Oct. Denny wrote on 22 Oct. that he thought the actual arrangement by which he published on commission, would be more advantageous for Newman than the payment of a royalty. See letter of 25 Oct. to Denny.

[2] Shaw wrote on 21 Oct. saying that he had repeatedly tried to discover when Newman would be preaching, and asking whether he would be doing so at Christmastime. Shaw, whose father lived at West Bromwich, was matriculated at Oxford, non-Collegiate, on 13 Oct. 1883, aged nineteen. He had now transferred to St John's College. In his letter he said that he had 'read with the most intense eagerness all your Eminence's writings to which I have had access — especially the "Apologia" and the "Difficulties felt by Anglicans."'

Shaw took his B.A. and entered the Middle Temple in 1887, but in 1890 when he was made a B.C.L., took Orders and was from 1895 to 1937 a clergyman in Manchester. He died in 1948, aged eighty-six.

Oct. 24. 1884

My dear Child

Your news is great indeed, and ought to keep us from despondency. On the other hand one must not forget St Philip's rule, to recollect that convalescents are not well.[1]

I am glad you are going to so nice a wintering place as the Isle of Wight.

You have nothing to tell me of yourself — and your tidings about your brother are very sad. I suppose such dejection is very difficult to meet and to succeed with. He has my earnest prayers for this great cross being removed from him.

I have nothing to say. I am very weak, but nothing is the matter with me, except that I cannot get rid of an affection of the throat which now is of a year's standing, but cannot be called a cold

Ever Yours affectly J.H. Card. Newman

P S.   I have burned your letter

TO THE EDITOR OF THE DAILY NEWS (I)

Private   Bm Oct. 24. 1884
Sir

I hope I may ask to be allowed the insertion in the Daily News of the inclosed answer to Lord Malmesbury.

I am sorry it has been delayed, but I had hoped it would have been superseded by some words from Lord Malmesbury himself.

I am, Sir, Your obedient servant, John H. Card. Newman

The Editor of the Daily News

TO THE EDITOR OF THE DAILY NEWS (II)

Oct. 24. [1884]

Sir

As Lord Malmesbury has not made any sign of the impression which my friend Lord Blachford's letter was calculated to make upon him, I consider he wishes to receive an answer from myself, which I proceed to give in as few words as I can.[2]

I am sorry that, at the end of nearly sixty years, he should not let bygones be bygones. I have never said a word against him, and his account of me is as discourteous as it is utterly unfounded. If I was as cowardly as he represents I never ought to have been a college tutor.

[1] Emily Bowles's brother John died early in Jan. 1885. What follows, however, probably refers to her brother the priest, F. S. Bowles.
[2] For Lord Blachford's letter to the *Daily News* see last note to letter of 8 Oct. to Lord Blachford.

The truth is, that when I came into office the discipline was in a very lax state, and I, like a new broom, began sweeping very vigorously, as far as my opportunities went. This aroused the indignation of certain high and mighty youths, who, relying on the claims of family and fortune, did their best to oppose me and to spread tales about me. I don't consider that on the whole I got the worst of it in the conflict; and what Lord Malmesbury calls 'helpless resignation' and 'painful tolerance,' I interpret to have been the conduct of a gentleman under great provocation.

Lest I be misapprehended, I add that the bad behaviour I have described was confined to a minority. Most of those whom I came across were perfectly well conducted. I recall the memory of many, both living and dead, with great respect. One of them, shocked at what was brought home to him,[1] had several years earlier taken the unusual step of printing a pamphlet to protest against the compulsory reception of the Sacrament by undergraduates, and one of the Tutors answered it in support of the existing rule. My own similar remonstrance to the same effect in 1826–7 had the same unsuccessful issue.

As to Lord Malmesbury's instances, Lord Blachford has disposed of the table-moving, and I, if I must condescend to notice it here, deny it absolutely.[2]

As to the 'bell-rope,' it was not the bell-rope, but the bell-wire outside my room. A clever youth mounted a ladder and performed the feat at midnight, when I was in bed; but I suppose it was an insipid joke, for it was not done again.

Lastly, as to the haunch of venison. I did not recollect that we had such generous fare, even at the Provost's table. Lord Malmesbury says he witnessed — What? That I was 'nearly' driven. How could he see me 'nearly driven'? He may take my word for it, I should either have been driven out and out, or not driven at all. So much, however, may be true — not that the statement is a fact, but that it is a mythical representation of what was the fact — viz., that I was not supported in my reforms by the high authorities of the college.

Your obedient servant, John H. Card. Newman[3]

TO EDWARD HAYES PLUMPTRE

Oct 24. 1884

Dear Dean Plumptre

I wish I was in a condition to answer your letter, but my normal state is not quite up to what those who see me once or twice would think, and my memory is getting worse and worse. This I say to excuse the great barrenness

[1] There are a number of drafts of this letter. One had 'shocked at the profanation he witnessed.' See second note to letter of 22 Oct. to Lord Blachford for what follows.
[2] In a draft Newman wrote 'it is an old story, of which the victim had already been a Tutor before my time ...'
[3] This letter was published in the *Daily News* (28 Oct.), together with a leading article critical of Lord Malmesbury. See also *A.W.* p. 89 note.

of this letter. As to the Monk and the Bird, I knew more about it once than I do now. I never possessed Ken's Poems. I recollect handling four volumes, I suppose at my friend S. Rickards's house. He, a great admirer of Ken, thought the volumes admitted of much criticism. Thank you for your offer to copy for me K's Monk and Bird, but for several reasons I will not accept it.[1] 2. The Article on Sacred Poetry in the Quarterly in 1825 is Keble's.[2] My only difficulty about it is a question of date, which I can very easily be shown my memory is wrong about. John Coleridge the Father of the present Lord Chief Justice, became Editor of the Quarterly, and Arnold and Keble wrote Articles, as being great friends of his, to support him. I had fancied this was in 1827. Anyhow I think he wrote it under Coleridge's Editorship.[3] 3. I have not seen a page of it since I published it, but there is no manner of doubt that the office on Ken is mine.[4] I thank you very much for what you say about Mr Spender, and what you are led to add.[5]

With my kindest remembrances to Mrs Plumptre

Most truly yours John H Card. Newman

TO ALEXANDER DENNY

Oct 25. 1884

Dear Mr Denny

I have no reason to think you do not fully enter to the offer which I am wishing to gain for my volumes,[6] but, since it is possible I may not fully have

---

[1] See *G.A.*, Note III, p. 502.

The legend of the Monk and the Bird was used by Ken in 'Eternity', a poem in his *Hymnarium*, ii, p. 10;

> 'I thought on the Recluse, perplex'd,
> As he at Matines sang the Text,
> That one short Day in Godhead's Eyes,
> A thousand Years would equalize;
> Till a winged Envoy from the Airy Sphere
> Was sent by Heaven, the Mystery to clear.
>
> The Bird by his harmonious Note,
> Allured him to a Wood remote;
> Three centuries her song he heard,
> Which not three Hours to him appear'd,
> While God to his dim-sighted, doubtful Thought,
> Duration boundless, unsuccessive, taught.'

E.H. Plumptre, *The Life of Thomas Ken*, London 1888, II, pp. 248–9.

Ken's poems were published in four volumes in 1721.

[2] This was a review of *The Star in the East, with other Poems*, by Josiah Conder, London 1824, 'Sacred Poetry', the *Quarterly Review* (June 1925), pp. 221–32, reprinted in Keble's *Occasional Papers and Remains*, Oxford 1877.

[3] '. . . during the interregnum in 1824, between the retirement of Gifford and the appointment of Lockhart, he [J. T. Coleridge] acted as editor for three or four months.' *DNB* on J. T. Coleridge. cf. *Ess.* I, p. 27.

[4] Specimen offices were given in *Tracts for the Times*, Number LXXV, 'On the Roman Breviary . . .', published 24 June 1836. See pp. 16 and 135–45. cf. *The Life of Thomas Ken*, II, p. 268.

[5] Plumptre, who was Dean of Wells, must have referred to John Kent Spender, well known Bath doctor, and his wife Lilian, who was a novelist. One of their sons was J. A. Spender, and another Hugh Frederick, also a journalist, became a Catholic in 1894.

[6] Denny wrote on 24 Oct. that it would take a few days to calculate the royalties he could offer Newman.

expressed myself, I will say that I am wishing to find what would be the value of a royalty on all my works, which would apply to each of them and not to a selected few, taken as the most saleable. I write this to you because an instance has occurred in which the misunderstanding has occurred

J H N

TO WILFRID OATES

Oct 25. 1884

in substance
Dear Mr Oates

I understand that you offer me £50 for 1000 copies of Callista, that is, one third of the neat profit on sale. This I calculate thus: a thousand copies at 5/ will be £250, and the cost will be at least £100. This leaves £150 as gain and £50 is a third of this.

You offer me then a third of the profit—But it must be recollected that this offer is not on an average of my volumes, but on one which is the most saleable. The offer then which I must ask from you now [must] have respect to my 36 volumes I should add that it is for all 36 volumes that the offer is made to me and this brings me to another consideration, that it is for my Protestant as well as for my Catholic works[1]

TO LORD BLACHFORD

Oct. 26. 1884

My dear Blachford

Alas! my letter to the Daily News went on Friday, before your letter came. Else I should certainly have left out 'high and mighty'. I did not really understand your strong feeling against it.[2]

There is a literary pleonasm, stuck in hastily at the last moment, 'similarly'![3]

Yrs affectly J H Card. Newman

I recollect Amon well[4] — also the 'noble wōman'.[5] I fancied Robert Wilberforce was a *witness*

---

[1] Oates replied on 27 Oct. that in fact his profit on a thousand copies of *Callista* would be £26. 5s. He was prepared to take over all Newman's works.

[2] This refers to Lord Blachford's letter of 24 Oct., quoted in third note to that of 22 Oct. to him.

[3] Last sentence of fourth paragraph of letter of 24 Oct. to the *Daily News*.

[4] Blachford wrote: 'Do you remember Froude's dry comment, coming home from a University Sermon of Tyler's on Manasseh and Amon — Amon was "the poor gown man" — so ill brought up etc. [2 *Kings*, 21]

F. "Old Tyler went on talking about Amon as if he had been one of his own gentlemen-commoners". He said it either to me or to you.'

[5] i.e. 'noble Roman', in an anecdote Blachford told about William James, the Oriel Fellow who could not pronounce his 'r's, and to whom belonged some of the legends Lord Malmesbury attributed to Newman. See last note to letter of 8 Oct. to Lord Blachford.

Oct. 29. 1884

My dear Dean

I wish my fingers would write a long letter.

What would you like? should I buy Anselmo of you? I am quite ready so to do, and more than ready. I can't conceive what you can wish to spend 16/ upon it for.[1]

The case is a very curious one, and, were I not here to answer for myself, the probability of it being mine would be strong on *internal* evidence. Both poems[2] are written in the style of Pope and [Erasmus] Darwin and I think Byron's Corsair, Lara etc. There is a sort of parallelism of plots — and one is laid in France, the other about Spain.

I send you a copy of St Bartholomew's Eve together with Anselm. History and the graphic and picturesque parts are Bowden's — mine are the theology, the antithesis, the plot and the notes![3]

Yours affectly J. H. Card. Newman.

TO THE EDITOR OF THE ACADEMY

Oct 29. 1884

Private

Sir

May I request the favour of the insertion of the following paragraph in the Academy.

For publication

We are requested by Cardinal Newman to contradict the statement that 'a Tale called Anselmo, with other Poems', Mondy [sic] and Slatter Oxford 1816 (made in Messrs Bull and Auvache's book Catalogues) is his writing

They note ⟨add⟩ 'This Tract is of the utmost interest and importance, being the first publication of Cardinal Newman and is excessively rare.'

The publication neither in whole nor in part is the Cardinal's writing, and he never heard of its existence, till a friend informed him of its place in Messrs B and A's Catalogue. It is well perhaps to add, that, whereas there it is dated Oxford 1816, he never was in Oxford till December 1816 when he matriculated, nor came into residence till June 1817, and then only for three weeks.

He considers the mistake has arisen from a confusion between the above Tale published before he knew Oxford, with a metrical composition of his

---

[1] See letter of 17 Oct. to Messrs Bull and Auvache. Dean Church had made them reduce the price of their pamphlet, fixed on the erroneous supposition that Newman was its author. Church suggested that Newman should send a correction to 'some paper like the "Athenaeum", or "Academy".'

[2] i.e. Newman and John Bowden's *St Bartholomew's Eve* and *Anselmo*.

[3] Dean Church replied on 30 Oct. thanking for the copy of *St Bartholomew's Eve*, 'These little bits of the past are very valuable to me.'

friend Mr Bowden and himself jointly, printed and published by the same well known firm in the years 1818, 1819.[1]

TO LORD BLACHFORD

Oct 30. 1884

My dear Blachford

I sent you just now a hasty telegram, knowing you were leaving the Deanery tomorrow. Else, I should have reflected that I ought to see Lord M's treatment of your letter before I wrote to him.[2] I have no doubt you will tell me so, if you write to me this evening — even if you don't, I feel it would be making peace without your positive consent, which cannot be.

Yrs affly J H Card. Newman

NB 'candour and generosity' are too strong.[3]

[1] Newman's letter appeared in the *Academy* on 1 Nov.

[2] Lord Malmesbury wrote to Newman on 29 Oct. from Heron's Court, Christchurch, Hants

'My Lord Cardinal,

I think it due to the sincere respect which I entertain for your high character and position to address you in person, rather than through a newspaper, on the subject of your letter [of 24 Oct,] to the "Daily News" of yesterday, relating to my "Memoirs".

Y.E. seems to have expected a notice from me of some letter written by Lord Blachford on a passage in the above publication. To this I must reply that I have never seen his Lordship's letter, which he probably sent to some newspaper not taken in by me, and therefore could not answer his remarks. But what I can do is to assure Y.E. with perfect truth, that I greatly regret my account of days long past should have annoyed you. They had not in the remotest way any *animus* of an unfriendly nature, nor is there one word, which as Y.E. says, could imply "cowardice".

It was intended as a contrast between the past and the present. We are, if you will excuse a comparison between us, changed since the days of Oriel. The too-indulgent and patient tutor has since become one of the most vigorous literary athletes of the age, and a Prince of the Church, while the idle pupil has in his time incurred duties as responsible as any Englishman can be charged with.

Nothing offensive, therefore, occurred to me, in the passage that has annoyed you, although, as it has had that effect, I regret having written it.

As to its spirit I would call your attention to the expression preceding the account of our tricks, which says they were "to our shame". These words are omitted by the Daily News, although surely they are an apology.

I feel certain that, in your sacred profession, you will agree that the spirit of our actions makes a great difference in their nature.

I would not wait till I happened to see Lord Blachford's letter before writing to Y.E. as I was anxious to express my regret at having unintentionally offended you.

I remain, with respect,

Y.E. obedient servt. Malmesbury

I have sent a copy of this letter to "The Globe".'

There it was published on 30 Oct. Newman's telegram to Lord Blachford was intended to inform him of this. Lord Blachford's letter was that in last note to letter of 8 Oct. to him. The words 'to our shame' were not omitted in the *Daily News*.

[3] Newman drafted on 30 Oct. and sent to Lord Blachford an answer to Lord Malmesbury, on which he wrote: 'This was my first impression but not sent to Lord Malmesbury. J H N.' It began: 'My dear Lord

I hope I am not taking a liberty thus to address you; but what I feel to be the ⟨candour and⟩ generosity ⟨language and tone⟩ of your Lordship's letter of this morning makes it difficult to write to you in more formal language.'

On the morning of 31 Oct. Lord Blachford telegraphed to Newman, 'You must not think of me   I am all right the words you mention are certainly too strong there being no withdrawal'

TO LORD BLACHFORD (I)

Oct 31. 1884

My dear Blachford

I am ashamed of my selfishness, which arose from my belief that you were leaving the Deanery and that I ought not to delay above a post or two my answer to Lord M. [Malmesbury]. My unhappy telegram intended to say 'M's letter is in today's Globe.'

I said in it nothing about *you*, not knowing what you would think best. Now I venture to propose something to your better judgment

viz 'I have to apologize to your Lordship as well as to Lord B. for not having sent you a copy of his letter to the Daily News. I send one now.'

Since he has already made his amende to me (I may consider it so?) he need not answer you (need he?) and your letter will remain an unanswered powerful statement in my favour.

My words 'candour and generosity' seem to me now too strong. By candour I meant to imply that he virtually withdrew the table turning[1]

Yours affectly J H Card Newman

Thus

My dear Lord

I hope it is not taking a liberty ⟨I am not too free⟩ thus to address your Lordship but the language and tone of your letter make it difficult in me to write to [you] in a less [more] formal manner.

I am no politician but I can truly say I have followed your public life with great interest and a feeling of the most sincere good will. And now you have done me a kindness in restoring to me that habitual sentiment towards your Lordship which to my sorrow was rudely disturbed according to my reading ⟨as I read⟩ your remarks upon me.

I am, J.H.N.

TO LORD BLACHFORD (II)

Oct 31. 1884

My dear Lord Blachford

I am sorry to plague you with letters.

As to Lord M. I thought I could not ask him directly to eat his words —

[1] Lord Blachford wrote on 31 Oct. from The Deanery of St Paul's:
'I do not see why you should take any thought of me in your matter. To use your own phrase "I don't think I have got the worst of it." I have struck a blow, so to call it, and it has not been returned. His "*some* letter of Lord Blachfords" — may be set off against my "ordinary impertinence." And the statement of an author that he has not seen a letter of which he knows that it charges him (not ill-naturedly) with injurious inaccuracy, is, it appears to me a statement which may be left to take care of itself.
I hope you will be handsome in your acceptance of his statement that he meant no offence — which I doubt not is true. But I do not see that his letter requires any effusive acknowledgment. The word "athlete" has a certain amount of sting and I do not see that he admits any inaccuracy of representation though of course he disclaims the expression of "cowardice".
A handsome but measure acknowledgment is what I should liked, with perhaps the slightest possible indication that you are letting him off easy.'

he *did* deny their offensive meaning. The question is whether his having explained away helpless incapacity ⟨?⟩ into over-indulgence is not virtually a retractation. But I see that the Daily News, as you, calls attention to the fact that there is no retractation.[1] And I am ashamed myself of having been so good-natured.

Would, instead of the draft letter of last night, I sent you, the following be better

My Lord

I beg to acknowledge the receipt of your Lordship's Letter, assuring me that you had no unkind meaning when you spoke in your Memoir of my helpless resignation, painful tolerance and simple impassiveness. I understand your Lordship's letter as withdrawing these epithets in that sense in which I read them, and on that understanding I accept such explanation.

I am sorry I did not send your Lordship a copy of Lord Blachford's letter to the Daily News. I now repair the omission.

&c J H N

I see I have been in a hurry to get over the controversy — but it *will* take time   If you are with your Sister, remember me most kindly to her[2]

Yours affectly John H Card Newman

P.S.   At present I see no alternative between returning *no* answer, or ⟨and⟩ such a one as the above.[3]

TO CHARLES PHILIPPE PLACE, ARCHBISHOP OF RENNES

[November 1884]

Your Grace may be sure that it would be the greatest pleasure and gain to me, to find I could do you a service in any way.

Any one recommended by you would be sure to please me. But I am sorry for various reasons this particular service is not in my power

[1] The *Daily News* (31 Oct.) commented:
'We republish this morning from the *Globe* a letter which Lord Malmesbury has addressed to Cardinal Newman. It will be seen that Lord Malmesbury does not withdraw the statements which both Cardinal Newman and Lord Blachford have point-blank contradicted. He practically reasserts them in his reference to the "too indulgent and patient tutor." In the only quotation we made of Lord Malmesbury's remarks (in the review of his book in the *Daily News* of October 3) the words "to our shame" which he charges us with omitting were given. They seem to us not so much an apology as a part of the original affront, which consists in representing Cardinal Newman as a hapless and helpless imbecile whom it was a shame to tease and bully. But why did Lord Malmesbury boastfully record his exploits if he is ashamed of them? Why does he not now acknowledge that he has confounded two distinct tutors of Oriel in his confused Reminiscences? The Oxford man who mixes up Latona with Lucina may have easily mixed up Mr. Newman and Mr. James.'
[2] Lord Blachford was staying at Blackheath with his sister Mrs Legge.
[3] Lord Blachford replied on 1 Nov., 'I certainly think you *were* "too good natured". But partly the tone of Lord M's letter imposed on me for a time as it did on you — and partly, a fault on the side of good nature seemed a fault on the right and becoming side.
You will think me hard to please when I say that I should have preferred a slight relaxation of sternness somewhere in your present draft . . .'

We are more in number than when you knew us, and our room is not so great as it was.[1]

What is more important [is] that, as time has gone on, our forms are more fixed than when we began. We keep our rule more exactly than at first, and our rule does not contemplate the reception of guests

May I add that the Benedictine House a large body at Ampleforth in Yorkshire is not hindered taking guests. They have had a young French man from Ivetot not long ago. I would write to them to inquire, if you wished me.

I have had a letter lately from Sister Pia recounting your various kindnesses to her.[2]

TO LORD BLACHFORD

Nov 2/84

My dear Blachford

I trust the accompanying will be the end of your trouble.[3] You have seen nearly every word of it, I think, before — but don't scruple to criticize. I hope to send it off to Lord M at once.

My fingers and wrist are so stiff and weak, that I cannot well write. W Neville was gauche —; not only he, but Bellasis junior, is said to write like me[4]

Ever Yrs affly J H Card. Newman[5]

TO THE EARL OF MALMESBURY

The Oratory, Birmingham, November 3, 1884

My Lord,

I beg to acknowledge the receipt of your lordship's letter of October 29.[6] I can truly say that, in spite of the unsatisfactory Oxford reminiscences to which you refer, I have, from the day on which I presented you for your

---

[1] Place stayed at the Oratory in 1859. See diary for 7 and 10 Oct. 1859.

[2] Miss Giberne's letter of 7 Oct. 1884 to Newman described Place's visit and the presents he had given her.

[3] This was a copy of the letter of 3 Nov. to Lord Malmesbury.

[4] Newman's second letter of 31 Oct. was, except for the last few lines, entirely in William Neville's hand. He began it, 'My dear Lord Blachford'. The latter commented on 1 Nov., 'I was startled at the beginning of your letter by "My dear *Lord* Blachford" till I saw that it was your amanuensis. His hand was so like yours of fifty odd years ago that it was a moment before I saw how it was, and I thought for a moment "Have I said anything shocking?" It is the way in which some people snub you'

[5] On an earlier draft of his letter of 2 Nov. to Lord Blachford, on which he wrote 'won't do', Newman said, 'Your letter of Nov 1 is an important one, but it dismays me, as rendering another tactic necessary. My unhappy wrist and fingers! but I must get through it.

My great disadvantage is in having to prove a negative — or rather to *remember* a negative. . . .' Newman then went on to speak much as in the second half of his letter of 4 Nov to Lord Blachford.

[6] In note to that of 30 Oct. to Lord Blachford.

B.A. degree, thrown off from my mind every unfriendly thought of you, and have followed your public life with much interest and thorough good will.[1] And now that I have just cause to be displeased, I should have warmly welcomed any words from your lordship which were of a nature to restore to me that habitual feeling which has recently been so rudely disturbed. However, we must take things as we find them; and I readily accept your lordship's letter without insisting upon questions of fact. I take it as assuring me that you had no unkind meaning when you spoke in your 'Memoirs' of my helpless resignation, painful tolerance, and utter impassiveness. I understand your lordship's letter as withdrawing those epithets in that sense in which I was led to read them, and on that understanding I am glad to accept such explanation. I am sorry I did not send your lordship a copy of Lord Blachford's letter to the *Daily News* of October 13.[2] I now repair the omission. You will find that he bears witness that the legend, as he calls it, of the table-jerking attached in his time to another tutor named James. But what we are told of two we may assume belongs to neither.[3]

I am, &c., John H. Card. Newman[4]

TO LORD BLACHFORD

Nov 4. 1884

My dear Blachford

Your telegram came right,[5] and I wish I could send you a long letter, but, when I attempt a running hand, I become unintelligible.

You seem surprised I should rest so much on your letter to the Daily News — so let me explain myself

1. I have no scruple, which at first I had, about any personal wish of yours, after your setting me at ease by your assurance you had no wish in the matter[6]

---

[1] cf. Newman's letter of 15 Sept. 1858 to Ornsby, where he spoke of how he had 'so unmercifully snubbed Lord Malmesbury when he was in Lecture with me'.

[2] In last note to that of 8 Oct. to Lord Blachford.

[3] Lord Blachford wrote on 5 Nov., 'It seems to me that nothing could be better than your letter as I have just seen it in the Globe.
Waiving expressly the *discussion* of *facts*, is a great improvement.
And I am glad you have shortened the table jerking.
It quite fulfils my wish that you should have the attitude of consciously letting Lord M off easy.'

[4] Newman sent this letter to the *Daily News*, 'Cardinal Newman presents his compliments to the Editor of the *Daily News*, and hopes he is not encroaching on the space of the paper by asking to be allowed a place there for his enclosed reply to the letter addressed to him by Lord Malmesbury: —'
Newman also sent his letter to the *Globe*, which introduced it: 'We have been requested by Cardinal Newman to publish the following answer to Lord Malmesbury, which he has forwarded to that nobleman.'
The text is as printed in both newspapers on 4 Nov. According to one of the drafts, Newman added at the end, 'I have sent a copy of this letter to the Daily News and to the Globe'.

[5] Sent on 3 Nov. from Waterloo, when Lord Blachford was returning to Devon.

[6] See Lord Blachford's telegram of 31 Oct. quoted at end of second note to letter of 30 Oct. to him.

2 Then, thinking of myself, I felt it but courteous, since I referred Lord M [Malmesbury] to your letter to send it to him

3 Moreover, your letter was not known, as it seemed to me, as much as so important [a] letter should have been. The Catholic Paper which officiously called Lord M's account of me pathetic, delayed to insert yours, and when it did, mixed it up with the Editorial article of the Daily News.[1] The popular daily of this place, tho' with a Catholic on its staff and always civil to me, tho' it inserted Lord M's account of me, did not insert yours to the Daily News — and, though on my urging it they inserted it, complained at first that it was too late.[2] Again the Academy, in questioning Lord M about me, evidently had not seen your letter, for, wishing to befriend me, called me 'shy Newman'[3]

4 And further your letter was most important in two ways, first in your positive testimony in my favour, and next as witnessing that you had inherited no tradition, as at a *later* date Hardy had, (1833, 4) countenancing Lord M's statement.[4] As to Hardy, I think rustication etc had been impossible in Copleston's time. I think nothing strong could be done till a new Provost succeeded and for the first year of his reign Hawkins acted as a Trojan — (NB tho' he took to other game later!) It was natural then that, when under the new regime ⟨1828–29⟩ sharp punishments came in, so as to startle the men, they should imagine causes, such as tablejerking. Let me add what I never yet brought out, that it was a longing on my part for some stricter discipline which was the direct cause of Hawkins's election. He had the reputation of even sternness. 'He was just the man we wanted' I said. When Froude pleaded for Keble, I said to myself 'He cannot cope with the evil.' I recollect another speech of mine which made Jenkins laugh — 'If we were choosing an Angel, of course Keble would get it .. but we are only choosing a Provost.'[5]

5. There is another thought which came into my mind, when I read what you said about Lord C's (Hardy's) recollection of Oriel. It is unpleasant to have to depend on a sole personal assertion — I am only able to deny Lord M's accuracy, by my own counter assertion — and more than this, I depend

---

[1] The *Weekly Register* (4 Oct. 1884), p. 437, after quoting the passage about Newman in Lord Malmesbury's *Memoirs* . . . , remarked, 'The record is not without a deep interest and surely a certain pathos of its own.' Lord Blachford's letter of 9 Oct. and the *Daily News* leading article of 13 Oct. were printed together, (18 Oct.), pp. 502–4.

[2] John Alfred Feeny was the Catholic on the staff of the *Birmingham Daily Post*, which did not print until 23 Oct. Lord Blachford's letter which had been published in the *Daily News* on 13 Oct.

[3] The review of Lord Malmesbury's *Memoirs* . . . , in the *Academy* (18 Oct. 1884), p. 247, remarked that 'He went to Oriel when Newman was a tutor there, and relates how shy Newman was and how much put upon. At lecture his class would cut his bell-rope and steadily push the table in upon him till he was jammed into a corner.'

[4] Lord Blachford wrote on 1 Nov., 'I spoke to Lord Cranbrook (Gaythorne Hardy) about the correspondence. And he had a story about your bell which gave more importance to it than you do. — His legend (existing in 1833–4) was of various repetitions of the offence, ending — (not in passive sufferance on your part — but) in some rustications.

I merely say this (which he mentioned as against *my* letter, not as against yours which he had not seen) because on these questions of memory it is well to know all that is said.'

[5] See letter of 29 June 1882 to Pusey.

on a negative assertion and that in a question of memory. At first sight he is in a better position than I am, for I have to prove a negative. Now even a vague reminiscence from some contemporary witness like Lord Cranbrook has some effect against a negative assertion such as mine. Then I asked, Where shall I stand if Christopher Talbot, or Dillwyn (if alive) or Charles Murray, or your neighbour M. Parker, or (forbid it!) the Duke of Cleveland ⟨contemporaries⟩ was led to express a recollection such as Hardy's in 1834?[1] Well, I said, 'the less I speak of my own knowledge, clear as it is, the better. Blachford's letter is my best card.'

You must be tired of this elaborate performance, as my fingers are[2]

Yours affectly J. H. Card. Newman

TO CHARLES GORE

Nov 6. 1884

Dear Mr Gore

How could you think I did not recollect you, when, in addition to other acts of kindness on (I think) my first visit to Trinity, you were one of those (if I do not confuse) who saw me off when I had come as Cardinal? I saw with great interest the news that you were to be one of the Pusey Librarians, and I indulge the welcome thought, that, in promoting the interests of his School, you will eventually be advancing Catholic Truth as held and taught at Rome, tho' it is not your purpose.[3]

Pardon me this unnecessary effusion, which I had no intention of being betrayed into when I began.

I was led into it by thinking of Pusey, and by feeling that I would rather do a service to the Pusey Library than to a London Bookseller, however respectable.

I have one question to ask. I think he is looking for Tracts Number 81. Do you mean to bind up in Pusey's works the Catena accompanying his Introduction to it, or only the Catena?[4]

Sincerely Yours John H Card. Newman

[1] These were Gentlemen Commoners at Oriel. Christopher Talbot, 1803–90, at Harrow, B.A. 1824, M.P. for Glamorgan 1830 until death; John Dillwyn (1810–82), to Oriel 1828, High Sheriff of Glamorgan 1834, assumed the additional name of Llewellyn; Charles Murray 1806–95, at Eton, B.A. 1827, traveller, diplomat and author; Montagu Parker, 1807–58, at Eton, B.A. 1830, M.P. for South Devon 1835–41, of Whiteway, Chudleigh; the Duke of Cleveland, Harry Vane, 1803–91, at Eton, B.A. 1829, M.P. for South Durham 1841–59, succeeded to the title in 1864.

[2] Lord Blachford replied on 6 Nov., 'I am amused at your launching me, like light calvary, first to disorder the enemies' ranks and clear a way for the phalanx, and then to hang on his retreat.

As matters stand Lord M has made a statement — which has been first disputed and then directly contradicted and which in the face of contradiction he does not repeat.'

[3] Gore became a Fellow of Trinity College, Oxford, in 1875, and was the first Principal of Pusey House, opened on 9 Oct. 1884.

[4] *Tract LXXXI*, 'Catena Patrum IV', 'Testimony of writers of the later English Church to the doctrine of the Eucharistic Sacrifice, with an historical account of the changes made in the Liturgy as to the expression of that doctrine.' The historical introduction was Pusey's.

TO JOHN WILLIAM OGLE

Nov. 7 1884

Dear Dr Ogle

You have noticed before the mucus. The doctor here noticed it in May last; in 1850–60 Mr Babington noticed it — and Dr Evans here about the year 1866

I inclose Dr Evans's prescription. Mr Babington's was to the same effect.

Would it do me good now? Thank you for the pains you have been taking with me.

Yours most truly J. H Newman

TO MICHAEL FROST

Nov 10. 1884

Dear Sir

I thank you for your sincere kindness but I am sorry to say I cannot grant your request.[1] There has been far too much said about me already and enough often by men of name and I do not think good will come from saying more, even though by a friendly hand[2]

J H N

TO WILFRID OATES

Nov 11. 1884

Dear Mr Oates

I have given up at present the idea of a royalty, as it was proposed to me

I will accept your offer of printing a 1000 copies of Callista, you taking all the expenses, and giving me £50 for the 1000.

The printer will be your own choice, but I understand you to print it uniformly with the present edition.

However, I must add one condition — viz that you pay me the £50 before printing. I add this condition, because as I have sometimes shown you by my remarks, I am by no means satisfied with the degree of activity which prevails in your publishing department[3]

I mention, what you bear in mind doubtless, that Callista is not stereotyped

J H N

[1] Frost, a Catholic, was contemplating his first work, to be called 'Newmanism and the Anglican Church', and asked leave to dedicate it to Newman.
[2] Frost wrote again on 11 Nov. hoping to visit Newman 'to be able to discourse about many subjects, which will, I trust, be of interest to you as the great leader of the true Catholic opinion in England.' Newman answered on 13 Nov. that his occupations would not allow of an interview.
[3] See letter of 27 Nov. to Oates.

TO MESSRS RIVINGTON

Nov. 12 1884.

Cardinal Newman, in the letter to Messrs Rivington answered by them this morning, referred to the following passage in their letter to him of October 15

'Should your arrangements admit of it, we should be happy to consider the purchase of your interest in the works we publish.'[1]

In this proposal they took the initiative. As to *all* the Cardinal's works, he had in a former letter distinctly volunteered his understanding that Messrs Rivington could not undertake them.[2]

Perhaps Mr Lilly did not feel himself at liberty to inform Messrs Rivington that a publishing firm had taken the initiative in proposing to the Cardinal to take all his volumes off his hands, the necessary condition being that the Protestant volumes should be included.
Messrs Rivington

TO F. W. MOORHEAD

[13 November 1884]

Cardinal Newman begs to acknowledge Mr Moorhead's letter.[3] It is not the first he has had the honour to receive from Dublin on behalf of public Libraries. He hopes that he may not seem disrespectful to the persons advocating so good an object, if he states his wish not to act in the matter without the sanction of the Cardinal Archbishop.[4]

TO EDWARD HAYES PLUMPTRE

Nov 13. 1884

My dear Dean of Wells

I have just received your new Edition of 'the Spirits in Prison' with the Studies annexed to it, and I thank you for so learned and interesting a work[5]

Yours very truly John H Card. Newman

[1] Rivington and Co. wrote on 11 Nov., 'The suggestion that we should buy your interest referred only to the Works which we publish, and we made no calculation on which to make an offer.
We understood from Mr Lilly that the principal object in altering the existing arrangement would be that all your Works would be procurable in a uniform series: this, we suggested, might be effected by our supplying from our stock copies of the Books in sheets to be bound and issued by the Publisher of the other Works.'
[2] See letter of 13 Oct.
[3] On 11 Nov. Moorhead, Honorary Librarian of the University Philosophical Society of Trinity College, Dublin, asked to include Newman's name in the list of donors to the library they were starting. The list already included Ruskin, Lecky, G. O. Trevelyan, Professors Dowden, Mahaffy, Fowler and others.
[4] On 17 Nov. Moorhead replied: 'I regret to state that the Cardinal Archbishop of Dublin cannot see his way to sanctioning the advancement of any College Society.'
[5] See letter of 14 Sept. to Plumptre.

TO LORD BLACHFORD

Nov. 14 1884

My dear Blachford

It was very kind of you to send me the amusing letter of my clerical critic which encouraged me much, as well as the judgment of those about you.[1] I have just received a letter from Bloxam about Plumer, whom you must recollect and who was a familiar friend of James's. It runs thus:—

'Mr Plumer told me that the story, which Lord Malmesbury had transferred to you, did really belong to Mr James.' I doubt whether either one or the other of them had seen your letter to the Daily News.[2]

Bloxam's letter also mentions that the Dean has gone up to Copeland. Whether this means that there is some change in C. I could not make out.[3]

Yours affectionately John H. Card. Newman

TO THOMAS JEFFERSON JENKINS

Nov. 14. 1884

Dear Sir

You could not give me a gift more interesting to me than the work of the Hon B. J. Webb's.[4] I have the greatest pleasure in reading the accounts given by old priests here of the state of religion a century ago, when zealous and able missionaries saw in their lifetime no or little fruit of their labours; and the same mixed feelings of sympathy and triumph are excited by various parts of Mr Webb's narrative.

As I do not write with ease, I will not use many words — I will but refer you to the words of a hymn or song, which, when I was young, was popular in England 'We will praise Him for all that is past, and trust Him in all that is to come'.

Very truly Yours, with my blessing on you and Mr Webb

John H. Card. Newman

[1] Blachford wrote on 9 Nov., 'I am amused at the unmitigated satisfaction, not unmingled with chuckle, with which your letter is received by all my belongings.

Here is a comment from a critic, who admits, with a shade of regret, that you are right in letting him off so cheap.

"I like the word 'displeasure'. It is just the word superiors use towards inferiors. But the whole tone of the letter puts the two in their proper position so far.

It will be a long time I should think before that habitual feeling of complacency with which Lord M wrote and which N's letter must have 'so rudely disturbed' will be restored to him. After reading N's letter, I think a good strong glass of brandy and water would have been justifiable."

This is the view of a reputable country clergyman who does not undervalue the castigation which he still thinks a little insufficient.'

[2] See last note to letter of 8 Oct. to Blachford. Bloxam wrote on 12 Nov. C. J. Plumer was a Fellow of Oriel, 1821–30.

[3] W. J. Copeland was ill. He died on 26 Aug. 1885.

[1] Hon. Ben. [Benedict] J. Webb, *The Centenary of Catholicity in Kentucky*, Louisville, 1884.

TO WILLIAM ROBERT BROWNLOW

Nov. 16. 1884

My dear Canon Brownlow

I have read with much interest and pleasure your opportune and conclusive paper on St. Boniface's nationality.[1]

It does not become Archbishops to covet their neighbours' goods, like
their more excusable country people who convert Oakely into O'Kelly

Very truly yours, John H. Card. Newman.

TO COVENTRY PATMORE

Nov 16. 1884

My dear Mr Patmore

I hope you have not thought I neglected your present of St Bernard's
work, (so sacred from the associations of its translation, and so welcome to me,
as coming from you,) because I have not thanked you for it.[2]

I believe the simple reason is that what one is not obliged to do right off
at once, is hustled aside by those duties which cannot be delayed, and my
fingers are so stiff just now that I cannot write on one day as many letters as
I could wish.

Hoping you make allowance for me, I am,

Most truly yours John H Card. Newman

MEMORANDUM. MANNING'S CALL AT LITTLEMORE

Nov 18. 1884

In the Spectator Review of Dr James Mozley's Letters, in last Saturday,
(Novr 15, 1843)[3] after mentioning that Archdeacon Manning had preached
on Nov 5. 1884[4] in the University Pulpit in favour of the puritan party etc
in 1605 it is said that on this account, I, on his coming up to Littlemore I
would not see him.[5] Nor was it my way to talk on serious and private matters

[1] This was Brownlow's *Was St Boniface an Irishman?* in reply to Archbishop Patrick
Moran of Sydney. The question was asked in the *Irish Ecclesiastical Record* for Feb., by the
editor John Healy, and by him answered in the negative. This was followed (March 1884),
pp. 181–90, by a long letter from Archbishop Moran arguing that the Saint was an Irishman.
Brownlow wrote in refutation of this (April 1884), pp. 259–64.

[2] This was a translation of *St Bernard on the Love of God*, London 1881, begun by Patmore's wife Mary, who died on 12 April 1880, and completed by her husband.

[3] A slip for 1884.

[4] A slip for 1843.

[5] In its review of *Letters of the Rev. J. B. Mozley*, the *Spectator* (15 Nov. 1884), p. 1517,
described Manning's 'violent no-Popery' sermon of 5 Nov. and after quoting Mozley 'Yet he
went up to Littlemore and saw J.H.N. yesterday', added 'that is, on November 6th 1843.
Dr Manning did go up. But Newman had heard of the sermon with great disgust; and anticipating a visit from Manning, had given strict orders to the member of his little community
whose duty it was to act as door-keeper — a gentleman since then risen to eminence, but no
longer a follower of Newman — to tell Manning that Newman would not see him. And Newman did not see him, much to Manning's grief.'

See also letters of 21 and 23 Dec. 1884 and 4 Jan. 1885 to R. W. Church.

with younger men. For instance in a few days before in a confidential letter written to Manning, speaking of my own religious unsettlement I had said: 'No one in Oxf[ord] knows or here (Littlemore) but one near friend whom I felt I could not help telling it [word illegible] Is it in keeping with his character that he should 'show his grief' to a servant Further I find I have entered in my [diary] 'Manning called' This in itself tells neither for or against the story, but I will observe that I generally added a few words, e.g. I have ⟨recorded⟩[1]

TO HENRY JAMES COLERIDGE

Nov 23. 84

My dear Fr Coleridge

I have been wishing to write to you day after day for a long while. And now comes the shocking law proceedings, which never entered into my head.

If you can tell me any thing to lessen the misery, do[2]

Yours affly J H Card. Newman

TO JOHN WILLIAM OGLE

Nov 24 1884

My dear Dr Ogle

Thank you for your answer to me. I really think I ought to see a Surgeon — and, if it must be, the sooner the better, in order to get it over. If I got to you between 12 and 1 tomorrow, perhaps I could go on to him at once supposing, that is, you approved of it

Most truly Yours J H Card. Newman

P S   I am too old to make punctual appointments — do not wait for me.

TO JOHN HENRY WYNNE, S.J.

Bm Nov 24. 84

My dear Fr Wynne

Your letter is a most kind and considerate one. If there is any thing I need, it is the support of good friends making the prospect of death and

[1] The memorandum ends thus.

[2] Lord Coleridge's daughter Mildred, aged thirty-seven, had become engaged to Charles Warren Adams, son of Serjeant Adams. Her brother Bernard Coleridge, who was in his father's confidence, disapproved of the match, and some time before the engagement wrote to his sister that Adams was little short of a scoundrel and she a fool for wishing to marry him. On the strength of this letter Adams brought an action for libel. He refused to settle out of court, and the case began to be reported in *The Times* (22 Nov. 1884), p. 4. It attracted much attention since the son and daughter of the Lord Chief Justice were involved. On 23 Nov. judgment was given against Adams on the ground that Bernard Coleridge's letter was privileged, and that he had not acted out of malice. Adams appealed, and in June 1885 a settlement was arrived at, Lord Coleridge guaranteeing his daughter, who married Adams, £600 a year for life. In Nov. 1885 there was further dispute as to the terms of the settlement. There is one allusion to the affair in E. H. Coleridge, *Life and Correspondence of John Duke Lord Coleridge*, II, pp. 345–6.

judgment less awful, and your letter is an assurance to me that you do not, and will not, forget me, when by prayer you can do much.[1]

I send you two copies of W. Palmer's work[2]

Most truly Yours John H. Card. Newman

TO J. R. BLOXAM

Nov 25/84

My dear Bloxam

I am just suddenly starting from Birmingham
I cannot interpret the letter, which I return.[3]
Is Mr 'Pusey' the *elder* brother, Philip, M P for Birkeshire?
Excuse haste

J H Card Newman

Who is 'Young'?

TO LORD EMLY

Nov 25. 1884

My dear Emly

I have wished very much to hear from you — and hoped there was chance of seeing you

I am just starting on a sudden call from Birmingham   As soon as I am safe here again, you shall know

Fr Ryder has given me your letter

Yrs affectly J H Card Newman

TO HENRY JAMES COLERIDGE

Nov 27. 1884

Dear Fr Coleridge

Many thanks for your full and most sad account.

It is pretty much as I interpreted the course of things. A most strange and unusual trial. It must be sent for great good[4]

Yours affectly John H Card. Newman

[1] Wynne on 25 Nov. wrote to Newman of his 'deep gratitude to you for inestimable services which you have (unconsciously) rendered to me in former times when I was not personally known to you.' He then explained, 'it is to the John Henry Newman of my Oxford days that I want to make my special acknowledgments'.
[2] Wynne had asked for copies of William Palmer's *Commentatio in librum Danielis Prophetae* for a German Jesuit, Fr Boeselager and his brother Baron Philipp von Boeselager.
[3] This was a letter from Sir Robert Peel to J. W. Croker, of 1 Aug. 1835, published in *The Croker Papers*, London 1884, II, p. 282, about attacks on Pusey from his own party. 'There is nothing more intolerable than the tyranny of party, and nothing more insane than the excommunication of a man, because he differs on some one point from those with whom he is disposed generally to act.' Bloxam appears to have thought the reference was to E. B. Pusey, whereas, as Newman saw, it was to his brother Philip, M.P. for Berkshire 1835–52, and a close friend of Peel.
[4] See letter of 23 Nov. to Coleridge.

TO ALEXANDER DENNY

Nov 27. 1884

vid my letters of Jany 20. 1885
and 23 Jany
Dear Mr Denny

I am sorry I have not answered your last letter before today, but I could not do so till this morning[1]

I have now to say that I have given up the idea of letting my books on royalties, and therefore must decline your proposal.

As I am writing, I will say that I have sold a new edition of Callista to Messrs Burns and Oates

Some months back I told Messrs Gilbert and Rivington to send you a new title page for 'Difficulties' vol 2 to be used in the case of unbound copies

J H N

TO WILFRID OATES

Nov 27. 1884

Dear Mr Oates

I accept your offer with its conditions, for the purchase from me of a new Edition (1000 copies) of Callista, as stated in your letter of yesterday ⟨this morning⟩[2] It will quite satisfy me to have the £50 paid on the day of publication as you propose. I shall want to add a line to the Preface in proof. Several months back I told Messrs Gilbert and Rivington to send you a new Title page for unbound copies of 'Difficulties' vol 1

J H N

TO JOHN BEVERIDGE

Nov 28. 1884

Sir

I fear I must have seemed neglectful of your letter of May last, doing me the honour of asking me to contribute some of my volumes to the Dublin free Libraries, an object which you truly said, would be for various accounts so interesting to me.[3] I must therefore beg you to accept the apology which I

[1] Denny wrote on 30 Oct. 'I have made a calculation, and am prepared to make the following offer: — to take the responsibility of publication and to pay your Eminence the sum of 1/– (one shilling) for every volume sold. I think this royalty is very fair ...'
[2] See letter of 11 Nov. to Oates.
[3] Beveridge, Town Clerk of Dublin, wrote on 16 May on behalf of the Public Libraries Committee asking for donations of Newman's works for two Free Libraries then being established in Dublin. Authors who had already contributed copies of their works were 'the Right Hon. and Most Rev. Dr. Trench, Mr Trevelyan M.P., Lord O'Hagan, Professor Hull L.L.D., and others'.

now offer for my silence, a silence which has arisen from difficulties of several kinds, which still remain but which I had hoped might by delay in writing to you have ceased to be valid

I trust you will accept this tardy explanation and to believe me to be

TO J. F. X. O'CONOR, S.J.

Nov. 28, 1884

Dear Father O'Conor, S.J.,

I have so many letters to write, and am so old, that I cannot tell whether I answered your letter of Sept. 20 or not. Accordingly I send you these few lines, lest I should have been silent on the receipt of a letter so kind and gratifying to me.[1]

But you must excuse me saying much, for I write with difficulty.

Your faithful servant, John H. Card. Newman.

TO JOHN WILLIAM OGLE

Nov 29. 1884

Dear Dr Ogle

Please burn this.

You asked me whether I could be sure of recollecting all that occurred 20 years ago

This set me on thinking, and something occurred to my memory, which it is wonderful I did not tell you

Some one connected in my mind my case with the suggestion of stricture. And I once fell in with a medical book, which said that 'simple strictures' did *not* always arise from some criminal cause — and added, (I *think*), that they sometimes so arose from calculus.[2] I almost think Mr Stanley implied or asked me as to stricture, tho' without mentioning the word.

Moreover, I think I found that, if this evil is not checked, it tends to a fatal obstruction of the passage.

I understand now, why I was so anxious, tho' I had forgotten the ground of it

Most truly Yours J H Newman

[1] See letter of 3 Oct. to O'Conor.
[2] Newman had in his possession Robert Thomas, *The Modern Practice of Physic*, tenth edition, London 1834. There it is said, p. 678:
'We may rest assured that inflammation in the urethra is the usual source of all strictures, and for the most part this is excited by gonorrhoea; occasionally it has, however, arisen from some other cause producing continued irritation in the parts, as, for instance, from some previous disease in the bladder or prostate gland.'

TO WILFRID WARD

Dec 4. 1884

My dear Mr Ward

Thank you for your book.[1] It gratifies me exceedingly that you are aiding one main proposition of my Essay on Assent, which so much needed aid. Indeed I cannot aspire, or ever has aspired [sic], to do more than open a large subject, having a full conviction that at best I could only claim the merit of an experimental sketch.

I shall read as much of your book as ever I can, but reading fatigues me now

Very truly Yours John H. Card Newman

TO EYTON BOND

[5 December 1884][2]

In answer to Mr Bond's inquiry Cardinal Newman observes that in various places in his writings, both as Anglican and Catholic he has spoken of the punishment of impenitent sinners as eternal.

As far as he can recollect, he has not spoken of it as always a state of torment, or as incessant or continuous.

He has in his 'Grammar of Assent' referred with satisfaction to the Jesuit Father Pétau, who distinguishes between continuity and endlessness. In a note at p 501 he pursues the subject.[3]

TO ERNEST HARTLEY COLERIDGE

Decr 5. 1884

Dear Sir

It is from no want of reverence for the genius of Mr Coleridge as a poet and a philosopher, and no insensibility to the compliment you pay me in writing to me on this occasion, that I feel a difficulty in accepting the opportunity you give me of joining in the act of homage to a celebrated man to which you invite me.[4]

[1] Wilfrid Ward, *The Wish to Believe*, London 1884. He wrote on 3 Dec. that part of his book was a defence of the illative sense, 'the great principle developed in the *Grammar of Assent.*'
[2] This is the date on Newman's draft. Bond, who was a gun manufacturer in Birmingham, wrote on 1 Dec. that he had seen an article in a newspaper which mentioned Newman's name and Manning's 'as partakers of what is called the "larger hope."' He asked if Newman had treated the subject in any of his works.
[3] *G.A.*, Note III, 'On the punishment of the wicked having no termination', pp. 501–3.
[4] E. H. Coleridge wrote on 28 Nov. that a bust of his grandfather the poet was to be placed in Westminster Abbey. The Dean, G. G. Bradley, had suggested it should go in the baptistry, but the Poets' Corner was felt to be more appropriate. 'The Dean is anxious to have the opinions of a few who are qualified to speak on the subject. I have placed in his hands letters from the Head Master of Harrow School [Henry Montagu Butler], Principal Shairp of St

Various reasons, which it would be too long and irrelevant to do justice to, lead me to view the present state of the Abbey with little satisfaction. I think it no real honour to obtain a memorial there

I am, Dear Sir Your faithful Servant

John H Card. Newman

TO JOHN WILLIAM OGLE

Dec 11. 1884

My dear Dr Ogle

I have wanted to write to you for a week past — but during the last half year my fingers have got so stiff or feeble that I am as slow and awkward as a child.

This day week I submitted myself for examination — I felt it necessary to my peace of mind to know whether Mr Stanley had known more than he said, that is, if I could analyse the cause of my anxiety I was somewhat roughly treated — perhaps it could not be helped — but the result was very satisfactory. There is *no* calculus, *no* enlargement of the third lobe of the gland, *no* obstruction of any kind. The instrument used was of full size, and went (I think he said) easily.

I am surprised you should not have heard of Mr Maitland. He was a great friend of Hugh Rose, succeeded him as Editor of the British Critic, and was Librarian at Lambeth[1]

Most truly yours John H Card Newman

TO EYTON BOND

Dec. 12. 1884

Dear Sir

I thank you for the very kind tone of your letter. It is not worth while your getting the 'Grammar of Assent' That book has only 3 pages out of 503 on the subject of future punishment.

As to that doctrine, I think it should be borne in mind that a Revelation is necessarily a matter of *faith*. This St Paul is strong in insisting on. The only question is whether eternity of punishment is *in truth* inconsistent with the moral attributes of God. Before we say it is, we must know what eternity is. We only know the negative side, not the positive. 'Punishment *never* ends.' This proposition we *can* understand; but 'Punishment *ever* is —' this we *cannot* understand as a proposition. We cannot understand what eternity consists in, and in consequence we do not know what it adds, whether it adds

Andrews, Mr Aubrey de Vere, and Mr Matthew Arnold who are all strongly in favour of the bust being placed in the Poets' Corner. . . . Lord Coleridge is very anxious that the bust should be placed in the Poets Corner. I have told him that I proposed writing to your Eminence and he did not altogether dissuade me.'

[1] Samuel Roffey Maitland (1796–1866), the ecclesiastical historian.

any thing positive to the intensity of the punishment. For instance, whether *dates* be supposed to exist in eternity or not, it is plain how different time would be to us from what it is now, if it had no measurements.

I say all this as suggesting the rashness of dogmatizing on that [sic] is consistent with the divine attributes, and what is not.

Very truly Yours John H Card. Newman

P.S.   I wish my fingers would let me write better

TO ALEXANDER DENNY (PICKERING & CO.)

Decr 17. 1884

Dear Mr Pickering

Thank you for the annual statement of account.

I am sorry to see that I gave you the onus of paying for an edition of the 2nd vol. of 'H [Historical] Sketches'. I quite forget how it took place

Yours very truly J H N

P.S.   I think the balance satisfactory

TO MISS M. R. GIBERNE

Dec. 19 1884

My dear Sister M. Pia

Your letter has just come, and I think it best to send you my affectionate congratulations and Cardinalitian blessing by anticipation of the Feast, than to run the risk of engagements and over fatigue when the day comes.

I don't think any thing of your special mental trouble, for it does not argue any want of faith, but is merely that now you *realize* more exactly what lies before you, and your enemy takes advantage of what is really a meritorious state of mind to frighten you. I am reading with great interest Wilfrid Ward's (son of W G Ward) book 'The wish to believe',[1] and if, when I have finished it, I like it as much as I do when I am half way through it, I will send it to you.

What I *am* anxious about is your state of health. You have never, as I think, have realized that the misfortune you have had is very serious.[2] You do not now, I fear, protect yourself against what may happen as you ought. I have known cases, which, for want of proper *habitual* precaution, terminated in sudden death. Perhaps I am quite wrong in my fear that you neglect it, but, if so, I am doing no harm by my mistake.

You are, I know, in our Lord's loving hands. You have given yourself to a life of great penance for His sake, and He will not, does not forget it   'When

[1] See letter of 4 Dec. to Wilfrid Ward.
[2] Miss Giberne had a rupture.

thou shalt pass through the waters, He will be with thee, and when thou shalt walk in the fire, thou shalt not be burnt'[1] for you are one of those who have taken your purgatory in this life, and I rejoice to think that, when God takes you hence, I shall have one to plead for me in heaven. For me, I have no sign on me of dying yet.

Yours ever affecte John H. Card. Newman

P.S. I am much gratified and consoled by Monsignor Place's letter about my Essay and P S.[2]

TO WILFRID WARD

Decr 20. 1884

Dear Wilfrid Ward

I thus familiarly address you on the plea that I was familiar with your Father before you were born; also because when an old man feels, as I do after reading your book, great pleasure in the work of another, he may speak of its author and to its author, with a freedom not warranted by personal intimacy. But my fingers move slow, and by their slowness so puzzle my brain, that I lose the thread of what I want to say.

I do really think your Essay[3] a *very* successful one, and I have more to say of it than I have room or leisure to say it in.

First you are dramatic, which is a quality of great excellence in a dialogue. It would never do for your arguments to profess to be irrefragable, and your opponent simply to be convinced by them. Also, it is the only way in which you can secure a fair and complete hearing for him, and his side of the question debated.

Next, you are outspoken and bold. You are not afraid of enunciating what so many will consider a paradox. You have the advantage, (and this enables you to be bold) of knowing that you have no chance of hazarding any statement which a rigid Catholic critic could accuse as censurable. This is what makes controversy to a Catholic so difficult.

As to the matter and main argument of your Essay it seems to me you mean to say that the same considerations which make you wish to believe are among the reasons which, when you actually do inquire, *lead you prudently* to believe, thus serving a double purpose. Do you bring this out anywhere? On the contrary are you not shy of calling those considerations *reasons*? why?

You seem to me to insist with an earnestness for which I doubt not you have some good reason on the difference between believing and realizing

---

[1] *Isaiah* 43:2.
[2] The correspondence shows that the Essay was that *On the Inspiration of Scripture*, and the P.S., the *Postscript* in the Italian translation.
[3] *The Wish to Believe*. See letter of 4 Dec.

445

(which is pretty much, I suppose, what in the Grammar of Assent I have called 'Notional' and 'Real' assent) and to be unwilling freely to grant from the first that there *must* be more grounds in reason to a religious mind whereas in fact a religious mind must always master much which is unsure to the non-religious; (not that there is any real difference of view between us) — thus you allow of two men with the *same* evidence and *equal* reasoning powers, being primâ facie likely he came to the same conclusion whereas *I* should say to Darlington[1] 'Stop there — I can't allow that a religious man has no more evidence *necessarily*, than a non-religious.' I wonder whether I make myself intelligible. It is only the *mode* of your stating and arguing on this point which I do not comfortably follow. And you may have reasons I do not know. I am very tired.

Yours affect J H Card Newman

You have expressed just what I want you at p 92 'A man who looks' etc[2]

P S   A happy Christmas to you

TO R. W. CHURCH

Decr 21. 1884

My dear Dean

I was going to wish you and yours a happy Christmas, when I saw a paragraph in the papers about your health.[3] However, I shall interpret it of Ogle's proper caution about you, unless I am to be made anxious by hearing from you to the contrary. I hope you will not be pressed to go to Lincoln. I always fancy that county unhealthy, and then Nottingham is a formidable undertaking.[4]

Perhaps you can help me in explaining a passage in the Spectator. In a review of James Mozley's letters the reviewer refers to p. 149 to his saying that Manning called on me, after his University Sermon, at Littlemore, and, (true enough) I note in my own Journal 'Manning called.' But the reviewer says that I gave orders to my young door keeper not to let him in — to Manning's distress. What does this mean? I recollect nothing about it — and, if I did give such a message, I don't think I should have given a young door keeper my real reason.[5]

[1] A character in the dialogue.

[2] 'Firstly, to take the Christian evidences alone. A man who looks at them for the purposes of religious inquiry must necessarily feel their strength to be supplemented by those very considerations in his own mind which prompted the inquiry. The need he has for a religion, the completeness of satisfaction which Christianity affords to that need, the powerful appeal of Christ's character to his moral nature, here are specimens of the supplementary personal evidences which an individual inquirer has over and above the historical evidences viewed on their own merits'. op. cit., p. 192.

[3] Church replied on 22 Dec., 'the newspapers have been needlessly disturbing my friends'.

[4] Church replied, 'I am not going to Lincoln or anywhere else, unless I can retire from St Paul's and Mr Gladstone 'has been good enough before now to talk to me of such things . . .'

[5] See the Memorandum of 18 Nov. 1884, and letter of 23 Dec. to Church, for his reply.

All through the last summer I have been meaning and trying to call on the Pagets — but Rednall is a difficult place to start from, — now that I cannot walk.[1]

Yours affectionately, John H. Card. Newman

TO W. J. COPELAND

Dec. 21. 1884

My very dear Copeland

It did not require your kind Christmas present, just arrived, to make us think of you. You are ever in my mind, and in William Neville's, indeed of all us who can count the years of your affectionate act, by which you have been used to signalize this sacred season. We in turn send you back all Christmas benedictions.

God be your strength and life, my dear Friend

Yours affectly John H Card Newman

TO THOMAS FORD

Dec 21/84

My dear Thomas Ford

I was shocked yesterday to hear of the great trial which had come upon you; and I said Mass for your dear wife's soul this morning. I pray God to comfort you under this affliction with His best blessings. My fingers will not let me write more[2]

Yours ever affectionately John H Card. Newman

TO J. R. BLOXAM

Dec 22. 1884

My dear Dr Bloxam

Thanks for your Christmas congratulations to me and Fr Wm [William] which I return with all my heart

I hope the Newspaper cuttings include those against me which used to be many more than those for me — I was used to say that I was the best-abused person in the world after O'Connell.[3]

---

[1] Francis Paget, who had married Church's daughter Helen, was Vicar of Bromsgrove 1883–5.
[2] Thomas Ford had become a member of the choir at the church of the Birmingham Oratory by 1855.
[3] Bloxam replied on 27 Dec., 'With respect to my Volume of Newspaper Cuttings, they are mostly if not all after the tide had turned, and you began to be spoken of with respect and eulogy . . .' Bloxam's collection is now at Magdalen College, Oxford.

I forget the Article in the Edinburgh. Have you seen James Mozley's letters? I hear Bishop Coffin is very ill[1]

Yrs affly John H Card. Newman

TO R. W. CHURCH

Decr 23. 1884

My dear Dean

Private

Thank you for your various informations in answer to my questions. Those about yourself are pleasant, but as to the one personal to myself, while I stare at it, I am quite defenceless, for I simply recollect *nothing* about it.[2]

I cannot *of course* deny M's [Manning] *own* witness if his 'account' is a personal testimony, but, that I should have made J. A. F. [Froude] my confidant is the queerest turn up I ever could have fancied! J.E. [sic] F. I never took to; the next year, 1844, he accused me of trying indirectly by means of the Lives of the Saints to hook him into the Tractarian party and to him is addressed my reply to the charge in the letter, part of which is inserted in Apologia p. 211 'November 1844.'

It is remarkable that I had, just before Guy Faux day, 1843, written three successive and most free letters to M. with the dates of Oct. 14. Oct. 25 and Oct. 31 (Apolog. pp. 219, 221, 223) and, though I gave him full leave to make what use he pleased of them and felt it a relief to have done so, yet of all the men I know down to this day there is no one so merciless and successful a pumper as M. and the only hypothesis for my refusing to see him, if *I did* — the only (hypothetical) reason at *the bottom* of my mind, was my fear of being pumped on and on, till I had given up my secret suspicions about Dalgairns, St John, Coffin, Ward, etc, conscious as I was of my helpless weakness.

However, this is simply an hypothesis — and I have nothing to say in answer especially since M. is a principal of it (nor am I accused of any great crime.) Was not Mr Paul an Exeter man? was not J.A.F. also at that time[3]

---

[1] Coffin died on 6 April 1885.

[2] In reply to Newman's question about the story that he had rebuffed Manning in 1843, Dean Church wrote on 22 Dec. that he had seen C. Kegan Paul, who had first published it in the *Illustrated Century Magazine* (May 1883), p. 129. In this version the doorkeeper at Littlemore was James Anthony Froude, 'who had to convey to the Archdeacon the unpleasant intimation that Dr. Newman declined to see him. So anxious was the young man to cover the slight, and to minimize its effect, that he walked away from the door with the Archdeacon, bare-headed as he was, and had covered half the way to Oxford before he turned back, unaware, as was his companion of his unprotected state, under a November sky.' Church understood that Kegan Paul had heard the story from Manning himself, but this he later corrected. See letter of 4 Jan. 1885 to Church.

[3] Kegan Paul went up to Exeter in 1846, when J. A. Froude was a Fellow of the College.

You and J. Mozley seem not to have heard it, being at Oriel. It is odd that the 'account' has been bottled up till now. I mean, that it has not been in print. The oddest part of it perhaps is that in November 1843 I should have the spirits and party feeling strong enough to do battle for any Anglican party (I forget J. Mozley's words)[1]

Ever yours affectly John H. Card. Newman.

P.S. I should be much surprised to find J.A.F. ever once slept in our house — or even that he ever was in it except for a call. I half recollect his once coming to me at Oriel or my going to him to talk over his own matters. Has he not shown me up in a Tale? perhaps I am quite wrong.[2]

TO ANNE MOZLEY

Dec 24. 1884

My dear Anne Mozley

I send you all best Christmas blessings, and give you notice that the Memoir is ready, when you tell me where and when to send it to you[3]

Also, I write to congratulate you on the success of your Volume.[4] One remarkable instance of it has occurred here in the last day or two. George Ryder's son, one of our Fathers, has just now seen your book, and has been marvelously taken with it, and is reading it through

Yrs affectly J. H. Card. Newman

TO MARIANNE FRANCES, CHARLOTTE AND WILLIAM BOWDEN

1884

To you, Maggie and Chattie
   and to dear Willie
of whom I should like to hear
   a better account
The best blessings of Christmas

J. H. Card. Newman

---

[1] This implies that Newman felt he would have objected, not so much to the violent anti-Catholicism of Manning's sermon, as to what J. B. Mozley expressed thus: 'He [Manning] seemed so really carried away by fear of Romanism that he almost took under his patronage the Puritans and the Whigs of 1688, because they had settled the matter against the Pope. He did not indeed commit himself into a direct approval of them and the means they used, but talked of the whole movement as having had a happy event and being providential.' *Letters of the Rev. J. B. Mozley*, p. 149.

[2] *The Nemesis of Faith*, London 1849. cf. letter of 15 March 1849 to J. M. Capes.

[3] See letter of 20 Oct. to Anne Mozley for this Memoir. She replied on 28 Dec. 'I can hardly tell you how much I value the permission to read it and how I look forward to it.'

[4] *Letters of J. B. Mozley.*

TO CATHERINE BOWDEN, SISTER MARY ALBAN

Decr 29. 1884

My dear Child

All best Christmas blessings come down on you and all your surroundings. The Bishop's [Ullathorne] recovery is a great grace, almost a miracle. Excuse a short letter, my fingers are so stiff

Yours affectly J H Card. Newman

How sad about Welby

TO AUGUSTA THEODOSIA DRANE

Dec 30. 1884

My dear Mother Provincial

I wish I could return you and Sister Gabriel [Du Boulay] suitable answers to your kind and pleasant letters. Yes, the Bishop's present recovery is most wonderful, and should encourage us in prayers. We are too apt to think ourselves as not worthy, for He has *made* us worthy. What should I do if you treated me in this fashion? I am wonderfully *well*, and I have no way of accounting for it, but that you give me your prayers, and not you only, but all of you, and others like you. My brain and my fingers move very slowly; I can't walk or speak, or hear as I should like. But my health is at present perfect, and I am puzzled why. I say it is certainly the prayers of good friends.

I am too tired to write more. God has ever helped me, and will help me still. My blessing on yourself, on Sister Gabriel, and all of you. I heard lately from the Bishop a tolerable account of yours Sisters in Australia. They must expect some rough experience at first[1]

Yours affectly in Jesus Xt   John H Card. Newman

TO CATHERINE ANNE BATHURST

Decr 31. 1884

My dear Child

Thank you for your affectionate letter and your good prayers — My stiff fingers write so slow, that I can only send you a few lines. I am, and have been, sorry you were sent to Harrow   Of course Watford is a better place. All Christmas blessings be on you and your surroundings

Ever Yours affectionately John H Card. Newman

[1] Mother Margaret Hallahan's nuns made a foundation at Adelaide in 1883.

TO WILLIAM MASKELL

Dec 31. 1884

My dear Mr Maskell

Thank you for your letter which has just come. I heartily return your and Mrs Maskell's good wishes for the New Year. For myself I am thankful to say that I appear to be quite well, excepting only the necessary infirmities of old age. I write very slowly, and think slowly — and read, hear and walk with difficulty — but I have no pain, and no foreboding of complaint or illness, which is a great mercy. Nor do I feel heat or cold — but one does not know what a day may bring forth.

Here is an egotistical letter but the coming of the New Year has drawn it from me

Very sincerely Yours John H Card. Newman

W. Maskell Esq

List of Letters by Correspondents

Abbreviations used in addition to those listed at the beginning of the Volume:

A.	Original Autograph.
Bodleian	Bodleian Library, Oxford.
C.	Copy, other than those made by Newman.
D.	Draft by Newman.
Georgetown	The University of Georgetown, Washington, D.C.
H.	Holograph copy by Newman.
Harrow	Dominican Convent, Harrow, Middlesex.
Keble	Keble College, Oxford
Lond.	London Oratory.
Magd.	Magdalen College, Oxford.
Oriel	Oriel College, Oxford.
Pr.	Printed.
Pusey	Pusey House, Oxford.
S.J. Dublin	The Jesuit Fathers, 35 Lower Leeson Street, Dublin.
S.J. Lond.	The Jesuit Fathers, 114 Mount Street, London.
Stoke	The Dominican Convent, Stoke-on-Trent.
Stone	The Dominican Convent, Stone.
Todhunter	John Todhunter, Beccles.

The abbreviation which describes the source is always the first one after the date of each letter. This is followed immediately by the indication of its present location or owner. When there is no such indication, it means that the source letter is preserved at the Birmingham Oratory. It has not been thought necessary to reproduce the catalogue indications of the Archives at the Oratory, because each of Newman's letters there is separately indexed, and can be traced at once.

After the source and its location have been indicated, any additional holograph copies (with their dates) or drafts are listed, and then, enclosed within brackets, any reference to previous publication in standard works.

Lastly, when it is available, comes the address to which the letter was sent.

Correspondent	Year	Date	Source	Location, Owner, Address
Acland, Henry	1882	21 Sept	Pr	J. B. Atlay, *Henry Acland, A Memoir*, London 1903, pp. 419–20
Alimonda, Cardinal	1883	15 Feb	D	(two)
Allies, T. W.	1881	26 Nov	C	
	1882	21 May	C	
	1883	22 July	C	
	1884	24 Feb	C	
Allies, Mrs T. W.	1884	24 Feb	C	
Amherst, William	1883	23 Aug	Pr	Mary Francis Roskell, O.S.B., *Memoirs of Francis Kerril Amherst*, London n.d., p. 374
Archer, William Henry	1883	2 May	A	University of Melbourne Archives
Argyll, Duke of	1884	6 Feb	A	Catholic Chaplaincy, Oxford
Avery, Thomas	1882	2 June	Pr	The *Weekly Register*, (10 June 1882)
Bacchus, Francis Joseph	1881	6 Oct	A	
Baines, Miss	1883	15 May	A	Dawson's of Pall Mall
Ball, Thomas Isaac	1881	5 Nov	A	Holy Cross College, Worcester, Mass. *Ad.* The Revd Thos J. Ball/15 Forrest Road/Edinburgh
Barrett, George Slatyer	1882	13 Oct	C	
Bartolini, Cardinal	1882	26 Sept	A	*Ad.* Emo e Revmo Sig. Mio Ossmo/Il Cardinale Domenico Bartolini/Palazzo della Fabbrica/Via d'Aracoeli i.
	1883	15 Feb	C	
			D	
Bath and Stewart, Messrs	1883	17 Oct	D	
Bathurst, Catherine Anne	1881	30 Dec	C	
	1882	29 May	C	
	1884	1 Jan	A	Harrow
		31 Dec	A	Harrow
Bedford, Henry	1882	29 Jan	C	
		13 Nov	C	
	1883	4 April	C	
	1884	23 Jan	C	
		1 April	C	
		5 June	C	
		9 June	C	
Bellairs, Henry Spencer Kenrick	1882	21 Mar	A	Newman Preparatory School, Boston
Bellasis, Edward, Junior	1882	26 April	A	*Ad.* Edward Bellasis Esqr/College of Arms/London E C
		8 Oct	A	*Ad.* the same
		10 Oct	A	*Ad.* the same
		13 Oct	A	*Ad.* the same
		19 Oct	A	*Ad.* the same
	1884	4 Feb	C	
		18 Mar	A	*Ad.* the same
		31 Mar	C	
Bellasis, Mrs Edward	1882	20 Dec	A	
	1883	12 Mar	A	
		17 June	A	
		22 June	A	
		13 Nov	A	
	1884	24 Jan	A	
Bellingham, Henry	1883	12 June	D	
Bennoch, Francis	1882	11 Sept	D	
Beveridge, John	1884	28 Nov	D	
Bittleston, Henry	1881	26 Oct	A	
	1882	26 April	A	
		14 June (I)	D	
		14 June (II)	Pr	The *Tablet* (17 June 1882), p. 937
Blachford, Lord	1882	2 Jan	C	

Correspondent	Year	Date	Source	Location, Owner, Address
		23 Feb	C	
		1 April	C	
		4 April	A	St John's Seminary, Camarillo, California
		16 Nov	C	
	1883	2 Jan	C	
		29 Jan	C	
		24 Mar	C	
		14 Aug	C	
	1884	19 Jan	A	St John's Seminary, Camarillo, California
		8 Feb	A	
		8 Oct	A	
		12 Oct	A	
			D	
		14 Oct	A	
		16 Oct	A	
		19 Oct	A	
			D	
		20 Oct	A	
		22 Oct	A	
		26 Oct	A	
		30 Oct	A	
		31 Oct (I)	A	
		31 Oct (II)	C	
		2 Nov	A	
			D	
		4 Nov	A	
		14 Nov	A	
Blackmore, R. W.	1881	16 Dec	D	
	1882	1 Feb	C	
Blake, Robert J.	1883	21 Feb	C	
	1884	10 Jan	A	
Blennerhasset, Sir Rowland	1882	12 Oct	A	Cambridge University Library, Add. MS. 7486
Bloxam, J. R.	1881	2 Oct	A	Magd. MS. 307
		28 Dec	A	Magd. MS. 307
	1882	23 Jan	A	Magd. MS. 307
		17 Feb	A	Magd. MS. 307
		26 April	A	Magd. MS. 307
		21 Sept	A	Magd. MS. 307
		7 Oct	A	Magd. MS. 307 (*Newman and Bloxam*, p. 16)
		21 Nov	A	Magd. MS. 307
	1883	6 Feb	A	Magd. MS. 307
		20 Feb	A	Magd. MS. 307
		16 Aug	A	University of Sussex Library *Ad*. The Rev. Dr Bloxam/Beeding Priory/Hurstpierpoint/Sussex
		11 Oct	A	Magd. MS. 307
	1884	27 Sept.	A	Magd. MS. 307
		7 Oct	A	Magd. MS. 307
		25 Nov	A	Magd. MS. 307
		22 Dec	A	Magd. MS. 307
Bond, Eyton	1884	5 Dec	A	
			D	
		12 Dec	A	
Borlase, Mrs William	1883	31 Dec	A	University of Texas Library *Ad*. Mrs Borlase/Farnham Rectory/Bishop's Stortford/Essex
Bowden, Catherine, Sister Mary Alban	1883	27 Dec	A	Stone
	1884	13 Feb	A	Stone
		29 Dec	A	Stone
Bowden, Charles	1882	26 Dec	A	Lond.

Correspondent	Year	Date	Source	Location, Owner, Address
Bowden, Marianne Frances	1882	26 Nov	A	*Ad.* Miss Bowden/32 Thurloe Square/ London S W
Bowden, Marianne Frances, Charlotte and William	1884	Christmas	A	
Bowden, Mrs J. W.	1884	24 Aug	A	*Lond.* Mrs Bowden/11 Cromwell Road/London S W/*to be forwarded*
Bowles, Emily	1881	9 Oct	A	
		24 Dec	A	
	1882	5 Jan	A	(*Ward* II, pp. 477–8)
		13 April	A	(*Ward* II, pp. 519–20)
		29 May	A	
		15 June	A	
		20 June	A	
		16 Nov	A	
	1883	10 Mar	A	
		31 Dec	A	
	1884	5 Jan	A	
		8 Jan	A	
		12 Mar	A	(*Trevor* II, pp. 596–7)
		12 May	A	
		7 July	A	
		24 Oct	A	
Boys of the Oratory School	1884	12 Mar	A	Oratory School, Woodcote
Bramston, John	1882	10 July	C	
Braye, Lord	1882	9 Oct	A	Canons Regular of the Lateran, St Augustine's, Datchet, Slough.
		29 Oct	A	St Augustine's, Datchet (*Ward* II, pp. 485–6) *Ad.* The Lord Braye/ Stanford Park/Rugby
		2 Nov	A	St Augustine's, Datchet (*Ward* II, pp. 486–7; Thomas Murphy, *The Position of the Catholic Church in England and Wales during the last two Centuries*, London 1892, pp. 7–8; *Trevor* II, pp. 600–1)
		10 Nov	A	St Augustine's, Datchet *Ad.* The Lord Braye/Stanford Park/Rugby
		15 Nov	A	St Augustine's, Datchet
		17 Nov	A	St Augustine's, Datchet *Ad.* The Lord Braye/Stanford Park/Rugby
	1883	7 Jan	A	St Augustine's, Datchet, *Ad.* the same
		4 Feb	A	St Augustine's, Datchet *Ad.* the same
		9 Feb	A	St Augustine's, Datchet
		12 Feb	A	
		10 Mar	A	St Augustine's, Datchet *Ad.* the same
		2 May	A	St Augustine's, Datchet *Ad.* the same
		6 May	A	St Augustine's, Datchet
		11 May	A	St Augustine's, Datchet *Ad.* the same
		20 May	A	St Augustine's, Datchet
		6 June	A	St Augustine's, Datchet *Ad.* The Lord Braye/40 Grosvenor Street/ London W
		12 June	A	St Augustine's, Datchet *Ad.* The Lord Braye/40 Grosvenor Street/ London W
		23 June	A	St Augustine's, Datchet

Correspondent	Year	Date	Source	Location, Owner, Address
		26 June	A	St Augustine's, Datchet *Ad*. The Lord Braye/40 Grosvenor Street/ London W
		29 June	A	St Augustine's, Datchet
		3 July	A	St Augustine's, Datchet
		31 July	A	St Augustine's, Datchet *Ad*. The Lord Braye/Stanford Park/Rugby
		8 Sept	A	St Augustine's, Datchet
		14 Dec	A	St Augustine's, Datchet
	1884	30 May	A	St Augustine's, Datchet *Ad*. The Lord Braye/Stanford Park/Rugby
		4 June	A	St Augustine's, Datchet (*Trevor* II, p. 601)
		13 June	A	St Augustine's, Datchet *Ad*. The Lord Braye/Stanford Park/Rugby
		7 July	A	St Augustine's, Datchet *Ad*. the same
Bright, William	1883	1 April	C	
		3 April	C	
		25 July	C	
Brosnan, Timothy	1883	22 May	C	
Brown, David	1882	21 April	A	Oriel
		20 June	A	Oriel (W. G. Blaikie, *David Brown, A Memoir*, London 1898, p. 246)
		21 June	A	Oriel (op. cit., pp. 246–7)
		27 Nov	A	Oriel
		12 Dec	A	Oriel
Brownlow, William Robert	1883	5 May	C	
		10 May	C	
	1884	16 Nov	C	
Bruce, P. Studholm	1881	end of Nov	D	
Bull and Auvache, Messrs	1884	17 Oct	D	
Bunting, Percy William	1883	14 May	A	University of Chicago Library
Burns and Oates, Messrs	1882	10 July	D	
Capes, J. M.	1882	16 Aug	C	
Casey, James	1882	14 May	Pr	
Charlton, Ulrich	1883	4 Sept	C	
			D	
		2 Oct	C	
Chesson, Frederick William	1883	8 May	A	Newman Preparatory School, Boston (The *Daily News* (14 May 1883) p. 5; Walter N Arnstein, *The Bradlaugh Case*, Oxford 1965, p. 230; *Trevor* II, p. 602) *Ad*. F. W. Chesson Esqr/Devonshire Club/ St James's/London S W
			D	
Chief Inspector of General Post Office, Birmingham	1884	30 July	A	Stephen Walker
Christie, Mrs	1881	20 Dec	C	
		29 Dec	C	
	1882	23 Oct	C	
Church, R. W.	1881	21 Dec	A	Pusey
	1882	6 Mar	A	Pusey
	1883	25 Feb	A	Pusey
		28 Mar	Pr	*Ward* II, pp. 520–1 (B.A. Smith, *Dean Church*, London 1957, p. 302)
		29 April	A	Pusey
		5 Nov	C	
	1884	29 Oct	C	
		21 Dec	C	
		23 Dec	C	

457

Correspondent	Year	Date	Source	Location, Owner, Address
Clarke, Richard Frederick	1882	5 Nov	C D	
Clifford, William	1883	7 Jan	A	Clifton Diocesan Archives (Shane Leslie, *Henry Edward Manning*, London 1921, p. 284; J. H. Newman, *On the Inspiration of Scripture*, edited by J. D. Holmes and R. Murray, London 1967, p. 28)
		20 Jan	A	Clifton Diocesan Archives (Shane Leslie, op. cit., p. 284)
		7 Feb	A	Clifton Diocesan Archives
		13 April	A	Clifton Diocesan Archives
		10 Sept	A	Clifton Diocesan Archives
		25 Sept	A	Clifton Diocesan Archives
		3 Oct	A D	Clifton Diocesan Archives (three)
		13 Oct	A	Clifton Diocesan Archives (Shane Leslie, op. cit., pp. 284–5)
		25 Oct	A D	Clifton Diocesan Archives
	1884	8 Feb	A	Clifton Diocesan Archives
		18 Mar	A D	Clifton Diocesan Archives
		29 July	A	Clifton Diocesan Archives
Cole, Sir Henry	1882	22 Mar	A	
		26 Mar	H	
Cole, a daughter of Sir Henry	1882	11 Aug	A	Newman Preparatory School, Boston
Cole, a son of Sir Henry	1882	20 April	A	The late Sir Shane Leslie
Coleridge, Edward	1883	24 Feb	C	
Coleridge, Ernest Hartley	1884	5 Dec	A	University of Texas Library
Coleridge, Henry James	1882	24 Nov	A	S.J. Lond.
	1884	24 April	A	S.J. Lond.
		6 May	A	S.J. Lond.
		24 May	A	S.J. Lond..
		23 Nov	A	S.J. Lond.
		27 Nov	A	S.J. Lond.
Coleridge, Lord	1884	18 Mar	C	
		29 April	D	
		17 May	H	
Colyar, Henry de	1883	9 Aug	A	Lond. Vol. 10
	1884	25 Feb	A	Lond. Vol. 10
		15 Mar	A	Lond. Vol. 10
		19 Mar	A	Lond. Vol. 10
Connelly, Pierce	1882	3 Mar	D	
Cope, Sir William Henry	1883	22 Feb	C	
	1884	23 Feb	C	
Copeland, W. J.	1881	21 Dec	C	
	1882	22 July	A	Pusey
		6 Dec	A	Pusey
	1883	31 Jan	A	Pusey
		26 Feb	A	Pusey
		18 Dec	A	Pusey
	1884	21 Dec	A	Pusey
Czacki, Cardinal	1882	Oct	C	
Davies-Cooke, Mrs	1884	9 Oct	A	St John's Seminary, Camarillo, California
Day, Shirley	1884	27 Sept	A	Rev. John R. Day *Ad*. Shirley Day Esqr/Overton Cottage/Water Orton/Birmingham
Deane, Louisa Elizabeth	1881	2 Nov	C	
		27 Dec	C	
	1882	16 April	C	
		14 Nov	C	

Correspondent	Year	Date	Source	Location, Owner, Address
	1883	21 Feb	C	
	1884	26 Jan	C	
		7 May	C	
		1 Aug	C	
		8 Sept	C	
		14 Oct	C	
Deane, Miss Louisa	1884	1 Sept	C	
Delany, William	1884	4 Feb	A	S.J. Dublin
De Lisle, Margaret	1882	10 June	A	St Mary's Abbey, Mill Hill *Ad.* Miss de Lisle/care of Messrs Burns and Oates/17 Portman Street/London W
	1883	12 Jan	A	St Mary's Abbey, Mill Hill *Ad.* Miss de Lisle/Mitford House/ Bournemouth/Hants
		27 May	A	St Mary's Abbey, Mill Hill
		6 Dec	A	St Mary's Abbey, Mill Hill
	1884	25 June	A	St Mary's Abbey, Mill Hill
		22 July	A	St Mary's Abbey, Mill Hill
Denbigh, Countess of	1884	16 Sept	A	
Denison, George Anthony	1884	4 July	D	
Denny, Alexander	1884	19 Feb	D	
		8 Mar	D	(two)
		17 Mar	D	
		7 June	D	
		16 July	D	
		9 Oct	D	
		23 Oct	D	
		25 Oct	D	
		27 Nov	H	
		17 Dec	D	
De Vere, Aubrey	1882	28 June	C	
	1884	1 Feb	A	National Library of Ireland
Devine, Joseph Pierse	1883	24 May	D	
Donnet, James	1883	5 May	C	
			D	
Drane, Augusta Theodosia	1881	16 Oct	A	Stone (Bertrand Wilberforce, O.P., *A Memoir of Mother Francis Raphael*, second edition, London 1897, p. 111)
		27 Oct	A	Stone
		3 Nov	A	Stone
	1883	4 May	C	
	1884	30 Dec	C	
Du Boulay, Sister Mary Gabriel	1881	15 Oct	C	
		27 Nov	C	
Duchesne, Louis	1883	16 April	C	
Eaglesim, Paul	1882	5 Aug	A	
Editor of the Academy	1881	12 Nov	Pr	The *Academy* (19 Nov. 1881), p. 385
			D	
	1884	29 Oct	Pr	The *Academy* (1 Nov. 1884), pp. 287–8)
			D	
			H	Pusey
Editor of the Athenaeum	1881	12 Nov	Pr	The *Athenaeum* (19 Nov. 1881), p. 666
			D	
		17 Nov	D	
Editor of the Birmingham Daily Gazette	1881	5 Nov	Pr	The *Birmingham Daily Gazette* (7 Nov. 1881)
			D	

Correspondent	Year	Date	Source	Location, Owner, Address
Editor of the Daily News	1884	24 Oct (I)	A	Archbishop Corrigan Memorial Library, Dunwoodie Seminary, Yonkers
		24 Oct (II)	A	Newman Memorial High School, Mason City, Iowa (The *Daily News*, 28 Oct. 1884)
Editor of the Fortnightly Review	1883	14 June	C	
Editor of the Guardian	1881	16 Nov	Pr	The *Guardian* (16 Nov. 1881), p. 1644
Editor of the Literary World	1881	12 Nov	D	
Editor of the Manchester Examiner	1883	23 May	D	
Editor of the Morning Post	1881	14 Nov	Pr	The *Morning Post* (14 Nov. 1881), p. 6
			D	
Editor of the Nonconformist and Independent	1882	2 Jan	Pr	The *Nonconformist and Independent* (5 Jan. 1882)
			D	
Editor of the Revue des Sciences Ecclésiastiques	1883	15 Feb	C	
			D	
Editor of the Spectator	1883	5 May	Pr	The *Spectator* (5 May 1883), p. 576
			D	(two)
Editor of The Times	1883	14 Feb	C	
			D	
Edwards, George T.	1881	30 Dec	A	St John's Seminary, Camarillo, California
	1882	15 Feb	A	St John's Seminary, Camarillo, California
		17 Sept	A	St John's Seminary, Camarillo, California (Wilson Harris, *Caroline Fox*, London 1944, p. 46)
		23 Sept	A	St John's Seminary, Camarillo, California (op. cit., p. 46; *Ward* II, p. 333)
		8 Nov	A	St John's Seminary, Camarillo, California (Wilson Harris, op. cit., p. 46)
		14 Dec	A	St John's Seminary, Camarillo, California (Wilson Harris, op. cit., p. 47)
	1883	2 Jan	A	St John's Seminary, Camarillo, California
		8 Feb	A	St John's Seminary, Camarillo, California
		24 Feb	A	St John's Seminary, Camarillo, California
		15 April	A	St John's Seminary, Camarillo, California
			D	
		2 May	A	St John's Seminary, Camarillo, California
		2 June	A	St John's Seminary, Camarillo, California
			D	
		9 June	A	Edward F. Hayes, New York; (enclosure) St John's Seminary, Camarillo, California
	1884	1 Jan	A	St John's Seminary, Camarillo, California
		22 Feb	A	St John's Seminary, Camarillo, California

Correspondent	Year	Date	Source	Location, Owner, Address
		26 Feb	A	St John's Seminary, Camarillo, California
		29 Aug	A	St John's Seminary, Camarillo, California
Ellacombe, Henry Thomas	1882	16 Jan	A	Bodleian
Emly, Lord	1881	5 Dec	A	
	1882	26 Nov	A	*Ad.* The Lord Emly/Tervoe/Limerick/Ireland
	1883	9 April	A	
		17 April	A	
			D	
		29 July	A	
	1884	29 Jan	A	
		30 May	A	
		11 July	A	
		25 Nov	A	
Fawcett, J.	1883	4 Oct	D	
Fish, James Leonard	1884	12 Feb	C	
Fisher, John Cowley	1883	10 Mar	A	Holy Cross College, Worcester Mass. *Ad.* J. Cowley Fisher Esqr/ Wood Hall/Cockermouth
Fitzgerald, Geraldine Penrose	1882	17 Mar	A	
		8 July	A	*Ad.* [Miss G.] Fitzgerald/19 Norfolk Square/London W
		13 July	A	
Ford, Thomas	1884	21 Dec	A	Olton Monastery *Ad.* Mr Thomas Ford/Selly Park /(near the Convent) /Birmingham
Fortey, Emily	1882	6 July	C	(*The Times*, 31 Jan. 1883)
	1884	3 Oct	C	
Fortey, Henry	1883	12 Feb	D	
		16 Feb	D	
Fourdrinier, Eliza	1882	6 Dec	C	(*Ward* II, p. 484)
Fraülein M	1883	27 Nov	C	
Freeman, James	1882	4 Jan	H	
			D	
Freer, Miss	1883	17 Oct	A	Newman Preparatory School, Boston
Frost, Michael	1883	17 May	Pr	The *Tablet* (6 April 1940), p. 336 *Ad.* Michael Frost, Esqr/Dunlemey/Plymouth
	1884	20 Mar	D	
		23 Mar	A	St John's Seminary, Camarillo, California *Ad.* Michael Frost Esqr/ Dunlewey/Plymouth
		10 Nov	D	
Fullerton, Alexander	1882	16 June	A	Maryfield Convent, Roehampton
	1884	20 Mar	A	Maryfield Convent, Roehampton
			D	
		4 June	A	Maryfield Convent, Roehampton
Giberne, Miss M. R.	1881	31 Oct	A	
	1882	5 Jan	A	(*Ward* II, pp. 483–4)
		26 April	A	
		3 July	A	(*Ward* II, p. 520)
		29 Nov	A	
	1883	8 Jan	A	
		9 Mar	A	
		14 May	A	
		22 June	A	(*Ward* II, p. 521)
		17 Sept	A	
		24 Dec	A	
	1884	12 Sept	A	
		19 Dec	A	(*Ward* II, p. 523)

Correspondent	Year	Date	Source	Location, Owner, Address
Gilbert and Rivington,	1882	8 July	D	
Messrs	1884	15 Mar	D	
		16 July	D	
Gladstone, William	1881	13 Dec	A	British Museum
Ewart		23 Dec	A	British Museum (V. A. McClelland, *Cardinal Manning*, London 1962, p. 81; Francis Hackett, *The Story of the Irish Nation*, Dublin 1922, p. 326)
			D	(two)
	1882	2 Jan	A	British Museum
	1883	3 Jan	A	British Museum
Goodwin, William Henry	1884	13 Aug	A	Oriel
Gordon, Dr	1882	14 Jan	A	Newman Preparatory School, Boston
Gordon, William Philip	1882	21 Mar	A	Lond. Vol. 10
		9 June	A	Lond. Vol. 10
	1883	17 Oct	A	Lond. Vol. 10
	1884	19 Mar	A	Lond. Vol. 10 (*Trevor* II, pp. 608–9)
			D	
		21 Mar	A	Lond. Vol. 10 (*Trevor* II, p. 609)
			D	
		25 Mar	A	Lond. Vol. 10
			D	
		3 April	A	Lond. Vol. 10
			D	
Gore, Charles	1884	6 Nov	A	Pusey *Ad*. The Rev. C Gore/ Pusey House/61 St Giles/Oxford
Gower, Lord Ronald	1884	30 July	C	
Grant, Sir Alexander	1884	25 Feb	A	
			D	
Grant, Ignatius	1882	23 Dec	Pr	Privately printed by the English Jesuits
Gray, Richard	1882	31 Dec	D	
Griffin, Arthur Sandes	1883	31 Jan	C	
		5 Mar	A	Cambridge University Library
	1884	28 Feb	A	Cambridge University Library
		21 May	A	Cambridge University Library
		1 July	A	Cambridge University Library
		5 July	A	Cambridge University Library
Hall and English, Messrs	1883	17 July	A	Oscott College, Warwickshire
Hamilton, Adam	1884	15 Mar	A	Buckfast Abbey
Hanmer, A. J.	1882	17 April	A	S.J. Lond. (*Mrs Sophia Ainsworth. A Memoir*, by her brother Anthony John Hanmer, privately printed 1899, p. 54) *Ad*. A. J. Hanmer Esqr/(chez Lesage) Maison Ferrier/ Rue Florestine Condamine/Principalité de Monaco
Harford, Frederick K.	1882	4 Aug	D	
Harper, Thomas	1884	28 July	A	S.J. Lond.
Hart, John	1883	15 July	D	
Hawkins, Mrs Edward	1882	21 Nov	A	Oriel
			D	
Healy, John	1884	3 July	Pr	John Healy, *Papers and Addresses* p. 445 (J. Seynaeve, *Cardinal Newman's Doctrine on Holy Scripture*, Louvain and Oxford, 1953, p. 79; J. D. Holmes and R. Murray (editors) *The Inspiration of Scripture*, London 1967, p. 47)
			D	
Hennin, Bernard	1882	11 Nov	C	

Correspondent	Year	Date	Source	Location, Owner, Address
	1883	9 Oct	C	
Herbert of Lea, Lady	1884	26 Jan	A	
		14 Feb	A	
Heslop, Thomas Pretious	1882	6 July	A	Birmingham University Library
Hewit, Augustine Francis	1884	19 June	C	
		26 June	C	
		22 Oct	C	(*Ward* II, p. 505 note)
Hibernian Bank	1884	12 July	D	
Higgins, Michael	1884	24 May	A	J. J. Wilson, Cork
Hopkins, Gerard Manley	1882	22 Feb	A	Campion Hall, Oxford (C. C. Abbott, *Further Letters of Gerard Manley Hopkins*, second edition, London 1956, p. 411) *Ad*. The Revd Fr Hopkins S J/St Wilfrid's Catholic Church/Preston
	1883	27 Feb	A	Campion Hall, Oxford (C.C. Abbott, op. cit., p. 412) *Ad*. The Rev. Fr Hopkins S J/Stonyhurst College/Blackburn
		26 April	A	Campion Hall, Oxford (C. C. Abbott, op. cit., p. 412) *Ad*. The Rev Fr Hopkins/Stonyhurst College/Blackburn
	1884	29 Feb	A	Campion Hall, Oxford (C. C. Abbott, op. cit., p. 413) *Ad*. The Rev. Fr Hopkins/85, 86 Stephen's Green/Dublin
Houghton and Co., Messrs	1881	26 Oct	D	(two) The *Weekly Register*, (12 Nov. 1881), p. 602)
Hughes, Dr	1883	15 Aug	A	St John's Seminary, Camarillo, California
Hughes, P. J.	1884	25 June	D	
Hutton, Arthur Wollaston	1881	24 Oct	D	
		21 Nov	D	
	1883	15 Nov	D	(two)
		27 Nov	A	Pierpont Morgan Library
			H	
Hutton, Richard Holt	1883	8 Oct	C	
			D	(two)
		12 Oct	C	
	1884	14 Jan	C	
		6 May	C	(*Ward* II, p. 522)
		11 May	C	(*Ward* II, p. 523)
Jenkins, Robert Charles	1882	7 May	C	
		21 July	C	
	1883	30 Mar	C	
		13 Nov	C	
		16 Dec	C	
	1884	1 Jan	C	
		24 Feb	D	
		24 April	C	
Jenkins, Thomas Jefferson	1884	3 Oct	A	American Catholic Historical Society of Philadelphia, St Charles Seminary, Overbrook, Philadelphia
		14 Nov	A	American Catholic Historical Society of Philadelphia
Keane, Augustus Henry	1882	11 Mar	D	
Keating, W. H.	1884	23 April	A	
			D	
Kegan Paul, Trench and Co., Messrs	1884	3 May	D	
		26 July	A	Donald F. Winslow, Philadelphia Divinity School
			D	
		30 July	D	

Correspondent	Year	Date	Source	Location, Owner, Address
		5 Sept	D	
Kehoe, Lawrence	1884	8 Feb	D	
Kenyon, Mrs John	1884	13 Feb	C	Todhunter
Keon, Mrs	1882	29 May	C	
	1883	24 Feb	C	
		27 May	C	
		21 Oct	C	
Kerr, Lady Henry	1882	12 Jan	C	Todhunter
		9 Mar	C	Todhunter
		25 May	C	Todhunter
	1883	1 Mar	C	Todhunter
Kerr, William Hobart	1882	30 Mar	C	Todhunter
King, Mr	1882	22 Feb	A	St Hugh's Charterhouse, Parkminster
Knowles, James	1884	2 April	D	
		4 April	D	
		6 April	D	
		23 April	D	
		30 April	C	
		1 May	D	(three)
		3 May	D	
Lady A [?]	1882	15 Sept	C	
Lake, William Charles	1881	18 Aug	C	(Katharine Lake, *Memorials of William Charles Lake*, London 1901, pp. 259–60)
			D	
La Serre, H.	1881	28 Dec	C	
Lavigerie, Cardinal	1882	4 April	C	
Law, the Hon. William Towry	1882	29 Jan	A	S.J. Lond. (W. T. Law, *A Memoir of the Life and Death of Rev. Father Augustus Henry Law*, II, London 1882, Introd.)
		1 Dec	A	S.J. Lond.
Lee, Mrs Frederick George	1882	22 April	A	Mrs Bond *Ad.* Mrs Lee/All Saints Vicarage/Lambeth/London
Leo XIII	1883	25 Nov	D	
Liddon, H. P.	1882	25 Sept	A	Keble *Ad.* The Rev/Canon Liddon/3 Amen Court/St Paul's/London E C
	1883	22 May	A	Keble *Ad.* The Rev./Canon Liddon/Ch Ch/Oxford
		24 May	A	Keble *Ad.* The Rev. Canon Liddon/Ch Ch/Oxford
		11 June	A	Keble *Ad.* The Rev. Canon Liddon/Ch Ch/Oxford
		13 June	A	Keble *Ad.* The Rev./Canon Liddon/Ch Ch/Oxford
		5 July	A	Keble *Ad.* The Revd Canon Liddon/Ch Ch/Oxford
		14 Aug	A	Keble *Ad.* The Rev./Canon Liddon./St Paul's/London E C
		21 Aug	A	Keble
		10 Sept	A	Keble *Ad.* The Rev./Canon Liddon/St Paul's/London E C
		15 Oct	A	Keble *Ad.* The Revd Canon Liddon/Amen Court/St Paul's/London E C
		29 Nov	A	Keble *Ad.* The Rev Canon Liddon/Ch Ch/Oxford
	1884	24 Feb	A	Keble *Ad.* the same
		19 Mar	A	Keble *Ad.* the same
Lilly, W. S.	1882	14 May	D	
		12 June	D	(two)
		27 June	Pr	The *Fortnightly Review* (Sept. 1890), p. 434

Correspondent	Year	Date	Source	Location, Owner, Address
		7 Dec	Pr	The *Fortnightly Review* (Sept. 1890), pp. 434–5; the *Guardian* (10 Sept. 1890), p. 1416
		13 Dec	Pr	The *Fortnightly Review* (Sept. 1890), p. 435
		18 Dec	A	Cashel Archdiocesan Archives
	1883	12 Aug	D	
	1884	17 Aug	Pr	The *Fortnightly Review* (Sept. 1890), pp. 435–6
		10 Oct	A	
		15 Oct	C	(A of P.S.)
			D	
Lindsay, Hon. Colin	1884	6 Jan	A	
Linton, W. J.	1883	30 Oct	A	Yale University
Liverziani, Achille	1881	17 Oct	D	
Lockhart, William	1881	2 Oct	A	
Londonderry, Marchioness of	1882	Nov	Pr	George Sexton, Brighton, Catalogue 55
Longman, Charles James	1884	21 May	D	
		7 June	D	
		11 June	D	
		16 June	D	
		4 July	D	
Loughnan, Francis	1882	21 Dec (I)	D	(two)
		21 Dec (II)	Pr	The *Bath Journal* (23 Dec. 1882)
			D	
MacCabe, Cardinal	1882	4 April	C	
Macchi, Monsignor	1883	31 Jan	A	Pembroke College, Oxford (*D R*, 1955, p. 455)
MacColl, Malcolm	1883	16 April	C	(*Malcolm MacColl, Memoirs and Correspondence*, edited by G. W. E. Russell, London 1914, p. 305)
		26 April	C	(op. cit., p. 305)
		28 April	C	(op. cit., p. 306)
		3 May	C	(op. cit., p. 307)
	1884	6 Feb	C	(op. cit., p. 307)
McInrow, John P.	1884	20 Mar	C	*Ad.* Rev. J. P. McInrow/St Mary's/Amsterdam/New York
McKenna, Arthur	1882	15 June	C	
McLoughlin, Patrick	1882	7 Sept	A	Littlemore (The *Tablet*, 14 Jan. 1928)
Macmillan, Messrs	1882	28 July	A	Newman Preparatory School, Boston
Malmesbury, Earl of	1884	3 Nov	Pr	The *Daily News* (4 Nov. 1884)
			D	(several)
Manning, Cardinal	1884	9 May	A	
Maskell, William	1884	31 Dec	A	British Museum
Matthews, Henry	1884	5 Jan	D	
		16 Feb	D	
Maxwell-Scott, the Hon. Mrs	1882	15 Feb	A	Abbotsford
		27 Feb	A	Abbotsford
		17 Mar	A	Abbotsford
		23 Sept	A	Abbotsford
	1883	9 Mar	A	Abbotsford *Ad.* The Hon./Mrs Maxwell Scott/Abbotsford/Melrose N B
		25 July	A	Abbotsford *Ad.* The Hon/Mrs Maxwell Scott/Abbotsford/Melrose N B
	1884	18 Jan	A	Abbotsford *Ad.* The Hon./Mrs Maxwell Scott/Abbotsford/Melrose N. B.
		20 Jan	A	Abbotsford *Ad.* The Hon./Mrs Maxwell Scott/Abbotsford/Melrose/N B

Correspondent	Year	Date	Source	Location, Owner, Address
		24 Jan	A	Abbotsford
		26 April	A	Abbotsford *Ad.* The Hon/Mrs Maxwell Scott/9 Place S.Eugene/ Biarritz/France
		20 Sept	A	Abbotsford
Mayall, John	1883	14 April	H	
Mayor and Mayoress of Wolverhampton	1884	May	D	
Meynell, Wilfrid	1883	23 May	D	
	1884	23 Jan	D	
Mills, Austin	1883	18 Sept	A	
Milward, R. H.	1882	24 Aug	A	
Mivart, St George Jackson	1882	12 Mar	C	
	1883	17 Aug	C	
		30 Oct	C	
		11 Nov	C	
	1884	6 Mar	A	(Jacob W. Gruber, *A Conscience in Conflict*, New York 1960, pp. 158–9)
		9 Mar	A	(op. cit., p. 160)
		11 Mar	A	(op. cit., p. 161)
		25 Mar	C	
		8 May	A	(op. cit., p. 163)
		9 May	A	(op. cit., p. 163)
		11 May	A	(op. cit., pp. 163–4)
Monteith, Joseph	1884	31 Mar	A	Major J. B. Monteith
Montgomery, Hon. Frances Charlotte	1884	end of Mar	D	
Moorhead, F. W.	1884	13 Nov	H	
Morgan, Francis	1882	22 Aug	A	*Ad.* The Rev. Francis Morgan/ Puerto de Sta Maria/Andalucia/ Spain
Morris, William B.	1882	7 May	A	Lond.
Mossman, Thomas Wimberley	1882	2 Jan	D	
Mozley, Anne	1881	28 Dec	A	
	1882	11 Jan	A	
		8 July	A	
		24 Sept	A	
		9 Nov	A	
		13 Nov	A	
	1883	26 Feb	A	
		7 Aug	A	
		3 Sept	A	
		28 Sept	A	
	1884	7 Jan	A	
		23 Mar	A	(*Trevor* II, p. 614)
		29 April	A	(*Trevor* II, p. 615)
		4 May	A	
		10 July	A	
		22 Sept	A	
		20 Oct	A	Oriel
			D	
		24 Dec	A	Oriel
Mozley, Edward Newman	1881	Christmas	A	Ernest Mozley
	1882	27 Dec	A	Ernest Mozley
Mozley, Henry Williams	1881	29 Oct	A	
		3 Nov	A	
		27 Nov	A	
	1883	5 Jan	A	
	1884	14 Mar	A	(*Moz.* II, p. 482)
Mozley, Herbert Newman	1883	14 Aug	D	
Mozley, Ida and Edward	1883	31 Dec	A	Ernest Mozley

Correspondent	Year	Date	Source	Location, Owner, Address
Mozley, Jane	1882	1 Mar	A	
		5 Oct	A	
		10 Oct	A	
	1883	8 Jan	A	
		21 July	A	
		26 Dec	A	
	1884	26 Feb	A	
Mozley, John Rickards	1881	20 Oct	C	(*Ward* II, pp. 517–8)
		24 Oct	C	(*Ward* II, pp. 518–9)
		3 Nov	C	
	1884	14 Mar	C	(*Moz.* II, p. 482)
Mozley, Mrs John Rickards	1882	July	C	
Mozley, Thomas	1881	21 Oct	A	Oriel *Ad.* The Revd T Mozley/ 7 Lansdown Terrace/Cheltenham
			D	
	1882	9 June	C	*Ad.* Revd T. Mozley/care of Messrs Longman and Co./34 Paternoster Row E.C.
		end of year	D	
Mullins, J. D.	1882	11 Dec	A	Reference Library, Birmingham
Munro, Miss	1882	4 Aug	A	Lond.
Neville, William	1881	6 Oct	A	
	1883	21 April	A	
	1884	29 May	A	
Newman, Francis William	1882	13 June	C	
			D	
	1883	8 April	A	
		26 June	A	Newman Preparatory School, Boston
	1884	22 Oct	A	St Mary's Abbey, Colwich, Staffs.
Norfolk, Duke of	1882	23 Jan	A	The Duke of Norfolk
		9 Feb	D	
		10 Feb	A	The Duke of Norfolk
		13 May	C	
			D	
	1883	9 Mar	A	The Duke of Norfolk
			D	
	1884	9 Jan	A	The Duke of Norfolk
		19 Mar	A	The Duke of Norfolk
			D	
		21 Mar	D	(not sent) (*Trevor* II, p. 610)
		21 Mar	A	The Duke of Norfolk
		23 Mar	A	The Duke of Norfolk (*Trevor* II, p. 610)
			D	
		3 April	D	(*Trevor* II, p. 613)
Northcote, J. Spencer	1881	25 Nov	A	Stoke
		11 Dec	A	Stoke
	1883	21 July	A	Stoke
	1884	5 Mar	A	Stoke
Oates, Wilfrid	1883	27 Aug	D	
	1884	12 Jan	D	
		8 Feb	D	
		16 Feb	D	
		10 Mar	D	
		14 Mar	D	
		29 April	D	
		9 June	D	
		16 July	D	
		13 Sept	D	
		18 Sept	D	
		9 Oct	D	
		13 Oct	D	
		25 Oct	D	

Correspondent	Year	Date	Source	Location, Owner, Address
		11 Nov	D	
		27 Nov	D	
O'Callaghan, Malachy	1882	15 Nov (I)	A	Castleknock College *Ad.* The Very Rev./Father O'Callaghan/Castleknock/Dublin
		15 Nov (II)	A	Castleknock College
O'Conor, Joseph F. X.	1884	3 Oct	A	Georgetown University *Ad.* The Rev. Father J. F. X. O'Conor, S.J./Woodstock College,/Md., U.S.A.
		28 Nov	Pr	privately printed by the English Jesuits
Ogle, John William	1882	4 Jan	D	*S.E.*, p. 107; J. W. Ogle, *Harveian Oration*, 1880, London 1881[1882], p. 161)
	1884	2 Mar	A	Wellcome Institute Library
		7 Nov	A	Wellcome Institute Library
		24 Nov	A	Wellcome Institute Library
		29 Nov	A	Wellcome Institute Library
		11 Dec	A	Wellcome Institute Library
O'Hagan, John	1881	28 Dec	A	S.J. Dublin
	1883	10 Aug	A	S.J. Dublin
O'Hagan, Lord	1884	15 Mar	A	S.J. Dublin
O'Neill, Simeon Wilberforce	1882	end of Aug	D	(two)
Oram, P. Sprague	1884	6 May	A	
Ornsby, Robert	1882	22 April	A	
		23 Sept	A	
	1883	7 Jan	A	*Ad.* Professor Ornsby/Verona/ 5 Univershall? [Summerhill] Road/Kingstown/Co Dublin
		18 Mar	A	
		4 May	A	
		16 Oct	A	
		22 Oct	A	
		24 Oct	A	
		23 Nov	A	
	1884	24 Jan	A	
		23 April	A	
		28 April	A	
		30 April	A	
		2 May	A	
O'Sullivan, Michael	1881	21 Nov	A	Birmingham Diocesan Archives
Palmer, Edwin	1881	9 Oct	A	Bishop of Peterborough
	1882	11 Jan	A	Bodleian MS Selborne 225 item B
		18 Mar	A	Bishop of Peterborough
		20 Mar	A	Bishop of Peterborough
		22 Mar	A	Bishop of Peterborough
		12 April	A	Bishop of Peterborough
		4 Aug	A	Bishop of Peterborough
		8 Aug	A	Bishop of Peterborough
		4 Sept	A	Bishop of Peterborough
		27 Sept	A	Bishop of Peterborough
	1883	13 Aug	A	Bishop of Peterborough
			D	
		27 Sept	A	Bishop of Peterborough
Parker, John Henry	1883	3 Jan	A	Pusey
Patmore, Coventry	1884	16 Nov	A	S.J. Lond. (Basil Champneys, *Memoirs and Correspondence of Coventry Patmore*, London 1900, II, p. 377)
Pattison, Mark	1883	25 Dec	A	
		27 Dec	A	(*Ward* II, p. 481; *Trevor* II, p. 619)
	1884	2 Jan	A	
			D	

Correspondent	Year	Date	Source	Location, Owner, Address
		4 Jan	A	(*Ward* II, p. 482)
			D	
		5 Jan	A	
			D	
		8 Jan	A	(*Ward* II, p. 483; Henry Tristram, *Newman and his Friends*, London 1933, p. 22)
			D	
Paul, Charles Kegan	1882	30 May	D	
		27 Oct	D	
Pecci, Cardinal	1882	26 Sept	A	
Penedo, Baron de	1881	29 Nov	C	
Penrose, F. C.	1881	6 Dec	D	
Percival, John	1884	May	D	
Pereira, Hon. Mrs	1882	17 April	C	
		25 April	C	
		2 May	C	
		16 May	C	
	1883	9 Aug	C	
Pincott, F. G.	1882	13 Mar	C	
Place, Charles Philippe, Archbishop of Rennes	1884	Nov	D	
Plumer, Charles John	1883	10 June	C	
Plummer, Alfred	1882	25 Feb	A	Pusey *Ad.* The Revd. A. Plummer/ Master of University College/ Durham
	1884	15 Jan	A	Pusey (F. L. Cross, *John Henry Newman*, London 1933, pp. 180–1) *Ad.* The Rev Dr Plummer/University College/Durham
Plumptre, Edward Hayes	1883	8 May	C	
	1884	14 Sept	C	
			D	
		22 Sept	C	
		24 Oct	C	
		6 Nov	C	
		13 Nov	C	
Pollen, John Hungerford	1881	8 Nov	C	
		14 Nov	A	S.J. Lond. *Ad.* J H Pollen Esqr/ 11 Pembridge Crescent/Bayswater/ London W
	1884	1 April	C	
		6 April	C	
		9 April	C	
		25 April	C	
		11 July	C	
		15 Sept (I)	C	
		15 Sept (II)	C	
Pollen, Mrs John Hungerford	1883	31 Dec	C	
	1884	1 Aug	C	
Pope, Annie Golightly	1881	31 Dec	A	
Pope, Launcelot John	1884	2 June	C	*Ad.* L. Pope Esqr/Stonyhurst College/Blackburn
Pope, Richard	1883	20 Aug	H	
		19 Sept	D	
Pope, Thomas Alder	1881	5 Oct	A	
	1882	10 Sept	A	
	1883	24 May	A	
Powell, John Hardman	1883	28 Aug	A	Mary H. Watts
	1884	24 Aug	A	Mary H. Watts
Provost of the Bologna Oratory	1883	28 Sept	C	
			D	
Publishers	1881	8 Nov	D	
Pusey, E. B.	1882	12 Jan	C	Pusey
		27 Jan	C	Pusey

Correspondent	Year	Date	Source	Location, Owner, Address
		29 June	C	Pusey (Liddon's *Pusey* I, p. 139; *Newman at Oxford*, p. 35)
		4 Aug	C	Pusey (Liddon's *Pusey* I, p. 139)
Raymond-Barker, Mrs Frederic Mills	1883	20 Feb 24 Feb	A C	
Reader, J.	1883	27 April	A	The Duke of Norfolk
Reffé, Edouard	1882	Mar	A	(facsimile)
Rende, Siciliano di	1883	9 Feb	H	
Renouf, Peter le Page	1884	24 Aug	A	Pembroke College, Oxford (*D R* (1955), p. 456) *Ad*. P. le P. Renouf Esqr/Grove Lodge/Drayton Gardens/London S W
Richmond, George	1883	3 June	D	
Riddell, Arthur	1883	25 Aug	Pr	Mary Francis Roskell, O.S.B., *Memoirs of Francis Kerril Amherst*, London n.d., pp. 373–4
Ring, W. M. J.	1883	end of April	D	
Ripon, Marquis of	1883	at 1 Jan	D	
Rivington, John	1881	22 Dec	A D	
	1882	2 Jan	D	
Rivington, Messrs	1884	29 Sept	D	
		13 Oct	D	
		16 Oct	H	
		12 Nov	D	
Roberts, Miss	1882	8 Dec	A	St Rose Priory, Dubuque, Iowa
Russell, Matthew	1881	6 Nov	A	S.J. Dublin
Ryder, Henry Ignatius Dudley	1883	4 Nov	A D	(*Trevor* II, pp. 595–6)
	1884	Jan	A	
Sanfelice, Guglielmo	1881	Dec	D	
Sconce, Mrs	1881	30 Dec	C	
Scott, Christopher	1884	29 Aug (I)	D	
		29 Aug (II)	D	
		12 Sept	D	
Scott, George Gilbert	1881	9 Oct	A	British Museum
Scratton, Thomas	1881	9 Oct	A	S.J. Dublin *Ad*. Thomas Scratton Esqr/Catholic University/86 Stephen's Green/Dublin
Seaton, Robert Cooper	1882	24 Aug	D	
Seccombe, John T.	1884	23 April	C	
Secretary of the Catholic Young Men's Societies	1882	7 Aug	Pr	Report of General Conference, 1882, p. 23
	1883	31 July	Pr	Report of General Conference, 1883, p. 7
	1884	26 July	Pr	Report of General Conference, 1884, p. 30
Secretary of St George's Club	1883	26 Aug	D	
Secretary of the Sydney Literary Society	1883	Sept	D	
Shadwell, Charles Lancelot	1882 1883	5 Dec 30 June	A D	Oriel
Shairp, John Campbell	1881	25 Nov	Pr	W. Knight, *Principal Shairp and his Friends*, London 1888, pp. 370–1
Shaw, Herbert James	1884	23 Oct	A	Miss A. M. C. Shaw *Ad*. Herbert Jas. Shaw Esq./St John's College/Oxford
Shipley, Orby	1882	3 Jan	D	
		5 Jan	D	
		7 Jan	D	
		13 Mar	D	
	1883	9 Dec	D	
Simeon, Lady	1882	21 Mar	C	

Correspondent	Year	Date	Source	Location, Owner, Address
	1884	25 April	C	
		16 May	D	
Simon, Oswald John	1882	19 Jan	D	
Smith, S. B.	1882	Oct	D	
Smyth, Albert Henry	1883	at 1 Jan	D	
Spooner, Miss E.	1884	13 June	D	
Stang, William	1883	13 April	C	
Stanton, Richard	1883	2 Mar	A	
	1884	12 June	A	
Stewart, James	1884	26 Jan	C	
Stonor, Edmund	1882	15 Feb	A	
		16 April	A	
	1884	10 April	A	
Tabb, John Bannister	1882	11 June	A	Fairfield University Library, Fairfield, Conn.
Taylor, J. P.	1882	8 Jan	A	Lond.
Teeling, George	1882	22 Nov	D	
Tennyson, Alfred	1882	18 Aug	A	Tennyson Research Centre, Lincoln City Library (Hallam Tennyson, *Materials for a life of Alfred Tennyson*, n.d., IV, pp. 27–8)
		23 Aug	A	Tennyson Research Centre, Lincoln City Library (Hallam Tennyson, op. cit., IV, pp. 27–8)
Thompson, Edward Healy	1882	20 May	A	Catholic Record Society
		25 May	A	Catholic Record Society
		12 June	A	Catholic Record Society
Thynne, Lord Charles	1884	23 Jan	A	Yale University Library
Trevelyan, Edwin	1884	21 Mar	A	(The *Weekly Register* (19 April 1884), p. 498)
			D	
Trübner and Co., Messrs	1883	16 Aug	A	William C. Bruce, Wanwatosa
		27 Aug	A	Newman Preparatory School, Boston
			D	
Tucker, Marion A.	1882	4 Sept	C	
Ullathorne, Bishop	1882	9 Oct	A	
		Dec	D	
	1883	31 July	A	
	1884	23 Feb	A	
		10 Sept	A	
Unknown	1881	12 Oct	H	
Correspondents	1882	28 Jan	A	Shrewsbury School Library
		17 Feb	D	
		13 Sept	A	Georgetown
		23 Sept	D	
		17 Nov	A	
	1883	at 1 Jan	D	
		at 1 Jan	D	
	1884	7 Oct	A	Rev. Denis G. Murphy
Unwin, Thomas Fisher	1884	19 Aug	D	
Vaughan, Edward Thomas	1883	27 Aug	C	
Vaughan, Jerome	1882	17 June	A	Fort Augustus Abbey
		9 Dec	A	Fort Augustus Abbey
Von Hügel, Baron Friedrich	1884	21 July	A	St Andrews University (*Ward* II, p. 504)
Von Hügel, Baroness Anatole	1882	26 Mar	A	
	1884	20 Feb	C	
Voysey, Charles	1884	4 Mar	D	
Waldron, James H.	1883	1 Oct	C	
Walford, John Thomas	1882	3 June	A	Stonyhurst College
	1883	13 April	C	

Correspondent	Year	Date	Source	Location, Owner, Address
	1884	7 Jan	A	S.J. Lond. *Ad.* The Rev Fr Walford S J/St Bueno's College/St Asaph/N Wales
Walsh, William J.	1881	19 Dec	D	
	1884	6 Feb	D	
Ward, F. R.	1883	20 Mar	A	
Ward, Mrs F. R.	1882	7 Oct	A	
	1883	31 Mar	A	
		1 Dec	A	
	1884	3 Oct	A	
Ward, Wilfrid	1882	13 Oct	A	The late Mrs Sheed
	1884	3 Aug	A	The late Mrs Sheed (W. Ward, *The Clothes of Religion*, London 1886, pp. xix–xx)
		4 Dec	A	The late Mrs Sheed
		20 Dec	A	The late Mrs Sheed (*Ward* II, pp. 488–9; Maisie Ward, *The Wilfrid Wards and the Transition*, London 1934, pp. 91–2)
Waring, F. Mercedes	1882	18 July	C	*Ad.* Miss Waring/St John's Road,/Clifton/Bristol
Watt, Mrs F. J.	1882	11 April	C	
	1884	27 Jan	C	
		7 Feb	C	
		8 July	C	
		13 Sept	C	
Wheble, James St Lawrence	1884	29 Jan	A	Newman Preparatory School, Boston
Whitaker, Joseph	1884	15 May	D	
		6 June	H	
		23 June	D	
		5 July	D	
Whitty, Robert	1882	2 Mar	A	S.J. Lond.
		16 Oct	A	S.J. Lond.
	1884	26 Jan	A	S.J. Lond.
		23 July	A	S.J. Lond.
Whyte, Alexander	1883	15 Dec	A	New College, The Mound, Edinburgh (Alexander Whyte, *Newman: An Appreciation*, London 1901, pp. 249–50; G. F. Barbour, *Life of Alexander Whyte*, eighth edition, London 1925, p. 244)
		21 Dec	A	New College, The Mound, Edinburgh (Alexander Whyte, op. cit., pp. 250–1; G. F. Barbour, op. cit., p. 245) *Ad.* The Rev. Alexander Whyte D D/52 Melville Street/Edinburgh
		26 Dec	A	New College, The Mound, Edinburgh (Alexander Whyte, op. cit., pp. 251–2; G. F. Barbour, op. cit., p. 245) *Ad.* The Rev. Dr Whyte/52 Melville Street/Edinburgh
			D	
		31 Dec	A	New College, The Mound, Edinburgh (Alexander Whyte, op. cit., pp. 252–3; G. F. Barbour, op. cit., p. 246) *Ad.* The Rev. Dr Whyte/52 Melville Street/Edinburgh
	1884	2 Jan	A	New College, The Mound, Edinburgh (Alexander Whyte, op. cit., frontispiece; G. F. Barbour, op. cit., p. 247) *Ad.* The Rev. Dr Whyte/52 Melville Street/Edinburgh

Correspondent	Year	Date	Source	Location, Owner, Address
Whyte, Mrs Alexander	1881	12 Nov	A	New College, The Mound, Edinburgh (G. F. Barbour, *Life of Alexander Whyte*, eighth edition, London 1925, pp. 241–2) *Ad.* Mrs Alexander Whyte/52 Melville Street/Edinburgh
		18 Nov	A	New College, The Mound, Edinburgh (G. F. Barbour, op. cit., p. 242) *Ad.* Mrs Whyte/52 Melville Street/Edinburgh
	1882	26 Nov	A	New College, The Mound, Edinburgh (G. F. Barbour, op. cit., p. 243) *Ad.* Mrs Whyte/Bonskeid/Pitlochry/N B
Wilberforce, Arthur Bertrand	1882	17 June	A	*Ad.* The Revd Fr Wilberforce/Catholic Church/Seaham Harbour/Seaham
Wilberforce, Henry Edward	1882	14 June	A	(photostat)
Williams, J.	1882	12 Dec	D	(two)
Willis, Helen P.	1884	4 Oct	D	
Wilson, Mrs	1882	22 Feb	C	
		20 April	C	
	1883	1 Feb	C	
	1884	25 Feb	C	
Wolseley, Sir Charles	1883	27 May	C	
		7 June	C	
		11 June	C	
Wolseley, Lady	1883	6 Sept	A	*Ad.* Lady Wolseley/Wolseley/Stafford
	1884	22 Oct	A	
Wood, Shakespere	1883	3 July	A	English College, Rome *Ad.* Shakespere Wood Esqr/Palazzo Thomazini/Via Nazionale 89/Roma/Italia
Wood, Hon. Charles Lindley	1884	3 Oct	A	Hickleton Papers *Ad.* The Hon C. L. Wood/Hickleton/Doncaster
		7 Oct	A	Hickleton Papers *Ad.* The Hon./Charles Wood/Hickleton/Doncaster
Woodgate, Henrietta	1881	26 Oct	A	Pusey *Ad.* Miss Woodgate/Oldbury/Bridgnorth/
		28 Oct	A	Pusey *Ad.* Miss Woodgate/Oldbury/Bridgenorth
	1882	1 Nov	A	Pusey *Ad.* Miss Woodgate/Oldbury/Bridgnorth
Woodlock, Bartholomew	1882	7 Nov	A	Georgetown
Woolner, Thomas	1881	21 Dec	A	Bodleian
	1884	24 July	A	Bodleian
Wordsworth, Charles	1882	13 Nov	A	Bodleian (Charles Wordsworth, *Annals of my Life, 1847–56*, edited by W. Earl Hodgson, London 1893, p. 82)
			D	
Wynne, John Henry	1884	24 Nov	A	S.J. Lond.
Yeatman, John Pym	1884	5 Oct	D	

MEMORANDA, ETC.

Date		Source	Subject
1881	4 Dec	A	Copyrights
1882	22 May	D	Temporal Power of the Pope
1884	18 Nov	A	Manning's Call at Littlemore

LETTERS TO NEWMAN

		From	*Inserted before Newman's of*
1881	12 Dec	W. E. Gladstone	13 Dec
	28 Dec	George T. Edwards	30 Dec
1882	20 Aug	Alfred Tennyson	23 Aug
	31 Dec	W. E. Gladstone	3 Jan 1883
1883	28 Dec	Mark Pattison	31 Dec (*Trevor* II, pp. 619–20)
1884	4 Jan	Mark Pattison	5 Jan
	13 Jan	Richard Holt Hutton	14 Jan
	20 Feb	Gerard Manley Hopkins	29 Feb
	1 July	Baron Friedrich von Hügel	21 July

Index of Persons and Places

The index to Volume XXI contains notices of almost all the persons who occur in that volume, and the indexes to subsequent volumes notices of those who occur in them for the first time. These are not repeated, and so, for persons and places already mentioned in those volumes, reference back is here made by a (XXI) or (XXII) etc. inserted after such names.

References are given in the case of persons mentioned for the first time in this volume, to *The Dictionary of National Biography* or *The Dictionary of American Biography*, and failing them, to Frederick Boase, *Modern English Biography*, or Joseph Gillow, *Bibliographical Dictionary* of the English Catholics; also occasionally to other printed works. Much of the information is derived from the correspondence and other material in the archives of the Birmingham Oratory, and from various private sources.

Abbott, Jacob (1803–79), American Congregationalist minister, author of many works, one of the first being *The Corner Stone*, Boston and London 1834, which was accused of Arian leanings. Newman criticised it in *Tract 73*, and in later editions Abbott modified some of the equivocal passages. He had a friendly meeting with Newman in 1843. (*D A B* I, 21), 211–12.

Acland (XXIX), Sir Henry Wentworth (1815–1900), 127.

Addis (XXII), William Edward (1844–1917), 138–9, 272.

Ainsworth, Sophia (1819–82), sister of A. J. Hanmer, was married to John Lees Ainsworth in 1839, and was received into the Church by Newman at King William Street, Strand, on 14 June 1850. Her husband became a Catholic before he died in 1871, and their five surviving children were also Catholics. In 1875 Mr Ainsworth became a Redemptorist nun, 78.

Alimonda, Gaetano (1818–91), a renowned preacher, became Bishop of Albenga in 1877, a Cardinal in 1879, and Archbishop of Turin in 1883, 183.

Alleguen, Edmund Henry, English master at the Oratory School, 1862–94. He died in 1909, 54.

Allies, (XXI), Eliza Hall Newman, Mrs T. W. Allies (1822–1902), 313.

Allies (XXVIII), Mary Helen (1852–1927), 239.

Allies (XXI), Thomas William (1813–1903), 26, 89, 123.

Amherst, Francis Kerril (1819–83), related to several old Catholic families was educated at Oscott and ordained priest there on 6 June 1846. He was Bishop of Northampton 1858–79. (*DNB*, I, 357), 249–50.

Amherst (XXVIII), William Joseph (1820–1904), 52, 249.

Antoine (XXVII), Julius (1826–1900), 16, 49.

Archer (XXVI), William Henry (1825–1909), 210

Argyll (XXV), George Douglas Campbell, eighth Duke of (1823–1900), 304, 346.

Arnold Thomas (1796–1842) (*DNB*, I, 585), 424.

Austin, see Mills, Henry Austin.

Avery, Thomas (1813–94), head of a well-known firm of scale makers, was a Birmingham alderman 1868 to death, and mayor 1867–8 and 1881–2. On 28 May 1882 he opened the new Birmingham Reference Library. (*Boase*, IV, 211), 93.

Awdry (XXVIII), Sir John (1795–1878), 107, 157.

Babington (XXV), George Gisborne (1794–1856), 349, 434.

Bacchus (XXIX), Francis Joseph (1860–1937), 5.

Baelemanns, F., 338.

Baines, Miss, 219.

Barrett, George Slatyer (1839–1916), Congregationalist author, born in Jamaica son of a missionary, was at University College, London, the Independent College, Manchester, and a D.D. of St Andrews. He was pastor of Princes Street Congregational Church, Norwich and in 1894 Chairman of the Congregational Union of England and Wales, 137.